Women in Spanish America: An Annotated Bibliography from pre-Conquest to Contemporary Times

Meri Knaster

G. K. HALL & CO., 70 LINCOLN STREET, BOSTON MASS.

Copyright © 1977 by Meri Knaster

Library of Congress Cataloging in Publication Data

Knaster, Meri
   Women in Spanish America.

   Includes bibliographical references and indexes.
   1. Women--Latin America--Bibliography. I. Title.
Z7964.L3K525 (HQ1610.5)   016.30141'2'098   76-46413
ISBN 0-8161-7865-8

This publication is printed on permanent/durable acid-free paper
MANUFACTURED IN THE UNITED STATES OF AMERICA

This book is dedicated to my sisters, of all
nationalities, who care about each other and
strive to be liberated human beings; *a mis
queridas amigas colombianas* Luc María y
Clara Inés; and to Larry, for sharing the
joys and pains of it all with me.

Contents

CONTENTS

Note: Countries are listed in the following order:

   Spanish America - General   South America:
                                     Venezuela
   Middle America: Colombia
     Mexico   Ecuador
     Guatemala   Peru
     El Salvador   Bolivia
     Honduras   Paraguay
     Nicaragua   Chile
     Costa Rica   Argentina
     Panama   Uruguay

                                  Caribbean:
                                  Puerto Rico
                                  Cuba
                                  Dominican Republic

Preface

The concatenation of events which led up to the undertaking and carrying out of a bibliographical project on women in Spanish America gives rise to a personal history of the enjoyment, frustrations, pitfalls, labors, and satisfactions experienced by one researcher intent on unearthing information about Latin American women. However, because that story is a long-winded account, the preface will only briefly recount the background of this bibliography.

The origins of this bibliography can be traced to a period prior to my graduate studies at Stanford, to the time when I lived and taught in Colombia. I did not know it then, but my friendships with Colombian women, my observations of women's lives in Latin America, and my own experience there as a woman provided the seed of interest which later germinated into academic work on women in Latin America. The bibliography itself was born of a personal need for references and subsequently coupled with a collective need for sources communicated by researchers in my immediate environment and elsewhere through correspondence. At that time, no bibliography, index, guide or catalogue of the relevant literature on women in Latin America existed.[1]

It was only when I was free to devote my energies to compiling the bibliography on, at minimum, a full-time basis that the project began to pick up momentum. It was then that I discovered that despite lamentations over the dearth of material on women in Latin America, there actually was, and still is, a wealth of sources, but only a systematic search would produce worthwhile results. I undertook to do that, beginning with the most basic task of consulting the card catalogues of the libraries at Stanford and at Berkeley with a list of the most obvious terms in English and in Spanish which refer to

---

Notes

[1] At that time, the only work dealing with the issue of research on women in Latin America was Ann Pescatello's essay, "The Female in Ibero-America: An Essay on Research Bibliography and Research Directions," Latin American Research Review 7:2 (1972):125-41 (see item 2318), which included a limited, partially annotated bibliography.

the female sex (e.g., woman/women), continuing with those institutions with which the subject is commonly associated (e.g., marriage
and the family), but also searching for its appearance beyond the
domestic sphere of activities (e.g., politics). One word precipitated
another, one publication cited others, one bibliography or index sig-
nalled additional sources. Often, while looking for a particular
item on a shelf in the stacks, I would chance upon five more. And
so on.

As indicated in the Appendix of Works Consulted, entire series of
periodicals and guides were gleaned for information on women. However, despite the systematic as well as serendipitous search that I
did carry out, I believe I have only scratched the surface. There
are many works I could not locate because they were either unavailable
in the United States, inaccessible through inter-library loan, impossible to find due to incomplete publishing data, or simply reported
as missing in a given library. Probably the single most important
factor which limited the comprehensiveness of the bibliography was
time. For every work I consulted, there were hundreds more waiting
on the shelves. Rather than pursue the search for years--perhaps
even a lifetime--I decided to make available at least the minimal
bibliography I have compiled as a beginning resource to the growing
field of studies on women in Latin America. Therefore, I stress that
this bibliography is neither complete nor definitive. However, until
all printed matter is computerized and readily accessible mechanically,
bibliographies will continue to serve as primary keys for entrance
into a subject. This bibliography was prepared with that objective
in mind.

Introduction

I think I never did anything else in my life which brought
me such hearty praise "in mouths of wisest censure"--imme-
diate and almost universal recognition, at home and abroad,
from ornithologists who knew that Bibliography was a necessary nuisance and a horrible drudgery that no mere drudge
could perform. It takes a sort of inspired idiot to be a
good bibliographer, and his inspiration is as dangerous a
gift as the appetite of the gambler or dipsomaniac--it grows
with what it feeds upon, and finally possesses its victim
like any other invincible vice.

> Elliott Coues, "Dr. Coues'
> Column," The Osprey, 2
> (november 1897), p. 39*

The purpose of this bibliography is to facilitate access to a
topic which for years has been neglected by some; by others given
attention in a limited, minor, and unsatisfactory way, fraught with
a biased perspective, and written mostly from a male viewpoint. Increased interest in women, of whatever continent, as a vital field of
study, as well as recognition of the need for more accurate research
on this subject, have been important by-products of the contemporary
women's movement. Incorporating female and feminist perspectives
helps to balance out our picture of society. By providing a minimal
list of references and suggesting complementary research to broaden
the base of information, this bibliography, as the first of its kind,[1]
strives to serve as a catalyst for the development of scholarly work
on women in Spanish America.

---

*Quoted by Richard H. Shoemaker, in Bibliography: Current State and
Future Trends, ed. by Robert B. Downs and Frances B. Jenkins (Urbana,
Ill.: University of Illinois Press, 1967), p. 5. I am grateful to
Mary Lombardi for giving me this quotation in October of 1974, and for
her help in resolving subject classification and bibliographical ques-
tions throughout the second half of the project.

WOMEN IN SPANISH AMERICA

I SCOPE

Libraries Consulted. Between late 1972 and the end of 1974 I
consulted the holdings of the libraries of Stanford University, the
University of California at Berkeley (including the Bancroft Library)
and at Los Angeles, the Latin American Collection of the University
of Texas at Austin, the Library of Congress, and the New York Public
Library. Additional publications were obtained from other University
of California campuses and out-of-state libraries through inter-
library loan. Information and publications were also gathered during
a three-month trip through South America (Argentina, Bolivia, Chile,
Ecuador, Colombia, Peru, Venezuela) and a two-week trip to Mexico City,
both in 1974. Due to various circumstances, only limited investigation of library and institutional holdings was possible during those
trips. Consequently, almost all of the publications cited in this
bibliography are available in libraries located in the United States.
Publications were also obtained from bookstores and book exhibits at
professional association meetings and individual authors, who were
kind enough to share their own bibliographies.

Countries and Ethnic Groups. For the purpose of linguistic, historical, cultural, and political homogeneity, only the Spanish-
speaking countries of Latin America have been considered for this
bibliography. For South America: Argentina, Bolivia, Chile, Uruguay,
Paraguay, Ecuador, Peru, Colombia, Venezuela. For Middle America:
Mexico, Guatemala, Costa Rica, Honduras, Nicaragua, El Salvador,
Panama. For the Caribbean: Cuba, the Dominican Republic, and Puerto
Rico.[2] Entries do not cover women in Spain, except for those Spanish
women who migrated to America, or as background information. Neither
do they cover other foreign-born women, except for those who achieved
prominence or notoriety in Spanish American history (e.g., Empress
Carlotta, Eliza Lynch, Flora Tristán, Catalina de Erauso); nor
Mexican-American or Latin American women in the United States or in
other countries, unless as part of a comparative culture study. They
do cover women of various indigenous and other ethnic groups, whether
Spanish-speaking or not, located within Spanish America.

Time Periods. The entries cover references to women from pre-
Conquest to contemporary times. The earliest publications are from
the 17th century; nothing published after 1974 is included.[3] While
some works were originally written and published in the 16th century,
modern reprints are usually cited here, and the annotation indicates
the date or era of the original.

Languages. This bibliography is comprised of only those works
published in Spanish or English. If editions are available in both
languages, the entry reflects this whenever possible. Some periodicals issue both a Spanish and an English edition (e.g., Revista
Internacional de Trabajo/ International Labor Review, Bulletin of the
Pan American Union/ Boletín de la Unión Panamericana). Other periodicals and books are published bilingually; the annotation notes the
latter variation. Virtually everything written before 1920 was

produced in Spanish. Approximately fifty percent of the total number
of items was written in Spanish. All annotations are written in English, but Spanish words are occasionally employed within the annotation
when an English translation does not adequately convey its meaning.
Those words or expressions appear in italics. The Spanish names of
institutes or organizations in Spanish America are retained to facilitate location of further information on that entity.

Kinds of Publications. Entries reflect mainly secondary sources,
some of which contain primary material. They include books, separate
chapters in books, articles and pamphlets. They range from full-
length studies to sketchy accounts. They may be memoirs, *tesis* and
memorias of schools and academies, columns, notices, bibliographies,
constituciones and *reglas* of institutions and organizations, travel
accounts, or correspondence.

Some government decrees and documents and publications of international agencies are included, but no attempt has been made to encom-
pass all the publications of the many government bureaus of the Spanish
American countries or of the United States, nor of all the commissions
of inter-American (e.g., Organization of American States) or international (e.g., United Nations), organizations. The items listed here
are but a sampling of what could constitute a separate bibliography
of official documents, bulletins, newsletters, and other periodicals.[4]
Neither does it endeavour to gather together all the publications of
the innumerable women's organizations which exist (e.g., Inter-
American Commission on Women, Federation of Cuban Women).

Statistical data are included when they comprise a separate publication or appear in a published study. Sources such as correspondence, and church and court records are invaluable for primary
research, but they are not included unless reproduced or transcribed
into a publication. Bulletins and journals (*revistas*) of national
academies of history or national archives have yielded much of this
material. Although valuable for their insight into female life and
psychology and women writers themselves, fiction and poetry are not
included separately or in anthologies. Some exceptions are those
works which use the novel or verse form to impart a sense of morality
to girls and women and convey ideas on what should constitute their
education (e.g., items 431, 569, 1594). Neither is literary criticism included. However, both criticism and literary pieces may appear
as part of a study on a writer's life and works. Novelized biographies
are included, particularly when sources are indicated, but historical
novels are not. Biographies of men are not included but may be a
useful source of information on the women in their lives. If the
focus of the publication is on the woman(-en) in a man's life, that
work is included (e.g., Porfirio Fariña Núñez, *Los amores de Sarmiento*,
item 79).

Entries do not include unpublished papers,[5] but a list of doctoral
dissertations cites, whenever possible, the availability of an ab-
stract in Dissertation Abstracts International. An unannotated list

of Master's theses is also included. Foreign theses and dissertations are included and annotated only when they appear in a periodical or as a separately published item.

Not included are newspaper items, except when they are reprinted in a periodical or other publication; neither are Sunday magazine sections of dailies. Popular magazines such as Novedades or El Hogar are not included, although a few items do analyze such periodicals for their appeal to and effect on female readers. However, several nineteenth-century periodicals directed at a female audience are listed for historical perspective. Although valuable for their incisive and timely commentary on women in contemporary Latin American society, published comic strip material, such as the Mafalda series in Argentina or collections by Rius in Mexico, are not included. Unless they contain a fair share of observations on women, few chronicles of the Conquest and early colonization period and travel accounts are included.[6]

Subject Matter and Disciplines. The entries in this bibliography consider aspects of women's lives ranging from the reproductive cycle to political participation as officeholders, from economic activity as market vendors to university training in medicine, from worship as goddesses to abuse as servants. There are fourteen major single or collective subject categories and one general section, each one preceded by scope notes which describe the contents of that particular section and also indicate what other sections should be consulted for additional information. The table of contents lists these categories. Limitations on a certain subject are indicated within the scope notes, and additional reference sources are suggested. The majority of publications listed in the bibliography cover disciplines of the social sciences and humanities (the arts, literature, history, education, political science, law, economics, psychology, sociology, theology), but also consider medicine, psychiatry, and physiology.

Selection of Material. The range of material is broad. The objective has been to provide a comprehensive rather than specialized survey; to include factual and scientific accounts, as well as reportage which has fostered stereotypes; to serve the interested reader as well as the academician; and to illustrate the possibilities of good source material as well as the difficulties in locating adequate or substantive references. In light of the growing general consensus that women do not fit neatly into the structures and models set up by social scientists, and thus are not measurable by their standards, there is a necessity to expose ourselves to other, perhaps unorthodox and innovative, methods, perspectives, and sources disclosing and analyzing data on women. Therefore, in agreement with Wilgus,[7] publications have not been omitted because they are inaccurate, unscientific, exaggerated, romanticized, novelized or written in verse; or reflective of political, religious, social, racial, cultural, or national prejudices; or just plain dull. As a result, the quality of publications ranges from excellent to poor, from scholarly to popular, from scientific to impressionist.[8] The purpose of including both "good" and "bad" material is to demonstrate the diversity of sources available. Some articles, though not especially informative or objective, were included not for the quality of the text, but for the illustrations and/or point of view.

On the whole, items were selected on the basis of the amount or kind of information on or related to women (e.g., only those studies on *machismo* and national character which indicate the male attitude toward women or describe the female character as well), the inclusion of women in the sample (even though the study may not be on women <u>per se</u>), or as reflections or examples of women's efforts and activities (e.g., letters written by women, though not necessarily about female life). In general, only publications specifically about women were reviewed. Some exceptions are ethnographic monographs and histories of slavery which include notes on female members of an indigenous group and consider female slaves and slaveowners, respectively. Some items containing only scattered references to women are included where little information is available on that topic or ethnic group. Further explanation of choice of material can be found in the scope notes which introduce the subject categories.

The number of entries which comprise a subject or country category reflects either of two situations: the choice of material included in the bibliography, or the actual state of published information for that topic or geographical area. Unless a wider, more exhaustive search is undertaken, it is impossible to state whether the references in this bibliography are truly representative of the total picture of studies on women in Spanish America.

II ORGANIZATION

Categories. Overall organization of the material has been done by major subject categories, as witnessed in the table of contents. The categories reflect women's activities not only in the domestic or private sphere, that domain within which women's roles is consistently defined, but also in the public sphere, in which women, as social actors, participate as well, even if only marginally. Consequently, an attempt was made to unearth information about women in their many capacities and functions which go beyond reproduction of the species-- their role as worker, student, politician, religious devotee, revolutionary, and so on.

Several major categories have been divided into subcategories: e.g., HISTORY BEFORE 1900 is broken down into four historical periods (pre-Conquest; Conquest and Colony; Independence; Republic or Nineteenth Century) and one general subcategory for those works which consider women in two or more historical epochs; LAW is broken down into three subsections (General Legal Status; Employment Legislation; Female Delinquency and Penal Institutions). Every category or subcategory is then divided by country, preceded by a Spanish America division for items referring to three or more countries; and finally, entries are listed alphabetically by author, or by title if author is unknown. If the topic of the item does not clearly fall into one of the major subject categories, it is located in the GENERAL section.

Because any one item may relate to several subject categories, there is much cross-referencing throughout, as indicated in the subject index. For the same reason, the reader is strongly advised to consult several categories, even when looking for a specific topic, and to check the scope notes for additional explanations of organization.

The Entry. All entries are numbered consecutively. Complete citation and publishing information is given whenever possible. Not all libraries follow the same rules; entries may reflect this inconsistency. Dates are located to the left of the entry. If more than one work by an author appears in a subject category, they are listed in descending order with the latest date first. Author's name is given in full except when not known, in which case initials are used if provided. Real name is also provided when a pseudonym is used, but cited under pseudonym if best known in that form (e.g., Gabriela Mistral rather than Lucila Godoy Alcayaga). Women's surname before marriage is retained when indicated in the publication. Corporate authors are indicated for material which would otherwise be difficult to locate (e.g., Mexico. Law, statutes, etc.). Titles, even lengthy ones, are given in full, with the exception of several which read as follows:

FERRER, GABRIEL
   1881 La mujer en Puerto-Rico. Memoria premiada en el
        Certámen de "El Buscapié" celebrado el 9 de octubre de 1880.
        San Juan, P.R.: Imp. de "El Agente." 72 p.

In this case, everything after La mujer en Puerto-Rico would not be included in the title because it does not contribute information about the subject itself, only that the work won a prize in a literary contest. Edition, series or collection number is given when indicated in the publication. If the publisher is unknown, but the printer's name is provided, the latter is used. Uncertainty as to accuracy of date or place of publication or other such facts is demonstrated by a question mark. Only Arabic numbered pages are indicated. If an introduction is especially lengthy and informative, that is indicated in the annotation. If there are additional unnumbered or separately numbered appendices, illustrated sections, etc., which are especially relevant, these too are noted in the annotation. Entry listing also indicates whether the publication is illustrated, contains tables, graphs, portraits, plates, bibliography of bibliographical notes. The term illustrated may signify pictures, photographs, drawings, figures, or diagrams. If a periodical is listed as a separate entry, whenever possible, place of publication, editor or director, and inclusive years of publication are cited. Lastly, each entry bears an annotation, with the exception of several biographies in the LITERATURE, MASS MEDIA AND FOLKLORE section, doctoral dissertations (which include a DAI citation), and Master's theses.

Introduction

Abbreviations are used throughout except for title and author's name when known in full. The reader should consult the list of abbreviations for terms as well as for periodicals. If three or more countries are covered within one item, the entry is located in the Spanish America group rather than listed individually three times. An entry dealing with women in two countries is cited in full under both countries; however, only one entry contains the annotation while the other indicates which other country to consult for the annotation.

An entry of an article appears as follows:

ACOSTA de SAMPER, SOLEDAD
    1957 "Las esposas de los conquistadores. Ensayo histórico."
    AHVC/B 25:108:140-54.

DAVIDSON, MARIA
    1969 "Some Demographic and Social Correlates of Fertility
    in Venezuela." IASI/E 27:105:587-601. tables.

An entry of a book appears as follows:

BARRETT, SAMUEL A.
    1925 The Cayapa Indians of Ecuador. Indian Notes and
    Monographs, 40. N.Y.: Museum of the American Indian,
    Heye Foundation. 2 vols. illus., map, tables, plates.

ALEGRÍA, JUANA ARMANDA
    1974 Psicología de las mexicanas. Serie: Cuarta Dimensión.
    Mex., D.F.: Edit. Samo. 187 p.

An entry of a section or chapter in a book appears as follows:

PHELAN, JOHN LEDDY
    1967 "The Sinners and the Saint." In his The Kingdom of
    Quito in the Seventeenth Century; Bureaucratic Politics
    in the Spanish Empire, pp. 177-95. Madison, Wis.: Univ.
    of Wis. Press. bibl. notes.

The Annotation. The purpose of the annotations in this bibliography is to provide a summary or description of the contents of the works compiled. The annotation attempts, whenever possible, to identify the various topics and/or individuals treated in a work, dates of research, methodology, hypotheses and conclusions, attitude or perspective; and to add information perhaps not available in the work itself but contributing to an understanding of the subject. Therefore, for the most part, the annotations are basically descriptive rather than evaluative. However, glaring generalizations or biases, lack of sources, substantiveness or merit, and profession of the author may also be noted. With approximately 2500 entries covering over a dozen disciplines, it is impossible to prepare a thoroughly researched annotation pointing out any or all faults in sources, data, methodology, and conclusions of every single work. Specialized bibliographies will assume that task.

Annotations are of varying length, depending on the publication itself--size, content, interest, value, etc. Annotations are based on examination of the publication, except for approximately a dozen items, where annotations are based on a secondary source and noted. Long phrases or sentences in quotation marks are taken from the text of the work itself, and in a very few instances, from another source, in which case that source is indicated.

Scope Notes. Scope notes introduce each subject category, describe its contents and any further division into subcategories, explain the rationale behind the choice and/or division of material in that section, and suggest other sections and/or reference guides for additional information.

IV OTHER MATERIAL

Doctoral Dissertations and Master's Theses. Doctoral dissertations and Master's theses are listed as an additional, but limited source. Most universities do not order copies of these references as a matter of course, but dissertations are available on microfilm. All the volumes of Dissertation Abstracts International (DAI) through 1974 were checked for doctoral dissertations specifically on women in Spanish America or their appearance in studies on a related subject such as the family, research which included a female sample, or a separate chapter on women. Abstracts of those dissertations are not repeated in this bibliography, but they can be consulted by using the DAI citation which follows the author, title, date, university and number of pages of the dissertation. For example:

HOLLANDER, NANCY CARO
    1974 "Women in the Political Economy of Argentina." University of California, Los Angeles. 357 p. DAI 35:10:6637-A.

However, not all universities have consistently listed with DAI (e.g., University of California and Harvard). Some dissertations of the University of California at Berkeley were obtained through a catalogue at its Main Library. Dissertations obtained through other sources and not cited in DAI are listed only with author, title, date, and university where submitted.[9]

A limited list of Master's theses cites only author, title, date, university where submitted, and whenever possible, number of pages. Foreign theses are not included in this group. The Catalogue of the University of Texas Latin American Collection cites many UNAM theses under various subject headings for women.

Appendix of Works Consulted. A list of the works consulted in the search for bibliographical entries is provided. Each item is cited with dates of the particular issues examined.

Introduction

Indexes. An author index lists all the authors of items in the
bibliography. A subject index serves the purpose of cross-referencing
and detailing those items which contain information on several topics
or persons. The indexes cite entry number rather than page number
for locating an item.

Orthography. Standard English spelling is used. Variations in
Spanish spelling within a title are retained. Place of publication
is given in its English spelling.

Abbreviations. There are two lists of abbreviations. One contains a system of abbreviations for the periodicals in which articles
reviewed appear. It follows the abbreviation system employed by the
Handbook of Latin American Studies but contains additional abbreviations for those periodicals not listed in HLAS. Another list contains
abbreviations of words, countries, and other proper nouns (e.g.,
states, institutes, organizations) used in the entries and annotations.

In conclusion, it should be pointed out that the search for references on women in Spanish America has disclosed many examples of
industrious, clever, forceful and lively women who clearly defy the
stereotype of Latin American women which pervades so many North American texts. The investigation has also revealed where such notions
originated. If myths about women are to be challenged and dispelled,
women's history must be reconstructed. A new perspective on the
existing literature, one which questions heretofore accepted assump-
tions, is a step in that direction. And, research which interprets
women's role in society more broadly and more equitably will then
serve to propagate different, less prejudicial attitudes toward women.
This bibliography endeavors to help others engaged in promoting that
objective.

---

[1] For a review of other bibliographical efforts, see section I of
my article: "Women in Latin America: The State of Research, 1975,"
Latin American Research Review 11:1(1976):3-74.

[2] Despite its extremely close economic and political ties with
the United States, Puerto Rico is here considered part of the Latin
American community.

[3] For a bibliography including 1975 publications as well, see my
article: "Women in Latin America: The State of Research, 1975,"
Latin American Research Review 11:1(1976):3-74.

[4] For some additional listings see the bibliography in Ann
Pescatello's Female and Male in Latin America (Pittsburgh, Pa.:
University of Pittsburgh Press, 1973) (item 2317).

[5] For a partial listing of unpublished papers presented at conferences, see my article: "Women in Latin America: The State of
Research," Latin American Research Review 11:1(1976):3-74.

[6] See instead Nancy O'Sullivan-Bear, Las mujeres de los conquistadores: la mujer española en los comienzos de la colonización americana (aportaciones para el estudio de la trasculturación) (Madrid: Cía. Bibliográfica Española, 1956) (item 1725) and A. Curtis Wilgus, Latin America in the Nineteenth Century: A Selected Bibliography of Books of Travel and Description Published in English (Metuchen, N.J.: Scarecrow Press, 1973).

[7] A. Curtis Wilgus, Latin America in the Nineteenth Century: A Selected Bibliography of Books of Travel and Description Published in English (Metuchen, N.J.: Scarecrow Press, 1973), p. ix.

[8] For example, Norte, published in Mexico, is not on a par with the Boletín de la Academia Nacional de la Historia (Caracas), but one issue does contain an interesting, albeit very brief, account of an intrepid Spanish woman who reached Asuncion in 1556 after a five-year journey which included a shipwreck at sea and a trek along the jungled coast of Brazil (item 1803).

[9] Some dissertations have also been published, in the original or revised version. Check author index. See also the Comprehensive Dissertation Index, 1861-1972 (Ann Arbor, Mich.: Xerox University Microfilms, 1973). There are 32 volumes covering 23 subjects and 5 volumes for the author index. The listing of a dissertation includes its location in Dissertation Abstracts International or another source.

Acknowledgments

During the course of the research project which has culminated in this bibliography on women in Spanish America, many individuals and institutions supported, advised, and encouraged me, as well as provided bibliographical information, copies of their work and useful suggestions. To all of them I am deeply grateful. More specifically, I want to express my sincere thanks to the following persons and agencies:

To the Ford Foundation, for financially supporting this research endeavour; and especially to Dr. Robert G. Myers, my liaison with the Foundation. Throughout the trials and tribulations of the project and the red tape of a research grant, he was always a cooperative, understanding, and amiable person to work with.

To the Center for Latin American Studies at Stanford University; in particular, to Dr. Bernard J. Siegel, its director during the time I was a graduate student there and during the course of the project, for his recommendation and continued support. Dr. Siegel served as a flexible, accepting, and encouraging guide in my desires to focus my graduate studies and subsequent research efforts on women in Latin America. I would also like to thank his staff at the Center--Ursula Spector and Margaret Herlin and, later, Josette Perrenoud and Marcia Erickson--who were always cooperative and efficient in attending to the necessary but thankless tasks which helped to oil the bureaucratic machinery at Stanford in the administration of the grant.

To the Center for the Continuing Education of Women (CCEW) on the Berkeley campus of the University of California; to Dr. Margaret Wilkerson, the Director, Helene Wenzel, Associate Director, and especially to Diana Gong, Administrative Assistant, for her personal touch in making me feel welcome there; and to all the other women who worked at CCEW during the two and a half years I maintained an office there. They were part of my second home, providing a congenial and feminist atmosphere to work in, giving me understanding and cooperation, taking endless messages, and bearing with me during crises.

To Dr. Elsa Chaney, one of the warmest, most positive, and giving persons I know, someone who displayed enough confidence in me in the earliest stages of the project to get the ball rolling along the right track. To Elsa and other members of the Women's Committee of the Latin American Studies Association, of which Dr. Nancie Gonzalez was then president, for their efforts in encouraging the Ford Foundation to finance the project. To Drs. Helen Safa and June Nash for their generous invitation to participate in the Buenos Aires conference on "Feminine Perspectives in Social Science Research in Latin America," which was the starting point of my research trip through Latin America. And to Dr. Nora Scott Kinzer, the wittiest *mala hada* anyone could wish for.

To Dr. May Diaz, now provost of Kresge College at the University of California in Santa Cruz, a wonderful teacher and warm human being, for her recommendation, successful efforts as then Director of CCEW in obtaining office space for me on the Berkeley campus, and participation, constructive advice and criticism as a member of my advisory committee. To James Breedlove, curator of Latin American materials at the Stanford University library, for helping to lay the original foundation in his bibliography class, for his recommendation, and helpful comments as a member of my advisory committee. I would also like to thank his staff--Marcia Dias Tchen and Mimi Zaugg--for acquiring and informing me of publications I needed for the bibliography. And to the other members of my advisory committee for taking time out of their busy schedules to contribute their expertise at workshops held to resolve questions which arose during the course of the project: Professors Mary Lowenthal Felstiner, Richard Fagan, Beverly Chiñas, Louisa Hoberman, Jane Jaquette, and graduate students Silvia Arrom and Jamie Felner.

To Mary Lombardi, for her conscientious preparation of the detailed subject index which accompanies this bibliography, assistance in resolving subject classification problems during the second half of the project, and friendly understanding and sharing of bibliographical work.

To Jill Immerman, for her tireless efforts, unstinting dedication, and excellent editing and typing skills during the long and weird hours of preparing the manuscript.

To the innumerable individuals who shared their personal bibliographies with me and/or sent me copies of their own research. To the staff of the many institutes, universities, libraries, centers, and governmental agencies in Latin America and the United States who granted me interviews and provided me with information and publications.

To those Latin Americans who opened their homes to me and made me feel welcome, like a *paisa*. To those Latin American women who shared with me their own personal journeys living as females in a Latin American society.

Acknowledgments

To all my friends, who stood by me during the years when I was working hard and could not come out to play with them.

And last, but never least, to Larry Jacobs, to whom mere words of gratitude are an inadequate means to express what I feel for an individual who provided a loving and supportive environment which helped make it possible for me to get through the long haul. For him, more than anyone else, are reserved and conveyed with love my deepest and sincerest thanks.

Abbreviations

ann.	annotated	Del.	Delaware
abr.	abridged	dept.	department
Ala.	Alabama	depto.	departmento
Arg.	Argentina	div.	division, división
Ariz.	Arizona	doc.	document
Ark.	Arkansas	Ecua.	Eucador
asoc.	asociación	ed(s).	edition(s),
assoc.	association		edición(es),
b.	born		editor(es),
B.A.	Buenos Aires		editor(a), edited
bibl.	bibliography,	edit.	editorial
	bibliographic	e.g.	for example
Bol.	Bolivia	El Sal.	El Salvador
Bra.	Brazil	est.	establishment,
bros.	brothers		establecimiento
c.	century, centuries	et al.	and others
CA	Central America	fac.	faculty, facultad
Ca.	California	facsim(s).	facsimile(s)
CELADE	Centro Latinoamer-	Fla.	Florida
	icano de Demo-	FMC	Federación de Mujeres
	grafía (Santiago)		Cubanas
cía.	compañía	f/note(s)	footnote(s)
CIDHAL	Comunicación, Inter-	fold.	folded
	cambio y Desarrollo	Ga.	Georgia
	Humano en América	gen.	general
	Latina.	geneal.	genealogical
	(Cuernavaca, Mex.)	govt.	government
CIDOC	Centro de Documenta-	Guat.	Guatemala
	ción (Cuernavaca,	Hond.	Honduras
	Mex.)	hnos.	hermanos
clr.	colored	IACW	Inter-American
col(s).	collection(s),		Commission on
	colección(es)		Women
Col.	Colombia	i.e.	that is
Conn.	Connecticut	Ill.	Illinois
corp.	corporation	illus.	illustrated,
C.R.	Costa Rica		illustration
d.	died		

ILO	International Labour Organization	Okla.	Oklahoma
		Oreg.	Oregon
incl.	including	p(p).	page(s)
Ind.	Indiana	Pa.	Pennsylvania
int'l	international, internacional	Pan.	Panama
		Par.	Paraguay
intro.	introduction	port(s).	portrait(s)
Jam.	Jamaica	P.R.	Puerto Rico
Kans.	Kansas	pseud.	pseudonym
Ky.	Kentucky	rev.	revised, revisada, revista
l.	leaves		
La.	Louisiana	R.I.	Rhode Island
LA	Latin America	SA	South America
L.A.	Los Angeles	S.C.	South Carolina
lic.	licenciado	S.Dak.	South Dakota
ltda.	limitada	ser.	series
Mass.	Massachusetts	st.	saint
Md.	Maryland	Tenn.	Tennessee
Mex.	Mexico	Tex.	Texas
Mex., D.F.	Mexico City	trans.	translated, translator
Mich.	Michigan		
Minn.	Minnesota	UN	United Nations
Miss.	Mississippi	UNAM	Universidad Nacional Autónoma de México (Mexico City)
NA	North America		
N.C.	North Carolina		
n.d.	no date	UNELAM	Unidad Evangélica Latinoamericana
N.Dak.	North Dakota		
Nebr.	Nebraska	univ.	university, universidad
Nev.	Nevada		
N.H.	New Hampshire	Uru.	Uruguay
Nic.	Nicaragua	US	United States of America
N.J.	New Jersey		
N. Mex.	New Mexico	Va.	Virginia
no(s)	number(s), número(s)	Ven.	Venezuela
n.p.	no place, no publisher, not paginated	vol(s).	volumes
		Vt.	Vermont
		Wash., D.C.	Washington, D.C.
numb.	numbered	Wis.	Wisconsin
N.Y.	New York	Wyo.	Wyoming
OAS	Organization of American States (Washington, D.C.)	WWI	World War I
		WWII	World War II

Periodical Abbreviations

A	<u>América</u>. Asociación de Escritores y Artistas Americanos. Havana.
AA/MSC	<u>Memorias de la Sociedad Científica "Antonio Alzate"</u>. Mexico, D.F.
AAA/AA	<u>American Anthropologist</u>. American Anthropological Association. Washington, D.C.
AAC/AJ	<u>Anthropological Journal of Canada</u>. Anthropological Association of Canada. Quebec.
AAFH/TAM	<u>The Americas</u>. Inter-American Cultural Agency. Academy of American Franciscan History. Washington, D.C.
AAH/RH	<u>Repertorio Histórico</u>. Academia Antioqueña de Historia. Medellin, Col.
AAHS/K	<u>The Kiva</u>. Journal of the Arizona Archaeological and Historical Society. Tucson, Arizona.
AAPSS/A	<u>The Annals of the American Academy of Political and Social Science</u>. Philadelphia.
AAUW/J	<u>Journal of the American Association of University Women</u>. Ithaca, N.Y.
ABN/R	<u>Revista del Archivo y Biblioteca Nacionales</u>. Tegucigalpa.
AC	<u>Acta Sociologica</u>. Copenhagen.
ACH/B	<u>Boletín de la Academia Chilena de la Historia</u>. Santiago.
ACSR	<u>American Catholic Sociological Review</u>. American Catholic Sociological Society. Chicago.
AE	<u>América Española</u>. Cartagena, Colombia.
AEE	<u>Anales de Economía y Estadística</u>. Departamento Administrativo Nacional de Estadística. Bogota.
AEST	<u>Estudios</u>. Revista argentina de cultura, información y documentación. Buenos Aires.
AFS/JAF	<u>Journal of American Folklore</u>. American Folklore Society. Austin, Texas.
AFSM/APPAL	<u>Acta Psiquiátrica y Psicológica de América Latina</u>. Buenos Aires.
AH	<u>Artes Hispánicas</u>. (<u>Hispanic Arts</u>). MacMillan Co. for Indian University. New York.
A/H	<u>Historia</u>. Revista bi-mensual. Buenos Aires.
AHVC/B	<u>Boletín de la Academia de Historia del Valle del Cauca</u>. Cali, Colombia.
AI/A	<u>Anthropos</u>. International Zeitschrift für Völkerkunde. St. Augustine, FRG.

AIP/C	Cuaderno de la Agencia de Informaciones Periodísticas. Miami, Florida.
AJCL	The American Journal of Comparative Law. American Association for the Comparative Study of Law. University of California. Berkeley, California.
AJES	The American Journal of Economics and Sociology. New York.
AJP	American Journal of Psychiatry. American Psychiatric Association. Utica, N.Y.
ALA	Action Latin America. Cambridge, Massachusetts.
ALMA	Alma Latina. Revista mensual de arte ilustrada. San Juan, Puerto Rico.
AMH/M	Memorias de la Academia Mexicana de la Historia. Mexico, D.F.
ANDMO	Andean Monthly. Instituto Chileno-Norteamericano de Cultura. Santiago.
ANH/B	Boletín de la Academia Nacional de la Historia. Buenos Aires.
ANH/BJHNA	Boletín de la Junta de Historia y Numismática Americana. Academia Nacional de la Historia. Buenos Aires.
APH/B	Boletín de Academia Panameña de la Historia. Panama.
APR/R	Revista de Agricultura de Puerto Rico. San Juan, Puerto Rico.
APRH/B	Boletín de la Academia Puertorriqueña de la Historia. San Juan, Puerto Rico.
ARMEX	Artes de México. Frente Nacional de Artes Plásticas. Mexico, D.F.
ASS/ASR	American Sociological Review. American Sociological Society. Manasha, Wisconsin.
AU	América Unida. Instituto Hondureño de Cultura Interamericana. Tegucigalpa.
AU/P	Phylon. Review of race and culture. Atlanta University. Atlanta, Georgia.
AVF	Archivos Venezolanos de Folklore. Universidad Central de Venezuela, Facultad de Filosofía y Letras. Caracas.
B/DRA	Desarrollo Rural en las Américas. Instituto Interamericano de Ciencias Agrícolas. Bogota.
BA/NR	Nueva Revista de Buenos Aires. Buenos Aires.
BA/RA	Revista Americana de Buenos Aires. Buenos Aires.
BAWM/B	Boletín de la Biblioteca Artigas-Washington. Montevideo.
BCB	Boletín Cultural y Bibliográfico. Banco de la República, Biblioteca "Luis-Angel Arango". Bogota.
BDSLM/CIDHAL	Boletín Documental Sobre la Mujer. Comunicación, Intercambio, y Desarrollo Humano en América Latina. Cuernavaca, Mex.
BIND	Boletín Indigenista. Instituto Indigenista Interamericano. Mexico, D.F.
BJS	British Journal of Sociology. For the London School of Economics and Political Science. London.

BSHCP/B	Boletín Bibliográfico de la Secretaría de Hacienda y Crédito Público. Mexico, D.F.
CA/RF	Revista del Foro. Colegio de Abogados. Lima.
CAM	Cuadernos Americanos. Mexico, D.F.
CATW	The Catholic World. A monthly magazine of general literature and science. New York.
CC	Cuba Contemporánea. Havana.
CCE/NAR	Revista del Núcleo del Azuay. Casa del Cultura Ecuatoriana. Cuenca, Ecuador.
CCP/J	Journal of Cross-Cultural Psychology. Center for Cross-Cultural Research; Department of Psychology. Western State College. Bellingham, Washington.
CCY	Christian Century. Chicago.
CCHE/HIDHC	Health Information Digest for Hot Countries. Central Council for Health Education. London.
CDAL	Cahiers des Amériques Latines. Paris.
CDJ	Community Development Journal. Manchester, Eng.
CDLA	Casa de las Américas. Revista. Casa de las Américas. Havana.
CEE/DS	Dinámica Social. Centro de Estudios Económico-Sociales. Buenos Aires.
CEF/R	Revista Chilena de Educación Física. Universidad de Chile. Instituto de Educación Física y Técnica. Santiago.
CEH/AHDE	Anuario de Historia del Derecho Español. Junta para ampliación de estudios e investigaciones científicas. Centro de Estudios Históricos. Madrid.
CEHA/NH	Nuestra Historia. Revista del Centro de Estudios de Historia Argentina. Buenos Aires.
CEHMP/R	Revista del Centro de Estudios Histórico-Militares del Perú. Lima.
CEM/ECM	Estudios de Cultura Maya. UNAM, Centro de Estudios Maya. Mexico, D.F.
CEMS	Educación Médica y Salud. Pan American Sanitary Bureau in collaboration with ASCOFAME. Washington, D.C.
CEPD/EPD	Estudios de Población y Desarrollo. Centro de Estudios de Población y Desarrollo. Lima.
CEST	Estudio. Centro de Historia de Santander. Bucaramanga, Col.
C/F	Familia. Centro Nacional de la Familia. Santiago.
CFS/J	Journal of Comparative Family Studies. Calgary, Alberta, Canada.
CFS/WF	Western Folklore. University of California Press for the California Folklore Society. Berkeley, California.
CGR/EC	Economía Colombiana. Departamento de Contraloría. Bogota.
CH	Cuadernos Hispanoamericanos. Seminario de problemas hispanoamericanos. Madrid.
CIAAP/RS	Revista del Ateneo Paraguayo: Suplemento Antropológico. Ateneo Paraguayo, Centro de Investigaciones Antropológicos. Asuncion.

CIF/FA   Folklore Americano. OAS, Instituto Panamericano de
Geografía e Historia, Comisión de Historia, Comité
Interamericano de Folklore. Lima.

CIH/B   Boletín del Centro de Investigaciones Históricas.
Guayaquil.

CJ/RF   Razón y Fe. Revista mensual hispanoamericana de
cultura. Los Padres de la Compañía de Jesús.
Madrid.

CJSR   Cornell Journal of Social Relations. Cornell University, Department of Sociology. Ithaca, New York.

CLEH   Cuadernos Latinoamericanos de Economía Humana. Centro
Latinoamericano de Economía Humana. Montevideo.

CLR   California Law Review. University of California,
Boalt School of Law. Berkeley, California.

CM/D   Diálogos. El Colegio de México. Mexico, D.F.

CM/DE   Demografía y Economía. El Colegio de México.
Mexico, D.F.

CM/HM   Historia Mexicana. El Colegio de México. Mexico, D.F.

CM/SS   La Cultura en México. Suplemento de Siempre!
Mexico, D.F.

CP/F   El Farol. Creole Petroleum Corporation. Caracas.

CPC/R   Revista de Criminología y Policía Científica. Santiago.

CPES/RPS   Revista Paraguaya de Sociología. Centro Paraguayo de
Estudios Sociológicos. Asuncion.

CPPR/P   Pedagogía. Universidad de Puerto Rico. Colegio de
Pedagogía. Rio Piedras, Puerto Rico.

CPS   Comparative Political Studies. Sage Publications.
Beverly Hills, California.

CR   Cuba Review. Cuba Resource Center. New York.

CRC/N   Cuba Resource Center Newsletter. New York.

CRCA   Crónica de Caracas. Caracas.

CRCA/A   Anthropologica. Canadian Research Centre for Anthropology. St. Paul University. Ottawa

CRED   Educación. Ministerio de Educación Pública. San Jose,
Costa Rica.

CRN/CEREN   Cuadernos de la Realidad Nacional. Universidad
Católica de Chile. Santiago.

CRW/A   America. A Catholic review of the week. New York.

CSDI/M   The Center Magazine. Center for the Study of Democratic
Institutions. Santa Barbara, California.

CSN/BESC   Cuban Studies Newsletter/Boletín de Estudios Sobre
Cuba. University of Pittsburgh. Center for Latin
American Studies, University Center for Inter-
national Studies. Pittsburgh, Pennsylvania.

CSSH   Comparative Studies in Society and History. Society
for the Comparative Study of Society and History.
The Hague.

CUA/AQ   Anthropological Quarterly. Catholic University of
America, Catholic Anthropological Conference.
Washington, D.C.

CUAG   Cuadernos del Guayas. Casa de la Cultura Ecuatoriana.
Guayaquil.

CUCO	Cursos y Conferencias. Buenos Aires.
CUDOC	Cuadernos Dominicanos de Cultura. Ciudad Trujillo.
CUVE	Cultura Venezolana. Revista mensual. Caracas.
DANE/BME	Boletín Mensual de Estadística. Departamento Administrative Nacional de Estadística. Bogota.
DCP/R	Revista de Derecho y Ciencias Políticas. Universidad Nacional Mayor de San Marcos, Facultad de Derecho y Ciencias Políticas. Lima.
DEF/F	Folk. Dansk Etnografisk Forening. Copenhagen.
DERIN/R	Revista de Derecho Internacional. Instituto Americano de Derecho Internacional. Havana.
DH	Divulgación Histórica. Mexico.
DHL/R	Revista de Derecho, Historia y Letras. Buenos Aires.
DJA/R	Revista de Derecho, Jurisprudencia y Administración. Montevideo.
DP/R	Revista de Derecho Penal. Buenos Aires.
DR	The Dominican Republic. Embassy of the Dominican Republic. Washington, D.C.
DS	Diálogo Social. Panama.
E/BIESE	Boletín de Informaciones y de Estudios Sociales y Económicos. Instituto Nacional de Previsión. Quito.
EANH/B	Boletín de la Academia Nacional de Historia. Quito.
ECA	Eca. Revista del Instituto Superior de Ciencias Administrativos. Universidad Nacional de la Plata. La Plata, Argentina.
ECAR/R	Revista de Economía Argentina. Buenos Aires.
ED	Estudios Dominicanos.
EE/R	Revista Ecuatoriana de Educación. Casa de la Cultura Ecuatoriana, Sección de Ciencias Filosóficas y de la Educación. Quito.
EEHA/AEA	Anuario de Estudios Americanos. Consejo Superior de Investigaciones Científicas and Universidad de Sevilla, Escuela de Estudios Hispano-Americanos. Seville.
EF	Encuentro Femenil. San Fernanco, California.
EHNH	Estudios de Historia Novo-hispana. UNAM. Mexico, D.F.
EJPS/R	Revista de Estudios Jurídicos, Políticos y Sociales. Universidad Técnica de Oruro, Centro de Estudiantes de Derecho. Oruro, Bolivia.
EQ	Eugenics Quarterly. American Eugenics Society. Baltimore; New York. (becomes Social Biology)
E/R	Revista de Educación. Ministerio de Educación Pública. Santiago.
ESFIL	Estudios Filológicos. Universidad Austral de Chile, Facultad de Filosofía y Letras. Valdivia, Chile.
ESMO	España Moderna. Madrid.
ESTAM	Estudios Americanos. Universidad de Sevilla, Escuela de Estudios Hispano-Americanos. Seville.
ET/T	Trabajo. Ministerio de Trabajo. Tegucigalpa.
FAH/N	Norte. Revista hispano-americana. Frente de Afirmación Hispanista. Mexico, D.F.

FCE/R	Revista de la Facultad de Ciencias Económicas. Universidad Nacional de Colombia. Bogota.
FICA	Ficción. Editorial Goyanarte. Buenos Aires.
FL	Filosofía y Letras. UNAM, Facultad de Filosofía y Letras. Mexico, D.F.
FLW	Free Labour World. International Confederation of Free Trade Unions. Brussels.
FSU/NA	Notes in Anthropology. Florida State University, Department of Anthropology and Archaeology. Tallahassee, Florida.
GAGG/B	Boletín del Archivo General del Gobierno. Guatemala.
GIIN/GI	Guatemala Indígena. Instituto Indigenista Nacional. Guatemala.
GM	The Geographical Magazine. London.
GPM	Genetic Psychology Monographs. Clark University. Worcester, Mass.
GRLO	Grace Log. New York.
GUAT/R	Revista de Guatemala. Guatemala.
HA/B	Boletín de Historia y Antiguedades. Organo de la Academia Colombiana de la Historia. Bogota.
HAHR	Hispanic American Historical Review. Conference on Latin American History of the American Historical Association. Duke University Press. Durham, N.C.
HH	Hora del Hombre. Revista mensual de cultura. Lima.
HIAM/R	Revista de Historia de América. Instituto Panamericano de Geografía e Historia. Mexico, D.F.
HISTO	Historium. (Istonio). Revista mensual, ilustrada de cultura. Buenos Aires.
HUDE	Human Development. Basel, Switzerland.
HURE	Human Relations. A quarterly journal of studies towards the integration of the social sciences. Tavistock Institute of Human Relations. Research Center for Group Dynamics. London; Cambridge, Massachusetts.
IAL/R	International Anthropological and Linguistic Review. Miami, Fla.
IASI/E	Estadística. Journal of the Inter-American Statistical Institute. Washington, D.C.
IBE/B	Bulletin of the International Bureau of Education. Geneva.
IBEAS/EA	Estudios Andinos. Instituto Boliviano de Estudio Acción Social. La Paz.
ICA/RCA	Revista Colombiana de Antropología. Ministerio de Educación Nacional, Instituto Colombiano de Antropología. Bogota.
ICAS/A	Antropológica. Instituto Caribe de Antropología y Sociología, Fundación La Salle de Ciencias Naturales. Caracas.
ID/R	Revista Internacional y Diplomática. Mexico, D.F.
IDRL/R	Revista del Instituto del Derecho Ricardo Levene. Universidad Nacional de Buenos Aires, Instituto de Historia del Derecho Argentino y Americano. Buenos Aires.

Periodical Abbreviations

IFIH/A   Anuario del Instituto Femenino de Investigaciones Históricas. Asuncion.

IGFO/RI   Revista de Indias. Consejo Superior de Investigaciones Científicas Instituto Gonzalo Fernández de Oviedo. Madrid.

IHGU/R   Revista del Instituto Histórico y Geográfico del Uruguay. Montevideo.

IIE/A   Anales del Instituto de Investigaciones Estéticas. UNAM. Mexico, D.F.

III/A   Anuario Indigenista. Instituto Indigenista Inter-americano. Mexico, D.F.

III/AI   América Indígena. Instituto Indigenista Interamericano. Mexico, D.F.

IILI/RI   Revista Iberoamericana. Organo del Instituto Inter-nacional de Literatura Iberoamericana. University of Pittsburgh. Pittsburgh, Pennsylvania.

IJAYE   International Journal of Adult and Youth Education. UNESCO. Paris.

IJP   International Journal of Psychology. (Journal Inter-nationale de Psychologie). International Union of Psychological Studies. Paris.

IJSP   International Journal of Social Psychiatry. London.

IL/ILO   Industry and Labour. International Labour Office. Geneva. (continues Industrial and Labour Information)

ILINFO   Industrial and Labor Information. International Labour Office. Geneva. (incorporated into International Labour Review)

ILO/R   International Labour Review. International Labour Office. Geneva.

INAH/A   Anales del Instituto Nacional de Antropología e Historia. Secretaría de Educación Pública. Mexico, D.F.

INNO   Indian Notes. Museum of the American Indian. New York.

INS   Insula. Revista bibliográfica de ciencias y letras. Madrid.

IP/J   Journal of Individual Psychology. Burlington, Vermont.

IPA/AP   Allpanchis Phuturinqa. Universidad de San Antonio de Abad, Seminario de Antropología, Instituto de Pastoral Andina. Cuzco, Peru.

ISR   International Socialist Review. New York.

IT/R   Revista Internacional del Trabajo. International Labour Office. Geneva.

ITAT/R   Revista del ITAT. Secretaría de Trabajo y Previsión Social, Instituto Técnico y Administrativo del Trabajo. Mexico, D.F.

JARES   Journal of Anthropological Research. University of New Mexico. Albuquerque, New Mexico (formerly UNM/SWJA)

JBS/SS   Servicio Social. Escuela de Servicio Social de la Junta de Beneficencia. Santiago.

JGP   Journal of Genetic Psychology. Worcester; Provincetown, Massachusetts.

JHE	Journal of Home Economics. American Home Economics Association. Baltimore, Maryland.
JMFL	Journal of Marriage and Family Living. (becomes WRU/JMF)
JRAI	Journal of the Royal Anthropological Institute of Great Britain and Ireland. London.
JSI	Journal of Social Issues. Society for the Psychological Study of Social Issues. New York.
JSP	Journal of Social Psychology. The Journal Press. Provincetown, Massachusetts.
JW	Journal of the West. Los Angeles, California.
KAS/P	Kroeber Anthropological Society Papers. University of California. Berkeley, California.
L/RH	Revista Histórica. Instituto Histórico del Perú. Lima.
LAP	Latin American Perspectives. A journal on capitalism and socialism. Riverside, California.
LARR	Latin American Research Review. Latin American Studies Association. University of North Carolina. Chapel Hill, North Carolina (formerly at the University of Texas in Austin)
LATR	Latin American Theatre Review. A journal devoted to the theatre and drama of Spanish and Portuguese America. University of Kansas, Center of Latin American Studies. Lawrence, Kansas.
LDA	Labor Developments Abroad. US Bureau of Labor Statistics. Washington, D.C.
LEEC	Letras del Ecuador. Periódico de literature y arte. Casa de la Cultura Ecuatoriana. Quito.
LJ/RG	Revista General de Legislación y Jurisprudencia. Colegio de Abogados. Madrid.
LNB/L	Lotería. Organo de la Lotería Nacional de Beneficencia. Panama.
LP/R	Revista de Legislación Peruana. Lima.
LSE/PS	Population Studies. A journal of demography. London School of Economics, The Population Investigation Committee. London.
MAAE/N	Notes on Middle American Archaelogy and Ethnology. Carnegie Institution of Washington, Department of Archaeology. Washington, D.C.
MAGN/B	Boletín del Archivo General de la Nación. Mexico.
MAN	Man. The Royal Anthropological Institute of Great Britain and Ireland. London.
MAR	Mexican-American Review. American Chamber of Commerce of Mexico. Mexico, D.F.
ME/RE	Revista de Educación. Dirección General de Escuelas. La Plata, Argentina.
MEC	Monitor de la Educación Común. Consejo Nacional de Educación. Buenos Aires.
ME/J	Journal of Medical Education. Association of American Medical Colleges. Chicago.
MEPE/E	Educación. Revista del Ministerio de Educación Pública del Ecuador. Quito.

MF	Mexican Folkways. Legends, festivals, art, archaeology. Mexico, D.F.
MH	Mundo Hispánico. La revista de veintitrés países. Madrid.
MIIN/NI	Nicaragua Indígena. Instituto Indigenista Nacional. Managua.
ML	Mexican Life. Mexico, D.F.
MLR	Monthly Labor Review. US Bureau of Labor Statistics. Washington, D.C.
MMFQ	Milbank Memorial Fund Quarterly. New York.
MN	Mundo Nuevo. Instituto Latinoamericano de Relaciones Internacionales. Paris.
MNAHE/A	Anales del Museo Nacional de Arqueología, Historia y Etnografía. Mexico, D.F.
MP	Modern Philology. University of Chicago. Chicago.
MPM	Mid-Pacific Magazine. Honolulu.
MPSQ/PS	Previsión Social. Boletín del Ministerio de Previsión Social. Quito.
MR	Monthly Review. An independent Socialist magazine. New York.
MRW	Missionary Review of the World. Princeton, New Jersey.
MSA/BM	Boletín Mensual del Museo Social Argentino. Buenos Aires.
MSBJ	Michigan State Bar Journal. Michigan State Bar Association. East Lansing; Ann Arbor, Michigan.
MSEP/LP	El Libro y el Pueblo. Secretaría de Educación Pública, Departamento de Bibliotecas. Mexico, D.F.
MSTPS/R	Revista Mexicana del Trabajo. Organo oficial de la Secretaría del Trabajo y Previsión Social. Mexico, D.F.
MTBS/R	Revista del Ministerio de Trabajo y Bienestar Social. Guatemala.
N/UNICEF	UNICEF News. United Nations. New York.
NACLA/LAER	NACLA's Latin American and Empire Report. North American Congress on Latin America. Berkeley, California; New York.
NAGH/R	Revista de la Academia de Geografía e Historia de Nicaragua. Managua.
NBW	National Business Woman. National Federation of Business and Professional Women's Clubs. Washington, D.C. (incorporates Independent Woman)
ND	La Nueva Democracia. New York.
NRCUB	Nueva Revista Cubana. Dirección General de Cultura. Havana.
NT	Nuestro Tiempo. Revista mensual. Ciencias y artes, política y hacienda. Madrid.
NUED	Nueva Educación. Lima.
NYAS/A	Annals of the New York Academy of Science. New York.
OAS/AM	Américas. Organization of American States. Washington, D.C.

OAS/CSNI	Ciencias Sociales. Notas e Informes. Pan American Union. Office of Social Sciences, Department of Cultural Affairs. Washington, D.C.
OC	Open Court. A quarterly magazine. Chicago.
PA	Political Affairs. A magazine devoted to the theory and practice of Marxism-Leninism. Chicago; New York.
PAA/D	Demography. Population Association of America. Chicago.
PANAM	Pan American. Magazine of the Americas. New York.
PASUS/PAR	Pan American Review. Pan American Society of the US. New York.
PAU/B	Bulletin of the Pan American Union. Washington, D.C.
PAU/Bs	Boletín de la Unión Panamericana. Washington, D.C.
PC	Punto Crítico. Mexico, D.F.
PED	Educación. Universidad Nacional Mayor de San Marcos. Facultad de Educación. Lima.
PHR	Public Health Reports.
PM	Primitive Man. Catholic Anthropological Conference. Washington, D.C.
PP	Past and Present. London.
PP/ASB	Archives of Sexual Behavior. Plenum Press. New York.
PP/R	Revista Penal y Penitenciaria. Dirección General de Institutos Penales. Buenos Aires.
PPP	Pan-Pacific Progress. Seattle; Los Angeles.
PR/E	Educación. Departmento de Instrucción de Puerto Rico. San Juan, Puerto Rico.
PRAM	Practical Anthropology. Tarrytown, New York. (becomes Missiology)
PRL/B	Boletín del Patronato de Recluídas y Liberadas. Buenos Aires.
PSR	Pacific Sociological Review. Pacific Sociological Association. Eugene, Oregon.
PUC/H	Humanidades. Pontificia Universidad Católica del Perú. Facultad de Letras. Lima.
PUFIN	Punto Final. Ediciones Punto Final Ltda. Santiago.
Q	Quetzalcoatl. Sociedad de Antropología y Etnografía de Mexico. Mexico, D.F.
RBC	Revista Bimestre Cubana. Sociedad Económica de Amigos del País. Havana.
RC	Revista de Cuba. Periódico mensual de ciencias, derecho, literatura y bellas artes. Havana.
RCE	Revista de Ciencias Económicas. Universidad Nacional de Buenos Aires. Buenos Aires.
RCPC	Revista Conservadora del Pensamiento Centroamericano. Managua.
RCT	Revista de Correos y Telecomunicaciones. Ministerio de Comunicaciones. Buenos Aires.
RDP	Revista de Derecho Puertorriqueño. Universidad Católica de Puerto Rico, Escuela de Derecho. Ponce, Puerto Rico.

REJAV	Revista Javeriana. Publicación mensual católica de interés general. Bogota.
RENAC	Revista Nacional. Literatura, arte, ciencia. Montevideo.
REPA	Repertorio Americano. Seminario de prensa castellana y extranjera. San Jose, Costa Rica.
REPB	Repertorio Boyacense. Centro de Historia de Tunja. Tunja, Col.
REVA	Revista de América. Bogota.
RHM	Revista Hispánica Moderna. Instituto de las Españas en los Estados Unidos. New York.
RI	Revista Interamericana/Interamerican Review. Universidad de Puerto Rico. Rio Piedras, Puerto Rico.
RIB	Revista Interamericana de Bibliografía/Inter-American Review of Bibliography. OAS. Washington, D.C.
RI/CUAD	Cuadernos de Ruedo Ibérico. Paris.
RIS	Revista Internacional de Sociología. Consejo Superior de Investigaciones Científicas, Instituto "Balmes" de Sociología. Madrid.
RLP	Revista Latinoamericana de Psicología. Editorial ABC. Bogota.
RMP	Revista Mexicana de Psicología. Instituto Tecnológico de Estudios Superiores de Occidente. Guadalajara, Mexico.
RPE/R	The Review of Radical Political Economics. Union for Radical Political Economics. Ann Arbor, Michigan.
RRP	The Review of the River Plate. Buenos Aires.
RSS/RS	Rural Sociology. Rural Sociological Society. New York State College of Agriculture. Ithaca, New York.
S/HM	Hechos Mundiales. Santiago.
SA	The South American. A journal for all interested in Latin American affairs. New York.
SAA/HO	Human Organization. Society for Applied Anthropology. New York.
SAQ	South Atlantic Quarterly. Durham, North Carolina.
SBV/R	Revista de la Sociedad Bolivariana de Venezuela. Caracas.
SCHG/R	Revista Chilena de Historia y Geografía. Sociedad Chilena de Historia y Geografía. Santiago.
SCHM/R	Revista de la Sociedad Cubana de Historia de la Medicina. Havana.
SCM/B	Boletín del Seminario de Cultura Mexicana. Secretaría de Educación Pública. Mexico, D.F.
SCNLS/M	Memoria de la Sociedad de Ciencias Naturales La Salle. Caracas.
SCSO	School and Society. New York.
SEHF/B	Boletín de la Sociedad Española de Historia de la Farmacia. Madrid.
SEM/E	Ethnos. Statens Etnografiska Museum. Stockholm.
SEND	Senderos. Biblioteca Nacional. Bogota.

SF	Social Forces. University of North Carolina Press by the Williams and Wilkins Co. Baltimore, Maryland.
SFP	Studies in Family Planning. Population Council. New York.
SGHG/A	Anales de la Sociedad de Geografía e Historia de Guatemala. Guatemala.
SGHH/R	Revista de la Sociedad de Geografía e Historia de Honduras. Tegucigalpa.
SGS/B	Boletín de la Sociedad Geográfica de Sucre. Sucre, Bolivia.
SIDI	Siete Días. Lima.
SIP/RIP	Revista Interamericana de Psicología. (Interamerican Journal of Psychology). Sociedad Interamericana de Psicología (Inter-American Society of Psychology). Austin, Texas.
SOBIO	Social Biology. New York.
SOSOR	Sociology and Social Research. Southern California Sociological Society. University of Southern California. Los Angeles, California.
SR/J	The Journal of Sex Research. Society for the Scientific Study of Sex. New York.
SS	Servicio Social. Escuela de Servicio Social del Perú. Lima.
SS/A	Servicio Social. Organo de la Escuela de Servicio Social del Museo Social Argentino. Buenos Aires.
SS/BBN	Boletín de la Biblioteca Nacional. San Salvador.
SS/RBN	Revista de la Biblioteca Nacional. San Salvador.
SSR	Social Service Review. A quarterly devoted to the scientific and professional interests of social work. University of Chicago, Graduate School of Social Service Administration. Chicago.
TDM	Tierra y Dos Mares. Panama.
TWCS/T	Transactions of the Third World Congress of Sociology. London.
UA/ED	Estudios de Derecho. Universidad de Antioquia, Facultad de Derecho y Ciencias Políticas. Medellin, Colombia.
UA/REH	Revista de Estudios Hispánicos. The University of Alabama Press. University, Alabama.
UA/U	Universidad de Antioquia. Medellin, Colombia.
UBAIA/R	Runa. Archivo para las Ciencias del Hombre. Universidad de Buenos Aires, Facultad de Filosofía y Letras, Instituto de Antropología. Buenos Aires.
UC/A	Anales de la Universidad de Cuenca. Cuenca, Ecuador.
UC/AJS	American Journal of Sociology. University of Chicago. Chicago.
UC/B	Boletín de la Universidad de Chile. Santiago.
UC/CA	Current Anthropology. University of Chicago. Chicago.
UC/EDCC	Economic Development and Cultural Change. University of Chicago, Research Center in Economic Development and Cultural Change. Chicago.

UC/RD	Revista de Derecho. Universidad de Concepción, Facultad de Ciencias Jurídicas y Sociales. Concepción, Chile.
UCAU/R	Revista de la Universidad del Cauca. Popayan, Colombia.
UCC/FT	Finis Terrae. Universidad Católica de Chile, Departamento de Extensión Cultural. Santiago.
UCE/A	Anales de la Universidad Central del Ecuador. Quito.
UCR/R	Revista de la Universidad de Costa Rica. San Jose, Costa Rica.
UH/U	Universidad de la Habana. Havana.
UJSC/ECA	Estudios Centro-Americanos. Revista de extensión cultural. Universidad José Simeón Cañas. San Salvador.
UM/JIAS	Journal of Inter-American Studies and World Affairs. University of Miami Press for the Center for Advanced International Studies. Coral Gables, Florida.
UM/R	Revista de la Universidad de Mexico. Mexico.
UM/REAA	Revista Española de Antropología Americana. Universidad de Madrid, Facultad de Filosofía y Letras, Departamento de Antropología y Etnología de América. Madrid.
UMEX	Universidad de México. Revista mensual. UNAM. Mexico, D.F.
UMSA/RD	Revista de Derecho. Universidad Mayor de San Andrés, Facultad de Derecho. La Paz.
UNAM/AA	Anales de Antropología. UNAM, Instituto de Investigaciones Históricas. Mexico, D.F.
UNAM/BIDCM	Boletín del Instituto de Derecho Comparado de México. UNAM. Mexico, D.F.
UNAM/CPS	Ciencias Políticas y Sociales. UNAM. Mexico. (incorporates Revista Mexicana de Ciencia Política)
UNAM/DPC	Derecho Penal Contemporánea. UNAM, Facultad de Derecho, Seminario de Derecho Penal. Mexico, D.F.
UNAM/ECN	Estudios de Cultura Náhuatl. UNAM, Instituto de Historia, Seminario de Cultura Náhuatl. Mexico, D.F.
UNAM/RMS	Revista Mexicana de Sociología. UNAM, Instituto de Investigaciones Sociales. Mexico, D.F.
UNAM/U	Los Universitarios. UNAM. Mexico, D.F.
UNAR/R	Revista de la Universidad de Arequipa. Arequipa, Peru.
UNC	Universidad Nacional de Colombia. Bogota.
UNC/BFDCS	Boletín de la Facultad de Derecho y Ciencias Sociales. Universidad Nacional de Córdoba. Cordoba, Argentina.
UNC/R	Revista de la Universidad Nacional de Córdoba. Cordoba, Argentina.
UNCFL/RL	Revista de Letras. Universidad Nacional de Cuzco, Facultad de Letras. Cuzco, Peru.
UNCH/A	Anales de la Universidad de Chile. Santiago.
UNESCO/BT	Boletín Trimestral. UNESCO. Pátzcuaro, Mexico.

UNESCO/I	Impact of Science on Society. UNESCO. Paris.
UNFFL/BIIH	Boletín del Instituto de Investigaciones Históricas. Universidad Nacional de Buenos Aires. Facultad de Filosofía y Letras. Buenos Aires.
UNI	Universitas. Bogota.
UNIPOB	Universidad Pontificia Bolivariana. Medellin, Colombia.
UNL/U	Universidad. Universidad Nacional del Litoral. Santa Fe, Rosario, Argentina.
UNLIIH/A	Anuario del Instituto de Investigaciones Históricas. Universidad Nacional del Litoral, Facultad de Filosofía, Letras y Ciencias de la Educación. Santa Fe, Rosario, Argentina.
UNLP/RF	Revista de Filosofía. Universidad Nacional de la Plata, Departamento de Filosofía. La Plata, Argentina.
UNM/SWJA	Southwestern Journal of Anthropology. University of New Mexico. Albuquerque, New Mexico. (becomes JARES)
UNMSM/RC	Revista de Ciencias. Universidad Nacional Mayor de San Marcos, Facultad de Ciencias. Lima.
UNT/RIE	Revista del Instituto de Etnología de la Universidad Nacional de Tucumán. San Miguel de Tucuman, Argentina.
UNT/RJ	Revista Jurídica. Universidad Nacional de Tucumán, Facultad de Derecho y Ciencias Sociales. San Miguel de Tucuman, Argentina.
UO/BA	Books Abroad. University of Oklahoma. Norman, Oklahoma.
UP/E	Ethnology. University of Pittsburgh. Pittsburgh, Pennsylvania.
UPR/CS	Caribbean Studies. Universidad de Puerto Rico, Institute of Caribbean Studies. Rio Piedras, Puerto Rico.
UPR/RCS	Revista de Ciencias Sociales. Universidad de Puerto Rico, Colegio de Ciencias Sociales. Rio Piedras, Puerto Rico.
UPR/RJ	Revista Jurídica de la Universidad de Puerto Rico. Rio Piedras, Puerto Rico.
UPR/T	La Torre. Revista general de la Universidad de Puerto Rico. Rio Piedras, Puerto Rico.
URL/ES	Estudios Sociales. Revista de ciencias sociales. Universidad Rafael Landívar, Instituto de Ciencias Político-Sociales. Guatemala.
USC/U	Universidad de San Carlos. Guatemala.
USDLWB/WW	The Woman Worker. US Department of Labor, Women's Bureau. Washington, D.C.
USDS/B	Department of State Bulletin. US Department of State. Washington, D.C.
UU/WPQ	Western Political Quarterly. The Western Political Science Association; Pacific Northwest Political Science Association; and Southern California Political Association. University of Utah, Institute of Government. Salt Lake City, Utah.
UWI/SES	Social and Economic Studies. University of the West Indies. Mona, Jamaica.

Periodical Abbreviations

UY/R	Revista de la Universidad de Yucatán. Merida, Mexico.
VA	Voces de América. Cartagena.
VANH/B	Boletín de la Academia Nacional de la Historia. Caracas.
VED	Educación. Revista para el magisterio. Ministerio de Educación. Caracas.
VFA/R	Revista de las Fuerzas Armadas. Ministerio de la Defensa Nacional. Caracas.
VME/R	Revista Nacional de Cultura. Ministerio de Educación, Instituto Nacional de Cultural y Bellas Artes. Caracas.
WLJ	Women Lawyers' Journal. National Association of Women Lawyers. New York.
WOM/JL	Women, A Journal of Liberation. Baltimore, Maryland.
WORED	World Education. World Federation of Education Associations. Washington, D.C.
WRU/JMF	Journal of Marriage and the Family. Western Reserve University. Cleveland, Ohio.
WSU/HB	Human Biology. A record of research. Wayne State University Press. Detroit, Michigan.
YU/IJCS	International Journal of Comparative Sociology. York University, Department of Sociology and Anthropology. Toronto.

Unabbreviated Periodicals

Abril. La Paz.
Abside. Revista de cultura mexicana. Mexico, D.F.
América. Revista...ilustrada de literatura, arte, ciencias. Quito.
Arco. Revista de las Areas Culturales Bolivarianas. Bogota.
Asomante. Asociación de graduadas. Universidad de Puerto Rico.
   San Juan, P.R.
Atenea. Revista mensual de ciencias, letras y bellas artes.
   Universidad de Concepción. Santiago.
Ateneo. Revista del Ateneo de El Salvador. Revista de ciencias,
   letras y artes. San Salvador.
Atlas. A select literary and historical journal. New York.
Bohemia. Havana.
Caretas. Lima.
Combate. Instituto Internacional de Estudios Político-Sociales.
   San Jose, C.R.
Comment. London.
Commonweal. A weekly review of literature, the arts and public
   affairs. New York.
Comunidad. Universidad Iberoamericana. Mexico, D.F.
Criminalia. Academia Mexicana de Ciencias Penales. Mexico, D.F.
Cuadernos. Congreso por la Libertad de la Cultura. Paris.
Era. Magazine. New York; Philadelphia.
Espejo. Colección del pensamiento económico moderno. Instituto de
   Investigaciones Sociales y Económicas. Mexico, D.F.
The Family. Also known as Social Casework. New York.
Fichas de ISAL. Movimiento de Iglesia y Sociedad en América Latina.
   Montevideo.
Flash. Bogota.
El Grito. Quinto Sol Publications, Inc. Berkeley, Ca.
Hispania.
Independent. New York.
The Inter-American. Washington, D.C.
Istmo. Revista del Centro de América. Mexico, D.F.
El Libertador. Sociedad Bolivariana del Ecuador. Quito.
Literary Digest. New York.
Matrix. Magazine for all women who write. Chicago.
Mentor. New York
The Militant. Communist Party of U.S.A. New York.

Ms. New York.
Nation. New York.
Norte. Revista continental. New York.
Nosotros. Revista mensual de letras, arte, historia, filosofía y
    ciencias sociales. Buenos Aires.
Peruanidad. Organo antológico del pensamiento nacional. Lima.
Plexus. Berkeley, Ca.
The Progressive. Madison, Wisc.
Psychiatry. William A. White Psychiatric Foundation. Baltimore;
    Washington, D.C.
Psychology Today. Del Mar, Ca.
Ramparts. Layman's Press. Menlo Park, Ca.
Registro Municipal. Bogota.
Revista Chilena. Santiago.
Revista Cubana. Havana.
Revista Jurídica. Universidad Autónoma "Simon Bolívar". Facultad
    de Derecho, Ciencias Sociales, Políticas y Económicas.
    Cochabamba, Bol.
Revista Nueva. Ciencias, literatura y artes. Panama.
Revista Shell. Shell Caribbean Petroleum Co. Caracas.
Rikchay Perú. Editorial Horizonte. Lima.
Science and Society. An independent journal of Marxism. New York.
Sic. Revista venezolana de orientación. Caracas.
Social. La revista para todos. Lima.
Society. Washington University. Fulton, Mo. (See Transaction)
Sociologus. Berlin.
Summa. Caracas.
Sur. Buenos Aires.
Survey. New York.
Technos. American Society for Engineering Education. International
    Division. Stanford, Ca.
Tlalocan. A journal of source materials on native cultures of
    Mexico. Sacramento, Ca.
Transaction. Washington University. Fulton, Mo. (See Society)
Travel. New York.
Turismo. Touring Club Peruano. Lima.
Turquino. Organización Nacional de Bibliotecas Ambulantes y
    Populares. Mariano, Cuba.
Vida. Compañía Colombiana de Seguros; Compañía Colombiana de Seguros
    de Vida. Bogota.
Yermo. Cuadernos de historia y de espiritualidad monásticas.
    Sociedad de Estudios Monásticos. Madrid.

Works Consulted*

Bibliographies

Aldous, Joan and Hill, Reuben. International Bibliography of Research in Marriage and the Family. Minneapolis, Minn.: University of Minnesota Press for the Minneapolis Family Study Center and the Institute of Life Insurance, 1967-74. 2 vols.

Bayitch, S. A. Latin America and the Caribbean: A Bibliographical Guide to Works in English. Coral Gables, Fla.: University of Miami Press, 1967.

"A Bibliography: Life Phases of Mestizo and Indian Women of Peasant Mexico." Berkeley, Ca.: University of California, Anthropology Department, n.d. 13 p.

Bird, Augusto. Bibliografía puertorriqueña de fuentes para investigaciones sociales, 1930-1945. Río Piedras, P.R.: Universidad de Puerto Rico, Centro de Investigaciones Sociales, 1946. vol. 1

Bellisimo, Yolanda. Untitled list of articles and books on women in Latin America. Los Angeles, Ca.: University of California, History Department, n.d. 14 unnumb. pages

Birdsall, Nancy. "An Introduction to the Social Science Literature on Woman's Place' and Fertility in the Developing World." Annotated Bibliography 2:1(1974): 39 p. Washington, D.C.: Smithsonian Institution, Interdisciplinary Communications Program.

Buvinić, Myra L.; Adams, Cheri Storton and Edgcomb, Gabrielle Simon. "Women in Development. Preliminary Annotated Bibliography, 1975." Washington, D.C.: American Association for the Advancement of Science, 1975. 63 p.

---

*Due to an unfortunate theft of data, this is only a partially reconstructed list of the many works consulted during the course of the project. Additional reference sources are cited in the introductory essay and the scope notes of each category section. Not listed are the bibliographies of all the articles and books which comprise the entries of the entire work.

Centro de Estudios sobre la Mujer in México. La mujer en México.
    Bibliografía 1. Mexico, D.F.: Centro de Estudios sobre la
    Mujer en México, 1974?; 94 p.

Chiñas, Beverly L. "Bibliography. Anthropology of Women." Chico,
    Ca.: Chico State College, Anthropology Department, 1970.
    39 unnumb. pages

"A Classified International Bibliography of Family Planning Research."
    Demography 5:2: (1968):977-1001.

Comas, Juan. Cien años de Congresos Internacionales de Americanistas.
    Ensayo histórico-crítico y bibliográfico. Mexico, D.F.:
    Instituto de Investigaciones Históricas, Instituto de Investiga-
    ciones Antropológicas, 1974.

_____. Los Congresos Internacionales de Americanistas. Síntesis
    histórica e índice bibliográfico general, 1875-1952. Ediciones
    especiales del Instituto Indigenista Interamericano, 19.
    Mexico, D.F.: Instituto Indigenista Interamericano.

Comisión Episcopal de Misiones y Cooperación entre las Iglesias.
    "Boletín bibliográfico iberoamericano." Madrid: Centro de
    Información y Sociología de la OCSHA, n.d. 11 p.

Committee on Women in Development. "Women's Role and Development
    Policies. A Bibliographic Index." Washington, D.C.: Society
    for International Development, 1974. 8 p.

Elton, Charlotte. "Bibliografía de la mujer en Panamá." Panama:
    1973. 9 p. Revised as "Bibliografía sobre la mujer en Panamá."
    Panama: 1975. 6 unnumb. pages.

Felstiner, Mary Lowenthal. "Bibliography on Women in Colonial
    Mexico." San Francisco, Ca.: California State University,
    Department of History, 1973. 10 p.

Géigel y Zenón, José and Morales Ferrer, Abelardo. Bibliografía
    puertorriqueña. Escrita en 1892-1894. Barcelona: Editorial
    Araluce, 1934.

Geoghegan, Abel Rodolfo. Obras de referencia de América Latina.
    Repertorio selectivo y anotado de enciclopedias, diccionarios,
    bibliográficas, repertorios biográficos, catálogos, guías,
    anuarios, índices, etc. Buenos Aires: Imprenta Crisol, 1965.

Griffin, Charles C., ed. and Warren, J. Benedict, asst. ed. Latin
    America: A Guide to the Historical Literature. Austin and
    London: University of Texas Press, 1971.

Gropp, Arthur E., comp. A Bibliography of Latin American Bibliog-
    raphies. Metuchen, N.J.: Scarecrow Press, 1971. Earlier
    edition, 1968.

Hartfiel, Ann. "II. A Partially Annotated Bibliography of Recent
    Publications in the Social Sciences." Washington, D.C.: Inter-
    American Foundation, 1974. 25 p.

Jacobs, Sue-Ellen. Women in Perspective: A Guide for Cross-Cultural
    Studies. Chicago and Urbana: University of Illinois Press, 1974.

Jones, Cecil Knight. A Bibliography of Latin American Bibliographies.
    2nd ed. rev. and enl. by the author with the assistance of
    James A. Granier. Latin American Series no. 2. Washington, D.C.:
    U.S. Government Printing Office, 1942.

Latin American Research and Publications at the University of Texas
    at Austin, 1893-1969. Guides and Bibliographies Series, 3.
    Austin, Tx.: University of Texas, Institute of Latin American
    Studies, 1971.

Lear, Julia Graham. "The Impact of Economic Development and Social
    Change on the Status of Women." Washington, D.C.: Committee on
    Women in Development, Society for International Development,
    1973. 8 unnumb. pages

Lavrín, Asunción Irigoyen. Bibliography of "Religious Life of
    Mexican Women in the 18th Century." Unpub. Ph.D. disser.
    Harvard University, 1963. pp. 276-92.

Marshall, Judith M. "Studies Relating Women's Non-Familial Activity
    and Fertility." Bibliography Series 1(1972):1-6. Chapel Hill,
    N.C.: Technical Information Service, Carolina Population Center,
    University of North Carolina.

Matos Mar, José and Ravines, Rogger. Bibliografía peruana de
    ciencias sociales (1957-1969). Lima: Campodónico Ediciones,
    1971. Part II: Cultura y Sociedad.

Mota de Ortega, Vivián. "Annotated Bibliography of the CIDAL
    Collection." Cuernavaca, Mex.: CIDHAL, n.d. 27 p.

Mounce, Virginia. "Mexican Women During the Porfiriato, 1877-1911:
    An Essay and Annotated Bibliography." Edinburgh, Tx.: n.d.
    34 p.

Nicolas, Suzanne. Bibliography on Women Workers/Bibliographie sur le
    travail des femmes (1861-1965). International Labour Office,
    Central Library and Documentation Branch, Bibliographical con-
    tributions, no. 26. Geneva: International Labour Office,
    Central Library and Documentation Branch.

North American Congress on Latin America. "Bibliography on Latin America." NACLA's Latin America and Empire Report 3:3(1973): 20-22.

O'Leary, Timothy J. Ethnographic Bibliography of South America. New Haven, Conn.: Human Relations Area Files, 1963.

Olien, Michael D. Appendix A through E of Latin Americans: Contemporary Peoples Their Cultural Traditions. New York: Holt, Rinehart and Winston, 1973. pp. 45-96.

Pedreira, Antonio S. Bibliografía puertorriqueña (1493-1930). Madrid: Imprenta de la Librería y Casa Editorial Hernando, 1932.

Pescatello, Ann, ed. "Bibliography." In Female and Male in Latin America: Essays. Pittsburgh, Pa.: University of Pittsburgh Press, 1973. pp. 293-334.

_____. "The Female in Ibero-America: An Essay on Research Bibliography and Research Directions." Latin American Research Review 7:2(1972):125-41.

Posada, Eduardo. Bibliografía bogotana. Bogota: Imprenta Nacional. vol. II

Sable, Martin H. A Guide to Latin American Studies. Reference Series no. 4. Los Angeles, Ca.: University of California, Latin American Center, 1967. 2 vols.

Uribe de Fernández de Córdoba, Susana. "Bibliografía histórica mexicana." Historia Mexicana 8(1958-59):557-600.

UNICEF. "Bibliography on Women." Santiago: UNICEF, n.d. 3 p.

Valdés, Nelson P. "A Bibliography of Cuban Women in the Twentieth Century." Cuban Studies Newsletter/ Boletín de Estudios sobre Cuba 4:2(1974):1-31.

Vivó, Paquita. The Puerto Ricans: An Annotated Bibliography. New York: R.R. Bowker and Co., 1973.

Wilgus, A. Curtis. Latin America in the Nineteenth Century. A Selected Bibliography of Books of Travel and Description Published in English. Metuchen, N.J.: Scarecrow Press, 1973.

Serial Abstracts, Guides, and Indexes

Abstracts in Anthropology: 1-5 (1970-74)
Advanced Bibliography of Contents: 1969-1972
Dissertation Abstracts International (formerly Dissertation Abstracts): 12-35 (1952-74)

Economic Abstracts: 1-21 (1953-74)
Education Index: 1-46 (1929-74)
Handbook of Latin American Studies: 1-36 (1936-74)
Historical Abstracts: 1-20 (1955-74)
Index to Latin American Periodical Literature: 1-8 (1929-60); 1st
    supplement, 1-2 (1961-65)
Indice General de Publicaciones Periódicas Latinoamericanas: 1-10
    (1961-70)
International Bibliography of the Social Sciences: Sociology, 5-23
    (1955-73); Political Science, 1-21 (1953-72); Economics, 1-22
    (1955-73)
International Bibliography on Crime and Delinquency: 1-8 (1963-72)
    (becomes Crime and Delinquency Abstracts)
International Political Science Abstracts: 1-20 (1951-74)
Journal of Economic Abstracts: 1-6 (1963-68)
Master's Abstracts: 1-11 (1962-73)
P.A.I.S.: 38-61 (1952-75)
Psychological Abstracts: 1-52 (1927-74)
Reader's Guide to Periodical Literature: 1-74 (1890-75)
Social Sciences Citation Index: 1973-74
Sociological Abstracts: 1-22 (1952-74)
Women Studies Abstracts: 1-3 (1972-74)
World Agricultural Economics and Rural Sociology Abstracts: 1-6
    (1959-74)

Periodicals

Acción Social. (La Caja de Seguro Obligatorio. Santiago) nos.
    90-141 (1940-1949)
América Indígena. vols. 1-34 (1941-1974)
Américas (OAS, Washington, D.C.) vols. 1-27 (1949-1974)
The Americas. (American Franciscan Society, Washington, D.C.)
    vols. 1-31 (1944-1974)
American Anthropologist. vols. 1-76 (1899-1974)
American Journal of Sociology. vols. 1-80 (1895-1974)
American Sociological Review. vols. 1-39 (1936-1974)
Anales de la Academia de la Historia de Cuba. vols. 1-30 (1919-1948)
Anthropological Quarterly. vols. 1-47 (1928-1974)
Antropológica. (Sociedad de Ciencias Naturales La Salle. Caracas).
    nos. 1-15, 25-32 (1958-1973)
Anuario de Estudios Americanos. (Escuela de Estudios Hispanoamericanos.
    Universidad de Sevilla. Seville) vols. 1-29 (1944-1972)
Anuario Indigenista. vols. 22-34 (1962-1974)
Boletín Cultural y Bibliográfico. (Banco de la República. Bogota)
    1958-1973
Boletín de Historia y Antiguedades. (Academia Colombiana de la
    Historia. Bogota.) vols. 1-58 (1902-1971)

Boletín de la Academia Chilena de la Historia. (Santiago)
    nos. 1-81 (1939-1969)
Boletín de la Academia de Historia del Valle del Cauca. (Cali)
    nos. 1-142, 150-155 (1932-1970)
Boletín de la Academia Nacional de la Historia. (Buenos Aires)
    vols. 1-45 (1924-1972)
Boletín de la Academia Nacional de la Historia. (Caracas) vols.
    1-56 (1912-1973)
Boletín de la Academia Nacional de la Historia. (Quito) vols. 21-52,
    56-57 (1941-1973)
Boletín de la Academia Panameña de la Historia. nos. 1-20 (1933-1939)
Boletín de la Academia Puertorriqueña de la Historia. vols. 1-3
    (1968-1973)
Boletín del Centro de Investigaciones Históricas. (Guayaquil).
    vols. 1-8, 21-28 (- 1958)
Boletín Histórico. (Fundación John Boulton. Caracas) nos. 1-21,
    25-36 (1962-1974)
Boletín Indigenista. vols. 1-21 (1941-1961)
Casa de las Americas. nos. 1-81 (1960-1973)
Clío. (Academia Dominicana de la Historia. Santo Domingo) vols.
    3-30, 33, 36, 39-41 (1935-1973)
Cuadernos Americanos. vols. 1-197 (1942-1974)
Cuadernos de Historia y Arqueología. (La Casa de la Cultura
    Ecuatoriana. Núcleo del Guayas. Guayaquil) nos. 1-33
    (1951-1967)
Current Anthropology. vols. 11-15 (1960-1974)
Demography. vols. 1-11 (1964-1974)
Estudios Andinos. vols. 1-3 (1970-1973)
Ethnology. vols. 1-13 (1962-1974)
Eugenics Quarterly (Social Biology). (1-21) 1954-1974
Guatemala Indígena. vols. 1-7 (1961-1972)
Hispanic American Historical Review. vols. 1-53 (1918-1973)
Historia. (Buenos Aires). 1-49 (1955-1967)
Educación. (Universidad Nacional Mayor de San Marcos. Organo de
    Facultad de Educación. Lima) 1-29 (1946-1966)
Educación. (Revista de orientación pedagógica. Organo del Consejo
    Nacional Técnico de la Educación. Secretaría de Educación
    Pública. Mexico) 1-6 (1959-1961)
Educación. (Pan American Union. Washington, D.C.) 1-14 (1956-1970)
Educación. (La revista del maestro peruano. Ministerio de
    Educacion Publica. Lima) 1-12 (1970-1974)
Educación. (Revista para el magisterio. Ministerio de Educación
    Nacional. Caracas) 40-132 (1945-1969)
Educación. (Departamento de Instrucción Pública. Puerto Rico)
    9-33 (1963-1971)
Educación Hoy. (Perspectivas Latinoamericanas. Revista de la
    Asociación de Publicaciones Educativas del Departamento de
    Educación de CELAM, CLAR, and CIEC. Bogota). 1-24 (1971-1974)
Educación Nacional. (Revista mensual. Secretaría de Educación
    Pública. Mexico) 1-3 (1944-1946)

Educación y Ciencias Humanas. (Universidad Nacional Federico
    Villarreal. Facultad de Educación y Ciencias Humanas. Lima)
    1-3 (1963-1965)
Historia Mexicana. vols. 1-24 (1951-1974)
Iberoamericana. nos. 1-45 (1932-1963)
International Congress of Americanists.
Journal of Interamerican Studies and World Affairs. 1-16 (1959-1974)
Journal of Marriage and the Family. vols. 1-36 (1939-1974)
Latin American Research Review. vols. 1-9 (1965-1974)
El Maestro. (Revista de orientación pedagógica. Ministerio de
    Educación. Guatemala) 14-22 (1968-1972)
El Maestro. (Secretaría de Educación Pública. Dirección General de
    Divulgación. Mexico.) 1-24 (1969-1970)
Milbank Memorial Fund Quarterly. 1-52 (1923-74)
Nicaragua Indígena. 1-47 (1946-1969)
Nueva Educación. (Tribuna de los jóvenes educadores del Peru. Lima)
    1-48 (1945-1969)
Pan-American Union Bulletin. 1-82 (1893-1948)
Population Studies. vols. 1-28 (1947-1974)
Practical Anthropology. vols. 1-19 (1953-1972); becomes Missiology
    vols. 1-2 (1973-1974)
Previsión Social. (Boletín del Ministerio de Previsión Social,
    Trabajo, Agricultura e Industrias. Quito) nos. 1-20 (1936-1947)
Publicaciones de la Academia Dominicana de la Historia. vols. 1-27
    (1955-1970)
Repertorio Boyacense. nos. 155-182, 203-218 (1950-1961)
Revista Chilena de Historia y Geografía. vols. 1-92, 101-136
    (1911-1968)
Revista Colombiana de Antropología. vols. 1-16 (1953-1974)
Revista de Indias. vols. 1-31 (1940-1971)
Revista de la Academia de Geografía e Historia de Nicaragua.
    vols. 1-7 (1936-1945)
Revista de Educación. (Ministerio de Educación Pública de Chile.
    Santiago) 1-7 (1928-1929); 1-47 (1941-1974)
Revista de Educación. (Ministerio de Educación de la Provincia de
    Buenos Aires. La Plata) 1-24 (1956-1969)
Revista de Servicio Social. (Colegio de Trabajadores Sociales de
    Puerto Rico. Santurce) vols. 5-12, 19-22 (1944-1961)
Revista del Instituto Histórico y Geográfico del Uruguay. vols. 1-24
    (1921-1958)
Revista Histórica. (Instituto Histórico. Lima). vols. 1-29
    (1906-1966)
Revista Interamericana de Bibliografía. vols. 1-23 (1951-1973)
Revista Interamericana de Psicología. vols. 1-8 (1967-1974)
Revista Latinoamericana de Psicología. vols. 1-6 (1969-1974)
Revista Javeriana. vols. 33-80 (1956-1973)
Revista Mexicana de Sociología. vols. 1-36 (1939-1974)
Servicio Social. (Escuela de Servicio Social del Museo Social
    Argentino. Buenos Aires). vols. 2-8 (1938-1944)
Servicio Social. (Escuela de Servicio Social del Perú. Lima).
    vols. 5-17 (1947-1964)

Servicio Social. (Santiago) vols. 24-39 (1950-1966)
Social Forces. vols. 1-53 (1922-1974)
Sociological Quarterly. vols. 1-16 (1960-1974)
Sociology and Social Research. vols. 1-59 (1916-1974)
Southwestern Journal of Anthropology. (becomes Journal of Anthro-
    pological Research). 1946-1974
Studies in Family Planning. 31-60 (1968-1970); vols. 205 (1971-1974)
Universidad. (Santa Fe, Arg.) vols. 1-76 (1935-1968)
Universidad de Antioquia. nos. 1-171, 184 (1935-1972)
Universidad Pontificia Bolivariana. vols. 1-31 (1937-1970)
Universitas. (Bogota). nos. 1-19 (1951-1960)

Libraries Consulted

United States

Stanford University

University of California: Berkeley, Davis, Los Angeles; Bancroft Library

University of Texas, Austin (Latin American Collection)

Tulane University (Latin American Collection Printed Catalogue)

New York Public Library

Library of Congress

Latin America

Buenos Aires, Argentina
    Biblioteca Nacional
    Biblioteca de la Facultad de Filosofía y Letras de la Universidad
    Nacional de Buenos Aires

La Paz, Bolivia
    Biblioteca Municipal Andrés de Santa Cruz
    Biblioteca Universitaria de la Universidad Mayor de San Andrés

Bogota, Colombia
    Biblioteca de la Universidad Nacional de Colombia
    Biblioteca de la Universidad de los Andes

Cuernavaca, Mexico
    Biblioteca de CIDHAL

Lima, Peru
    Biblioteca de CEPD
    Biblioteca de la Universidad Católica del Perú
    Library of the Ford Foundation

Caracas, Venezuela
    Biblioteca de la Facultad de Sociología de la Universidad
    Central

Women in Spanish America:
An Annotated Bibliography

BIOGRAPHY AND AUTOBIOGRAPHY

For the category of biography I have followed Library of Congress classification, which states that subject biography which is illustrative of any specific subject and contributes to an understanding of the respective subject field is classed by subject.[1] Therefore, biographies of Independence heroines will be found in HISTORY BEFORE 1900; of educators, in EDUCATION; of writers, in LITERATURE, MASS MEDIA, AND FOLKLORE; of nuns and saints, in MAGIC, RELIGION, AND RITUAL; and so on. Biographies of Sor Juana and la Madre Castillo, although both nuns, are located in LITERATURE, MASS MEDIA, AND FOLKLORE because of their contributions to that field. The memoirs of la Madre Conchita, also a nun, are located in POLITICS AND 20th CENTURY REVOLUTIONARY MOVEMENTS because they were written as a result of the political persecution and imprisonment she suffered. Biographies of Eva Perón are located in POLITICS AND 20th CENTURY REVOLUTIONARY MOVEMENTS. Notes on the wives of viceroys and presidents prior to the 20th century can be found in HISTORY BEFORE 1900; notes on wives of politicians after 1900 can be found in POLITICS AND 20th CENTURY REVOLUTIONARY MOVEMENTS. Biographies of women who participated in the conquest and colonization as well as Republican era of America are located in HISTORY BEFORE 1900. Biographical data on the women in the lives of famous men such as Hostos or O'Higgins are included here (e.g., Los amores de Sarmiento, item 79). This section, then, for the most part, includes collective biographies: notes on women who have contributed to a variety of fields during the history of Spanish America from pre-Conquest to contemporary times. It includes some correspondence and individual biographies of such women as Flora Tristán, French born of a Peruvian father, renowed for her political activities in favor of workers' and women's rights;

---

[1] Richard H. Schimmelpfeng and C. Donald Cook, eds. The Use of the Library of Congress Classification; Proceedings. Chicago: American Library Association, 1968, pp. 22-23.

1

la Quintrala, infamous in the criminal annals of colonial Chile; and
the Nun-Ensign, Catalina de Erauso, Spanish-born adventurer who spent
most of her life in various parts of Spanish America. La Perricholi,
well known actress and lover of Viceroy Amat in 18th century Lima,
can be found in THE ARTS, along with other actresses, dancers, etc.
See other categories for much additional biographical information.
See Hilton's[2] and Kay's[3] works for 20th century figures and various
national biographical dictionaries[4] or *semblanzas* which consider
both men and women.

There is a tendency in the biographical literature, in whichever
section it appears, to be superfluously laudatory and uncritical; or,
at the other extreme, to be overly vituperative and subjective in a
negative way. Biographies of Eva Perón provide a good example of
this problem in references. She is either unabashedly worshipped as
an angel of mercy--the fairy godmother of Argentina--or caustically
invalidated as an untalented actress who schemed her way into political power. Hagiographic accounts tend to dwell on the saintly virtues, ghastly mortifications, or miraculous feats of a nun, *beata*,
or other female religious figure, while leaving much to be desired
in terms of documented facts. Biographies of Manuela Sáenz express
gratitude for her having saved the Liberator's life, while censuring
her passionate or "licentious" nature. Wives of male public figures
are invariably praised as faithful companions, while little is mentioned of their role outside their functions as a wife and mother.
There are, however, several quite readable and well-researched
studies on Sor Juana.

----

[2] Ronald Hilton, ed. Who's Who in Latin America: A Biographical
Dictionary of Notable Living Men and Women in Latin America. 3rd
ed. Stanford, Ca.: Stanford University Press, 1945-51. 7 vols.

[3] Ernest Kay, gen. ed. Dictionary of Latin American and Caribbean
Biography. 2nd ed. London: Melrose Press Ltd., 1971.

[4] For an international bibliography of collective biographies, bio-
bibliographies, dictionaries of anonyms and pseudonyms, historical
and specialized dictionaries, biographical materials in government
manuals, bibliographies of biography, biographical indexes, and
selected portrait catalogs, see Robert Bigney Slocum, Biographical
Dictionaries and Related Works. Detroit, Mich.: Gale Research Co.,
1967; with a supplement in 1972. Almost 2000 pages contain universal
bibliographies, national or area biographies, and biographies by
vocation. See individual countries for their Who's Who and *diccio-
narios biográficos*; e.g., Cesareo Rosa-Nieves and Esther M. Melon,
Biografías puertorriqueñas: perfil histórico de un pueblo. Puerto
Rico: realidad y anhelo, 12. Sharon, Conn.: Troutman Press, 1970
or 71. It contains more than 300 biographical sketches of notable
Puerto Rican men and women.

[5] See also Biography Index, beginning with volume 1 in 1946; it lists
published materials on individuals such as Gabriela Mistral.

2

SPANISH AMERICA - GENERAL

1 ARCINIEGAS, GERMÁN
    1961 América mágica. II. Las mujeres y las horas.
    Buenos Aires: Edit. Sudamericana. 255 p. plates,
    ports.
       In chronological order presents chatty sketches of
    notable women in Latin American history and literature:
    Inés de Suárez, Sor Juana Inés de la Cruz, la Perricholi,
    Policarpa Salavarrieta, Manuela Sáenz, Flora Tristán,
    Marietta de Veintemilla, Eliza Lynch, Laura Montoya,
    Gabriela Mistral, and *las Juanas* (*soldaderas* of 19c.
    Colombian civil wars who cooked and performed rudimen-
    tary first aid for and had other relations with soldiers).

1a D'ALESIO de CARNEVALE BONINO, ROSA C.
    1968 "La mujer y la farmacia en el mundo." SEHF/B
    19:73:25-29.
       According to Historical Abstracts 19A (1973):376,
    "reports on the first women pharmacists in various
    countries of the world, including Spain and the Latin
    American nations, in the 19th and 20th centuries."

2 D'AUVERGNE, EDMUND BASIL FRANCIS
    1927? "The Nun Ensign (Catalina de Erauso)." In his
    Adventuresses and Adventurous Ladies, pp. 15-44.
    New York: J. H. Sears and Co. port.
       Combines what is supposedly Catalina's version of her
    life with statements by her contemporaries to authen-
    ticate her existence. Agrees with Ferrer that her auto-
    biography is apocryphal and may be a literary piece
    written by someone else. Does not agree with N. León
    that she was a physiological freak; she was merely ill-
    suited to fulfill roles open to women during 16c. and
    17c. No bibliography.

3 ERAUSO, CATALINA de
    1959 Historia de la monja Alférez doña Catalina de Erauso
    escrita por ella misma con la última y tercera relación
    en que se hace historia de los últimos años y muerte de
    este personaje. Prologue by J. Berruezo. Col. Ipar, 6.
    Pamplona, Spain: Edit. Gómez. 142 p. port.
       The introduction to this edition of Catalina de
    Erauso's life history makes it the most interesting and
    enlightening to date. Discusses dissenting opinions on
    the validity of the autobiography, various editions, and
    other publications about her. Reproduces documents which
    attest to her existence and offers an explanation of
    discrepancies in dates.

Biography and Autobiography

4   ERAUSO, CATALINA de
      1918 Historia de la Monja Alférez (D.ª Catalina de Erauso).
      Illus. with notes and documents by D. Joaquín M.ª de
      Ferrer. Prologue by D. José María de Heredia. Madrid:
      Tipográfica Renovación. 138 p. f/notes.
         This autobiography of Catalina de Erauso was first
      published by Ferrer in French (Paris, 1820) in the pub-
      lishing house of Julio Didot. Of the many editions pub-
      lished, this is considered to be the most erudite,
      replete with detailed footnotes explaining dates, places
      and persons and proven documentation which validates her
      existence. Her life story reads like a picaresque novel.

5   GONZÁLEZ OBREGÓN, LUIS
      1946 "The Nun Alférez." ML 22:1:25-26, 64.
         Relates various incidents in the life of Catalina de
      Erauso, focusing on episode in which she was charged
      with accompanying a young woman to a convent. Despite
      Catalina's protestations and promises of providing a
      dowry, the young woman marries an hidalgo instead, with
      whom Catalina quarrels and fights. No documentation.

6   JARPA GANA de LASO, SARA
      1960 La Monja Alférez. Santiago: Edit. del Pacífico.
      40 p.
         Brief study traces Catalina de Erauso's life, based on
      her supposed autobiography and several historical
      references.

7   KRESS, DOROTHY M.
      1935 "Catalina de Erauso." MSEP/LP 13:2:84-89.
         Believes Catalina de Erauso was a real personality and
      not a literary creation, comparing and contrasting her
      life of adventures with that of the rogue portrayed in
      picaresque novels. Additional comparisons are made with
      real and fictitious Spanish adventurers of the 17c. and
      18c.

8   LANZAROTTI, JULIO
      1954 "With Her Dagger, Sword, and Harquebus. The Strange
      Tale of Catalina de Erauso." OAS/AM 6:10:9-11, 44-45.
      illus., ports.
         Narrative of a woman who fled convent life in Spain
      and journeyed to America, where she participated in
      military expeditions, moving from one viceroyalty to
      another until circumstances forced her return to Spain;
      but she died in Mexico in 1650 as a mule driver. Does
      not provide documented sources attesting to validity of
      her extraordinary life.

9 LEÓN, NICOLÁS
   1973 Adventuras de la Monja Alférez. Col. Metropolitana,
   3. Mex., D.F.: Complejo Edit. Mexicano. 135 p.
   illus., bibl.
       Recapitulation of the life of Cataline de Erauso
   (1592-1650) based on existing biographical narrations
   attributed to her with additional testimony by a *padre*
   and notes on her name, bibliography, psychology, physiology. Speculative data.

10 _____.
       1923 "La Monja Alférez Catalina de Erauso. ¿Cuál será su
   verdadero sexo?" MNAHE/A 2:71-110. illus., facsims.,
   port.
       First cites various publications and documents related
   to Catalina de Erauso and summarizes her life history.
   Then attempts to determine her real sex by analyzing
   psychological details in autobiographical text, her
   portrait, and descriptions of her by other persons.
   Does not provide convincing argument that she was a man
   with abnormal sexuality and that her behavior was natural
   only to a man.

11 ROMERO de VALLE, EMILIA, ed.
       1948 Mujeres de América. Biblioteca Enciclopédica
   popular, 3ª época, 196. Mex., D.F.: Secretaría de
   Educación Pública. 84 p.
       A kind of primer of 33 famous women (educators, writ-
   ers, heroines, singers, nuns, etc.) in LA since colonial
   times--from St. Rose of Lima to Javiera Carrera and
   Clorinda Matto de Turner--by various authors (some
   biographers).

12 ROMERO de VALLE, EMILIA
       1945 "Mujeres famosas de América." Social 14:299:3-6.
       Brief paragraphs on Doña Marina, la Perricholi,
   la Quintrala, Sor Juana, Santa Rosa, Francisca Reyes
   del Palacio.

13 SUÁREZ, JOSÉ BERNARDO
       1878 Plutarco de las jóvenes. Rasgos biográficos de
   mujeres célebres de América; escritos, traducidos i
   estractados para el uso de las jóvenes. 2nd ed.
   Biblioteca de la Juventud. Paris: Librería de
   C. Bouret. 173 p.
       Brief sketches of more than 50 heroines, writers,
   educators, nuns, etc. in Latin American history, intended
   for school age girls.

Biography and Autobiography

14   TAPPEN, KATHLEEN B. and MORRIS, BERENICE T.
         1944 Prominent Women in Latin America. Wash., D.C.:
         Office of the Coordinator of Inter-American Affairs.
         25 p.
            Mimeographed list with biographical data on Latin
         American women painters, educators, journalists, lawyers,
         feminists, etc.

15   TRENTI ROCAMORA, J. LUIS
         1945 Grandes mujeres de América. B.A.: Edit. Huarpes.
         165 p. bibl.
            One of the better collections of vignettes of 11
         Latin American women from the 16c. - 19c., famous as
         heroines in the independence movements, religious fig-
         ures, writers, etc. Also includes section containing
         very brief biographical data on 91 additional note-
         worthy women. Considers all of these women exceptions
         to the rule that woman's exclusive mission in life lies
         in the home. Based on secondary sources.

16   XIMÉNEZ de SANDOVAL, FELIPE
         1951 "Diez mujeres hispánicas." MH 37:31-35. ports.
            Includes brief portraits of Manuelita Sáenz, Sor Juana,
         Santa Rosa, and Doña Marina de Jaramillo. Not espe-
         cially informative.

MIDDLE AMERICA

Mexico

17   ACOSTA, HELIA d'
         1971 Veinte mujeres. Mex., D.F.: Eds. Asociados,
         S. de R. L. 282 p.
            Collection of chatty interviews with 19 Mexican and
         1 Costa Rican women by Mexican journalist originally
         appeared in Impacto, 1969-70: Esther Chapa, champion
         of women's rights for more than 25 years; writers,
         including poets--Rosario Sansores, Victoria Urbano,
         Indiana Nájera, Teresa Tallían, Graciana Alvarez del
         Castillo de Chacón; painter Sofía Bussi; archaeologist
         Eulalia Guzmán; folklorist Amalia Millán; et al.

18   CHUMACERO, ROSALÍA d'
         1961 Perfil y pensamiento de la mujer mexicana. Mex.,
         D.F.: Ed. de la Autora. 2 vols.
            Costa Rican journalist residing in Mexico provides
         biographical sketches of 50 Mexican and 5 Central
         American women--chemists, singers, ambassadors,

WOMEN IN SPANISH AMERICA

Middle America - Mexico

politicians, writers, doctors, etc.--accompanied by
portrait and thoughts of each woman in her own words.

19 COLÓN R., CONSUELO
    1944 Mujeres de México. Mex., D.F.: Imprenta Gallarda.
    316 p. ports.
       Biographical sketches of 30 Mexican women well known
    in education, the arts, and public life.

20 ESCOBEDO, RAQUEL
    1967 Galería de mujeres ilustres. Libro primero. Mex.,
    D.F.: Eds. Mexicanos Unidos. 272 p. illus., ports.,
    bibl.
       Biographical sketches of 25 illustrious women during
    the pre-Cortesian epoch and early 16c.: queens and
    heroines of Mexican tribes and empires; and the first
    Mexican woman historian.

21 FERNÁNDEZ y FERNÁNDEZ, AURORA
    1958 Mujeres que honran a la patria. Mex., D.F. 244 p.
    illus.
       Biographical sketches of women representing different
    states of Mexico: e.g., Leona Vicario (Quintana Roo),
    Rita Cetina Gutiérrez (Yucatán), María Hernández Zarco
    (Chiapas), etc. Also includes sketches of Sor Juana
    and wife of President López Mateos, and political plug
    for López Mateos.

22 FLORES MURO, IGNACIO
    1969 La verdadera Juana Gallo. Mex., D.F.: Edit.
    Progreso. 222 p. illus., plates, bibl.
       Based on interviews with persons who knew her and some
    documentation, offers biographical account of the legen-
    dary Juana Gallo. Born as Angela Ramos in a poor *barrio*
    of Zacatecas, Mexico in 1876, she spent most of her life
    selling *tacos* and *aguas frescas* to support herself and
    her mother. Contrary to her film portrait, she was
    never a revolutionary, *soldadera*, or *coronel* in the
    Revolution of 1910; rather, she defended her religious
    convictions, the Catholic Church and its priests against
    the Carranzistas. She died in 1958.

23 GERSTEL, ALICE RUHLE
    1942 "Mexican Profiles." NBW 21:11:330-32. illus.
       Brief portrait of prominent career women in Mexico,
    their educational background and current activities.

Biography and Autobiography

24 GÓMEZ, MATHILDE
    1942 Cartas biográficas de madres célebres para los niños
    mexicanos en ocasión del día de la madre. Mex., D.F.:
    Eds. de la Secretaría de Educación Pública. 43 p.
    illus., ports.
        Biographical sketches of 5 Mexican women--heroines of
    Independence movement and mothers of famous men; and of
    the mothers of Pasteur, Napoleon et al.

25 HERNÁNDEZ, CARLOS
    1918 Mujeres célebres de México. San Antonio, Tex.:
    Casa Edit. Lozano. 188 p. ports.
        Sketches political, cultural, social or religious
    participation of 35+ women in 4 periods of Mexican
    history: before the Conquest, Spanish rule, wars of
    Independence, and Independence.

26 OTRANTO, duque de
    1958 Familias de México. Mex., D.F.: 981 p. ports.
        Biographical sketches with photographs of 500 women
    from illustrious Mexican families.

27 RODRÍGUEZ RIVERA, VIRGINIA
    1967 Mujeres folkloristas. Estudios de folklore, 3.
    Mex., D.F.: UNAM, Inst. de Investigaciones Estéticas.
    219 p. illus., ports., bibl.
        Collection of biographical, bibliographical and
    technical notes on women folklorists who have researched
    traditional culture in Mexico. Also considers folk-
    lorists of US, Spain, England, Santo Domingo, Panama,
    Puerto Rico and Venezuela.

28 UROZ, ANTONIO
    1972 "La mujer al servicio de México." In his Hombres y
    mujeres de México, pp. 249-72. Mex., D.F.: Edit. Lic.
    A. Uroz. illus., ports., maps.
        Biographical dictionary with several sketches of
    heroines in the Mexican revolutions of 1812 and 1910.
    Elite women as well as soldaderas are included, along
    with President Echeverría's wife and María Lavalle
    Urbina, well-known lawyer, educator and former senator.

29 VALLE-ARIZPE, ARTEMIO de
    1959 La Güera Rodríguez. 8th ed. Biblioteca Mexicana,
    2. Mex., D.F.: Edit. Porrúa. 284 p. port., bibl.
        Biography of María Ignacia Rodríguez de Velasco
    (1778-1850), well-loved upper-class woman who became a
    legend in Mexico City. She was divorced in early years
    of 19c., married 3 times, adored by Humboldt and

Iturbide and denounced to the Inquisition (but she
talked them out of sentencing her). Replete with
unending praise and flattery.

30 WRIGHT de KLEINHAUS, LAUREANA
    1910 Mujeres notables mexicanas. Mex., D.F.: Tipografía
Económica. 546 p. front., illus., ports.
    Biographical sketches of varying lengths on more than
155 women in Mexico of the pre-Conquest, colonial,
Independence and contemporary (1820-1910) periods:
royalty of indigenous groups, nuns, heroines, writers,
teachers, singers, etc.

Guatemala

31 OSBORNE, LILLY de JONGH
    1930 "Prominent Women in Central America." PPP 13:2:48-50.
    Generalized observations on the life of women in CA.
Sketches several prominent Guatemalan women: wife of
Minister to US, socialite, writer, 1st female university
graduate, educator, et al.

Nicaragua

32 ORTEGA de HUEZO, JOSEFA
    1967 "La mujer de ayer y la mujer de hoy." RCPC
86:75-76.
    Very brief biographical sketches of 19c. Nicaraguan
women.

Panama

33 COLLANTE de TAPIA, LOLA
    1964 "Vivimos en el ciclo radiante de la mujer." LNB/L
9:109:22-33. ports.
    Names and includes the portraits of women in 20c.
Panama who have contributed to the nation as educators,
musicians, poets, lawyers, etc.

Women in Spanish America

Biography and Autobiography

SOUTH AMERICA

Venezuela

34 OLLER de MULFORD, JUANA
    1963 "Valores femeninos panameños: Dra. Lidia Gertrudis
    Sogandares." TDM 3:14:10-11.
    Biographical sketch of the first female Panamanian
    doctor.

35 "LAS ARISTEGUIETA."
    1950 VANH/B 33:131:313-18.
    Based on data from personal archive of General
    Clemente Zárraga, provides notes on women and marriage
    in upper-class colonial Venezuelan society. For each
    of 9 daughters (also known as the 9 muses) of Miguel
    Jérez Aristeguieta and Josefa María Blanco y Herrera
    (Venezuelan aristocrats who married in 1752 and later
    supported Independence movement), cites when and whom
    she married, number of children, and participation in
    Venezuelan society and history.

36 COLL, PEDRO EMILIO
    1945 "La novia caraqueña de Sucre." VANH/B 28:109:51-53.
    Does not develop theme of Manuela White as Sucre's
    fiancée, but quotes from her letters (1820's) to her
    father Guillermo. Includes sketchy paragraph about her,
    and people and incidents around her. See also "Cartas
    de mujeres" (#1818).

37 FRANCIA, FELIPE
    1946 "Las Aristeguietas." VANH/B:116:393-96.
    Genealogical table on 11 Aristeguieta women, an im-
    portant family of 18c. and 19c. Caracas society:
    parents, siblings, spouses; where and when born, bap-
    tized, married, died.

38 LECUNA, VICENTE
    1951 "Mariana Camacho." VANH/B 34:136:380-82. port.
    From interview with daughter of Bolívar's older sis-
    ter María Antonia, Mariana Camacho Clemente, in 1915
    (then 92 years old), provides notes on other women of
    the Bolívar family. Some brief biographical data on
    interviewee.

39 _____.
    1946 "Las nueve musas." VANH/B 29:116:386-92. bibl.
    With a brief introduction on society in late 18c.
    Caracas, presents a kind of genealogical portrait of

the women of some of the most distinguished families of
Venezuela: 9 daughters of Aristeguieta Blanco, their 6
cousins of Palacios Blanco and many of their descendents.
(Concepción Palacios was Bolìvar's mother.) Documented.
See also Francia, Felipe (#37).

40 MÉNDEZ M., LEOPOLDO, transcriber
        1962 "Un autógrafo de la señora Dominga Ortiz, esposa del
        General Páez." CRCA 10:51/54:176-77.
            Reproduced and transcribed facsimile of personal letter
        (1822) belonging to Martín Pérez Matos.

Colombia

41 CÁRDENAS ACOSTA, PABLO E.
        1958 "Doña Barbarita Niño y familia Acosta Berbeo."
        REPB 44:196/197:445-51.
            Brief sketch of aristocratic patroness and director
        of the Tunja Hospital, Bárbara Josefa Apolinaria Niño
        Camacho (1794-1868). Reproduces her baptismal and death
        certificates and quotes a secondary source regarding her
        arrest in 1854 when Pedro Neira Acevedo governed the
        province of Tunja. She forsook conventual life of the
        Carmelites and dedicated her life to charity work.

42 MARQUÉZ de LAVERGNE, AURA
        1961 Mi vida en Colombia. Santiago: Edit. Del Pacífico.
        162 p. illus.
            A Chilean woman's account of a 5-year stay in various
        parts of Colombia in the late 1940's. Married to a
        French banker and scornful of lower-class behavior and
        customs, she presents negative impressions of black
        domestic servants and Indian market women which reflect
        little understanding of exploited groups.

43 MELO LANCHEROS, LIVIA STELLA
        1966 Valores femeninos de Colombia. Bogota: Carvajal
        Hnos. 1244 p. ports.
            Extensive who's who of Colombian women since colonial
        times. Three parts are subdivided into fields in which
        the women distinguished themselves: law, architecture,
        literature, civic action, heroism, religion, journalism,
        education, etc. Each biographical sketch focuses on the
        noteworthy activities of the individual woman.

44 ROMERO de NOHRA, FLOR and PACHÓN CASTRO, GLORIA
        1961 Mujeres en Colombia. Bogotá: Edit. Andes. 287 p.
        ports.

Biography and Autobiography

> Biographical sketches of more than 250 Colombian educators, artists, journalists, politicians, lawyers, etc. of the 20c.

Ecuador

45 CARVAJAL, MORAYMA OFYR
     1949 Galería del espíritu: mujeres de mi patria. Quito: Edit. "Fr. Jodoco Ricke." 300 p. ports.
     Biographical sketches of 48 Ecuadorian women, beginning with the Indian Paccha and the mystic Mariana de Jesús. The others are grouped in history, social service, as prose writers, pedagogues, artists, and poets, accompanied by portraits.

46 MOSCOSO DÁVILA, ISABEL
     1969 Abanico de recuerdos. Cuenca, Ecua. 182 p. illus., ports.
     Biographical sketches of 30 upper-class Ecuadorian women born in the 19c. (except for 2 born in 1900 and 1910) accompanied by portraits, with genealogies provided for some. Inclusion appears to be based more on membership in the aristocracy than on individual noteworthy accomplishments. Does not indicate sources.

Peru

47 ARCINIEGA, ROSA
     1948 "Flora Tristán, la precursora." CAM 42:6:190-202.
     Sketches life and works of Flora Tristán (1803-44), precursor of the international worker's movement (or utopian socialism) who strove for women's and workers' rights. Born in France to a Peruvian father and French mother.

48 BARROS, TOBÍAS
     1949 "Los parientes de O'Higgins en el Perú." ACH/B 16:41:5-10.
     Antonia Isabel O'Higgins (b. 1856) was the illegitimate daughter of Demetrio O'Higgins, illegitimate son of Bernardo O'Higgins, who was the illegitimate son of the man who rose through ranks of Intendent of Concepción to Captain General to Governor of Chile and finally to Viceroy of Peru.

49 BERMEJO, VLADIMIRO
1945 "Flora Tristán." UNAR/R 17:22:19-49.
Born in Paris (1803) of a Peruvian father and French
mother, Flora Tristán married an unknown artist when she
was 17, traveled to Peru (1833-34), and died a crusader
in 1844. Apparently based on her Peregrinaciones de una
paria (#56), discusses her family background, early
years in Paris, unsuccessful marriage, impressions of
Peru, activities for the proletariat, experiences with
men, and defense of women.

50 GARCÍA Y GARCÍA, ELVIRA
1924-25 La mujer peruana a través de los siglos; serie
historiada de estudios y observaciones. Lima: Imprenta
Americana. 2 vols. illus., plates, ports.
Extensive compendium of brief biographical sketches
of hundreds of Peruvian heroines, women writers and
poets, benefactors, professionals et al. belonging to
7 historical epochs--from the Tahuantisuyo (Mama-Occllo
in 12c) to early 20c. (Volume 2 is completely dedicated
to contemporary figures.) Also describes women's organizations and educational institutions.

51 MANGIN, WILLIAM
1971 "Autobiographical Notes on a Rural Migrant to Lima,
Peru." Sociologus 21:1:58-76. illus., bibl.
Important contribution to literature on migrants and
squatter settlements, which has generally not focused
on women. Case history of Olimpia Gonzales (born in
Cuzco, 1930), a married woman living in a Lima barriada,
is a composite picture of a typical migration experience.
Based on formal and informal interviews (1958-59),
narrates Olimpia's life in the province, Lima, and the
barriada: family, marriage, work, children's future,
attitudes toward the city and her neighborhood. Lengthy,
descriptive footnotes further explain various subjects
touched upon in text: domestic servants, education,
language, clothing, drunkenness, envy, wife-beating, etc.

52 RECAVARREN de ZIZOLD, CATALINA
1946 La mujer mesiánica, Flora Tristán. Lima: Eds. Hora
del Hombre. 32 p. port.
After a rambling apologetic introduction, presents
Flora Tristán's (1803-44) biography as a synthesis of
2 definitive events: the circumstances of her birth
(illegitimate) and her marriage (which she abandoned).
Includes 15 letters reflective of the woman and how she
thought.

Biography and Autobiography

53 SÁNCHEZ, LUIS ALBERTO
    1961 Una mujer sola contra el mundo. (Flora Tristán, la
    paria). Escritores Latinoamericanos. Lima: Eds. Nuevo
    Mundo. 214 p.
        Novelized biography of Flora Tristán y Moscoso
    (1803-44), born of a Peruvian father and French mother,
    who championed for women's and worker's rights. Purports
    to be based on documentation but there are no reference
    notes or bibliography.

54 SEEGERS, SCOTT
    1950 "Rebeca and the Mummy." OAS/AM 2:1:6-10, 40-41.
    illus.
        Featured as Peru's only female archaeologist and
    director of Lima's National Museum of Archaeology,
    Rebeca Carrión Cachot helped Julio C. Tello to build and
    equip the museum. Traces her activities in this field.

55 TISOC LINDLEY, HILDA
    1971 La agonía social de Flora Tristán y el movimiento
    feminista. Lima. 75 p. bibl.
        Based on an interpretation of Tristán's Peregrinaciones
    de una paria (#56) and secondary sources, attempts to
    present socio-economic causes which subjugate women, with
    Tristán as an example of not allowing cultural barriers,
    which fence off women, to strangle her historical role
    and revolutionary attitude. Suggests that she became a
    precursor in the struggle for women's and workers'
    rights as a result of her agonized personality, due to
    multiple frustrations experienced in her short lifetime.
    Analyzes her ideology of feminism and socialism, uniting
    women and workers in a single movement in International
    Workers' Unions.

56 TRISTÁN y MOSCOSO, FLORA
    1971 Peregrinaciones de una paria. 2nd ed. Trans. by
    Emilia Romero. Lima: Moncloa-Campodonico. 554 p.
        Daughter of Mariano de Tristán y Moscoso, a member of
    a wealthy Peruvian family, and a French woman, traveled
    to South America from France to try to obtain her inheri-
    tance and position in society, neither of which she
    achieved because she could not fully prove her legiti-
    macy. Narrates her trip and impressions of Peru during
    a several months' stay (1833-34): revolution, aristo-
    cratic society of Arequipa, conventual life and nuns'
    customs, slavery, Francisca de Gamarra. First published
    in France, 1838.

Women in Spanish America

Bolivia

57 PAREDES de SALAZAR, ELSSA
    1965 Diccionario biográfico de la mujer boliviana.
    La Paz: Eds. "Isla." 309 p. ports., bibl.
       Provides brief, uneven biographical notes on approxi-
    mately 200 18c., 19c., and 20c. (emphasizing latter)
    Bolivian women writers, educators, benefactors, patriots,
    artists, dancers, professionals and feminists. Some
    sketches lack even birthdate.

Chile

58 AMESTI, LUIS de
    1954 "Notas genealógicas y biográficas. Doña Carmen
    Arriagada de Gutike." ACH/B 22:5:87-90.
       Determines which of 3 Carmen Arriagada's was the
    friend and confidante of German painter Juan Mauricio
    Rugendas, who spent 11 years in Chile (1834-1845).
    Provides genealogical/biographical notes on Carmen
    Arriagada de Gutike and her family.

59 BALBONTÍN MORENO, MANUEL G. and OPAZO MATURANA, GUSTAVO
    1964 Cinco mujeres en la vida de O'Higgins. Santiago:
    Arancibia Hnos. 161 p. illus., bibl.
       Well-researched with primary and secondary sources
    from archives and libraries of Santiago, provides
    genealogical data on the women and the role they played
    in the life of Bernardo O'Higgins: María Isabel
    Riquelme de la Barrera Meza (1759-1839), his mother;
    Rosa Rodríguez Riquelme (1787-1850) and Nieves Puga y
    Riquelme (1790-1868), his sisters; Carlota Eels (1780-
    1803), an English love of his youth; and María de
    Rosario Puga y Vidaurre (1796-1858), his lover and
    mother of his son.

60 DÍAZ MEZA, AURELIO
    1927 "La Quintrala y los augustinos." SCHG/R 54:58:324-
    30.
       Ex-dramatist and journalist defends himself against
    Fray Alfonso Escudero's critical attack on En plena
    colonia, the second part of his work called Leyendas y
    episodios chilenos (1926). Refers especially to those
    passages regarding Catalina Lisperguer and her associa-
    tion with an Augustine cousin, Father Juan Lisperguer,
    who supposedly aided her after she poisoned Ribera,
    Governor of Chile, and la Quintrala's association with
    Augustine sculptor Pedro de Figueroa in the early 17c.
    See documented account by J. Eyzaguirre (#63).

Biography and Autobiography

61   ESCUDERO, ALFONSO
        1927 "Al margen de En plena colonia." SCHG/R 53:57:284-
        96.
           Augustine priest accuses A. Díaz Meza of falsifying
        history and plagiarizing historians in collection of
        Chilean legends and episodes of colonial times, En plena
        colonia (1926). Contends that material on the episode
        involving la Quintrala, the Lisperguer family and
        Augustines in first half of 17c. is inaccurate, providing
        data to dispute it. See Díaz Meza's retort (#60) and
        documented account by J. Eyzaguirre (#63).

62   EYZAGUIRRE, JAIME
        1945 "Correspondencia de D. Demetrio O'Higgins con Doña
        Rosario Puga y Doña Isabel Vidaurre." ACH/B 12:33:34-55.
           Bernardo O'Higgins sired an illegitimate child of
        Rosario Puga y Vidaure, Demetrio, who after losing con-
        tact with his mother for many years, reestablishes
        communication with her in 1846. Her letters are charged
        with emotion, affection, love and much joy at being
        recognized as his mother. Isabel Vidaure, Rosario's
        mother, with whom she was living in Santiago, encourages
        the communication. Correspondence covers 1847 to 1852.

63   _____.
        1945 "La Quintrala en lucha con la iglesia." ACH/B
        12:32:5-16. bibl. f/notes.
           Well-documented clarification of the disputes and
        scandals of la Quintrala, Catalina de los Ríos, with
        Father Venegas, vicar of the valley of La Ligua, where
        she was a property owner, and with the Bishop of Santi-
        ago, Francisco de Salcedo in 1633. La Quintrala is a
        celebrated case of criminal behavior in 17c. Chile.
        Detailed footnotes challenge and discuss controversial
        points.

64   _____.
        1942 "La muerte de Doña Isabel Riquelme." ACH/B 9:23:
        51-54. illus., port.
           Laments lack of homage to Bernardo O'Higgins' mother,
        who died in Lima in 1839 where she was in exile with her
        son. Suggests that her remains and tombstone be brought
        to Chile to occupy a place of honor.

65   HOLMES, OLIVE
        1944 "Women Pathbreakers of Chile." NBW 23:3:68, 85-86.
           Reports on the activities and background of Gabriela
        Mistral, Amanda Labarca, Carlotta Andrée (founder of the
        Society for the Distributor of Home Industry Products),

Alicia Canas (mayor of Providencia), Irma Salas and Graciela Mandujano.

66 KELLER, CARLOS
    1958 "El pintor Rugendas y doña Carmen Arriagada."
    ACH/B 25:59:98-133. illus., port.
       Biographical notes on the German painter Juan
    Mauricio Rugendas who spent many years living and
    traveling in LA in the 19c. and his friendship with
    Chilean Carmen Arriagada de Guticke (a relative of
    O'Higgins), whom he considered his spiritual sister,
    from 1835 to 1851. Essay based principally on Gertrud
    Richert's 1952 monograph on the painter.

67 MIRANDA, MARTA ELBA
    1940 Mujeres chilenas. Santiago: Edit. Nascimento.
    150 p. bibl.
       Brief accounts of outstanding women in Chile from
    Inés de Suarez and 5 others during the colonial period,
    to 9 women during the struggle for independence, 11 of
    the Republican era, and concluding with 9 women of con-
    temporary times; they represent fervent patriots,
    charity workers, writers, a feminist, etc.

68 OPAZO MATURANA, GUSTAVO
    1941 "Los amores de don Diego Portales." ACH/B
    8:19:47-87. illus., port.
       Traces the women who figured in the life of Diego
    Portales (1793-1837), Chilean statesman, beginning with
    his wife Chepita Portales y Larraín who left him a
    widower in 1821, his affairs in Peru which resulted in
    scandal, and his illicit and uncomfortable relationship
    with Constanza Nordenflicht y Cortés, with whom he sired
    3 illegitimate children, until they both died in 1837.
    Provides details on her background and portrays her
    sympathetically and him as somewhat cold and inconsid-
    erate. Quotes correspondence.

69 "Representative Chilean Women."
    1936 PAU/B 70:4:317-21. illus., ports.
       Brief notes on outstanding Chilean women and their
    contributions to education, philanthropy, literature,
    music, etc.

70 VICUÑA MACKENNA, BENJAMÍN
    1950 Los Lisperguer y la Quintrala (doña Catalina de los
    Ríos). 2nd critical ed. by J. Eyzaguirre. Biblioteca
    de Escritores Chilenos. Santiago: Edit. Zig-Zag.
    346 p.

17

Biography and Autobiography

Originally published in 1877, scholarly edition includes ample, detailed footnotes based on new documentation. Recounts legend of heinous acts committed by Catalina de los Ríos y Lisperguer in 17c. Chile. Based on archival research, correspondence, papers from various families and bishop, et al. 80-page appendix of documents.

71   WEEKS, ELSIE
        1940 "Great Chilean Women. I." ANDMO 3:4:174-81.
            Part 1 of a series on women who made valuable contributions to the development of Chile begins with 2 directors of girls' schools in the 1870's whose petition for the admission of women to the University, resulted in the Amunátegui Decree of 1877. Also sketches activities by women during the Independence movement--Luisa Recabarren de Marín, Javiera Carrera, Paula Jara Quemada, Antonia Salas.

72   _____.
        1940 "Great Chilean Women. II. Women in Medicine. Women in Music." ANDMO 3:5:211-18.
            Part 2 of a series on women who made valuable contributions to the development of Chile. Sketches 4 women doctors, 2 of whom were the first to receive medical degrees in Chile (and possibly in SA as well): Eloísa Díaz Inzunza (1886) and Ernestina Pérez Barahona (1887). Briefly mentions 9 women musicians of that period.

73   _____.
        1940 "Great Chilean Women. III. Women in Industry. Women in Law. Women in Art." ANDMO 3:6:293-98.
            Part 3 of a series on women who made valuable contributions to the development of Chile. Very briefly sketches women with their own businesses, the first 2 women to receive a law degree from the University of Chile--Matilde Throup Sepúlveda (1892) and Matilde Brandau (1898); and 2 sculptors.

74   _____.
        1940 "Great Chilean Women. IV. Literary Women." ANDMO 3:7:329-39. ports.
            Part 4 of a series on women who made valuable contributions to Chile. Beginning with Sor García de la Huerta of the colonial period, Luisa Recabarren de Marín of the revolutionary period and her daughter Amelia Solar de Claro, briefly considers Chilean writers Rosario Orrego de Uribe, Gabriela Mistral, Inés Echeverría de Larraín (Iris), Elvira Santa Cruz Ossa, Sarah Hübner de Fresno, Amanda Labarca Hubertson.

Argentina

75 CARNEVALE BENINO, ROSA C. D. de
      1967 "Elida Passo, la primera farmacéutica argentina."
      SEHF/B 18:72:180-84. facsim., bibl.
        Based on documents found in the Archives of the Fac-
      ulty of Medicine (Buenos Aires) and publications at the
      end of the 19c., determines who was first female grad-
      uate in pharmacy in Argentina: Elida Passo, 1885.
      Includes notes about the epoch, her life, and other
      graduates.

76 CARRANZA, ADOLFO P.
      1910 Patricias argentinas. 2nd ed. B.A.: Sociedad
      Patricias Argentinas "Dios y Patria." 176 p. illus.,
      ports.
        Provides minimal biographical data on more than 40
      patriotic and/or aristocratic Argentine women, noting
      also the financial contributions of some to their
      country's liberation movement in 1810, and citing
      similar donations by dozens of other women. Reproduces
      correspondence and other documents.

77 CORDERO, HÉCTOR ADOLFO
      1963 María de los Santos Sayas, carretera y correo del
      viejo Buenos Aires. Buenos Aires: Eds. Delta. 61 p.
      map.
        Brief notes on María de los Santos Sayas de Bengochea
      (1787?-1868), the Argentine woman who succeeded her
      mother and grandmother in transporting persons, goods,
      and mail in an ox-drawn cart between Buenos Aires and
      the Canal of San Fernando during the late 18c. and 19c.
      Relates 2 anecdotes about her and her work, derived from
      secondary sources. Undocumented.

78 DOMÍNGUEZ, MARÍA ALICIA
      1937 Mariquita Sánchez (biografía novelada). Buenos
      Aires: "El Ateneo." 330 p.
        Novelized biography of aristocratic Argentine woman,
      María Sánchez de Mendeville (1786-1868), renowned for
      her intellectual, cultural and philanthropic activities.
      See A. Dellepiane (#2002).

79 FARIÑA NUÑEZ, PORFIRIO
      1935 Los amores de Sarmiento. Eds. Argentinas "Condor."
      Las grandes biografías contemporáneas, 12. Buenos
      Aires: Edit. Tor. 248 p.
        Documented history of the role several women played in
      the life of Domingo Faustino Sarmiento (1811-88). Part 1

Biography and Autobiography

deals with his relationship with Dalmacio Vélez
Sársfield and his daughter Aurelia; part 2 with his wife
Benita Martínez Pastoriza, daughter Faustina, and niece
Sofía Lenoir de Klappenbach. Part 3 analyzes Sarmiento's
attitudes toward women, as revealed in his writings and
letters, and includes more information on his long-
standing friendship with Aurelia Vélez Sársfield.

80 GONZÁLEZ ARRILI, BERNARDO
    1950 Mujeres de nuestra tierra. B.A.: Eds. La Obra.
    143 p. ports., bibl., f/notes.
      Brief sketches of 40 Argentine women: heroines of the
    Independence movement, as well as 19c. and early 20c.
    women poets, educators, artists, journalists, relatives
    of famous public figures, etc.; based on secondary
    sources.

81 MARÍN, RUFINO
    1941 Perfiles de mujer: 21 temperamentos femeninos
    vistos a través de la comprensión rápida, certera y
    elegante de un croniqueur de jerarquía. B.A.: Edit.
    "Amistad." 168 p.
      Mosaic of personal impressions of various contemporary
    women interviewed by journalist. Out of 21 portraits,
    only 12 are of Latin American women, mostly Argentine:
    e.g., Lola Nucífora, painter; Olga Bettino, singer and
    poet.

82 MENDOZA, ANGÉLICA
    1941 "El itinerario de Cecilia Grierson - la primera
    médica argentina." PAU/Bs 65:10:577-80.
      Brief notes on Cecilia Grierson (1859-1934), well
    known for her activities as an educator, as the first
    woman doctor in Argentina (1889), and as the founder of
    several organizations and institutions (e.g., Consejo
    Nacional de Mujeres).

83 PEERS de PERKINS, CARMEN
    1969 Eramos jovenes el siglo y yo. Col. Cómo nos ven.
    Buenos Aires: Edit. Jorge Alvarez. 126 p. illus.,
    ports.
      Memoirs of Carmen Peers de Perkins, Argentine-born, of
    a noble European father and upper-class Argentine
    mother—her childhood and youth spent in Argentina and
    Europe during first quarter of 20c. Includes comments
    on the women on her mother's side of the family and
    social customs—female frivolity as well as cultural
    leadership.

84   SÁNCHEZ de MENDEVILLE, MARÍA
       1952 Cartas de Mariquita Sánchez, biografía de una época.
       Compilation, prologue and notes by C. Vilaseca. B.A.:
       Eds. Peuser. 426 p. ports., fold. plan, bibl.
         Excellent primary source, the epistolary collection
       (covering 1804-1868) of cultured aristocratic Argentine
       woman (1786-1868) admired for her salon in Buenos Aires
       as an intellectual and social center, and for her philan-
       thropic activities as one of the founders of the
       Sociedad de Beneficencia. Footnotes and introduction
       provide overview of her life. Appendix includes repro-
       duction of her diary from 1839-1840. Letters located in
       several private and public archives.

85   SOIZA REILLY, JUAN JOSÉ de
       1924? Mujeres de América. Buenos Aires: Librerías
       Anaconda. 227 p.
         Collection of journalistic fragments about women in
       Argentina (and several from Chile and Brazil), beginning
       with anecdotes about women in the 19c. and continuing
       with many 20c. writers, artists, singers, educators,
       actresses, etc., using their verses or their letters to
       author: for example, "habla la doctora Cecilia Grierson,"
       or "hablan las mujeres deportistas."

86   SOSA de NEWTON, LILY
       1972 Diccionario biográfico de mujeres argentinas. Col.
       "Diccionarios Biográficos Argentinos." B.A.: the
       author. 414 p. bibl.
         Brief biographical sketches of hundreds of Argentine
       women writers, artists, educators, philanthropists,
       heroines, etc.; emphasis on 19c. and 20c.

Uruguay

87   CARREL, JOSÉ
       1970 Hilda, protesta contra una madre. Montevideo:
       Tierra Nueva. 161 p. bibl.
         A very poor Uruguayan woman narrates her life of pri-
       vation, punishment, and lack of warmth, kindness and
       affection. Born in Montevideo in 1920, but abandoned
       soon after, she was shunted between orphanages and fam-
       ilies and she also led the life of a street urchin,
       dressed as a boy. At 13 she married and proceeded to
       have many children, all of whom she loved and never
       abandoned. Reproaches her own mother for leaving her.
       Emotional account of hardship illustrates dehumanizing
       and cruel treatment of disadvantaged members of society.

Biography and Autobiography

88 MORATORIO, ARSINOE
     1946 Mujeres del Uruguay. Montevideo: Edit.
     Independencia. 123 p. bibl.
        Personal and uncritical impressions, with some bio-
     graphical data, of 29 Uruguayan woman poets, educators,
     artists, musicians, and other professionals of 19c. and
     20c. Based in part on interviews.

CARIBBEAN

Puerto Rico

89 BOSCH, JUAN
     1939 Mujeres en la vida de Hostos, conferencia. 2nd ed.
     San Juan, P.R.: Asoc. de Mujeres Graduadas de la Univ.
     de P.R. 52 p.
        In celebration of the 100th anniversary of birth of
     Eugenio María de Hostos y Bonilla (1839-1903)--Puerto
     Rican educator, social philosopher, and promoter of Pan
     Americanism who won for Chilean women the right to uni-
     versity education and professional training in law and
     medicine--discusses the influence of women (mother,
     sister, aunt, lovers, etc.) in his life.

90 CARRERAS, CARLOS N.
     1961 Hombres y mujeres de Puerto Rico. Mex., D.F.:
     Edit. Orión. 256p. ports.
        Includes 4 biographical sketches of famous Puerto
     Rican women: Lola Rodríguez de Tío (1843-1924)--her
     devotion to the home, poetry and political involvement;
     Pilar Defillo Amiguet de Casals (1853-1931)--mother of
     world-renowned Pablo Casals, violincellist, composer and
     director; Rosario Andraca de Timothée (1873-1946)--edu-
     cator; and María Cadilla de Martínez (1886-1951)--educa-
     tor, poet, essayist, historian and painter. No
     references.

91 NEGRÓN MUÑOZ, ANGELA
     1935 Mujeres de Puerto Rico, desde el período de
     colonización hasta el primer tercio del siglo XX. San
     Juan, P.R.: Imprenta Venezuela. 266 p. ports., bibl.,
     f/notes.
        Briefly sketches more than 100 women who have collab-
     orated in the civic, social and cultural life of Puerto
     Rico since Indian women helped the Spaniards in the 16c.
     Includes founder of the first religious institution for
     women (1646), philanthropists, educators, writers,

suffragists, participants in the Revolution of Lares
(1868), etc. Useful index.

92   No Entry

Cuba

93   ESTÉNGER, RAFAEL
      1953 Amores de cubanos famosos. Col. "Más Allá," 103.
      Madrid: Afrodisio Aguado. 195 p.
         A dozen lively journalistic anecdotes, which are not
      passed off as historically factual accounts, of various
      and sundry romances experienced by well-known Cubans in
      19c. One recounts the story of the relationship between
      2 women, one of whom pretended to be a male doctor.

94   FIGAROLA CANEDA, DOMINGO
      1928 La Condesa de Merlín (María de la Merced Santa Cruz
      y Montalvo): estudio bibliográfico e iconográfico.
      Paris: Eds. Excelsior. 391 p. illus., plates, music,
      ports., facsims., fold. geneal. table, coat of arms.
         According to the Hispanic American Historical Review
      13:2 (1933):222-23 this is a thorough work on the bio-
      graphical and literary work of the Cuban-born Countess
      of Merlín (1789-1852) by a noted Cuban historian who
      once headed the National Library in Havana. She spent
      most of her life in Europe, particularly Paris, but de-
      rived much pleasure from that which was Cuban, on which
      she published at least 2 books. However, because she
      wrote second-hand information and in an inaccurate roman-
      tic style, her works displeased many Cubans.

95   GARCÍA ALONSO, AIDA
      1968 Manuela la mexicana. Col. Premio. Havana: Casa de
      las Américas. 444 p. graphs, bibl.
         Biographical monograph of Manuela Azcanio Alias (born
      in 1890 in Tabasco, Mexico) who lived for 31 years in
      the Havana barrio of Las Yaguas which was eradicated in
      the 1960's. Uses her history as a vehicle to reflect
      daily life of marginal population.

96   LARA MENA, MARÍA JULIA de
      1964 Laura Martínez de Carvajal y del Camino. (Primera
      graduada de medicina en Cuba). Cuadernos de Historia de
      la Salud Pública, 28. Havana: Ministerio de Salud
      Pública. 120 p. illus., ports., bibl.

Biography and Autobiography

> Biography in commemoration of the 75th anniversary of first Cuban woman's graduation in medicine from University of Havana (1899). Based on data collected from her daughters and other individuals, some documents, and secondary sources, considers her family life, friendships, education, marriage, professional career, etc. to understand why and how she became the first Cuban woman doctor to practice.

97 MARTÍNEZ GUAYANES, MARÍA ANUNCIA
    1955 Efigies femeninas en los sellos de Cuba. El
    Centenario del primer sello postal, 1855-1955. Havana.
    108 p. illus., bibl. notes.
       Includes brief sketches of women who have appeared on Cuban postage stamps--La Avellaneda, Marta Abreu, María Luisa Dolz--known for their contributions to poetry, education, philanthropy, patriotism.

98 MERLÍN, MARÍA de las MERCEDES SANTA CRUZ y MONTALVO, COMTESSE de
    1922 Mis doce primeros años e Historia de Sor Inés.
    Havana: Imprenta "El Siglo XX." 249 p. port.
       Charming account of first 12 years of the life of Countess of Merlín (1789-1852) written in retrospect from Europe. Provides an interesting though limited view of upper-class society, convent life, education of girls, and the plight of slaves in late 18c. Cuba. Part 2 claims to be the story of 2 upper-class girls who meet in a convent: one condemned to unhappiness, the other to joy. Interesting for what it reveals about possibilities for women in late 18c. and early 19c. Cuba: to marry a man one didn't like or to enter a convent. Reflects on the torment of emotions, hardships of the nunnery, strain on male-female relationships, unexplained female illnesses. Originally written in French and published in Paris, 1831 and 1832; also known as Memorias de una criolla.

Dominican Republic

99 STENGRE, CARMEN
    1943 Mujeres dominicanas (semblanzas). Santiago, D.R.:
    Edit. El Diario. 157 p. plate, port.
       Brief, uninformative, personal impressions of 26 women in 20c. Dominican Republic lack even minimal biographical data.

THE ARTS

This section considers women acclaimed as painters, sculptors, singers, actresses, musicians, dancers and other artists. Publications on la Perricholi, Lima's well known actress of the 18th century, are included here even though she is also remembered for her historical relationship with Viceroy Amat. See BIOGRAPHY AND AUTOBIOGRAPHY for additional notes on women cited in collective biographical works.

This section also includes entries on Fashion and Native Costume, which considers female clothing and adornments (hair style, body painting, jewelry, etc.) as well as weaving. Costumes, almost invariably the product of women's technical and artistic skill in weaving, sewing, and embroidery, are viewed here as an art form. Well-illustrated publications on this aspect of a group's material culture afford a different kind of source. As a visual aid, they may indicate sex differences, stratification among groups or within a group, values, and esthetic appreciation. For much additional information on women's costumes and crafts, see ETHNOGRAPHIC MONOGRAPHS/COMMUNITY STUDIES.

SPANISH AMERICA - GENERAL

100 GARCÍA CISNEROS, FLORENCIO
     1970 Maternity in Pre-Columbian Art. La maternidad en
           el arte precolombiano. Photography by R. Llerena.
           N.Y.: Cisneros Gallery of N.Y. 147 p. illus, plates.
           English and Spanish texts introduce 96 plates depict-
           ing motherhood in ceramic and terracotta figures from
           the pre-Columbian cultures of Meso-America, Ecuador and
           Peru.

101 HUBERMAN, BETTY
     1969 "Las realizaciones de la mujer en las artes
           plásticas." UNC/R 10:1/2:395-410.
           University lecture very briefly describes 19 Latin
           American women artists, the periods they belong to, and
           the reaction to request for information on female artists
           in various Latin American countries.

The Arts

MIDDLE AMERICA

<u>Mexico</u>

102   ARENAL, ROSE B.
        1962 "Lady Artists in Mexico." <u>OAS/AM</u> 14:8:24-29. illus.
           Brief history of the development of art in Mexico and
        the emergence of Mexican women as artists, 9 of which
        are featured along with their art.

103   CARRASCO PUENTE, RAFAEL
        1969 <u>Antolobibliografía del rebozo mexicano</u>. Puebla,
        Mex.: Eds. del Centro de Estudios Históricos de Puebla.
        243 p. illus.
           Anthology of selected texts and annotated bibliography
        of 127 items which deal with the *rebozo*, a typical arti-
        cle of clothing used by Mexican women since pre-Conquest
        days.

104   _____.
        1961 "Indumentaria mexicana. (Fichas hemero-
        bibliográficas)." Suplemento del <u>BSHCP/B</u> 223:1-6.
        illus.
           Useful, partially annotated guide to over 200 pub-
        lished items on the origin and use of typical Mexican
        clothing and adornment--*el rebozo*, *la china poblana*, *el
        huipil*--located in Mexico City libraries and archives.

105   _____.
        1950 <u>Bibliografía de Catarina de San Juan y de la China</u>
        <u>Poblana</u>. Monografías Bibliográficas Mexicanas,
        Serie 2, no. 3. Mex., D.F.: Secretaría de Relaciones
        Exteriores, Depto. de Información para el Extranjero.
        149 p. illus., plates.
           Beautifully illustrated and amply annotated bibliog-
        raphy on traditional and typical *china poblana*, whose
        figure originated with Catarina de San Juan, who died
        in Puebla in 1688. 151 items refer to poetry, histor-
        ical studies, newspaper and periodical articles, monu-
        ments, travel accounts, illustrations, etc., located in
        libraries in Mexico and Spain. Quotes extensively from
        works cited.

106   CARRILLO y GARIEL, ABELARDO
        1959 <u>El traje en la Nueva España</u>. Dirección de Monumentos
        Coloniales, Publicaciones, 7. Mex., D.F.: Instituto de
        Antropología e Historia. 207 p. illus., ports.
           Traces history of clothing, hairstyles, and adornments
        in New Spain from 16c. to 18c. in their relationship to

colonial Mexican society. Scattered references to women
of all classes and occupations. Appears to be based on
primary sources and archival research but lacks
bibliography.

107 CASTELLO YTURBIDE, TERESA, et al.
1971 "El rebozo." ARMEX 18:142:3-96. illus., plates,
bibl.
Very beautifully illustrated issue depicts ubiquitous
garment, characteristically *mestiza*, worn by Mexican
women--the *rebozo* or shawl. Accompanying commentaries
discuss its origins, appearance in literature, weaving
techniques, and silk industry. Useful also for depic-
tion of women in all kinds of activities since 16c.
Some French and English translations.

108 CASTELLO YTURBIDE, TERESA and MAPELLI MOZO, CARLOTTA
1965-68 El traje indígena en México. Mex., D.F.: Inst.
Nacional de Antropología e Historia. 2 vols. illus.,
clr. plates.
Beautifully illustrated description of traditional
clothing of indo-colonial origin presently worn by indigenous groups throughout Mexico; volume 2 deals specifically with the Nahua and Maya groups. Includes comments
on women's handicraft, English and Spanish texts, 60
color plates, 90 sheets of embroidery, weaving and
clothing designs and illustrations of jewelry.

109 CORDRY, DONALD BUSH and CORDRY, DOROTHY M.
1968 Mexican Indian Costumes. Tex. Pan American Series.
Austin: Univ. of Tex. Press. 373 p. illus., map,
plates, bibl.
Approximately 300 illustrations accompany much information on indigenous women of Mexico through their costume
and weaving. Part 1 discusses pre-Hispanic and contemporary costume, specific women's clothing and accessories,
loom and its processes, weaving beliefs. Part 2 covers
native costumes from Sonora to Chiapas. Based on fieldwork, primary and secondary texts.

110 _____.
1941 Costumes and Weaving of the Zoque Indians of
Chiapas, Mexico. Southwest Museum Papers, no. 15.
Los Angeles. 130 p. illus., plates, map, bibl.
Based on field research in state of Chiapas (1940),
includes data and illustrations on Zoque women weavers
and women's costume, with additional notes on family
life, legends and beliefs, historical background,
disease, etc.

The Arts

111　CORDRY, DONALD BUSH and CORDRY, DOROTHY M.
1940　<u>Costumes and Textiles of the Aztec Indians of the</u>
<u>Cuetzalán Region, Puebla, Mexico</u>. Southwest Museum
Papers, no. 14. Los Angeles. 60 p. illus., plates.
Dedicates half of monograph to women's costume (gar-
ments, ornaments, footwear, baskets, bags) and includes
data on their weaving. Based on research in state of
Puebla.

112　DESMOND, ALICE CURTIS
1930　"Señoritas of Mañana Land." <u>Mentor</u> 18:2:32-35, 69.
illus.
American visitor describes clothing and social customs
of women in different classes in South America. In some
cases, briefly notes their education and views on
fidelity.

113　DU SOLIER, WILFRID
1950　<u>Ancient Mexican Costume</u>. Trans. by W. Du Solier and
J. G. Roberts. Mex., D.F.: Eds. Mexicanas. 99 p.
illus., plates, bibl.
Includes section on female apparel, based on Sahagún's
writings and the Vindobonensis codex. 14 illustrations
depict noble women, priestesses et al. Each costume is
described. Notes "very little factual basis for study
on the apparel worn by women in pre-Hispanic times."

114　LUNA ARROYO, ANTONIO
1959　<u>Ana Mérida en la historia de la danza mexicana</u>
<u>moderna</u>. Publicaciones de Danza Moderna. Mex., D.F.:
Imprenta Técnica Gráfica. 341 p. illus., ports., bibl.
Biography of Mexico's leading exponent of modern dance
(born 1924) includes documents of her work, reprints of
programs, etc.

115　MARÍA y CAMPOS, ARMANDO de
1944　<u>Angela Peralta, el ruiseñor mexicano</u>. Vidas
mexicanas, 15. Mex., D.F.: Eds. "Xochitl." 185 p.
plates, ports., facsim., bibl. f/notes.
Based on primary and secondary sources, traces the life
and successful career in Europe and Mexico of the "Mexican nightingale," from her humble birth in 1845 to her
death in 1883. Also discusses her talent as a composer.

116　MONTOYA, MARÍA TERESA
1956　<u>El teatro en mi vida</u>. Mex., D.F.: Eds. Botas,
365 p. illus., ports.
Chatty memoirs of María Teresa Montoya demonstrate much
enthusiasm for her 40-year career in Mexican theatre.

Middle America - Mexico

117 PULIDO, ESPERANZA
1958 La mujer mexicana en la música (hasta la tercera
década del siglo XX). Ed. de la Revista Bellas Artes,
7. Mex., D.F.: Ed. de la Revista Bellas Artes. 126 p.
illus.
Traces participation of Mexican women in music (including dances) from the pre-Hispanic epoch, through
colonial and Independence days; and includes famous
female musicians of the 20c.

118 _____.
1956 "La mujer mexicana en la música." FL 30:61/62/63:
119-33.
Briefly recounts the participation of Mexican women in
the field of music since pre-Cortesian times. Remarks
that Aztec and Mayan women were never depicted as musicians and that during colonial times girls began to
receive some instruction in music; describes several
institutions where this was possible. Names 20c. women
pianists, violinists, musicologists, composers, etc.

119 RIVAS, GUILLERMO
1963 "New Names in Mexican Art." ML 39:2:30-32. illus.
Reviews works by 3 new painters, 2 of them women—
Pilar Sánchez Cast and Julia López—with pictures of
their work.

120 _____.
1963 "Women in Mexican Art." ML 39:1:30-32. illus.
A few paragraphs on Mexican women painters in this
century with 7 photographs of their work.

121 VILLAURRUTIA, JAVIER
1932 "María Izquierdo." MF 7:3:138-42. illus.
Critical review of Mexican painter María Izquierdo,
with 2 examples of her work.

122 WIESSE, MARÍA
1944 "María Izquierdo: color y fragancia de México."
HH 2:14:16-17. illus.
Brief notes on exhibit of Mexican painter's works in
Lima and interview with her. Includes illustrations of
3 of her paintings, all of women, photograph of painter,
and discourse given at banquet for her.

The Arts

Guatemala

123   BOGGS, STANLEY H.
      1973 "Pre-Maya Costumes and Coiffures." OAS/AM
      25:2:19-24. illus.
         See EL SALVADOR for annotation.

124   ORTIZ MALDONADO, JOSÉ PATRICIO
      1972 "El traje en una comunidad indígena: telar, tejido
      y algunas motivaciones psico-sociales acerca de la
      conducta del indígena." GIIN/GI 7:1/2:161-226. illus.
         Based on field research (1970-71), describes native
      costume worn in San Ildefonso Ixtahuacán in department
      of Huehuetenango, Guatemala, where every item is manu-
      factured by women. Describes male and female outfits
      and relates them to social categories. Notes changes
      over the centuries as well as variations according to
      climate. Weaving is a source of pride for women, who
      occupy an inferior position to Indian men and Ladino
      women.

125   OSBORNE, LILLY de JONGH
      1965 Indian Crafts of Guatemala and El Salvador.
      Norman, Okla.: Univ. of Okla. Press. 278 p. illus.,
      plates, bibl.
         Includes much information on textiles and weaving, in
      which Indian women are particularly involved; a chapter
      on women's clothing and accessories; and notes on other
      crafts. 82 plates illustrate women in their native
      costumes and activities.

126   _____.
      1963-64 "Breves apuntes de la indumentaria indígena de
      Guatemala." CIF/FA 11/12:11/12:22-57. illus., bibl.
         Describes and explains the components of indigenous
      clothing worn by women and men in Guatemala. Includes
      some information on weaving, carried out by Indian women.

127   _____.
      1945 "Costumes and Wedding Customs at Mixco, Guatemala."
      MAAE/N 2:48:148-52. Wash., D.C.: Carnegie Institution
      of Wash., Div. of Historical Research. illus.
         Describes women's costumes and courtship procedures
      in a Pokoman-Maya village near Guatemala City. Notes
      considerable change in everyday garb but adherence to
      traditional outfits for ceremonies.

Women in Spanish America

128 WOOD, JOSEPHINE and OSBORNE, LILLY de JONGH
       1966 Indian Costumes of Guatemala. Graz, Austria:
       Akademische Druck u. Verlagsanstalt. 154 p. fold. map,
       plates, bibl.
           Describes women's activities of carding, spinning,
       dyeing, weaving, and embroidery in the preparation of
       indigenous clothing in Guatemala. Includes sections on
       women's, men's, children's, and ceremonial costumes.
       40 beautiful color plates depict women of different
       villages.

El Salvador

129 BOGGS, STANLEY H.
       1973 "Pre-Maya Costumes and Coiffures." OAS/AM
       25:2:19-24. illus.
           Well-illustrated, detailed description of physical
       features, clothing, hair styles, and ornaments of girls
       and women in eastern Guatemala and western El Salvador
       as evidenced by 1967 discovery of clay figurines dated
       to approximately 500-300 B.C.

130 OSBORNE, LILLY de JONGH
       1965 Indian Crafts of Guatemala and El Salvador. Norman,
       Okla.: Univ. of Okla. Press. 278 p. illus., bibl.
       See GUATEMALA for annotation.

Panama

131 HOYOS SANCHO, NIEVES de
       1963 "La pollera panameña." IGFO/RI 23:93/94:513-17.
       illus., plates
           Description of female costume native to Panama--the
       pollera--a term which refers not only to the skirt but
       also to the blouse. Describes festive as well as daily
       common examples, including accompanying jewelry and hair
       style. Originating from outfit worn by women in 17c.
       Spain, today it is used almost exclusively for special
       occasions.

132 KEELER, CLYDE
       1969 "The Mola Blouse." In his Cuna Indian Art: The
       Culture and Crafts of Panama's San Blas Islanders,
       pp. 71-96. Jericho, N.Y.: Exposition Press. illus.,
       plates, bibl.
           Well-illustrated chapter on typical garment artis-
       tically fashioned and worn by San Blas Cuna women.

31

The Arts

Other chapters briefly remark on women and jewelry, the hurricane goddess, music, dance, and children's play.

133 KORSI de RIPOLL, BLANCA
1962 "El hechizo de la pollera." TDM 2:8:2-3, 25. bibl.
History of the traditional costume worn by Panamanian women since colonial times. Includes a bibliography of other works on the *pollera*.

134 REYES, ROMÁN B.
1954 Origen e historia de la pollera. Disertación patriótica. Panama: Imprenta de la Academia. 88 p. illus., music, ports.
Bi-lingual (Spanish and English) edition traces history of typical garment of Panamanian women, from the colonial period to contemporary times. Describes kinds of *polleras*, how worn, origin of name; includes verses, lyrics, and anecdotes.

135 SPICER, DOROTHY GLADYS
1944 "In Panama It's the Pollera." PANAM 5:3:30-32.
Briefly describes traditional costume, *la pollera*, worn by Panamanian women during colonial times, but now used only as a fancy dress costume. Briefly mentions costumes of indigenous groups.

136 ZÁRATE, DORA P. de
1972 "No se ha logrado todavía la evolución histórica de nuestro traje nacional, desde la colonia hasta nuestros días." TDM 10:60:8, 36, 42.
Briefly discusses historical evolution of national costume worn by Panamanian women since colonial times, but today used as a festive garment--the *pollera*--; and materials and designs for its construction.

SOUTH AMERICA

Venezuela

137 SEKELJ, TIBOR
1952 "Pintura facial de la mujer guajira." AVF 1:1:157-58. illus.
Among the Guajiro Indians of Colombia and Venezuela, the women continue to dress in traditional costume and paint their face. Differences in color and design denote social status and age (child, married woman, mother, etc.). 2 pages of photographs follow text.

Colombia

138   SEKELJ, TIBOR
      1952 "Pintura facial de la mujer guajira." AVF 1:1:157-58.
      illus.
      See VENEZUELA for annotation.

139   TORRES MÉNDEZ, RAMÓN
      196-? Cuadros de costumbres. Bogota: Banco Cafetero.
      14 p. port. clr. plates.
          Album containing 55 colored plates of sketches and
      paintings of Bogota painter Ramón Torres Méndez depict-
      ing rural and urban scenes from mid-19c.; they show
      women of different classes in different outfits engaged
      in a variety of activities: e.g., fighting, selling
      chickens, buying meat.

Peru

140   LAVALLE, JOSÉ ANTONIO de
      1968 La Perricholi. Estudios de Teatro Peruano. Serie
      IV, no. 52. Lima: Univ. Nacional de San Marcos. 8 p.
          Sees la Perricholi as a personification of the limeña
      of 18c. Peru, in terms of physical and moral aspects,
      virtues and defects. Micaela Villegas was a well-known
      actress during last third of 18c. and mistress of
      Viceroy Amat. Mimeo reprint of article which appeared
      in El Ateneo (Lima), 4:39 (1887) and taken from author's
      Estudios Históricos (Lima, 1935), pp. 411-21.

141   MIRÓ QUESADA LAOS, CARLOS
      1958 "Vida y muerte de la Perricholi." In his De Santa
      Rosa a la Perricholi (Páginas peruanas), pp. 287-325.
      Lima: Talleres Gráficos P. L. Villanueva.
          Micaela Villegas (1746?-1819) was a mestiza of poor
      origins who became a famous actress in Lima, where she
      scandalized society by her love affair with Viceroy Amat,
      who sired her son. Places her in the context of Lima
      society during the era of "saya y manto," and includes
      notes on the possible origin of her nickname, insinua-
      tions of other love affairs, her house, marriage to an
      actor (1795), will, etc. Based on historical and liter-
      ary sources, this is final chapter of impressions of
      Peru during several centuries of Spanish domination,
      beginning with a saintly woman (see his "Santa Rosa")
      and ending with a "sinner-lover" for contrast.

The Arts

142 SÁNCHEZ, LUIS ALBERTO
      1963 La Perricholi. 4th ed. Serie: biografías. Lima:
      Univ. Nacional Mayor de San Marcos, Depto. de Publica-
      ciones. 172 p. illus., plates, facsims.
        Recounts life of Micaela Villegas (1748-1819) within
      the context of the historical/political scene and the
      theatre of 18c. Peru. Her affair with Viceroy Amat,
      with whom she had a son (1769), scandalized Lima.
      Although documented to some extent (includes her will),
      and based on several primary and secondary sources, the
      story of this actress' life is projected or suggested
      more than verified by fact and includes more information
      on other scenes and persons than on her.

143 TAMAYO VARGAS, AUGUSTO
      1968 Vieja y nueva historia de Micaela Villegas.
      Estudios de Teatro Peruano, serie IV, no. 51. Lima:
      Univ. Nacional Mayor de San Marcos. 18 p.
        Sees Micaela Villegas (la Perricholi), a mestiza, as a
      representative of a social class and the average woman
      of Lima during the last third of 18c. Uses secondary
      sources, romances and other literary forms to provide
      social/moral context and biographical data (1748-1819)
      on well-known Peruvian actress and her illicit affair
      with Viceroy Amat.

144 TORRE REVELLO, JOSÉ
      1961 "Las mujeres limeñas." HIAM/R 52:521-26. bibl.
      f/notes.
        Interesting and informative description of women's
      controversial dress style--"la saya y manto"--in colo-
      nial Lima which elicited so much commentary and debate
      that legislation was passed to prohibit it. Quotes
      travel accounts and verses on "las tapadas," the women
      who dressed in this style and refers reader to paintings
      depicting them.

145 UNGARO de FOX, LUCIA
      1969 "The Tapada." OAS/AM 21:1:2-7. illus.
        Presents portrait of controversial fashion adopted by
      women in colonial Peru who dressed with a veil that
      earned them the name "tapada" (covered one). A custom
      inherited from Arab population in Spain, it was de-
      nounced by several writers as dissimulation of who and
      what a woman really was. Suggests 2 Baroque elements--
      stylization and paradox--as an explanation. Illustrates
      with verses and paintings.

Bolivia

146   FALCÓN, JORGE
        1946 "Marina Nuñez del Prado." HH 4:37:28-33. illus.
        Interprets Bolivian sculptor's works of male and
        female Indian workers, as seen in a N.Y. exhibit, as a
        social accusation of their national and imperialist
        exploiters.

Paraguay

147   GONZÁLEZ, GUSTAVO
        1967 Ñandutí. Biblioteca del Centro de Estudios
        Antropológicos del Ateneo Paraguayo. Asunción: Artes
        Gráficas Zamphirópolos. 92 p. illus., plates, bibl.
        Also in: 1966 CIAAP/RS 2:1:77-142.
        Well-researched and illustrated monograph on fine
        cotton lace work woven by Paraguayan women. Ñandutí
        means spider web in Guaraní and originated in town of
        Itaugua in 18c. Considers history and development of
        this native art, poetic and symbolic interpretation of
        it, representative motifs, economic aspects, and its
        appearance in folklore and literature. Based on primary
        and secondary sources.

Chile

148   HUASI, JULIO
        1971 "Violeta de América." CDLA 10:65/66:91-104.
        Admiring and respectful portrait of Violeta Parra
        (1917-67), Chilean singer, composer, and folk artist of
        humble origins, who fought against hypocrisy of the
        bourgeoisie. She founded and directed Museum of Popular
        Art at the University of Concepción. Integrates verses
        from her songs, statements by her children, and commen-
        tary by José María Arguedas.

Argentina

149   ALVA NEGRI, TOMÁS
        1972 "Raquel Forner, Space Age Artist." OAS/AM
        24:9:25-30. illus., port.
        Brings together various critiques of paintings by
        contemporary Argentine artist Raquel Forner and repro-
        duces 10 works.

The Arts

150   Argentine Republic. Ministerio de Cultura y Educación.
       1972   Conferencia Interamericana Especializada sobre
       Educación Integral de la Mujer, Buenos Aires, 1972.
       Muestra Cultural. Buenos Aires. 1 vol. plates.
          According to the Handbook of Latin American Studies
       36(1974):402, this is a catalogue of an all-woman plas-
       tic arts show held in Buenos Aires 21-25 August, 1972.

151   BALESTRERI de DEVOTO, ORNELLA
       1969   "Realización de la mujer en el campo de la música."
       UNC/R 10:1/2:459-64.
          Briefly synthesizes female participation in different
       fields of music in 20c. Argentina, considering the works
       of Hilda Dianda and Graciella Castillo in particular.

152   CAMPRA, ROSALBA
       1969   "Participación de la mujer en el teatro." UNC/R
       10:1/2:427-57. bibl.
          Traces the participation of women in Argentine theater
       as a dramatic character and as a playwright. Analyzes
       in detail evolving female role from object in love and
       patriarchal authority to a more liberated being with her
       own will, from Siripo (1789) to 20c. plays. Also names
       actresses, directors, and playwrights, focusing on the
       works of Marta Lehmann and Griselda Gámbaro.

153   CAPDEVILA, ARTURO
       1951   La Trinidad Guevara y su tiempo. Col. Vertice.
       Buenos Aires: Edit. Guillermo Kraft. 187 p. port.
          Biography of famous 19c. creole actress (1798-1873) of
       Platine region, Trinidad Guevara, based mostly on peri-
       odicals and some documents, which are partially repro-
       duced in text.

154   CARIDE, VICENTE P.
       1970-1971 "La mujer en el proceso histórico de la pintura
       en Argentina." Sur 326/327/328:147-53.
          Overview of women artists in Argentina, beginning with
       group from Colegio de Santa Rosa in the 19c. and ending
       with vanguards of contemporary times, naming persons in
       each trend.

155   CLARENC de SUÁREZ, NORMA
       1969   "Participación de la mujer en las artes plásticas:
       escultura." UNC/R 10:1/2:411-25.
          Cites 3 problems women had to overcome in order to
       become sculptors: 1) struggle of sculpture to be con-
       sidered on same level as painting; 2) belief that women
       are inferior to men in creativity and productivity in

work, art, and intellect; and 3) archaic beliefs and
taboos which restricted female activity to particular
fields. Believes a difference exists between nature of
art as a vocation in women and in men in terms of psychological attitude toward the artistic task. Names
several artists. Discusses Pop Art and happenings.

156 IÑIGO CARRERA, HÉCTOR
     1972 La mujer argentina. La historia popular, 91.
     Buenos Aires: Centro Ed. de América Latina. 116 p.
     illus., plates, bibl. notes.
        Based on traveler's observations on Argentine women's
     activities, dress, and behavior and on secondary sources,
     provides a history of female styles followed by women of
     different classes from the 16c. to 20c. Quotes travel
     accounts and literature.

157 SQUIRRU, RAFAEL
     1968 "Raquel Forner." OAS/AM 20:8:6-12. illus.
        Considers Argentine painter Raquel Forner "one of the
     most important figures in pictorial art of our time" in
     her treatment of space. Illustrates with 7 of her
     paintings and a photo of the artist.

158 URIBE, BASILIO
     1972 La mujer argentina en las artes visuales de hoy.
     B.A.: Ministerio de Cultura y Educación, Centro Nacional
     de Documentación e Información Educativa. 11 p.
        Commissioned by Ministry of Culture and Education for
     Inter-American Conference on Integral Education of Women
     (Buenos Aires, 21-25 August 1972), briefly cites 6 women
     artists in Argentina. Generally uninformative.

159 WAISMAN, MARINA
     1969 "La mujer en la arquitectura." UNC/R 10:1/2:379-93.
        With brief, general overview of architecture as a
     profession in Argentina, describes female participation
     in this field since 1940 and concomitant problems.

CARIBBEAN

Puerto Rico

160 VALLE, ANA del
     1969 "María Rodríguez Señeriz: personalidad artística de
     una pintora boricua." PR/E 22:27:107-18. illus., port.

WOMEN IN SPANISH AMERICA

The Arts

Very general and brief comments on Puerto Rican woman
painter who represents the tribulations of the Puerto
Rican people in her art and illustrations of 5 of her
works, 3 on women.

LITERATURE, MASS MEDIA, AND FOLKLORE[1]

This section considers women in their capacity as writers, readers, and characters or themes of poetry, novels, short stories, plays, legends, myths, etc. It includes material on women and journalism as well as 19th century periodicals directed at a female audience. The items are divided by country and by individual writers within a country when the number of entries (five or more) warrants it. For example, a group of entries on Gabriela Mistral follows a general group of entries on Chile. Bibliographical articles on individual writers are included. Nineteenth century periodicals for women comprise a separate subcategory and are listed alphabetically without being divided by country.

Because there are thousands of Spanish American women writers (poets, novelists, essayists, etc.) and because there are thousands of articles and full-length studies on their literary works as well as on their personal lives, it is impossible to present but a very minimal picture of this subject, given the scope of the bibliography.[2] Preference is given to publications of a more personal nature rather than to those which are strictly literary criticism. My concern here is not with analyses of verse form or narrative style, but with the women themselves and their perception of femaleness. However, it is often the case that a publication contains both biographical data as well as literary criticism, with a selection of the writer's work. Many publications listed in this section are collective, i.e., mentioning at least three writers, as a way of introducing more Spanish

---

[1] My decision to include folklore and mythology in the literary section is based on Bronislaw Malinowski's consideration that "myth is above all a cultural force; but it is not only that. It is obviously a narrative, and thus it has its literary aspect. . ." in Magic, Science and Religion (New York: Doubleday, Anchor Books, 1954) p. 143.

[2] Kathleen O'Quinn is preparing Latin American Women Authors: A Bio-Bibliography, which will include publishing information and biographical data on approximately 1,000 women authors from colonial to contemporary times of all of the Spanish-speaking countries of Latin America plus Brazil, to be published by G. K. Hall & Co. in Boston.

American women writers. Those items which are specific to one writer
were selected because they deal with the writer's life and/or work
with respect to her position as a woman, because of their relevance
to contemporary women's issues, or because I have found so little
material on women writers for the particular country that the few
cited serve as a minimal representation.

Those writers who are also known as nuns are included in this
section rather than in MAGIC, RELIGION, AND RITUAL. For writers such
as Sor Juana and Gabriela Mistral, about whom so much has been published, only a sampling of works is listed, including bibliographies
for further references; several of these entries are unannotated.
For additional items which may refer to women as writers see EDUCA-
TION, BIOGRAPHY AND AUTOBIOGRAPHY, and GENERAL. For studies on women
and language see PSYCHOLOGY.

For additional information and references see the following works.
Although these bibliographies and histories are limited in their coverage of women writers, they are useful guides to begin exploration
of this subject. For a comprehensive bibliographical guide to primary and important secondary research sources, see Foster and Foster's
manual,[3] which includes guides to libraries and collections, periodicals and periodical literature, theses and dissertations, for Spanish
and Spanish American literature and Spanish American national bibliographies for eighteen countries. Although dated, another useful
guide is Grismer's[4] reference index to 12,000 Spanish American authors.
Rela's[5] unannotated but helpful bibliographical guide to Hispanic
American literature from the 19th century to 1970 contains 6023 separate items referring to general, national and individual bibliographies and anthologies; general and national literary histories;
essays, history and criticism; collective and individual biographies;
and dictionaries. For a general introduction to Hispanic American
literature, see Anderson Imbert's history.[6] For a general history

---

[3] David W. Foster and Virginia Ramos Foster, compilers. Manual of
Hispanic Bibliography. University of Washington Publications in
Language and Literature, 18. Seattle, Wash.: University of
Washington Press, 1970.

[4] Raymond L. Grismer. A Reference Index to Twelve Thousand Spanish
American Authors. A Guide to the Literature of Spanish America.
Inter-American Bibliographical and Library Association Publications,
series 3, vol. 1. N.Y.: H. W. Wilson Co.

[5] Walter Rela. Guía bibliográfica de la literature hispanoamericana
desde el siglo XIX hasta 1970. B.A.: Casa Pardo, 1971.

[6] Enrique Anderson Imbert. Historia de la literatura hispanoamericana.
5th ed. Brevarios del Fondo de Cultura Económica, 89, 156. Mexico,
D.F.: Fondo de Cultura Económica, 1964-65. 2 vols.

of the Hispanic American novel, see Alegría's,[7] which includes an overall bibliography plus a bibliography at the end of each subsection of each chapter. For more recent works, see Schwartz'[8] history of Spanish American fiction, which has an excellent bibliography divided into general works on Spanish American fiction and on fiction in different countries, and works about particular authors. An even more recent edition, covering only 20th century Spanish American novels, is Brushwood's[9] work, which contains a very useful, briefly annotated bibliography. For a general history of Hispanic American theatre, see Dauster's[10] recent publication, which includes a final bibliography as well as shorter bibliographies within and at the end of each chapter. For a general history of the Hispanic American short story, see Leal's,[11] which includes bibliography at the end of sub-sections in each chapter as well as a final bibliography of critical studies, bibliographies, anthologies, and theoretical works. Ferro's history of Hispanic American poetry (item 165) considers female poets as a separate group rather than integrating them into the various cultural movements; and covers only poets of the 20th century. Although dated, the bibliography of Rosenbaum's Modern Women Poets of Spanish America (item 175) is very useful. It is divided into general works (studies and anthologies) and authors (works and studies): María Enriqueta, Juana Borrero, María Eugenia Vaz Ferreira, Delmira Agustini, Gabriela Mistral, Alfonsina Storni, Juana de Ibarbourou. For Argentine women poets, see the extensive bibliography of Percas' work on La poesía femenina argentina, 1810-1950 (item 359). The latter three works are annotated below.

---

[7] Fernando Alegría. Historia de la novela hispanoamericana. 3rd. ed. Historia literaria de Hispanoamérica, 1. Mexico, D.F.: Ediciones de Andrea Edison, 1966.

[8] Kessel Schwartz. A New History of Spanish American Fiction. Coral Gables, Fla.: University of Miami Press, 1972.

[9] John S. Brushwood. The Spanish American Novel, A Twentieth Century Survey. The Texas Pan American Series. Austin, Tex.: University of Texas Press, 1975.

[10] Frank Dauster. Historia del teatro hispanoamericano, siglos XIX-XX. 2nd ed. Historia literaria de Hispanoamérica, 4. Mexico, D.F.: Ediciones de Andrea Edison, 1972.

[11] Luis Leal. Historia del cuento hispanoamericano. Historia literaria de Hispanoamérica, 2. Mexico, D.F.: Ediciones de Andrea Edison, 1971.

WOMEN IN SPANISH AMERICA

Literature, Mass Media, and Folklore

SPANISH AMERICA - GENERAL

160a ACOSTA de SAMPER, SOLEDAD
      1895? La mujer en la sociedad moderna. Paris: Casa
      Edit. Garnier Hnos. 429 p.
        General survey of notable women in 19c. Europe and Amer-
      ica. Part 6 discusses the role of women in society before
      Independence, women writers before and during the 19c.,
      and the education of women. Lacks depth but early work
      by probably the most prolific woman writer of 19c. LA.

161 CARRERA, JULIETA
      1956 La mujer en América escribe . . . Semblanzas.
      Mex., D.F.: Eds. Alonso. 332 p.
        Collection of sketches of 53 Latin American women
      writers, briefly introducing their works with summary
      comments on content and style, quoting verses of some.
      Beginning with María Eugenia Vaz Ferreira and ending
      with Dulce María Loynaz, the writers are grouped as
      initiators; essayists and novelists; surrealists; revo-
      lutionaries; neo-romantics.

162 CONDE ABELLÁN, CARMEN, comp.
      1967 Once grandes poetisas américohispanas. Col. La
      Encina y El Mar; poesía de España y América, 34.
      Madrid: Eds. Cultura Hispánica. 631 p. illus., ports.,
      facsims.
        Anthology of poetry by 11 20c. poets of LA, including
      bio-bibliographical sketches preceding the poetry of
      each one and discussing more than a dozen other poets
      in the prologue, providing examples of their work.

163 CONDE ABELLÁN, CARMEN
      1951 "Poesía femenina hispanoamericana (Nómina
      incompleta)." MH 37:19-26. illus.
        Notes considerable increase in women poets after 1939 and
      the denominator of their poetry as serious and transcen-
      dental. Includes selections from 14 LA women poets, accom-
      panied by very brief critical or bibliographical remarks.

164 FENOCHIO FURLONG, AMAPOLA
      1955? Poetisas de América. México, D.F.? 120 p. bibl.
        Alphabetical presentation of brief biographical notes,
      accompanied by poetry, on 56 Latin American women poets
      from Margarita Abella Caprile to Wally Zenner.

165 FERRO, HELLÉN
      1964 "Las mujeres en la poesía de América." In her
      Historia de la poesía hispanoamericana, pp. 313-43.
      N.Y.: Las Americas Publishing Co.
        Considers 20c. Latin American women poets in a group
      rather than in separate literary movements because the
      principal theme of their poetry is love, although they

were inspired by other subjects as well, and because
they dared to enter territory previously only occupied
by men: they inverted the love poetry of men, by con-
verting themselves from desired into desiring, from
accused into accusatory, from humiliated into dominant.
In addition, almost without exception, they led dramatic
lives, some ending in tragedy. Considers María Eugenia
Vaz Ferreira, Delmira Agustini, Alfonsina Storni, Juana
de Ibarbourou, Gabriela Mistral, Julia de Burgos, Clara
Lair, several modern mystics and cites many others.

166   FIGUEIRA, GASTÓN
      1948 "Perfiles: escritoras iberoamericanas." IILI/RI
      14:27:125-38.
         Brief profiles on María Enriqueta, Delmira Agustini,
      Alfonsina Storni, María Alicia Domínguez, et al.

167   FLORA, CORNELIA BUTLER
      1971 "The Passive Female: Her Comparative Image by Class
      and Culture in Women's Magazine Fiction." WRU/JMF
      33:3:435-44. tables, bibl.
         Content analysis of 202 examples of women's magazine
      fiction in LA and the US to test hypothesis of passivity
      as ideal of women regardless of culture or class. Latin
      American and middle-class fiction were found to stress
      passivity more. Concludes that the passive female type
      is reinforced across class and culture.

168   GIANELLO, LEONCIO
      1959 Musas de amor. Col. Ensayos, 12. Sante Fe, Arg.:
      Librería y Edit. Castellví. 41 p.
         Considers women as the inspiration for love expressed
      in poetry of Jose Martí (María, "la niña de Guatemala");
      Ruben Darío (Stella); Amado Nervo (Ana Cecilia Luisa
      Dailliez); and Manuel Acuña (Rosario de la Peña).

169   GONZÁLEZ y CONTRERAS, GILBERTO
      1941 "Interpretación de la poesía femenina." VME/R
      2:25:84-104.
         Believes women of his time created poetry from sexual
      sublimation, but without modifying the sexual ethic, only
      dramatizing female insatisfaction for poetic ends. Lengthy
      discussion of eroticism in poetry, illustrating with ex-
      amples from Juana de Ibarbourou, whom he considers the
      principal representative of lyrics by Latin American women,
      Blanca Luz Brum, Isa Caraballo, Alfonsina Storni, Rosario
      Sansores, Emilia Bernal et al. Draws comparisons between
      men and women: sex for men is nothing more than a source
      of desire while for women it is a biological tragedy.

169a GREGOIRE, MENIE
      1970 "La responsabilidad de la mujer como periodista."
      Comunidad 5:23:88-92.

Literature, Mass Media, and Folklore

Translated from French, speech given at first World
Meeting of Women Journalists (Mexico, May 1969), compares situation of women in journalism between Europe
and LA. Emphasizes responsibility of women journalists
to inform more, and to force society's attention toward
its problems of everyday life, which only women know so
well.

170   GUTIÉRREZ, JUAN MARÍA
       "Poetisas sud-americanas durante el régimen colonial."
       BA/R 20:80:568-607.
          Recognizes high level of feminine culture, at least in
       literature, in colonial America. Brings to light some
       obscure names and provides historical notes on nuns and
       convents as well.

171   "The Latin American Woman: Image and Reality"
       1974 Special edition of RI 4:2.
          Collection of 10 articles and 2 book reviews exploring
       Hispanic Caribbean female as seen through literary
       media. Includes: analysis of female archetypes in
       historical literature, image of women in magazines, the
       news, novels and poetry, feminist perspective of Latin
       American writers, etc.

172   OTERO MUÑOZ, GUSTAVO
       1940 "El amor indígena en la colonización." AE 8:28:7-16.
          Although more paragraphs are devoted to a discussion
       of the presence of Indian women and their relationship
       with Spanish conquistadors in several historical novels,
       true cases of interracial relationships in the 1500's
       are also pointed out. Early miscegenation often resulted
       in future generations of famous Latin Americans, such as
       Francisco de Paula Santander.

173   PESCATELLO, ANN
       1974 Preface to "The Special Issue in Perspective: The
       Hispanic Caribbean Woman and the Literary Media." RI
       4:2:131-35.
          As guest editor for special issue on the Hispanic
       Caribbean woman and the literary media, Pescatello ex-
       plains purpose of issue and briefly reviews the 10 essays
       included. To explore roles and perceptions of and by
       Caribbean women, literary media are examined. Pescatello
       considers this collection of articles a challenge to the
       dearth of studies on Latin American women.

Women in Spanish America

174   REDONDO, SUSANA
        1954 "Proceso de la literature femenina hispanoamericana."
        Cuadernos 6:34-38.
           Sketches trajectory of Hispanic American literature
        written by women from "Amarilis" and Sor Juana of the
        17c. to many poets and novelists of the 20c., briefly
        taking into account different trends.

175   ROSENBAUM, SIDONIA CARMEN
        1945 Modern Women Poets of Spanish America: The Precur-
        sors, Delmira Agustini, Gabriela Mistral, Alfonsina
        Storni, Juana de Ibarbourou. N.Y.: Hispanic Inst. of
        the US. 273 p. bibl.
           Although Delmira Agustini--her life and character,
        works, themes, and styles--is the pivotal post-modernist
        poet of this study, the introduction briefly traces the
        role of women in Hispanic American life from the Conquest
        to Independence and a survey reviews female literary
        contributions from Amarilis to the forerunners of
        Modernism (1888-1905): María Enriqueta, Juana Borrero,
        and María Eugenia Vaz Ferreira. Part 3 focuses on
        Agustini's influence on 3 outstanding and original poets
        in their own right: Gabriela Mistral, Alfonsina Storni
        and Juana de Ibarbourou. Extensive bibliography.

176   SUÁREZ CALIMANO, E.
        1931 "El narcisismo en la poesía femenina de Hispano-
        américa." Nosotros 72:264:27-55.
           Women's function in society is characterized by altru-
        ism and externalization of the ego; her destiny is always
        to project herself outwardly. That's why narcissism in
        women, even in a field as inoffensive as poetry, appears
        contrary to nature and sense. Discusses the myth of
        Narcissus in ancient and contemporary times; psycholog-
        ical characteristics, degeneration, and complexes of
        narcissistic individual; and major female proponents of
        narcissism in Latin American poetry--Delmira Agustini,
        and María Eugenia Vaz Ferreira. Criticizes them for
        going against women's mission in life as a moderating
        power and considers their egocentrism an evil. Cites
        Argentine women poets whom he considers inspired with
        noble sentiments which are more appropriate for women!

177   UGARTE, MANUEL
        1931 "Women Writers of South America." UO/BA 5:3:238-41.
        port.
           Believes women have to surmount even greater obstacles--
        hostile opinions and suspicion--than men in order to
        write. Identifies women writers in 6 Latin American

Literature, Mass Media, and Folklore

countries whom he considers to have been inspired by
vocation rather than dilettantism.

178 URIBE MUÑOZ, BERNARDO
1934 Mujeres de América. Medellín, Spain: Imprenta
Oficial. 460 p. illus., ports.
Collection of very brief autobiographical and biographical sketches of 150 women writers (poets, novelists,
journalists, etc.) of 16 Latin American countries,
accompanied by portraits and examples of their work.

179 VALENCIA LAPATA, ALFONSO
1944 "La poesía femenina en América." UA/U 65:147-50.
Except for the Venezuelan poet, Luz Machado de Arnao,
feminine poetry of LA holds no charm or excellence.
Sentiments and impressions of life appear in rudimentary
construction in poems filled with clichés and repeti-
tions, lacking originality. Quotes verses.

180 VALENZUELA, VICTOR M.
1974 Grandes escritores hispanoamericanos. Poetisas y
novelistas. Bethelehem, Pa.: Lehigh Univ. 133 p.
bibl.
Examination of contributions made to Hispanic American
literature by 4 women poets (Sor Juana, Agustini,
Ibarbourou, Mistral) and 5 novelists (Matto de Turner,
Brunet, Bombal, Bullrich, Hernández). Emphasizes expression of "feminine soul" and sexual, social and
intellectual frustrations. Lists 36 other writers and
their works.

181 VIDAL, MARÍA ANTONIA
1947 "Romanticismo, modernismo y actualidad de la poesía
femenina." VA 7:39:101-04.
Brief comments on several romantic, modernist and
contemporary Latin American women poets. Notes differences between Latin American and Spanish women poets.

182 ZARDOYA, CONCHA
1953 "La muerte en la poesía femenina latinoamericana."
CAM 71:5:233-79.
Discusses Spanish literary influences and the preoccupation with death and its relationship to love in an
analysis of poetry by Agustini, Mistral, Storni and
Ibarbourou.

MIDDLE AMERICA

Mexico

183   ACOSTA, HELIA d'
         1956 "La mujer y el periodismo." UNAN/CPS 2:4:85-100.
         bibl. f/notes.
            Briefly traces history of journalism in general and in
         Mexico, citing Leona Vicario as first woman journalist
         during Independence era. Defines social function of the
         press, the journalist and the vocation, concluding that
         there is limited number of women in journalism because
         it is a male-run monopoly which keeps women out. Pro-
         poses solving conflict facing journalism in Mexico--i.e.,
         between private and public interests--through national
         congress and formation of a Press Council with specific
         functions and integrated with both sexes.

184   ACOSTA, MARICLAIRE
         1973 "Los estereotipos de la mujer mexicana en las
         fotonovelas." CM/D 9:53:29-31.
            An analysis of *fotonovelas* popular in Mexico reveals
         4 female stereotypes: erotic object (fiancée, lover);
         wife/mother; older woman (grandmother, mother-in-law,
         professional woman); "devourer of men." Women are de-
         fined in limited and rigid characteristics and behavior
         and presented as emotionally and physically dependent
         on men. *Fotonovelas* serve as vehicle to formalize and
         perpetuate myth that women are fulfilled only through
         sexual and/or maternal love, and not through independence
         and self-sufficiency.

185   No Entry

186   AGOGINO, GEORGE A.; STEVENS, DOMINIQUE E.; and CARLOTTA, LYNDA
         1973 "Doña Marina and the Legend of la Llorona." AAC/AJ
         11:1:27-29.
            Reviews versions of the Crying Woman legend and
         attempts to identify her original as Doña Marina.
         Briefly traces her role in the conquest as Cortez'
         linguist and mistress.

187   ANDERSON, LOLA
         1934 "Mexican Women Journalists." PAU/B 68:5:315-20.
            Brief history of the development of journalism for
         women in Mexico, citing and describing the activities of
         several journalists, editors, publishers and printer-
         journalists, as well as publications for women, since
         the 19c.

Literature, Mass Media, and Folklore

188   BRANN, SYLVIA J.
       1973 "El fracaso de la voluntad en las comedias de
       Luisa Josefina Hernández." <u>LATR</u> 7:1:25-31. bibl.
       notes.
         Analyzes 6 plays in which female protagonists find
       themselves trapped in a crisis which they have created,
       obliged to resolve their problems and destiny.

189   CARDOZA y ARAGÓN, LUIS
       1964 "María Lombardo de Caso." <u>CAM</u> 136:5:216-23.
         Upon rereading 3 works of Mexican novelist who had
       recently died, presents personal impressions: believes
       they demonstrate her fervor for Mexican life, recreating
       emotions of childhood in state of Puebla.

190   CARRERA, JULIETA
       1955 "La novela femenina mexicana." <u>ND</u> 35:4:32-41.
       Also in 1953 <u>Cuadernos</u> 3:101-104.
         Good synthesizing introduction to the works of 27 20c.
       Mexican women novelists and short story writers, many
       of which focus on the lives of women.

191   CASTELLANOS, ROSARIO
       1973 <u>Mujer que sabe latín . . . .</u> Mex., D.F.: Sep
       Setentas. 213 p. illus.
         Collection of short essays by well-known Mexican
       writer and feminist looks at image of women and several
       Latin American women writers--Clarice Lispector, María
       Luisa Bombal, Silvina Ocampo, et al.--but emphasis is
       more on European and North American writers. Briefly
       considers historical reasons why women have not been
       educated in Mexico and generally writes in favor of
       education for women.

192   _____.
       1967 "Autobiography." Trans. by L. Kemp. <u>AH</u> 1:66-70.
         Text appears in English and Spanish in parallel
       columns. Mexican writer's life and intellectual/
       literary development briefly outlined in her own words;
       notes that in her youth literature was not considered a
       profession, even less so for a woman.

193   CASTILLO LEDÓN, AMALIA C. de
       1940 "Poetisas modernas de México." <u>PAU/Bs</u> 74:10:645-56.
         Names dozens of Mexican women poets since Sor Juana,
       with brief notes on and verses of several contemporaries
       included (e.g., Concha Guerrero Kramer, Chayo Uriarte,
       María del Mar, Caridad Bravo Adams).

Women in Spanish America

194   CERVANTES de CONDE, MARÍA TERESA
        1970 "El romanticismo, la mujer y el libro. Romanticism,
        Women and Books." ARMEX 17:131:43-64. illus.
          Beautiful illustrations from books, manuals and calen-
        dars of 19c. Mexico accompany Spanish/English text deal-
        ing with literature aimed at female audience.

195   COLL, EDNA
        1964 Injerto de temas en las novelistas mexicanas
        contemporáneas. San Juan, P.R.: Eds. Juan Ponce de
        León. 283 p. bibl.
          University of Florida Ph.D. dissertation (1963) states
        objective as bringing to light greatest possible number
        of female novelists of 20c. (from 1910 on) Mexico.
        Divides discussion according to kind of novel: sen-
        timental, *ranchera*, introspective, adventure, Mexican
        Revolution, fantasy, humorous, cosmopolitan, evocation
        of infancy; several individual writers: María Luisa
        Ocampo, Asunción Izquierdo Albiñana, Rosa de Castaño,
        Magdalena Mondragón; and a separate chapter on the win-
        ners of the Lanz Duret Prize. Believes subjectivism
        and the sublime sentiment expressed toward motherhood
        are the common denominators of all these novelists; their
        contribution lies in the emphasis on their femininity.
        Criticizes their lack of polish in terms of grammar and
        style.

196   CONSTANTINO, ALBERTINA
        1934 Galería de escritoras y poetisas mexicanas. Mex.,
        D.F.: Imprenta Mundial. n.p. ports.
          Sixty-eight portraits of Mexican women writers are
        accompanied by the briefest of notes. Begins with Sor
        Juana, jumps to late 19c., and ends with 1931.

197   ESQUIVEL, FERNANDO
        1960 "La mujer en la poesía de López Velarde." Abside
        24:2:206-32. bibl.
          Contradicts what other literary critics have said
        about image of women in poetry of Ramón López Velarde.
        Contends that only 3 poems can be classified as "carnal"
        while other poems were inspired by the spiritual rather
        than material aspect of women. Analyzes poet's percep-
        tion of women's physical parts; the 3 poems regarded as
        inspired by passion; and 2 poems using women for concepts
        of fatherland and hope. Discusses 2 loves in poet's
        life.

Literature, Mass Media, and Folklore

198 FERNÁNDEZ, SERGIO E.
        1968 "Las de abajo." In his Retratos del fuego y la
        ceniza, pp. 81-93. Letras Mexicanas, 91. Mex., D.F.:
        Fondo de Cultura Económica.
           Analyzes female characters, Camila and La Pintada in
        Mariano Azuela's novel about the 1910 Revolution, Los
        de abajo. Introduction to book, a collection of com-
        mentaries on female protagonists, is by Rosario
        Castellanos.

199 FLORA, CORNELIA BUTLER
        1973 "The Passive Female and Social Change: A Cross-
        Cultural Comparison of Women's Magazine Fiction." In
        Female and Male in Latin America: Essays, ed. by
        A. Pescatello, pp. 59-85. Pittsburgh, Pa.: Univ. of
        Pittsburgh Press. tables, bibl.
           See COLOMBIA for annotation.

200 GÓMEZ, MATHILDE
        1944 "La mujer mexicana en las letras." SCM/B 2:3:77-85.
           Based on several biographical collections, cites Rosa
        Carreto, Mexican writer of fables, and discusses 2
        female historians of Mexico: María Bartola, daughter
        of Indian governor of Texcoco in 16c., who learned Span-
        ish, gathered data, and wrote about events she witnessed
        during Conquest; and Emilia Beltrán y Puga, who was much
        appreciated for her many donations of books, especially
        of history, around the country and for her own histor-
        ical writings in the 19c.

201 GONZÁLEZ SALAS, CARLOS
        1967 "Poesía femenina mexicana del siglo XX." Abside
        31:3:230-32.
           General survey of 20c. Mexican female poets according
        to theme: love, God, man and his social condition, pure
        poetry.

202 No Entry

203 HERRICK, JANE
        1957 "Periodicals for Women in Mexico During the Nine-
        teenth Century." AAFH/TAM 14:2:135-44.
           Examines 8 periodicals (discussing 2 in detail) for
        appeal made to Mexican women in the 19c. Concludes
        that, because of recurrent failure of these periodicals,
        there was not yet a large enough audience for them.

204 HIDALGO y MONDRAGÓN, BERTA
        1947 La mujer en el periodismo. Mex., D.F. 32 p.

Uninformative pamphlet discusses Mexican women's
ability to be journalists for the various kinds of
reportage and columns of a newspaper or magazine. They
need not be limited to page on social events.

205 HORCASITAS, FERNANDO and BUTTERWORTH, DOUGLAS
      1963 "La llorona." Tlalocan 4:3:204-24.
      Reconstruct prototype of Mexican legend about a noc-
      turnal apparition who is heard crying for her lost
      children: La Llorona or the Weeping Woman. Using
      historical-geographical system called "mythochronology,"
      authors collected 120 variants of folk tale to trace it
      to original form and suggest that theme is pre-Hispanic.
      Also discuss its social functions in historical context.

206 IBARRA de ANDA, FORTINO
      1937 Las mexicanas en el periodismo. In his El periodismo
      en Mexico, vol. 2. 2nd ed. Mex., D.F.: Edit.
      "Juventa." illus.
      Interesting and informative little book on women's
      participation in journalism in Mexico, beginning with
      Leona Vicario, heroine of the Independence Movement, as
      first woman journalist. Includes sketches of reporters
      and writers since early 19c. and a section on literature
      published for a female audience. Last chapter, by
      Concepción de Villarreal, discusses 60 20c. social writ-
      ers (Margarita Robles de Mendoza et al.)--what they have
      written and done as "social fighters."

207 JACKSON, MARY H.
      1971 The Portrayal of Women in the Novels of José Joaquín
      Fernández de Lizardi. Northwest Missouri State College
      Studies, 32:4; Northwest Missouri State College Bulletin,
      65:8. Maryville, Mo.: 53 p. bibl.
      Analyzes portrayal of women in early 19c. Mexico in
      Lizardi's 4 novels. Considers his and society's atti-
      tude toward women. Discusses women in terms of classi-
      fication ("good" and "bad"), descriptions, traits and
      characteristics; in contrast to men, and in love and
      marriage. Concludes that, on the whole, women are cast
      as types rather than individuals, as inferior beings,
      and as objects of both derision and compassion.

208 JAQUETTE, JANE
      1973 "Literary Archetypes and Female Role Alternatives:
      The Woman and the Novel in Latin America." In Female
      and Male in Latin America: Essays, ed. by A. Pescatello,
      pp. 3-27. Pittsburgh: Univ. of Pittsburgh Press.
      bibl. notes.
      See COLOMBIA for annotation.

Literature, Mass Media, and Folklore

209 KEARNEY, MICHAEL
1972 "*La Llorona*: Symbol of Family and Interpersonal
Relations." In his The Winds of Ixtepiji: World View
and Society in a Zapotec Town, pp. 110-15. Case Studies
in Cultural Anthropology. N.Y.: Holt, Rinehart and
Winston. illus., maps, bibl.
Analyzes unconscious logic of widespread Mexican folk-
tale theme about the Weeping Woman. Views the legend,
divided into a sequence of 4 events which reflect simple
structural relationship of male to female, as an elegant
and economical expression of multiple underlying, covert
values and perceptions about family and interpersonal
relations. *La Llorona* is significant as a concatenation
of roles: wife, mother, victim of fate, and deceiving
seductress. Monograph contains scattered references to
women in discussions about *susto*, *aire*, envy and anger,
dreams, sharing food and raising children which are re-
ferred to in analysis of legend. Based on fieldwork
(1965-67; with follow-up visits, 1969, 1970, 1972).

210 LEDDY, BETTY
1950 "La Llorona Again." CFS/WF 9:4:363-65.
Relates version of the "Weeping Woman" as told to
María Luisa Flores, a native of Nogales, Sonora, by her
uncle. Also refers to play based on the legend and
collection of variations on it.

211 LLACH, LEONOR
1934 "Tres escritoras mexicanas." MSEP/LP 12:4:165-74.
Brief biographical sketches of Laura Méndez de Cuenca,
Isabel Prieto de Landázuru and Dolores Correa Zapata,
19c. Mexican writers of poetry and prose. Quotes verses
to demonstrate emotional themes: enthusiasm for Mexican
landscape, defense of women, lamentation for women's
condition as a beautiful but useless flower.

212 MacLACHLAN, COLIN M.
1974 "Modernization of Female Status in Mexico: The Image
of Women's Magazines." RI 4:2:246-57. bibl. f/notes.
Examination of image of modern middle-class women as
reflected in several women's magazines available in
Mexico City; preceded by discussion of stereotypical
traditional sex roles patterned after *machismo* and its
feminine counterpart *marianismo*. Believes "crucible for
change in women's status is within the expanding middle
class." Concludes that Mexican middle-class women are
in an inferior position, status modification through
modernization has been limited, and lack of ideology of
change impedes radical transformation.

213 MONSIVÁIS, CARLOS
       1973 "Soñadora, coqueta y ardiente: notas sobre sexismo
       en la literature mexicana." CM/SS 579 (14 March):
       II-VII. illus.
          Woman's fundamental role in Mexican literature is that
       of background and as an instrument, while man is the
       center. Discusses various images of women (pure sweet-
       heart, crazy lover, mother, etc.), noting that female
       characters are not described organically but are con-
       ceived in a mythical way, as "a vast utopian project."
       Cites Sor Juana as exceptional woman who opted to exer-
       cise her intelligence; Lizardi's La quitotita y su prima
       (1818-19) as a reflection of "liberal" mentality of early
       19c. Mexican society and as an implacable code of behav-
       ior for women; and failure of novels of the Revolution
       to portray women's advances in participation. Almost
       all authors treat women with scorn or philanthropic
       paternalism. Despite relaxation of anti-sexuality in
       Mexican literature, believes rigid mores prevail and
       sexism continues to portray woman as dominated and
       dominable object—as passive scenery.

214 "Las mujeres y los medios de comunicación social."
       1972 BDSLM/CIDHAL 2:3:8-19.
          Collection of data, extracts and summaries of articles
       and talks related to role of mass media with respect to
       women. One part discusses influence of television on
       working class women, especially domestics.

215 MUNK BENTON, GABRIELE von
       1959 "Women Writers of Contemporary Mexico." UO/BA
       33:1:15-19.
          Referring to literary generation from 1930 on, briefly
       discusses 9 women poets and prose writers and mentions
       others in passing. The novelists are known more for
       their description of the country, its people and prob-
       lems while the poets probe into general human experience
       with a personal theme or tone.

216 Los narradores ante el público.
       1966 Mex., D.F.: Edit. Joaquín Mortiz. 267 p. ports.,
       bibl.
          In 1965, 20 Mexican writers were invited to speak
       about their life and literary work in a series at the
       National Institute of Fine Arts. The women writers
       included Rosario Castellanos (pp. 87-98); Inés Arredondo
       (pp. 119-26); Amparo Dávila (pp. 127-34); Irma Sabina
       Sepúlveda (pp. 197-208); and Beatriz Espejo (pp. 209-20).

Literature, Mass Media, and Folklore

217 OCAMPO de GÓMEZ, AURORA M. and PRADO VELÁZQUEZ, ERNESTO
    1967 Diccionario de escritores mexicanos. Mex., D.F.:
    UNAM, Centro de Estudios Literarios. 422 p. illus.,
    bibl.
        Brief biographical sketches, including bibliographical
    data on each author's works as well as reference sources.
    Out of several hundred Mexican writers, covers 60-odd
    women. Preceded by an overview of Mexican literature.

218 PERAZA LANDERO, ROCÍO
    1972 "Imágenes y anti-imágenes de la mujer mexicana."
    CM/SS 558 (18 October): VII-VIII.
        Describes diffusion of sexist ideology in stereotyp-
    ical images of women conveyed through the mass media,
    especially films: femme fatale, self-abnegating wife
    and mother, the brave and beautiful indigenous woman,
    the North American perfect spouse, etc. Names the roles
    and cites actresses who play them.

219 RAMBO, ANN MARIE REMLEY
    1968 "The Presence of Woman in the Poetry of Octavio Paz."
    Hispania 51:2:259-64.
        Examines 3 forms in which woman appears in poetry of
    Octavio Paz and determines role of each. Basic philoso-
    phy is that woman and her relationship to man through
    love represents means whereby man can communicate with
    all life.

220 RUIZ CASTAÑEDA, MARÍA del CARMEN
    1956 "La mujer mexicana en el periodismo." FL
    30:60/61/62:207-21.
        Informative outline of women's role in publishing and
    journalism in Mexico from the first printers during the
    colonial period to writers since independence was gained.
    Names many women, as well as publications organized by
    and/or for them, especially during the 19c. and early
    20c., describing their particular orientation.

221 TORRES de ENRÍQUEZ, JOSEFINA
    1969 "Comunidad en la primera Reunión Mundial de Mujeres
    Periodistas." Comunidad 4:20:563-66.
        Report on 7-day conference attended by female journal-
    ists from all over the world. At final session the con-
    stitution of the World Association of Women Journalists
    was signed, establishing Mexico as its base.

Sor Juana Inés de la Cruz

222 ABREU GÓMEZ, ERMILO
1934 Sor Juana Inés de la Cruz. Bibliografía y
biblioteca. Monografías bibliográficas mexicanas, 29.
Mex., D.F.: Imprenta de la Secretaría de Relaciones
Exteriores. 455 p. illus., facsims.
Pages 389-421 contain a partially annotated
bibliography.

223 ARROYO, ANITA
1952 Razón y pasión de Sor Juana. Mex., D.F.: Porrúa
Obregón 439 p. bibl.
Contains a good bibliography.

224 BARDIN, JAMES C.
1941 "Three Literary Ladies of Spain's American Colonies:
III. Sor Juana Inés de la Cruz." PAU/B 75:3:150-58.
illus., port.
Brief biography of LA's most famous woman poet describes her childhood, life at the viceregal court, the
literary environment of the 17c., her life in the convent,
and many accomplishments. Some verses quoted.

225 CHÁVEZ, EZEQUIEL A.
1972 Ensayo de psicología de Sor Juana Inés de la Cruz y
de estimación del sentido de su obra y de su vida para
la historia de la cultura y de la formación de México.
2nd ed. Mex., D.F.: Asoc. Civil "Ezequiel A. Chávez."
559 p.

226 GÓMEZ ALONSO, PAULA
1956 "Ensayo sobre la filosofía en Sor Juana Inés de la
Cruz." FL 30:60/61/62:59-74.
Describes the epoch in which Sor Juana lived (second
half of 17c.), quotes the opinions of other writers on
her philosophical talent, reflects on her literary talent
and encyclopedic knowledge, and demonstrates her philosophical formation within her own work. Concludes that
under more propitious circumstances Sor Juana would have
developed a systematic work on philosophy.

227 JIMÉNEZ RUEDA, JULIO
1951 Sor Juana Inés de la Cruz en su época. Mex., D.F.:
Porrúa. 131 p. port., bibl. notes.

228 LEONARD, IRVING A.
1959 "A Baroque Poetess." In his Baroque Times in Old
Mexico: Seventeenth-Century Persons, Places, and

Literature, Mass Media, and Folklore

Practices, pp. 172-92. Ann Arbor: Univ. of Mich. Press.
port., bibl. notes.
Intellectual portrait of Sor Juana Inés de la Cruz
interprets conflict between her "feminine" emotions and
"masculine" intellectuality in light of Baroque era in
which she lived, a time when dedication to intellectual
pursuits was considered sinful for women. Discusses her
mental development and role as an early champion of
women's intellectual rights by way of example.

229 MÉNDEZ PLANCARTE, ALFONSO
1951 "Tríptico de la Fénix." Abside 15:4:453-89. illus.,
ports., bibl.
In celebration of 300th anniversary of Sor Juana's
birth, synthesizes life and works of "10th Muse" or
"Phoenix of Mexico." Although not an in-depth study,
contains much information, an excellent bibliography,
and detailed footnotes.

230 PAZ, OCTAVIO
1951 "Homenaje a Sor Juana Inés de la Cruz en su Tercer
Centenario (1651-1695)." Sur 206:29-40.
Looks at significance of Carta Athenagórica as
possibly Sor Juana's only theological work; her crisis
in life during public calamities of 17c. Mexican
society, without deducing a cause-and-effect relationship; theme of love in her poetry; importance of Primer
Sueño as poem about act of knowing rather than knowledge.
Sees her entrance into convent as neither due to absence
of love with a man nor a divine calling, but rather an
expedient measure offering her refuge and solitude.

231 PFANDL, LUDWIG
1963 Sor Juana Inés de la Cruz, décima musa de México. Su
vida. Su poesía. Su psique. Trans. by J. A. Ortega y
Medina. Estudios de Literatura, 2. Mex., D.F.: UNAM,
Inst. de Investigaciones Estéticas. 380 p. port.,
facsim., bibl.
Prologue indicates that this is a psychoanalytical
study of Sor Juana, considering her more as a woman and
less a nun, more human and less mysterious. The appendix cites biographical and critical studies from 1873
to 1935; an addition to it brings the bibliography up
to date from 1936. Original German edition published in
1937.

232 PITTALUGA, GUSTAVO
1946 "La sociedad mexicana en tiempos en Sor Juana Inés
de la Cruz." REVA 7:20:230-34.

Middle America - Mexico/Sor Juana Inés de la Cruz

Interesting biographical anecdotes about Sor Juana,
but no reference notes.

233 RAMÍREZ ESPAÑA, GUILLERMO, ed.
1947 La familia de sor Juana Inés de la Cruz. Documentos
inéditos. Mex., D.F.: Imprenta Universitaria. 121 p.
   Thirty-one documents amplify biographical information
on Sor Juana and her family. Her mother's will reveals
she never married; Sor Juana was therefore illegitimate,
although acknowledged by her father.

234 ROYER, FANCHÓN
1952 The Tenth Muse: Sor Juana Inés de la Cruz. Pater-
son, N.J.: St. Anthony Guild Press. 179 p. illus.,
facsims., bibl.
   First biography of Sor Juana (1651-95) written in
English provides documented and scholarly approach
rather than romantic and highly subjective interpretation. Appendix (pp. 139-75) includes selection from
her poetry.

235 SALAZAR MALLÉN, RUBÉN
1952 Apuntes para una biografíe de sor Juana Inés de la
Cruz. Mex., D.F.: Edit. Stylo. 67 p.

236 SCHONS, DOROTHY
1926 "Some Obscure Points in the Life of Sor Juana Inés
de la Cruz." MP 24:2:141-62. bibl. f/notes.
   Laments limited material available, but attempts to
answer several questions concerning Sor Juana's life,
utilizing primary and secondary references since 17c.
Explains her motives for choosing conventual life in
light of social and moral climate of her epoch. Argues
in favor of surname Asbaje rather than Ramírez. Believes
she renounced fame in exchange for martyr role because of
a series of tragic circumstances and the suffering which
existed in Mexico. Very readable, interesting, and
documented study.

237 _____.
1925 Some Bibliographical Notes on Sor Juana Inés de la
Cruz. Univ. of Tex. Bulletin, 2526. Austin: Univ. of
Tex. Press. 30 p. bibl.
   Valuable early guide to work by and about Mexico's
leading poet in 17c. Brief historical survey of published material on Sor Juana indicates that 18c. was
not a prolific period, while 19c. produced a great deal,
with several notable contributions in early 20c.

Literature, Mass Media, and Folklore

> Appended bibliography supplements Pedro Henríquez Ureña's list of her works in Revue Hispanique 40:97 (1917):161-214, cites manuscripts and 1st editions, reprints, contemporary and early material, articles and studies, brief notices and reviews, literary works based on Sor Juana, general and bibliographical works.

238   SCHULTZ CAZENEUVE de MANTOVANI, FRYDA
      1951 "La décima musa." Sur 206:41-60.
      Views Sor Juana in her condition as woman, in her monastic life, and in her historical epoch as an image of contradictory synthesis. Discusses her verbal dexterity, love of learning, sense of humor, persecution, etc. Illustrates with verses.

239   THURMAN, JUDITH
      1973 "Sister Juana: The Price of Genius." Ms. 1:10:14-21.
      Short, concise biography of Sor Juana covers her precocious start as an intellectual and traces it through her popularity at the viceragal court in New Spain; her life in the convent; her constant struggle between the desire to please others and to be loyal to herself; her defeat and untimely death. Points out Sor Juana's understanding which is of contemporary importance: "that intelligence has been defined in sexist terms, and that it is necessary to redefine it--to stop accepting women as the 'instinctual' and man as the 'rational' being."

240   XIRAU, RAMÓN
      1967 Genio y figura de Sor Juana Inés de la Cruz. Biblioteca de América. Col. Genio y Figura, 16. Buenos Aires: Edit. Universitaria de Buenos Aires. 175 p. illus., facsims., ports., plan, bibl.

El Salvador

241   CARRERA, JULIETA
      1941 "Claudia Lars." IILI/RI 3:5:85-94.
      Discussion of Salvadorean poet: symbolism, neo-romanticism, and daily world of a woman reflected in her verses. No biographical notes.

242   TORUÑO, JUAN FELIPE
      1946 "La mujer salvadoreña en las letras y en el arte." SS/BBN 70/81:14-28.

Brief, not very informative sketches of almost 40
Salvadorean women writers, artists, and musicians since
1860, with an emphasis on writers.

Honduras

243 ATUÑEZ CASTILLO, RUBÉN
      1967 "La Alondra de Chaiguapa." Vida y obra literaria de
      Teresa Morejón de Bográn. *20 octubre, 1860. +4
      febrero, 1929. In vol. 2 of his Biografía del
      matrimonio Bográn-Morejón. Tegucigalpa?: Edit.
      Nacional. 154 p. ports., bibl. in vol. 1.
      Biography of life and literary achievements of the
      wife of Honduras' president from 1883 to 1891. Teresa
      Morejón de Bográn (1860-1929) lived on her family's
      estate Chaiguapa where she was born, Santa Barbara,
      and San Pedro Sula. Includes her poetry and other
      works in verse and traces her genealogy to an artisto-
      cratic Spanish family.

Costa Rica

244 [SÁENZ ELIZONDO, CARLOS LUIS]
      1956 Costarriqueñas del 56. San José, C.R.: Imprenta Las
      Américas. 46 p.
      Tribute to Costa Rican women on 100th anniversary of
      War of '56. Collection of short stories about various
      Costa Rican women--a President's wife who constructed
      1st flag, a peasant woman, a soldier-woman, etc.

245 URBANO, VICTORIA
      1968 Una escritora costarricense: Yolanda Oreamuno;
      ensayo crítico. Col. Orosí. Madrid: Eds. Castilla de
      Oro. 246 p. bibl.
      Analysis of literary career of Costa Rican novelist
      Yolanda Oreamuno (1916-1961) includes biographical and
      bibliographical data; and discusses themes, especially
      a predominant sexual theme; male and female characters;
      and influences on her work.

Panama

246 MIRANDA de CABAL, BEATRIZ
      1963 "Ida Belli, el Meteoro." TDM 3:13:37, 39, 45.
      Brief biographical sketch of Ida Belli, Panama-born
      poet of Italian parents.

Literature, Mass Media, and Folklore

247   NIVAR de PITTALUGA, AMADA
          1969 "María Olimpia de Obaldía y Esther Neira de Calvo:
          poesía y acción de la mujer en América." TDM 8:47:8-9,
          26, 52.
             Dominican poet discusses 2 illustrious Panamanian
          women: one a poet; the other, a woman of social action
          (educator, fighter for women's rights, participant in
          women's organizations, such as IACW).

248   OLLER de MULFORD, JUANA
          1966 "Valores femeninos panameños: María Olimpia de
          Obaldía." TDM 5:29:10-11, 28, 35.
             Discusses Panamanian poet's works and activities.

249   _____.
          1963 "Valores femeninos panameños: María T. Recuero."
          TDM 3:15:14-15.
             Biographical sketch of a female pioneer in journalism
          and national literature born in 1869.

250   _____.
          1962 "Valores femeninos panameños: Amelia Denis de
          Icaza." TDM 2:10:8-9.
             Biographical sketch of Panamanian poet of the 19c.,
          Amelia Denis de Icaza, including an example of her
          literary effort.

251   _____.
          1962 "Valores femeninos panameños: Nicole Garay." TDM
          2:11:10-11.
             Biographical sketch of Panamanian poet born in 1873.
          Includes examples of her literary efforts.

SOUTH AMERICA

Venezuela

252   CERTAD, AQUILES
          1945 "Valores femeninos venezolanos." REPA 42:5:71.
             Names 18 women who figure in the literary tradition
          of Venezuela as poets, novelists, short story writers,
          historians, etc., singling out Luz Machado de Arnao as
          a fighter for women's rights as well as writer. Very
          brief.

253 CORREA, LUIS
1936 "Teresa de la Parra" and "Bolívar y Teresa de la
Parra." VANH/B 19:76:491-513. port.
Following short tribute to Teresa de la Parra, famous
for her autobiographical novel Iphigenia, 11 letters
written to noted Venezuelan historian Vicente Lecuna
discuss her desire to write a biography of Bolívar as a
lover more than as a hero and her efforts toward that
goal; and record her emotions (self-doubt, excitement,
curiosity), observations of people and places around
her, and anecdotes about other women in her family
during Independence movement (she was a distant relative
of Bolívar). Correspondence dates from Panama, 1930 to
France, 1932.

254 ESCALA, VÍCTOR HUGO
1952 "Cartas de Teresa de la Parra." VANH/B 35:139:282-
83.
Reports that National Library in Caracas received
collection of 36 letters of Teresa de la Parra,
Venezuelan writer famous for her autobiographical novel
Iphigenia, written from Europe to Vicente Lecuna, Luis
Zea Uribe and Rafael Carias. Correspondence includes
comments on social and literary incidents in Paris after
WWI, family affairs, problems related to her personal
income, and efforts toward writing a biography of
Bolívar. For her letters to Lecuna, See Correa, Luis
(#253).

255 GRAMCKO, IDA
1960 "La mujer en la obra de Gallegos." Revista Shell
9:37:33-40.
Considers female figures in the writings of several
authors and in the novels of former president of
Venezuela, Romúlo Gallegos. Interprets Doña Barbara
as a synthesis for defining the vast stretches of unex-
plored and wild territory of Venezuela.

256 HERNÁNDEZ CHAPELLÍN, JESÚS M.
1959 Falconianas ilustres. Eds. del Ministerio de
Relaciones Interiores, 3. Caracas. 355 p. illus.,
plates, ports.
Collection of comments on 7 19c. Venezuelan writers
and 1 educator of early 20c. and on the first cultural
society organized by women in Coro (1889), the founding
of another one, plus the literary journals they edited.
Includes some biographical data, notes on literary
career, examples of work, correspondence, and commentaries from newspapers and other sources. Documented.

Literature, Mass Media, and Folklore

257   NIETO CABALLERO, LUIS EDUARDO
        1952 "Recuerdo de Teresa de la Parra." VANH/B 35:140:
        396-401. illus., ports.
            Fond remembrance of Venezuelan writer Teresa de la
        Parra, by Colombian writer followed by a collection
        of 3 letters from her to him, sent from Europe in the
        early 1930's, in which she mentions aspects of her
        travels, familiar figures of their intellectual circle,
        and her thoughts of Colombia.

258   NUCETI-SARDI, JOSÉ and PÉREZ DÍAZ, LUCILA L. de
        1929 "Women in Venezuelan Literature." PAU/B 63:5:467-74.
        illus., ports.
            Very brief notes on life and literary works of 11
        Venezuelan women writers of late 19c., early 20c. with
        accompanying portraits.

259   PÉREZ GUEVARA, ADA
        1941 "Cooperación femenina en la evolución literaria de
        Venezuela." PAU/Bs 65:12:707-14.
            Brief review of female literary figures in Venezuela
        from the colonial period to contemporary times. For
        the 20c. names writers of history, poetry, novels, etc.
        Notes only one figure, a nun, until the end of the 19c.

260   ROJAS WETTEL, CLAUDIO
        1956 "La presencia de la madre en tres poesías
        venezolanas." UCV/CU 55:79-90. ports.
            Analyzes the presence of Mother, in terms of filial
        feelings, in the poetry of Cecilio Acosta (1818-1881),
        Juan Antonio Pérez Bonalde (1846-1892) and Andrés Eloy
        Blanco (1898-1955). Unclear image of women; appears to
        be more of a longing for or remembrance of childhood,
        innocence and Nature.

Colombia

261   ARANGO FERRER, JAVIER
        1940 "Breve noticia de la mujer en la literatura
        colombiana." In his La literatura de Colombia, pp.
        97-104. Buenos Aires: Imprenta y Casa Edit. "Goni."
            Sketchy presentation of female writers in Colombia
        from the colonial nun la Madre Castillo to 20c. poet
        Laura Victoria, citing several essayists, short story
        and other writers.

262   CAYCEDO, BERNARDO J.
      1952   "Semblanza de doña Soledad Acosta de Samper." HA/B
      39:452/454:356-79.
         Pays tribute to Colombia's most prolific woman writer
      of the 19c. and to her work. Quotes selections from
      her diary; discusses literary influence as well as
      influence of particular individuals and travels.

263   FLORA, CORNELIA BUTLER
      1973   "The Passive Female and Social Change: A Cross-
      Cultural Comparison of Women's Magazine Fiction." In
      Female and Male in Latin America: Essays, ed. by A.
      Pescatello, pp. 59-85. Pittsburgh, Pa.: Univ. of
      Pittsburgh Press. tables, bibl.
         Utilizes women's magazine fiction in the US, Mexico
      and Colombia to examine the ideal of the passive female
      and her relationship to change in a cross-class compari-
      son. Suggests that such literature is counterrevolution-
      ary and that there is a need to overcome the values
      expressed in it in order to mobilize women for radical
      change.

264   HARKESS, SHIRLEY and FLORA, CORNELIA B.
      1974   "Women in the News: An Analysis of Media Images
      in Colombia." RI 4:2:220-38. bibl.
         Using data gathered from 2 Colombian newspapers
      (1970-73), 2 sociologists set up a 4-fold typology,
      composed of 2 dimensions--manifestation of the tradi-
      tional ideal of a woman and the approach to that ideal--
      for the purpose of comparing and conceptualizing 4 key
      images of women which are manipulated by the establish-
      ment press: saintly mother, beauty queen, altruist,
      politician. Conclusion is that deviance from traditional
      ideal in a passive way and an active approach to tradi-
      tional ideal are positively sanctioned if there is
      conformity to idea. Politician image, both deviant and
      active, does not guarantee human liberation.

265   JAQUETTE, JANE
      1973   "Literary Archetypes and Female Role Alternatives:
      The Woman and the Novel in Latin America." In Female
      and Male in Latin America: Essays, ed. by A.
      Pescatello, pp. 3-27. Pittsburgh, Pa.: Univ. of
      Pittsburgh Press. bibl. notes.
         Examines literary images of women in 20c. Peruvian
      novels; and draws 3 female archetypes (mother, witch,
      wife/concubine) from Cien años de soledad by Colombian
      writer Gabriel García Márquez. Concludes that avail-
      ability of strong female roles in Latin American culture

Literature, Mass Media, and Folklore

> indicates viability of role differentiation, which is
> rejected by North American feminists.

266 JARAMILLO MEZA, J. B.
    1956 "La verdadera 'María' de Isaacs." AHVC/B
    24:105:245-48.
        Speculates on woman who served as inspiration for
    María, protagonist of Jorge Isaacs' familiar romantic
    novel of Colombia (1867). Clementina Isaacs, the only
    survivor of his children, relates what she heard from
    her mother and a servant--that Isaacs' cousin Esther,
    brought from Jamaica to live with his family on their
    estate "El Paraíso," was probably the original María.

267 MARTÍNEZ DELGADO, LUIS
    1950 "Quién fué la "María" que inspiró a Jorge Isaacs?"
    REPB 37:157/158:2205-20.
        Based on primary and secondary sources, agrees with
    Velasco Madriñán that inspiration for Isaacs' romantic
    novel María (1867) came from Pedro Vicente Martínez and
    Mercedes Cabal Borrero, Efraim and María respectively.
    Relates upper-class family histories (marriages) which
    served as models for the story. Ample footnotes.

268 MEJÍA B., WILLIAM
    1967 "La mujer en la obra riveriana." BCB 10/11:158-63.
        Discusses image of women on a symbolic level in crea-
    tions of nature (star, palm tree, etc.), on a real level,
    and on an ideal level in the poetic and prose works of
    José Eustasio Rivera. Concludes that the writer always
    wished for an ideal woman but could never find her in
    any concrete individual, so he escaped in nature.

269 OTERO MUÑOZ, GUSTAVO
    1964 "Soledad Acosta de Samper." BCB 7:6:1063-69.
        Discusses the extensive literary career of Soledad
    Acosta de Samper, prolific 19c. woman writer who divided
    her time between Colombia and Europe; and identifies the
    influence of other writers in her works.

270 _____.
    1937 "Soledad Acosta de Samper." HA/B 24:271:257-83.
    ports., bibl.
        Biographical notes on the most prominent and prolific
    19c. woman writer of Colombia, Soledad Acosta de Samper
    (1833-1913). Considered a "precursor of the modern type
    of intellectual Colombian woman," this well-educated,
    upper-class woman held a salon, spoke many languages,
    traveled and lived abroad. Includes list and commentary

of her written works, which ranged from scientific,
religious, and historical studies to novels.

271 _____.
   1933 "Doña Soledad Acosta de Samper." HA/B 20:229:169-75.
   Known as "the most notable [female writer] of Colombia,
   and one of the most glorious figures of feminine intellectuality in America," Soledad Acosta de Samper (1833-
   1913) wrote articles, novels, biographies, historical
   pieces, and edited periodicals. Born to an English
   mother and Colombian father, she lived abroad on and off.
   Provides chronological account of her prodigious literary output. Introduction on women in Colombia, especially in literature, from the Conquest to the 19c.,
   considers attitudes toward women, romantic scandals,
   political action, intellectual life.

272 PARDO de HURTADO, ISABEL
   1940 Mujeres colombians (desfile de escritoras y poetisas).
   Quito: Edit. de "El Comercio." 94 p.
   Very brief notes on 20c. Colombian writers, grouped by
   city or department, accompany selections from their
   works. Cites some journalists at end.

Sor Francisca Josefa del Castillo

273 ACHURY VALENZUELA, DARÍO, ed.
   1968 Obras completas de la Madre Francisca Josefa de
   Castillo, según fiel transcripción de los manuscriptos
   originales que se conservan en la Biblioteca Luis-Angel
   Arango. Bogota: Talleres Gráficos del Banco de la
   República. 2 vols. clr. port., facsims., bibl.
   f/notes.
   Long introduction discusses Tunja, birthplace of literary nun Madre Castillo (1671-1741), at the end of the
   17c., her lineage, birth, infancy and adolescence, conventual life, religious experiences, confessors, similarities and differences between her and Santa Teresa
   and Sor Juana, the Inquisition, her Erasmian nature;
   analyzes her works and provides chronological table of
   her life. Volume 1, her Vida, is her spiritual autobiography; volume 2, her Afectos espirituales, continues
   her religious experience.

274 _____.
   1967 "De las hablas o lucuciones divinas en la obra de
   la Venerable Madre Castillo." BCB 10:9:17-28. bibl.
   f/notes.

Literature, Mass Media, and Folklore

Reproduces passages from the Vida of Sor Francisca, in
which her sensations, visions, dreams, and spiritual
states are recorded, and compares them to the supernatural graces of Santa Teresa. Concludes that the latter very much influenced the Madre Castillo in expressions
and literary phrases.

275 _____.
1967 "Tunja en tiempos de Sor Francisca Josefa de la
Concepción de Castillo." BCB 10:6:1276-82.
Describes the city of Tunja, birthplace of Colombia's
most famous nun, Sor Francisca, when she lived there,
conjecturing about her activities and the people she
related to.

276 _____.
1967 "Sor Francisca y el brazo largo de la Inquisición."
BCB 10:4:770-72.
Explains why Sor Francisca, famous literary nun of
colonial Colombia, was able to read and write while the
prohibitions of the Inquisition deprived Santa Teresa of
mystical works. Exportation of books from the Iberian
Peninsula was an important economic activity for the
Spanish Crown.

277 ANDRADE GONZÁLEZ, GERARDO
1968 "Algunos aspectos de la sociedad neogranadina. La
vida conventual y social tunjana, en los escritos de la
Madre Castillo." BCB 11:1:5-11.
Based on the autobiography of the Madre Castillo, provides a portrait of colonial society and conventual life
in Tunja, Colombia from 1671 to 1742. Includes observations on women's situation.

278 _____.
1967 "La Madre Castillo una mística de la colonia." BCB
10:3:500-06. bibl.
Discussion of Sor Francisca as a mystic in colonial
America, illustrated with selections from her poetry.
Some comparison made with Sor Juana and Santa Teresa.

279 BEJARANO DÍAZ, HORACIO
1958-59 "La Madre Castillo." UNIPOB 23:82:17-21.
Briefly comments on literary output and influences of
one of the first women writers during the colonial period,
a nun from Tunja. Contrasts Santa Teresa and Sor
Francisca Josefa del Castillo (1671-1742), while most
writers draw parallels between the two. No biographical
data.

South America - Colombia/Sor Francisca Josefa del Castillo

280 CARRASQUILLA, RAFAEL MARÍA
    1957 "La Madre Castillo." UNIPOB 22:79:183-97. bibl.
        1890 talk on Francisca Josefa de la Concepción Castillo
    y Guevara (1671-1742), the famous nun of Tunja, reflects
    on mysticism and analyzes her 2 works--Vida and Afectos
    espirituales--including some brief biographical notes. Her
    literary works are surprising because of their mystical
    nature at a time (late 17c.) when everyone was reading
    and/or writing in the Góngora style.

281 CASTILLO y GUEVARA, SOR FRANCISCA JOSEFA del
    1942 Mi vida. Biblioteca Popular de Cultura Colombiana,
    16. Clásicos Colombianos. Bogotá: Imprenta Nacional.
    226 p.
        Autobiography of famous nun reflects her religious
    states and convent life in 17 and 18c. Tunja, Colombia.
    A primary source.

282 CORREA, RAMÓN C.
    1963 "La monja colonial Sor Francisca Josefa del Castillo."
    CEST 32:266:51-58. Also in 1966 REPB 52:246/247:2587-94.
    illus.
        Utilizing quotations from her Vida, provides biograph-
    ical sketch of the Madre Castillo (1671-1742, the Clare
    nun of Tunja who became famous as a mystic writer and
    who has been compared to Santa Teresa.

283 _____.
    1935 "Francisca Josefa del Castillo." AE 2:7:295-98.
        Also known as the Colombian Santa Teresa, the Madre
    Castillo (1671-1742), born in Tunja, entered its convent
    of the Clares when she was barely able to read but de-
    veloped intellectually there and wrote the 2 works for
    which she is famous: Vida and Afectos espirituales
    (both begun in 1690 and concluded in 1728).

284 GÓMEZ RESTREPO, ANTONIO
    1971 "Una gran escritora en la colonia." UPB
    32:110:347-78.
        Notes on the life, mysticism, and literary achievements
    of the Madre Castillo based principally on her autobiography,
    Vida, and her Sentimientos espirituales (Tunja, 17c.)

Literature, Mass Media, and Folklore

285 SAMPER ORTEGA, DANIEL
      1930 "La madre Castillo." In his Al galope, pp. 39-75.
      Bogota: Edit. Minerva. Also in 1951 REPB
      38:161/162:2358-73.
      Biography of Colombia's well-known literary nun of
      Tunja, Josefa del Castillo y Guevara (1671-1742) dis-
      cusses the ambiance of colonial Tunja, her home, life
      in the convent of Santa Clara, her literary personality
      and religious struggle. No references.

Ecuador

286 ANDRADE COELLO, ALEJANDRA
      1942 Cultura femenina; floración intelectual de la mujer
      ecuatoriana en el siglo XX. Quito: Talleres Gráficos
      del Ministerio de Educación. 74 p. bibl. f/notes.
      Poorly organized overview of women writers--poets,
      educators, journalists, etc.--in Ecuador during first
      4 decades of 20c.

287 ARIAS, AUGUSTO
      1946 "La mujer en la letra del hombre." América
      22:85/86:328-45.
      Superficially traces the presence of women in
      Ecuadorian letters, particularly in biography, but also
      in other literary forms.

288 CORYLE, MARY
      1952 "Tres mujeres máximas en la literatura nacional."
      UC/A 8:2:153-63.
      Chatty, praising sketches of 3 19c. and 20c. Ecuador-
      ian writers--Dolores Veintimilla, Zoila Ugarte de
      Landivar, Aurora Estrada y Ayala--taken from her book
      20 hombres y mujeres del Ecuador.

289 RENDÓN, VICTOR MANUEL
      1936 "Escritoras ecuatorianas." CIH/B 4:4/6:112-14.
      Also in 1935 "Women Writers of Ecuador." UO/BA
      9:4:380-82.
      Extremely brief information on the life and works of
      Ecuadorian women writers from Teresa de Jesús Cepeda
      (1566-1610), educated in a Carmelite convent in Spain
      and known for her letters, to A. Raquel Verdesoto, a
      Modernist poet.

Peru

290 BARDIN, JAMES C.
1941 "Three Literary Ladies of Spain's American Colonies:
II. 'Amarilis'." PAU/B 75:1:19-24.
Pictures young novitiate in 17c. Peru, believed to be
María Tello de Lara, so moved by Lope de Vega's writings
that she composed and had smuggled out of the convent a
poem to him. It is reproduced here with comments and
excerpts from Lope de Vega's reply.

291 BAZÁN MONTENEGRO, DORA
1967 La mujer en las Tradiciones peruanas. Madrid:
Maribel. 124 p. bibl.
Detailed analysis of portrayal of women in the
Tradiciones peruanas of Ricardo Palma (1833-1919). Sets
up a typology of female protagonists by nationality and
race, civil status, physical attributes, social and moral
class, and discusses how they are presented and characterized. Considers women with respect to male personages
and the author and as a reflection of ideological problems in Palma's work. Concludes that woman, the central
character of the Tradiciones, appears in an infinite
variety of characters, in different epochs, and of different moral and social conditions, although certain
constants or themes can be denominated. Woman is not
only an active character, but an alterative element,
especially in matters of love and marriage. Believes
notion that Palma is antifeminist because of certain
defects with which he characterizes woman is counter-
balanced by his use of adjectives, diminutives, etc.,
which demonstrate a sympathetic attitude.

292 Claridad, no. 294
1935? Magda Portal, su vida y su obra. B.A.: Edit.
Claridad. 47 p.
Collection of short pieces praising Magda Portal as a
writer and political activist plus several of her own
writings (e.g., "La mujer aprista"). Published while
she was in jail.

293 CUADROS ESCOBEDO, MANUEL E.
1949 Paisaje i obra, mujer e historia: Clorinda Matto de
Turner. Cuzco: Edit. H. G. Rozas Sucesores. 160 p.
illus., port., facsims., bibl.
Analyzes the writings of Peruvian poet, tradicionista,
essayist, playwright and novelist known for her criticism of 19c. Peruvian society. Provides biographical
data (1852-1909) as well.

Literature, Mass Media, and Folklore

294   DELGADO, JAIME
          1969 "El amor en la América prehispánica." IGFO/RI
          29:115/118:151-71.
          See MEXICO for annotation.

295   FOX, LUCÍA UNGARO
          1968 "La mujer como motivo en la poesía peruana."
          Abside 32:1:75-91. bibl. notes.
          Looks at the variations in which women are presented
          as a subject in Peruvian poetry--from the verses of
          anonymous pre-Columbian poets and of 7 poets from Juan
          del Valle Caviedes (17c.) to César Vallejo (20c.):
          passive indigenous woman; ordinary (i.e., not the Virgin
          or a saint) colonial woman; heavenly or damned angel;
          American muse; mother and lover.

296   GIRALDO JARAMILLO, GABRIEL
          1938 "Amarilis, supuesta santafereña." HA/B
          25:289/290:846-50.
          Agrees that one of the most notable injustices of
          Western civilization has been women's secondary position
          in intellectual activities. Attempts to shed light on
          Peruvian woman, María de Alvarado (born during colonial
          epoch), who wrote a letter/poem to Spanish playwright
          Lope de Vega, whose works she read with much admiration.
          Quotes verses.

297   GORRITI, JUANA MANUELA
          1892 Veladas literarias de Lima. 1876-1877. Tomo primero.
          Veladas I a X. Buenos Aires: Imprenta Europea. 486 p.
          port.
          See ARGENTINA for annotation.

298   JAQUETTE, JANE
          1973 "Literary Archetypes and Female Role Alternatives:
          The Woman and the Novel in Latin America." In Female
          and Male in Latin America: Essays, ed. by A. Pescatello,
          pp. 3-27. Pittsburgh, Pa: University of Pittsburgh
          Press. bibl. notes.
          See COLOMBIA for annotation.

299   REEDY, DANIEL R.
          1970 "Magda Portal: Peru's Voice of Social Protest."
          UA/REH 4:1:85-97. bibl. f/notes.
          Examines theme of social protest in poetry of Magda
          Portal; important Peruvian writer whose popularity and
          political influence through APRA was greatest from the
          1920's to 1940's. Traces her literary development of
          revolutionary thesis and her political career, including
          persecution and exile, until the 1960's.

300 TAMAYO VARGAS, AUGUSTO
       1940 "Las novelas de la Carbonera." Turismo 15:155:3
       p. unnumbered. illus., port.
          Summarizes 6 novels of Mercedes Cabello de Carbonera,
       who won gold medal for novel in literary contest of
       Ateneo de Lima in 1886. Describes female protagonists.

301 TEMPLE, ELLA DUNBAR
       1939 "Curso de la literatura femenina a través del
       período colonial en el Perú." 3 (Tres) 1:25-56.
          Based on primary and secondary sources, not only names
       the many women writers of colonial Peru, but sets them
       within the political/cultural context of their particular
       epoch (e.g., foreign influences, the Inquisition) and
       provides historical background (royal legislation
       affecting women's position: passage to America, inheri-
       tance, ability to own land and Indians; and active
       female participants in the Conquest and colonization).
       Section 3 discusses character of the 3 types of litera-
       ture written by women during colonial times: devout
       (emerging from conventual life); aristocratic (poetry
       by upper-class women); and visionary (vulgarized mysti-
       cism by lower-class women).

302 WEISSE, MARÍA
       1944 "La mujer limeña en las "Tradiciones." HH 2:15:18-
       20. illus., port.
          Of the many kinds of women in the colonial society of
       Lima portrayed in Ricardo Palma's Tradiciones peruanas,
       chooses the seductive and picaresque *tapada* and her
       scandalous fashion and convent women for very brief
       discussion.

Bolivia

303 URQUIDI, JOSÉ MACEDONIO
       1918 Bolivianas ilustres. Estudios biográficos y
       críticos. Segunda parte. La cultura femenina en
       nuestra evolución republicana. La Paz: Escuela
       Tipográfica Salesiana. 216 p. ports.
          Sketches provide some biographical and literary data
       on 19c. Bolivian women writers (poets, educators,
       novelists): María Josefa Mujía, Mercedes Belzu de
       Dorado, Lindaura Anzoátegui de Campero, Adela Zamudio,
       Hercilia Fernández de Mujía, Sara Ugarte de Salamanca;
       plus a paragraph apiece on 16 others, into early 20c.
       Includes examples of their poetry and prose.

WOMEN IN SPANISH AMERICA

Literature, Mass Media, and Folklore

Paraguay

304 RODRÍGUEZ-ALCALÁ, HUGO
1968 "Josefina Plá, española de América, y la poesía."
CAM 159:4:73-101. illus., bibl. notes.
Introductory essay on Paraguayan poet contains biographical data, evaluation of intellectual and artistic
nature of the writer, analysis of fundamental themes in
her work, and commentary on a few representative poems.

Chile

305 ALLEN, MARTHA E.
1952 "Dos estilos de novela: Marta Brunet y María Luisa
Bombal." RI 18:35:63-91.
Analyzes 2 novels of each of these Chilean writers
from the point of view that each takes a conscious but
different direction: Brunet writes regional, realistic,
dramatic social novels in which the reader is a specta-
tor, while Bombal writes subjectively, immersing the
reader within the protagonist's perception.

306 CONTRERAS O., CONSTANTINO
1966 "Mitos de brujería de Chiloé (estudio linguistico-
folklórico)." ESFIL 2:161-98. map, bibl.
Analyzes various myths of witchcraft of Chiloé for
linguistic aspects and roots in indigenous or Hispanic
tradition. Few women are dedicated to witchcraft there,
but one myth is about la voladora or mensajera, a daughter of witch parents who is able to transform herself
into a bird.

307 GARDENER, MARY A.
1972-1973 "Press Woman's Role in Chile." Matrix 58:2:
6-7, 22-23. illus., ports.
Synthesis of 8 top women journalists in Chile--their
political positions (when Allende was elected) and professional activities--and the antecedents of their
contemporary success.

308 GEEL, MARÍA CAROLINA
1964 "Chile." In El hombre en la literatura de la mujer,
ed. by E. Hoppe, trans. by I. Durruty, pp. 418-22.
Madrid: Edit. Gredos.
Examines varying image of men in the literary works of
Chilean women writers beginning with Mercedes Marín del
Solar of the 19c. Concludes that man serves as a source
of inspiration and an element of subtle speculations.

309 LATCHAM, RICARDO A.
       1955 "Literatura imaginativa y novela femenina en Chile."
       ESTAM 10:48:337-49.
         Only pages 346-49 deal with Chilean women novelists.
       Cites authors and titles of their works since 1932 and
       very briefly notes style.

310 LEVINE, LINDA GOULD
       1974 "María Luisa Bombal from a Feminist Perspective."
       RI 4:2:148-61. bibl. f/notes.
         In an examination of the novels and short stories of
       Chilean writer María Luisa Bombal, notes passive image
       of women's role despite panoply of female characters:
       "woman is obsessed by man and contemplates her existence
       always in relationship to him." Discusses emphasis on
       physical beauty rather than intelligence, machistic
       attitude of men toward women, eroticism, suicide. Even
       in the one work which slightly deviates from Bombal's
       consistent image of relations between the sexes, the
       woman's life is ultimately marked by frustration and
       despair.

311 MATTELART, MICHÈLE
       1973 "Apuntes sobre lo moderno: una manera de leer las
       revistas femeninas." CDLA 13:77:112-25.
         Using popular women's magazines, demonstrates manipu-
       lative aspects of the medium to convey false sense of
       modernity which actually repudiates rather than promotes
       change. Mechanism employed reaffirms myth of femininity
       by conferring new validity upon it; uses rhetoric of
       fantasy to simulate alliance with liberating ideologies;
       and reinforces dependence and static structure of
       bourgeois order. Women derive status from conforming to
       way of life and consuming products presented.

312 _____.
       1970 "El nivel mítico en la prensa pseudoamorosa." CRN/
       CEREN 3:221-83. bibl.
         Detailed, incisive analysis of 103 issues of Chilean
       fotonovela Cine Amor on 2 levels: 1) semantic-
       structural, pointing out archetypal elements in dramatic,
       plastic and linguistic form and substance; 2) mythical-
       content, decoding the messages communicated in this
       popular form of literary/pictorial mass media. Reveals
       manipulative mechanisms used to dilute social conflicts,
       including women's liberation.

Literature, Mass Media, and Folklore

313 MEDINA, JOSÉ TORIBIO
    1933 "Las mujeres de 'La Araucana'." SCHG/R 74:464-78.
        Discusses female characters--both Spanish and Indian--
        that appear in La Araucana, Alonso Ercilla y Zúñiga's
        16c. epic poem about the Spanish attempt to conquer the
        Araucanians in Chile. Doña Mencia de los Nidos, a
        Spanish woman who actually existed, is presented as a
        strong woman. The Indian women are portrayed as active,
        devoted, patriotic and passionate.

314 _____.
        1923 La literatura femenina en Chile. (Notas bibliográ-
        ficas y en parte críticas). Santiago: Imprenta
        Universitaria. 334 p.
            Valuable, if dated, annotated bibliography (642 items)
        of women's literary contributions in Chile in poetry,
        religion, translation, pedagogy, fiction, travel,
        theatre, journalism, law, medicine, pharmacy, and
        dentistry since the colonial period, including some
        examples. Serves as a supplement to L. Zanelli Lopez'
        Mujeres chilenas de letras (#320), which does not
        describe the women's works.

315 OYARZÚN, MILA
    1943 "La poesía femenina en Chile." Atenea 73:218:168-94.
        In an examination of women's poetry in Chile, takes
        into account epoch in which each poet lived as the prin-
        cipal factor for evaluating her verses. Begins with
        Mercedes Marín del Solar, whose first poem appeared in
        1837, and Rosario Orrego de Uribe, who in 1879 became
        the first member of Santiago's Academia de Bellas
        Letras, and briefly mentions 4 other 19c. poets. For the
        20c., covers Gabriela Mistral, Whinett de Rokha, María
        Monvel, Olga Acevedo, Gladys Thein; mentions 5 others
        briefly; and lists 15 more. No references.

316 RODRÍGUEZ FERNÁNDEZ, MARIO
    1962 "Imagen de la mujer y el amor en un momento de la
        poesía de Pablo Neruda." UNCH/A 120:125:74-79.
        Analyzes the image of woman in Los veinte poemas de
        amor y una canción desesperada of 20c. Chilean poet
        Pablo Neruda: a godwoman of carnal strength and divine
        powers; an integration of elements which express the
        purest sensuality of the earth or sea; a tool or weapon
        to help affirm life against solitude and pain; a
        revealer or seer; hope and the capacity to show the way,
        to overcome anguish and anxiety. Neruda turns to women
        to help him in his liberation. However, in "la canción
        desesperada," the poet recognizes the impossibility of

communication and the inadequacy of physical possession--
woman is no longer possessed of divine powers.

317 SILVA CASTRO, RAÚL
1965 "Mujeres en las letras chilenas." Cuadernos
94:75-80.
Discusses growing appearance of women writers in
Chile since 1945. States that there is no difference
between women and men in their function as writers, but
introduces several woman writers by remarking on their
physical appearance first. Notes that but for a few
exceptions, women in Chile have not written literary
criticism; most of the women writers are partial to
realism, the countryside, careful style, and prose over
verse.

318 URZÚA, MARÍA and ADRIASOLA, XIMENA
1963 La mujer en la poesía chilena, 1784-1961. Santiago:
Edit. Nascimento. 239 p. bibl.
Series of 36 very brief biographical-bibliographical
sketches of Chilean women poets accompanied by selections
of their verses. Begins with Sor Tadea de San Joaquín,
whose romance (1784) narrates the inundation of the
Convent San Rafael by the Mapocho River, considered the
oldest poem by a Chilean woman and ending with Ximena
Sepúlveda, whose work was published in the 1950's.

319 VICUÑA CIFUENTES, JULIO
1914-15 "Mitos y supersticiones recogidas de la tradición
oral chilena." SCHG/R 9:13:399-453; 10:14:294-333;
11:15:307-71; 12:16:415-38; 13:17:415-74; 14:18:412-59;
15:19:369-422.
Extensive, well-researched compendium of myths and
popular beliefs based on many other collections and
informants' narrations. Although not specifically
about women, refers to witches, figures such as la
calchona, las sirenas, la viuda, la voladora, reproductive cycle, marriage, courtship, romance and love, etc.

320 ZANELLI LÓPEZ, LUISA
1917 Mujeres chilenas de letras. vol. 1. Santiago:
Imprenta Universitaria. 203 p. ports.
Based on references in Chile's Biblioteca Nacional,
interviews, and visits to various institutions, traces
parallel evolution of women in education and literature
in Chile. Cites first university graduates, schools,
programs, and women's social and literary organizations.

Literature, Mass Media, and Folklore

Gabriela Mistral

321 ALBANELL, NORAH and MANGO, NANCY
      1958 "Los escritos de Gabriela Mistral y estudios sobre
      su obra." In Gabriela Mistral, 1889-1957, pp. 49-90.
      Wash., D.C.: Pan American Union.
        Bibliography of 506 items divided by works of Gabriela
      Mistral, critical studies and biographies on her, and
      bibliographies.

322 ALEGRÍA, FERNANDO
      1966 Genio y figura de Gabriela Mistral. Biblioteca de
      América. Col. Genio y Figura, 7. Buenos Aires: Edit.
      Universitaria de Buenos Aires. 191 p. illus., bibl.

323 ARCE de VAZQUEZ, MARGOT
      1964 Gabriela Mistral: The Poet and Her Work. Trans. by
      H. M. Anderson. The Gotham Library. N.Y.: N.Y. Univ.
      Press. 158 p. bibl.
        Close friend and companion of Gabriela Mistral provides
      personal discussion of her life as a teacher, writer,
      diplomat, and traveler. Includes a useful bibliography
      of books by and about this Nobel Prize winner.

324 BATES, MARGARET J.
      1946 "Gabriela Mistral." AAFH/TAM 3:2:168-89. bibl.
      f/notes.
        Biographical notes and literary criticism on Gabriela
      Mistral, Chile's foremost woman poet, with illustrations
      from her work, and 98 footnotes.

325 DONOSO LOERO, TERESA
      1967 "Gabriela Mistral y la maternidad frustrada." UCC/
      FT 14:60:7-15.
        Limited view of Gabriela Mistral as a woman, trauma-
      tized by the loss of her father and lover, who achieves
      a cosmic motherhood. She gives tenderness to children
      as a teacher because of an unattainable maternity within
      herself. Illustrates emotions of frustrated motherhood
      in her poetry.

326 ESPINOSA, AURELIO MACEDONIO
      1951 "Gabriela Mistral." AAFH/TAM 8:1:3-40.
        Includes biographical notes on Gabriela Mistral,
      summaries of important publications, analysis and
      criticism of some of her poems (e.g., themes of religious
      spirit, humanitarianism, universal love, maternity and
      motherhood, death, teaching, nature, modernism, and
      comments on versification. Illustrates with verses from
      her poetry.

South America-Chile/Gabriela Mistral

327 FIGUEIRA, GASTÓN
1970 "Páginas desconocidas u olvidadas de Gabriela
Mistral." RIB 20:2:139-56. bibl. f/notes.
Brings together various selections from Mistral's
prose, including a meeting with Juana de Ibarbourou and
Alfonsina Storni in 1938 and her impressions of them,
travel notes, etc. Presents her life and opinions
through her prose rather than poetry.

328 _____.
1959 De la vida y la obra de Gabriela Mistral.
Montevideo. 68 p. illus.

329 IDUARTE, ANDRÉS
1958 "Gabriela Mistral, santa a la jineta." CAM 100:427-
61. illus.
Reflections on long friendship with Gabriela Mistral,
including letters he wrote when he first stayed with her
in Bédarrides, France in 1929, in which he gives a daily
account of activities and observations of her. Considers
her America's greatest woman.

330 _____.
1946 "En torno a Gabriela Mistral." CAM 26:2:240-56.
Personal impressions based on time spent with
Gabriela Mistral in France. Includes verses from her
poetry.

331 LADRÓN de GUEVARA, MATILDE
1962 Gabriela Mistral, rebelde magnífica. Biblioteca
Contemporánea. Buenos Aires: Edit. Losada. 189 p.
bibl.
Reproduces conversations and correspondence between
two Chilean women writers.

332 OCAMPO, VICTORIA
1957 "Y Lucila, que hablaba a río . . . Gabriela Mistral,
1889-1957." Sur 245:75-82. Reprint from 1957
Nación (Buenos Aires, 2 March 1957).
Personal portrait of Gabriela Mistral through recollections of time spent with her since 1930. Anecdotes
reveal particular traits or habits of the famous Chilean
poet, Nobel Prize winner.

333 _____.
1945 "Gabriela Mistral y el Premio Novel." Sur 14:134:
7-15. port.

Literature, Mass Media, and Folklore

Personal recollections of relationship with Gabriela
Mistral since their first encounter in Madrid in 1930.
Believes in her well-deserved earning of the Nobel Prize;
evocation of America in her poetry (obsessive preoccupation with land and race, love of children); solution to
problems of language. Quotes verses to illustrate.

334 PINILLA, NORBERTO
      1940 Bibliografía crítica sobre Gabriela Mistral.
      Santiago: Ed. de la Univ. de Chile. 69 p.
        Though dated, very useful, briefly annotated bibliog-
      raphy of Gabriela Mistral: works and prologues; poetry
      put to music; translations; anthologies which include
      her; studies and biographies; publications which refer
      to her, her winning the Nobel Prize; and articles about
      books about her.

335 SZMULEWICZ, EFRAÍN
      1967 Gabriela Mistral (biografía emotiva). 2nd ed.
      Col. Esencia. Santiago: Edit. Universitaria. 171 p.
      bibl.

Argentina

336 ALONSO PIÑEIRO, ARMANDO
      1957 Poetisa mística de América: María Raquel Adler.
      B.A.: Edit. Prestigio. 48 p.
        Analysis of mysticism in Argentine poet, María Raquel
      Adler, considered by Fermín Arenas Luque to be the suc-
      cessor of Sor Juana. Includes anthology of her poetry.

337 Amigos de Herminia Brumana, Buenos Aires
      1964 Ideario y presencia de Herminia Brumana. Buenos
      Aires. 176 p. ports., bibl.
        Collection of ideas and thoughts excerpted from the
      writings of Herminia Brumana, 20c. Argentine writer and
      teacher, along with 6 selected essays (which won
      prizes) and brief articles by other figures in the
      Argentine literary world, which discuss her life and
      work.

338 BARALIS, MARTA
      1964 Contribución a la bibliografía de Alfonsina Storni.
      Compilaciones especiales, 18. Buenos Aires: Fondo
      Nacional de las Artes. 66 p.

339   BECK, VERA FISHEROVÁ
      1944   "Las heroínas en la novelística argentina." RHM
      10:3/4:231-50.
         Heroines do not appear in Argentine literature until
      the beginning of the 19c., during the Romantic era,
      but thereafter are developed during the periods of
      realism and naturalism. Describes typical examples of
      heroines (historical figures, teachers in the provinces,
      the campesina, middle-class women of Buenos Aires, etc.).
      Considers the works of Mármol, Wast, Blómberg, López,
      Gorriti, Sarmiento, Hudson, Ocantos, Gálvez, Burgos,
      Lynch, Güiraldes, Mansilla, Gutiérrez, de la Barra,
      Leumann, Mallea, whose principal interest lies in
      women's love affairs. Notes influence of European and
      North American literature. Provides useful summaries
      of female characters and plots of novels and short
      stories of 19c. and first 4 decades of 20c.

340   BONET, CARMELO MELITON
      1962   Margarita Abella Caprile. Biblioteca del
      Sesquicentenario. Col. Antologías. Buenos Aires: Eds.
      Culturales Argentinas. 97 p. illus., plates.
         Biographical sketch of 20c. Argentine poet Margarita
      Abella Caprile (1901-61) and analytical study of her
      poetry--its themes and style--followed by an anthology
      of her work. She was a member of the well-known Mitre
      family.

341   BULLRICH PALENQUE, SILVINA
      1972   La mujer argentina en la literature. B.A.:
      Ministerio de Cultura y Educación, Centro Nacional de
      Documentación e Información Educativa. 21 p.
         Thoughts and impressions of Argentine novelist: being
      a writer; early women writers of 20c.; portrayal of
      women by women different than by men; timid entry of
      women into literature; lack of feminism in women's
      literature of last 25 years; writing as a vocation for
      women; etc.

342   CARRERA, JULIETA
      1944   "Tres poetisas argentinas." RI 8:15:31-47.
         Short study on Argentine poets Alfonsina Storni,
      Elvira de Alvear and Norah Lange and their literary
      output.

343   _____.
      1939   "Una notable escritora argentina." A 3:2:37-40.
         Discusses feminine literature and notes that more
      women have emerged as poets than as prose writers because

Literature, Mass Media, and Folklore

poetry is a better medium to serve egoism and vanity.
Suggests Herminia Brumana as one of the few women writers
in prose to emerge as a witness of her environment and
20c. epoch. Reviews her literary output and praises her
style--executed with understanding, exactitude, forceful-
ness, sharp and realistic observations. Discusses her
Cartas a las mujeres argentinas, a collection of letters
which reflect on women and her problem as female,
suggesting consciousness, responsibility and action.

344   CARVALHO, JOAQUIM MONTEZUMA de
      1973 "Alfonsina Storni: fundadora de la emancipación
      femenina hispoamericana." FAH/N 253:44-52. illus.
         Exclaims and agrees with other critics that she was
      a precursor, but does not explain why except by recount-
      ing her tragic life as a poor woman of Italian heritage
      who gave birth to an illegitimate child and committed
      suicide. Verses quoted.

345   CHACA, DIONISIO
      1940 Historia de "Juana Manuela Gorriti". B.A.: Imprenta
      y Libreria "El Centenario" de Bruno Iaria. 146 p.
      ports.
         Ex-director of "Juana Manuela Gorriti" School in
      Buenos Aires, provides biography of Juana Manuela
      Gorriti (1818-1892), an Argentine woman who spent many
      years in Lima, where she founded a school for girls,
      a literary salon, and developed her own literary career,
      publishing widely and founding a magazine. Quotes
      primary and secondary sources. See #350.

346   CHERTUDI, SUSANA
      1971 "Martina Chapanay: un personaje legendario." In
      Veinticinco estudios de folklore; homenaje a Vicente T.
      Mendoza y Virginia Rodríguez Rivera, pp. 141-48.
      Estudios de Folklore, 4. Mex., D.F.: UNAM, Inst. de
      Investigaciones Estéticas. bibl.
         Demonstrates the persisting appearance of female
      bandit Martina Chapanay in Argentine oral traditions and
      beliefs of those who relate her story. An analysis of
      22 versions of the legend offers data on her place of
      birth, physical appearance and garb, activities, death,
      comparisons, etc. Transcribes recording of version 22
      from native informant of province of San Juan. Classi-
      fies these narrations as historical legends of an
      outstanding personality.

347 GALARZA, PEDRO IGNACIO
1970 Presencia de la mujer en el Martín Fierro.
Cuadernos de Cultura, 3. Catamarca, Arg.: Dirección
General de Cultura. 35 p. illus.
According to the Handbook of Latin American Studies
36(1974):6643, this is a collection of those passages
from José Hernández' poem about the Argentine *gaucho*
(1872, 1879) which refer to woman, wife, and mother
and their qualities.

348 GIUSTI, ROBERTO F.
1937 "Letras argentinas: la protesta de las mujeres."
Nosotros 3:10:87-93.
Reviews 1936 publications of Victoria Ocampo and
Margarita Abella Caprile, Argentine writers who "without
renouncing being intimately feminine, translate in their
conduct and thinking the strong proposal of being
intellectually equal to men and treated as such." Both
share a spiritual attitude with respect to certain questions on women's role in society, a protest against
those who ignore women's right to express themselves with
freedom and against social limitations imposed on women.

349 GONZÁLEZ TUÑÓN, RAÚL
1952 "El caso de Madame Victoria Ocampo." GUAT/R 4:4:
212-15.
Criticizes Victoria Ocampo's politics as manifested in
her writings, activities as editor of Sur, speeches, and
foreign intellectual friends. Describes her as an
admirer of Yankee imperialism, possessing an allergy to
communism. Reproaches her position vis-a-vis fascism
during WWII.

350 GORRITI, JUANA M.
1892 Veladas literarias de Lima. 1876-1877. Tomo
primero. Veladas I a X. Buenos Aires: Imprenta
Europea. 486 p. port.
Introduction (41 p.) by Pastor S. Obligado provides
a biographical sketch of Juana M. Gorriti (1818-92),
19c. literary and feminist figure who, like Juana Manso,
spent much time outside of Argentina for political
reasons. She was the wife of a president of Bolivia,
and mother-in-law of another, and an educator who
founded a *colegio* in La Paz, teaching there and in Lima.
She held a salon in Lima, 10 sessions of which are
reproduced. Attended by married and unmarried women and
men (including Ricardo Palma), they consisted of readings and music, which are reproduced in this collection,
along with newspaper critiques. For 19c. ideas on

Literature, Mass Media, and Folklore

women's education expressed at the *veladas*, See A. de la
E. Delgado (#496), M. Eléspuru y Lazo (#497), T. G.
de Fanning (#500), and B. Alamos González (#493).

351 LÓIZAGA, ELVA de
1960 "Sarmiento, Virginia Woolf y las revistas femeninas."
FICA 24/25:91-98.
Concurs with Sarmiento that Argentina is still a desert
and with Virginia Woolf that marriage is the only profession open for women, i.e., Argentine women are professors
of marriages. Wonders why so many magazines are specifically directed at women instead of at both sexes, and
why almost all of them are directed by men, many of whom
do so with condescension. Sets up typology of women's
magazines: 1) technical, for "feminine" crafts (e.g.,
embroidery); 2) technical, serials like *fotonovelas*;
3) literary--a) for women, b) for women in the family;
and 4) literary, for "cultured" women. Describes typical
list of contents for types 3a and 3b and discusses predominant themes, particularly love. Type 4 is for women
who do not have time to read entire books about different
topics. Also mentions deficient writing style.

352 MARENGO de CAMINOTTI, DELIA
1969 "La mujer: personaje en la novela." UNC/R 10:1/2:
339-61.
Discusses debate over "feminine literature," different
kinds of heroines in Argentine novels since the 19c.,
and several themes (solitude; women in society, in relation to men and to the world) reflected in female
characters in 20c. Argentine novels. Believes "feminism
is, in reality, 'anti-feminism'."

353 MIGUEL, MARÍA ESTHER de
1969 "La mujer en su literatura y su responsabilidad como
escritora." UNC/R 10:1/2:321-37.
A novelist's mission is to witness and judge or point
out causes with respect to society's problems and
members--to detect problems, not to solve them. Focuses
on Enero by Sara Gallardo (about a country girl) and
Aire tan dulce by Elvira Orphée (about life in the
provinces). Does not believe in separate masculine and
feminine literatures.

354 MORALES GUIÑAZÚ, FERNANDO
1943 "La mujer mendocina en la literatura." In his
Historia de la cultura mendocina, pp. 409-38. Biblioteca
de la Junta de Estudios Históricos. Mendoza, Arg.:
Best Hnos. bibl.

Overview of women in the culture of Mendoza since the 18c., focusing mostly on writers, some musical composers, and educators. Mentions first convent/school (1778).

355 NALÉ ROXLO, CONRADO
1964 Genio y figura de Alfonsina Storni. Biblioteca de América. Col. Genio y Figura, 4. Buenos Aires: Edit. Universitaria de Buenos Aires. 191 p. illus., facsims., ports., bibl.

356 NÚÑEZ, MIRTA GRISELDA
1973 "La mujer en Martín Fierro." In José Hernández: estudios reunidos en conmemoración del centenario de El Gaucho Martín Fierro, 1872-1972, pp. 141-55. Trabajos, communicaciones y conferencias, 14. La Plata, Arg.: Univ. Nacional de La Plata, Facultad de Humanidades y Ciencias de la Educación, Dept. de Letras, Inst. de Literature Argentina e Iberoamericana.
Analyzes the role of women in José Hernández' famous 19c. poem about *gaucho* life on the Argentine pampa. In the first part women appear as very secondary--as an occasional companion and possession; in the second part, they are elevated to a prominent, almost heroic position as the focal point of family life and social organization.

357 PASTORIZA de ETCHEBARNE, DORA
1964 "Argentina." In El hombre en la literature de la mujer, ed. by E. Hoppe, trans. by I. Durruty, pp. 367-92. Madrid: Edit. Gredos.
Sees literary creations as an escape from one's environment or epoch, but for women even more as an escape from their condition as women. In the poetry of Argentine women is an omnipresent preoccupation with men. Briefly traces development of literature by Argentine women in the 19c. and illustrates theme of men in the poetry of Alfonsina Storni et al. through the 20c. Concludes that as women become more liberated, their feeling of not being understood increases; as a result, men appear less as a theme of direct inspiration while unfulfilled love predominates.

358 PERCAS PONSETI, HELENA
1960 "Ciento cincuenta años de poesía femenina argentina." ME/RE 5:5/6:53-62.
Argentine poetry did not emerge until the 19c., the first verses of a female poet appearing in print in 1824. Outlines trends and characteristics which women's poetry followed in Argentina during the 19c. and first half of the 20c. and their major representative exponents from

Literature, Mass Media, and Folklore

the political ardor of Juana Manso to the neo-classicism
of María de Villarino. Points out common denominators
of expression among several poets.

359 _____.
1958 La poesía femenina argentina, 1810-1950. Madrid:
Eds. Cultura Hispánica. 738 p. bibl.
Originally a Ph.D. dissertation, this lengthy study of
more than 150 female Argentine poets and their works,
grouped by themes or generation (e.g., postmodernism),
consists more of literary analysis than biographical
notes. Includes a valuable extensive bibliography of
primary works and studies.

360 _____.
1953 "María Dhialma Tiberti, promesa para la Argentina."
RI 18:37:361-68. bibl. notes.
Brief discussion of young untra-modernist Argentine
poet, María Dhialma Tiberti: literary influences in
her work, critiques by other writers, and themes in her
poetry. Illustrates with selections.

361 ROJAS, RICARDO
1922 "Las mujeres escritoras." In his Historia de la
literatura argentina. IV Los modernos, pp. 538-56.
Buenos Aires: Librería "La Facultad" de J. Roldán.
ports., bibl. f/notes.
Chapter on Argentine women who held salons and wrote,
mostly novels, in the 19c., focuses on Mariquita Sánchez,
Josefina Pelliza, Eduarda Mansilla, Juana Manso, and
Juana Manuela Gorriti, and is preceded by a brief discussion of remarkable women in Argentina's history since
the Conquest.

362 SCHULTZ CAZENUEVE de MANTOVANI, FRYDA
1963 Victoria Ocampo. Biblioteca del Sesquicentenario.
Serie Argentinos en las Letras. Buenos Aires: Eds.
Culturales Argentinas, Ministerio de Educación y
Justicia, Dirección General de Cultura. 113 p. illus.,
ports., facsims.
Portrait of Victoria Ocampo (b. 1891) in her adult
years as a writer, editor of Sur, and cultural leader in
Buenos Aires, through her writings to and about such figures as Gabriela Mistral, Gandhi, T. E. Lawrence, Valéry,
Ortega y Gasset, Groussac, Tagore, Virginia Woolf et al.,
as well as through their comments. Brief biographical
data precede an anthology of some of her writings, a
bibliography of her works, and another of works written
on her.

363 _____.
1960 "La mujer en la Argentina hasta fin de siglo."
FICA 24/25:111-18.
Brief sketches of Mariquita Sánchez (1768-1868), well-
known aristocratic woman for her involvement in the May
Revolution, sheltering patriots in her home, holding a
salon, and acting as secretary and president of the
Society of Beneficence; Juana Manuela Gorriti (1818-92),
and César Duyen (Emma de la Barra de Llanos, 1860-1947).

364 TUNINETTI, BEATRIZ T.
1962 Contribución a la bibliografía de Victoria Ocampo.
Guías bibliográficas, 6. Buenos Aires: Univ. de Buenos
Aires, Facultad de Filosofía y Letras, Inst. de Literatura Argentina "Ricardo Rojas." 32 p.
Contains 304 bibliographical items on the books, translations, articles, and interviews of Victorio Ocampo,
well-known figure of 20c. Argentine literary circles and
editor of Sur, as well as publications about her.

365 VERGARA de BIETTI, NOEMI
1962 "La poesía de Margarita Abella Caprile." UNL/U
53:113-26.
Discusses poetry (first published in 1919) of
Margarita Abella Caprile (d. 1961), who was also a
journalist for 25 years for the Buenos Aires daily
La Nación.

366 WAPNIR, SALOMON
1957 Perfil y obra de Herminia Brumana. Buenos Aires:
Eds. Librería Perlado. 127 p. illus., port., facsim.
Personal interpretation of the works of Herminia
Brumana, 20c. Argentine writer, points out that she was
audacious in her ideas and writings because she wanted
women to be educated and cultured, to read and not be
exploited, to be true to their human, social, and spiritual functions. Few biographical data; no in-depth
analysis.

Uruguay

367 FIGUEIRA, GASTÓN
1950 "Daughters of the Muses." OAS/AM 2:11:28-31, 39.
illus., ports.
Brief discussion, accompanied by verses, of several
famous Uruguayan poets--María Eugenia Vaz Ferreira,
Delmira Agustini, Juana de Ibarbourou, Esther de Cáceres,
Sara Iglesias de Ibañez, Selva Márquez, Dora Isella

Literature, Mass Media, and Folklore

Russel et al. Contrary to other Latin American countries, Uruguay has produced great poems by Uruguayan women in the present century, beginning with an anthology published in 1905.

368 GANDOLFO, MIRTHA
1957 "Voz de mujer en la poesía uruguaya." LEEC 13:109:17, 26. port.
Passes over Uruguay's prestigous female poets to describe works of 4 women poets of the "new generation": Paulina Medeiros, Dora Isella Russell, Lucy Parrilla, Orfila Bardesio.

369 LABARCA, EUGENIO
1924 "Poetisas uruguayas." Atenea 1:60-62.
Very brief notes on 5 Uruguayan women poets from Adela Castell (b. 1864) to Luisa Luisi, with verses quoted from Agustini and Ibarbourou.

370 LERENA ACEVEDO, JOSEFINA
1939 "Mis compatriotas. Juicio crítico sobre las mujeres intelectuales uruguayas." UA/U 32:577-81.
Cannot explain origin of women's tendency to be romantics and mystics "by nature," but believes it is obvious in women's intellectual production as it appears in newspapers, magazines, and radios. It is rare to find female prose writers, painters, sculptors or musicians since women who dedicate themselves to art let poetry absorb all their attention. Names several Uruguayan poets (Sarah Bollo, Esther de Cáceres, et al.).

371 SILVA, CLARA
1968 Genio y figura de Delmira Agustini. Biblioteca de América. Col. Genio y Figura, 18. Buenos Aires: Edit. Universitaria de Buenos Aires. 215 p. illus., facsims., ports., bibl.
Biography of famous Uruguayan poet (1886-1914), who was killed by her husband because she filed for divorce after year of marriage and 5 years of courtship. Includes anthology of her poetry, opinions by well-known literati, and other writings about her. Discusses eroticism in her poetry and her "double personality," using correspondence to narrate her life and psyche. Based on archival research.

CARIBBEAN

Puerto Rico

372   CORTÓN, ANTONIO
        1883 La literata. Madrid: Tipografía de Manuel G.
        Hernández, Impresor de la Real Casa. 56 p.
           According to Bibliografía puertorriqueña (Barcelona,
        1934) of Géigel y Zenón and Morales Ferrer, this curious
        little book is accompanied by a letter from Julio Nombela
        to the author, in which he defends women authors against
        rude attacks made by the Puerto Rican critic. Says
        Cortón is not an adversary of literary women, he's their
        enemy incarnate.

373   COULTHARD, G. R.
        1958 "La mujer de color en la poesía antillana."
        Asomante 14:1:35-50.
           Reviews praise of colored, black and mulatto women as
        a general theme in Antillean literature. Indicates
        appearance of women in various poems. Although predom-
        inant in the non-Spanish-speaking island, the theme
        shows up in 2 Puerto Rican poets, and Afro-Cuban poetry
        stereotypes the black woman as a sensual object.

374   LEE, MUNA
        1934 "Puerto Rican Women Writers: The Record of One
        Hundred Years." UO/BA 8:1:7-10.
           Briefly considers Puerto Rican writers, from Bibiana
        Benítez--the island's first dramatist in 1833--to Ana
        Roqué de Duprey--founder and editor of 5 magazines de-
        voted to advancement of women, writer of treatises on
        botany, textbooks in geography and grammar, novels and
        short stories in the 20c. Mentions contributors to
        educational literature, poetry, etc.

375   NEGGERS, GLADYS
        1974 "Clara Lair y Julia de Burgos: Reminiscencias de
        Evaristo Ribera Chevremont y Jorge Font Saldaña." RI
        4:2:258-63. bibl.
           Personal recollections by 2 prominent men in Puerto
        Rican cultural life on 2 famous Puerto Rican women
        poets--Mercedes Negrón Muñoz and Julia de Burgos: appear-
        ance, manner, personality, love life. Concludes that
        both poets were examples of confident, independent, in-
        telligent and creative women who led sad and dramatic
        lives.

Literature, Mass Media, and Folklore

376 TIO, AURELIO
1971 "Semblanza de Lola Rodríguez de Tío." APRH/B
2:7:99-119.
Biographical sketch of upper-class (descendant of
Juan Ponce de León) woman (1843-1924), a prolific Puerto
Rican poet. Notes her cultural and political activities,
travels, and exile. Cites others' comments on her poetic
achievements. Considers her precursor of feminism in
Puerto Rico because of her civic and intellectual participation at a time when women were relegated to the home.
"La Borinqueña," national hymn, originated from her
early musical verses. Includes correspondence and list
of her works (p. 97).

Cuba

377 AROCENA, BERTA
1953 "Mujeres en el periodismo cubano." In Album del
Cincuentenario 1902-1952, by Asociación de Reporteros
de la Habana, pp. 114-16. Havana: Edit. Lex. port.
Lists many women journalists of Cuba since late 19c.,
the periodicals they founded and directed, and/or wrote
in.

378 CARABALLO, ISA
1945 "Poetisas de América: Dulce María Borrero de Luján."
AU 3:37:1, 8.
Tribute to Cuban poet soon after her death. Includes
some notes on her family and her life (she was Director
of Culture in the Ministry of Education) and quotes from
her poetry.

379 GARCÍA de CORONADO, DOMITILA
1926 Album poético-fotográfico de las escritoras cubanas.
3rd ed. Havana: Imprenta de "El Figaro." 256 p.
illus., ports., facsim.
Biographical sketches, accompanied by selections from
their works, of 27 Cuban writers, from the Countess of
Merlin (18c.) to the end of the 19c.

380 HARRISON, POLLY F.
1974 "Images and Exile: the Cuban Woman and her Poetry."
RI 4:2:186-219. bibl.
Viewing culture as a system of symbols, explores images
in categorizing experience and expressing values in poetry by 15 Cuban women, beginning with la Avellaneda of
the 19c. Concludes that there are classes of essences
of lo Cubano, whose emphasis has fluctuated according to

historical moments. Draws a classification system of
the symbols, attributes and values, using woman as the
central category from which radiate Nature, Culture and
Destiny. Points out centrality of the exile condition
in the Cuban ethos; the sea serves as the synthetic
metaphor for that condition.

381 MARQUINA, RAFAEL
1959 La mujer, alma del mundo; censo femenino en la obra
de Martí. Havana: Edit. Librería Martí. 606 p.
Definitive analysis of José Martí's works for poet's
ideas and beliefs about women's role in society. Gathers together and comments on those texts which refer to
particular women; to the specific temperament of women
in various countries; to concepts about love, the loved
one, the home, etc.; and to woman as a woman, mother,
wife, daughter, etc.

Gertrudis Gómez de Avellaneda

382 CASTILLO de GONZÁLEZ, AURELIA
1887 Biografía de Gertrudis Gómez de Avellaneda y juicio
crítico de sus obras. Havana: Imprenta de Soler,
Alvarez y cía. 78 p.
Early biography and critical commentary on literary
works of la Avellaneda (1814-73), well-known Cuban
writer. Remarks on her intense desire and eventual ful-
fillment to live in Spain.

383 GUITERAS, PEDRO JOSÉ
1877 "Poetisas cubanas. Gertrudis Gómez de Avellaneda.
(Dedicada al bello sexo de Cuba). RC 2:481-502.
Early study of the life and works of Cuba's prominent
Romantic poet, with examples of her literary efforts.

384 GUTIÉRREZ, JUAN MARÍA
1865 "Gertrudis Gómez de Avellaneda." BA/R 8:29:71-80.
Biographical notes on well-known Cuban poet (1814-73);
critique by Juan Nicacio Gallego in which he compliments
la Avellaneda's verses as masculine rather than feminine;
and letter to Juan Thompson (1864), a friend in Spain,
in which she expresses her state of low spirits and
health.

385 KELLY, EDITH L.
1945 "La Avellaneda's Sab and the Political Situation in
Cuba." AAFH/TAM 1:3:303-16. bibl. f/notes.

89

Literature, Mass Media, and Folklore

Sab, anti-slavery novel of 19c. Cuban novelist, was
branded "subversive." Discusses writing and banning of
the work, literary criticism of it, and Cuban situation
as it influenced La Avellaneda. Includes document which
banned Sab (pp. 350-53), and excellent footnotes.

386 _____.
1935 "Bibliografía de la Avellaneda." RBC 35:1:107-39;
35:2:261-95. bibl. f/notes.

387 LAZO, RAIMUNDO
1972 Gertrudis Gómez de Avellaneda, la mujer y la poetisa
lírica. Col. "Sepan Cuantos," 226. Mex., D.F.: Edit.
Porrúa. 106 p. port., bibl.

388 MANZANARES de CIRRE, MANUELA
1953 "Doña Gertrudis Gómez de Avellaneda." UA/U
114:311-22. bibl.
Notes on life and some works of 19c. Cuban writer,
citing verses and passages from correspondence. Attempts
to understand Cuba's greatest female poet through her
lyrical poetry as a representative of her time--
Romanticism.

389 MARQUINA, RAFAEL
1939 Gertrudis Gómez de Avellaneda, la peregrina. Biografías Cubanas, 10. Havana: Edit. Trópico. 241 p. port.
Detailed, intimate biography of famous 19c. Cuban
writer.

390 MILLER, BETH KURTI
1974 "Avellaneda, Nineteenth-Century Feminist." RI
4:2:177-83. bibl. f/notes.
Discussion of Cuba's Romantic poet Gertrudis Gómez de
Avellaneda as a 19c. feminist, as evidenced in her literary and autobiographical works. She created strong female characters; leveled criticism at the cultural
definitions of masculine/feminine, the double standard,
and patriarchy; and undertook the direction of a journal
for women, the Album Cubano.

391 PERCAS PONSETI, HELENA
1962 "Sobre la Avellaneda y su novela Sab." IILI/RI
28:54:346-57. bibl. notes.
Discusses psychological richness of la Avellaneda's
19c. anti-slavery novel for its analysis of male and
female characters from a woman's vision of humanity,
one which is distinct from that conceived by a man.

392   SCHULTZ CAZENUEVE de MANTOVANI, FRYDA
         1959 "Gertrudis Gómez de Avellaneda." CUCO 54:285/286:
         148-62. Also in 1961 UH/U 25:151/153:147-63.
         Reflections on works of 19c. Cuban Romantic poet
         (1814-73) coupled with biographical notes.

Dominican Republic

393   BARDIN, JAMES C.
         1940 "Three Literary Ladies of Spain's American Colonies:
         I. Doña Leonor de Ovando." PAU/B 74:12:828-30.
         Brief notes on the first native-born (Santo Domingo)
         woman poet, Leonor de Ovando, whose work is included in
         the Silva of Eugenio de Salazar de Alarcón, a Spanish
         gentleman sent to the colony as a judge in 1573. One
         sonnet is reproduced in translation.

394   LAMB, RUTH S.
         1957 "La poesía de Salomé Ureña de Henríquez." IILI/RI
         22:44:345-51.
         Brief biographical notes accompanied by verse selec-
         tions to illustrate her philosophy--love of her country,
         liberty, perfection of man. Poet belonged to generation
         which flourished after the Independence of the Dominican
         Republic was achieved in 1844.

395   MEJÍA de FERNÁNDEZ, ABIGAIL
         1939 "La mujer dominicana en la literatura." A 4:2:42-44.
         Very brief history of Dominican women of letters, be-
         ginning with first female poet of America, Sor Leonor de
         Ovando, from the colonial period, including several 19c.
         writers, and citing at least 20 more (novelists,
         teachers, etc.).

396   VALLDEPERES, MANUEL
         1969 "Salomé Ureña, poetisa y educadora." RIB
         19:1:23-38. bibl.
         Notes on Dominican educator and poet (1850-97) includes
         selections on major themes in her poetry, bibliography
         of her works and one of works about her.

Nineteenth-Century Periodicals

397   EL ÁLBUM
         1882 Biweekly. Matanzas, Cuba. Director: Catalina
         Rodríguez de Morales.

Literature, Mass Media, and Folklore

> Women's magazine of literature, sciences, fine arts, and articles of general interest. Eight issues were published between 15 July and 31 October, 1882.

398 ÁLBUM CUBANO DE LO BUENO Y LO BELLO
> 1860 Biweekly. Havana: La Antilla. Director: Gertrudis Gómez de Avellaneda.
> Women's magazine of morals, literature, fine arts, and fashions. In its 12 issues included a polemical series "Woman," written by Gertrudis Gómez de Avellaneda, along with her biographies of famous women, contemporaneous with writing, speeches, and political activities of pioneer North American feminists.

399 EL ÁLBUM DE LA MUJER
> 1883-90 Mexico. Editor: Concepción Gimeno de Flaquer.
> Well-illustrated weekly periodical for women in Mexico, edited by Spanish woman. The 1883 issues include articles in praise of Mexican women's virtues as priestess of the home and devotee of maternal role, the influence exercised by women in Spain, the origin of music; short pieces on Santa Teresa, Sor Juana, Angela Peralta; a novel in serial form; columns for society, fashion, and hygiene; and poetry. A series of engravings called "The Animated Flowers" showed women dressed as flowers. Attempts to contribute to the education of women in late 19c. Mexico, but also reinforces traditional behavior.

400 ÁLBUM DE LAS DAMAS
> 1894-95 Weekly. Matanzas, Cuba: Galería Literaria.
> Editor: Pablo Peniche.
> Literary periodical of plays and varieties directed to the "fair sex" of Matanzas, Cuba.

401 EL ÁLBUM DE LAS NIÑAS
> 1877 Weekly. Buenos Aires.
> Publication of semi-serious literary pieces.

402 ÁLBUM DE SEÑORITAS
> 1853-54? Buenos Aires. Editor: Juana Paula Manso de Noronha.
> Periodical of literature, fashions, fine arts, and theater, directed by well-known Argentine educator, feminist, writer, and friend of Sarmiento.

403 LA AZUCENA
> 1870-77 Biweekly. Puerto Rico. Founder and editor: Alejandro Tapia y Rivera.

Magazine of literature, sciences, arts, travel and customs, exclusively directed at the Puerto Rican "fair sex." Tapia y Rivera was a male feminist.

404   BIBLIOTECA DE SEÑORITAS
        1858-59? Weekly. Bogota.
        This weekly periodical for women included column "Revista parisiense" by Soledad Acosta de Samper, Colombia's most well-known and prolific 19c. woman writer.

405   LA CAMELIA
        1853 Semanario de literatura, variedades, teatros, modos, etc., dedicado a las señoritas mejicanas. vol 1. Mex., D.F.: Imprenta de J. R. Navarro. 447 p. plates (incl. music).
        Introduction states purpose of weekly is to contribute to women's education, by providing not only novels and poetry for entertainment, but also pieces on history, geography, physics, language, etc.

406   EL CORREO DE LAS SEÑORAS
        1883-93 Weekly. Mexico. Director: José Adrián M. Rico.
        Similar to the women's section of newspapers today, this weekly periodical for women included fashions, hygiene rules, cooking recipes, norms of sexual education, poetical compositions and religious notes.

407   LA FAMILIA
        1884-? Bogota: Imprenta de "La Luz." Editor: Soledad Acosta de Samper.
        Periodical devoted to a variety of topics: biography, literature, moral instruction, history. One example (2(1885):10-12) contains a biography of General Manuel Serviez, a translation of an English work about persecution in Ireland, the continuation of Acosta de Samper's historical novel La familia de Tío Andrés, about the Independence era (1812-21), critiques of Spanish writers Pedro Antonio de Alarcón and José María de Peredia. A great deal of the writing is by Acosta de Samper--this magazine serving perhaps as a vehicle for her prodigious capacity to write.

408   LA GUIRNALDA PUERTO-RIQUEÑA
        1856-57 Puerto Rico.
        Magazine directed exclusively at female audience; founded by male feminist Ignacio Guaso.

Literature, Mass Media, and Folklore

409 LA MUJER
        1878-1881 Bi-weekly. Bogotá.
        First Colombian periodical for and by women founded by
        Soledad Acosta de Samper. Includes historical studies,
        novels, poetry, and didactic articles.

410 PANORAMA DE LAS SEÑORITAS
        1842-? Mexico: published by Vincente García Torres.
        Picturesque, scientific and literary periodical; con-
        taining drawings, engravings, prints, and music. Prologue
        (1842) states: "I want to give young women a book of pure
        entertainment which does not bore them, but, rather the
        contrary, which serves as a diversion in their leisure."

411 PRESENTE AMISTOSO DEDICATO A LAS SEÑORITAS MEXICANAS
        1840-? Mex., D.F. ports. Editor: Ignacio Cumplido.
        A beautifully illustrated example of books published
        in 19c. Mexico devoted to the "honest entertainment of
        the fair sex." Published annually, beginning in 1840,
        it contained an advice column, poems, engraved portraits
        of young ladies, etc. Editions numbered an average of
        slightly over 400 pages.

412 LA SEMANA DE LAS SEÑORITAS MEJICANAS
        1851-52 5 vols. Mexico.
        Literary publication dedicated to the "fair sex" con-
        cerned with moral rectitude. Included much translated
        literary material, advice, information for "domestic
        economy" (i.e., recipes), puzzles, instructions in games,
        music and handiwork, and fashion illustrations.

413 SEMANARIO DE LAS SEÑORITAS MEJICANAS
        1841-42 3 vols. Mexico: Imprenta de Vicente G. Torres.
        Editor: Isidro Rafael Gondra.
        Useful for understanding the ideal which women were
        expected to fulfill at that time. The articles were
        intended to educate female readers in history, music,
        literature, religion, science, handiwork (e.g., em-
        broidery), domestic economy, etc. Included were trans-
        lated selections from European works (e.g. Ivanhoe),
        all destined to make fine young ladies, creatures of
        femininity, of the readers. Illustrated. Divided into
        fine arts, physique, literature, morality.

414 LA SIEMPREVIVA
        1870 Yucatan, Mexico.
        Periodical founded, edited, and staffed by early
        feminist society in Mérida, Mexico; dedicated to fur-
        thering the education of females.

EDUCATION

This section contains published material on the education of females in Spanish America since colonial times. It considers primary school to university, vocational as well as academic programs, urban as well as rural instruction. The entries refer to individual educators, the history of institutions of learning and training of a secular or religious nature, the first university graduates, concern for women's role as mother/educator, literacy rates, educational legislation, 19th century ideas on what women's education should consist of, and institutionalized child care.

For additional information on convents as centers of learning, see entries on nuns and nunneries in MAGIC, RELIGION AND RITUAL. See BIOGRAPHY AND AUTOBIOGRAPHY for collective compilations which cite educators. See 19th Century Periodicals, a subsection of LITERATURE, MASS MEDIA, AND FOLKLORE, for periodical literature as an educational vehicle for women in the 19th century. See ETHNOGRAPHIC MONOGRAPHS/ COMMUNITY STUDIES for notes on education within a specific indigenous or ethnic community. For the relationship between women's educational level and fertility, see HUMAN SEXUALITY, REPRODUCTION AND HEALTH. For the education, or socialization, of girls within the family, see MARRIAGE AND THE FAMILY. For statistics and notes on women's education in studies which cover a variety of topics, see the GENERAL category.

SPANISH AMERICA - GENERAL

415   AROSEMENA de TEJEIRA, OTILIA
        1967 "La educación de la mujer." LNB/L 12:140:45-48.
        Believes education should be equal in content and
        quality for both sexes and coeducation should prevail.
        Whether women will work as professionals or as
        housewives/mothers, they need to be capacitated to con-
        front modern life. Reproduces some comparative educa-
        tional statistics from UNESCO for 1960's.

Education

416 BAYLE, CONSTANTINO
      1941 "Educación de la mujer en América." CJ/RF
      124:526:206-25. bibl. f/notes.
      Good contribution on the education of women during
      colonial times, especially in Mexico and Peru. Identi-
      fies related legislation, institutions and individuals.
      Makes a case for early education because of the number
      of women writers then. Contends that although boys'
      level of instruction was higher, girls' education did
      exist and was similar to that provided in Europe. Docu-
      ments and secondary sources cited in 72 footnotes.

417 COWPER, MARY O.
      1920 "Education of Women in Latin America." SAQ
      19:4:350-59. bibl.
      Brief but informative survey of education for women
      in LA in late 19c. and early 20c. General indifference,
      actual opposition, Spanish/Moorish attitudes toward
      women and discrimination against the lower class combine
      to hinder progress in women's education. Cites differ-
      ences among women according to class. Normal schools,
      liceos and universities are described with some histori-
      cal data about their founding.

418 FURLONG CARDIFF, GUILLERMO
      1951 La cultura femenina en la época colonial. B.A.:
      Edit. Kapelusz. 264 p. ports., facsims., bibl.,
      f/notes.
      Valuable contribution on the education of women in
      colonial America which refutes false picture presented
      by others. Scrupulously researched, it provides back-
      ground data on the education of women in Spain from the
      16c. through 18c. and chapters on female education in
      Mexico, Guatemala, Santo Domingo, Nueva Granada, Peru,
      Chile and the La Plata region. Includes information on
      women writers as well as colonial society and much more.
      Detailed footnotes.

419 HERRADORA A., MARÍA LUISA
      1938 Temario: trabajo desarrollado . . . para enviarlo
      al primer Congreso centroamericano femenino de
      educación, que se reunirá en San José de Costa Rica,
      del 8 al 15 de septiembre de 1938. Biblioteca de la
      Sociedad de Geografía e Historia. Tegucigalpa:
      Talleres Tipográficos Nacionales. 30 p.
      Concludes that education for women in CA should be
      geared toward the effective application of arts and
      sciences in the home, development of handiwork as an
      economic source for women, and preparation in the art of

running a house and educating one's children. Suggests
that technical schools be founded so that women can earn
a living instead of turning to prostitution and that
servants be instructed for their work too.

420   Inter-American Commission of Women (IACW)
       1949 Report presented by Amalia de Castillo Ledón
       Chairman [sic] of the Inter-American Commission of
       Women, to the Consultative Conference on Obstacles
       Confronting Women's Access to Education, Convened by
       UNESCO. Paris, France. December 5-7, 1949. Wash.,
       D.C.: Pan American Union. 33 p.
          Based on information gathered prior to 1947 and
       additional data contributed by IACW delegates, summarizes
       the status of women in each Latin American country from
       the perspective of education and professional qualifica-
       tions. Recommendations are made to abolish discrimina-
       tion and inequality.

421   International Bureau of Education (IBE)
       1952 Access of Women to Education. XVth International
       Conference on Public Education. UNESCO, International
       Bureau of Education, Publication no. 141. Geneva.
       207 p.
          Consists of responses by 47 Ministries of Education
       to a questionnaire from the IBE regarding legislation on
       women's rights to education, teacher training, factors
       affecting women's access to education. Statistics indi-
       cate number of schools and students by sex and number of
       teachers by educational level.

MIDDLE AMERICA

Mexico

422   ALDANA, MARÍA A.
       1902 Dos palabras acerca de la educación femenina.
       Puebla, Mex.: Imprenta Artística. 24 p.
          Professional examination for Instituto Normalista of
       the State of Puebla suggests manner in which girls
       should be educated physically, morally, intellectually,
       and domestically so that they can carry out their roles
       as housewife and mother. However, female heads of
       household also need to be trained so they can work to
       support their family.

Education

423   Arquisterio; o, Casa de ejercicios para honesto recreo de las
       señoras grandes. Fundada en el año de 1882. Documentos
       inéditos, restaurados y publicados por un anticuario de esta
       capital.
              1945 Biblioteca Aportación Histórica. Mex., D.F.:
              Vargas Rea. 128 p.
                   Reprint of 1897 collection of anecdotes and satire
              which ridicule women. Includes details drawn up for
              founding a school or house of charm, culture and recrea-
              tion for older, unmarried women. Interesting reflection
              of Mexican males' contempt for women.

424   BONILLA, TRINIDAD
              1903 Algunas consideraciones acerca de la importancia de
              la educación de la mujer. Puebla, Mex.: Imprenta de la
              Escuela de Artes y Oficios del Estado. 48 p.
                   Professional examination for Instituto Normalista of
              the State of Puebla studies necessity of providing
              women with a sound physical, intellectual and moral
              education in order to fulfill their role as educators
              at home and at school. Says tendency toward motherhood
              is noticeable in girls almost immediately.

425   BOPP, MARIANNE O. de
              1956 "La mujer en la universidad." FL 30:60/61/62:147-63.
                   Includes several pages on growing number of female
              university graduates in Mexico since Mathilde P. de
              Montoya entered medical school in Puebla (1870). How-
              ever, small percentage of women university students
              graduate and then only 12% of graduates practice their
              profession.

426   BROWN, WILLIAM
              1952 "Emancipating Mexico's Women: Education Seen as the
              Answer to Demands of Equal Rights for Mexican Women;
              Women's University Leads Way to Goal." MAR 20:5:12-14,
              32, 34.
                   Cites efforts of Adela Formoso de Obregón Santacilla
              to obtain political and economic independence for
              Mexican women through education, specifically her
              founding of the Universidad Feminina de México in 1943.
              Discusses University curriculum, students, faculty,
              goals, etc.

427   Cartas sobre la educación del bello sexo, por una señora
       americana.
              1851 Mex., D.F.: Tipografía de Rafael y Vila. 228 p.
                   Originally published in London, 1824, 12 letters written
              by Mexican woman who sought asylum in Europe, communicate

her observations on education of women there and moral, domestic, intellectual, artistic, physical and religious reasons for such education.

428 CASTELLANOS, ROSARIO
1972 "La participación de la mujer en la educación formal." CM/D 44:4-10.
General remarks on women's position, changes in education of women, citing contemporary statistics for Mexico. Poses series of questions--what pushes Mexican woman to break with traditional mold and attempt to fulfill herself?--and makes several points about relation between education and economic independence, consciousness-raising to awaken critical spirit and reject dogma, etc.

429 CENICEROS y VILLAREAL, RAFAEL
1891 Páginas para mis hijas. Obra destinada a la educación católica de la mujer. Zacatecas, Mex.: Imprenta y Encuadernación de "La Rosa." 198 p.
19c. counsel to young women on the education they should have and behavior they should exhibit, reflecting very traditional attitudes. Instills readers with such "virtues" as submission, obedience, chastity, religious devotion, resignation, etc. Advises them how to dress, keep house, converse, deal with servants, etc.

430 CORTÉS, GONZALO del ANGEL
1915 Feminismo en acción. San Juan Bautista, Tabasco, Mex.: Talleres Tipográficos Royados y Encuadernación del Gobierno Constitucionalista. 13 p.
Women should reign in the home, where the education of children begins, with words from the father and affection from the mother. Teachers are a symbol of love and, like mothers, should profess an infinite amount of love for children and others.

431 FERNÁNDEZ de LIZARDI, JOSÉ JOAQUÍN
1831 La Quijotita y su prima. Historia muy cierta con aparencias de novela. Escrita por el Pensador Mexicano. 2nd ed. 4 vols. Mex., D.F.: Imprenta de Altamirano. fronts., illus.
Mexico's first novelist portrays the disastrous consequences of frivolous instruction and the manner in which women ought to be taught in the contrasting educations of 2 girls, Pomposa and Pudenciana. Reflects the general thinking of Lizardi's time (late colonial Mexican society) and the inadequacy of education for women.

Education

432 FLORES, MARÍA D.
     1894 Educación de la mujer. Puebla, Mex.: Tipografía
     Moneda. 24 p.
        Professional examination presented to Instituto
     Normalista of the State of Puebla sees need for women
     to be educated because of their role as director and
     educator in the family and as companion to a husband
     but also in case of critical circumstances which leave
     them unsupported. Cites professions particularly suit-
     able for women and outlines means to be employed to
     develop moral, physical and intellectual education of
     women.

433 GALINDO y VILLA, JESÚS
     1900-1901 "La educación de la mujer mexicana al través
     del siglo XIX." AA/MSC 15:9/10:289-312. bibl. f/notes.
        Traces education of women during the 19c. Advocates
     that women be better educated and prepared to exercise
     certain professions but not to the detriment of their
     primordial role as mother. Draws distinction between
     working class and elite women, encouraging increased
     opportunities for the female.

434 _____.
     1897-1898 "Breves consideraciones sobre la educación de
     la mujer mexicana." AA/MSC 11:109-36.
        Reviews the pros and cons of women's education and
     liberation as voiced by 19c. European thinkers.
     Believes women have the right to an adequate education,
     especially in light of economic pressures which require
     that they be able to earn a living; but once married,
     women should give up their careers and become queens
     of their household. Also reproduces part of a work by
     another Mexican in which similar ideas are expressed re
     women's roles, "natural" functions and aptitudes.

435 GAOS, JOSÉ
     1960 "En torno y como anejo a la educación de las
     mujeres." In his Sobre enseñanza y educación, pp. 85-
     124. Eds. Filosofía y Letras, 47. Mex., D.F.: UNAM,
     Dirección General de Publicaciones.
        Includes "Conversation, Matrimony and Democracy," talk
     given to 1948 graduating class of the Feminine University
     of Mexico; "Illusions and the Interesting Woman," talk
     given at closing of academic year 1951 at the same
     university, on what makes an interesting woman; and
     "Women in History," reflections on women's absence in
     History as an aspect of their historical/social situation
     of inferiority.

436 GARCÍA ICAZBALCETA, JOAQUÍN
     1896 "El Colegio de Niñas, México." In his Obras, vol.
     2, pp. 427-34. Mex., D.F.: Imprenta de V. Agüeros.
       Short history of founding, in 1548 (or earlier), of a
     school for mestizas as well as Spanish girls in New
     Spain. Beatas (devout, pious women) were sent from
     Spain to instruct daughters of Indian caciques. In
     1861, the students were transferred to the Colegio de
     las Vizcaínas.

437 HERNÁNDEZ, GUADALUPE
     1904 Educación de la mujer. Puebla, Mex.: Imprenta
     Gilberto Carrillo. 61 p.
       Professional examination at the School for Teachers of
     the Instituto Normalista of the State of Puebla discusses
     deficiency of and diverse opinions on the education of
     women, the manner in which women should be educated,
     its importance and relation to their primordial role in
     the family. Describes stereotypical differences between
     boys and girls. If women do not marry, they should be
     prepared to sustain themselves through work; otherwise,
     a career for women is as absurd as ignorance is
     disastrous.

438 LARROYO, FRANCISCO
     1954 "Sor Juana Inés de la Cruz y la defensa de la
     educación femenina superior." FL 55/56:197-202.
       Sees Sor Juana as a defender of higher education for
     women by example of her own intellectual life and actual
     support in her famous response to Puebla's Bishop's
     censure of her ideas. Discusses state of education for
     women in 17c., Sor Juana's educational ideal and back-
     ground, and her considerable influence.

439 LAVALLE URBINA, MARÍA
     1974 "La mujer y su situación legal y de facto. Me daban
     el asiento pero no el lugar." UNAM/U 29 (15 July):8.
     port., tables.
       Magistrate appointed by Alemán in 1946 recounts her
     own education and entrance into field of law, difficul-
     ties encountered by her and other women as individuals
     and as a group struggling for women's rights. States
     her position regarding feminism. Pages 8, 12, 16 have
     tables comparing male and female student population at
     different levels in Mexico, 1972.

440 LLANO CIFUENTES, CARLOS
     1968 "La educación superior femenina como tarea
     específica." Istmo 58:24-28, 30-35. bibl.

Education

After superficial history of women and education,
discusses women's difficult attainment of higher education because the university is a masculine and mascu-
linized institution. Focuses on problems to be resolved
regarding curriculum and applicability of programs to
differences between women and men.

441 LÓPEZ VALLEJO, EVA
1902 Ligeras consideraciones acerca de la influencia que
la mujer ejerce en la educación. Puebla, Mex.: Imprenta
Artística. 15 p.
Professional examination for Instituto Normalista of
the State of Puebla sees moral education as the task
of mothers more than of the school. Therefore, it is
necessary that women be given solid instruction to
carry out their domestic role, which requires that they
guide their children toward virtue and good.

442 Mexico (City). Colegio de la Paz.
1890 Reglamento del Colegio de la Paz, año de 1890.
Mex., D.F.: Imprenta de Ignacio Cumplido. 54 p.
Reproduces the regulations governing the internal
organization of the Colegio de la Paz, originally
founded in Mexico City in 1732 as the Colegio de San
Ignacio de Loyola for the civil education of girls.
Covers objectives of the school, examinations, punish-
ments and awards, etc.

443 _____. _____.
1766 Constituciones del Colegio de S. Ignacio de Loyola
de México, fundado por la ilustre congregación de Ntra.
Señora de Aranzazu de la misma ciudad para la manuten-
ción, enseñanza de niñas huérfanas, y viudas pobres.
2nd ed. Madrid: Impr. de Juan Antonio Lozano. 56 p.
Primary source explains organization of early school
(established in 1766) for girls in Mexico: who is to
be admitted, each job to be fulfilled and how, economy,
etc.

444 MISTRAL, GABRIELA (pseud.)
1961 Lecturas para mujeres. San Salvador: Ministerio de
Educatión, Depto. Edit. 521 p.
Originally published by Mexico's Secretariat of Education in 1923, gathers together prose and poetry used by
Mistral when teaching women students in Mexico in
early 1920's. Writings divided into categories of home
and family, LA and Mexico, spiritual themes, work,
nature.

445 MÖRNER, JULIA
1945 Memorias de una colegiala. Mex., D.F.: Colegio de
las Vizcaínas. 176 p. plates, plan, ports.
Recollections of life as a student in the Colegio de
las Vizcaínas, Mexico City, early educational establishment for women. Begins with December 1877 and ends with
homage paid to its founders in 1941. Lists rectors,
vice-rectors, directors and secretaries since the 18c.
and discusses administrative aspects, based on her experience as director of the school during the 1920's.

446 MURIEL de la TORRE, JOSEFINA
1968 "Notas para la historia de la educación de la mujer
durante el virreynato: Colegio de Niñas de Oaxaca,
Oaxaca." EHNH 2:25-33.
Discusses first convents and feminine institutions
founded in latter part of 16c. and 17c., especially
history of Colegio de Niñas de Oaxaca, and their role
in education of girls in colonial Mexico. Education
consisted of religious and moral training, preparation
for austere convent life, reading, writing, arithmetic,
needlework. Teachers were always married women, widows
or single women, but never nuns.

447 OBREGÓN, GONZALO
1949 El Real Colegio de San Ignacio de México (Las
Vizcaínas). Mex., D.F.: El Colegio de México. 190 p.
illus., plans, bibl. f/notes.
Very readable, valuable contribution to history of
female education in colonial Mexico, based on archival
research. Covers history of the brotherhood that
founded Colegio de las Vizcaínas in 18c.; status of
women in colonial Mexico; origin, organization and
defects of 2 other colegios established in 16c. and 17c.;
complete history of Las Vizcaínas (how it functioned,
admission rules, regulations, convent life, monetary
problems, repercussions of revolutionary movement,
changes in internal government, the building as a monument, etc.) from 18c. to contemporary times; kind of
education provided; educational innovations introduced
by Sor María Ignacia; suppression of colegios; etc.
Appendices include the constitutions of the school and
a chart of students' daily activities (1875).

448 OLAVARRÍA Y FERRARI, ENRIQUE de
1889 El real colegio de San Ignacio de Loyola, vulgar-
mente Colegio de las vizcaínas en la actualidad Colegio
de la Paz; reseña histórica. Mex., D.F.: Imprenta de
F. Díaz de León. 244, 130 p. illus., ports., fold. plan.

Education

Based on primary sources, valuable first history of
Colegio de las Vizcaínas, founded in 18c. to provide
secular education for girls, discusses governing structure of school and laws affecting its existence rather
than the education itself.

449   PERER ÁLVAREZ, EDUARDO
      1967 "La evolución profesional de la mujer en la
      Universidad." Espejo 3:55-68. tables.
         Examination of annual UNAM statistics indicating dis-
      tribution of women in professions according to degrees
      granted between 1910 and 1964. In 1910 women graduated
      as 9 midwives, 3 singers and 2 dentists. By 1964 they
      were graduating in at least 13 other fields. Makes
      some comparison with US and Europe.

450   PORRAS MUÑOZ, GUILLERMO
      1969 "esdai = oportunidad para la mujer." Istmo 65:29-32.
         Reflections upon reading pamphlet put out by a civil
      association, "Hogar y Cultura," announcing organization
      ESDAI (Escuela Superior de Administraciones de
      Instituciones), which attempts to train women on a
      university level for the administration of institutions--
      hotels, restaurants, airlines, hospitals, schools, public
      health organizations, etc. Lacks details on professional
      training itself.

451   REYES L., JOSEFINA
      1903 La mujer en el hogar y en la sociedad. Puebla,
      Mex. 27 p.
         Professional examination for Instituto Normalista
      of the State of Puebla sees the education of women as
      very important because woman forms the basis of the
      home, which in turn is the foundation of society.
      Describes the ideal wife but also felicitously notes
      women's professional advances, debunks myth of women's
      inferiority, and encourages women's liberation through
      education and work.

452   RIVERA y SANROMÁN, AGUSTÍN
      1899 Pensamientos filosóficos sobre la educación de la
      mujer en México, escojidos de muchos autores
      célebres . . . . Lagos de Moreno, Mex.: Imprenta de'
      Ausencio López Arce e Hijo. 41 p. Also 1908 Mazatlan,
      Mex.: Tipografía y Casa Edit. de Valadés y Cía.
         Pamphlet of quotations from famous writers (e.g. Fray
      Luis de León) and other sources on what a woman should

be taught; women without education; importance of education for women; physical, literary or intellectual, and
moral education for women, etc. Interesting collection
as reflection of 19c. ideas of feminine education.

453 Santa Sofía. Colegio de instrucción elemental y superior,
para niñas y señoritas.
1870 Veracruz: Imprenta del "Progreso." 14 p.
Letter written to parents in Veracruz regarding the
education their daughters could receive at the *colegio*
Santa Sofía. Attached to letter by directors (2 women)
are a list of the personnel and a prospectus for admission of pupils (i.e., regulations and costs).

454 SCHULZ, ENRIQUE E.
1898-99 "La educación de la mujer y la profesión de la
farmacia." AA/MSC 12:461-65.
Suggests that women be educated in pharmacy so that
they would have a means of subsistence, especially if
they become the head of household. Concludes that normal
schools should continue to prepare women for teaching
and that preparatory schools for other professions
should open their doors to women. Enlightened view for
19c.

455 STECK, FRANCIS BORGIA, ed.
1946 "La cofradía del santísimo sacramento y caridad."
AAFH/TAM 2:3:369-76.
Reproduces document which contains regulations of
confraternity, which made a bequest in a letter to
Viceroy Velasco (1555) to sponsor a school and home for
orphan girls of Spanish parents, and of the charitable
institution as well. Believes that since there are
many records of various other institutions and groups
which cared for *mestizo* children but not of this one,
the document is important and interesting.

456 ZAMORA PALLARES, DIONISIA
1956 "La mujer en la educación." FL 30:60/61/62:75-82.
Sketchy notes about women in elementary education in
Mexico with a portrait of Sor Juana to illustrate her
defending the right to be herself and for women to
cultivate their intellect. Academic preparation of
teachers was formalized in the 19c.

Education

Guatemala

457 "Escritura de dotación y fundación del Colegio de Recogimiento
de Doncellas, otorgada por Francisco de Santiago, Juan de
Cueto y Cristóbal de Solís, el 5 de julio de 1591."
1943 GAGG/B 8:4:395-402.
Reproduces 2 documents related to founding of a school
for girls, to be directed by a mother superior, with
the option of becoming nuns or getting married, and only
for daughters of true Christians, in early 17c.
Guatemala.

458 Guatemala. Secretaría de Educación Pública.
1940 Programas para las escuelas de artes y oficios
femeniles. Guatemala: Tipografía Nacional de Guatemala.
36 p.
Program outlines for female education at primary level
in Guatemala as approved by the government in 1939.
Useful as indication of orientation and training for
girls. Includes cooking, housekeeping, sewing, needlework, etc., in addition to basic mathematics, history,
etc.

Honduras

459 CÁCERES, MARIANA de
1940 "Women of the Americas: III. María Francisca Reyes,
Honduras." PAU/B 74:7:500-503.
Very brief biographical sketch of María Francisca
Reyes (1835-1906), a teacher who pioneered in the introduction of public primary schools in Honduras and who
was the first principal of the Tegucigalpa school for
girls.

460 CID, MARÍA TRINIDAD del
1947 "Mujeres de América. María Cristina Valentine de
Martínez." ABN/R 26:3/4:181-87.
Biographical sketch of pioneering educator of the
deaf and mute in Honduras in 20c.

461 JÉREZ ALVARADO, RAFAEL
1957 La educación de la mujer en Honduras. Col. Ramón
Rosa, 5. Tegucigalpa: Ministerio de Educación Pública
de la República de Honduras. 250 p.
Author discusses more than scholastic education.
Charts the life of a woman in terms of what she learns
in the home, in schools, and her role in society
(class, marriage, activities).

WOMEN IN SPANISH AMERICA

Nicaragua

462   AGUERRI, JOSEFA TOLEDO de
      1940 (Reproducciones) Educación y feminismo, Sobre
      enseñanza, Artículos varios. Managua: Talleres
      Nacionales. 71 p. port.
         Collection of articles, lectures and speeches by
      Nicaraguan reflecting her position on education and
      feminism. Also includes a petition to the government
      to recognize women's rights as citizens, a brief review
      of the goals of a women's organization, and an explana-
      tion of the necessity of providing courses for working
      women.

Costa Rica

463   Colegio Superior de Señoritas
      1939 Album del cincuentenario, 1888-1938. San José,
      C.R.: Imprenta y Librería Lehmann. 313 p. illus.,
      ports., music.
         School album contains articles, photos, poems, songs,
      etc. recording 100 year history of the Colegio Superior
      de Señoritas in San José.

464   LUROS, PABLO
      1938 La educación de las jóvenes. San José, C.R.:
      Imprenta Borrase Hnos. 100 p.
         Reactionary attack on modern education for leading
      women astray from their fundamental mission as house-
      wife and mother and training them to compete profes-
      sionally with men, to the detriment of their "feminine
      nature." Describes what he considers to be ideal educa-
      tion for women, so that women are not alienated from
      their primordial role, and family and society do not
      break down.

Panama

465   DUNCAN, JEPTA B.
      1919 "La mujer ante la democracia." Revista Nueva
      6:2:88-95.
         Speech given to graduating class of Panama's Escuela
      Normal de Institutoras advises that the education of
      women be broadened to encompass knowledge of social
      problems beyond vague training in domestic obligations,
      family relations and some community duties because
      women's role in society has expanded beyond salon
      activities since WWI.

Education

466   PÉREZ-VENERO, MIRNA M.
          1973   "The Education of Women on the Isthmus of Panama."
          JW 12:2:325-34. bibl. f/notes.
          First attempt in English to shed some light on the
          education of women in 19c. Panama, based mostly on Juan
          Antonio Susto's 1966 pamphlet, La educación de la mujer
          panameña en el siglo XIX. Concludes that basic assump-
          tions about women's primary role as mothers had hardly
          changed since 1832, when it was urged that schools for
          girls be established.

467   SUSTO, JUAN ANTONIO
          1966   La educación de la mujer panamaña en el siglo XIX.
          Panama: Ministerio de Educación, Dirección Nacional de
          Cultura. 63 p. bibl. f/notes. Also in: 1965 LNB/L
          10:119:91-96; 10:120/121:57-71.
          Briefly discusses state of education for women in 17c.
          and 18c. Viceroyship. For 19c. Panama itemizes 103
          dates (from 1821 to 1904) on which laws were passed,
          schools founded, directors appointed, etc., all relevant
          to development of education of Panamanian girls.

SOUTH AMERICA

Venezuela

468   PUCHI ALBORNÓZ, EMIRO
          1955   "La educación de la mujer en Venezuela." VED
          16:75:38-54. bibl.
          Well-documented contribution to study of female educa-
          tion in Venezuela traces history of 1 particular insti-
          tution, Colegio de Niñas Educandas "Jesús, María y
          José," founded by Father Simón Marciano de Malpica in
          Caracas during second half of 18c., in order to protect
          and educate orphaned and unsheltered girls. Reproduces
          documents related to founding, functioning during colo-
          nial and republican times, changes and reforms.

469   RUDDLE, KENNETH and CHESTERFIELD, RAY
          1974   "The Venezuelan 'Demonstradora del Hogar': An
          Example of Women in Nonformal Rural Education." CDJ
          9:2:140-44. bibl.
          Notes problems of nonschool educational and training
          programs in rural LA but describes a successful one in
          Venezuela, that of the home demonstrator, who visits and
          instructs individual housewives in their homes and in
          classes. Concludes that women's important economic role
          in traditional societies may be exploited to bring women
          into modern sector.

Colombia

470 CARDOZO SERRANO, ANTONIA
1961 "Monografía de la Escuela Normal de Señoritas de
Bucaramanga." CEST 30:263:217-29.
History of a public school for girls founded in
Bucaramanga in 1875 lists events, activities and persons
(teachers, directors, students) until 1959 and includes
decree by which public school instruction is organized
and school's official hymn. Information derived from
Escuela Primaria, a publication of the Inspección
General de Instrucción Pública of the Department of
Santander. Alludes to what the girls had to bring to
school, the food they ate, lack of comfortable facilities,
etc. at end of 19c.

471 COHEN, LUCY M.
1973 "Women's Entry to the Professions: Selected Characteristics." WRU/JMF 35:2:322-30. tables, bibl.
Presents data from larger study (See #472) on innova-
tion among the first women to graduate from Colombian
universities, in which patterns of persistence and change
in dominant value orientations were analyzed. Based on
interviews and participation with 100 professional
women (1965-68), describes their social and educational
background, patterns of professional practice, and role
adjustment in combining marriage and work. Concludes
that influence of family, teacher or significant other,
mutual agreement between husband and wife, and role
flexibility allowed for greater female participation in
educational and occupational opportunities.

472 _____.
1971 Las colombianas ante la renovación universitaria.
Col. "Tribuna Libre," 4. Bogota: Eds. Tercer Mundo.
149 p. tables, bibl. notes.
Investigates social and cultural factors influencing
innovative activity among the first generation of women
who graduated from Colombian universities between 1935
and 1954. Based on interviews with 100 women in Bogota,
Medellin, and Cali (1965-68), presents data on the social,
educational and occupational background of their family
experience; the influence of their family, teachers, peer
group; their professional and married lives, especially
the combined role of professional with that of wife and
mother, and interpersonal relations between spouses.
Chapter 2 provides a brief overview of education for
women from the 16c. ideas of Juan Luis Vives to universities in 20c. Bogota.

Education

473 COHEN, LUCY M.
1968 "Patrones de práctica profesional en mujeres."
CEMS 2:1:1-22. tables.
Reports on the social and cultural patterns of the
first women doctors, pharmacists and dentists of Colombia and describes traditional and new values in their
positions as professional workers and as wives/mothers.
Interviews were conducted with 56 women who had completed their studies before 1955 for information in 4
general areas: identity and background; influential
factors in the decision to undertake university studies;
patterns of home life and professional activities;
opinions on specific problems. Concludes that this is
a "transitional" generation among urban Colombian women.

474 CUERVO, LUIS AUGUSTO
1942 "Homenaje a la memoria de doña Clemencia Caycedo."
HA/B 29:335/336:808-10. port.
Pays tribute to María Clemencia Caycedo (1707-79), the
woman who founded Colombia's first *colegio* for girls,
the famous convent of the nuns of La Enseñanza (1770).

475 DÍAZ DÍAZ, OSWALDO
1962 "Una educadora de la colonia." BCB 5:1:25-27.
Less than 2 centuries ago, there was no educational
establishment for girls and women were not taught to
read and write (the Madre Castillo, Josefa Acevedo,
Soledad Acosta were exceptions). Doña Clemencia Caicedo
went to Spain to acquire legal means for founding a
colegio, under the auspices of the order of María or
Nuestra Señora de la Enseñanza (1770), which would
accept boarding as well as daily students and include a
section for poor girls to study free. It finally opened
in 1783. When Clemencia died in 1779, her sister continued to work with the school, the only one for women
for more than 30 years.

476 "The Education of Women in Official Training Schools."
1941 WORED 6:2:190-91.
Condensed from Gaceta Cultural (October 1940) of
Colombia's Ministerio de Educación, discusses establishment of the Liceo Nacional Femenino and the Ministry's
decision to provide, in addition to preparatory courses
for university studies, training for office management
(secretary, bookkeeper, business machine operator) and
laboratory technology.

South America - Colombia

477   FILELLA, JAMES F.
      1960 "Educational and Sex Differences in the Organization
      of Abilities in Technical and Academic Students in
      Colombia, South America." GPM 61:115-63. tables,
      graphs, bibl.
         Abridgement of Ph.D. thesis (Fordham Univ., 1957).
      Differential battery of standardized tests administered
      to urban group of 300 boys from technical and public and
      private academic high schools and 90 girls from private
      academic high schools. Findings suggest influence of
      experiential factors in the organization of abilities,
      with socio-economic and sex factors appearing related
      to the degree of trait organization.

478   "Higher Education for Women in Colombia."
      1934 SCSO 39:603.
         Very brief notice announces Universidad del Cauca's
      (Popayan) acceptance of women for the first time in
      Colombia and program set up for them.

479   JIMÉNEZ de TEJADA, SONNY
      1964 "Surgimiento y desarrollo de la educación femenina
      en Antioquia." UA/U 41:158:609-24.
         Documented but limited history of the development of
      women's education in the department of Antioquia, begin-
      ning with the founding of the Colegio de María (1906).
      Cites various other institutions and persons connected
      with their founding and direction, education laws, and
      letters which indicate attitudinal climate regarding
      female education. Describes the Instituto Central
      Femenino and Centro Educacional Femenino de Antioquia.

480   MARTÍNEZ NARANJO, MERCEDES
      1969 "Helena Arenas Canal." CEST 30:263:209-16.
         For centennial celebration of her birth (1859), traces
      the education and role as educator of Helena Arenas
      Canal. Mentions the various girls' schools where she
      taught as well as other teachers and students. She
      founded (1915) and directed Colegio de la Merced, the
      first establishment in Colombia to have a female basket-
      ball team and to be the site of the first game (1928).

481   ORTIZ, SERGIO ELÍAS
      1963 "Una educadora colonial olvidada, Sor Petronila de
      Cuellar." BCB 6:1:41-44.
         Discusses history of school for girls, supposedly
      founded in Bogota in 1783, 13 years after the first
      female educational center La Enseñanza, by one of the
      first pupils of that convent school. Includes some

Education

  details about the life of the religious community which
directed the institution. <u>See</u> M. G. Romero (#484) for a
refutation.

482 RESTREPO CANAL, CARLOS
   1962 "El Colegio de la Merced al cumplir los ciento
   treinta años de su fundación." <u>BCB</u> 5:6:760-62.
   Brief history of the second school established for
  women in Colombia in 1832, directed by Salesian nuns.
  Still functioning today, it provided a traditional
  education.

483 RODRÍGUEZ, MANUEL del SOCORRO
   1957 <u>Fundación del Monasterio de la Enseñanza. Epigramas
   y otras obras inéditas o importantes.</u> Biblioteca de la
   Presidencia de Colombia, 44. Bogotá: Empresa Nacional
   de Publicaciones. 566 p.
   Primary source traces the history of the oldest center
  of education for girls in Santa Fe de Bogotá and first
  group of Benedictine nuns in America. The Monasterio de
  la Enseñanza was founded through the beneficence of María
  Clemencia Caycedo in the latter half of 18c. Reproduces
  relevant documents.

484 ROMERO, MARIO GERMÁN
   1963 "Una comunidad religiosa que no existió." <u>BCB</u>
   6:5:702-08.
   Refutes Ortiz' (#481) claims about a school for girls
  directed by a religious community in late 18c. Bogota.
  Proves it never existed; refers to 2 sources which indicate it was actually La Enseñanza. Describes life at the
  convent school, education, founding, pupils, and Sor
  Petronila Cuellar. Documented.

485 TERESA de la INMACULADA, SISTER
   1960 <u>Quién ha educado la mujer colombiana?</u> Bogota.
   351 p. illus., plates, ports., tables, bibl.
   Published Ph.D. thesis which traces the history of
  education for women in Colombia since colonial times.
  Considers many educational institutions, especially religious ones, outstanding educators and the founding of
  normal schools. Based on primary and secondary sources.

486 "Training Girls for Professions."
   1944 <u>IBE/B</u> 18:72:86-87.
   Very brief notice on Colegio de las Hijas de María de
  las Esclavas, a high school for girls in Teusaquillo,
  Colombia, founded (1939) by daughter of former President
  López.

487 ZAPATA, RAMÓN
1934 "Granjas populares para la educación agrícola de la
mujer." SEND 2:7/8:65-76.
Points out lack of schools oriented toward economic
development in Colombia, and the social and economic
need to establish them. Argues for founding rural
schools to provide women with technical competence to
manage their households and perhaps develop cottage
industries. Decries paucity of female teachers trained
to direct such schools and suggests how they can be
prepared to instruct and how the schools could be
organized.

488 ZULUETA, LUIS de
1945 "La educación de la mujer: Eva en la universidad."
REVA 4:12:417-24.
Discusses psychology of women, their social transformation in the 20c., their influence and ability to modify
customs, and "scientific" differences between men and
women (according to several European writers). Describes
kind of education "suitable" to the female character:
disciplines related to general culture--philosophy and
letters, natural sciences, arts--since women's education should be less specialized than men's. Exercising
a profession (medicine, law, engineering, architecture)
is incompatible with home life and primordial obligations of maternity.

Ecuador

489 ALBORNOZ, VÍCTOR MANUEL
1963 "El Colegio de los Sagrados Corazones de la Ciudad
de Cuenca en el primer centenario de su fundación,
1862-1962." CCE/NAR 10:17:122-74.
Traces the founding of the Colegio de Sagrados
Corazones in Cuenca in 1862, an establishment for educating girls, first run by Sacred Heart nuns from France
and Chile. Includes brief biographical notes on the
first 73 students, who married or became nuns.

490 BAZANTE, JULIA
1964-1965 "Notas para un planteamiento de la educación
de la mujer ecuatoriana." EE/R 54/55:168-80.
Attempts to give general idea as to complex implications of education for women in Ecuador, discussing
concepts about nature of women and its influence in
education, educational and social situation of Ecuadorian women resulting from those concepts, social function

Education

of women and national economic structure. Recommends
equal education for both sexes and an orientation particular to women.

491 MORETTA CLAVIJO, FABIOLA
1971 "Ecuador: falta la investigación sobre la situación
actual de la mujer." BDSLM/CIDHAL 1:1:52-56.
Excerpts from talk given at National Congress of Women
in Ecuador (July 1970), briefly describe generally
marginal situation of Ecuadorian women in terms of illiteracy and job opportunities. Sees education as best and
most efficacious tool for improving one's lot.

492 ORTIZ B., EMMA
1934 "Reflexiones sobre la educación de la mujer
ecuatoriana." MEPE/E 9:90/97:61-68.
Teacher from Normal School states her personal views
on education for women. It should not be different from
that of boys, for girls need professional technical
training for economic liberation; however, their education should be supplemented with special facilities where
they can learn the ways of making a home. Quotes
Gregorio Marañón on the question of sex education and
Luis Araquistan on average family and need to deal with
separate problems of distinct socio-economic groups.

Peru

493 ALAMOS GONZÁLEZ, BENICIO
1892 "Enseñanza superior de la mujer." In Veladas
literarias de Lima. 1876-1877. Tomo primero. Veladas
I a X, by J. M. Gorriti, pp. 347-85. Buenos Aires:
Imprenta Europea.
Advanced ideas on women's education in 19c. Peru.
Women should enrich themselves with all kinds of knowledge and not hide their intellect behind washing clothes,
dusting furniture, saying sweet things and cooking.
Offers a "plan of studies for the higher instruction of
women"; discusses timeworn arguments against educating
women as much as men; and argues why women should be
better educated for beneficial effects on men, family
and society. However, also cautions against moving too
quickly--i.e., woman cannot have all her rights nor be
prepared for all professions just yet. Reviews kinds of
education and instruction needed and suggests that certain studies be undertaken: e.g., the history of women,
in order to appreciate the importance of their influence.

494 ARAOZ, MARÍA ROSARIO
1953-54 "La orientación profesional femenina en el Perú."
SS 11/12:11/12:139-59.
Director of School for Social Work in Peru discusses
professional orientation of women, citing pertinent
legislation, describing National Psychopedagogical
Institute, and reporting on investigations carried out
at the Special Institute of Feminine Technical Education
No. 1. Presents data on hundreds of students in 1954
who wished to continue their education, listing schools,
professional aspirations and vocational specialties.
Concludes that definite ascending interest in professions
exists among Peruvian women; however, much is still lacking, especially in the provinces, in terms of coordination among different groups and between professional
formation and practical life activities. Makes 10
suggestions for improvement.

495 D'BROT, CARMELA
1973 "La mujer triunfa en las universidades." SIDI
23:782:60-61. illus.
Cites 1969 statistics on male/female student population of the University of San Marcos in Lima. Except
for several fields (such as obstetrics), where women
predominate, and others (such as pharmacy, psychology,
education), where women are in equal proportion to men,
women continue to lag behind men. Of approximately
100,000 university students in Peru, about 30,000 were
female.

496 DELGADO, ABEL de la E.
1892 "La educación social de la mujer." In Velades
literarias de Lima. 1876-1877. Tomo primero. Velades
I a X, by J. M. Gorriti, pp. 27-39. Buenos Aires:
Imprenta Europa.
Reflection of 19c. attitudes toward women's education
and role in society. Believes women's participation in
literary circles--e.g., that of Gorriti in Lima--signi-
fies a true revolution over 2 erroneous notions held
about women: that they should not have access to higher
learning and that their education should terminate at
the *colegio* level. Woman should not be kept in ignorance;
her influence, without physical involvement, is needed
in business and politics as a moral force. The great
secret of educating woman lies in counseling her "to be
prudent, to suffer, to be still, and to moderate and
ultimately to teach her the way of governing wills and
estates." Decries social education imported from Europe--
called *buen tono*, as frivolous and insufficient.

Education

497 ELÉSPURU y LAZO, MERCEDES
1892 "La instrucción de la muger." In Veladas literarias
de Lima. 1876-1877. Tomo primero. Veladas I a X, by
J. M. Gorriti, pp. 145-49. Buenos Aires: Imprenta
Europea.
Reflects advanced 19c. ideas on education for women.
Decries notion that women's science be in the kitchen,
her arms the needle and scissors, and her mission in
life confined to pot and broom. Challenges belief that
educating women will result in a repugnant excess of
female pedantry. Points out abysmal backwardness of
women's education and makes a plea for women's preparation in a skill or profession. Also suggests that a
library be formed for women.

498 GARCÍA y GARCÍA, ELVIRA
1928 Actividad femenina. Fascículo I. Lima: Casa
Editora "La Opinión Nacional." 136 p.
Discusses capability of women to be educated and to
educate, inequality between male and female education,
and reasons why it is imperative that women be well-
educated or prepared. Considers all levels and kinds
of education. Counteracts resistance to women's education by explaining, for example, that an advancement in
women's knowledge will not masculinize them. Also discusses charity work, philanthropy, various occupations,
kindergartens, feminism in Buenos Aires, and contemporary
(i.e., 1920's) situation. Makes suggestions for upgrad-
ing women's status.

499 GLICERIO MANRIQUE, MARIO
1946 "Crisis de la educación femenina." NUED 1:4:37-39.
Women have their own distinct mission in life: the
full expression of their femininity as perpetuators of
the human species. More classes should be offered to
prepare women to be able to carry out their responsibility as mothers: e.g., preventive medicine, sexual
education, child psychology, etc. Deplores increasing
influence of film industry in women's irreligiosity and
unconcern with respect to their "true" role in life.
The spiritual abandonment in which majority of women
live causes today's problems of uncertainty and
disorientation.

500 GONZÁLEZ de FANNING, TERESA
1892 "Trabajo de la muger." In Veladas literarias de
Lima. 1876-1877. Tomo primero. Veladas I a X, by
J. M. Gorriti, pp. 286-93. Buenos Aires: Imprenta
Europea.

Advanced 19c. argument for women's education and work.
Requests that women, like men, be taught a skill or profession consistent with their sex and social position so
that they can develop their intelligence and a certain
amount of independence. If women were educated into an
occupation, they would not have to rely on fathers and
husbands to support them completely; they could fend for
themselves and/or contribute to the family income. Education and work are important elements in a woman's
happiness, complementing rather than destroying marriage.
Women have only 2 roads open to them--the convent or
marriage--but not every woman can marry, and those who
don't become victims of scorn and jest. Every woman has
the right to aspire to independence and the need to fulfill it in times of economic straits.

501 PRIETO de ZEGARRA, JUDITH
        1965 "Teresa González de Fanning, precursora de la
        educación femenina en el Perú." NUED 36:180:28-29.
          Teresa Gonzalez de Fanning was a 19c. Peruvian educa-
        tor who wrote school textbooks as well as novels. Edu-
        cación femenina, her collection of journalistic articles,
        revealed ideas considered audacious then but which are
        fundamental in female education today. Lists 9 points:
        e.g., adult education, a break with rote learning, sci-
        entific learning free of prejudices; but also, women
        need to be educated as mothers and managers of their
        household.

502 SILVA de SANTOLALLA, IRENE
        1954 "La educación familiar de la mujer peruana." NUED
        14:72:17-32.
          Women are attracted to public sphere of activities
        where they become engaged in careers and jobs for which
        they are not physically or psychologically prepared.
        They are drawn to the latest fad rather than their
        spiritual formation. Fundamental task of education is
        to teach women to harmonize their activities with their
        "natural" qualities: i.e., beginning of a new culture
        for women must be founded in their special capacity as
        mother/educator.

Bolivia

503 CODEX. Comité Coordinador de Promoción Femenina.
        1973 Organizaciones de promoción femenina. La Paz.
        100 p. illus.

Education

        Inventory of national, regional, and local organizations in Bolivia which are dedicated to the education or advancement of women: location, objectives, programs, recourses, work methods, etc.

504 ICHASO VÁSQUEZ, RAQUEL
      1927 La enseñanza nacional femenina. La Paz: Imprenta Intendencia de Guerra. 189 p. tables.
      Educator reports her observations on various aspects (teaching personnel, student population, library, discipline, program, etc.) of schools for girls in 6 Bolivian cities and draws up a detailed plan for a uniform program in female education.

505 VILLANUEVA y SAAVEDRA, ETELVINA
      1970 Acción socialista de la mujer en Bolivia. La Paz: 188 p. port.
      Collection of documents, correspondence and newspaper items on the Legión Femenina de Educación Popular América, founded in Bolivia (1935) by Etelvina Villaneuva y Saavedra, who also edited its newsletter Vocero. In its educative, cultural and social welfare service for mothers and children, this women's organization fought for women's civil rights, organized night schools for women, created a professorship in sexual education, and child care centers in factories and markets, disseminated information through the press or its newsletter, etc.; other actions of social assistance are planned.

Paraguay

506 MOLINA, RAÚL A.
      1948 "La instrucción pública en tiempos de Hernandarias." In his Hernandarias, el hijo de la tierra, pp. 301-12. Buenos Aires: Edit. Lancestremere.
      See ARGENTINA for annotation.

507 Paraguay. Dirección General de Escuelas.
      1920 Reglamento de las academias de corte y confección aprobado por el Consejo Nacional de Educación en su sesión del 8 de octubre de 1919. Asunción: Imprenta "El Arte." 7 p.
      States regulations governing schools of sewing in Paraguay with respect to authorization, obtaining diploma, exams, technical personnel, incorporation, courses, reports to Council, etc.

508 RODRÍGUEZ ALCALÁ de GONZÁLEZ ODDONE, BEATRIZ
1970 Rosa Peña. Asunción: Academia Paraguaya de la
Historia. 30 p. plates.
According to the Handbook of Latin American Studies
36(1974):3376, this is a brief sketch of the "mother
of Paraguayan education" Rosa Peña (1843-99), a disciple
of Argentina's prominent educator Sarmiento, who established a normal school in Asunción.

509 URBIETA ROJAS, PASTOR
1944 La mujer en el preceso cultural del Paraguay.
Buenos Aires: Edit. Ayacucho. 54 p.
Briefly sketches history of female education and
teachers in Paraguay, beginning with the "Casa de
recogidas y huérfanas" (1603) for daughters of the
conquistadors. Part 2 cites women who have held high
posts in education, musicians, singers, writers, poets.
No references.

Chile

510 BARAHONA y VEGA, CLEMENTINA
1904 "La educación de la mujer . . ." In her Algo sobre
educación nacional, pp. 17-27. Santiago: Impresa de
Enrique Blanchard-Chessi.
Speech given at Liceo de Señoritas (Santiago, 1898)
reflects traditional 19c. ideas on education of women.
Although a woman's mission in life is to be the companion
of a man, it is necessary that she be educated, docile
without abjectness, and modest without pedantry.

511 BARBIERI, M. TERESITA de
1972 Acceso de la mujer a las carreras y ocupaciones
tecnológicas de nivel medio. Santiago: ELAS-UNESCO.
121 p. tables.
Exploratory investigation of the factors which favor
or impede women's access to careers and occupations of
a middle technological level, analyzing level, type
and content of education; career choices; occupational
possibilities; and promotion, in 3 Chilean cities
(Valparaiso, Tolca, Valdivia), based on interviews with
teachers, students, employers, and employees.

512 BRANDAU de ROSS, MATILDE
1934 "Education of Women in Chile." MPM 47:5:453-58.
illus.
Brief history of women's education in Chile before
1877, when the first two women doctors received their

Education

degrees. Notes first school for girls and the individuals involved in pushing for female education. Continues
with the 20c. and 11 outstanding professional women in
medicine, law, education, engineering, who were
precursors.

513   Cien profesiones y oficios para la mujer chilena.
      1950 Col. Orientación, 1. Santiago: Imprenta Chile.
      96 p. tables.
      Part 1 catalogues basic information on many schools
      which prepare women for employment: objectives, require-
      ments, uniform, degree, etc.; includes nursing, child
      care, office skills, teaching, social work, etc. Part
      2 discusses kind of work women are or could be engaged
      in, describing activities in commerce, industry, etc.

514   GAETE PEQUEÑO, DORA
      1948 "La escuela granja femenina." E/R 8:50:258-60.
      illus.
      Founding director of first rural school (granja) for
      women in Chile discusses role of such an establishment,
      very briefly reviewing history of rural education since
      1938. Lacks concrete information about the school and
      instruction provided there.

515   GISSI BUSTOS, JORGE
      1973 "Prejuicios en la educación de la mujer." C/F
      1:2:92-95.
      Prejudices exist with respect to what careers women
      may pursue. They differ according to social class and
      are in part caused by the scarce and false information
      which Chile receives as a victim of capitalism.

516   GURRIERI, ADOLFO
      1966 "Situación y perspectivas de la juventud en una
      población urbana popular." UNAM/RMS 28:3:571-602.
      tables, bibl.
      Attempts to provide general picture of situation of
      268 youths in the marginal population of Cardenal Caro
      in Santiago, using 98 from the middle class of
      Providencia as a control. Contrary to the stereotype,
      the majority works and/or attends school. Tables pro-
      vide breakdown according to sector and sex for work,
      education, obstacles against continuing studies, level
      of aspirations, relations with parents and professors,
      social involvement, means of attaining goals, etc. Con-
      cludes that young people are in a state of perplexity or
      disorientation.

517 GUTIÉRREZ, FERMÍN ESTRELLA
       1957 "Gabriela Mistral, maestra." ND 37:4:46-49.
       Briefly recounts the positions Gabriela Mistral held
       as educator, and quotes statements and verses which
       reflect her attitudes toward teaching. Suggests that
       her frustrated desire to be a mother in part explains
       her tremendous love for and dedication to children.

518 HOSTOS, EUGENIO MARÍA de
       1873 La educación de la mujer. Santiago: Imprenta del
       Sud-América. 29 p.
       Puerto Rican who helped advance women's education in
       Chile speaks in favor of the "scientific" education of
       women, to remove them from the state of moral anarchy
       in which male egoism has had them submerged. Women
       should be educated not so that they can function in
       social life but rather to be human beings who practice
       reason, whose conscience is alive, and whose faculties
       are cultivated and developed. This pamphlet is anno-
       tated in Bibliografía puertorriqueña (Barcelona, 1934)
       of Géigel y Zenón and Morales Ferrer.

519 LABARCA HUBERTSON, AMANDA
       1939 Historia de la enseñanza en Chile. Santiago:
       Imprenta Universitaria. 399 p. illus., bibl.
       Notes on women's education appear throughout this
       history of education in Chile from colonial times to
       the 1930's by Chile's foremost female educator. An
       appendix includes various decrees regarding the founding,
       curriculum, and administration of educational centers
       for women. Based on secondary sources, national statis-
       tics and documents. Basically repeats information of
       her 1925 article.

520 _____.
       1925 "La educación femenina en Chile." UNLP/RF 11:1:37-73.
       bibl. f/notes.
       Beginning with the Dominican theologist, Fray
       Bartolomé Rodríguez González, who taught Inés de Suárez
       how to read and write in the 16c., Chile's foremost
       female educator presents a history of the education of
       women in Chile from colonial times to the first quarter
       of the 20c., when the "feminine movement" of Gabriela
       Mistral and other professional women demonstrated
       women's capacity to flower culturally. Provides informa-
       tion on educators, institutions and curricula based on
       primary and secondary sources.

Education

521 MENDOZA D., MARÍA
      1965 "Razón de ser de la cátedra de vestuario." CEF/R
      31:124:48-50.
         Member of the Departmento de Alimentación y Educación
      para el Hogar of the Instituto de Educación Física y
      Técnica (Santiago) discusses her function as a teacher
      of sewing to young women and comments that while research
      on other topics has touched upon it, no thesis has been
      written entirely on sewing. Lists theses from 1936 to
      1964 with a brief summary of each; e.g., "Influence of
      the Chilean Woman in the Economic Improvement of the
      Nation," "Instruction of Feminine Manual Arts and of
      Domestic Economy and Its Influence in Family Life."

522 SCHMIDT de ALVAREZ, ADELA
      1903 Enseñanza artística de la mujer. Informe presentado
      al Ministerio de instrucción pública en cumplimiento de
      una comisión del supremo gobierno. Santiago:
      Encuadernación y Litografía Esmeralda. 50 p.
         Reports to Minister of Public Education in Chile on an
      investigative visit to girls' schools, recommending,
      in her estimation, the best plan of action for educating
      girls. In an attached study, proposes the establishment
      of a school to develop the artistic potential of upper
      class girls.

523 SEWARD, GEORGENE H. and WILLIAMSON, ROBERT C.
      1969 "A Cross-National Study of Adolescent Professional
      Goals." HUDE 12:4:248-54. tables, bibl.
         Approximately 500 adolescents (16 to 19 years old)
      of each sex, attending public schools in the US,
      Germany, Chile, Poland and Turkey recorded their voca-
      tional goals, which were then sorted between major and
      minor professional. Findings for Chile reveal that
      girls chose minor goals, irrespective of social class,
      while boys attending private schools chose major pro-
      fessions exclusively. Attributes findings to different
      motivational pressures exerted in the various groups.

524 SOIZA REILLY, JUAN JOSÉ de
      1924? Mujeres de América. Buenos Aires: Librerías
      Anaconda. 227 p.
         See ARGENTINA for annotation. Considers Chilean poet
      and educator Gabriela Mistral and educator Amanda
      Labarca Hubertson.

525 VERA MANRÍQUEZ, SERGIO
      1968 "Situación de la educación para la mujer campesina."
      E/R 11:14-15.

Briefly describes state of education for women in
rural Chile since 1952, naming programs and schools and
their objectives in preparing peasant women. Also
explains organization of the Instituto de Educación
Rural, established in 1958.

Argentina

526   AMADEO, TOMÁS
      1947 La redención por la mujer. 2nd ed. B.A.:   Guillermo
      Kraft. 224 p. illus., plates, bibl. f/notes.
          Argues for adequate and appropriate education for
      women in the countryside, which he calls "hogar
      agrícola," describes it, recommends a program of action,
      and comments on existing schools and commissions.
      Includes a chapter on a rural women's organization and
      much complementary material on agricultural instruction
      for women.

527   _____.
      1942 "La acción de la mujer en el mejoramiento agrario
      argentino." SS/A 5:1/4:8-20.
          Appeals to women of Buenos Aires to act in favor of
      their sisters in the provinces in order to better the
      life of rural families; offers outline of action.
      Because of abysmal conditions, initiated campaign in
      1909 to organize instruction in countryside--Enseñanza
      del Hogar Agrícola--because educating women means
      creating more educators. Discusses some of the
      programs--very traditional--directed at women.

528   Argentine Republic. Ministerio de Cultura y Educación.
      1972 Encuesta. Conferencia Interamericana Especializada
      sobre Educación Integral de la Mujer. (Buenos Aires,
      21-25 de agosto de 1972). B.A.: Centro Nacional de
      Documentación e Información Educativa. 58 p. tables.
          In response to a request by the IACW for information
      on the position of women in America, the National Office
      of Women of the Ministry of Labor collaborated with the
      Ministry of Social Welfare and Ministry of Culture and
      Education to prepare this basic document for the Inter
      American Conference on Women's Integral Education.
      Comprised of answers to 64 questions on labor force
      participation, politics, volunteer work, and education,
      emphasizing latter. Appendix of statistics and
      additional data on education.

Education

529   Argentine Republic. Ministerio de Justicia e Instrucción
      Pública.
         1924 Plan de estudios, programas y reglamentos para las
         escuelas profesionales de artes y oficios de mujeres.
         B.A.: Talleres Gráficos de la Penitenciaría Nacional.
         53 p.
            Reproduces the plan of studies, programs, and regula-
         tions set up by presidential decree in 1912 to regulate
         technical education for women in Argentina. Primary
         source for knowing in what trades and arts women were
         being trained.

530   _____. Secretaría de Estado de Trabajo. Dirección Nacional
      de Recursos Humanos. Oficina Nacional de la Mujer.
         1970 Evolución de la mujer en las profesiones liberales
         en Argentina, años 1900-1965. 2nd ed. Suplemento de
         Boletín de la Oficina Nacional de la Mujer, Serie A -
         "La mujer economicamente activa." Buenos Aires. 160 p.
         tables, graphs.
            Update on first edition (1965) which covered 1900-1960.
         Presents detailed data from 8 national universities in
         Argentina to illustrate women's gains in the professions
         through the number of university degrees granted to them
         from 1900 to 1965 in the fields of medicine, law, archi-
         tecture, mathematics, engineering, chemistry, etc. Many
         comparative statistics with men.

531   BARILARI, SUSANA S. de
         1943 "Asociación femenina de acción rural (A.F.A.R.).
         Memoria (1942-1943)." MSA/B 31:257/258:350-58.
            The A.F.A.R. was founded for the purpose of educating
         rural women. Reports on first year's activities: names
         and describes 16 committees formed to fulfill various
         needs; lists publications of the association; and points
         out scarcity of teachers specialized in instruction for
         the rural home and lack of institute to train teachers
         in the field.

532   "Breve instrucción de la fundación de la Santa Caridad,
      Colegio de Niñas Húerfanas, Hospital de Pobres Enfermas de
      esta ciudad de Buenos Aires."
         1870 BA/R 23:90:161-92.
            Unedited manuscript on the founding of the Hermandad
         de Santa Caridad which, in turn, helped found the
         Colegio de Niñas Huérfanas to provide shelter, instruc-
         tion, and doctrine for 12 orphans under the direction
         of 3 sisters (Buenos Aires, 1755). Includes notes on
         rules governing daily activities and on the history and

problems of this charitable institution, in which girls
were taught sewing and other skills to help sustain it.
Complements early article by V. G. Quesada (#547),
which provides a documented history of the school.

533 CABRERA, PABLO
1928 "Educación de la mujer." In his Cultura y
beneficencia durante la colonia, vol. 1, pp. 53-137.
2nd ed. Tesoros del pasado argentino. Córdoba, Arg.:
Talleres Gráficos de la Penitenciaría. bibl. f/notes.
Based on documents and secondary sources, traces the
evolution of education for women in Argentina, from
the Colegio de Recogidas, founded in Asunción, Paraguay
in very early 1600's, to 19c. establishments. Concludes
that all education was eminently religious, provided by
secular and regular clerics. Footnotes are ample,
detailed, and informative.

534 CHANETÓN, ABEL
1942 "La educación de la mujer." In his La instrucción
primaria en la época colonial, 2nd ed., pp. 313-28.
Biblioteca de la Sociedad de Historia Argentina, 12.
Buenos Aires: Talleres gráficos de Guillermo Kraft
Ltda. bibl. f/notes.
Brief but informative chapter (based on documents and
secondary sources) recounts the development of schools
for women in Argentina from 1653 to 1811, citing establishments founded in Buenos Aires, Córdoba, Catamarca,
Mendoza, Salta and San Juan. Wonders, if instruction
for females was so limited during colonial epoch, where
the many intelligent and cultured women (some of
whom he names) became versed in letters, arts and sciences. Includes appendix of documents.

535 EICHELBAUM de BABINI, ANA MARÍA
1972 "La desigualdad educacional en Argentina." In
Argentina conflictiva: seis estudios sobre problemas
sociales argentinos, ed. by J. F. Marsal, pp. 19-57.
Buenos Aires: PAIDOS. tables, bibl.
Analyzes unequal distribution of educational opportunities in Argentina, emphasizing disparities according
to 3 variables: socio-economic status, degree of urbanization, and sex. Using 1960 national census data and
data from government agencies, discusses differences in
education for men and women on all levels. Notes
probability of increased sex differentiation in certain
careers. Draws brief comparison with world situation
and concludes that progress made in women's education in
Argentina is not exceptional.

Education

536   ESTANY, ADELINA A.
        1936 "Juana Manso." MEC 55:760:42-47. port.
          Recounts Juana Manso's (1819-75) history as an educator
        in Uruguay, Brazil, and especially in Argentina, where
        she worked with Sarmiento to found the first co-
        educational school. She was also a writer, initiator of
        Album de Señoritas (19c. periodical for women), and first
        woman to occupy a seat in the council of Public
        Instruction.

537   FIORILLI, LETICIA
        1967 "Coeducación de los sexos." AEST 582:202-16. bibl.
          Suggests that a scientific investigation be undertaken
        to resolve problem of co-education. Points out differ-
        ences between boys and girls and pro and con opinions
        on educating the sexes together. There is a fear of
        possible early sexual relations. Part 2 outlines 6
        stages of development--from embryo to post-adolescence--
        discussing traditionally accepted physical and psycho-
        logical differences between the sexes.

538   GRIERSON, CECILIA
        1902 Educación técnica de la mujer. Informe presentado
        al Sr. Ministro de Instrucción Pública de la República
        Argentina. B.A.: Tipografía de la Penitenciaría
        Nacional. 244 p.
          First Argentine woman doctor reports observations on
        technical education for women in various European
        countries and then summarizes the development of educa-
        tion for women in 19c. Argentina, recommending programs
        to capacitate women at home, in business and in agricul-
        ture, with special emphasis on training in the
        "Domestic sciences" (pp. 167-242).

539   GUAGLIANONE de DELGADO FITO, MANÓN V.
        1968 Juana Manso: una vida al servicio de la cultura
        argentina. Buenos Aires. 153 p.
          According to the Handbook of Latin American Studies
        32(1970):2554, this is a sensitive biography of a leading
        Argentine feminist, writer, and educator (1819-75) who
        was also a close friend of Sarmiento, Argentina's well-
        known 19c. educator.

540   _____.
        1939 "Women of America: II. Juana Manso de Noronha,
        Argentina." PAU/B 73:12:721-26. illus., port.
          A brief account of Juana Manso's, Sarmiento's favorite
        disciple, life-long struggle to promote modern public

education, primarily in 19c. Argentina. She was the
first principal of the first coeducational primary
school (Buenos Aires, 1859).

541 GUERRERO, CÉSAR H.
     1960 Mujeres de Sarmiento. Buenos Aires: Artes Gráficas
     Bartolomé U. Chiesino. 332 p. ports.
     Sketches of varying length of the women in the life of
     Domingo Faustino Sarmiento, Argentina's greatest educator
     who contributed to the development of women's education
     by establishing schools where they could learn and teach.
     Begins with his mother Paula Albarracín and his godmother/
     aunt, Paula de Oro, and covers other female relatives as
     well as other educators (Juana Manso, Mary Mann) and
     women who were influential in his life (Aurelia Vélez
     Sarsfield plus 26 more). Good notes about a group of
     people who contributed to Argentina's educational system
     for women.

542 JALÓN, ANA MARÍA
     1969 "La mujer y su papel de educadora." UNC/R 10:1/2:
     305-18.
     Cites comparative statistics for female students and
     teachers in Argentina and other Latin American countries;
     briefly traces establishment of education institutions
     and notable educators in Argentina; and considers ques-
     tions related to women's function as an educative agent.

543 LUIGGI, ALICE HOUSTON
     1959 Sesenta y cinco valiantes. Sarmiento y las maestras
     norteamericanas. Trans. by R. Ottolenghi. Buenos Aires:
     Edit. Agora. 250 p. ports., map, bibl.
     Although essentially an account of the contributions
     to Argentina's public educational system made by 65
     Protestant schoolteachers brought from NA by President
     Sarmiento from 1869 to 1883, indirectly there is also
     information on the education available for girls during
     second half of 19c. Documented.

544 MOLINA, RAÚL A.
     1956 "La educación de la mujer en el siglo XVII y
     comienzo del siguiente. La influencia de la beata
     española Da. Marina de Escobar." A/H 2:5:11-32.
     facsims., bibl. notes.
     Documented attempt to complete information on women's
     education in the 17c. in G. Furlong Cardiff's study
     (#418). Challenges other historians who maintain that
     marriage or the convent were colonial women's only

Education

possibilities. Contends that women's education was at
the same level as men's. Through a history of *beatas*,
beginning with Marina de Escobar in Spain and tracing
the appearance of others in Buenos Aires, associated
with the Company of Jesus and other religious groups,
claims that indeed scholastic education was available
to women in the 17c., but it was intimately tied to
religion. Facsimiles attest to women's ability to
write.

545   MOLINA, RAÚL A.
      1948 "La instrucción pública en tiempos de Hernandarias."
      In his Hernandarias, el hijo de la tierra, pp. 301-12.
      Buenos Aires: Edit. Lancastremere.
         Hernandarias (1561-1634) was the *Adelantado* and Gover-
      nor of Río de la Plata, known for his interest in and
      development of education in this region.   Discusses his
      founding of 2 *casas de recogimiento* for women, one in
      Asunción, the other in Santa Fe, with the intention of
      teaching women how to earn a living.   Unfortunately,
      documents relate that it became more of a sweatshop than
      a simple workshop for instruction in spinning.   Relates
      the escapes of 2 women.

546   PROBST, JUAN
      1940 "La educacion de las mujeres."   In his La instrucción
      primaria durante la dominación española en el territorio
      que forma actualmente la República Argentina, pp. 11-13.
      Inst. de Didáctica, Facultad de Folosofía y Letras de la
      Univ. de Buenos Aires.   Trabajos de investigación y de
      tesis, 5.   Buenos Aires: Imprenta López.   bibl.
      f/notes.
         Briefly states that educating girls so that they could
      become mothers who collaborated in the education of their
      children and women with their own intellectual life was
      unknown in colonial Argentina.   Wealthy families had
      their daughters instructed in handiwork, a little reading
      and signing their name at home, in convents, orphanages
      and private schools.   Based on primary and secondary
      sources.

547   QUESADA, VICENTE GREGORIO
      1863 "Fundación del Colegio de Huérfanas en Buenos Aires."
      BA/R 2:6:207-24.
         Documented history of the Colegio de Huérfanas since
      1699.   Originally under the direction of the Hermandad
      de Santa Caridad, this charitable institution came under
      the umbrella of the Sociedad de Beneficencia in 1823.

It was founded as a home and place of spiritual as well
as practical education for orphaned girls. See #532.

548   RABINOVICH de PIROSKY, ROSA
        1969 "Participación de la mujer en la investigación
        científica." UNC/R 10:1:363-78.
           Barely includes some statistics on female graduates
        in the sciences in Argentina (1950-60) and cites some
        women scientists.

549   REISSIG, LUIS
        1948 "La educación de la mujer en la Argentina. I-IV."
        CUCO 33:196:189-251.
           Series of 4 lectures discussing education as a social
        and moral problem and women in urban and rural areas.
        Considers changes in women's education, family life,
        society and public life. Sees a need for women to be
        educated in the problems of public and domestic spheres
        in order to have a political consciousness. Domestic
        life is the concern of everyone, not merely of women.

550   RIGALT, FRANCISCO
        1969 "La mujer rural y el Instituto Nacional de
        Tecnología Agropecuaria." UNC/R 10:1/2:217-20.
           Describes function of the INTA with respect to rural
        families especially to capacitate women in their role
        as housewife, mother, wife and community member through
        Rural Home Clubs.

551   SARMIENTO, DOMINGO FAUSTINO
        1944 "Sarmiento y la educación de la mujer." In
        Antología del pensamiento democrático Domingo Faustino
        Sarmiento, ed. by P. de Alba, pp. 191-93. Mex., D.F.:
        Imprenta Universitaria.
           Argentina's leading educator of the 19c. expresses his
        thoughts on women's role in society, especially in educa-
        tion. Women, through instinct and natural disposition
        alone, know how to educate and care for children.
        Maternity is their most powerful instinct. If society
        wants great and virtuous men, women have to be taught
        greatness and virtue; it all lies in their hands as
        mothers/educators. They too are capable of studying;
        they have reason, a will and passions, just like men do.

552   SCHULTZ CAZENEUVE de MANTOVANI, FRYDA
        1960 "La mujer en los últimos treinta años." Sur 267:
        20-29.
           Suggests that Argentine women were able to move out
        of an absolute patriarchy sooner than their Latin

Education

American sisters and into the arts, music and literature,
perhaps because men dedicated themselves more to politics
and women to education, especially the Normal School.
Discusses women's overwhelming participation in teaching
and why; and comments on their political involvement
(struggle for suffrage; political party participation,
especially Socialist; Eva Perón, etc.) Considers women
neither conservative nor progressive, but rather innovative because they're attracted to change. Provides some
statistics on population, voting, and education
(1959-60).

553 TANZI, HÉCTOR JOSÉ
1963 "La educación femenina a través de un periódico de
antaño." AEST 550:750-52.
A weekly Buenos Aires periodical of political persua-
sion, El Observador Americano, during 1816 dedicated some
space to the subject of women's education. Using quota-
tions from different columns, demonstrates that education
has not fallen into complete oblivion, as is generally
thought for the colonial epoch. Briefly discusses public
reaction incurred by these opinions and advice in correspondence subsequently received by periodical: one woman
expressed her frustration at attention given to her
beauty rather than to her intelligence.

554 VELASCO y ARIAS, MARÍA
1937 Juana Paula Manso: vida y acción. B.A.: Talleres
Gráficos Portes. 419 p. illus., ports., facsim.,
bibl. f/notes.
Biography of Juana Paula Manso de Noronha (1819-1875),
indefatigable Argentine educator, feminist, and writer;
includes epistolary collection, travel account, and other
writings in appendix. Appears well-researched, using
much correspondence.

Uruguay

555 P. S.
1925 "Rasgos biográficos de Emma Catalá de Princivalle."
IHGU/R 4:2:573-88.
Biographical notes on Uruguayan teacher (1860-1924),
emphasizing the development of her education and pedagog-
ical contributions. Includes data on her family,
marriage and children. No references, but quotes extensively from her texts.

CARIBBEAN

Puerto Rico

556   ARRIVÍ, FRANCISCO
      1965 "Doña Antonia Sáenz, ceiba." PR/E 15:16:66-81.
      Biographical sketch of well-known Puerto Rican educator
      and writer upon her death with excerpts from her memoirs.
      Professor Emeritus at the University of Puerto Rico and
      recipient of the Institute of Puerto Rican Culture award,
      she wrote on Puerto Rican theatre and language.

557   Asociación de Damas para la Instrucción de la Mujer.
      1886 Reglamento de la Asociación de Damas para la
      Instrucción de la Mujer. San Juan, P.R.: Tipografía de
      González y cía. 16 p.
      Reproduces project of regulation approved by Governor
      General of Puerto Rico in 1885 for Association of Ladies
      for the Education of Women by which to rule themselves.
      Main objective was to give daughters of poor families
      the means to acquire an education or professional
      instruction as well as the title or degree necessary to
      direct a private or public school.

558   BENÍTEZ, JAIME
      1966 "Actualidad de la educación en Puerto Rico. I, La
      mujer universitaria en la vida puertorriqueña." UPR/T
      14:53:11-18.
      President of the University of Puerto Rico tells
      female graduating class of University College of Sacred
      Heart (1966) about their mission as women in a new
      society and the meaning of private education, especially
      of a religious nature.

559   BERIA, FELICIA
      1942 Cuidado diurno para niños de madres que trabajan;
      establecimientos de casas cunas en Puerto Rico. San
      Juan, P.R.: Dept. del Trabajo, Servico de Supervisión
      del Trabajo de Mujeres. 25 p. tables.
      1,060 working mothers were interviewed in sewing shops
      and laundries in 13 Puerto Rican towns in 1941 by the
      Servicio de Supervisión del Trabajo de Mujeres. Includes
      information on salaries and work hours of the mothers,
      living conditions, who cares for the children. Briefly
      describes 5 established child care centers. Makes
      specific recommendations for a child care program to be
      instituted.

Education

560   BRAU, SALVADOR
      1886 La campesina. (Disquisiciones sociológicas). San
      Juan, P.R.: Imprenta de José González Font. 54 p.
         According to Bibliografía puertorriqueña (Barcelona,
      1934) of Géigel y Zenón and Morales Ferrer, this work
      is a generous argument in favor of instructing the pro-
      letarian women of Puerto Rico's countryside and creating
      rural schools for children. "Let us dignify that
      [i.e., peasant] mother through education" in order to
      see our society regenerated from its deepest foundations.

561   COLLAZO-COLLAZO, JÉNARO
      1969 "Participación de la mujer en la fase educativa de
      la vida puertorriqueña." PR/E 22:27:41-53. tables.
         Report prepared for Governor's Commission on the Status
      of Women presents statistical data revealing women's
      participation in different educational levels in Puerto
      Rico (1960-68). Concludes that rates of female participa-
      tion as students did not significantly vary between 1960
      and 1967 and do not increase as educational level rises.
      On a university level women participate less than men in
      teaching and non-teaching tasks. Data from Department
      of Public Instruction, 2 colleges and 3 universities.

562   DÍAZ, JOSÉ FRANCISCO
      1888 Memoria relative a la fundación, trabajos, medios
      con que cuenta y recursos que peuden aportarse para la
      mejor marcha de la Junta de Damas, para la instrucción
      y educación de la mujer en nuestra provencia. San Juan,
      P.R.: Tipografía El Comercio de J. Anfosso y Cía. 8 p.
         According to the Bibliografía puertorriqueña
      (Barcelona, 1934) of Géigel y Zenón and Morales Ferrer,
      Díaz edited this memoria in compliance with article 22
      of the Reglamento interior and in agreement with the
      board of directors in the January 15, 1888 session.
      President at the time was doña Rafaela Dolz de Contreras;
      secretary, doña Belén Zequeira de Cuevas.

563   FERRER, GABRIEL
      1881 La mujer en Puerto-Rico. San Juan, P.R.: Imprenta
      de "El Agente." 72 p.
         According to Bibliografía puertorriqueña (Barcelona,
      1934) of Géigel y Zenón and Morales Ferrer, this
      memoria is by an "apostle of progress and partisan of the
      moral equality of the two sexes" who favors the regenera-
      tion of women through an ample and solid education in
      harmony with their qualities as human beings. Even in
      their state of intellectual slavery, women have many
      features which make them superior to men. Includes

selections from celebrated authors of their thoughts
on women and a poem in their defense by Sor Juana.

564   GIL de TABOADA, ELVIRA
        1851 Plan del Colegio de Ninas bajo la invocación de
        Santa Filomena. San Juan, P.R.: Imprenta del Boletín
        Mercantil. 7 p.
           According to Bibliografía puertorriqueña (Barcelona,
        1934) of Géigel y Zenón and Morales Ferrer, this pamphlet
        lists kinds of classes given in this school for girls
        founded in 1851: religion, reading, writing, arithmetic,
        French and English, drawing, embroidery, piano, etc.

565   ROSARIO, JOSÉ C.
        1927 "Home Economics in the Rural Schools." PAU/B 61:
        7:685-92. illus.
           Discusses what girls in Puerto Rican rural schools
        need to be taught in order to have a better home. Con-
        siders house improvements, child care, health instruction,
        food preparation, and sewing.

Cuba

566   AGUAYO, ALFREDO MIGUEL
        1937 "María Luisa Dolz, educadora de la mujer cubana."
        In his Tres grandes educadores cubanos: Varona,
        Echemendía, María Luisa Dolz, pp. 51-64. Havana:
        "Cultural."
           Demonstrates that liberal ideas about education for
        women in Cuba existed earlier than late 19c. Reviews
        pedagogical career and ideas of María Luisa Dolz, famous
        Cuban educator of women and proponent of feminism in
        latter third of 19c. Quotes from her discourses.

567   DOLZ y ARANGO, MARÍA LUISA
        1955 La liberación de la mujer cubana por la educación.
        Homenaje de la ciudad de la Habana en el centenario de
        su nacimiento, 1854--4 de octubre--1954. Havana:
        Oficina del Historiador de la Ciudad. 151 p.
           Collection of talks given by well-known Cuban educator,
        María Luisa Dolz y Arango (1854-1928). She dedicated
        her life to providing an "integral education" for women
        and defending their emancipation. In her own colegio,
        purchased in 1879, she introduced physical education,
        and secondary school courses considered innovative for
        those times. Preceded by biographical data. One
        speech, given in 1894, was entitled "Feminismo.
        Injusticia de los Códigos."

Education

568 EDREIRA PAZ, NOEMÍ
     1949 "¿Con qué tendencias y para qué fin debe educarse la
     mujer (de acuerdo con el concepto martiano)." UH/U
     14:82/87:329-32.
           According to an interpretation of Jose Martí's
     writings, women's role par excellence is that of mother.
     Female education should teach woman to be a "treasure
     of abnegation" and a "fountain of consolation," both
     "innate" female characteristics.

569 HIERRO, CASTOR
     1877 Enseñanzas femeninas. Cuadros de instrucción
     tomados de la historia y de las costumbres. Havana:
     Imprenta de E. Valdés. 212 p.
           Women's education is even more important than men's
     because, as mothers, women educate the next generation.
     To instruct Cuban girls and instill in them moral
     rectitude, offers maxims, apothegms and principles of
     good doctrine in a series of rhymed verses; divided
     into 2 parts: preliminary (historical-traditional) and
     moral (infancy-adolescence, youth, marriage, old age).

570 HOPKINS, DEE
     1974 "Ya brotan las semillas." CR 4:2:32-34. illus.
           Description of childcare in revolutionary Cuba, based
     mostly on Marvin Leiner's Children are the Revolution:
     Day Care in Cuba (#571). Notes growing consciousness
     among Cubans with respect to sexual division in sociali-
     zation. Few lament the absence of men from day care
     centers.

571 LEINER, MARVIN
     1947 Children Are the Revolution: Day Care in Cuba.
     N.Y.: Viking Press. 213 p. tables, bibl. f/notes.
           Based on interviews and personal observations
     (1968-69), traces development of early-childhood education
     from pre-revolutionary days to the present. Reports on
     the women who work in day care centers, educational
     techniques, socialization of children in these centers,
     their mothers, role of child's family, etc. Cites day
     care program, directed by the FMC, as a governmental
     goal to deal with issue of women's roles and to free
     women from traditional constraints of the past. Includes
     excerpts from diary of author's 14-year-old daughter,
     who was a volunteer at a center, and update from a 1971
     visit.

572 MANZANO, MATILDE
      1963 "Apuntes de una alfabetizadora." CDLA 3:19:91-117.
      Personal account of one woman's efforts toward eradi-
      cating illiteracy in a Cuban community, problems she
      encountered, and observations on her female students,
      and on women's inability to participate because of
      child care.

573 MESA RODRÍGUEZ, MANUEL ISAÍAS
      1954 María Luisa Dolz, educadora y ciudadana . . . .
      Havana: Imprenta "El Siglo XX." 20 p. port.
      Speech given at centennial commemoration of birth of
      María Luisa Dolz is an homage to this precursor in
      education for women in 19c. Cuba. Includes some bio-
      graphical data and notes on her career.

574 PERERA, HILDA
      1962 "Women in a New Social Context in Cuba." IJAYE 14:
      3:144-49. Spanish version: 1962 "La mujer y el nuevo
      contexto social en Cuba." UNESCO/BT 14:152-57.
      Reports on results of 3 years' efforts of Cuban
      revolutionary government in the field of women's educa-
      tion. Discusses dressmaking classes for rural women,
      schools for domestic servants and their teachers,
      courses for the female staff of child care centers and
      for art teachers.

Dominican Republic

575 RODRÍGUEZ DEMORIZI, EMILIO
      1960 Salomé Ureña y el Instituto de Senoritas. Para la
      historia de la espiritualidad dominicana. Academia
      Dominicana de la Historia, 9. Ciudad Trujillo:
      Impresora Dominicana. 427 p. illus.
      Collection of writings on Salomé Ureña (1850-97),
      poet, educator and founder/director of first institution
      of higher education for women in the Dominican Republic
      (1881), and documents related to the school: documented
      genealogical data; tributes, odes, sonnets, eulogies,
      reprints, etc.; course programs, correspondence, lists
      of students, speeches on education of women, reports
      on exams and teacher training, etc.

575a VALLDEPERES, MANUEL
      1969 "Salomé Ureña, poetisa y maestra." RIB 19:1:23-38. bibl.
      Biographical sketch of Salomé Ureña de Henríquez
      (1850-97) traces her career as a poet and as an educator
      of women in late 19th c. Dominican Republic. Quotes
      verses and provides useful bibliography of her works as
      well as works written about her.

MAGIC, RELIGION, AND RITUAL

This section is comprised of studies on women and their relationship to church and clergy, religious beliefs and practices, and participation in religious-denominated organizations; on saints, goddesses, female shamans and witches; on the cult of the Virgin Mary; on nuns and nunneries. Entries consider the founding of individual convents, the social, cultural and economic role of convents, conventual life, and biographies of nuns.

Literary nuns, such as Sor Juana or the Madre Castillo, are located in the LITERATURE, MASS MEDIA, AND FOLKLORE category. For the relationship between the Virgin Mary as a symbol of womanhood and female behavior, see studies on *marianismo*, and the Virgin as a surrogate mother figure, see PSYCHOLOGY. For notes on women's participation in the religious life of indigenous groups and other subcultures, see ETHNOGRAPHIC MONOGRAPHS/COMMUNITY STUDIES and the pre-Conquest period of HISTORY BEFORE 1900. For rituals related to the female reproductive cycle, see HUMAN SEXUALITY, REPRODUCTION, AND HEALTH. For other educational institutions and programs founded and directed by nuns, see EDUCATION.

While there is good primary and secondary source material on convents and conventual life, hagiographies of nuns and saints border on an exaggeration of Christian devoutness, miraculous feats, and masochistic behavior (e.g., extreme mortification). These *vidas* are often written by other clerics, with no documentation or reference sources cited.

SPANISH AMERICA - GENERAL

576   BARBER, NATALIE
         1967 "Latin America's Methodist Women." CCY 84:8:247-48.
              Brief statements from participants in Latin American
              Methodist Women's Confederation in Bolivia regarding the
              need for change in the structure of the Church and
              women's organizations.

Spanish America - General

577   BAYLE, CONSTANTINO
      1928 Santa María en Indias: la devoción a Nuestra
      Señora y los descubridores, conquistadores y pobladores
      de América. Madrid: Apostolado de la Prensa. 369 p.
      illus.
         Deals with the importance of the Virgin in America.
      Cites examples of devotion to her worship among the
      conquistadors, native peoples, et al.

578   CARILLO CAZARES, ALBERTO
      1971 El diaconado femenino. La traición eclesial y las
      perspectivas ante el problema del clero latinoamericano.
      Bilbao: Mensajero. 226 p. bibl.
         Reviews the absence and presence of women in liturgical
      action; theological and socio-cultural prejudices which
      have alienated women; arguments from the 4c. and the
      Middle Ages against female participation in liturgical
      service of the Church; and linguistic, anthropological
      and Biblical premises to understand the cultural roots
      of degrading ideas about women. Concludes that there is
      no dogmatic, exegetic or consistent argument for impeding
      women's access to the ministry and that an adequate form
      of *diakonia* of women in the Church be restored.

579   COMBLIN, JOSÉ
      1971 "Las religiosas y los altos estudios de teología."
      BDSLM/CIDHAL 1:1:41-42.
         Brazilian theologist decries lack of women trained in
      theology and lack of action on part of Church in the
      cultural promotion of women. Suggests sending female
      students to Europe for intellectual preparation, espe-
      cially in theology, so that they can teach in the
      ecclesiastical faculties.

580   DOTSON, FLOYD
      1953 "A Note on Participation in Voluntary Association
      in a Mexican City." ASS/ASR 18:4:380-86. tables, bibl.
      f/notes.
         230 women and 185 men were interviewed in Guadalajara
      for exploration into development of formally organized
      voluntary associations in urban areas. Concludes that
      less women than men participate and their membership is
      overwhelmingly concentrated in church-affiliated asso-
      ciations, and secondarily in society clubs.

581   Equipo de Monjas de Santa Escolástica, Argentina
      1968 "Aspecto sociológico de las vocaciones monásticas
      femeninas en el cono sur de América Latina." Yermo
      6:1:17-34.

Magic, Religion, and Ritual

>Lecture discusses women in religious orders in Latin
>America from the colonial epoch to after WWII: character-
>istics of religious foundations, 3 types of women found
>in them reflecting 3 social classes, differences between
>earlier and contemporary times. Concerned with repercus-
>sion of socio-economic problems in female monastic voca-
>tions and validity of latter in today's world. Suggests
>that bishops fully integrate religious women into local
>church in order to help in problems of third world.

582   HODGE, KATHERINE A.
>1915 "Women's Rights and Women's Wrongs in South America."
>MRW 28:8:599-604. illus.
>   Missionary's pity for the spiritual and physical state of
>South American women. Notes dreadful work conditions, es-
>pecially in factories, the white slave traffic, seductions by
>priests, high rate of illiteracy, scarcity of doctors and
>nurses and sound medical and health practices. Appeals
>to readers to give their South American sisters the Gospel.

583   Jornadas Ecuménicas Latinoamericanas
>1968 El rol de la mujer en la iglesia y en la sociedad.
>Conclusiones y recomendaciones. Montevideo: UNELAM.
>123 p. bibl.
>   Results of a consultation held in Piriápolis, Uruguay,
>December 1967, to discuss and recommend solutions to the
>concerns expressed about women's role in the ecumenical
>movement and social changes in LA. Includes presenta-
>tions on the position of women, psychological analysis
>of it, mission of the Church, and an evaluation of
>organized female Church activities. Participants and
>addresses listed.

584   MARTÍNEZ DELGADO, LUIS
>1954 "La Santísima Virgen en la historia." HA/B 41:481/
>482:722-42. bibl.
>   God created the perfect woman in the Vigin Mary, in
>whom he sanctified all women. Traces cult of and devo-
>tion to Mary and other virgins from 16c. navigators to
>obsequium by US Ambassador to Chile in 1949.

585   NIDA, EUGENE A.
>1957 "Mariology in Latin America." PRAN 4:3:69-82.
>Reprinted in Supplement, 1960, pp. 1-15.
>   Reviews reasons for greater attention showered upon
>Mary than on Christ and considers 3 underlying factors
>to understand the relationship between Roman Catholic
>Church and Latin American society: female--rather than
>sex--orientation of the culture; mother as emotional

center of family; and well-defined relationship of rein-
forcement between position of the Church and status of
women. Loyalty to the Virgin reflects emotional patterns
in Latin life. Makes comparisons to other religions.

586 PEREIRA LEITE, SOR INÉS
1970 "America Latina y los institutos religiosos."
BDSLM/CIDHAL 1:1:41-50.
Addresses question of what LA expects of its female
religious institutions and of its religious women,
particularly nuns. Among other things, calls for less
rigid structures and more active participation in
contemporary community problems.

587 SÁNCHEZ MORALES, AURELIA GUADALUPE
1974 "Archetypes and Religious Stereotypes: Their Impact
on Man-Woman Relations." In An Anthology on Women in
Latin America, pp. 15-31. First special issue of BDSLM/
CIDHAL. illus., bibl. Original version: "Arquetipos y
estereotipos religiosos. Su impacto en las relaciones
hombre-mujer." BDSLM/CIDHAL 4:1 (1974):4-22.
Discusses contemporary religious stereotypes (Great
Mother and Child-God) and stereotypes (God-Father and
Virgin-Mother) as determined by Catholic Church in LA,
and their influence on the life of women, their role in
society, and male/female relationships. Specific illustrations provided for Mexico.

588 SCHILLING, REV. GERALD J.
1915 "Our Sisters in South America." MRW 28:10:756-58.
illus.
Missionary of Methodist Episcopal Church criticizes
article by Hodges (#582) in August issue of same magazine. Notes large wave of immigrants in 1913 into
Buenos Aires, strides toward emancipation in the form
of education and employment, the independent Bolivian
chola, Argentine home-lover, etc. Concludes that "South
American women are not sinners above all others."

589 SEVERINO de SANTA TERESA, FATHER
1954 "Instituciones concepcionistas en la América
Española." In his La Inmaculada en la conquista y
coloniaje de la América Española, pp. 197-212. Vitoria,
Spain: Eds. El Carmen. illus., bibl. f/notes.
Based on archival research and secondary sources,
traces early founding of convents of Conceptionist nuns
in LA, beginning with first establishment in 1530 in
Mexico; and also discusses brotherhoods. Entire book
dedicated to the history of the multiple manifestations
of devotion to the Virgin Mary in LA since the Conquest.

Magic, Religion, and Ritual

MIDDLE AMERICA

Mexico

590 BAEZ, EDUARDO
1968 "Fundaciones de religiosas carmelitas en
Querétaro." IIE/A 37:55-69. illus., plans, plates.
Recounts origins of *beaterio* of San José de Gracia,
founded (late 18c.) by small group of women who, unable
to enter a regular convent, joined together to imitate
monastic life as much as possible, and of a Carmelite
convent, founded in 1802.

591 BLAFFER, SARAH C.
1972 The Black Man of Zinacantan: A Central American
Legend. The Tex. Pan American Series. Austin, Tex.:
Univ. of Tex. Press. 194 p. illus., photos, tables,
maps, diagrams, bibl.
Analyzes a legendary Maya demon and other spooks in
the myth and ritual of the Zinacantecos in Chiapas,
Mexico. Considers many spook themes in terms of contrasts between male and female. Includes much detail
throughout on women as victims of spooks and as spooks
themselves, and notes on menstruation, rape, pregnancy,
and sexuality. Based on the field work of others and
secondary sources.

592 BORDA, ANDRÉS de
1708 Práctica de confessores de monjas, en que se explican
los cuatro votos de obediencia, pobreza, casstidad y
clausura, por modo de diálogo. Mex., D.F.: F. de
Ribera Calderón. 88 p.
Kind of practical guide contains 13 examinations
related to vows taken by nuns, positions held in convents
(abbess, vicaress, teacher of novitiates et al.) and
various activities. Includes numbers in margin for
identification and index. Useful for understanding
regulations governing religious life of women.

593 BURLAND, COTTIE A.
1964 "The Goddess Chalchihuitlicue as an Expression of
an Archetype in Ancient Mexican Religion." 6th International Congress of Anthropological and Ethnological
Sciences, vol. 2, pp. 373-76. Paris: Musée de l'Homme.
Using pictorial documents from post-Conquest Mexico
(Codex Borbonicus, Aubin Tonalamatl et al.) and Sahagún's
writings, discusses importance of Aztec fertility goddess
Chalchihuitlicue (Lady Precious Jewel) as a projected
archetypal vision and describes ceremonial worship of
her.

594 BUTLER, MRS. JOHN W.
     1916 "The Women of Mexico." MRW 29:3:181-86. illus.
     General remarks on Mexican women of upper, middle,
     and "peon" (!) classes by missionary of Methodist
     Episcopal Church. Notes control and initiative taken
     by indigenous women of Tehuantepec. "White man's
     burden" perspective: "These poor people need wise and
     loving help, they need some one to take an interest in
     them . . . [to teach them] better ideas of morality."
     Protestant women are needed for great and glorious tasks.

595 DÁVILA GARIBI, JOSÉ IGNACIO PAULINO, comp.
     1968 Colección de documentos inéditos referentes a la
     fundación del Convento de Pobres Capuchinas de Lagos,
     del título de Señor San José, precedidos de una sucinta
     noticia histórica del mismo monasterio y seguidos de la
     serie cronológico-biográfico-genealógica de las
     religiosas que en él tomaron el hábito de capuchinas
     recoletas, según la regla de Santa Clara, desde 1756
     hasta 1859. Mex., D.F.: Edit. Cultura. 276 p.
     illus., coats of arms, facsims., ports., bibl. f/notes.
     As title indicates, collection of documents referring
     to founding of Convento de Pobres Capuchinas de Lagos,
     a brief history of the convent, and a series of biograph-
     ical sketches of its nuns from 1756 to 1859.

596 DÁVILA GARIBI, JOSÉ IGNACIO
     1959 Diligencias generalmente observadas en la Nueva
     Galicia para la fundación de conventos de monjas de
     vida contemplative. Mex., D.F.: Edit. Cultura. 32 p.
     1958 "Diligencias generalmente observadas en la Nueva
     Galicia para la fundación de conventos de monjas de vida
     contemplativa." AMH/M 17:4:358-67.
     Documented discussion of the red tape incurred when
     trying to establish a convent in colonial Mexico. Not
     only did the founders have to be influential persons,
     but the girls to enter such institutions were required
     to prove pure Christian ancestry and to provide a dowry.
     Illustrates with the case of Augustine nunnery in
     Guadalajara in the 18c.

597 DÍAZ de GAMARRA y DÁVALOS, JUAN BENITO
     1830 Ejemplar de religiosas. Vida de la muy reverenda
     madre sor María Josefina Lino de la Santísima Trinidad.
     Mex., D.F.: Imprenta del A. Valdés. 102 p.
     Biography of founder of Convento de la Purísima
     Concepción in San Miguel de Allende, Michoacán. Covers
     family, early childhood, adolescence, founding of
     convent, becoming a nun, teaching novitiates, virtues,
     death.

Magic, Religion, and Ritual

598   ECHEVERRÍA, AGUSTÍN, ed.
        1906 <u>Memorias religiosas y ejemplares noticias de la</u>
        <u>fundación del Monasterio de Nª Sª de la Soledad, en esta</u>
        <u>ciudad de Antequera, valle de Oaxaca. Escritas por las</u>
        <u>reverendas madres fundadoras y publicadoras por el</u>
        <u>Pbro Agustín Echeverría.</u> Oaxaca: M. M. Vazquez. 172 p.
        An assortment of notes on founding and other aspects
        of convent, Nuestra Señora de la Soledad, in Oaxaca,
        and on the nuns who lived there.

599   [FERNÁNDEZ CEJUDO, JUAN]
        1815 <u>Llave de Oro, para abrir las puertas del cielo.</u>
        <u>La regla y ordenaciones de las monjas de la Inmaculada</u>
        <u>Concepción de Nuestra Señora la Madre de Dios.</u> Mex.,
        D.F.: Imprenta de María Fernández y Jaúregui. 155 p.
        plate.
        Provides insight into convent life. Contains 4 brief
        compendiums on the origin of the Conceptionist order,
        12 rules to be followed by the nuns; additional regula-
        tions regarding prayer, silence and exercise; considera-
        tions to facilitate observance of rules; prayers;
        spiritual/moral self-examination prepared for nuns by
        Santa Juana Francisca.

600   GENOVESI, JOSÉ. MARÍA
        1753 <u>Carta del P. José María Genovesi religioso professo</u>
        <u>de la Cía de Jesús a la muy R. M. abadesa del</u>
        <u>religiosísimo Convento de la Encarnación de la ciudad</u>
        <u>de Mexico, que le da noticia de la virtudes de la M.</u>
        <u>María Josepha de la Encarnación, religiosa del mismo</u>
        <u>convento, que murió a 13 de septiembre de 1752.</u> Mex.,
        D.F.: Colegio Máximo de San Pedro. 47 p.
        Biography of abbess (1687-1752) of the Convento de la
        Encarnación in Mexico City and her devotion to God.

601   GONZÁLEZ y GONZÁLEZ, LUIS
        1952 "El siglo mágico." <u>CM/HM</u> 2:1(5):66-86. bibl.
        notes.
        Based on ecclesiastical and Inquisition documents,
        describes magic in 18c. Mexico related to love, hate,
        hunger, pain and ignorance. Names famous witches,
        noting that few men engaged in these activities as
        professional practitioners and that women were more
        affected than men by magical-erotic arts.

602   GUTIÉRREZ, CARMEN A.
        1964 <u>Mujeres presbiterianas de México.</u> Kingsville,
        Tex.: Imprenta de la Escuela Presbiteriana Panamericana.
        39 p.

Personal remembrances of author's conversion to
evangelism and Presbyterian women who were an influence.
Describes women's church work in Mexico through the
Unión Femenil Sinodica, Comisión de Labor Femenil, and
Unión Nacional de Sociedades Femeniles, reproducing
documents related to their organization. Awful style
but one of the few available publications on women's
activities in other than Catholic associations.

603 HELLBOM, ANNA-BRITTA
    1964 "Las apariciones de la Virgen de Guadalupe en México
    y en España. Un estudio comparativo." SEM/E 29:1/2:
    58-72. illus., bibl. f/notes.
    Compares Mexican and European legends about the Virgin
    of Guadalupe, noting similarities among various Marian
    legends.

604 LADRÓN de GUEVARA, BALTAZAR
    1771 Manifiesto, que el real convento de religiosas de
    Jesús María de México, de el real patronato, sujeto a
    el orden de la púrissima e immaculada concepción, hace
    a el sagrado concilio provincial de las razones que le
    assisten, para que se digne de declarar ser la que
    siguen vida comun, y conforme a su regla, y que no se
    debe hacer alguna novedad en el méthodo, que les
    prescribió el Illmo. y Excmo. Sr. D. Frai Payo Enríquez
    de Rivera. Mex., D.F.: Imprenta de D. Felipe de Zuñiga
    y Ontiveros. 217 p.
    Contains historical synopsis of the founding and prog-
    ress of Mexican convent from 1597 on, followed by 10
    points or considerations (e.g., 8: the vow of poverty
    is not offended if nuns have servants because they need
    help in carrying out their respective jobs.)

605 LAVRÍN, ASUNCIÓN
    1973 "La riqueza de los conventos de monjas en Nueva
    España: estructura y evolución durante el siglo XVIII."
    CDAL 8:91-122. tables, bibl. f/notes.
    Using archival documents and secondary sources,
    presents a picture of the nature and evolution of the
    wealth of Mexican nunneries, principally during the
    18c., but also referring to earlier part of colonial
    period. From 1744 on, the accumulation of urban prop-
    erty becomes a more important investment and socioeco-
    nomic ties with the elite of colonial society are again
    strengthened. Such ties originated in the founding of
    convents as centers of refuge and protection for women
    who were unable to marry appropriate to their social
    rank.

Magic, Religion, and Ritual

606 _____.
1972 "Mexican Nunneries from 1835-1860: Their Administrative Policies and Relations With the State." AAFH/TAM 28:3:288-310.
Continuation of 1971 article (#608).

607 _____.
1972 "Values and Meaning of Monastic Life for Nuns in Colonial Mexico." ACHA/CHR 58:3:367-87. bibl. f/notes.
Excellent summary of convent life in colonial Mexico includes motivating factors for entering a nunnery; qualifications for admittance; access for Indian women; dowries; values, in terms of vows practiced; general orientation; intellectual life, as reflected in the literary works of several nuns; innovations in an educational order. Concludes that monastic life of women remained basically static in its moral and religious principles during 3 centuries of colonial life in Mexico.

608 _____.
1971 "Problems and Policies in the Administration of Nunneries in Mexico, 1800-1835." AAFH/TAM 28:1:57-77.
Documented study deals strictly with financial aspects of nunneries in colonial Mexico and does not refer to actual convent life. See #606.

609 _____.
1966 "The Role of Nunneries in the Economy of New Spain in the 18th Century." HAHR 46:6:371-93. bibl. f/notes.
Based on primary and secondary sources, demonstrates how nunneries played an interesting and important role in the economic life of colonial Mexico. They declined in economic importance in late 18c. and early 19c. when the Bourbon kings legislated to subordinate the Church to State in temporal affairs so as to curtail power of clergy and to obtain funds for wars with the French and English. Insight into convents as more than religious and educational institutions.

610 _____.
1965 "Ecclesiastical Reform of Nunneries in New Spain in the Eighteenth Century." AAFH/TAM 22:2:182-203. bibl. f/notes.
Based on archival research, documents Spanish Crown's efforts to introduce reforms, especially with respect to restoring a more communal life in the convents and proper observance of their Rules and Constitutions, and the sustained and open protests by Mexican nuns to preserve their way of life.

611 LEÓN, NICOLÁS
1946 Catarina de San Juan y la china poblana. Estudio
etnográfico-crítico. Mex., D.F.: Ed. Vargas Rea.
113 p. illus., plates.
Refutes historical errors about the life of Catarina
de San Juan, who supposedly was born in Delhi, India in
early 17c. but spent most of her life in Puebla de los
Angeles, where she was known for religious works until
her death in 1688 and venerated as a saint. Concludes
that she had nothing to do with traditional and popular
outfit for women, the *china poblana*. Explains etymology
of *china*, origin of costume, and women called *poblanas*.
Well-researched.

612 LÓPEZ AMABILIS, MANUEL
1961 "El convento de las monjas concepcionistas." UY/R
3:15:83-98.
Account of Conceptionist convent in Mérida, Yucatán
from 1596 to 1866 discusses who could enter, how they
dressed and lived, penance and mortification, etc. Also
includes biographical notes on several nuns.

613 LÓPEZ de MENESES, AMADA
1952 "Dos nietas de Moteczuma, monjas de la Concepción de
México." IGFO/RI 12:47:81-100. bibl. f/notes.
Repeats some data from his 1948 article (#1740) and
continues with information on Moctezuma's daughter, her
descendents, and women of other aristocratic families
who became nuns: inheritance, dowries, founding of convents, qualifications for admittance to Conceptionist
order. Includes genealogical data and documents on
Catalina Cano Moteczuma, who renounced her rights to
Tacuba, and on Isabel and Catalina Cano Moctezuma
regarding their inheritances. Well-researched, with
amply explanatory footnotes.

614 MADSEN, WILLIAM and MADSEN, CLAUDIA
1970 "Witchcraft in Tecospa and Tepepan." In Systems
of North American Witchcraft and Sorcery, ed. by
D. E. Walker, Jr., pp. 73-94. Anthropological Monographs
of the Univ. of Idaho, 1. Moscow, Idaho: Univ. of
Idaho. map, bibl.
Describes structural metamorphosis of witchcraft from
Conquest to present times, explaining differences between
Indian (Nahuatl) and Mexican (*mestizo*) forms. Based on
historical sources and fieldwork in San Francisco
Tecospa and Tepepan (1952-53). Christian association
of witchcraft with sin links women with evil. In
Indian village, where witchcraft serves integrative

Magic, Religion, and Ritual

function, there are no female witches; in *mestizo* town,
where witchcraft serves as divisive mechanism and where
male preoccupation with sexual conquest is very strong,
there are female witches. Concludes that increase in
witchcraft reflects sexual anxieties and ambiguous social
relations resulting from acculturation.

615   MAZA, FRANCISCO de la
      1971 Catarina de San Juan. Princesa de la India y
      visionaria de Puebla. Mex., D.F.: Edit. Libros de
      México. 137 p. illus., bibl.
            Based primarily on 3 biographies written in 17c.,
      recounts story of Mirra, supposedly a princess in India
      who was kidnapped at age of 10 by pirates and sold as
      servant/slave boy in Manila (1621) to Captain Miguel de
      Sosa. She later became Catarina de San Juan, a Catholic
      visionary in Puebla, Mexico during 17c. and was
      condemned by the Inquisition, which also hounded her
      biographers. She died in 1688.

616   _____.
      1953 El guadalupanismo mexicano. Mexico y lo mexicano,
      17. Mex., D.F.: Porrúa y Obregón. 130 p. illus.,
      plates.
            Traces history of cult of Virgin of Guadalupe,
      analyzing several old sermons not previously treated
      by historians of this subject. Introduces work as
      intended for intellectuals, not general populace.

617   _____.
      1943 "La vida conventual de Sor Juana." DH 4:12:666-70.
      illus., bibl. f/notes.
            Based on the Regla y constituciones of the Jeronymite
      Order to which Sor Juana Inés de la Cruz belonged in
      Mexico City (1669-1695), constructs pictures of convent
      life, describing daily activities, nun's habit, peni-
      tence, etc. Abreu Gómez argues that Sor Juana's activi-
      ties contradicted the order's regulations.

618   MAZA y de la CUADRA, FRANCISCO de la
      1937 "La madre Agueda, escritora mística poblana." AE
      6:21:97-104.
            Sister Mariana Agueda de San Ignacio (1695-1756), a
      Dominican nun of humble origins, founded convent of
      Santa Rosa de Puebla, where she was born. Based on
      biography by José Bellido, a Jesuit, published together
      with her mystic works in 1756, briefly describes her
      childhood, religious life, efforts to found convent,
      death, and literary works.

619 MEIER, MATT S.
1974 "María Insurgente." CM/HM 23:3(91):466-82.
Demonstrates historical importance of Virgin of
Guadalupe as religious symbol used for political ends
of unification and nationalism during struggle between
royalists and insurgents in 1810. Traces this development since colonial times. Cites role of other virgins
as well. Based largely on secondary sources.

620 MENDOZA, VIRGINIA R. R. de
1967 "La bruja en México." In Acculturation in the
Americas. Proceedings and Selected Papers of the XXIXth
International Congress of Americanists, ed. by S. Tax,
pp. 285-91. N.Y.: Cooper Square Publishers.
Based on data from direct observation and information
about popular beliefs (some indigenous and others
European, interjected after Conquest) which persist in
Mexico, describes attributes, capabilities, activities,
methods, and location of witch, using Nahuatl terms.

621 Mexico (City), Convento de monias de San Geronymo vs. Segura,
Ana de.
1626 Por el convento de monias de San Geronymo desta
Ciudad, donde están professas, y viven las Madres
Agueda de S. Joseph, y Juana de S. Geronymo, hijas
legítimas del Afrérez Sebastián Ruyz de Nebro diffunto,
y de doña Ana de Segura, con La dicha D. Ana de Segura,
y Hernando de Segura, albaceas testamentarios del dichos
Alferez. Sobre que el dicho convento deve ser admitido
como heredero, a la división y partición de los bienes
del dicho Alferez, fin que las renunciaciones hechas
de dichas religiosas. Mex., D.F. 12 1.
Letter by Agueda de San Joseph, novitiate receiving
habit in convent of San Jeronimo in Mexico City is
legal statement upon profession. Refers to her dowry
among other things.

622 MORA, JUAN ANTONIO de
1729 Espejo crystalino de paciencia y viva imagen de
Christo crucificado en la admirable vida, y virtudes
de la venerable madre Sor María Ynés de los Dolores,
religiosa professa en el religioso convento de San
Lorenzo de la ciudad de Mexico. Mex., D.F.: M. de
Rivera Calderón. 325 p. port.
Biography of Sor María Ynés de los Dolores in which
he discusses her admirable virtues and life-long devotion
to God.

Magic, Religion, and Ritual

623   MURIEL de la TORRE, JOSEFINA, ed.
1963 Las indias caciques de Corpus Christi. Inst. de
Historia, Serie Histórica, 6. Mex., D.F.: Univ.
Nacional Autónoma de México. (UNAM, Publicaciones del
Inst. de Historia. 1. serie, no. 83). 401 p. illus.,
facsims., plates, ports., bibl.
    Paleographic version of original 18c. manuscript
which relates spiritual biographies of 8 young Indian
women, daughters of *caciques*, who became nuns in the
Convent of Corpus Christi. Introduction discusses
Spanish and *mestizo* society in 18c. Mexico: position
of *caciques*; transculturation process through marriage
between Indians and Spaniards; Spanish interest in con-
serving indigenous nobility; noble Indian women (birth,
education, position in Aztec society, different categories, protective legislation passed by Crown). It is
conjectured that the biographies were written by one of
the Indian girls from this first convent founded for
them in 18c.

624   _____.
1946 Conventos de Monjas en la Nueva España. Mex., D.F.:
Edit. Santiago. 553 p. illus., plates, ports., map,
plan, facsim., bibl.
    Using unpublished manuscripts in Mexican archives,
reconstructs establishment and social and financial
development of nunneries in Mexico City from 16c. until
their abolition in 1860. Covers founding, building,
decoration, festivities, organization, ceremonies,
emoluments, and daily life. Includes list of nuns
belonging to convents--dates of profession, parents.

625   _____.
1943 "El Convento de la Concepción." PUC/H 1:1:22-28.
bibl. notes.
    Based on archival research and secondary sources,
traces history of first convent (1541) in New Spain.
Explains its importance and describes conventual life,
finances, education, standing with the King and viceroys.
Lists convents which it gave rise to. Despite lack of
original documents and varying opinions as to origin,
believes a Franciscan friar brought several nuns with
him from Spain to Mexico.

626   _____.
1941 "El Convento de Corpus Christi de México:
institución para indias caciques." IIE/A 7:11-57.
illus., plates.

Based on archival research, traces history of first
convent for daughters of Indian chieftains. Idea of
providing a place for them to attain spiritual perfection
originated with Viceroy Baltazar de Zuñiga, Marquis of
Valero in 1720. Covers indigenous and Spanish antecedents, requirements for admittance, conventual life,
physical and artistic aspects of convent itself, which
later became a school for deaf-mutes (1861). Includes
list of women who entered convent since 1741--parents,
place of origin, lineage, father's occupation. Appendix
reproduces documents related to founding of convent
(1723-24).

627   MURIEL de la TORRE, JOSEFINA and GROBET, ALICIA
      1969 Fundaciones neoclásicas; la Marquesa de Selva
      Nevada, sus conventos y sus arquitectos. Cuadernos,
      serie histórica, 15. Mex., D.F.: UNAM, Inst. de
      Investigaciones Históricas. 131 p. illus., facsims.,
      plans, bibl.
         Useful for knowing which were last convents founded
      during viceroyalty of New Spain, just before becoming
      the Mexican Republic, and the change in ideas operating
      then regarding founding of such institutions. Includes
      partial biography of Josefa Gómez Rodríguez de Pedroso,
      founder of convents, wife, and mother, who at age of
      50 entered most austere religious order, the Discalced
      Carmelites.

628   NÚÑEZ, ANTONIO
      1712 Distribución de las obras ordinarias, y extraordinar-
      ias del día, para hacerlas perfectamente, conforme al
      estado de las señoras religiosas. Instruída con doze
      máximas substanciales, para la vida regular, y espiritual,
      que deben seguir. Mex., D.F.: Viuda de M. de Ribera
      Calderón. 160 p.
         Elaborates 12 maxims for nuns to follow and instruction
      of principel daily exercises (e.g., when to wake up,
      mental prayer, handiwork).

629   NÚÑEZ de HARO y PERALTA, ALONSO
      1774 Nos el d^r. d. Alonso Nuñez de Haro y Peralta por la
      gracia de Dios, y de la Santa Sede Apostólica del
      Consejo de S.M. Arzobispo de Mégico. A nuestras mis
      amadas hijas en el Señor las R.R.M.M. abadesas, prioras,
      vicarias, y demás religiosas de los diez sagrados
      conventos de calzadas, sugetos a nuestra filiación, y
      obediencia, salud, y paz en nuestro Señor Jesu Christo.
      Mex., D.F. 42 p.

Magic, Religion, and Ritual

> Pastoral letter regarding community life within the
> Carmelite convents under the Archbishop of Mexico's
> jurisdiction in 18c.

630 RAMÍREZ APARICIO, MANUEL
1861 Los conventos suprimidos en México. Estudios
biográficos, históricos y arqueológicos. Mex., D.F.:
J. M. Aguilar. 525 p. plates.
Architectural, historical, and some biographical notes
on Mexican convents and their nuns: La Encarnación,
La Concepción, Santa Clara, Santa Isabel.

631 RAMÓN MARTINEZ, J.
1963 Las carmelitas descalzas en Querétaro. Monografías
Históricas de la Diocesis de Querétaro. Col. Primer
Centenario, 1863–1963, no. 7. Querétaro, Mex.: Edit.
Jus. 162 p. illus., plates, ports.
Priest of the diocese of Querétaro, Mexico recounts
the history of the convent of Discalced Carmelites since
its founding in 1803, based on diocesan chronicles and
convent annals. Covers expulsion of the nuns under
Reform Laws of 1857 and 1859, restoration in 1910,
second expulsion in 1914, dispersion of the sisters to
other convents, and reestablishment in 1949.

632 Regla y constituciones que han de guardar las relígiosas de
los conventos de Nª Sª de la Concepción y la Santª Trinidad
de la ciudad de los Angeles.
1795 Mex., D.F.: M. de Zuñiga y Ontíveros. 121 p.
front.
Rules and regulations to be followed by Conceptionist
nuns in late 18c. in Puebla, Mexico on prayer, mass,
habit, modesty, dowries, food, number to be admitted to
convent, number of servants, illnesses, etc.

633 Regla y constituciones que han de guardar las religiosas del
Convento del glorioso padre San Geronymo de la ciudad de los
Angeles.
1773 Puebla, Mex.: El Seminario Palafoxiano. 212 p.
Rules and regulations governing convent life of
Jeronymite nuns in 18c. Puebla, Mexico with respect to
how long nuns should hold office, how dead nuns should
be buried, visits from Prelate, register or inquiry of
poverty, habit to be worn, places where speaking was
permitted, instruction of novitiates, etc.

634   Regla y constituciones de las religiosas descalzas de la Orden
      de la gloriosíssima Virgen María del Monte Carmelo.
         1733 Mex., D.F.: Imprenta Rl. del Superior Govierno de
         Doña María de Rivera. 126, 63 p.
            Tiny book (approximately 4" x 3") of rules and regula-
         tions governing life of discalced Carmelites in 18c.
         Mexico: with respect to obedience; election of supe-
         riors; eating; where, when and to whom to speak; guilt;
         reception and profession of novitiates; number of nuns
         in a convent; etc.

635   Regla y ordenaciones de las religiosas de la limpia, e
      Immacvlada Concepción de la Virgen Santissima Ñra Señora, que
      se an de observar en los conventos de la dicha orden de la
      ciudad de Mexico . . . .
         1635 Mex., D.F.: Iuan Ruyz. 39 numb. 1.
            Rules and regulations of Conceptionist nuns in 17c.
         Mexico regarding observance of poverty, election of
         abbess, habit, prayer, discipline, silence, fasting,
         sleeping, work, etc.

636   Representación que las señoras de Guadalajara dirigen al
      soberano congreso constituyente sobre que en la carta
      fundamental que se discute, no quede consignada la tolerancia
      de cultos en la República.
         1856 Guadalajara: Tipografía de Rodriguez. n.p.
            A plea, endorsed by nearly 500 women, and sent to the
         framers of the 1857 Mexican Constitution, for more
         church power.

637   ROSELL, LAURO E., et al.
         1931 México y la guadalupana; cuatro siglos de culto a
         la patrona de América. Mex., D.F.: La Enseñanza
         Objetiva Mexicana. 128 p. illus., ports., plans,
         facsims.
            Illustrated history of guadalupanismo, devotion to the
         Virgin of Guadalupe, begins with etymology and evolution
         of the name.

638   SÁNCHEZ MORALES, AURELIA GUADALUPE
         1974 "Archetypes and Religious Stereotypes: Their Impact
         on Man-Woman Relations." In An Anthology on Women in
         Latin America, pp. 15-31. First special issue of BDSLM/
         CIDHAL. Spanish version: 1974 "Arquetipos y
         estereotipos religiosos. Su impacto en las relaciones
         hombre-mujer." BDSLM/CIDHAL 4:1:4-22.
            See #587 for annotation.

Magic, Religion, and Ritual

639   SANTANDER y TORRES, SEBASTIÁN de
     1723 Vida de la venerable madre María de S. Joseph
     religiosa Augustina recoleta, fundadora en los conventos
     de Santa Monica de la ciudad de Puebla, y después en el
     de la Soledad de Oaxaca. Mex., D.F.: Herederos de la
     viuda de Miguel de Rivera. 407 p. port.
     Biography of Augustine nun (1656-1719) who founded 2
     convents: Santa Monica in Puebla and Soledad in Oaxaca.

640   THOMPSON, JOHN ERIC
     1966 "Ayopechtli, An Aspect of the Nahua Goddess of the
     Maguey." In XXXVI Congreso Internacional de American-
     istas, España, 1964, Actas y memorias, vol. 2, pp. 103-
     106. illus., plate.
     Argues for viewing Tezcacoac Ayopechtli and Tezcacoac
     Atlacoaya as either additional aspects of Mayauel, god-
     dess of the maguey plant, or as her sister goddesses.
     In support of his thesis, reviews evidence from
     Sahagún's writings and the Codices Bourbon, Borgia,
     Vatican A and B., Magliabecchi and the Aubin Tonalamatl.

641   _____.
     1939 "The Moon Goddess in Middle America, With Notes on
     Related Duties . . . With 5 Text-figures." In Contribu-
     tions to American Anthropology and History, vol. 5,
     pp. 121-73. Publication 509. Wash., D.C.: Carnegie
     Institution of Wash. illus., tables, bibl.
     Detailed, informative discussion of moon goddess in
     Middle America, with comparisons made between Maya and
     Mexican traditions. Explores facets of deity as wife of
     the sun, patroness of weaving, goddess of procreation,
     pregnancy and birth, etc.

642   TIBÓN, GUTIERRE
     1967 Mujeres y diosas de México; parviescultura pre-
     hispánica en barro. Mex., D.F.: Inst. Nacional de
     Antropología e Historia. 196 p. illus., bibl.
     Describes and illustrates 39 pieces of sculpture from
     different parts of Mexico chosen for their "feminine
     essence" and ritual purpose. Each female figure is a
     vehicle of magical attraction for fecundity, fertility
     of the earth, and supernatural protection; as such, each
     woman is a priestess or goddess.

643   Vida de la Reverendísima madre María Rosa de la Torre O.P.,
     fundadora y superiora general de las hermanas dominicanas de
     Santo Tomás de Aquino.
     1967 Mex., D.F.: Imprenta Aldina. 417 p. illus.,
     facsim., ports.

Biography of María Rosa de la Torre (1880-1958),
founder and mother superior of Dominican nuns of
St. Thomas Aquinas. Includes information on the birth
and development of the congregation, and the family and
nuns that lived with her in 2 convents--1 in Mexico,
another in the US.

644   WATSON, SISTER SIMONE
      1964 The Cult of Our Lady of Guadalupe: A Historical
      Study. Collegeville, Minn.: The Liturgical Press.
      87 p. illus., facsims., ports., bibl.
         Based on primary and secondary materials, analyzes
      ancient Indian sources and historical narratives in
      support of the Guadalupan cult and considers theological
      reflections on the Guadalupan message in terms of divine
      maternity, spiritual motherhood, and mediation. Possibly
      useful for study of religious symbolism behind mother
      role. Originally submitted toward an M.A. in Sacred
      Science, St. John's University.

645   WOLF, ERIC R.
      1958 "The Virgin of Guadalupe: A Mexican National
      Symbol." AFS/JAF 71:279:34-39. bibl. notes.
         Discusses Virgin of Guadalupe as a master symbol of
      the major hopes and aspirations of Mexican society and
      the ideology surrounding it. Briefly traces its history
      and considers its functional aspects in social relation-
      ships. Believes it ties together family, politics and
      religion as well as the colonial past and the indepen-
      dent present, and the Indian and Mexican. Guadalupe is
      a supernatural mother through which emotions can be
      expressed. Based mainly on secondary sources.

Panama

646   Congreso Nacional de la Mujer Católica de Panama. 1st.
      Panama, 1963.
         1963 Memoria. Panama. 119 p. illus., ports.
         Outlines speeches given at first National Congress of
      Catholic Women of Panama on such themes as women in
      primary and teacher education; Catholic women and the
      Church; influence of nuns in Panamanian life; profes-
      sional Catholic women and their influence in the
      community, etc.

647   OLLER de MULFORD, JUANA
      1963 "Valores femeninos panamenos: Rev. Madre Bethlemita
      María Dolores." TDM 3:13:10-11.

Magic, Religion, and Ritual

> Biographical sketch of María Luisa Sosa Medina, Bethlemite nun.

SOUTH AMERICA

Colombia

648   AYAPE, EUGENIO
         1939 "Monasterio de la Concepción de Tunja." HA/B
         26:291/292:48-77.
         Documented history of convent in Tunja, from the
         founding of the Conceptionist order in Spain (1484) and
         its establishment by 3 women who took the habit in 1600
         to canonical visits, abesses, vicissitudes, suppression,
         etc. until 1937.

649   GARCÍA, JOSÉ CÉSAR
         1959 "María en la historia de Antioquia." UNIPOB
         23:84:336-45.
         After briefly referring to Columbus' caravelle Santa
         María and Santa María la Antigua del Darién (founded in
         1510), traces faith in protection by Virgin Mary in
         Antioquia from the soldiers who first entered that ter-
         ritory through devotion in 19c. Documented.

650   JIMÉNEZ, GABRIEL
         1955 "Convento de Santa Clara de Asís (en Cartagena de
         Indias, Colombia)." AE 17:59:376-82.
         Based on documentation, relates history of the Convent
         of Santa Clara of Asisi, founded through generous dona-
         tions of Catalina de Cobrera before 1607.

651   LUCENA SALMORAL, MANUEL
         1964 "Vicisitudes de la fundación del Convento de
         Carmelitas de Sta Fe." BCB 7:1:40-43.
         Recounts troubled history of the Convent of Carmelites,
         which was founded in 1606 in Santa Fe de Bogotá without
         the Crown's authorization. Documented.

652   MIRAMÓN, ALBERTO
         1943 "La brujería en la colonia." HA/B 30:347/348:806-24.
         bibl.
         Brief history of witchcraft in colonial Colombia begins
         with some commentary by Spanish writers and describes
         fame and activities of Juana García, a black woman who
         arrived in Santa Fe de Bogotá in 1543 in the expedition
         of Adelantado Alfonso Luis de Lugo. In its auto da fe
         of 1614, the Inquisition in Cartagena accused at least
         2 women of witchcraft. Ends with 18c.

653 REICHEL-DOLMATOFF, GERARDO
1971 Amazonian Cosmos. The Sexual and Religious Symbolism of the Tukano Indians. Chicago: Univ. of Chicago
Press. 290 p. illus., plates, bibl.
Based on conversations with a Desana Indian informant
(1966) and a field trip to the Vaupés area (1967), includes women in study of sexual and religious symbolism
of the Tukano Indians: women in the creation myth and
its reflection in regular life (menstruation, sexual
relations, pregnancy, birth); encouragement of women to
practice birth control; principal rites, which center on
puberty and death; description of life cycle; women in
reunions and dances, other myths, disease and curing;
discussion of deities and demons, symbols and associations, cultural norms, sexuality, mythology, and economic situation. Appendix contains 24 myths.

Ecuador

654 JERVES, ALFREDO A.
1950 "La venerable Madre Herrera (1717-1795)." CIH/B
8:18/19/20:189-93.
Elegiac biographical notes on Sor Catalina Luisa de
Jesús María y José, teacher of novitiates and prioress
of convent Santa Catalina de Sena in Quito. Her autobiography, Secretos entre el alma y Diós, classifies her
as one of the few or first female writers of the colonial era.

655 KEYES, FRANCES PARKINSON
1961 "Book II. The Lily." In her The Rose and the Lily.
The Lives and Times of Two South American Saints,
pp. 151-230. N.Y.: Hawthorn Books. illus., ports.,
bibl.
Popular rather than scholarly biography of Mariana de
Jesús (1618-44), born into a family of noble rank in
Quito as Mariana Paredes y Flores, who made private vows
of poverty, chastity and obedience without entering a
convent but considering herself a member of the Company
of Jesus, but who later joined third Order of St. Francis.
Her philanthropic social work included first organized
effort at Acción Católica, first free clinic in Quito,
and a kindergarten. She became known as the Lily of
Quito because, according to legend, the flower grew from
where her blood had been spilled after an attempt to
reduce a fever. She was beatified in 1850, canonized in
1950.

Magic, Religion, and Ritual

656 MESA, CARLOS E.
     1973 Mercedes Molina, fundadora de las Marianitas.
     Quito: Edit. D. Bosco. 212 p. illus.
          Biography of Mercedes Molina y Ayala (1828-83),
     beatified by Pope Pius XII in 1946. She worked with
     Jesuit missionaries among the Jívaro Indians, directed
     an orphanage for girls, founded the Congregation of
     Sisters of the Beatified Mariana de Jesús in Riobamba
     (1873), in which she served as the mother superior,
     teacher of novitiates, and director of collegians.
     Based on her dictated autobiography, other biographies
     and secondary sources.

657 MONCAYO de MONGE, GERMANIA
     1950 Mariana de Jesús, Señora de Indias. Quito: La
     Prensa Católica. 312 p.
          Biography of Mariana de Jesús Paredes y Flores
     (1618-45), of noble Spanish ancestry. In Quito she tried
     her vocation as a religious but failed and thereafter
     lived as a solitary in her brother-in-law's home. She
     died shortly after offering herself as a victim for the
     people during Quito's earthquakes in 1645. Noted for
     her physical mortifications, she was canonized in 1950.

658 MORÁN de BUTRÓN, JACINTO
     1724? La azucena de Quito, que brotó el florido campo de
     la Iglesia en las Indias Occidentales de los reynos del
     Perú, y cultivó con los esmeros de su enseñanza. Madrid:
     Imprenta de Gabriel del Barrio. 465 p.
          First hagiographic account of Mariana de Jesús
     (1618-45) by Ecuadorian Jesuit, written in 5 books
     (i.e., parts) to correspond to the 5 petals of a lily,
     associated with her name. After she failed in her voca-
     tion as a religious, she lived as a solitary, subjected
     herself to physical moritification, and offered herself
     as a victim for the city of Quito during the earthquakes
     of 1645. She was canonized in 1950.

659 NAVARRO, JOSÉ GABRIEL
     1949 "Contribución a la historia del arte en el Ecuador:
     Monasterio del Carmen antiguo, Monasterio del Carmen
     moderno." EANH/B 29:73:5-43. illus.
          Well-documented account of founding of 2 Carmelite
     convents in 17c. Ecuador--El Antiguo or Alto in Quito
     and El Moderno or Bajo in Latacunga--indicates the women
     who contributed to the founding and the nuns who entered
     and directed the religious institutions, and the problems
     they encountered. Includes royal decrees, letters,
     declarations, etc.

660 ____.
1948 "Contribución a la historia del arte en el Ecuador:
Monasterio de Santa Catalina. Monasterio de la Concepción. Monasterio de Santa Clara." EANH/B 28:72:155-225.
illus., plans.
Well-documented history of 3 convents founded in 16c.
Quito includes notes on the women who contributed to
their founding and on those who inhabited the religious
institutions as well as on the growth of the nunneries.

661 TOBAR DONOSO, JULIO
1950 "Santa Mariana de Jesús." EANH/B 30:76:216-24.
In celebration of canonization of Mariana de Jesús,
makes comparison to other female saint of LA--St. Rose
of Lima. Says the Lily of Quito gave up her life for
the salvation of Quito and surrounding area, which in
1645 experienced earthquakes and other calamities.

662 VALVERDE, MIGUEL
1904 Conferencia sobre la clausura de la mujer . . . .
Quito: Tipografía de la Escuela de Artes y Oficios.
26 p.
Passionate argument presented to the Juridical-
Literary Society of Quito against the cloistering of
women in convents, which he considers imprisonment and
the inability to exercise those rights and liberties
accorded to all Ecuadorian citizens.

663 VILLASÍS TERÁN, ENRIQUE M.
1946 Mariana de Jesús, Azucena de Quito. Una gran figura
hispano-americana de los siglos de oro. Quito: Tipografía de "La Prensa Católica." 82 p. illus., bibl.
f/notes.
Hagiography of Mariana de Paredes relates miraculous
childhood events similar to those of Santa Rosa de Lima;
describes 17c. in which she lived (1618-1645), her
mortification and physical martyrdom, and life devoted
to Christ and charity.

Peru

664 ALPHONSUS, SISTER MARY
1968 St. Rose of Lima. Patroness of the Americas.
St. Louis: B. Herder Book Co. 304 p.
Biography of humble woman of second-class nobility in
17c. Lima who became a saint (1586-1617). No indication
of sources.

Magic, Religion, and Ritual

665   ANGULO P., DOMINGO
        1917 Santa Rosa de Santa María. Estudio bibliográfico.
        Lima: Sanmarti y cía. 249 p. ports.
        Valuable compendium of materials useful for studying
        St. Rose of Lima (1586-1617). Includes information on
        written and pictorial items and reproduces documents,
        correspondence, sermons and panegyrics; etc. Provides
        explanatory notes and location of materials. Text num-
        bers 241 items.

666   BERMÚDEZ, JOSÉ MANUEL
        1782 Sermón panegírico de la admirable virgen Santa Rosa
        de Santa María. Lima: Imprenta de los huérfanos. 80 p.
        Translation of 1781 eulogy in Latin of America's first
        woman saint, Rose of Lima (1586-1617), with extensive
        footnotes.

667   BUSTAMENTE de la FUENTE, MANUEL J.
        1971 La monja Gutiérrez y la Arequipa de ayer y de hoy.
        Lima: Gráfica Morson. 104 p. illus.
        After sentimental remembrances of Arequipa, relates
        with documentation the interesting story of Sor Dominga
        Gutiérrez Cossío, who in 1831, after 5 years of forced
        cloister in the Monasterio de Santa Teresa, escaped by
        having 2 young women set a substitute cadaver on fire
        in her cell so that she would be thought dead. Author
        believes her to have been a victim of the misunderstand-
        ing, intolerance and fanaticism of the epoch in which
        she lived.

668   CADIZ, LUIS M. de
        1944 Santa Rosa de Lima. Biblioteca Billiken. Col. Azul.
        Buenos Aires: Edit. Atlantida. 129 p. illus., ports.
        Short, undocumented biography of the patron saint of
        America, St. Rose of Lima (1586-1617), covers her back-
        ground; mortification; comparison to Catalina of Sienna;
        how she joined Dominican order rather than enter other
        convents; anecdotes about apparitions, prophecies and
        strange occurrences; process of beatification and canon-
        ization; celebrations of them.

669   CÓRDOVA SALINAS, DIEGO de
        1957 Crónica franciscana de las provincias del Perú.
        New edition with notes and introduction by Lino G.
        Canedo. Wash., D.C.: Academy of American Franciscan
        History. 1195 p. plates, bibl.
        17c. documented chronicle of Peru by Franciscan friar
        includes several sections on nunneries and nuns in sev-
        eral cities of colonial Peru. See Book 3, Chapter 5

(pp. 505-08) for a description of 8 convents in Lima.
See Book 5, Chapters 1-18 (pp. 831-914) for an account
of the founding, founders, and other nuns of the convent
of Santa Clara in Guamanga and Chapters 23-28 (pp. 938-
71) for an account of the founding and nuns of the convent of Santa María de Gracia la Real in Trujillo,
convents of Santa Clara in Cuzco, la Plata, and Lima,
and convent of Concepción in Lima.

670   DOBKIN de RÍOS, MARLENE
      1969 "La cultura de la pobreza y el amor mágico: un
      síndrome urbano en la selva peruana." III/AI 29:1:3-16.
        Discusses 4 categories of love magic (benign, malig-
      nant, preventive, restorative) in the barriada of Belén
      in Iquitos in an attempt to describe male/female rela-
      tionship in the community. Believes that despite or
      because of social disintegration there, an elaborate
      series of beliefs and a cognitive system set up certain
      expectations, values, and patterns of behavior between
      the sexes.

671   FABER, F. W., ed.
      1855 The Life of Saint Rose of Lima. 4th ed. Philadel-
      phia: Peter F. Cunningham and Son. 264 p. port.
        Translation of Father Jean Baptist Feuillet's (Domini-
      can friar and Missionary Apostolic in the Antilles) book,
      third edition published in Paris in 1671, when St. Rose
      of Lima was canonized by Clement X. It is interesting
      that preface warns Catholic readers not to pass judgment
      when startled by the strange mixture of natural and
      supernatural aspects of this 17c. woman's life.

672   GETINO, LUIS G. ALONSO
      192-? La patrona de las Américas, Santa Rosa de Lima,
      doctora, su personalidad intelectual. Madrid?:
      Talleres Gráficos de la Penitenciaría. 48 p. clr. plates.
        Not wanting St. Rose of Lima (1586-1617) to be left out
      of the pantheon of intellectual women saints (Ste. Catalina
      of Sienna, Ste. Teresa et al.), evaluates her intellectual
      stature through an examination of her drawings in the
      Convent of St. Rose of the Mothers in Lima. Corroborates
      her authorship by comparing these to her handwriting in
      2 letters.

673   GONZÁLEZ PRADA, MANUEL
      1904 El catolicismo y la mujer. Las esclavas de la
      iglesia. Asoc. de Propaganda Liberal, Montevideo.
      Folleto no. 52. Montevideo? 19 p.

Magic, Religion, and Ritual

> Scathing denunciation of Catholic Church's role in
> fomenting and sanctioning the canonical and civil servi-
> tude which women suffer. Women have always been the
> victim and weapon of priests, who morally or spiritually
> deflower them in confession.

674 KEYES, FRANCES PARKINSON
1961 "Book I. The Rose." In her The Rose and the Lily,
The Lives and Times of Two South American Saints,
pp. 51-150. N.Y.: Hawthorn Books. illus., ports., bibl.
More historical and realistic than most hagiographies
of St. Rose of Lima (1586-1617), plays down her gifts as
a prophet and raises those as a mystic and social worker;
and discusses her relationship with the viceregal court,
aristocratic circles, and her benefactors. Clement X
declared her not only a saint, but also the Patroness of
Lima, Peru, and America, the Philippine Islands, and
India.

675 MARECHAL, LEOPOLDO
1945 Vida de Santa Rosa de Lima. 2nd ed. Col. Buen Aire,
33. Buenos Aires: Emecé Eds. 99 p. illus., ports.
Without any reference notes, describes life of St. Rose
of Lima (1586-1617): her various names, infancy, education, hermitage cell in the garden, penitence and various
forms of mortification, charity, visions, etc. Appendix has
description of her funeral rites, sonnet to her by 17c.
Cordobés poet, several paragraphs from bull of
canonization.

676 MIRÓ, CÉSAR
1945 Cielo y tierra de Santa Rosa. Buenos Aires: Edit.
Schapire. 245 p.
Documented hagiography of St. Rose of Lima (1586-1617)
provides historical setting but reads like most of the
works on her life, narrating events from when she came
to be called Rose to her canonization (1671).

677 MIRÓ QUESADA LAOS, CARLOS
1958 "Santa Rosa." In his De Santa Rosa a la Perricholi.
(Páginas peruanas), pp. 11-38. Lima: Talleres Gráficos
P.L. Villanueva. bibl.
Brief biography of Isabel Flores de Oliva (1586-1617),
Patroness of America and better known as St. Rose, based
on secondary sources. Sets up traditional dichotomy of
madonna vs. whore by beginning his impressions of colonial Peru with a saintly woman of the 16c. and ending
with a "sinner-lover" of the second half of 18c.

678   SCANLAN, OLIVE MARY
      1957 Rose of Peru. Dublin: M. H. Gill and Son. 89 p.
      Written by a Tertiary of the Dominican order, this
      life history of St. Rose of Lima, born Isabel Flores,
      emphasizes a series of miracles which began when she was
      an infant and her constant mortification. Unsubstan-
      tiated, limited, unreferenced version.

679   STORM, MARIAN
      1937 The Life of Saint Rose. First American Saint and
      Only American Woman Saint. Santa Fe, New Mex.: Writers'
      Editions. 216 p. bibl.
      Another unscholarly hagiography of St. Rose of Lima
      (1586-1617).

680   VARGAS UGARTE, RUBEN
      1951 Vida de Santa Rosa de Santa María. 2nd ed. Lima:
      Talleres Gráficos de la Tipografía Peruana. 222 p.
      illus., ports.
      Yet another biography of St. Rose of Lima (1586-1617)
      uncorroborated by reference sources.

681   _____.
      1945 "El Monasterio de la Concepción de la Ciudad de los
      Reyes." IGFO/RI 6:21:419-44. illus., plates.
      Documented history of Conception, second convent
      founded in colonial Lima, from 1575 to the 19c., begins
      with the role of Inés Muñoz (and her daughter-in-law
      María de Chaves) in establishing it, professing vows,
      and taking the habit. Discusses finances; convent's
      role not only in terms of religious fervor but also in
      social well-being (it was an option against marriage and
      an opportunity for education); physical and esthetic
      aspects (as a museum of art).

682   WEISSE, MARÍA
      1950 "La mujer en el panorama histórico del país peruano."
      HISTO 12:137:45-46. illus.
      Briefly discusses women in Inca religion and mythology
      as goddesses (earth, sea, moon), especially the role of
      Mama Ocllo in founding the empire; in weaving and agri-
      culture. In women's role as farmers, Peru owes them
      more than men in the formation of rural property. In
      their role as mother, women guide, orient, and sustain
      the family. Mentions creoles and mestizas as well.

683   ZUIDEMA, R. T. and QUISPE, U.
      1973 "A Visit to God: The Account and Interpretation of
      a Religious Experience in the Peruvian Community of

Magic, Religion, and Ritual

Choque-Huarcaya." In Peoples and Cultures of Native South America: An Anthropological Reader, ed. by D. R. Gross, pp. 357-74. Garden City, N.Y.: Doubleday/The Natural History Press. illus., bibl.

Structural interpretation of a septagenarian widow's account of her ascent to God and return to earth because God had not called on her yet. Importance of experience lies in value as a reflection of centuries-old elements of Inca religion and social organization which have persisted in the present. Diagrams basic model to represent figures in her "dream," Inca cosmogony, pre-Hispanic and modern lineage system. Includes translation of Quechua text recorded in the Department of Ayacucho in 1966.

Chile

684 BICHON, MARÍA
     1946 "En torno a la cerámica de las monjas." SCHG/R 108:204-42. illus., bibl.

     Attempts to establish the origins of ceramic work attributed to nuns in colonial Chile and carried on secularly in the 19c. and 20c., by tracing the history of convents in Chile since the 16c., especially that of the Clares. Provides interesting data on conventual life (rules, economy, servants, activities and on the artwork). Based on documentation, oral tradition, and secondary historical sources from 19c. and 20c.

685 FARON, LOUIS C.
     1964 Hawks of the Sun: Mapuche Morality and Its Ritual Attributes. Pittsburgh, Pa.: Univ. of Pittsburgh Press. 220 p. illus., tables, map, bibl.

     Based on fieldwork among the Mapuche Indians in south central Chile (1952-54), provides much descriptive data on sorcery and shamanism, compares organizational aspects between shamanistic activities and those of the sisterhood of sorcerers, and attempts to explain historical shift of the profession of shaman from male dominance to almost exclusively female dominance. Describes the machi, female Mapuche shamans who are regarded as powerful, awesome persons (properties, purpose, passing on of lore among women). Also considers witches, goddesses, courtship and marriage, matrilateral system, and moral implications of certain economic, political, residential, marital and unilineal arrangements. Outlines Mapuche social structure and examines sorcery and shamanism in reference to institutional solidarity at local level of Mapuche society.

686 FONTECILLA LARRAÍN, ARTURO
1943 "Recuerdos del antiguo monasterio de las monjas
capuchinas." ACH/B 10:27:77-93. illus.
Based on Crónica del monasterio de Capuchinos
(Santiago, 1911) by Luis Francisco Prieto, recounts history of the convent of Capuchin nuns from its founding
in Santiago in 1722 by Margarita Carrión and licensing
by Phillip V in 1723, for young women of the nobility
who lacked dowries, until construction of a new building
in early 20c. Capuchin nuns were brought from Lima;
associated with the Jesuits, they led a life of poverty.
Includes information on the entering nuns and life in
the convent.

687 PRIETO del RÍO, LUIS FRANCISCO
1911 Crónica del Monasterio de Capuchinas. Santiago:
Imprenta de San José. 406 p. facsims.
A 21-page introduction provides a general history of
the Clares in Spain and in America. The text covers
1695 to 1911, the first Capuchins not arriving in
Santiago until 1726: the founding of and life in the
convent, abbesses, etc. Names all the women who entered
this convent in 184 years of existence. Based princi-
pally on books and papers of the convent and documents
from the Archivo de la Secretaria Arzobispal, Biblioteca
Nacional, and Chilean government.

688 VICUÑA MACKENNA, BENJAMÍN
1904 Historia de la Calle de las Monjitas. Biblioteca de
Autores Chilenos, 22. Santiago: G. E. Miranda. 66 p.
Based on primary and secondary sources, lively narrative recounts the troubled history of the Clare nuns
from the founding of their convent in Osorno (1573) by
Isabel de Plascencia to their final location in Santiago
in 1876 after 7 moves. Cabildo records relate a scandalous attack by Fray Alonso Cordero and his Franciscan
brothers on these nuns and their defense. Explains how
the street came to be called Calle de las Monjitas and
includes brief notes on some of the aristocratic women
who lived there.

Argentina

689 OYARZÚN, AURELIANO
1945 "La fiesta de la kina, o sea de la supresión del
derecho materno entre los yaganes." SCHG/R 106:126-153.
Excerpted and translated from Martin Gusinde's Die
Feuerland-Indianer, describes in detail a rite or

163

Magic, Religion, and Ritual

festival reserved exclusively for young men to initiate
them into manhood and dominance over women, as observed
in 1922 among the nomadic Yaganes of Tierra del Fuego.
It is based on their genesis myth, in which women held
sway over men through deceit, which when accidently discovered by a man, led to their downfall and subsequent
hegemony by men. Women understand their changed role
as victims of the male deceit (re. ties with the spirits)
and do not rebel. There is no indication that this rite
is a reflection of a true animosity between the sexes.
Some women are permitted to attend the ceremony.

690   PALAU, GABRIEL
        194? La mujer de acción católica. 4th ed. Biblioteca
      de la Mujer Católica. B.A.: Edit. Poblet. 340 p.
        Religious counsel and doctrine for women to be good
      Catholics written by Jesuit priest in Buenos Aires.

Uruguay

691   O'HARA, JOHN P.
        1921 "The League of Catholic Women in Uruguay." CATW
      113:674:217-24.
        Deplores religious bigotry, anti-clericalism and
      secularization of education witnessed in Uruguay (e.g.,
      divorce law of 1907). Contends that as a result of
      persecution of Church, the League of Catholic Women of
      Uruguay has developed into "one of the most efficient
      Catholic social organizations in the world," fighting
      against the divorce law and theatrical productions con-
      sidered salacious and detrimental to womanhood. Outlines
      their numbers, accomplishments, and establishments (e.g.,
      sewing circles for girls, libraries). Affirms that
      these noble women are neither nuns nor "queer."!

CARIBBEAN

Puerto Rico

692   DOHEN, DOROTHY
        1959 "Religious Practice and Marital Patterns in Puerto
      Rico." ACSR 20:3:203-18. tables.
        Examines religious practices of men and women in 2
      barrios of Ponce, Puerto Rico. Women, in consensual
      union or Catholic marriage, evidence greater religious
      practice than men of same marital status. Suggests that
      where religious practice is high, consensual unions are
      low.

693 PERPIÑÁ, JUAN
    1888 Jesucristo y la mujer. San Juan, P.R.: Tipografía
    del "Boletín Mercantíl." 44 p.
        According to Bibliografía puertorriqueña (Barcelona,
    1934) of Géigel y Zenón and Morales Ferrer, this pamphlet
    combats "two errors of rationalism which consist of pre-
    senting Christ in purely human form, destitute of the
    essential element of divinity, and woman, destitute of
    any idea of the supernatural order, without any affinity
    or inclination for the spiritual and divine . . ."

Cuba

694 DÍAZ de ESPADA y LANDA, JUAN JOSÉ
    1811 Carta pastoral que el ilustrísimo senor Don Juan
    José Díaz de Espada y Landa dirige a sus diocesanos
    sobre las falsas doctrinas contrarias a nuestros dogmas
    y costumbres christianos impresas en varios papeles del
    Correo de las damas de esta ciudad. Havana: en la
    empresa de la curia episcopal, por D. E. J. Boloña,
    18 p.
        Diatribe by Bishop of Havana against issues 47 and 48
    of Correo de las Damas, pamphlets in which the sexual
    act was discussed. Quotes from the Bible to confirm his
    opinion about sexual relations outside of marriage. Loss
    of virginity is the ultimate horror.

695 [Isla de Cuba]
    1837 Supresión de conventos: contribución extraordinaria
    de guerra: inconvenientes de estas medidas allí. Ideas
    sobre la que podría substituirse. Madrid: Imprenta de
    I. Sancha. 2 vols. in 1.
        Notes on monasteries of both sexes (5 nunneries) in
    Cuba: their financial condition and their purpose (e.g.,
    Ursulines were dedicated to the education of young girls).
    Makes plea for rectification of poor financial state of
    convents so that they are not entirely done away with.

ETHNOGRAPHIC MONOGRAPHS/COMMUNITY STUDIES

The object of this category is to provide a sampling of a particular genre of literature which regularly offers notes on women in
individual communities. It is comprised of those references which
contain information on women in various indigenous and other ethnic
groups. The studies do not consider only pure Indian communities,
but also black and mestizo populations.

Ethnographic literature generally focuses on women in the home.
It encompasses the life cycle (from pregnancy to death), marriage and
the family, daily round of activities, folk beliefs, practices, and
professionals (e.g., *curanderas*, witches, midwives), clothing and
adornment, crafts, socialization, sexual relations, division of labor,
goddesses, legends, and much more. Chapters entitled "social organization," "the life cycle," "the family," or "the domestic group"
usually offer the most notes. However, women are often mentioned,
even if briefly, in sections on economic life, religion and ritual,
and folk medicine. They may also appear in case history material and
photographs for illustration.

Chapters including information on women are noted in the annotation of each entry in this section; their contents are listed, but
not described in detail. When the information is very limited, the
annotation indicates this. Such items have been incorporated because
little or nothing else was found on women in that particular group,
Not all of the publications are full-length monographs; some are
brief articles, but specifically about women in a particular Indian
community or about indigenous women in general. General articles--
i.e., covering various aspects of women's lives in an indigenous
groups, such as "La mujer tzeltal"--are included in this section;
but articles on more specific topics, such as *curanderas* are placed
separately in the appropriate major subject category, since the bibliography concentrates on subject information rather than ethnic
composition.

While dated studies often lack sufficient data because either the
anthropologists did not deem women's activities worthy of much or
serious attention, or because male researchers were not expected or
allowed to get close to the women of the community, more recent

monographs, especially those prepared by female anthropologists, are expanding the information and perspective on female members of a group. Because much of the ethnographic literature in this bibliography was written in English, it is also limited by a North American perspective, whether male or female. In recent years, Latin Americans have become more and more engaged in anthropological study in their native countries and are producing ethnographies in Spanish. And, because of rapid modernization taking place all over Spanish America, the data also becomes limited as various groups assimilate into and become acculturated to the national culture of a country.

For notes on the position of women in Indian civilizations before the Spanish conquest, see HISTORY BEFORE 1900. For additional information on customs and ceremonies related to courtship and marriage, see MARRIAGE AND THE FAMILY; on female shamans, witches, goddesses, and ritual, see MAGIC, RELIGION, AND RITUAL; on legends in which women appear, see LITERATURE, MASS MEDIA, AND FOLKLORE; on the division of labor by sex, see ECONOMIC LIFE; on the female reproductive cycle, fertility and family planning, folk illnesses and curing, see HUMAN SEXUALITY, REPRODUCTION, AND HEALTH. For studies on *machismo* and national character which trace exaggerated sex role behavior to the clash between Indian civilizations and the Spanish culture, see PSYCHOLOGY; on race mixing, or mestizaje, see HISTORY BEFORE 1900. For notes on the daughters of Indian chieftains who were educated and/or became nuns during the colonial period, see EDUCATION and MAGIC, RELIGION, AND RITUAL.

An additional source for ethnographic information is the area handbook prepared by Foreign Area Studies of American University. Although designed for the use of military and other personnel as a source of basic facts about the social, economic, political and military institutions and practices of a country, the area handbooks, compiled by a group of authors and derived from an extensive bibliography of published materials, provide a useful description of contemporary society. They include information on marriage, the family, and divorce, birth control, religion, education, etc; and incorporate maps and tables. A separate handbook is published for each Spanish American country; they date from 1969 to 1974; e.g., Area Handbook for El Salvador. Washington, D.C.: US Government Printing Office, 1971.

Many of the monographs listed in this section were taken from Olien's useful bibliography[1]; see it for additional references. For

---

[1] Michael D. Olien. Latin Americans: Contemporary Peoples and Their Cultural Traditions. N.Y.: Holt, Rinehart and Winston, 1973, pp. 321-96. Following a list of references, Appendices A through E cite collections of articles, reference material, periodicals and monograph series, biographies and autobiographies, and monographs on Latin American societies and subcultures.

individual groups, consult the Handbook of Middle American Indians
(item 740) and the Handbook of South American Indians (item 699), and
Leary's bibliography.[2]

696   GAMIO de ALBA, MARGARITA
        1959 "The Indian Woman in Latin America." In Women's
        Role in the Development of Tropical and Sub-Tropical
        Countries. Report of the XXXIst Meeting, held in
        Brussels on 17th, 18th, 19th and 20th September 1958,
        ed. by International Institute of Differing Civiliza-
        tions, pp. 384-97. Brussels. bibl.
        Based on secondary sources and field work, synthesizes
        the situation of Indian women in LA according to 3 cate-
        gories of acculturation: "spontaneous," induced, and
        nonexistent; uses examples mainly from Mexico and Central
        America. Concludes that systematic acculturation has
        fomented a relatively advantageous position for women.

697   _____.
        1957-1958 "La mujer indígena de Centroamérica." MIIN/NI
        2:13/14:53-60; 2:19/20:31-50; 3:21:21-29; 3:23:25-38.
        bibl. notes.
        Abbreviated version of book with same title.

        _____.
        1957 La mujer indígena de Centro América, sumaria
        recopilación acerca de sus condiciones de vida. Inst.
        Indigenista Interamericano, Ediciones Especiales, 31.
        Mex., D.F. 90 p. illus., bibl.
        Discusses indigenous women in Guatemala, Honduras,
        Nicaragua, Costa Rica and Panama with respect to biology
        and health (maternity, food, witches and curers,
        illnesses); economy and work; inheritance and transfer
        of property; intellectual development; marriage and
        psycho-sexual relations; social life; and predominant
        pre-Columbian surviving customs.

698   KOCH GRÜNBERG, THEODOR
        1908-1909 "South America." In Women of All Nations. A
        Record of Their Characteristics, Habits, Manners, Cus-
        toms and Influence, ed. by T. A. Joyce and N. W. Thomas,

---

[2] Timothy J. O'Leary. Ethnographic Bibliography of South America.
New Haven, Conn.: Human Relations Area Files, 1963. Divided by
country and then separate indigenous groups, it includes literature
written in Spanish, English, German, French, Portuguese, and Italian.

vol. 1, pp. 360-92. London: Cassell and Co. illus., notes.

Potpourri of information on indigenous women of SA from the Caribbean coast to Tierra del Fuego: rites, marriage, conjugal fidelity, divorce, birth customs, children, economic aspects, crafts, clothing, division of labor, etc. Personal interpretations based on observations during travels (1903-05) plus comments of other writers. Refutes general representation of Indian women as degraded slaves. Interesting though questionable notes.

699 STEWARD, JULIAN HAYNES, ed.
        1946-59 Handbook of South American Indians. US Bureau of
        American Ethnology, Bulletin 143. Wash., D.C.: US
        Govt. Printing Office. 7 vols. illus., plates, maps,
        bibl.
        Covers wives, woman stealing, witches, virginity, weaving, sexual life and marriage, separation of the sexes, servants, matrilocal residence, prostitution, polygyny, polygamy, polyandry, matriarchate, marital relations, pregnancy, abortion, adultery, myths about mythical Amazon women, contraception, concubinage, etc. in marginal, circum-Caribbean and tropical forest tribes and the Andean civilizations.

MIDDLE AMERICA

Mexico

700 BAILEY, HELEN MILLER
        1958 Santa Cruz of the Etla Hills. Gainesville, Fla.:
        Univ. of Fla. Press. 292 p. illus., map.
        Collective biography tells story of Santa Cruz, village in Oaxaca, Mexico, through chapters on individual villagers. Part 2 covers women: landowner, curer, oldest grandmother et al. Part 3 deals with male and female teachers and students. Based on brief visits between 1934 and 1954.

701 BEALS, RALPH L.
        1946 Cherán: A Sierra Tarascan Village. Smithsonian
        Institution, Inst. of Social Anthropology, Publication
        no. 2. Wash., D.C.: US Govt. Printing Office. 225 p.
        illus., plates, bibl.
        Study carried out in 1940-41 in the mountain Tarascan village of Cherán, Michoacán, Mexico. Includes extensive notes on women's clothing, eating customs, division of

Ethnographic Monographs/Community Studies

               labor, conflict and law, witchcraft, midwifery, the life
cycle (birth, socialization, marriage and sexual
relations.)

702   _____.

        1945   Ethnology of the Western Mixe. Univ. of Ca. Publi-
cations in American Archaelogy and Ethnology 42:1:1-176.
Berkeley, Ca.: Univ. of Ca. Press. illus., plates,
maps, bibl.

          Based on brief fieldwork (1933) among the Western
Mixe near Oaxaca Valley, including female native informants, contains chapters on family and marriage and life
cycle and notes on women's dress, weaving, pottery
making, market trading, food preparation, curing and
religious participation.

703   BENNETT, WILLIAM C. and ZINGG, ROBERT M.

        1935   The Tarahumara, An Indian Tribe of Northern Mexico.
Univ. of Chicago Publications in Anthropology. Ethnological Series. Chicago: Univ. of Chicago Press.
412 p. illus., fold. table, bibl.

          Fieldwork carried out in Samachique, a high sierra
Tarahumara village (1930-31). Includes data on role of
women in animal husbandry, food preparation, housekeeping, manufacturing (basketry, weaving, pottery), ceremonial activities, marriage, extra-marital relations,
divorce, family unit, division of property, law cases,
birth, mourning, etc. Also describes women's clothing
and ornaments.

704   CARRASCO PUENTE, RAFAEL

        1961   "La Tehuana. (Fichas hemero-bibliográficas)."
Suplemento del BSHCP/B 219:1-4. illus.

          Guide to more than 70 published references containing
historical, artistic, musical and poetic material on the
women of the Isthmus of Tehuantepec.

705   CHIÑAS, BEVERLY LITZLER

        1973   The Isthmus Zapotecs: Women's Role in Cultural
Context. Case Studies in Cultural Anthropology. N.Y.:
Holt, Rinehart and Winston. 122 p. illus., map, bibl.

          Valuable contribution to growing body of anthropologi-
cal literature which focuses on female experience.
Demonstrates mutual dependence and complementarity of
male and female roles in the Zapotec economic and social
system in the Isthmus of Tehuantepec. Develops an
analytical model of roles to distinguish between formalized and non-formalized roles in the public and private
domains of society. Based on fieldwork in 1967.

706 COVARRUBIAS, MIGUEL
1954 <u>Mexico South: The Isthmus of Tehuantepec</u>. N.Y.:
Alfred A. Knopf. 427 p. illus., plates, map, bibl.
Originally appeared in 1946. In Part 2, chapters 8-10
deal with the people of the Isthmus--how they look, live,
work, think, speak and amuse themselves--and the Zapotec
family--sexual relations, childbirth, wedding. Women
also appear in other chapters with respect to their role
in fiestas, magic, and death ceremonies.

707 DÍAZ, MAY N.
1970 <u>Tonalá: Conservatism, Responsibility, and Authority
in a Mexican Town</u>. Berkeley, Ca.: Univ. of Ca. Press.
234 p. illus., bibl.
Although focus of study is on effect of industrialization on pottery village near Guadalajara, there is much
information on role of women in the context of family
life, work, and social or community life. Believes
women have little or no overt power or authority, but
in reality, women "maneuver" others in order to carry
out decisions.

708 ELMENDORF, MARY LINDSAY
1975 <u>Nine Mayan Women: A Village Faces Change</u>. Cambridge,
Mass.: Schenkman. Spanish version: 1973 <u>La mujer maya
y el cambio</u>. Trans. by C. Viqueira. SEP/SETENTAS, 85.
Mex., D.F.: Secretaría de Educación Pública. 173 p.
map, illus., plates, bibl. 1972 <u>The Mayan Woman and
Change</u>. CIDOC Cuaderno, 81. Cuernavaca, Mex.: Centro
Intercultural de Documentación. 257 p. bibl., chart.
Focuses on women in traditional Maya village of Chan
Kom. Explores the feelings of 7 women about their own
lives (work, recreation, dreams, marriage, family, sex,
birth control, etc.) and the possible effects that
changes may have on them as a new road links the village
with modern Mexico. Based on several brief field trips
in 1971 and 1972. Descriptive rather than analytical.

709 No entry.

710 FOSTER, GEORGE M.
1967 <u>Tzintzuntzan: Mexican Peasants in a Changing
World</u>. Boston: Little, Brown and Co. 372 p. illus.,
maps, graph.
Based on field work in mid-1940's and 1959-66 in
pottery-making village of Michoacán, Mexico. Includes
notes on occupations, daily round of activities, interpersonal relations, envy and pregnancy, bride's favors,

Ethnographic Monographs/Community Studies

limited good and *machismo*. Women figure throughout text.

711   GAMIO de ALBA, MARGARITA
        1960 "El Dr. Manuel Gamio y el Proyecto de la Mujer Indígena." III/AI 20:4:291-93.
           Describes action taken in favor of solving problems of indigenous women.

712   GRIFFEN, WILLIAM
        1959 Notes on Seri Indian Culture. Latin American Monographs, 10. Gainesville, Fla.: Univ. of Fla. Press, School of Inter-American Studies. 54 p. map.
           Based on brief fieldwork (1955) among the Seri Indians at Desemboque, Sonora, includes information on women as traditional housebuilders, costume, jewelry making, games, dances, religious lore, childbirth, puberty ceremony, courtship, marriage, divorce, division of labor, few employment opportunities. There is a separate chapter on the life cycle.

713   IWÁNSKA, ALICJA
        1971 Purgatory and Utopia: A Mazahua Indian Village of Mexico. Cambridge, Mass.: Schenkman Publishing Co. 214 p. illus., bibl. notes.
           Based on fieldwork (1962, 1963, 1965) in El Nopal, Toluca. Part 2, "Social Differentiation," covers sexual and generational differences, including division of labor, and conception of the supernatural, especially "the weeping woman" and the witch. "El Libro del Nopal," dictated by the villagers in 1962 and transcribed, relates their lives, activities and beliefs.

714   JOHNSON, JEAN B.
        1950 The Opata: An Inland Tribe of Sonora. Univ. of New Mex. Publications in Anthropology, 6. Albuquerque, New Mex.: Univ. of New Mex. Press. 50 p. illus., plates, bibl.
           Based on fieldwork (1940) among the Opata Indians in the Mexican state of Sonora as well as primary and secondary sources, briefly notes women's past assistance in cultivation, weaving, clothing, warfare, marriage and sex relations.

715   LEWIS, OSCAR
        1963 Life in a Mexian Village: Tepotzlán Restudied.
        Illinois Books, IB-9. Urbana: Univ. of Ill. Press. 512 p. illus., maps, bibl.

Fieldwork carried out in peasant village of Tepotzlán
near Mexico City in the 1940's. Contains information on
all aspects of village plus detailed descriptions of
women at various activities and stages of life cycle.
Part 2 discusses childbirth, childrearing, adolescence,
courtship and marriage, interpersonal relations.
Includes results of Rorschach tests given to 57 men and
47 women (5 - 75 years old), analyzed by age and sex,
with samples reproduced in appendix.

716 _____.
1960 Tepotzlán: Village in Mexico. Case Studies in
Cultural Anthropology. N.Y.: Holt, Rinehart and
Winston. 104 p. illus., map, bibl.
Based on fieldwork (1956-57) in village in state of
Morelos, Mexico, includes information on the division
of labor, husband/wife and parent/child relations, the
life cycle (from pregnancy through courtship, marriage
and death), body contact, sexual restraint, conflict
in sex roles and relations, clothing and midwifery.
There are separate chapters on the family and life
cycle.

717 LOMBARDO OTERO de SOTA, ROSA MARÍA
1944 La mujer tzeltal. Mex., D.F. 76 p. illus., plates
Commissioned by Mexican government and Interamerican
Indigenous Institute, author provides information for
Tzeltal-speaking Indian women of Oxchuc, Chiapas on
pregnancy and birth, child-naming, infancy, adolescence
and puberty, education, courtship and marriage, sexual
life, family role, division of labor, religion, public
life, inheritance, illness, etc.

718 MADSEN, WILLIAM
1960 The Virgin's Children. Life in an Aztec Village
Today. Austin: Univ. of Tex. Press. 248 p. illus.,
bibl.
Based on fieldwork in Nahuatl village of Tecospa
(1952-53), includes information on women taking care of
animals (including slaughter) and preparing food; folk
practices surrounding birth; birth, midwifery, child-
rearing and socialization; influence of virgin cults;
wife-beating; women and evil air; a curandera special-
izing in "evil eye" sickness; etc. Many illustrations
of women at different activities.

719 NADER, LAURA
1964 Talea and Juquila: A Comparison of Zapotec Cultural
Organization. Univ. of Ca. Publications in American

Ethnographic Monographs/Community Studies

Archaelogy and Ethnology 48:3:195-216. Berkeley, Ca.:
Univ. of Ca. Press. illus., maps, bibl.
Based on field research (1957-58, 1959-60) in 2
Zapotec communities north of Oaxaca Valley, including
female native informants. Provides information on the
family (authority and drinking patterns, marriage,
husband/wife and parent/child relations, residence and
spatial arrangements, interfamily relations); social
groups and division of labor; grievances and remedy
agents (court, supernatural and family systems), illustrating with cases involving women. There is a separate
chapter on the family.

720   NASH, JUNE
1970   In the Eyes of the Ancestors. Belief and Behavior
in a Maya Community. New Haven, Conn.: Yale Univ.
Press. 368 p. illus., tables, map, bibl.
Based on field trips between 1957 and 1967 to Mayan
community in Chiapas. Includes section on pottery production by women, behavior defined within the family
(socialization, birth, sexual division of labor and
play), women's role in rituals of life crisis (baptism,
betrothal and marriage, death and burial). Appendix
contains transcribed tape recorded cases on house
arrangement of separation (involving a woman who left
her husband's home), court arrangement of separation,
bloodletting in witchcraft, and observations of behavior
in church, school, etc.

721   NELSON, CYNTHIA
1971   The Waiting Village: Social Change in Rural Mexico.
A Latin American Case Study. Boston: Little, Brown
and Co. 160 p. illus., map, tables, bibl.
Based on fieldwork in Erongarícuaro, Michoacan
(1960-61). Includes information on occupations of
female heads of household, a social worker, a middle-
woman in the weaving industry, getting married, estab-
lishing a family, role models and role conflicts, other
interpersonal relations, and world-view and values as
reflected in TAT responses by men and women.

722   OWEN, ROGER C.
1959   Marobavi: A Study of an Assimilated Group in
Northern Sonora. Anthropological Papers of the Univ.
of Ariz., 3. Tucson, Ariz.: Univ. of Ariz. Press.
70 p. illus., maps, tables, bibl.
Based on brief fieldwork (1955) in village of north
central Sonora, Mexico, includes information on division

of labor, clothing, handicrafts; household and family,
marriage, status, and social behavior; religious organization, attitudes and participation (e.g., *cantoras*).
Tables indicate household composition and population by
age and sex.

723   PARSONS, ELSIE CLEWS
        1936   Mitla. Town of the Souls and Other Zapoteco-
        Speaking Pueblos of Oaxaca, Mexico. Univ. of Chicago
        Publications in Anthropology. Ethnological Series.
        Chicago: Univ. of Chicago Press. 590 p. illus., maps,
        bibl.
            Based on fieldwork (1929-33), includes great deal of
        information on women in chapter on family and personal
        life: beliefs and practices related to fertility
        (menstruation, pregnancy, abortion, midwives, breast
        feeding, child rearing, menopause); marriage (courtship,
        wedding, conjugal relations); sickness and *curanderas*;
        witches; death and burial. Provides many examples and
        comparisons with Aztec practices. Includes additional
        references to adultery, barrenness, birth rate, bride
        stealing, dress, divorce, goddesses, illegitimacy,
        intermarriage, division of labor, prostitution, promis-
        cuity, remarriage, sexual habits, separation of the
        sexes, weavers, widowhood.

724   PAUL, BENJAMIN D. and PAUL, LOIS
        1952   "The Life Cycle." In Heritage of Conquest: The
        Ethnology of Middle America, ed. by S. Tax, pp. 174-92.
        Glencoe, Ill.: The Free Press. bibl.
            See GUATEMALA for annotation.

725   PI-SUNYER, ORIOL
        1973   Zamora: Change and Continuity in a Mexican Town.
        Case Studies in Cultural Anthropology. N.Y.: Holt,
        Rinehart and Winston. 116 p. illus., bibl.
            Based on fieldwork (1957-58, 1971) in Zamora, a
        mestizo town in Michoacán, includes a chapter on inter-
        personal and intersexual relations, which considers
        ideology of male superiority, female image and conduct,
        vergüenza as an ideal womanly attribute, courtship and
        marriage, etc.

726   _____.
        1968 "Zamora: A Regional Economy in Mexico." In Studies
        in Middle American Economics, by R. A. La Barge, W. M.
        Clegren, and O. Pi-Sunyer, pp. 97-180. Middle American
        Research Inst. Publication 29. New Orleans: Tulane
        Univ. illus., bibl.

Ethnographic Monographs/Community Studies

In microstudy of economic change in a *mestizo* community
of Michoacán, discussion on status determinants considers
sex variable. Section on interpersonal and intersexual
relations discusses sex roles and ideology of male superiority, world of the female, courtship and marriage.
Interesting details on differences between male and
female positions, rather than useless generalizations.

727 POZAS ARCINIEGAS, RICARDO
1959 Chamula: Un pueblo indio de los altos de Chiapas.
Memorias del Inst. Nacional Indigenista, 8. Mex., D.F.:
Eds. del Inst. Nacional Indigenista. 206 p. illus.,
maps, bibl.
Based on fieldwork in 1944, with subsequent trips,
includes information on women as heads of households,
migrants, weavers, potters, and food preparers. Also
covers sexual attraction and beauty of women, marriage,
wedding day, sexual relations, conception and contraceptives, preference for male children, birth, women's
position in the family, bigamy, separation, education
of children at home, daily round of activities, division
of labor, property and inheritance, and women's roles in
religious functions.

728 REDFIELD, ROBERT
1950 A Village that Chose Progress: Chan Kom Revisited.
Chicago: Univ. of Chicago Press. 187 p. illus.,
table, maps.
Based on brief field trip (1948) to Indian village in
state of Yucatán, Mexico, updates earlier research.
Contains notes on women's clothing and activities,
marriage, sexual relations, behavioral changes, employment opportunities, participation in sports, education,
new life styles for women and sexual morality.

729 _____.
1941 The Folk Culture of Yucatán. Social Anthropology
Series. Chicago: Univ. of Chicago Press. 416 p.
illus., map, plates, bibl.
Data collected in early 1930's in Yucatán by Redfield
et al. Includes information on women in chapters on
money, land, and work and on family organization and
disorganization; with scattered references to *curandera,*
witchcraft, birth and marriage rituals, women as carriers
of culture and as prayer reciters.

730 _____.
        1930 Tepotzlán, a Mexican Village: A Study of Folk Life.
        Ethnological Series. Chicago: Univ. of Chicago Press.
        247 p. illus., plates, map, bibl.
            Fieldwork carried out in *mestizo* village of Tepotzlán,
        Morelos (1926-27). Includes notes on women's clothing,
        daily cycle of activity, participation in festivals,
        birth customs, marriage, division of labor, magic and
        medicine.

731 REDFIELD, ROBERT and VILLA ROJAS, ALFONSO
        1962 Chan Kom: A Maya Village. Phoenix Books. Univ. of
        Chicago Press. 236 p. illus., maps.
            Field research conducted in early 1930's among
        Yucatecan Maya. Includes information on domestic equip-
        ment, food and cookery, clothing and handicrafts;
        personal property and inheritance; division of labor by
        sex; midwife; family and household--marriage, divorce,
        desertion; sickness and cure; and the life cycle.
        Photographs show women at their activities.

732 Revista Mexicana de Sociología
        Volumes 1-5 (1939-43) and 23 (1961) include ethnographic
        data on both sexes of 16 indigenous groups in Mexico.

733 RITZENTHALER, ROBERT E. and PETERSON, FREDERICK A.
        1956 The Mexican Kickapoo Indians. Publications in
        Anthropology, 2. Milwaukee, Wis.: Milwaukee Public
        Museum. 91 p. illus., map, bibl.
            Based on very brief field trip among Kickapoo Indians
        in Mexican state of Coahuila, mentions women's dress,
        tasks, property, games, and role in religious life.
        Part 2 deals with the life cycle (pregnancy taboos and
        birth, childcare and training, courtship, marriage,
        divorce). Part 3 on material culture, discusses weaving
        and leatherwork by women and housebuilding (including
        a menstrual hut), a cooperative venture by women and
        men. Because of a language barrier, did not consult
        female informants.

734 ROMNEY, A. KIMBALL and ROMNEY, ROMAINE
        1966 The Mixtecans of Juxtlahuaca, Mexico. Six Cultures.
        Studies of Child Rearing Series, 4. N.Y.: John Wiley
        and Sons. 150 p. illus., maps, bibl. Reprint: 1973
        Huntington, N.Y.: Robert F. Krieger Publishing Co.
            Contribution to cross-cultural collection of monographs
        which explore relation between different patterns of
        child rearing and subsequent differences in personality.
        Part 1 is an ethnography of Mixtecan Indians in Santo

Ethnographic Monographs/Community Studies

Domingo *barrio* of Juxtlahuaca, Oaxaca (including daily routine, family organization, etc.). Part 2, on child training, begins with pregnancy and childbirth and ends with late childhood. Excerpts from field observations illustrate behavior responses by boys and girls, which vary according to particular behavior, such as nurturance or self-reliance. Based on interviews with mothers and with children, child TAT's, and observation of child behavior.

735 TERRY, G. CUNNINGHAM
1928 "Imperious Amazons of Mexico." Travel 50:4:23-27, 45. illus.
Well-illustrated article on Tehuantepec women, the "rulers" of the Isthmus. Description of their physical appearance, clothing, headdress, jewelry, morals, ceremonies, festivities, housework and dances. Women outnumber men 5-1 and control all family property; but they are illiterate, resorting to a male public letter-writer.

736 TOOR, FRANCES
1947 A Treasury of Mexican Folkways. N.Y.: Crown Publishers. 566 p. illus., plates, map, music, bibl.
Based on 25 years' residence in Mexico and 100 anthropological, historical and folkloric items, attempts a composite picture of life in Mexico among many ethnic groups: customs, myths, folklore, festivals, social and religious organization, economic life, music and dance. References to women in weaving, food preparation, division of labor, apparel, life cycle, marriage, weddings, love magic, healing, birth, pregnancy, virgin cults, stories of the wicked woman, and the legend of the *china poblana*.

737 TURNER, PAUL R.
1972 The Highland Chontal. Case Studies in Cultural Anthropology. N.Y.: Holt, Rinehart and Winston. 96 p. illus., bibl.
Fieldwork conducted in San Matías Petacaltepec, Oaxaca (1959-63, 1964-69). Includes data on family, courtship and marriage, birth, childhood, adolescence, adulthood, death, division of labor, socialization and an individual life account of one woman.

738 VILLA ROJAS, ALFONSO
1945 The Maya of East Central Quintana Roo. Carnegie Institution of Wash. Publication 559. Wash., D.C. 182 p. illus., maps, plates, ports., bibl.

178

Based on field work in the 1930's, includes information on population and division of labor by sex and age,
women's clothing and property rights, household composition, marriage and choice of spouse, temporary matrilocal residence, ceremonies and practices connected with
the life cycle.

739   VOGT, EVON Z.
      1970 The Zinacantecos of Mexico: A Modern Maya Way of
      Life. Case Studies in Cultural Anthropology. N.Y.:
      Holt, Rinehart and Winston. 113 p. illus., tables,
      map, bibl.
          Essentially a condensed version of Zinacantan: A
      Maya Community in the Highlands of Chiapas, (#741) with
      similar information on women.

740   _____, vol. ed.
      1969 Ethnology, part 1 and Ethnology, part 2. Vols. 7
      and 8 of the Handbook of Middle American Indians, ed.
      by R. Wauchope. Austin, Tex.: Univ. of Tex. Press.
      illus, maps, bibl.
          Provides descriptive summaries of contemporary indig-
      enous cultures of Middle America, covering the Maya,
      southern and central Mexican highlands and adjacent
      coastal regions, western and northwest Mexico. Includes
      notes on crafts, dress and adornment, processing and
      manufacturing, division of labor, specialization, prop-
      erty, trade and markets, family and kinship, myth and
      ritual, folklore, sickness and curing, gossip, life
      cycle/personality development, socialization, education,
      etc.

741   _____.
      1969 Zinacantan: A Maya Community in the Highlands of
      Chiapas. Cambridge, Mass.: The Belknap Press of Harvard
      Univ. Press. 733 p. illus., maps, tables, bibl.
          Based on fieldwork among Tzotzil-speaking Maya by
      Harvard-Chiapas project since 1957. Includes informa-
      tion on women in chapters 3 (tortilla making), 5
      (women's clothing and division of labor), 7 (domestic
      group, patterns of endogamy and exogamy), and 9 (beliefs
      and customs surrounding birth, socialization, marriage
      and death). Illustrations depict women at their
      activities.

742   WHETTEN, NATHAN L.
      1948 Rural Mexico. Chicago: Univ. of Chicago Press.
      671 p. illus., maps, tables, graphs, plates, bibl.

Ethnographic Monographs/Community Studies

Study in rural sociology based on residence, field-work, and statistical data from official sources. Information on women in part 3, "Standards and Levels of Living" (including housing, diet, clothing, health and mortality) and part 4, "Social Institutions" (including marriage and the family). Scattered references in other sections.

743   WHITEFORD, ANDREW HUNTER
        1964 Two Cities of Latin America. A Comparative Description of Social Classes. Anchor Books, A395. Garden City, N.Y.: Doubleday. 266 p. illus., bibl.
        See COLOMBIA for annotation.

744   WILKIE, RAYMOND
        1971 San Miguel: A Mexican Collective Ejido. Stanford: Stanford Univ. Press. 190 p. illus., plates, tables, bibl.
        Fieldwork carried out in 1953, 1966-67 in the San Miguel *ejido* of the Laguna region. Includes a chapter on "Social Life and the Family": courtship and marriage, husband-wife relations, control of family finances, leisure activities, etc.

Guatemala

745   BUNZEL, RUTH
        1952 Chichicastenango: A Guatemalan Village. Publications of the American Ethnological Society, 22. Locust Valley, N.Y.: J. J. Augustin. 438 p. plans, bibl.
        Fieldwork carried out in Quiché-speaking municipality near Lake Atitlán (1930-32). Chapter on economic life includes inheritance of land, marriage, and food preparation; chapter on family life covers pregnancy and childbirth, parents and children, growing up, education, betrothal, marriage ceremonies and ideals, husbands and wives, divorce, breakup of the family, sickness, curing and death.

746   GILLIN, JOHN
        1951 The Culture of Security in San Carlos: A Study of a Guatemalan Community of Indians and Ladinos. Middle American Research Series, Publication 16. New Orleans: Tulane Univ., Middle American Research Inst. 128 p. tables, bibl.
        Based on fieldwork (summers of 1942, 1946 and 1948) among Pokomám Indians and Ladinos in San Carlos (pseudonym), Guatemala, including female informants as well.

Provides information on women in both ethnic groups with
respect to clothing, economic activities (pottery making
and marketing), marriage and adultery, religious festivals, midwifery, etc.

747 LaFARGE, OLIVER II and BYERS, DOUGLAS
     1931 The Year Bearer's People. Middle American Research
     Series, Publication no. 3. New Orleans, La.: Tulane
     Univ., Middle American Research Inst. 379 p. illus.,
     map, plates, tables, bibl.
          Based on fieldwork (1927) among the Jacalteca Indians
     (Maya descendants), at Guatemala border, includes infor-
     mation on women's costume; work (food preparation,
     weaving, pottery); childbirth and marriage; the legend
     of doña Juana; and a soothsayer.

748 MEJÍA PIVARAL, VÍCTOR
     1972 "Características económicas y socioculturales de
     cuatro aldeas ladinas de Guatemala." GIIN/GI 7:3:3-300.
     illus., tables, maps.
          Fieldwork carried out in 4 Ladino communities in east-
     ern Guatemala as part of a larger longitudinal study on
     environmental, social and nutritional factors which
     affect mental development (INCAP), begun in 1965.
     Covers population figures, division of labor, family
     structure, life cycle, daily routine, clothing, religion,
     health, recreation, food, and education. Much informa-
     tion in tables.

749 MOORE, G. ALEXANDER
     1973 Life Cycles in Atchalán. The Diverse Careers of
     Certain Guatemalans. N.Y.: Teachers College Press.
     220 p. illus., tables, bibl.
          Based on 10 years of fieldwork, conceives of education
     as a lifelong process; therefore, one must examine all
     the events that mark the passage of an individual from
     1 station of life to another. Chapter 4 deals with an
     Indian woman's coming of age, which is marriage; describes
     courtship, engagement, wedding, ritual profit and diffu-
     sion. Chapter 3 deals with children and the household--
     the socialization process and home environment.

750 PAUL, BENJAMIN D. and PAUL, LOIS
     1952 "The Life Cycle." In Heritage of Conquest: The
     Ethnology of Middle America, ed. by S. Tax, pp. 174-92.
     Glencoe, Ill.: The Free Press. bibl.
          Based on field research, comparative data for 10 com-
     munities in Mexico and Guatemala, and Meso-American
     materials, provides survey of attitudes and practices

Ethnographic Monographs/Community Studies

surrounding life cycle for indigenous men and women:
conception, pregnancy, childbirth, child naming, infancy
rites, childhood, puberty, marriage, adulthood, death.

751 REINA, RUBEN C.
     1966 The Law of the Saints: A Pokoman Pueblo and Its
     Community Culture. N.Y.: Bobbs-Merrill. 338 p. illus.,
     maps, bibl.
        Based on field research (1955-56) conducted in Pokoman-
     speaking community of Chinautla. Includes information on
     women as potters; courtship, marriage, wedding, divorce
     and separation, attitudes of Ladino and Indian women
     after marriage; family relationships (husband/wife,
     parent/child); pregnancy and birth, growing up, old age,
     illness, death. Remarks on shift in relative position
     of men and women since latter began to market their own
     products and become more independent in the family.
     Cites 2 cases of marital differences and of a woman's
     problems with her children, all dealt with by the mayor.
     Discusses evil eye, *susto*, witches, diviners, envy and
     gossip. Relates personal story of male villager, in
     which he reveals attitudes toward women.

752 SAQUIC CALEL, ROSALÍO
     1973 "La mujer indígena guatemalteca." GIIN/GI 8:1:81-110.
        Describes various aspects of life cycle of Indian wo-
     men in Santa Lucía Utatlán, Sololá, Guatemala: child-
     hood, education, puberty, menstruation, courtship and
     formal request to marry, marriage, elopement, inheritance,
     pregnancy, birth, beliefs and practices, religious post.

753 WAGLEY, CHARLES
     1949 The Social and Religious Life of a Guatemalan Vil-
     lage. Memoir Series of the American Anthropological
     Assoc., 71. Menasha, Wis.: American Anthropological
     Assoc. 150 p. plates, bibl. Also in: 1949 AAA/AA
     51:4 (part 2).
        Based on field investigation in Mam-speaking community
     of Santiago, Chimaltenango in northwest Guatemalan high-
     lands (1937), includes information on family groups and
     a chapter on the life cycle (childhood, pre-marital sex-
     ual experience, marriage, divorce, death, household
     duties, socialization, conjugal relations, inheritance,
     etc.). Notes that men dress as women for certain fes-
     tivities. Appendix contains excerpts from diary of
     Juan de Dios Rosales, who visited the village in 1944;
     he describes women at their activities and the purchase
     of 13- or 14-year-old girls for marriage.

754 WHETTEN, NATHAN L.
1961 Guatemala: The Land and the People. Caribbean
Series, 4. New Haven, Conn.: Yale Univ. Press. 399 p.
illus., plates, tables, bibl.
Rural sociological study, similar to his Rural Mexico,
based on data gathered in 1944, 1952 and 1956, includes
scattered references to women: economic aspects, housing, clothing, diet and nutrition, health and mortality,
marriage and the family.

755 WISDOM, CHARLES
1940 The Chorti Indians of Guatemala. Chicago: Univ. of
Chicago Press. 490 p. illus., map, plates, bibl.
Based on fieldwork among the Chorti-speaking Indians
of eastern Guatemala (1931, 1932, 1933), including native women informants, mentions women's marketing,
clothing, food preparation, weaving and pottery; sexual
division of labor and professionalization; the family
and marriage; individual life cycle; sickness, sorcery,
and medicine; the supernatural and sacred.

Honduras

756 CONZEMIUS, EDUARD
1932 Ethnographical Survey of the Miskito and Suma Indi-
ans of Honduras and Nicaragua. Bulletin, 106. Wash.,
D.C.: Smithsonian Institution, Bureau of American
Ethnology. 191 p. illus., plates, bibl.
See NICARAGUA for annotation.

Nicaragua

757 CONZEMIUS, EDUARD
1932 Ethnographical Survey of the Miskito and Suma Indians of Honduras and Nicaragua. Bulletin 106. Wash.,
D.C.: Smithsonian Institution, Bureau of American
Ethnology. 191 p. illus., plates, bibl.
Includes data on physical appearance and clothing;
division of labor, craft work; punishment for adultery;
various aspects of birth and child care; myths; marriage
and sexual relations; menstrual seclusion; quarrels
among women; women in trade for tools.

Ethnographic Monographs/Community Studies

Costa Rica

758   BIESANZ, JOHN and BIESANZ, MAVIS
          1944   Costa Rican Life.   N.Y.:   Columbia Univ. Press.
          272 p.   illus., map, plates, bibl.
             General observations on life in Costa Rica by American
          couple on exchange professorship with University of Costa
          Rica in early 1940's.   Women mentioned throughout text
          (religion, play, education, class and everyday living),
          but especially in chapters on courtship, marriage and
          family life.

759   STONE, DORIS Z.
          1962   The Talamancan Tribes of Costa Rica.   Papers of the
          Peabody Museum of Archaeology and Ethnology, Harvard
          Univ., vol. 43, no. 2.   Cambridge, Mass.:   The Peabody
          Museum.   108 p.   illus., map, plates, bibl.   Spanish
          version: 1961   Las tribus talamanqueñas de Costa Rica.
          San José, C.R.:   Edit. A. Lehmann, 1961.   209 p.   illus.,
          bibl.
             Fieldwork carried out (1956-59) among the Cabécares
          and Bribi, 2 indigenous groups of Costa Rica divided
          into matrilineal clans.   Information on women in reli-
          gion and magic, myths, dress and adornment, life cycle,
          and social organization.

760   _____.
          1949   The Borica of Costa Rica.   Papers of the Peabody
          Museum of American Archaeology and Ethnology, Harvard
          Univ., vol. 26, no. 2.   Cambridge, Mass.:   The Peabody
          Museum.   50 p.   illus., maps, tables, bibl.
             Based on 4 visits to Boruca Indians in southeast Costa
          Rica in early 1940's, includes information on dress and
          ornaments; weaving and pottery; the life cycle (birth,
          puberty, education, marriage, death); curanderas and
          folk medical practices; and 4 myths in which women
          figure.

Panama

761   BIESANZ, JOHN and BIESANZ, MAVIS
          1955   The People of Panama.   N.Y.:   Columbia Univ. Press.
          418 p.   illus., bibl.   Spanish version: 1961   Panamá y
          su pueblo.   Trans. by V. Pérez.   Mex., D.F.:   Edit.
          Letras.   308 p.
             General survey on Panama and its people includes much
          information on women in chapters on daily life, the
          family (rural, urban, West Indian black).

762   TORRES, REINA C.
        1958   "Aspectos culturales de los indios cunas." EEHA/AEA
        15:515-47. plates, bibl.
            Based on field research and secondary sources on the
        Cuna Indians of the San Blas Islands off Panama. In-
        cludes information on women's clothing and adornments,
        sexual division of labor, family, female puberty rites,
        etc.

763   TORRES de IANELLO, REINA
        1957   La mujer cuna de Panamá. Eds. especiales del III.
        Mex., D.F.: Inst. Indigenista Interamericano. 54 p.
        illus. Also in: 1956-57 III/AI 16:4:277-302; 17:1:
        9-38.
            Describes in detail the position of women in Cuna
        society from the time of birth through marriage, their
        status within the culture and religion, and their social
        life. Covers division of labor, pregnancy, relations
        with whites, illness, etc.

764   YOUNG, PHILIP D.
        1971   Ngawbe: Tradition and Change Among the Western
        Guaymí of Panama. Ill. Studies in Anthropology, 7.
        Urbana: Univ. of Ill. Press. 256 p. illus., tables,
        maps, bibl.
            Fieldwork conducted among Ngawbe (Chibchan-speaking
        Guaymí Indians) of Chiriquí Province, Panama (1964-65).
        Includes notes on post-marital residence, tradition,
        ideals and practice; division of labor, basic economic
        unit, household routine; traditional marriage arrange-
        ments, choosing a spouse, polygyny, levirate, sororate,
        divorce, exchange marriage; and the cult of Mama Chi.

SOUTH AMERICA

Venezuela

765   ARMELLADA, CESÁREO de
        1957   "The Woman's Place Among the Pemon Indians." BIND
        17:1:82-91.
            Member of Capuchin mission among the Pemon Indians of
        Venezuela describes women in terms of different stages
        of their life cycle: sweetheart, wife, sister, daughter,
        mother. Paints idyllic picture in which male/female
        relations are conducted with understanding rather than
        violence. In Spanish and English.

Ethnographic Monographs/Community Studies

766   CARMENES, NICOLÁS de
       1957 "Some Aspects of the Guayquirí Indian Woman's Life."
       BIND 17:2:185-89.
       Member of Capuchin mission comments on information on
       Guayaquirí women provided by Father Joseph Gumilla, 18c.
       Jesuit explorer of the Orinoco region, who observed that
       they led an insufferable slave existence and frequently
       practiced female infanticide to prevent daughters from
       having to suffer same kind of life. In English and
       Spanish.

767   WILBERT, JOHANNES
       1970 "Goajiro Kinship and the Eïruku Cycle." In The
       Social Anthropology of Latin America: Essays in Honor
       of Ralph Leon Beals, ed. by W. Goldschmidt and H. Hoijer,
       pp. 306-57. Los Angeles: Univ. of Ca., Latin American
       Center. bibl.
       See COLOMBIA for annotation.

Colombia

768   FALS BORDA, ORLANDO
       1955 Peasant Society in the Colombian Andes: A Socio-
       logical Study of Saució. Gainesville, Fla.: Univ. of
       Fla. 277 p. illus., maps, plates, tables, bibl.
       Spanish version: 1961 Campesinos de los Andes: estudio
       sociológico de Saució. Monografías Sociológicas, 7.
       Bogota: Univ. Nacional, Facultad de Sociología. 340 p.
       illus., bibl.
       Based on field research (1949-51) in Andean village
       of Saució, northeast of Bogota, includes information on
       female migrants, literacy, education, property, marriage,
       socialization, birth, and economic activity.

769   MOREY, ROBERT V.
       1972 "Notes on the Sáliva of Eastern Colombia." UC/CA
       13:1:144-47. tables, bibl.
       Based on short field trip (1965) among the Sáliva
       Indians of the Colombian plains, briefly describes mar-
       riage system: trial marriage is still practiced. Tables
       offer data on distribution of family type, age, sex,
       residence (uxorilocal, neolocal, patrilocal), marriage
       cases and duration.

770   ORTIZ de CASTRO, BLANCA
       1972 "Consideraciones sobre la mujer indígena colombiana."
       III/AI 32:4:1233-36.

South America - Colombia

Colombian delegate at the Seminario Sobre la Situación de la Mujer Indígena (Mexico, June 1972) compares position of indigenous women in Colombian tribes today as inferior to men and to Chibcha women in pre-historic times. Suggests that living conditions of indigenous groups be improved through the creation of effective community development programs which would raise their consciousness level in terms of self-pride, solidarity and traditions rather than through direct incorporation into national society.

771 REICHEL-DOLMATOFF, GERARDO and DUSSAN de REICHEL-DOLMATOFF, ALICIA
1961 The People of Aritama. The Cultural Personality of a Colombian Mestizo Village. Chicago: Univ. of Chicago Press. 482 p. tables, plates.
Study of people and institutions of a small mestizo village in northern Colombia contains great deal of information on women with regard to health, motherhood, socialization (infancy to adolescence), sexual relations, formal schooling, household composition, marriage and free union, interpersonal family relations, economic activities, beliefs regarding the body, midwifery, beliefs in the supernatural, witches, myths, abortion, etc. Women figure throughout text.

772 RICHARDSON, MILES
1970 San Pedro, Colombia. Small Town in a Developing Society. N.Y.: Holt, Rinehart and Winston. 98 p. illus., maps, bibl.
Based on field research (1962-63) in San Pedro, a small town in Colombia's Cauca Valley, includes references to women throughout text: types of families, family life, attitudes, economic activities, religious life (especially devotion to the Virgin).

773 WALDE-WALDEGG, HERMANN von
1936 "Notes on the Indians of the Llanos of Casanare and San Martín (Colombia)." PM 9:3:38-45.
Notes from a field trip (1932-33) in the Colombian plains: discusses practices of the Sáliva Indians regarding birth, circumcision for male and female infants, monogamy, succession, prohibition of prostitution (severe punishment by fasting, having one's womb cut out, or dwelling burned down, etc.).

774 WILBERT, JOHANNES
1970 "Goajiro Kinship and the Eïruku Cycle." In The Social Anthropology of Latin America: Essays in Honor

Ethnographic Monographs/Community Studies

of Ralph Leon Beals, ed. by W. Goldschmidt and H. Hoijer,
pp. 306-57. Los Angeles: Univ. of Ca, Latin American
Center. bibl.
Useful for understanding women's position in Guajiro
society. Describes the eĩruku (matrilineage) cycle;
kinship terms and relations (e.g., a brother has legal
power over his sister because he is the nearest male
relative of the same eĩruku); socialization of girls;
menstruation and blanqueo (isolation stage during
menstrual cycle); marriage; menopause.

775   WHITEFORD, ANDREW HUNTER
      1964 Two Cities of Latin America. A Comparative Descrip-
      tion of Social Classes. Anchor Books, A395. Garden
      City, N.Y.: Doubleday. 266 p. illus., bibl. Also:
      1960 Beloit College, Beloit, Wis. Logan Museum. Pub-
      lications in Anthropology. Bulletin, no. 9. Spanish
      version: 1963 Popayán y Querétaro; comparación de sus
      clases sociales. Trans. by F. C. Gregory. Monografías
      latinoamericanas, no. 1. Bogota: Univ. Nacional de
      Colombia, Facultad de Sociología.
      Research carried out in Popayán, Colombia and
      Querétaro, Mexico intermittently between 1949 and 1958.
      For each city describes occupations, activities and
      recreation, residences, and divisions within the upper,
      middle and lower classes; and discusses social mobility
      and inter-class relationships. Covers all aspects of
      women's situation in each class (appearance, religious
      and charitable functions, strict chaperonage, employment,
      health, education, etc.)

Ecuador

776   BARRETT, SAMUEL A.
      1925 The Cayapa Indians of Ecuador. Indian Notes and
      Monographs, 40. N.Y.: Museum of the American Indian,
      Heye Foundation. 2 vols. illus., map, tables, plates.
      Early study of the Cayapa Indians in Ecuadorian prov-
      ince of Esmeraldas, based on field research (1908-1909),
      contains notes on daily life; dress, ornaments, hair-
      style, body painting, field work and harvesting, sugar
      cane milling, canoeing, and pottery making, basketry,
      spinning and weaving; birth and puberty, and marriage.

777   HARNER, MICHAEL
      1972 The Jívaro: People of the Sacred Waterfalls.
      Garden City, N.J.: Doubleday/Natural History Press.
      233 p. illus., maps, bibl.

188

Based on field research (1956-57) among Jívaro
Indians of eastern Ecuador, who successfully resisted
the Spanish Conquest; with an epilogue from a 1969
visit. Includes notes on division of labor, household,
child rearing, visiting, parties, poisoning of men by
women, sexual offenses, inheritance, rise in adultery,
shortening of temporary matrilocal residence, clothing.

778 PARSONS, ELSIE CLEWS
     1945 Peguche. A Study of Andean Indians. Chicago:
     Univ. of Chicago Press. 225 p. illus., plates, bibl.
        Field work conducted among the Otovalo Indians of
     highland Ecuador, 1940-41. Includes notes on women as
     agriculturalists, potters, weavers and market vendors;
     in ritual, the life cycle, sickness and curing, male/
     female relations, tales, etc. Details provided for 1
     woman and her family. An appendix offers additional
     notes on all aspects of life in a particular parish,
     including lore about the reproductive cycle and typical
     activities and practices.

779 STIRLING, MATTHEW W.
     1938 Historical and Ethnographical Material on Jívaro
     Indians. Smithsonian Institution, Bureau of American
     Ethnology, Bulletin 117. Wash., D.C.: US Govt.
     Printing Office. 148 p. illus., plates, map, bibl.
        Based on field research (1930-31) among the head hunt-
     ing Jívaro Indians of eastern Ecuador, contains notes on
     women's pottery making, weaving, greeting customs; body
     piercing and painting, clothing and jewelry; marriage,
     childbirth, death; women's end of the house; duties and
     purchase of wives; women as burden bearers; burial cus-
     toms and desirable traits for women; role in war and
     agriculture.

780 VÁZQUEZ FULLER, BEATRIZ
     1974 "La mujer indígena." III/AI 34:3:663-75. illus.
        Simple outline of the different life stages of the
     Quichua women of highland Ecuador from birth and child-
     hood to marriage and motherhood. Lists most outstanding
     aspects of indigenous women's social and economic con-
     tributions to the family unit and community, considering
     her the guardian of cultural values.

781 WHITTEN, NORMAN E., JR.
     1965 Class, Kinship, and Power in an Ecuadorian Town.
     The Negroes of San Lorenzo. Stanford: Stanford Univ.
     Press. 238 p. maps, plates, bibl.

Ethnographic Monographs/Community Studies

Field research conducted among black population of
San Lorenzo, port town of northwest Ecuador, in 1961 and
1963. Includes notes on education of girls in upper and
middle classes; cash and subsistence economics in lower
class (sewing, gathering mussels, washing, cooking,
ironing, prostitution, singing and playing music, midwifery), typical daily activities and life style; and
on family, household and kinship (courtship, marriage,
residence, taboos, marital restrictions, preferential
marriage, nuclear family, serial polygyny and ritual
expressions of it, monogamy, types of households, child
rearing).

Peru

782   ADAMS, RICHARD N.
      1959 A Community in the Andes: Problems and Progress in
      Muquiquayo. American Ethnological Society, monograph
      31. Seattle: Univ. of Wash. Press. 251 p. tables,
      maps, bibl.
         Field research carried out in central Sierran *mestizo*
      and Indian community in Huancayo (1949-50). Includes
      information on women as seamstresses, spinners, market
      vendors; women in the home and their activities; women's
      clothing and costume; life cycle; recreation and
      celebrations.

783   DOUGHTY, PAUL L. and DOUGHTY, MARY F.
      1968 Huaylas: An Andean District in Search of Progress.
      Cornell Studies in Anthropology. Ithaca, N.Y.: Cornell
      Univ. Press. 284 p. illus., maps, tables, bibl.
         Based on field research (1960-61, 1962-64) in the
      Callejón de Huaylas, a *mestizo* community in highland
      Peru, including interviews with women. There is no
      separate life cycle or family chapter; refers to women
      throughout (education, religion, marriage, clothing,
      etc.). Women figure in tables on fertility and sex
      ratio, marital status, population, residence, literacy,
      land ownership, reasons for arrest, occupations.

784   ESCOBAR M., GABRIEL
      1967 Organización social y cultural del Sur del Perú.
      Serie: Antropologia Social, 7. Mex., D.F.: Inst.
      Indigenista Interamericano. 250 p. tables, bibl.
         In collaboration with R. P. Schaedel and O. Nuñez del
      Prado, and based in part on fieldwork in department of
      Puno, studies values system and institutional factors in
      indigenous culture. Discusses socialization or informal

traditional education; concepts of masculinity and femininity according to class; attitudes toward sex differences, distinction between male and female occupations, subordination of women to men; socioeconomic position of women in the family and in social classes (e.g., women as a factor in social mobility and change).

785 GILLIN, JOHN
       1947 Moche, a Peruvian Coastal Community. Smithsonian
     Institution, Inst. of Social Anthropology, Publication
     3. Wash., D.C.: US Govt. Printing Office. 166 p.
     illus., plates, map, tables, bibl.
       Based on 6 months (1944) field trip to Peruvian coastal
     community, including female native informants. Contains
     an account of women's domestic activities, and notes on
     clothing, hairstyles and jewelry; division of labor, own-
     ership and inheritance of property, finance and business
     dealings, and marketing; sex, love magic, aberrent incest
     and witchcraft, courtship, marriage, family and house-
     hold, prestige, and godmothers; curandera, pregnancy and
     childbirth. Also refers to milk saleswomen, fish mar-
     keting, participation in religious life, eating and
     drinking, spinning and weaving.

786 LLANQUE CHANA, DOMINGO
       1974 "La campesina en el altiplano aymará." BDSLM/CIDHAL
     4:2:43-52. Longer version: 1972 "La mujer campesina
     en el altiplano aymará." IPA/AP 4:101-19.
       Seven points summarize present situation of Aymará wo-
     men: a cultural environment which fosters subordination,
     timidity, passivity and suffering as essential feminine
     virtues; restriction to domestic sphere of activities
     and consequent isolation from outside world; cultural
     traditionalism and conservatism manifested in illiteracy,
     low level of education, monolingualism and consequent
     resistance to change; secondary role in exercising
     authority in family matters; exploitation in urban cen-
     ters through domestic service; new consciousness among
     young women to break with traditional restrictions.
     Believes that liberation for these women is greater
     schooling and consequent integration into national cul-
     ture. May be based on interviews and surveys conducted
     by Church.

787 No Entry.

788 SISKIND, JANET
       1973 To Hunt in the Morning. N.Y.: Oxford Univ. Press.
     214 p. illus., map, bibl. notes.

Ethnographic Monographs/Community Studies

Field research conducted among the patrilineal, matrilocal Sharanahua Indians along Peru's Upper Purús River
(1966-67, 68). Does not separate women out for a chapter on family life, but integrates them into entire text.
As a female, author was able to spend more time with the
women, but her participation was also limited in this
forest hunting-and-agricultural society.

789   VADILLO de ROMANÍ, AÍDA
      1969 "Papel e intervención de la mujer en la tecnología
      de la cultura yagua (resumen)." In Mesa Redonda de
      Ciencias Prehistóricas y Antropológicas, vol. 1,
      pp. 161-66. Lima: Pontificia Univ. Católica del Perú,
      Inst. Riva-Agüero, Seminario de Antropología. illus.,
      map, bibl.
      Based on personal observations and secondary sources,
      reviews various tasks fulfilled by women of the Yagua
      tribe in upper Amazon area near Iquitos, their status in
      and importance to the group, birth and puberty rites.
      Yagua women are active in and significant to the social,
      cultural, spiritual and productive life of the group.
      Illustrates how they serve as a principal agent in
      actualizing and conserving technical knowledge and
      cultural patterns.

790   ZAMALLOA GONZÁLES, ZULMA
      1972 "Ciclo vital en Sayllapata. Estudio de la cultura
      campesina del Distrito de Sayllapata. Provincia de
      Paucartambo (Cusco)." IPA/AP 4:21-32.
      Briefly describes customs and people who practice cer-
      tain skills related to the life cycle, as observed in
      Indian community in highland Peru. Covers 4 major
      stages: pregnancy and birth; infancy and adolescence;
      selecting a spouse; different kinds of marriage. Con-
      siders abortion, infanticide, courtship, precautions
      during pregnancy, etc.

Bolivia

791   BUECHLER, HANS C. and BUECHLER, JUDITH-MARÍA
      1971 The Bolivian Aymará. Case Studies in Cultural
      Anthropology. N.Y.: Holt, Rinehart and Winston. 114 p.
      illus., map. bibl.
      Based on fieldwork (1961-69) among the Bolivian Aymará,
      especially of Compi, Lake Titicaca. Includes information
      on market women, pregnancy and birth, boys and girls,
      education, family relations, etc.

South America - Bolivia

792 KARSTEN, RAFAEL
     1923 The Toba Indians of the Bolivian Gran Chaco. Acta
     Academiae Aboensis. Humaniora 4:4. Abo, Finland: Abo
     Akademi. 126 p. bibl. f/notes.
        Based on fieldwork (1911-12) among the Toba of Bolivia
     and the Toba Pilagás of Jujuy, Argentina. Includes in-
     formation on courtship and marriage, birth customs, abor-
     tion and infanticide, puberty rites, myths about women,
     female sorcerers, curing, the "tiger-dance," funeral and
     mourning customs.

793 LaBARRE, WESTON
     1948 The Aymará Indians of the Lake Titicaca Plateau,
     Bolivia, ed. by J. A. Mason and D. C. Donath. Memoir
     Series of the American Anthropological Assoc., 68.
     Menasha, Wis.: American Anthropological Assoc. 250 p.
     illus. Also as 1948 AAA/AA new series, 50:1 (part 2).
        Based on fieldwork among the Aymará in La Paz, Oruro,
     and Cochabamba areas (1937-38), includes some notes on
     birth, childhood, courtship, marriage, division of labor,
     clothing and textiles.

794 LLANQUE CHANA, DOMINGO
     1974 "La campesina en el altiplano aymará." BDSLM/CIDHAL
     4:2:43-52. Also in: 1972 "La mujer campesina en el
     altiplana aymará." IPA/AP 4:101-19.
     See PERU for annotation.

795 METRAUX, ALFRED
     1935 "La mujer en la vida social y religiosa de los
     indios chiriguano." UNT/RIE 3:1:145-66. bibl. notes.
        Based on field notes, primary and secondary sources
     on the Indians of the Gran Chaco, covers physical appear-
     ance, clothing and ornaments; division of labor, marriage
     practices, sexual mores, pregnancy and birth; role in
     war activities and magic-religious beliefs and practices;
     daily activities, etc.

796 RAMÍREZ CANSECO, TERESA
     1972 "La mujer campesina en Bolivia." III/AI 32:3:1025-27.
        Attempts to show, in brief and general way, principal
     characteristics of indigenous woman of Bolivia in her
     social, political and economic situation. Supposedly
     based on field notes and sources which are not cited.
     Does not cite which ethnic groups, location or
     methodology.

Ethnographic Monographs/Community Studies

797   STEARMAN, ALLYN MacLEAN
        1974   San Rafael, Camba Town.   Center for Latin American
        Studies.   Latin American Monographs, Series II, vol. 12,
        Gainesville, Fla.:   Univ. of Fla. Press.   126 p.   illus.,
        map, bibl.
             Based on a 4-year Peace Corps experience in the 1960's,
        recounts life in the village and surrounding area of
        San Rafael in the tropical eastern lowlands of Bolivia.
        Includes many observations on women's behavior and
        activities within the town and in the countryside.

798   PANE, IGNACIO A.
        1946   "La mujer guaraní."   In his Ensayos paraguayos,
        2nd ed., pp. 99-119.   Col. Panamericana, 24.   Buenos
        Aires: W. M. Jackson.
             Compendium of brief notes, based on 17c. and 19c.
        writings, praising Guaraní women of Paraguay: physical
        beauty, valor, work, right to divorce, role in religion
        and militarism, sexual relations, sacred prostitution,
        etc.

Paraguay

799   SERVICE, ELMAN R. and SERVICE, HELEN S.
        1954   Tobatí: Paraguayan Town.   Chicago: Univ. of Chicago
        Press.   337 p.   illus., maps, plates, tables, bibl.
             Based on field research (1948-49) in a mestizo town
        and an extensive bibliography of primary and secondary
        sources, provides information on women in parts 2, 3,
        and 4:   economic specialization, commerce and industry,
        standards of living; marriage, illegitimacy, household
        composition, everyday social life, ritual kinship; so-
        cialization, sex education, formal education, witchcraft,
        curanderas, menstruation, birth control, midwives,
        courtship, wedding ceremonies.   Appendix cites folk
        medicine treatment for menstruation and pregnancy.

Chile

800   FARON, LOUIS C.
        1969   Los mapuche: su estructura social.   Eds. Especiales,
        53.   Mex., D.F.:   Inst. Indigenista Interamericano.
        284 p.   illus., maps, bibl.   Also: 1961   Mapuche Social
        Structure: Institutional Reintegration in a Patrilineal
        Society of Central Chile.   Ill.   Studies in Anthropology,
        11.   Urbana, Ill.:   Univ. of Ill. Press.   247 p.   illus.,
        maps, bibl.

Based on fieldwork (1952-54) among the Mapuche Indians
in south central Chile, includes information on women of
the patrilineage (whom and when they marry, claims to
property rights, their general position, with examples
of an unmarried woman and a widow), uxorilocal residence,
position of married women; types of family organization,
husband/wife, mother/child, father/child, and sibling
relations; sexual experiences and attitudes, illicit
love affairs and illegitimate children, marriage preparations, secondary unions, separation and divorce; structure of matrilateral marriage, incest and exogamy, donors
and recipients of wives, competition for wives, etc.
Appendix A contains case examples of the composition and
change of 26 domestic units from 1910 to 1953.

801 _____.
    1968 The Mapuche Indians of Chile. Case Studies in Cul-
    tural Anthropology. N.Y.: Holt, Rinehart and Winston.
    113 p. illus., map, table, bibl.
    Condensed version of her earlier work on the Mapuche
    in south central Chile covers uxorilocal residence, sta-
    tus of married and unmarried women, Chilean and Mapuche
    views on illicit sexual relations, courtship, matrilateral
    marriage, marriage negotiations, secondary marriage,
    separation and divorce, family types, family interrela-
    tionships, socialization of children, employment; status,
    practices and training of shamans and sorcerer-witches
    (generally women).

802 HILGER, M. INEZ
    1957 Araucanian Child Life and Its Cultural Background.
    Smithsonian Miscellaneous Cols., 133. Wash., D.C.:
    The Smithsonian Institution. 439 p. illus., map,
    plates, tables, bibl.
    Based on fieldwork in Alepúe, Chile (1946-47) and
    Territorio Neuquén, Argentina (1951-52), provides impres-
    sive collection of data on many aspects of Araucanian
    Indian life: reproductive cycle, family relationships,
    sex differences in child and adult behavior, attitudes
    and socialization, domestic handicrafts, health, marriage,
    education, religious beliefs, witchcraft, etc. Extensive
    bibliography.

803 LOTHROP, SAMUEL KIRKLAND
    1928 The Indians of Tierra del Fuego. Contributions from
    the Museum of the American Indian, Heye Foundation, 10.
    N.Y.: Museum of the American Indian. 244 p. illus.,
    map, tables, plates, bibl.

195

Ethnographic Monographs/Community Studies

Based on fieldwork (summer of 1924-25) in settlements
of the Ona, Haush, Yahgan and Alacaluf Indians of Tierra
del Fuego, contains very little information on women,
noting only physical features, clothing, fishing, marriage, female masked spirit, canoeing, childbirth, and
initiation rites.

804   TITIEV, MISCHA
      1951 Araucanian Culture in Transition. Occasional Con-
      tributions from the Museum of Anthropology of the Univ.
      of Mich., 15. Ann Arbor: Univ. of Mich. Press. 164 p.
      illus., tables, maps, plates, bibl.
      Based on fieldwork (1948) among the Araucanian Indians
      in Cholchol, Chile, includes information on women through-
      out text: food habits, daily activities, kinship behav-
      ior, uni-local households, social composition, life
      cycle (pregnancy, birth, infancy, childhood, adolescence,
      premarital sex customs, courtship and marriage), witch-
      craft and curing practices.

Argentina

805   HILGER, M. INEZ
      1957 Araucanian Child Life and Its Cultural Background.
      Smithsonian Miscellaneous Collections, 133. Wash., D.C.:
      The Smithsonian Institution. 439 p. illus., maps,
      tables, plates, bibl.
      See CHILE for annotation.

CARIBBEAN

Puerto Rico

806   BUITRAGO ORTIZ, CARLOS
      1973 Esperanza: An Ethnographic Study of a Peasant Com-
      munity in Puerto Rico. Viking Fund Publications in
      Anthropology, no. 50. Tucson: Univ. of Arizona Press.
      217 p. illus., tables, maps, bibl.
      Fieldwork carried out in La Esperanza, Arecibo,
      Puerto Rico, 1962-63. Includes chapters on organization,
      composition and economy of a peasant household: husband-
      wife public and private roles, conflict, and routines,
      and female heads of household; on the individual's life
      cycle (including sexual patterns); on marriage; and
      notes on women's role in vigils. Concludes that family
      patterns are likely to move in direction of more formal

and de facto equality for women as they abandon traditional role through education, employment in industry,
and migration.

807   LA RUFFA, ANTHONY L.
      1971 San Cipriano. Life in a Puerto Rican Community.
      N.Y.: Gordon and Breach Science Publishers. 149 p.
      illus., map, tables, bibl.
        Based on fieldwork (1963-64) in predominantly black
      community, includes information on women in chapters on
      economics; structure and organization of community life
      (especially interpersonal relations in household); life
      cycle (pregnancy, birth, child rearing, education, ado-
      lescence, courtship, marriage, death); traditional
      approaches to the supernatural (religious associations,
      spiritualism, witchcraft); Protestantism; and
      Pentecostalism.

MARRIAGE AND THE FAMILY

This section covers procedures leading to the formation of the family (customs and ceremonies related to courtship, weddings, trial marriages, etc.); family structure or organization (monogamy, polygamy, consensual union, matrifocality, etc.); family life or dynamics (interspousal relations, parent/child relations, family roles, socialization of children, child behavior, divorce, etc.) Historical and economic aspects of the family (e.g., dowries) are included. This section includes accounts of family life by Oscar Lewis, but does not comment on the controversy surrounding his "culture of poverty" thesis. See instead discussions by Leacock[1] and Paddock.[2]

For much additional information on the family in indigenous and other ethnic groups, see ETHNOGRAPHIC MONOGRAPHS/COMMUNITY STUDIES; for role conflict, see PSYCHOLOGY; for the reproductive role of women, family planning, and sexual relations, see HUMAN SEXUALITY, REPRODUCTION, AND HEALTH; for references on women's legal status as a wife, see LAW. Studies on marriage, family, and divorce law are not included.

SPANISH AMERICA - GENERAL

808   CAMISA, ZULMA C.
         1971 La nupcialidad femenina en América Latina durante el
         período intercensal, 1950-1960. Serie AS, no. 10.
         San José, Costa Rica: CELADE, Subsede. 44 p. tables,
         graphs.
            Using census data and statistics on registered marriages for 15 countries, presents a statistical analysis

---

[1] Eleanor Burke Leacock, ed. The Culture of Poverty: A Critique.
N.Y.: Simon and Schuster, 1971.

[2] John Paddock, ed. Mesoamerican Notes 6(1965):1-144. The entire issue is dedicated to reviews and critiques of Oscar Lewis' works.

of female nuptiality by age groups, distinguishing
between legal and consensual unions, and 3 types
according to geographical region.

809   CARLOS, MANUEL L. and SELLERS, LOIS
        1972 "Family, Kinship Structure, and Modernization in
        Latin America." LARR 7:2:95-124. tables, bibl.
        Analysis of family and kinship patterns among differ-
        ent socio-economic groups in urban and rural LA. Male
        and female dominance and the literature in which they
        appear as themes are discussed and presented in 3 tables.
        Extensive bibliography.

810   COLUCCIO, FÉLIX
        1954 "Costumbres relativas al matrimonio en América."
        OAS/CSNI 5:30:252-61.
        Brief compendium of indigenous and mestizo marriage
        customs in Argentina, Peru, Bolivia, the Dominican
        Republic, Mexico and Panama, with a glossary of terms.

811   CORREDOR RODRÍGUEZ, BERTA
        1962 La familia en América Latina. Serie Socio-económica,
        5. Bogota: Oficina Internacional de Investigaciones
        Sociales de FERES. 141 p. tables, graphs, bibl.
        Part of a larger study on social and religious change
        in LA carried out between 1958 and 1961 by research cen-
        ters in Europe and LA. Considers family structure,
        functions and problems in urban and rural areas. Based
        on census data, laws, and secondary sources. Conclu-
        sions regarding consensual unions and illegitimacy
        reflect religious concerns of investigation (e.g.
        although economic, cultural and social factors determine
        high rate of non-Church marriages, the scarcity of rural
        priests in also influential).

812   GONZÁLEZ, ELDA R. and MELLAFE, ROLANDO
        1965 "La función de la familia en la historia social
        hispano-americana colonial." UN-LIIH/A 8:57-71. bibl.
        f/notes.
        Based on archival research and primary and secondary
        sources, analyzes the interrelationship among the struc-
        tures of power, social strata and the family in colonial
        America. The integral role of women of all races and
        classes in this interaction is noted throughout. Point
        of departure is that the family is the nucleus which
        experiences the repercussions of significant economic
        and social changes.

Marriage and the Family

813   GUERRERO C., JULIÁN N.
        1958 "El matrimonio entre los aborígenes centroamericanos."
        MIIN/NI 3:21:31-39.
            Based on early chronicles, presents general picture of
        marriage among the indigenous peoples of Central Amer-
        ica: concept of, age at, impediments to, ceremony, and
        divorce. Notes that kings and chiefs practiced excep-
        tions to the rules.

814   MARTIN, M. KAY
        1969 "South American Foragers: A Case Study in Cultural
        Devolution." AAA/AA 71:2:243-60. tables, bibl.
            Using Steward and Faron's data on 33 hunting and
        gathering societies in SA, challenged typologies classi-
        fying such groups on the basis of patrilocal residence
        and/or patrilineal residence patterns by demonstrating
        high incidence of matriliny and matrilocality. The
        latter emphasizes economic predominance of women. Con-
        cludes that need exists to evaluate benefits and disad-
        vantages of patrilocal and matrilocal residence patterns
        according to ecological and inter-societal adaptation
        so that typology be universally applicable.

815   NUTINI, HUGO G.
        1967 "A Synoptic Comparison of Mesoamerican Marriage and
        Family Structure." UNM/SWJA 23:4:383-404. bibl.
            Presents "a synoptic comparison of marriage and the
        family in Mesoamerica, with special attention to house-
        hold composition, nuclear and extended family arrange-
        ments, marriage and divorce, polygyny and marriage
        regulations, and residence and the spatial components of
        marriage and the family." Consulted 49 sources (mono-
        graphs and articles); analyzed 27 for comparative pur-
        poses. Points out inadequacy of ethnographic coverage
        in this area of study.

816   STEPHENS, WILLIAM N.
        1963 The Family in Cross-Cultural Perspective. N.Y.:
        Holt, Rinehart and Winston. 460 p. tables, bibl.
            Based on an extensive bibliography of mostly anthropo-
        logical literature on family customs and interviews with
        ethnographers, presents comprehensive survey of various
        aspects of the family.

817   TERÁN, JUAN BAUTISTA
        1927 "La mujer y la familia en la conquista de América."
        In his El nacimiento de la América española, pp. 71-92.
        Tucumán, Arg.: M. Violetto y cía. bibl. notes.

Main point is that *mestizaje* took place as soon as the conquest began. Because of the lack of Spanish women, the formation of the American family became the responsibility of Indian, and then *mestizo* women. Chapter notes, revealing primary and secondary sources (documents, chronicles, etc.), yield much additional valuable information on the few early Spanish women, how many Spaniards married women of other races, kinds of relationships, etc.

818 TORRES-RIOSECO, ARTURO
     1959 "The Family in Latin America." In The Family: Its
     Function and Destiny, rev. ed. by R. N. Ashen, pp. 85-
     103. Science of Culture Series, 5. N.Y.: Harper and
     Bros.
        Notes on Iberian origins of the Latin American family
     since colonial times, powerful influence of the Catholic
     Church, and evolution of the modern (pre-World War II)
     family brought on by changing economic conditions since
     the 19c. Believes North American home will increasingly
     serve as LA's model for the future.

819 VEGA, JUAN RAMÓN
     1972 "El concubinato de la población indígena." BDSLM/
     CIDHAL 2:3:51-59.
        Excerpts from article in Estudios Centroamericanos
     (El Salvador, 1970) discuss free union relationships
     among the indigenous population of CA, citing historical-
     institutional factors and indigenous marriage practices,
     and suggesting a policy for family integration.

820 WILLIAMSON, ROBERT C.
     1970 "Role Themes in Latin America." In Sex Roles in
     Changing Society, ed. by G. H. Seward, pp. 177-200.
     N.Y.: Random House. bibl.
        Generalizations on courtship and mate selection,
     marriage patterns, sex roles as reflected in literature,
     kinship and occupational roles, *machismo*, attitudes,
     prevailing value orientations, etc., based on survey of
     works published from 1946 to 1968. Concludes that "the
     advance of women can only proceed with other basic
     changes . . ." which are enumerated.

821 YAUKEY, DAVID and THORSEN, TIMM
     1972 "Differential Female Age at First Marriage in Six
     Latin American Cities." WRU/JMF 34:2:375-79. tables,
     bibl.
        Based on CELADE fertility survey data (1964), notes
     that better-educated women state a later ideal age for

Marriage and the Family

first marriage with a corresponding pattern of marrying later. Consensual unions were associated with low education and rural origins, occurring at an earlier age than legal first marriages.

822 YAUKEY, DAVID; THORSEN, TIMM and ONAKA, ALVIN T.
1972 "Marriage at an Earlier Than Ideal Age in Six Latin American Capital Cities." LSE/PS 26:2:263-72. tables.
Reports same findings as article by Yaukey and Thorsen.

823 YOUSSEF, NADIA HAGGAG
1973 "Cultural Ideals, Feminine Behavior and Family Control." CSSH 15:3:326-47.
As an explanation of the discrepancy between ideal and real female behavior in LA, highlights the importance of the structural context in which family behavior takes place. Discusses impact of the Spanish conquest, influence of the Catholic clergy, and situational circumstances for lower and upper classes. Believes wider range of alternative patterns of behavior exists for and is utilized by Latin American women.

MIDDLE AMERICA

Mexico

824 BAER, PHILLIP and BAER, MARY
1949 "Notes on Lacandon Marriage." UNM/SWJA 5:2:101-06.
Data gathered in Pethá region of eastern Chiapas, Mexico among 3 families on courtship, marriage ceremony, permitted and nonpermitted marriages, general attitudes toward marriage, divorce and separation, family life. Polygymy is practiced. Includes English and Lacandon text of conversation between suitor and father for girl's hand.

825 BARBA de PIÑA CHAN, BEATRIZ
1960 "Bosquejo socio-económico de un grupo de familias de la ciudad de México." INAH/A 11:40:87-152. tables.
Detailed study on home and family life of 200 Mexican families concentrates on 4 aspects: economy, education of children, problem of hygiene, nature of family integration. Findings, presented in 56 tables, indicate women have a tendency to start and leave work sooner than men; more men than women are atheists; men are more mobile demographically than women.

826   BERMÚDEZ, MARÍA ELVIRA
        1955 La vida familiar del mexicano. Mexico y lo mexicano,
        20. Mex., D.F.: Antigua Librería Robredo. 142 p.
        Based on personal observations, literary and folkloric
        sources, studies family life among Mexican peasants,
        workers and members of the middle and upper classes,
        looking into the influence of history, economics, reli-
        gion and public opinion on attitudes and modes of behav-
        ior. Focuses on male/female relations and roles,
        especially the exaggeration of masculine and feminine
        traits in *machismo* and *hembrismo*.

827   BORAH, WOODROW and COOK, SHERBURNE F.
        1966 "Marriage and Legitimacy in Mexican Culture: Mexico
        and California." CLR 54:1:946-1008. tables.
        Examination of Mexican law and custom as well as of
        experience in California questions whether higher per-
        centage of informal unions among Mexican-Americans is a
        characteristic of poverty shared with other low-income
        groups or a carryover of patterns in Mexican culture.
        Part 1 is lengthy, historical investigation of marriage
        and legitimacy patterns in Mexico (origins, earlier
        forms, present-day features). Part 2 examines character-
        istics found among Mexican-Americans in Santa Clara
        County, California.

828   BRANDES, STANLEY H.
        1968 "Tzintzuntzan Wedding: A Study in Cultural Complex-
        ity." KAS/P 39:30-53.
        Examines interrelationship of ideals, expectations and
        reality in peasant wedding in Michoacán village. Dis-
        tinguishes predominant forces causing difference between
        ideals/expectations and reality of social life. Outlines
        outstanding features of a wedding, using one as a case
        study.

829   BUSHNELL, JOHN H. and BUSHNELL, DONNA D.
        1971 "Sociocultural and Psychodynamic Correlates of Poly-
        gyny in a Highland Mexican Village." UP/E 10:1:44-55.
        table, bibl.
        Based on fieldwork (1950-51, 1967) in San Juan Atzingo,
        a village in south central Mexico, examines several
        social, cultural, economic and historical variables rele-
        vant to state of polygyny there and considers some poten-
        tial determinants of it. Hypothesizes that polygyny
        serves as a "cultural arena for the re-enactment of" an
        individual's early psychological trauma in which a new-
        born sibling supplants child's central position with
        mother. On a symbolic level, polygyny insures men with

Marriage and the Family

constant mother figure. Epilogue provides additional
case studies from subsequent field trip in 1970 to
support hypothesis.

830   CANCIAN, FRANCESCA M.
1966   "Patrones de interacción en las familias
Zinacantecas." In Los zinacantecos: un pueblo tzotzil
de los altos de Chiapas, ed. by E. Z. Vogt, pp. 251-74.
Col. de Antropología Social, 7. Mex., D.F.: Instituto
Nacional Indigenista. tables, bibl. f/notes.
Spanish translation of article in American Sociological
Review 29:4(1964):540-50. See #832.

831   _____.
1965   "The Effect of Patrilocal Households on Nuclear
Family Interaction in Zinacantan." CEM/ECM 5:300-15.
tables.
Through a comparison of interaction patterns of 5
neolocal and 5 patrilocal households in Zinacantan,
Chiapas, Mexico, accurately predicted that mother and
children would react to paternal grandmother with more
hostility and authoritarianism in patrilocal than in
neolocal households. Proved that differences among 5
grandmothers were related to differences among 5 sets of
mother and children in patrilocal homes. Concludes that
residence rules significantly affect behavior patterns
in household. Reports additional unexpected findings
on dominance and affection among children and on social
contact among household members.

832   _____.
1964   "Interaction Patterns in Zinacanteco Families."
ASS/ASR 29:4:540-50. tables, bibl. f/notes.
Based on doctoral dissertation, "Family Interaction in
Zinacantan" (Harvard, 1963). Observed interaction patterns in 10 Indian families in Zinacantan, Chiapas,
Mexico to test 6 hypotheses of a theory on small group
research. Confirms predictions that within family
dyads 1) affection elicits affection; 2) dominance
elicits submission; and all members within family will
demonstrate 3) same degree of affection and 4) same
degree of dominance-submission. Does not confirm interaction role predictions. Describes typical household.

833   CARRASCO, PEDRO
1969   "Parentesco y regulación del matrimonio entre los
indios del antiguo Michoacán, México." UM/REAA 4:219-22.
bibl.

Provides Latin transcription and Spanish translation
from Fray Juan Focher's Enchiridion baptismi adultorum
et matrimonii baptisandorum (Tzintzuntzan, 1544) regarding marriage regulations in pre-Hispanic Michoacán: a
woman could marry her paternal or maternal uncle while
a man was not permitted to marry his aunt. Contrary to
the Relación de Michoacán, there is no evidence that
this rule is associated with either matrilineality or
patrilineality among the Tarascans.

834 CARSCH, H.
1957-1958 "The Family, Child Rearing and Social Controls
Among the Aztecs." IAL/R 3:1/2:8-21.
General notes on child rearing, family and social controls in Aztec society derived from secondary sources
and Bandelier English version of Sahagún's writings.
Briefly refers to women regarding breast feeding,
divorce, concubinage, polygyny.

835 COLLIER, JANE FISHBURNE
1968 "Courtship and Marriage in Zinacantan, Chiapas,
Mexico." In Contemporary Latin American Culture, by
M. S. Edmunson, C. Madsen, and J. F. Collier, pp. 139-
201. Middle American Research Inst., Publication 25.
New Orleans: Tulane Univ.
Report based on series of 18 formal interviews during
1961 with 8 Zinacantecan informants and on direct observation. Discusses the beginning of a courtship, the
paying of bride-price, house-entering and presentation
ceremonies, wedding preparations, wedding, other forms
of marriage, divorce and the breaking of courtship, and
practices in other Tzotzil and Tzeltal communities in
Chiapas. Appendix includes case studies.

836 _____.
1966 "El noviazgo zinacanteco como transición económica."
In Los zinacantecos: un pueblo tzotzil de los altos de
Chiapas, ed. by E. Z. Vogt, pp. 235-50. Col. de
Antropología Social, 7. Mex., D.F.: Instituto Nacional
Indigenista.
Based on field research (1961, 1963), describes long
(generally 2 years) process of courtship in Zinacantan,
Chiapas, Mexico, which is viewed as an economic transaction, especially by court which resolves disputes
occurring during it. Raising a girl is an investment
to be paid for by future spouse; when engagement is
broken, money must be returned by father.

Marriage and the Family

837   CROMWELL, RONALD E.; CORRALES, RAMÓN and TORSIELLO, PETER M.
      1973 "Normative Patterns of Marital Decision Making
      Power and Influence in Mexico and the United States:
      A Partial Test of Resource and Ideology Theory." CFS/J
      4:2:177-96. tables, bibl.
          Discusses major self-report studies, "resource theory"
      and "ideology theory," and normative expectations. Anal-
      yses selected cross-cultural self-report responses from
      husbands and wives in conjugal pairs in Mexico and US
      to test hypotheses about marital and family power struc-
      ture. Findings indicate general and consistent trend
      toward egalitarianism. Cites María Elu de Lenero's
      ¿Hacia donde va la mujer mexicana? (#844) as only major
      work on this subject to appear in Mexico.

838   de HOYOS, ARTURO and de HOYOS, GENEVIEVE
      1966 "The Amigo System and Alienation of the Wife in the
      Conjugal Mexican Family." In Kinship and Family Organi-
      zation, ed. by B. Farber, pp. 102-15. N.Y.: J. Wiley
      and Sons.
          Carried out among individuals of various classes in
      Ciudad Juárez, demonstrates how a husband's participation
      in the amigo (friend) system after marriage can alienate
      wife. Describes prevalence of some characteristics of
      conjugal families in which this system persists.

839   DELGADO, JAIME
      1969 "El amor en la América prehispánica." IGFO/RI 29:
      115/118:151-71.
          Based on Sahagún's writings, discusses differences in
      socialization of Aztec girls and boys. True love was
      impeded by pedagogical system and customs and is almost
      entirely absent as a theme in Nahuatl literature,
      although it does appear in 3 poems of the Cancionero
      Otomí and in process leading to marriage among Aztecs.
      Mentions several goddesses, courtesans, and polygamy.
      Compares Aztecs, Mayans and Incas, noting abundance of
      love lyrics on Quechua literature as indication of
      greater importance given to love and sexual relations
      among Incas. Secondary sources.

840   DÍAZ, MAY N.
      1964 "Opposition and Alliance in a Mexican Town." UP/E
      3:2:179-84.
          Examines how a political alliance is formed by a mar-
      riage. Describes and analyzes marriage procedures in
      pottery village near Guadalajara--abduction (robo) as
      well as traditional marriage--and how they lead to a
      temporary truce between opposing quarters of town.

841   DÍAZ-GUERRERO, ROGELIO
       1972   "Una escala factorial de premisas historico-
       socioculturales de la familia mexicana." SIP/RIP 6:3/4:
       235-44. tables, bibl.
          A principal axis factor analysis of the results of a
       questionnaire administered to 190 secondary school stu-
       dents divided by 3 age groups, 2 social classes and sex
       in Mexico City yielded only 1 factor--the traditionalism
       of the Mexican family. Typical questions included: Is
       your mother the person you love the most? Is woman's
       place in the home? In comparison to earlier studies
       girls appeared to respond more assertively.

842   _____.
       1955   "Neurosis and the Mexican Family Structure." AJP
       6:112:411-17. tables, bibl.
          Describes dominant Mexican family pattern, which is
       based on the unquestioned and absolute supremacy of
       father and necessary and absolute self-sacrifice of
       mother. Compares socialization of boys and girls and
       sex roles in the family, demonstrating that role playing
       closely follows role expectations.

843   "Divorce à la Yucatán"
       1929   Nation 129:3351:318.
          In spite of ease in obtaining a divorce in Yucatán and
       Morelos, tradition and religion play a more important
       role in binding marriage among the Mexican aristocracy
       and bourgeoisie. Women have shaky legal standing,
       difficulty in collecting alimony, and face hostile public
       opinion.

844   ELU de LEÑERO, MARÍA del CARMEN
       1969   ¿Hacia dónde va la mujer mexicana? Proyecciones a
       partir de los datos de una encuesta nacional. Mex.,
       D.F.: Inst. Mexicano de Estudios Sociales. 203 p.
       tables, bibl. f/notes.
          Reports results of survey conducted in 1966-67 among
       5,410 husbands and wives in 15 rural and urban Mexican
       communities, exploring variables of age, urban-rural
       residence, education, class, and religion. Discusses
       concept of "masculine" and "feminine" according to tra-
       ditional stereotypes, cultural values, family planning,
       decisionmaking, happiness of married women, etc. Con-
       cludes in favor of furthering women's total development
       for full participation in social life of Mexico, discuss-
       ing how it should be carried out. Important study.

Marriage and the Family

845 ESTEVA FABREGAT, CLAUDIO
1969 "Ethics of Authority in the Mexican Family." In
VIIIth International Congress of Anthropological and
Ethnological Sciences. Tokyo and Kyoto, 1968.
Proceedings, vol. 2, pp. 358-59. Tokyo: Science Council
of Japan.
Based on research carried out in the Federal District,
including Mexico City (1952-56), and in other parts of
Mexico, among different social groups, using a questionnaire related to character orientation and prevalent
values in family relationship. Concludes that pattern
of authority in family is patriarchal and internal organization is patrifocal; the natural role of women is
identified by weakness.

846 _____.
1969 "Familia y matrimonio en México: el patrón
cultural." IGFO/RI 29:115/118:173-278.
Attempts to present comprehensive cultural model of
family and marriage among several social classes in
Mexico, based on 16 years' residence there and data from
questionnaire administered to 88 men and women in 1952-
56. Lengthy discussion of family organization and structure includes much information on women: choice of
spouse, age at time of marriage, economic functions,
sexual relations, roles and status, power and prestige,
authority, etc. Concludes that social change is dimin-
ishing importance of family and marriage as forms of
living together while accentuating social and economic
functions which take place outside the home; result is
breakdown of strong family ties of obligation.

847 FERNÁNDEZ-MARINA, RAMÓN; MALDONADO SIERRA, EDUARDO D. and
TRENT, RICHARD D.
1958 "Three Basic Themes in Mexican and Puerto Rican
Family Values." JSP 48(2nd half):167-81.
Survey taken at University of Puerto Rico (1957)
among 494 middle class unmarried teenagers explores
extent to which family values in Puerto Rico have changed
from those in Mexico, as set forth by Díaz-Guerrero.
Primary themes include family values associated with
patterns of affection and of authority, and differential
evaluation of status of males and females.

848 FINLEY, GORDON E. and LAYNE, OTIS
1971 "Play Behavior in Young Children: A Cross-Cultural
Study." JGP 119:2:203-10. tables, bibl.
Explores 3 interdependent classes of children's early
play behavior. 8 boys and 8 girls were tested at age 1,

2 and 3 among Mayan Indians of Yucatán and in Cambridge, Mass. In terms of sex differences, results were not significant for play activity, visual exploration or mother contact and proximity. However, girls did touch their mothers more than boys did. Age differences were less systematic and significant than cultural differences.

849   FOLAN, WILLIAM J. and WEIGAND, PHIL C.
       1968 "Fictive Widowhood in Rural and Urban Mexico."
       CRCA/A 10:1:119-27.
          Preliminary report describes phenomenon of "fictive
       widowhood" (husband actually living) as practiced in
       rural areas of Jalisco and in Mexico City. 4 case his-
       tories demonstrate how women who want to start a new
       career or form of life, or single mothers, can do so by
       assuming role of widow.

850   FRIED, JACOB
       1961 "An Interpretation of Tarahumara Interpersonal Rela-
       tions." CUA/AQ 34:2:110-20.
          Based on fieldwork in Sierra Madre of Chihuahua in
       1971, describes patterning and texture of interpersonal
       processes in Tarahumara culture. Analyzes structural
       weaknesses and interpersonal stresses in nuclear family;
       tactics and style of inner-family conflict; wide situa-
       tional variability and need for flexibility in applying
       ideal norms; outstanding characteristics of Tarahumara
       temperament; conflict between group and individualistic
       orientations. At community level, culture appears work-
       able, but at interpersonal level unstable aspects of
       life situations lead to difficulties and conflicts
       through suspicion, hostility and insecurity.

851   _____.
       1953 "The Relations of Ideal Norms to Actual Behavior in
       Tarahumara Society." UNM/SWJA 9:3:286-95.
          Focuses on problem of variance from ideal norms among
       Tarahumara of Chihuahua. Illustrates with 3 common
       types of interpersonal conflicts with the family: sex-
       ual division of labor, divorce, child punishment. Con-
       cludes that latent concept of rigid legal aspect of
       ideal standards permits flexibility of behavior. Sanc-
       tion is incurred only for unresolvable problems: e.g.,
       if a man or woman deserts spouse for no valid reason,
       depriving other one of certain services, a complaint is
       made to native official to elicit direct action. Based
       on field research, 1950-51.

Marriage and the Family

852 HAYNER, NORMAN S.
         1954 "The Family in Mexico." JMFL 16:4:369-73.
         Summarizes old traditions and changing patterns in
         women's position in Mexico in terms of education, em-
         ployment, courtship, marriage and divorce, family cus-
         toms. Notes new attitudes and rural/urban differences.
         Male domination crosses class lines, though class
         differences exist.

853 _____.
         1942 "Notes on the Changing Mexican Family." JMFL
         7:4:489-97.
         Describes upper class family behavior in a provincial
         Mexican city; includes notes about agricultural village
         life and life in Mexico City. Three features of upper
         class Mexican life are subordination and domestication
         of women, chaperonage of unmarried girls, and keeping
         mistresses.

854 HORCASITAS, FERNANDO
         1965 "La boda en Ameyaltepec. Un texto guerrerense."
         UNAM/ECN 5:123-27.
         Transcription in Nahuatl and Spanish of an informant's
         brief account of courting practices and wedding proce-
         dures in his village (Ameyaltepec, Guerrero, 1964).

855 HOTCHKISS, JOHN C.
         1967 "Children and Conduct in a Ladino Community of
         Chiapas, Mexico." AAA/AA 69:6:711-18.
         In Teopisca children's behavior has an integral place
         in the community's system of conduct. Boys and girls
         run errands for adults concerned with maintaining their
         reputation, protecting their role, and ensuring privacy
         in their affairs: e.g., a woman who wishes to avoid
         embarrassment in borrowing food, can send a child. Older
         women often interrogate little girls for information.

856 HUMPHREY, NORMAN DAVID
         1952 "Family Patterns in a Mexican Middletown." SSR
         26:2:195-201.
         Study of sociocultural family patterns in Tecolotlán,
         Jalisco. Discusses family size, type of sanction for
         marriage, sex roles, children, extramarital relation-
         ships, pregnancy and childbirth, etc.

857 LEÑERO OTERO, LUIS
         1968 Investigación de la familia en México. Presentación
         y avance de resultados de una encuesta nacional. Mex.,
         D.F.: Inst. Mexicano de Estudios Sociales. 360 p. bibl.

Part 1 describes investigation from its theoretical
and methodological aspects to processing and analysis
of data. Part 2 presents findings of questionnaires
administered to Mexican families and public leaders on
marital integration, family planning, and development.
Provides data on family relations and problems. Appendix
includes questionnaire for women.

858   LEÓN-PORTILLA, MIGUEL
      1967 "La institución de la familia náhuatl prehispánica.
      Un antecedente cultural." CAM 64:5:143-61.
         Documented account of the family in pre-Hispanic
      central Mexico discusses ideal figures of mother and
      father, importance of children, etc.

859   _____.
      1961 "Consejos de un padre náhuatl a su hija." III/AI
      21:4:339-43. Also as: 1960 "La educación del niño
      entre los nahoas: consejos a una niña náhuatl."
      MIIN/NI 3:31:14-18.
         Spanish translation of complete version of one of the
      huehuetlatolli (moral counsel of elders), folios 74v-
      84r of Florentine Codex, compiled by Sahagún in 16c.
      Classic text contains 36 items of advice given to
      daughter by parents on her role in upper-class Aztec
      society as devout, virtuous, noble, and honorable woman.

860   LEWIS, OSCAR
      1964 Pedro Martínez: A Mexican Peasant and His Family.
      N.Y.: Random House. 507 p. illus.
         Tape-recorded account of Mexican peasant family as
      told by Pedro, the father, Esperanza, the mother, and
      Felipe, eldest son provides insight into thoughts, ac-
      tivities, and interaction of family members.

861   _____.
      1961 The Children of Sánchez: Autobiography of a Mexican
      Family. N.Y.: Random House. 499 p.
         Autobiography of a working-class family living in a
      Mexico City tenement slum related by family members
      themselves: Jesús Sánchez, father; Manuel and Roberto,
      his two sons; Consuelo and Marta, his two daughters.

862   _____.
      1959 "Family Dynamics in a Mexican Village." JMFL
      21:3:218-26.
         Compares internal structure, psychodynamics and person-
      ality development in the Rojas and Martínez families
      (of whom more extensive studies were made later on) in

Marriage and the Family

peasant community near Mexico City. One family is
strictly father-directed; the other family life revolves
around the mother.

863   _____.
1959 Five Families: Mexican Case Studies in the Culture
of Poverty. N.Y.: Basic Books. 351 p. illus., bibl.
An account of the daily lives of cross-section of
Mexican families, based on fieldwork (late 1940's,
1950's) in peasant village of Tepotzlán, and slum tenement, new working-class housing development, and upper-
class residential district, all in Mexico City. Narrates
intimate details of family members' activities, especially of the women.

864   _____.
1959 "La cultura de vecindad en la Ciudad de México."
UNAM/CPS 5:17:350-64. tables, bibl.
Preliminary observations of 2 working class neighborhoods in Mexico City (1956-57) illustrate common factors
as well as differences between them: physical and economic aspects, family structure, education, etc. Suggests women play crucial role in family relations in
spite of *machismo* cult and emphasis on male superiority
and dominance. Sees possible cause as frequent abandonment of women and prevalence of "*casa chica*," both
indicative of father's general absence.

865   _____.
1953 "Husbands and Wives in a Mexican Village: A Study
of Role Conflict." In Readings in Latin American Social
Organization and Institutions, ed. by O. Leonard and
C. Loomis, pp. 23-27. East Lansing: Mich. State College
Press. Also in: 1949 AAA/AA 51:4:602-10.
Points out discrepancy between ideal and actual behavior of women and men in peasant village of Tepotzlán and
conflict, tension, and maladjustment which characterize
interpersonal relations. Outward compliance by women is
somewhat superficial, conforming, and formal, for there
are actually few homes in which husband truly dominates
his family.

866   LEWIS, OSCAR and LEWIS, RUTH
1956 "One Day in the Life of a Mexican Family." JMFL
18:1:3-13.
Suggests intensive family studies as another approach
to presenting scientific data on people and their culture without losing a sense of the individual--ethno-
graphic realism. Describes one day in life of peasant

Mexican family based on family members' own autobiographical statements: interaction, activities, and problems.

867 LOMNITZ, LARISSA
     1973 "La mujer marginada de México." CM/D 9:6(54):29-31.
     General sketch of women who live in *barriadas* in
     Mexico. Describes daily round of activities (housework,
     social relations, tv and radio, visits to Church or
     relatives, shopping); conjugal relations; male/female
     roles. Concludes that because their role is essential
     to social and family structure and because their eco-
     nomic contribution gives them greater emotional and
     economic independence, working-class women appear less
     alienated than middle-class women.

868 LOVE, EDGAR F.
     1971 "Marriage Patterns of Persons of African Descent in
     Mexico City." HAHR 51:1:79-91.
     Using colonial parish records of Santa Veracruz, Mex-
     ico City, analyzes marriages in which one or both per-
     sons were of African descent from 1646 to 1746 to
     determine to what extent black slaves tended to marry
     other black slaves rather than persons of other ethnic
     groups or legal status; whether free blacks tended to
     marry within or outside their racial groups and from
     which racial groups mates were chosen; to what extent
     Spaniards and blacks married; etc.

869 McGINN, NOEL F.
     1966 "Marriage and Family in Middle-Class Mexico."
     WRU/JMF 28:3:305-13.
     Describes middle-class marriage and family roles in
     Mexico. Attempts to demonstrate how culturally defined
     ideals of male and female roles in courtship influence
     marital relations. Argues that break with such role
     expectations appears in child-rearing practices, which
     then lead to a male-female role dichotomy; that, in
     turn, perpetuates the cycle.

870 MADSEN, MILLARD C. and KAGAN, SPENCER
     1973 "Mother-Directed Achievement of Children in Two
     Cultures." CCP/J 4:2:221-28. table, bibl.
     Twelve mother-child (equal number of boys and girls)
     pairs engaged in 2 experiments in which mothers chose
     achievement goals or decided upon distribution of rewards
     for their child's achievement. No significant differences
     found between mother-daughter and mother-son pairs, but
     Los Angeles mothers encouraged motivation for high

Marriage and the Family

achievement by rewarding successes, withholding rewards
for failure, and choosing harder targets while Mexican
(Baja Californian) mothers rewarded children less con-
ditionally and geared their own expectations according
to child's ability. Socio-economic factors not
controlled.

871 MARTÍNEZ DOMÍNGUEZ, GUILLERMO
     1949 "La familia mexicana." UNAM/RMS 11:3:337-53.
     tables, graphs.
         Using 1930 and 1940 census data, computes average
     Mexican family. For 1940 2 tables indicate sex of head
     of household: women headed more households with fewer
     children, but men outnumbered women as household head
     on all levels; notes increase in former.

872 METZGER, DUANE and WILLIAMS, GERALD E.
     1963 "A Formal Ethnographic Analysis of Tenejapa Ladino
     Weddings." AAA/AA 65:5:1076-1101.
         Describes wedding ceremonies among Ladino population
     of Tenejapa, Chiapas, in terms of ways in which people
     perceive their weddings to differ in form, and kinds of
     inferences they draw on basis of one form occurring
     over another in a particular wedding. A wedding con-
     sists of a series of well-defined ceremonies which take
     place after initial *pedida* (request for hand of woman).

873 MINTURN, LEIGH, et al.
     1964 Mothers of Six Cultures - Antecedents of Child
     Rearing. N.Y.: John Wiley and Sons. 351 p. tables,
     bibl.
         Sequel to Six Cultures - Studies of Child Rearing,
     edited by B. Whiting, uses factor analysis to determine
     differences in socialization practices employed by
     mothers in 6 rural communities, 1 of them Juxtlahuacan,
     Mexico. Based on interviews with Mixtecan mothers, con-
     cludes that they evidence extreme positions on warmth
     and punishment for peer-directed aggression, possibly as
     a result of intimate social ties with other adult members
     of the Indian community. Other factors considered are
     responsibility training, emotional instability of mother,
     proportion of time mother cared for baby and cares for
     child, and training in mother-directed aggression. Notes
     that chores become sex-typed after age of 6 and girls
     are expected to be more responsible and obedient than
     boys and to help take care of younger children. See
     Romney (#734) for child rearing study.

874   MONTEIL, MARIE NOELLE
       1974 "Campesinas en el norte de México." BDSLM/CIDHAL
       4:3:32-34.
           Brief, personal description of proletarian family in
       Valley of Mexicali: their differences and gains and
       the situation which maintains woman in an oppressed
       state--by the Church, which along with her husband
       counsels her against birth control, by the State, by
       the family, and by society.

875   MOYA de MARTÍ, ANA CRISTINA
       1939 "La maternidad indígena." XXVIIth International
       Congress of Americanists. Actas de la 1ª sesión,
       celebrada en la ciudad de México en 1939, vol. 2,
       pp. 419-27. Mex., D.F.: Inst. Nacional de Antropología
       e Historia, Secretaría de Educación Pública. illus.
           In ancient Mexico, more ceremonies and rites were cele-
       brated for maternity than for any other function because
       of its social importance and religious transcendence.
       Notes practices and beliefs among the Aztecs, Maya,
       Totonac, Tarascans and Huaxtecas, as evidenced in their
       monuments, codices, and ceramics. Woman who died in
       childbirth of first male was considered as valiant as
       dead warrior. Links La Llorona to goddess Cihaupipiltin.

876   NÁJERA, INDIANA E.
       1967 Escuela práctica de novias (introducción al matri-
       monio; técnica y armonía conyugales; educación familiar,
       etc.). Para el medio mundo que quiere casarse y para
       el otro medio que quiere divorciarse. 2nd ed. Mex.,
       D.F.: Costa-Amic, Ed. 183 p.
           Mexican novelist turns to marital counseling. Taking
       into account the particular characteristics of Mexican
       women and men and the lack of training for matrimony,
       instructs women how to have a successful marriage, dis-
       cussing the major problems which arise most frequently
       and suggesting possible solutions: e.g., do not flaunt
       superior talent or intelligence before a husband, but do
       live in his shadow and foster his success so as to avoid
       professional jealousy.

877   NASH, JUNE
       1973 "The Betrothal: A Study of Ideology and Behavior in
       a Maya Indian Community." In Drinking Patterns in High-
       land Chiapas. A Teamwork Approach to the Study of Seman-
       tics Through Ethnography, ed. by H. Siverts, pp. 89-120.
       Bergen: Universitetsforlaget. illus., tables, graph.
           Analyzes betrothal as highly organized set of behaviors
       as performed in Tzeltal-speaking community of Amatenango

Marriage and the Family

del Valle, Chiapas. Uses 3 informants (2 men, 1 woman)
to elicit range of expectations concerning what should
be done; questions and responses listed in tables.
Makes comparison with responses of an elder from neigh-
boring town, where gaining a woman is not as difficult
and procedure is not as important because more emphasis
is placed on wedding ceremony itself.

878   NUTINI, HUGO G.
      1968   San Bernardino, Contla: Marriage and Family Struc-
      ture in a Tlaxcalan Municipio. Pittsburgh, Pa.: Univ.
      of Pittsburgh Press. 420 p. fold. map, tables, map,
      bibl.
          Based on fieldwork and historical research (1959-66).
      Includes information on women in division of labor,
      labor migration, life cycle, structure and functions
      of nuclear and extended family (e.g., basic patterns of
      male and female behavior, matrilocality), marriage and
      divorce, polygyny and family structure. Concludes with
      synoptic comparison of Mesoamerican marriage and family
      structure.

879   _____.
          1965   "Polygyny in a Tlaxcalan Community." UP/E 4:2:123-47.
          Demonstrates that polygyny in San Bernardino Contla
      has a social and economic function: it provides unmar-
      ried, divorced or widowed women with an opportunity to
      marry, but primarily for economic reasons. Describes
      kinds of unions (unitory bigamy, satellite bigamy, etc.)
      and their subtypes and how they relate to the social
      structure. Describes marriage, household and family
      organization.

880   OTERO, LUIS L.
      1968   "The Mexican Urbanization Process and Its Implica-
      tions." PAA/D 5:2:866-73. tables.
          Sees family as basic unit for analysis of demographic
      phenomena. Based on survey of family planning attitudes
      and opinions of 2,500 couples and approximately 300
      social, political and religious leaders in 3 urban and
      1 rural regions of Mexico (1966-68), compares attitudes
      and behavior in decision-making in family in general
      and in family planning field. Contrary to stereotyped
      statements about Mexican women and men, finds that re-
      sponsibilities and decision-making are jointly shared in
      conjugal structure, with a notable tendency for this to
      be linked to urbanization process. Conjugal dissatis-
      faction and acceptance of family planning varied accord-
      ing to degree of urbanization.

881 PAREJA SERRADA, ANTONIO
     1880 Influencia de la mujer en la regeneración social.
     Guadalajara: La Aurora. 219 p.
     Emotional history of women since the Creation does not
     deal specifically with Mexico, but reflects 19c. ideas.
     Discusses influence of women at home, over men, and in
     the education of children; women's roles as girl, young
     bride, resigned wife, martyr, mother, etc.

882 PARSONS, ELSIE CLEWS
     1932 "Casándose en Mitla, Oaxaca. Getting Married at
     Mitla, Oaxaca." MF 7:3:129-37. illus.
     Based on field observations in 1929 and 1930, describes
     customs before and during marriage ceremony in Mitla.
     Villagers believe in and practice trial marriage. In
     Spanish and English.

883 PAZ, LUCIANO de la
     1964 El fundamento psicológico de la familia. 2nd ed.
     Eds. Filosofía y Letras, 20. Mex., D.F.: UNAM,
     Dirección General de Publicaciones. 165 p. bibl.
     Generalized statements about women's traditional role
     as mother. "The primordial mission of woman is to be a
     mother." She is destined to mature with the fruit she
     bears. She is to be faithful to her nature and mission.

884 PEÑALOSA, FERNANDO
     1968 "Mexican Family Roles." WRU/JMF 30:4:680-89. bibl.
     f/notes.
     Synthesizes Mexican social science literature on the
     dynamics of Mexican family life for an understanding of
     changes in the Mexican-American family. Notes two basic
     approaches: 1) historical, and 2) male dominance and
     female submission. Describes role relationships between
     spouses, siblings, and parents and children. Sister-
     sister and mother-daughter relations are considered the
     closest.

885 PEROCHENA, ISABEL de
     1969 "Algunas reflexiones sobre el matrimonio." Istmo
     64:34-38.
     General discussion of marriage: why people get mar-
     ried, their disillusionment with it; characteristics
     of married life; husband/wife roles; need for
     communication.

886 PIKE, EUNICE V.
     1948 "Head-washing and Other Elements in the Mazateco
     Marriage Ceremony." III/AI 8:3:219-22.

Marriage and the Family

Based on fieldwork in Mazateco region of Oaxaca,
briefly describes "washing of the bride's hair," a ritual
performed by married godmother and groom's baptismal
godmother, and other aspects of marriage ceremony (dances,
banquets, etc.). Groom undergoes similar ritual.

887   RAMÍREZ, SANTIAGO and PORRAS, RAMÓN
      1957   "Some Dynamic Patterns in the Organization of the
      Mexican Family." IJSP 3:1:18-21.
         Brief preliminary report, based on psychosocial re-
      search among 635 urban proletariat families in Mexico
      City, with analytic treatment of 11 "typical" Mexicans,
      considers prototypical family organization. Notes 3
      basic dynamic patterns: intense mother-child relation-
      ship during first year of life; dilution of father-child
      relationship; traumatic rupture of mother-child relation-
      ship at birth of next sibling.

888   RAMÍREZ FLORES, JOSÉ
      1960   Matrimonio. Indígenas de Zacoalco. Jalisco en el
      arte. Guadalajara: Planeación y Promoción. 61 p.
      illus., music.
         Description in parallel texts of Spanish and English
      of traditional Indian marriage ceremony in Zacoalco,
      south of Guadalajara: courtship, preparations, betrothal,
      dowry, advice to bride, consent, costumes, wedding,
      party, first night.

889   REDFIELD, ROBERT
      1932   "Casamiento en un pueblo Maya. Marriage in a Maya
      Village." MF 7:3:154-59. illus.
         In parallel Spanish and English columns, describes
      process of getting married in Chan Kom, Yucatán. It
      begins with parents' decision that their son "now . . .
      needs a woman to serve him." Girl remains passive
      throughout.

890   ROMANUCCI-ROSS, LOLA
      1973   Conflict, Violence, and Morality in a Mexican Village.
      Palo Alto, Ca.: National Press Books. 203 p. illus.,
      tables, bibl.
         Based on fieldwork in mestizo peasant village in
      Morelos (1958-61). Contains interesting details on
      relations between women, men and women, mothers and their
      children; conflict in these relations; witchcraft and
      violence resulting from conflict; moral status; birth
      control. Women form temporary, unstable alliances
      against other women. Husband and wife form the most
      fragile familial link while greatest solidarity exists

between mother and children. That women leave more often than they are abandoned suggests much female independence. Illustrates with case histories.

891   SÁNCHEZ MORALES, AURELIA GUADALUPE
      1974 "La familia campesina . . . vista por el campesino."
      BDSLM/CIDHAL 4:4:41-45.
      Series of responses by Mexican peasants to questions posed in CIDAL seminars about their rural communities, family problems, communications between women and men and between parents and children, sexual relations, and family planning. Indicates low esteem for woman except when she bears many children.

892   STROSS, BRIAN
      1974 "Tzeltal Marriage by Capture." CUA/AQ 47:3:328-46.
      bibl.
      Examines bride theft among the Tzeltal of Tenejapa, Chiapas, Mexico in 1972 with regard to strict norms governing pre-marital cross-sex interaction, incest prohibitions, courtship and marriage traditions, and types of authority held by heads of household. Also discusses factors in mate selection, polygyny, personal attributes and material possessions, female reticence about marriage, orphans. Concludes that marriage by capture is on the decline because conditions for its presence are also waning (e.g., bride price complex now less severe—fewer beatings and less verbal abuse).

893   TERRY, LILLIE M.
      1904 "Courtship and Marriage in Mexico." Era 13:1:26-28.
      North American woman's impressions at the turn of the century of marriage customs among members of Mexican high society. Typical remark: "The women are content in their shut-in existences . . ."

894   TOOR, FRANCES
      1932 "Corte y casamiento. Courtship and Marriage." MF
      7:3:160-62. illus.
      Briefly summarizes marriage customs among several Indian groups in Mexico. Includes copy of a peasant's love letter. In Spanish and English.

895   VALDIVIESO, E. R.
      1929 "El matrimonio zapoteco." Q 1:1:21-22; 1:2:8-9.
      Discusses procedures for contracting marriage in Isthmus of Tehuantepec. Virginity is prized among the Zapotecs.

Marriage and the Family

896   WATTLES, JOAN DUDLEY
       1955   "Jalacingo Woman: An Individual and Her Society."
       AU/P 16:1:41-55.
          Based on 6-month stay (1952-53) in Mexican village and
       friendship with Esperanza Reyes de Murrieta. Describes
       work camp group, of which author was a member; village
       in Puebla; and Murrieta family, especially the wife and
       mother, Esperanza.

897   WOLGEMUTH, CARL
       1971   "Marriage Customs of Our Forefathers: Nahuat Text
       from Mecayapan, Veracruz." Tlalocan 6:4:347-73.
          Transcription, in Nahuat and literal and free English
       translations, of a tape recording in which 2 Isthmus
       Nahuat men (aged 15 and 22) narrate marriage customs of
       their grandparents. Describes changes in those proce-
       dures today. Many young people also elope.

Guatemala

898   BARRIOS PEÑA, JAIME
       1963   "Dimensión familiar (integración-desintegración)."
       USC/U 60:151-63.
          Deals with integration and disintegration of family as
       educative problem in formation of attitudes. Illustrates
       with examples of problems in family life and reasons for
       them, according to wife or husband.

899   CARRANZA R., LUIS FELIPE
       1971   "'Costumbres' o ceremonias matrimoniales indígenas
       en el departamento de Totonicapán." GIIN/GI 6:2/3:161-71.
          Describes courtship and wedding practices among the
       Indians of the Department of Totonicapán, Guatemala.
       Although young women initiate relationships through a
       series of coquetries, they play a minor role in the pro-
       ceedings and may even be returned to parents by husband
       if they prove sterile or negligent in house duties.

900   GONZÁLEZ, NANCY L. SOLIEN
       1969   Black Carib Household Structure: A Study of Migra-
       tion and Modernization. The American Ethnological Soci-
       ety. Monograph 48. Seattle: Univ. of Wash. Press.
       163 p. illus., maps, tables, bibl.
          Describes structure and function of consanguineal
       household among the Black Caribs of Livingston, Guate-
       mala (with additional observations on villages and towns
       in Belize and Honduras), and traces historical events
       leading to its development. Believes this household,

usually composed of a mother and children with no regularly present male as husband-father, arises as an alternate type of domestic group during the process of adaptation of neoteric societies to a modern economy in which primary mechanism of westernization is recurrent migratory wage labor with low remuneration.

901   MAYNARD, EILEEN
      1974   "Guatemalan Women: Life Under Two Types of Patriarchy."   In Many Sisters: Women in Cross-Cultural Perspective, ed. by C. J. Matthiason, pp. 77-98. N.Y.: The Free Press, A Division of Macmillan Publishing Co.
      Based on field research (1960-61), compares and contrasts Indian and Ladino women living under patriarchal system in Palín, Guatemala. Believes mythical patriarchy exists because it is actually the woman who wields power within the family and because in neither group can women generally be characterized as submissive. Ladino women have greater opportunities for individual achievement and economic roles but Indian women are afforded more economic and emotional security and less incongruity between ideal and real behavior and roles because Indian definition of masculinity includes responsibility to one's family.

902   ORDÓÑEZ CHIPÍN, MARTÍN
      1971   "Estudio sobre la poliginia en Santa María Chiquimula, municipio del departamento de Totonicapán."   GIIN/GI 6:2/3:154-59.
      The practice of polygyny among the Indians of Santa María Chiquimula, a Guatemalan village, began around 1930 when 2 businessmen obtained female helpers for their wives while they traveled. It remains as a privilege for those who can afford it, and only in this locale because it is considered an insult to traditional precepts.

903   PALOMINO, AQUILES
      1972   "Patrones matrimoniales entre los Ixiles de Chajul." GIIN/GI 7:1/2:5-159. illus., tables, maps, bibl.
      Peruvian anthropologist details marriage patterns among the Ixil in Chajul, Guatemala, based on fieldwork (1970-71). Considers concepts of, preconditions for, preliminaries to, forms of marriage, the ceremony, irregular unions, dissolution and secondary marriages. Provides case examples and statistics.

904   PAUL, LOIS and PAUL, BENJAMIN D.
      1963   "Changing Marriage Patterns in a Highland Guatemalan Community."   UNM/SWJA 19:2:131-48. Spanish version:

Marriage and the Family

1966 Cambios en los modelos de casamiento en una comu-
nidad guatemalteca del altiplano. Trans. by F. Rojas
Lima. Cuadernos del Seminario de Integración Social
Guatemalteca, Serie 3, no. 13. Guatemala: Depto. Edit.
"José de Pineda Ibarra," Ministerio de Educación. 38 p.
Reports on changes in forms of courtship and marriage
in San Pedro de la Laguna, Lake Atitlán, since 1900:
traditional, formal request; elopement (1900-50); and
Church marriage (1950-). At the same time, sees rela-
tively few changes in family life.

905 SIEGEL, MORRIS
1942 "Effects of Culture Contacts on the Form of the
Family in a Guatemalan Village." JRAI 72:55-68.
Describes Indian extended household and Ladino family,
forms of marriage, divorce and its causes, and culture
contact situation in municipality of San Miguel Atacán.
Includes sketches of 23 Ladino families and court records
for 24 divorce cases. Concludes that family instability
exists greatly in both family groups, but its effects
vary for each, especially with respect to female children.
Indian women are more fortunate than Ladino women because they are relatively more independent and have
alternatives when marriage disolves.

906 VAN DER TAK, JEAN and GENDELL, MURRAY
1973 "The Size and Structure of Residential Families,
Guatemala City, 1964." LSE/PS 27:2:305-22. tables,
graphs, bibl. f/notes.
Based on a 5% sample of Guatemala City private households (1964 census), examines variations in size and
structure of the residential family and prevalence of
family extension, controlling for age of family head,
presence/absence of spouse, marital status, education
of head, number of head's children in household, age
and relationship to head of other relatives present in
household. Concludes that perpetuation of extended
residential family is due to its particular importance
in families headed by males or females without a spouse.

El Salvador

907 LANDARACH, ALFONSO MARÍA
1961 "El noviazgo." UJSC/ECA 16:165:617-20.
Advice in Jesuit publication as to how engaged couple
should behave before marriage--how often to see one
another, permitted and forbidden physical affection,
different manners of kissing.

Middle America - Costa Rica

Honduras

908 HELMS, MARY W.
1970 "Matrilocality and the Maintenance of Ethnic Identity: the Miskito of Eastern Nicaragua and Honduras."
In XXXVIIIth International Congress of Americanists.
Stuttgart-Munich (12-18 August 1968). Proceedings,
vol. 2, pp. 459-64. Munich: Kommissionsverlag Klaus
Renner. bibl.
Sees matrilocality among Miskito Indians as positive
adaptation to economic demands. Traces historical roots
in commercial relations with Europeans since the 17c.
and explores whether uxorilocal residence was aboriginal
in origin or a postcontact development. Modifications
in the 20c. have not eliminated strong core of related
women who emphasize and conserve traditional culture.
Based on travel accounts, ethnographic studies, and
fieldwork.

Nicaragua

909 HELMS, MARY W.
1970 "Matrilocality and the Maintenance of Ethnic Iden-
tity: the Miskito of Eastern Nicaragua and Honduras."
In XXXVIIIth International Congress of Americanists.
Stuttgart-Munich (12-18 August 1968). Proceedings,
vol. 2, pp. 459-64. Munich: Kommissionsverlag Klaus
Renner. bibl.
See HONDURAS for annotation.

910 _____.
1970 "Matrilocality, Social Solidarity, and Culture Contact: Three Case Histories." UNM/SWJA 26:2:197-212.
bibl.
See PARAGUAY for annotation.

Costa Rica

911 BIESANZ, JOHN and BIESANZ, MAVIS
1943 "Mate Selection Standards of Costa Rican Students."
SF 22:2:194-99. tables.
Questionnaires administered to 171 girls and 103 boys
at the University of Costa Rica investigated their attitudes (economic rank, good looks, religious faith, age)
about persons they would consider marrying. Results
indicated general similarity between North American and

Marriage and the Family

Costa Rican college students but a more marked difference
along sex lines. Sample reflects traditional sex roles.

912   JIMÉNEZ J., RICARDO
      1961 "Marriage and Family in Costa Rica." IASI/E 19:71:
      297-304. tables.
      Cites 1950's statistics on number of marriages by
      Church, free unions, legitimate and illegitimate births,
      age of men and women at marriage, divorces and separa-
      tions, population control. Also looks at legal aspects
      of the family.

Panama

913   BIESANZ, JOHN
      1950 "Interamerican Marriages on the Isthmus of Panama."
      SF 29:2:159-63.
      Examines factors influential in exogamous selection
      and characteristics of those marrying exogamously--i.e.,
      Panamanian women and North American men. Ethnocentrism,
      racial prejudice and self-sufficiency of North American
      community in Panama deter intermarriage, but freedom of
      association, complementary imbalance in sex ratio,
      stereotypes of other group as good mates, disorganization
      of Panamanian family life and liberation of some North
      American men from social controls to implement endogamy
      all encourage intermarriage. Courtships are brief.

914   BIESANZ, JOHN and SMITH, LUKE M.
      1951 "Adjustment of Interethnic Marriages on the Isthmus
      of Panama." ASS/ASR 16:6:819-22.
      Interviewed 66 Panamanian women married to North Ameri-
      can men, considering 3 variables in adjustment of inter-
      ethnic marriages: prestige, informal-primary
      organization, and formal-secondary organization.
      Concludes that such adjustment depends not only upon
      general factors in marital adjustment, but also upon
      the intergroup situation and diverse norms of the 2
      ethnic groups.

915   FARON, LOUIS C.
      1962 "Marriage, Residence and Domestic Group Among the
      Chocó." UP/E 1:1:13-38.
      Discusses kinship and marriage and the domestic group
      of the Chocó Indians, who occupy the tropical forests
      of Darien.

South America - Venezuela

916   REVERTE COMA, JOSÉ MANUEL
          1966   El matrimonio entre los indios cuna de Panamá.
          Panama: Edilito. 52 p. illus., bibl. f/notes.
          Describes beliefs and practices of San Blas Cuna
          Indians of Panama with respect to the life cycle:
          pregnancy, birth, socialization, puberty ceremonies,
          adornments, marriage ceremony, different forms of mar-
          riage, divorce, ceremonial sacrifice of wives. Notes
          changes since colonial times.

SOUTH AMERICA

Venezuela

917   ARRIAGA, EDUARDO E.
          1968   "Some Aspects of Family Composition in Venezuela."
          EQ 15:3:177-90. tables, bibl.
          Using Venezuelan census data from 1950 and 1961 and
          vital statistics from 1907 to 1963, makes comparative
          analysis of family composition and change, discussing
          births, formation and dissolution of marriages and con-
          sensual unions. Notes rural/urban differences for
          family composition, age at marriage or consensual union,
          and fertility. Suggests recognition of consensual
          unions within Venezuelan law because of high rate of
          illigitimacy and lack of legal responsibility to such
          children; these unions dissolve 8 times more frequently
          than marriages. Statistics on women in 14 tables.

918   HEINEN, H. DIETER
          1972   "Economic Factors in Marriage Alliance and Kinship
          System Among the Winikina-Warao." ICAS/A 32:28-67.
          illus., fold. maps, bibl.
          Based on fieldwork, examines kinship terminology of
          the Winikina, a Warao subtribe of the Orinoco Delta in
          northeastern Venezuela; explores alternative models of
          marriage exchange based on kinship categories; and
          analyzes marriage alliances. "The way the kinship system
          is handled in actual interpersonal behavior--especially
          affinal kinship and rules of postmarital residence--shows
          considerable interplay with economic factors and the
          division of labor by sex."

919   _____.
          1972   "Residence Rules and Household Cycles in a Warao
          Subtribe: The Case of the Winikina." ICAS/A 31:21-86.
          fold maps, tables, bibl.

Marriage and the Family

Based on fieldwork among the Winikina, a Warao subtribe
of the Orinoco Delta in northeastern Venezuela, correlates census material with the stated ideal of this
matrilocal group that preferred post-marital residence is
with wife's parents. A first analysis indicated less
than 50% conformity to the norm, but a detailed analysis
of behavioral rules regarding residence in relation to
life cycle of households and resulting gamut of individual economic strategies showed only very minor deviation
from expected behavior, by marriages contracted in
mission centers.

920   PEATTIE, LISA REDFIELD
       1970   The View from the Barrio. Ann Arbor, Mich.: Ann
       Arbor Paperback, Univ. of Mich. Press. illus., map.
       As part of a team of planners, social anthropologist
       makes a personal analysis of the interaction between
       individuals and their environment in the *barrio* of La
       Laja, Ciudad Guayana (1962-64). Chapter on the kinship
       network discusses women in the household, noting differ-
       ence between legalized marriage with a male head and
       working-class families organized around a mother and her
       children. Sees female-headed families as a structural
       response in the "culture of poverty."

921   SCHWERÍN, KARL H.
       1963   "Family Among the Karinya of Eastern Venezuela."
       III/AI 23:3:201-09.
       Based on fieldwork conducted among 2 Karinya communi-
       ties--Mamo and Cachama--in eastern Venezuela. Compares
       the 2 in terms of changes in marriage customs and family
       structure: e.g., because of greater contact with modern
       Venezuelan culture, the Mamo group has undergone greater
       acculturation; their residence is neolocal while the
       Cachama group is still somewhat matrilocal. Girls and
       women almost never go anywhere alone; they are considered
       incapable of dealing with the world and in need of
       protection.

921a   WILBERT, JOHANNES
       1957   "Notes on Guahibo Kinship and Social Organization."
       UNM/SWJA 13:1:88-98. bibl. f/notes.
       Based on data collected from a native informant,
       describes various aspects of the matrilineal Guahibo
       Indians along the Vichada River in Venezuela: family,
       marital relations, female authority, divorce, kinship,
       menstrual rite.

922 WATSON, LAWRENCE C.
　　　　1970 "Urbanization and the Guajiro Matrifocal Family;
　　　　Consequences for Socialization and Personality Develop-
　　　　ment." ICAS/A 27:3-23. bibl.
　　　　　　Discusses family and socialization in traditional
　　　　Guajiro society, which is matrilineal, and structural
　　　　features and socialization patterns in the emergent
　　　　matrifocal family in an urban setting (Maracaibo). Using
　　　　social learning and psychoanalytic theory, predicts
　　　　significant results in the development of a novel person-
　　　　ality type among younger urban-reared Guajiro; and tests
　　　　them against evaluation of responses made by Guajiro
　　　　subjects to Rorschach and TAT tests. Notes incipient
　　　　establishment of an Oedipus complex.

Colombia

923 AITKEN, W. ERNEST
　　　　1946 "Lo que aportaba un matrimonio en el nuevo reino
　　　　en el siglo XVII." REVA 7:20:273-76.
　　　　　　Reproduces inventory of goods and their value which
　　　　Captain Ambrosio de Salazar of Villa de Timaná brought
　　　　to his marriage with Isabel de la Sarsa in 1639. A
　　　　portion of another document lists the dowry given to
　　　　Lucía de Herrera in 1704 by her husband Juan Palomino
　　　　de Salazar. See also M. J. Forero (#930).

924 ANGULO, ALEJANDRO
　　　　1969 "La familia colombiana, sus características."
　　　　REJAV 72:359:364-67.
　　　　　　Although there are several varieties of conjugal rela-
　　　　tions in Colombia, monogamy is the common type, sanc-
　　　　tioned by the Church and State. Single motherhood is
　　　　more predominant in rural zone of the Andes; free union
　　　　in urban zone. See instead V. Gutiérrez de Pineda
　　　　(#932).

925 BERNAL A., HERNANDO
　　　　1965 "Ritmos de vida en Buenaventura." ICA/RCA 12:329-
　　　　55. bibl.
　　　　　　Based on a survey among families of several socio-
　　　　economic groups in the port city of Buenaventura, on
　　　　Colombia's southwest coast, analyzes their daily sched-
　　　　ules for both men and women in terms of time spent at
　　　　home, in transit, at work, and in recreation. One of
　　　　the few available studies which provide a detailed break-
　　　　down of how women spend their day, and in relation to

Marriage and the Family

other family members. Concludes that the morning hour
for marketing is important for female social interaction
because it's the time of day when women cross geographical limits of their home. *Radionovelas* (soap opera
series) play an important recreational role in a woman's
day, for in general possibilities for entertainment,
especially for women, are limited. Provides good breakdown on how a woman spends her day.

926 BETANCUR, CAYETANO
1975 "La madre soltera." Arco 171:9-12.
Ten or more years ago in Colombia, unmarried mothers
were absolutely rejected; today, they're considered a
triumph over the crime of abortion and no longer an
offense to the established order because patriarchal
family structure has weakened.

927 CALLE RESTREPO, ARTURO
1964 Conflictos familiares y problemas humanos. La
familia en zonas de rápida urbanización. Estudio
sociológico en tres barrios populares de Pereira
(Colombia). Univ. Católica de Lovaina. Coll. del
Inst. de Ciencias Políticas y Sociales, 178. Madrid:
Escuelas Profesionales "Sagrado Corazón." 239 p.
tables, fold. maps, plates, bibl.
Based on interviews and observation in 6 rural communities near and 3 barrios in the city of Pereira, analyzes social, cultural, religious and economic change in
rural-urban migrant families, focusing specifically on
family conflicts. Includes comparative data for men and
women on demographic and socio-economic-cultural-
religious characteristics; and motivations and attitudes
related to migration. Notes changes for women in an
urban setting, related to their economic role.

928 DUSSAN de REICHEL-DOLMATOFF, ALICIA
1959 "La estructura de la familia en la Costa Caribe de
Colombia." XXXIIIrd International Congress of Americanists. San José, 20-27 July 1958. Acts, vol. 2,
pp. 692-703. San José, C.R.: Lehmann. bibl.
Describes family structure and function among 3 subcultures along the Caribbean coast of Colombia. Divides
family into 2 basic categories: nuclear (man is generally the economic provider and central figure) and
extended (women play very central role and are economic
sustainers). Concludes that matrifocal character and
extended matrilineal ties of 3 generational domestic
units result from instability of conjugal unions.

929 FLINN, WILLIAM L.
1974 "Family Life of Latin American Urban Migrants.
Three Case Studies in Botogá." UM/JIAS 16:3:326-49.
tables, bibl.
Examines the life of urban migrants through a description of the migratory process, family structure, economic, educational and value systems of 120 families interviewed in 2 pirate and 1 squatter settlements in Bogotá (1964-66). Findings indicate standard nuclear family is most common type with relatively few female-headed households, common law marriages or separations. 3 tables present statistics indicating differences in educational level between males and females.

930 FORERO, MANUEL JOSÉ
1938 "Unas capitulaciones matrimoniales en el nuevo reino." HA/B 25:289/290:802-05.
Reproduces articles of marriage from colonial New Granada of Luis Trujillo and Justa Pastora Mutiens, both considered white and of first distinction; certification by Fray Ignacio López of Cartagena that he knew Trujillo; and document in which Trujillo states that he has married Mutiens and received from her parents a dowry of jewels, goods, and money (listed with their value).

931 GUTIÉRREZ de PINEDA, VIRGINIA
1973 Tradicionalismo y familia en Colombia. Trasfondo familiar del menor con problema civil, Bogotá. Bogota: ASCOFAME, División de Medicina Social y Población. 128 p. illus., tables, graphs, bibl.
In an analysis of the family background of minors who have been brought to juvenile court in Bogota, considers historical evolution of Colombian family structure and changes in sex roles, particularly women's break with traditional norms once in an urban area, and how these changes are affecting the socialization of children. Provides statistics.

932 _____.
1968 Familia y cultura en Colombia: tipologías, funciones, y dinámica de la familia; manifestaciones múltiples a través del mosaico cultural y sus estructuras sociales. Bogota: Coeditions of Tercer Mundo and Depto. de Sociología (Sección Investigaciones), Univ. Nacional de Colombia. 415 p. illus., plates, fold. maps, bibl.
Most comprehensive study to date on the family in Colombia, divided according to 4 cultural zones and

Marriage and the Family

based on participant observation, interviews, biographies, historical sources, and statistical data. For
each family group describes habitat, economy, religion,
structure, typology, status, and function. Includes a
great deal of information on women's lives, describing
psychology, roles, relations, socialization, single
motherhood, cultural images (e.g., the old maid, the
religious, the prostitute), and much more.

933 _____.
1962 La familia en Colombia, estudio antropológico.
Estudios Sociológicos Latino-Americanos, 15. Fribourg,
Switz.: Oficina Internacional de Investigaciones
Sociales de FERES. 86 p. maps, tables, graphs.
Statistical and descriptive portrait of the Colombian
family within 5 cultural zones considers women's position, especially as mother and notes salaries of female
agricultural workers (1951). Early version of her more
comprehensive and detailed work, Familia y cultura en
Colombia (#932).

934 OSPINA R., MARIANO
1884 Carta a la senorita María Josefa Ospina, en la
víspera de su matrimonio. Bogota: Imprenta de
Silvestre y cía. 16 p.
Reprint of letter written from Guatamela (21 October
1864) which first appeared in El Heraldo of Cartagena.
Father counsels his daughter on the eve of her wedding:
happiness depends on exercising such Christian virtues
as humility, patience, resignation, abnegation, pru-
dence, discretion; prime object of a wife's attention,
care and concern is her husband, with everyone else
taking second and third place; a wife should always show
deference to her husband, especially in public, and
should not contradict nor impose her will on him; in
order to keep a husband's love alive, a wife must always
comport herself with the modesty of a virgin; etc.
Reflects 19c. instruction in female behavior.

935 PIEDRAHITA ECHEVERRI, MARTA
1956 "El divorcio." UNIPOB 21:75:47-71. bibl.
Useful only as a reflection of very conservative and
traditional attitudes toward women's role as wife and
mother: e.g., with the implantation of divorce laws,
woman has retroceded several centuries. She has become
a licentious being available only for satisfying carnal
appetite as an instrument for men's passion. Nature has
been violated to such a degree that women now renounce
their children with the same ease as rejecting a dress.

936 ROSENTHAL, CELIA STONICKA
1960 "Lower Class Family Organization on the Caribbean
Coast of Colombia." PSR 3:1:12-17. bibl.
Claims to be first systematic study of Colombian
coastal family (department of Bolívar), based on research
among predominantly black lower-class residents of
Cartagena (1953-56). Attempts to explain different
organizational and structural types of families--conjugal
(Catholic and consensual) and consanguineous (female-
centered); using functionalist approach, describes and
analyzes. Concludes that the female-centered family
fulfills function of care and socialization of children
more adequately than discontinuous conjugal families.
Discusses male/female relations (exaggerated hostility).

937 SICARD CHAVES, IGNACIO
1966 "Matrimonio civil y divorcio en Colombia?" REJAV
66:329:374-79.
Opposes civil marriage and divorce as the solution to
problems surrounding institution of marriage and is
aghast that members of the Colombian clergy have sanc-
tioned them. Argues that natural divine right rejects
divorce. It is those atheistic, neo-pagan countries
which scorn the supreme norms that govern human race and
which approve divorce to the opprobrium of women, tor-
ture of innocent children, and ruin of family and
society!

938 SMYTH, CLIFFORD
1903 "Love-making in Colombia." Independent 55:2859:
2328-33. illus.
A young enamoured Colombian man describes with humor
and some regret the elaborate courtship customs in his
country: letter writing, serenading, the balcony watch,
sitting with the family, etc.

939 SOLAÚN, MAURICIO and KRONUS, SIDNEY
1973 Discrimination Without Violence: Miscegenation and
Racial Conflict in Latin America. N.Y.: John Wiley.
240 p. tables, bibl.
Although study was conducted in Cartagena, background
information deals with Latin America as a whole and
generalizations are extrapolated from this participation
case study on miscegenation; intermarriage, interracial
sexual relationships. Although a questionnaire was
applied equally to men and women, there is almost no
breakdown according to sex variable within the
discussion.

Marriage and the Family

Ecuador

940   JARAMILLO J., ALFREDO
       1972 Estructura familiar. (Estudio sobre los sectores
       populares de Quito, Ecuador). Cuadernos del Instituto
       Latinoamericano de Planificación Económica y Social.
       Serie 2: Anticipos de Investigación, no. 16. Santiago:
       ILPES. 115 p. tables, graphs, bibl.
           Provides demographic data on male/female population
       of 1960's in Ecuador as a whole, Quito, and province of
       Pichincha. Reports findings of survey conducted among
       457 women and 483 men of popular classes in Quito: basic
       socio-economic characteristics, power structure in
       family, socialization of children, and more. Notes dis-
       criminatory treatment of girls in family socialization,
       but concludes that there are signs indicating patriarchal
       family structure is now in transition toward a less
       authoritarian system in which women's situation changes.

Peru

941   ALTMANN SMYTHE, JULIO
       1967 "La familia como realidad social." Criminalia 33:
       2:80-90.
           Briefly summarizes origins of the family, distinguish-
       ing between conjugal and paternal-filial societies and
       noting changes in evolution of both. Short section on
       indigenous family of Peru sees some predominant charac-
       teristics of primitive family groups reflected in con-
       temporary indigenous groups: e.g., trial marriage.
       Believes marriage among Indians is a matter of posses-
       sion and economics; concept of love, as defined by
       modern western society, does not exist, even in relation
       to children, who are elements of production and capital.
       Nevertheless, notes that their marriage is stable.

942   BARRIONUEVO, ALFONSINA
       1973 Sirvinakuy. Un ensayo sobre el matrimonio de
       prueba. Lima. 64 p. illus.
           Brief essay on sirvinakuy, a system of trial marriage
       practiced among the Andean Indians of Peru. Uses
       Conquest and colonial chronicles and secondary sources
       to describe marriage practices during reign of the Incas
       and trial marriage in 7 Peruvian highland communities
       today.

943 BOLTON, RALPH
     1973 "*Tawanku*: Intercouple Bonds in a Qolla Village
     (Peru)." AI/A 68:1/2:145-55. bibl.
          Based on fieldwork among Quechua-speaking Qolla at
     Lake Titicaca (1968-70), describes household, marriage
     and family in this atomistic-type society and practice
     of mate-swapping among married couples. Concludes that
     tawanku, an institution distinct from marital arrange-
     ments, has important psychological and social functions
     in addition to sexual motivation. Provides a comparative
     list of 6 variable characteristics of such a practice
     among several societies.

944 CARAVEDO M., CARMEN
     1963 "Influencia de la madre en la vida del niño."
     Nueva Educación 33:160:8-18.
          Discusses the important role a mother exercises in the
     development of her child as the first contact, as a
     figure of protection, as mediator in his/her difficul-
     ties. Based on standard texts in English on love, child
     development, etc.

945 Conferencia Nacional sobre la Familia, la Infancia, y la
     Juventud en el Desarrollo Nacional.
          1968 Informe final de la conferencia celebrada en Lima,
          Perú, del 14 al 20 de mayo de 1967. Lima. 592 p.
               Collection of more than 20 papers presented at national
          conference on the family, childhood and adolescence in
          Peru. See Ismodes Cairo (#1612) and Hernández Aguilar
          (#1611) for reports on prostitution.

946 DOLE, GERTRUDE E.
     1974 "The Marriages of Pacho: A Woman's Life Among the
     Amahuaca." In Many Sisters: Women in Cross-Cultural
     Perspective, ed. by C. J. Mathiasson, pp. 3-35. N.Y.:
     Free Press, Macmillan. illus.
          Based on fieldwork among Amahuaca Indians in southeast
     Peru (1960-61), narrates series of events culminating in
     marriage of Pacho in order to illustrate female role as
     child, wife and mother, and touches upon other aspects
     of Amahuaca life (kinship, rites, economic activities,
     sexual relations, death and mourning, family, witchcraft,
     ceremonies, etc.). Women's generally dominant role is
     in contrast to women's generally passive or integrative
     role in interfamilial and intergroup relations despite
     great amount of physical strength which women must have.
     Pacho's nontraditional behavior created enough tension
     to temporarily split the community. Concludes that
     Amahuaca women enjoy moderately high status in relatively
     egalitarian society.

Marriage and the Family

947   GILLIN, JOHN
        1949   "Marriage Among the Mocheros." JMFL 11:2:70-71, 92.
        Describes marriage customs and attitudes toward sex
        among the *mestizo* population in the district of Moche in
        northern Peru. Marriage can be common law, civil or
        religious; divorce is not permitted for the latter. Sex
        is natural and to be indulged in without secrecy or
        shame. Lack of female virginity, masturbation and ille-
        gitimacy are all taken in stride. Abortion is practiced
        but mechanical and chemical means of birth control are
        not.

948   HAMMEL, EUGENE A.
        1964   "Some Characteristics of Rural Village and Urban
        Slum Populations on the Coast of Peru." UNM/SWJA 20:
        4:346-58. bibl.
        Offers comparative data on fertility, age and sex dis-
        tribution, nature and frequency of conjugal unions,
        housing, occupations, and family composition of rural
        and urban populations of Ica Valley. Analysis of data
        reveals nonconformities: e.g., urban areas are generally
        believed to have a heavy concentration of women over age
        50, but here rural area has a marked excess of adult
        females over 45 and slum has lowest number of such
        women; and whole cities generally accumulate women over
        age 15 but the Ica slum does not have a greater propor-
        tion of these women than the rural district. Concludes,
        among other things, that slum families are more matri-
        focal than rural ones.

949   _____.
        1964   "Territorial Patterning of Marriage Relationships in
        a Coastal Peruvian Village." AAA/AA 66:1:67-74. map,
        tables.
        Based on 1957 census data, marriage records (1937-57),
        and field research (1957-58) in San Juan Bautista in
        Ica Valley, "attempts to specify (1) the degree of
        endogamy occurring at several levels of territorial
        specification, (2) the nature and direction of exogamous
        unions, (3) the relationship between marriage and other
        forms of social intercourse, and (4) the changes that
        have occurred in these phenomena over time."

950   _____.
        1961   "The Family Cycle in a Coastal Peruvian Slum and
        Village." AAA/AA 63:5:989-1005. graphs, tables.
        Describes various types of family structure and ana-
        lyzes census data for a slum in Ica and a neighboring

village, San Juan Bautista, to determine what development
patterns exist in rural-urban conditions. Notes differences between both places, especially in terms of women's
role in family life.

951 MAC-LEAN, ROBERTO
     1941 "El sirvinacuy. Matrimonio de prueba entre los
     aborígenes peruanos." UNAM/RMS 3:1:25-33. bibl.
         "*Sirvinacuy*" or "*tinkunakuspa*" is a prematrimonial
     institution originating in pre-Inca times. Finds histor-
     ical references to it in the writings of a viceroy,
     visitador, and missionaries in 16c. and 17c. Describes
     the practice of trial marriage and regional variations.

952 NÚÑEZ del PRADO, OSCAR
     1969 "El hombre y la familia: su matrimonio y
     organización político-social en Q'ero." IPA/AP 1:5-27.
     illus. Also in: 1964 His Estudios sobre la cultura
     actual en el Perú, pp. 273-97. Serie Problemática del
     Perú, 2. Lima: Univ. Nacional Mayor de San Marcos.
     1957 El hombre y la familia, su matrimonio y organiza-
     ción político-social en Q'ero. Cuzco: Edit. Garcilaso.
     23 p. plates, bibl.
         Describes field study made by group from National
     University of Cuzco in 1955, which includes 7 pages on
     marriage among Kechua population of Q'ero: sexual
     freedom before marriage; qualities a woman should
     possess in order to be chosen as a wife; consultation
     with a diviner and other procedures; female fidelity
     once married.

953 PRICE, RICHARD
     1965 "Trial Marriage in the Andes." UP/E 4:3:310-22.
     bibl.
         Briefly sketches pre-Columbian marriage practices in
     highland Peru and describes them in the Quechua community
     of Vicos today. Suggests that a basic relatively
     unchanged pattern has persisted since before the Inca
     empire: Inca and Roman Catholic ceremonies differ, but
     their sociological function does not. Explains 5 major
     functions of *watanki* ("having a year together") within
     cultural context of Vicos.

954 SCHULLER, RUDOLF
     1930 "Trial Marriage in South America." INNO 7:4:522-34.
     bibl. notes.
         Traces references to trial marriage ("prenuptial con-
     cubinage") among ancient Peruvians since 1550. Strongly

Marriage and the Family

condemned as a vice by Catholic missionaries, *pantanaco*
or *tincunacuspa* is a prenuptial arrangement by which a
couple lives together for a certain period of time so
that the man can learn whether the woman is suitable to
be a good wife. Very briefly describes variations of
this practice today.

955   VIVANCO FLORES, CARLOS A.
      1972 "El matrimonio indigena." IPA/AP 4:33-42.
      Describes the 9 phases of marriage as practiced by the
      indigenous community in the province of Andahuaylas
      (Apurímac): *rimaykukuy*, asking for the hand of a girl;
      willana, announcement of the upcoming marriage; marriage
      ceremony; *aynikuy*, collaboration of unmarried relatives
      and neighbors; *ramada*, *urpi kuchuy*; *wawa tusuchiy*; *ramada
      vendey*; *kutichiy*, return of expenses by boy's parents
      to girl's if there is difficulty in culminating the
      marriage. Includes verses (Spanish and Quechua) of
      songs from the wedding.

Bolivia

956   BARRIONUEVO, ALFONSINA
      1973 Sirvinakuy. Un ensayo sobre el matrimonio de prueba.
      Lima. 64 p. illus.
      See PERU for annotation.

957   CISNEROS C., ANTONIO
      1970 Estudio exploratorio sobre actitudes prematrimon-
      iales. Diciembre, 1969. La Paz: Centro Nacional de
      Familia (CENAFA). 37 p. illus., tables, graphs, bibl.
      Presents findings of survey among 27 couples attending
      a course on prematrimonial orientation given by
      Movimiento Cristiano Familiar in La Paz. Explores pref-
      erences for solutions to conjugal conflicts, opinions
      on divorce and birth control, attitudes toward family
      structure and decision making, religious beliefs, etc.
      Concludes that the double standard is very pronounced,
      with concomitant subordinate status of women, marital
      problems, and family disorientation; that marital roles
      are in a process of change because female intervention
      in such areas as work and family decisions is now
      accepted, but men still prevail in traditional role of
      breadwinner and decision maker. Virginity was prized by
      70% of sample.

South America - Paraguay

958 PANTELIS, FANNY GIDE
      1974 "¿La igualdad? Ni un sueño para las bolivianas."
      BDSLM/CIDHAL 4:3:26-31. illus.
      Originally published in Response (1973), considers 3
      groups of Bolivian women: peasants, *mestizas*, middle
      class, and briefly describes their economic activities
      and role as wives and mothers. Believes middle-class
      women have the most traditional and restricted role,
      but they also are the only ones questioning their posi-
      tion in family and society.

Paraguay

959 HELMS, MARY W.
      1970 "Matrilocality, Social Solidarity, and Culture
      Contact: Three Case Histories." UNM/SWJA 26:2:197-212.
      bibl.
      Using data on 3 seminomadic-semisedentary bilateral
      societies--Apache, Miskito of eastern Nicaragua, Mbayá
      of Paraguayan Gran Chaco--analyzes functional value of
      matrilocality. Suggests that cultural stability and
      continuity provided by uxorilocal residence patterns
      among simpler societies experiencing culture contact with
      more complex ones may be an adaptable form of social
      organization compatible with bilaterality. Based on
      available ethnographic and travel literature, considers
      hypothesis within historical context of colonial and
      early Republican LA.

960 NÚÑEZ CARVALLO, GABRIEL
      1962 "La familia en el Paraguay: organización y función."
      UNC/BFDCS 26:4:161-75.
      General summary of Paraguayan family--from the Guaraní
      at the time of the Spaniards' arrival to the mestizos
      of today. Peasant women prefer free union to legal mar-
      riage because it makes separation easier. No references.

960a RIVAROLA, DOMINGO M.
      1971 "Apuntes para el estudio de la familia en el Para-
      guay." CPES/RPS 8:21:84-104. tables, bibl. notes.
      Using mostly census data, presents descriptive profile
      of the structure and situation of the Paraguayan family
      in Asuncion and in the interior. Considers legal and
      socio-demographic aspects, attitudes toward number of
      children, kinds and distribution of conjugal unions,
      illegitimacy, etc.

Marriage and the Family

Chile

961 ALVAREZ ANDREWS, OSCAR
1958 "El problema de la familia en Chile." UNAM/RMS
20:2:413-28.
Compares the supposedly matriarchal family structure
of the Mapuche Indians of Chile with the patriarchy
transplanted by the Spaniards and characteristics of
the Chilean family in 19c. and 20c. Suggests a tendency
exists toward polygamy and treatment of women as inferior
to men. Distinguishes among 3 classes: greatest "natural disorganization" of family is found among the
poorest classes; while greatest "legal disorganization"
exists among the bourgeoisie and upper classes. Physical
factors of family disintegration are malnutrition, alcoholism, poor housing, illiteracy. Also cites factors of
family cohesion and legislation conducive to it. Cites
1900 and 1940 statistics on birth rate, nuptiality,
illegitimate birth, dissolution of family, divorce, and
abortion.

962 "Carta de dote de Doña María Bárbara Mayo."
1938 ACH/B 5:10:383-90.
An interesting document (1811) reveals certain legal
aspects of marriage with respect to the bride's dowry.
Lists her goods and their values, which the husband
states he has received.

963 FARON, LOUIS C.
1962 "Matrilateral Marriage Among the Mapuche
(Araucanians) of Central Chile." Sociologus 12:1:54-66.
illus., bibl.
Essentially a condensed version of Chapter 8 of
author's study Los mapuche: su estructura social
(Mexico, 1969). Describes some of the features of
Mapuche matrilateral marriage, beliefs regarding incest
and exogamy, wife-givers and wife-receivers.

964 IRARRÁZAVAL V., MARÍA T.
1973 "Conflictos en el matrimonio." C/F 1:2:96-103.
tables.
Considers certain factors present in matrimonial conflict among Chilean couples: variables related to
family structure, personality, couple relations. Tables
give responses by men and women on manifestation of
affection, reason for marriage, affective substitutes,
etc.; collected from 400 cases handled by the Family
Counseling Service of CENFA between 1969 and 1971.

Argentina

965   AMADEO, TOMÁS
       1929   "Función social de la madre." In his La función
       social, pp. 35-59. Buenos Aires: Imprenta Oceana.
       Encomium to women on Mother's Day by president of
       Argentine Social Museum. Within the family it is the
       mother who has the greatest opportunities to exercise
       an educational influence as the guiding light for her
       children. Woman's social conscience is more developed
       than man's, as a consequence of her feminine nature and
       extension of maternal feelings. Her abnegation lasts a
       lifetime. Feminism is antinatural and masculinizing and
       therefore must disappear. Woman's social function must
       be and is fulfilled within the home itself, bearing and
       raising children as her most fundamental service to
       humanity. Also comments about women without children
       and children without mothers.

966   CHAMORRO GRECA, EVA
       1969   "La madre que sale a trabajar." UNC/R 10:1/2:241-65.
       tables.
       Discusses findings of interviews with 90 working
       mothers of 3 occupational levels in Cordoba, Argentina
       with respect to their opinions about working, decision-
       making on income expenditure, individual and social
       factors creating role conflict, husband-wife collabora-
       tion and child assistance in household tasks, family
       relations as a source of dissatisfaction, and masculine/
       feminine tasks.

967   FORNI, FLOREAL HOMERO
       1962   "Familia y sociedad rural en la Argentina." CLEH
       5:13:59-69. tables, bibl.
       Makes several hypotheses regarding family structure
       in Argentina, according to region and social group, in
       order to point out problem of social disintegration
       among poor families in rural areas. There is greater
       single motherhood among salaried landless workers. Uses
       1947 and 1957 census data.

968   GARCÍA, JUAN AGUSTÍN
       1900   "La familia." In his La ciudad indiana (Buenos
       Aires desde 1600 hasta mediados del siglo XVIII),
       pp. 83-99. Buenos Aires: Angel Estrada y cía. bibl.
       f/notes.
       General portrait of family life in colonial Argentina.
       In the patriarchal unit woman occupied an inferior
       legal position but constituted principal factor for

Marriage and the Family

> success or failure of a home. Children were often
> raised by blacks or *pardas*. Religion was a continuous
> preoccupation.

969 GRENÓN, PEDRO
> 1958 "Nuestros divorcios históricos." A/H 3:11:5-19.
> Interesting material from the Archive of the Archbishop
> for the province of Buenos Aires: transcribes 10 out of
> 250 divorce and annulment cases covering early 17c. to
> 19c. In most instances, suit was filed by the woman;
> all the cases were effected on the basis of cruelty by
> the husband or adultery by either spouse. Summarizes
> 17 other cases. Sheds light on marital relations and
> woman's ability to act legally in her own interest.

970 PADILLA, FRANCISCO E.
> 1957 "Evolución de la familia en la Argentina." UNT/RJ
> 1:45-93. bibl. f/notes.
> Traces evolution of Argentine family from the indig-
> enous groups before the arrival of the Spaniards, through
> the colonial period into contemporary times, remarking
> on women's position, legal and otherwise.

971 POGODIN, PEDRO E.
> 1969 Una agencia matrimonial en Buenos Aires. Memorias
> de su director. Buenos Aires: Talleres Gráficos
> "Cultura." 191 p.
> Director of a marriage agency (operating since 1934)
> offers his general impressions on Argentine women, love,
> marriage, divorce and family as well as specifics about
> the agency itself (how it is run, who uses it and why).
> Men turn to it because they have no time to find a wife,
> are looking for more than a playmate, or want someone
> outside of their circle; women recur to it because they
> are alone in the big city, have lost time in a relation-
> ship which did not lead to marriage, have little social
> contact, or face family objections at losing their help
> at home. Uses case examples from clientele. Includes
> notes on family law (civil marriage, rights and obliga-
> tions of spouses, women's civil capacity, divorce, sepa-
> ration, illegitimate children, adoption, etc.).

972 SAN MARTÍN, JOSÉ de
> 195-? Máximas redactadas por el general San Martín para
> su hija Mercedes Tomasa de quien fue el verdadero
> formador de conciencia moral. Buenos Aires: Peuser.
> 5 p. port., facsim.
> Facsimile and transcription of document (1825), in the
> Mitre Museum, which lists 11 maxims by General San Martín

to help build the moral character of his daughter: for
example, by inspiring her to love truth and hate lies,
feel charity for the poor, respect another's property,
keep a secret, be sweet with servants, poor and old
people, etc.

973   SEDRÁN, FERINO
      1968 "Relaciones entre novios." AEST 547:516-25.
      Defines courtship from the perspective of the Catholic
      Church. Discusses its 3 stages, relations between
      fiancés (e.g., demonstrations of affection, visits), and
      the necessity of educating young people in the meaning
      and function of courtship. Women have the duty of main-
      taining relations on a spiritual and erotic level with-
      out going beyond the boundaries of their mission in life
      (i.e., family and home), while men have the responsibility
      of contributing their strength of will and lucidness of
      mind!

Uruguay

974   GANÓN, ISAAC
      1964 "Sobre la familia uruguaya." UNAM/RMS 26:1:173-90.
      tables, bibl.
      Defines family, using Murdock's scheme. Based on
      statistical data from 1954, provides information on
      family size; nuptiality (1881-1960); divorce (1935-1960);
      birth (legitimate and illegitimate, 1910-1954). Small
      family size is the norm in Uruguay.

CARIBBEAN

Puerto Rico

975   BODARSKY, CLIFFORD J.
      1964 "Chaperonage and the Puerto Rican Middle Class."
      WRU/JMF 26:3:347-48. bibl. f/notes.
      Despite increasing influence of North American culture,
      custom of chaperonage persists in Puerto Rico. In a
      sample of 20 high school seniors, equally divided by
      sex, of middle-class families (1960-62), favorable
      attitudes toward chaperonage predominated while ideology
      of freedom of mate selection did not appear characteris-
      tic of the group. Concludes that custom may have become
      a status symbol representing aspirations of participants
      in their society.

Marriage and the Family

976   BRYCE-LAPORTE, ROY SIMÓN
      1970 "Urban Relocation and Family Adaptation in Puerto
      Rico: A Case Study in Urban Ethnography." In Peasants
      in Cities: Readings in the Anthropology of Urbanization,
      ed. by W. Mangin, pp. 85-97. Boston: Houghton Mifflin.
        Based on research on family life of working mothers in
      a low income housing project in San Juan (early 1960's),
      also observes way of life--social relations and events--
      of the housing project. Explores matrifocal nature of
      family organization among shanty-town dwellers in new
      residence, citing case example of female head of
      household.

977   CUCHÍ COLL, ISABEL
      1945 Mujer. Mex., D.F.: Talleres de la Edit. Cultura.
      139 p. port.
        Puerto Rican writer's personal opinions about women--
      as wives and mothers--interspersed with comments and
      verses by other writers, male and female. Some of her
      suggestions: be feminine and weak for therein lie
      women's happiness and strength; be indispensable and
      agreeable company to a man so that he won't look for
      another woman. Compendium of advice and counsel on how
      to be a successful woman in traditional terms.

978   FERNÁNDEZ-MARINA, RAMÓN; MALDONADO-SIERRA, EDUARDO D. and
      TRENT, RICHARD D.
      1958 "Three Basic Themes in Mexican and Puerto Rican
      Family Values." JSP 48(2nd half):167-81. tables, bibl.
      See MEXICO for annotation.

979   FERNÁNDEZ MÉNDEZ, EUGENIO
      1955 "La familia puertorriqueña de hoy: como la ve el
      antropólogo social." CPPR/P 3:2:35-51.
        Reviews characteristics of the Puerto Rican family
      according to anthropological and sociological studies.
      Notes cults of machismo and female virginity; women's
      contribution to family income; and greater economic
      independence of middle-class women over lower-class
      women. Concludes that the economic forces of industrial
      capitalism lead toward breakdown of the old order of
      commercial and agrarian capitalism, which fostered the
      double standard.

980   GREEN, HELEN B.
      1960 "Comparison of Nurturance and Independence Training
      in Jamaica and Puerto Rico, With Consideration of the
      Resulting Personality Structure and Transplanted Social
      Patterns." JSP 51:1st half:27-63. bibl.

Bi-cultural study of child-training in areas of similar
economic conditions reveals important differences resulting from transplanted cultures of England and Spain:
Puerto Ricans are strong in continuity of encouragement,
extensive social relationships, and ideals of acceptance
and fatalism, but weak in anxiety over male dominance,
female martyrdom and the weight of social obligations.
Compares for background (historical, religious, sexual
and socio-economic aspects), rural and urban regions
and sub-cultures by class, personality structures of
adults and of migrants. Based on secondary sources,
describes socialization of Puerto Rican girls and
female roles.

981   HERNÁNDEZ ALVAREZ, LILIA INÉS de
      1971 Matrimonio en Puerto Rico: Estudio sociodemográfico,
      1910-1968. Río Piedras, P.R.: Edit. Edil. 177 p.
      graphs, tables, bibl.
      Considering nuptiality as a socio-demographic concept,
analyzes unmarried and married populations according to
sex, age, race, and residence and compares Puerto Rico
with other countries. Discusses legal and consensual
unions--differences in terms of education, race, family
structure, economics, and number of children. Provides
historical perspective of legal matrimony in Puerto Rico.
Notes an increase in number of individuals, particularly
women, who marry; an increase in legal unions; young age
at which people marry; and second marriages because of
divorce, all of which reflect fundamental ideological
changes between 1910 and 1968.

982   HILL, REUBEN
      1955 "Courtship in Puerto Rico: An Institution in
      Transition." WRU/JMF 17:1:26-35. Spanish version:
      1958 "El noviazgo en Puerto Rico: período de transición."
      Trans. by A. Pego. UPR/RCS 2:1:87-104. table, bibl.
      f/notes.
      Based on observation and studies (1951-54) in metro-
politan San Juan, examines courtship system within context of rapid social change--i.e., mingling of
Hispanic-Catholic and North American cultures. Discusses
courtship as it was transplanted from Spain, contemporary
patterns, stages of involvement and commitment. Concludes that Puerto Rican pattern is still predominantly
more Spanish than North American, although both systems
merge at a number of points. Outlines role of both
girls and boys.

Marriage and the Family

983 _____.
1955 "Impediments to Freedom of Mate Selection in Puerto Rico." JHE 47:3:189-97. tables.
According to survey conducted among students at the University of Puerto Rico, traditional patterns of Hispanic-Catholic courtship system persist and lean toward a serious commitment to marriage. However, a discrepancy exists between now largely accepted goal of freedom of mate selection, based on experience with and knowledge of opposite sex, and objective of marrying chaste and innocent women.

984 HILL, REUBEN; STYCOS, J. MAYONE and BACK, KURT
1955 The Family and Population Control. A Puerto Rican Experiment in Social Change. Chapel Hill, N.C.: Univ. of N.C. Press. 481 p. illus., tables.
Chapter 3 is an overview of urban and rural family life in Puerto Rico: patterns of affection, dominance, sexual orientations, recreation, stability; marital and family organization (marital relations, authority patterns, communication).

985 LANDY, DAVID
1959 Tropical Childhood: Cultural Transmission and Learning in a Rural Puerto Rican Village. Chapel Hill, N.C.: Univ. of N.C. Press. 291 p. tables, bibl.
Intensive study of family, childhood, and cultural transmission among 18 lower-class families in Valle Caña, a sugar cane area of eastern Puerto Rico, based on interviews with mothers and fathers, objective and projective tests of children, and demographic statistics. Chapter 4 covers types of marriage, tenure and responsibility, duty and independence, division of labor by sex and age, balance of authority, responsibility for discipline, child-bearing, interspousal communication, economics of fertility, birth control, preferences for boy or girl, marital relationships, role evaluation and self-esteem. Other chapters consider culture and society, bringing up children, and coming of age. Compares child training and behavior in Valle Caña and New England community.

986 LEWIS, OSCAR
1969 "The Death of Dolores." Transaction 6:7:10-19.
Relates the experiences of a poor family in San Juan, focusing especially on those events before and after the death of Dolores, a mother who was responsible for maintaining her children and other household members.

987 _____.
 1966 La Vida: A Puerto Rican Family in the Culture of
 Poverty - San Juan and New York. N.Y.: Random House.
 669 p.
 "Culture of poverty" study of a Puerto Rican family
 living in San Juan and New York as told by the mother
 and her children.

988 NERLOVE, MARC and SCHULTZ, T. PAUL
 1970 Love and Life Between the Census: A Model of Family
 Decision Making in Puerto Rico, 1950-1960. RAND Report
 RM-6322-AID. 105 p. tables, bibl.
 Under AID sponsorship, a simultaneous-equations model
 was developed to explain demographic-economic behavior
 related to family formation process in Puerto Rico,
 using 1950 and 1960 census data for 75 municipalities.
 Looks at female labor force participation, marriage,
 income, and migration.

989 ROSARIO, CHARLES
 1958 "Dos tipos de amor romántico: Estados Unidos y
 Puerto Rico." UPR/RCS 2:3:349-68.
 The principal function of romantic love is to achieve
 very stable male/female relations, "so as to overcome
 the tensions and anxieties that characterize the process
 of submission of the personality of the woman to that of
 the man." Wifely submission permits survival of marriage.

990 SAFA, HELEN ICKEN
 1974 The Urban Poor of Puerto Rico: A Study in Development and Inequality. Case Studies in Cultural Anthropology. N.Y.: Holt, Rinehart and Winston, Inc. 116 p.
 illus., tables, map, bibl.
 Contains much information on woman living in a shantytown of San Juan as well as later on in public housing.
 Helps to understand the changes that lower-class women
 are experiencing in relationships with men and their
 families; education and employment; aspirations; self-
 concept; and sex. Discusses matrifocal structure of
 many households, especially in public housing, and
 socialization process, which stresses dichotomy of sex
 roles. Based on interviews with male and female
 residents.

991 _____.
 1965 "The Female-Based Household in Public Housing: A
 Case Study in Puerto Rico." SAA/HO 24:2:135-39. tables.
 The modern welfare state provides a condition--public
 housing--which weakens economic role of men in lower-class

Marriage and the Family

households by giving institutional support to female-
based households. Describes matrifocal families in
this context and compares them to similar project in
Syracuse, New York. Suggests that policy makers in
public welfare design their programs so as to rehabilitate rather than merely sustain fatherless family.

992 _____.
1964 "From Shantytown to Public Housing: A Comparison of
Family Structure in Two Urban Neighborhoods in Puerto
Rico." UPR/CS 4:1:3-13. tables.
Based on fieldwork in San Juan (1959-60) to analyze
basic family structure in shantytowns and public housing,
finds matrifocality as the dominant form and as the
final stage in the atrophy of a man's authority in his
family. Other contributing factors are economic insecurity, strictly dichotomized conjugal roles, and strong
emotional ties between a mother, her children and female
relatives. Public housing and other forms of public
welfare undermine male authority and seem to strengthen
women's position by providing her with a home, a source
of income, and better employment opportunities by living
in an urban center.

993 SÁNCHEZ HIDALGO, EFRAÍN
1960 "¿Desorganización o reorganización del hogar?"
CPPR/P 8:2:7-17.
Continues theme of and repeats passages from his 1954
speech (#994) in same journal. Reviews current North
American opinions on the subject and notes changes from
a patriarchal to "biarchal" authority pattern; economic
support provided by both spouses; economic, political
and intellectual equality of women; sharing of functions
and responsibilities by spouses, etc.

994 _____.
1954 "Posibles efectos de la industrialización rápida
sobre la familia puertorriqueña." CPPR/P 2:1:17-28.
Hypothesizes on positive and negative effects of industrialization on the Puerto Rican family: greater
marital stability, women's economic independence and
consequent liberation, decreasing number of children
per family, diminution of domestic servants, but also
problems at home when the mother works. Does not agree
with generally held opinion that the family is in a
state of disorganization; rather, it is in a process of
reorganization toward better integration.

995 SEDA BONILLA, EDUARDO
1973 Social Change and Personality in a Puerto Rican
Agrarian Reform Community. Evanston, Ill.: Northwestern
Univ. Press. 187 p. bibl.
Chapter 5, "The Family," discusses virginity before
marriage, changes in marriage, and the family structure;
sex and contraception; child-rearing practices. Verses
from folk songs and games illustrate the traditional
pattern of male-female relations and girls' play.
Includes questionnaire.

996 _____.
1968 "Toro Bravo: una comunidad tradicional de pequeños
agricultores en el centro montañoso de Puerto Rico."
UPR/RCS 12:2:239-54.
In the traditional agricultural community of Toro
Bravo, woman is a "social unit corruptible by the per-
version and lasciviousness of man and therefore must be
protected from the omnipresent danger of masculine
'instincts'." Describes courtship, family life, notions
of birth control, religious practice, etc. Notes female
timidity and resignation vs. male dominance.

997 STEWARD, JULIAN HAYNES, et al.
1956 The People of Puerto Rico. A Study in Social
Anthropology. Urbana, Ill.: Univ. of Ill. Press.
540 p. illus., maps, graphs, bibl.
A collection of studies on different subcultures in
Puerto Rico includes information on women, male-female
relationships, courtship, marriage, the family, etc.
throughout.

998 WOLF, KATHLEEN L.
1952 "Growing Up and Its Price in Three Puerto Rican
Subcultures." Psychiatry 15:4:401-33.
Analysis of the Puerto Rican family and process of
socialization in 3 subcultures--rural sugarcane proletariat, workers on a coffee farm, a town's middle class--
includes much information on women (norms of adult behavior and actual behavior patterns) and child training.

Cuba

999 AMES, DAVID W.
1950 "Negro Family Types in a Cuban Solar." AU/P
11:2:159-63.
Data from residents of tenement house (solar) "Miami"
in Havana indicate 2 principle patterns of family

Marriage and the Family

organization: 1) woman--grandmother, mother, aunt or older sister--as head of household; 2) *arrimado*--institutionalized common-law form of marriage. Attributes patterns to historical experience of slaves in America and socio-economic conditions of Cuban blacks.

1000   CASTILLO de GONZÁLEZ, AURELIA
        1918 "Mujeres antes que hombres." CC 17:2:89-94.
        Criticizes frivolous manner in which girls are raised, arguing for domestic and social reforms. Women, not only men, need to be fortified with useful knowledge, because they are weak and hysterical and the family needs them to be strong, serene and responsible.

1001   FOX, GEOFFREY E.
        1973 "Race, Sex, and Revolution in Cuba." In Interracial Marriage: Expectations and Realities, ed. by I. R. Stuart and L. Abt, pp. 293-308. N.Y.: Grossman Publishers. bibl.
        Considers political aspect of marriage as an instrument of the State for regulating sexual relations as well as those pertaining to property. Discusses interracial relations in pre- and post-revolutionary Cuba: heritage of feudalism and slavery; race and sex (interracial marriage considered as a status loss for white person); slow but potential impact of revolution on race relations. Conflicts between old traditions and customs and new social and ethical order exist.

1002   MARTINEZ-ALIER, VERENA
        1974 Marriage, Class and Colour in Nineteenth-Century Cuba. A Study of Racial Attitudes and Sexual Values in a Slave Society. London: Cambridge Univ. Press. 202 p. tables, bibl.
        Based on archival research in Cuba and Spain, well-documented anthropological/historical monograph uses marriage as a focal point for assessing 19c. Cuban society, which was divided along racial lines. Brings to light conflicts and norms to single out deviations from ideal behavior as reflected in administrative and judicial proceedings of cases of parental opposition to a marriage, of marriage through elopement, and of interracial marriage. Sees virginity and chastity as a structural rather than cultural feature of a highly stratified society. Concludes with analytical comparisons with the Mediterranean, Caribbean, and India. Appendix includes 3 Cuban genealogies, detailed notes, and extensive bibliography.

1003   _____.
    1972 "Elopement and Seduction in Nineteenth Century Cuba."
    PP 55:91-129.
       Abbreviated version of larger study Marriage, Class
    and Color in Nineteenth-Century Cuba (1974) (#1002).
    focuses on marriage as a reflection of social structure.
    Covers marriage in canon and civil law in Spain, elope-
    ment by whites, reasons for eloping and for parental
    opposition, efficacy of elopement, seduction, elopement
    by people of color, interracial elopement, honor of
    women of color, and analytical comparisons with Medi-
    terranean concept of honor and shame and Caribbean
    matrifocality.

1004   _____.
    1971 "Virginidad y machismo: el honor de la mujer en
    Cuba en el siglo XIX." RI/CUAD 30:51-79. bibl. f/notes.
       Abbreviated version of larger study Marriage, Class
    and Colour in Nineteenth-Century Cuba (1974) (#1002)
    Sees elopement in 19c. Cuba as an institutionalized
    mechanism to overcome parental dissent to marriage
    between a man and woman of different social status.
    Protection of female honor (especially virginity) was
    directly related to maintaining family integrity along
    class lines, rather than to Catholic morality. Machismo
    is thus a secondary element derived from a system of
    values. Concludes that contemporary Cuban policy favors
    marriage even though marriage is interrelated to social
    structure and supposedly would lose its raison d'etre in
    an egalitarian social system.

1005 NELSON, LOWRY
    1951 Rural Cuba. Minneapolis, Minn.: Univ. of Minn.
    Press. 285 p. tables, graphs, bibl.
       Based on fieldwork (1945-46), discusses status of
    women and women in education. Chapter on the Cuban
    family mentions women throughout: historical background,
    male dominance, position of children, decline of aristo-
    cratic family, black family, interracial unions, con-
    temporary class and rural-urban differences, and marital
    statistics (age at marriage, family composition and size,
    marriage rates and sex ratios, divorce, illegitimacy, etc.

1006 OLESEN, VIRGINIA
    1971 "Context and Posture: Notes on Socio-Cultural Aspects
    of Women's Roles and Family Policy in Contemporary Cuba."
    WRU/JMF 33:3:548-60.

Marriage and the Family

Focuses on the socio-cultural context of women's roles
in a changing society and considers types of emergent
institutions relevant to the family. Using an indexical
survey of *Granma* and reports of travelers, journalists
et al., analyzes Cuban women's roles and public position
on the family.

1007 RODRÍGUEZ, ANÍBAL C.
1962 "Sobre la familia cubana." <u>UH/U</u> 26:156:7-29.
tables, bibl.
Concerned with the influence of socio-economic factors
on the Cuban family and changes in women's roles. Includes results of interviews with family members with
respect to ideal characteristics of family roles: e.g.,
qualities a good father, mother, husband, wife, son and
daughter should have (broken down by class).

1008 SÁNCHEZ, MEGALY
1974 "Rights and Duties Go Together." <u>CR</u> 4:2:13-14.
illus.
Title is slogan of XIIIth Congress of Cuban Workers
(November 1973). Series of 3 interviews with married
couples, adapted from Cuban women's magazine <u>Romances</u>
(November 1973) and translated by Center for Cuban
Studies, deals with issue of sharing household responsibilities when both wife and husband work. Responses
given by folk singers, journalist and 2nd grade teacher,
president of dock labor board and secretary.

1009 STEFFENS, HEIDI
1974 "A Woman's Place . . . <u>CR</u> 4:2:29-30. illus.
General comments on the process of change in Cuban
society since the Revolution, specifically those relating to women: divorce, sharing of household responsibilities, *machismo*, child care, Family Code.
Redefinitions are being formulated for family relations,
womanhood and manhood.

Dominican Republic

1009a BROWN, SUSAN E.
1973 "Coping with Poverty in the Dominican Republic:
Women and their Mates." <u>UC/CA</u> 14:5:555.
Briefly outlines major findings of doctoral research
(1969-71) on domestic organization of lower-income sector of a rural village in the Dominican Republic. Comparing 2 mating patterns among women in terms of

relative value for dealing with stress-laden socio-economic situations, concludes that women following single-mate pattern are more successful in traditional measures of wealth but women following multiple-mate pattern do better in terms of various indices of well-being.

1010 _____.

1973 "La mujer pobre en Santo Domingo." ED 1:5:67-82.

Describes ideals for women in a rural community in the Dominican Republic and why even women who wish to embody them are unable to. Explains why monogamy is not economically feasible for lowest income sector and why women prefer serial unions. Suggests that women following multiple mating pattern have more advantages and that this pattern serves as positive mechanism of subsistence and domestic organization. Based on field research.

HUMAN SEXUALITY, REPRODUCTION, AND HEALTH

This section includes those publications which deal with various aspects of sexuality (attitudes, behavior, and sex education); reproduction (menstruation, pregnancy, childbirth, breast-feeding, midwifery, puberty rites); fertility (its relationship to educational level, labor force participation, migration, religious observance, type of conjugal union, and other factors); family planning (interspousal communication; knowledge of, attitudes toward, and use of contraceptive methods; abortion); and health (illnesses, beliefs, practices, and practitioners, whether folk, psychiatric or otherwise: e.g., *susto*, alcoholism, *curanderas*).

Since all the topics in this section are so closely interrelated--reproductive cycle affects fertility; contraception affects health; sexual relations affect family planning; health affects birth; and so on--they have not been divided into sub-sections, but are grouped together for each country in alphabetical order by author. For facility in handling the quantity of material on fertility, all studies on this topic are located in this section and cross-referenced into EDUCATION, ECONOMIC LIFE, MARRIAGE AND THE FAMILY, etc., according to the respective factor influencing fertility level.

This section is not a forum for discussing the polemics of population control. Instead, emphasis is placed on those studies which are directly concerned with women's experiences--attitudes and behavior--regarding birth control. Therefore, only a few studies on attitudes and opinions held by national leaders with respect to family planning have been included.[1]

Studies dealing with abortion in legal terms, i.e., as a crime, and with women as the object of sexual crimes, can be found in the LAW category. For a general guide to more medical studies on specific

---

[1] Barry Edmonston (Food Research Institute, Stanford University) is preparing an unannotated bibliography of all population studies on Latin America through 1975, to be published in 1976 by Arizona State University Press as part of its reference series.

illnesses, consult the Index Medicus.[2] For biographical sketches of
women doctors, see BIOGRAPHY AND AUTOBIOGRAPHY. For much additional
information on the female life cycle, health, and sexual practices,
see ETHNOGRAPHIC MONOGRAPHS/COMMUNITY STUDIES. For additional entries
on sexuality and psychological health, see also PSYCHOLOGY. For items
which may consider sexual relations as part of family dynamics, see
MARRIAGE AND THE FAMILY.

SPANISH AMERICA - GENERAL

1011   ARGUMOSA, J. A. de
            1965 "La circuncisión femenina en los aborígenes de la
            región neotropical." MIIN/NI 6:40:3-10. bibl.
                Reproduces interesting, if brief, notes on rites of
            female circumcision among indigenous groups of tropical
            SA from chronicles and anthropological literature.

1012   ARIAS, EULOGIA R. de
            1970 "Sexto Laboratorio de Dinámica de Población,
            Fisiología de la Reproducción y Planificación Familiar."
            TDM 8:48:6-7, 20, 22, 32-33, 43, 51, 53.
                Reports on seminar held in El Salvador 24-29 November
            1969: population problems in Central America and pos-
            sible solutions; planning programs; sexual education and
            its goals.

1013   BERELSON, BERNARD et al., eds.
            1966 Family Planning and Population Programs: A Review
            of World Developments. Proceedings of the International
            Conference on Family Planning Programs, Geneva, August,
            1965. Chicago: University of Chicago Press. 848 p.
            illus., plates, tables, graphs.
                For LA, includes 3 articles reviewing the achievements
            and problems of national family planning programs, 2 on
            specific contraceptive methods; 1 on misconceptions
            regarding variables associated with fertility behavior;
            and several which refer to LA in a discussion about the
            world situation.

---

[2] Index Medicus. Washington, D.C.: National Library of Medicine.
It is a monthly and classified record of the current medical literature of the world. The subject index includes such topics as abortion, pregnancy, and menstruation. From 1960 on there is an annual
cumulative index.

Human Sexuality, Reproduction, and Health

1014   BERG, ALAN
      1972 "La economía del amamantar." BDSLM/CIDHAL 3:2:17-22.
      Translated excerpts from Saturday Review of the Sci-
      ences (March 1973) descry alarming and detrimental de-
      crease in breast-feeding, resulting from new social
      values. Quotes statistics for Chile, Colombia, El
      Salvador, Guatemala and Mexico.

1015   BOYD, MONICA
      1973 "Occupational Mobility and Fertility in Metropolitan
      Latin America." PAA/D 10:1:1-17. tables, bibl.
      Re-examines relationship between wife's fertility and
      husband's occupational mobility in Bogota, San José,
      Mexico City, Panama City, and Caracas, using data from
      CELADE 1963-64 surveys. Concludes that process of
      career mobility is not a significant factor in explaining
      differential reproductive behavior. Also critiques
      theory and methodology in mobility-fertility research.

1016   BROWN, JUDITH K.
      1963 "A Cross-Cultural Study of Female Initiation Rites."
      AAA/AA 65:4:837-53. tables, bibl.
      Using Murdock's "World Ethnographic Sample," (including
      16 South American indigenous groups) notes presence or
      absence of female initiation rites and discusses the
      relationship between rites and residence after marriage
      and female participation in subsistence activities, and
      between painful rites and sex identity conflict. Con-
      cludes that rites occur in societies in which girls re-
      main in parents' home even after marriage, early
      conditions result in conflict of sex identity, and women
      make a significant contribution to subsistence.

1017   CARLETON, ROBERT O.
      1965 "Fertility Trends and Differentials in Latin America."
      MMFQ 43:4/Part 2:15-35. tables, bibl.
      Discusses fertility trends and differentials in LA
      with respect to education and urban/rural residence,
      using child-woman ratio. In all age groups in 5 coun-
      tries, urban fertility is definitely and uniformly lower
      than rural fertility.

1018   CARLUCI, MARÍA ANGÉLICA
      1953/54 "La couvade en Sudamérica." UBAIA/R 6:1/2:133-74.
      maps, bibl. f/notes.
      Based on travel accounts and ethnographies cited in
      209 footnotes, this detailed study attempts to put in
      order the extensive literature which deals with the

couvade as manifested among 100 indigenous groups in SA.
Discusses methodology; problems of classification and
definition; and the magical, psychological, utilitarian,
physiological, economic, and legal interpretations of
this practice by other writers. Provides a map and
descriptive list of the distribution of *couvade* in SA
and another map for comparison with the rest of the
world.

1019 CORREA HENAO, ALFREDO
      1967 "Folklor de menstruación." UA/U 164:321-33. bibl.
      Professor of pathology provides interesting compendium
      of popular beliefs and practices related to menstruation,
      citing many examples from ancient times to the present,
      from all over the world. Mentions different terms to
      indicate menstruation in several regions of Colombia,
      causes and cures of amenorrhea, uses of menstrual
      blood, etc. Sources listed in 38 footnotes.

1020 CURRIER, RICHARD L.
      1966 "The Hot-Cold Syndrome and Symbolic Balance in
      Mexican and Spanish-American Folk Medicine." UP/E 5:3:
      251-62. bibl.
      Describes folk medical beliefs and practices in terms
      of "hot" and "cold." Hypothesizes that this syndrome
      functions as a logical system for dealing with disorder
      and disease on one level, but on a subconscious level
      it is a model of social relations, acting as a kind of
      projective system. Illustrates with examples as to how
      syndrome operates with respect to the processes of
      reproduction (menstruation, fertility, pregnancy,
      nursing).

1021 ELAM, EDGAR H.
      1971 "Opinion Profiles of Seven Cities." In Ideology,
      Faith and Family Planning in Latin America, ed. by
      J. M. Stycos, pp. 260-95. New York: McGraw Hill.
      tables, graphs, notes.
      Uses 1963/1964 CELADE survey data measuring knowledge,
      attitudes and practices (KAP) related to fertility among
      representative samples of 2000 women aged 20-50 currently
      or previously mated, from Bogotá, Buenos Aires, Caracas,
      Mexico City, Rio de Janeiro and San José. Concludes
      that young women with higher education are most favorable
      to low fertility and older women with lower education
      are least favorable; and inter-city variation was greater
      than intra-city variations by age and education with
      regard to several measures of fertility.

Human Sexuality, Reproduction, and Health

1022   FOCK, NIELS
       1967   "South American Birth Customs in Theory and Practice."
       In Cross-Cultural Approaches: Readings in Comparative
       Research, ed. by C. S. Ford, pp. 126-44. New Haven,
       Conn.: Human Relations Area Files. Reprinted from
       DEF/F 2(1960):51-69. illus., map, bibl.
          Discusses existing research and conflict of theories
       on the *couvade*. Clarifies term: women and men both
       take part in post-natal customs in South American indig-
       enous groups. Cites practices for Guayakí in Paraguay,
       Yahgan in Tierra del Fuego, et al.

1023   GASLONDE, SANTIAGO
       1973   Análisis preliminar de algunos datos sobre aborto
       provenientes de encuestas en América Latina. Serie A,
       no. 118. Santiago: Centro Latinamericano de Demografía.
       102 p. tables, graphs, bibl. f/notes.
          Reports on the results of a comparative studies program
       on abortion and the use of contraceptives in LA, begun
       in 1967 by CELADE. Provides much statistical
       information.

1024   GÓMEZ, VÍCTOR
       1972   Argentina, Costa Rica, Mexico y Venezuela: Algunos
       resultados de las encuestas comparativas de fecundidad
       en América Latina relacionados con la participación
       femenina en actividades económicas. Serie C, no. 145.
       Santiago: Centro Latinoamericano de Demografía. 49 p.
       tables, graphs, bibl.
          Using census and survey data, delineates notable
       characteristics of the 4 female populations under con-
       sideration (marital status, occupation, age, etc.) and
       suggests functional relations between those socio-
       economic variables and fertility levels and differen-
       tials. Reveals inverse association between economic
       activity of women and fertility and notes limitations of
       data.

1025   GUERRA, FRANCISCO
       1971   The Pre-Columbian Mind. A Study into the Aberrant
       Nature of Sexual Drives, Drugs Affecting Behavior, and
       the Attitude Towards Life and Death, With a Survey of
       Psychotherapy, in Pre-Columbian America. N.Y.: Seminar
       Press. 335 p. illus., map, plates, bibl.
          Post-Hispanic codices, pre-Columbian pottery and post-
       Hispanic 16c., 17c., and 18c. chronicles are used to illus-
       trate practices and beliefs related to sin, virginity,
       rape, prostitution, matrimony, polygamy, lesbianism,
       lust, incest, sexual aberration, divorce, fornication,

adultery, abortion, and sodomy. Considers pre-Columbian
and Spanish traditional morals and colonial acculturation. Extensive bibliography.

1026   HASS, PAULA H.
        1972 "Maternal Role Incompatibility and Fertility in
        Urban Latin America." JSI 28:2:111-27. tables, bibl.
           Summarizes Ph.D. thesis based on 1963-64 CELADE
        fertility surveys in 7 major Latin American cities.
        Hypothesis that wives employed outside the home, full
        time or in white collar jobs have lower fertility was
        not consistently supported in all 7 samples. Motivation,
        education and preferred role of women appear to be
        greater influences. Concludes that ecological conditions
        and variations among them are important operatives.

1027   HEER, DAVID M.
        1964 "Fertility Differences Between Indian and Spanish-
        Speaking Parts of Andean Countries." LSE/PS 18:1:71-84.
        tables, bibl.
           Findings suggest that lower fertility rates in Indian-
        speaking areas (Ecuador, Peru, Bolivia) may be due to
        involuntary causes. Computes child-woman ratio using
        1950 census data for Bolivia and Ecuador and concludes
        that Stycos' evidence and explanation for Peru are inade-
        quate. Suggests that female labor force participation is
        probably a more important variable than sex ratio in
        explaining variance in Peruvian fertility.

1028   HEER, DAVID M. and TURNER, ELSA S.
        1965 "Areal Differences in Latin America's Fertility."
        LSE/PS 18:3:279-92. tables.
           Child-woman ratio was computed for 18 Latin American
        nations from 1940's and 1950's census data. In 318
        areal units 8 variables (sex ratio, female labor force
        participation, literacy, et al.) were utilized to measure
        the relationship between the level of economic develop-
        ment and fertility. Analysis revealed positive associa-
        tion between rapid increase in economic development and
        higher than expected fertility. In the long run,
        however, a high level of economic growth depresses
        fertility level.

1029   KINZER, NORA SCOTT
        1973 "Priests, Machos and Babies: Or, Latin American
        Women and the Manichaean Heresy." WRU/JMF 35:2:300-12.
        bibl.

Human Sexuality, Reproduction, and Health

> Reviewing social science and popular literature since
> the 1950's, concludes that Latin America's high birth
> rate cannot be attributed merely to *machismo* and Church
> opposition to contraceptives. Considers female unemploy-
> ment and illiteracy more significant factors. Extensive
> bibliography.

1030 MATTELART, ARMAND
     1967 "América Latina: la anticoncepción es un mal menor."
     In his ¿Adónde va el control de la natalidad?, pp. 150-
     75. Col. Problemas de Nuestro Tiempo, 1. Santiago:
     Edit. Universitaria. bibl. notes.
     Good overview of population growth, fertility and
     birth control in LA since indigenous groups practiced
     contraception and abortion when the Spaniards conquered
     and enslaved them in the 16c. Considers economic, polit-
     ical, cultural, psychological, religious, and physical
     aspects of these controversial issues.

1031 MINTURN, LEIGH; GROSSE, MARTIN and HAIDER, SANTOAH
     1969 "Cultural Patterning of Sexual Beliefs and Behavior."
     UP/E 8:3:301-18. tables, bibl.
     Cross-cultural investigation of interrelationships of
     some forms of sexual behaviors and beliefs concerning
     sex. Scales measure kinds of marriage arrangements or
     dissolutions, extent of sexual segregation among unmar-
     ried adolescents, homosexuality and rape as deviance,
     aphrodisiacs and love charms, and sexual anxiety. Based
     on Human Relations Area Files.

1032 MIRÓ, CARMEN A. and MERTENS, WALTER
     1968 "Influences Affecting Fertility in Urban and Rural
     Latin America." MMFQ 46:3/part 2:89-120. tables, bibl.
     Using CELADE comparative fertility survey data, con-
     cludes that age at marriage, education, and family plan-
     ning practices are significant variables in explaining
     fertility differentials between rural and urban areas in
     LA. Age distribution, work of the woman and husband's
     occupation are considered inadequate factors.

1033 MIRÓ, CARMEN A. and RATH, FERDINAND
     1965 "Preliminary Findings of Comparative Fertility Sur-
     veys in Three Latin American Cities." MMFQ 43:4/part 2:
     36-68. tables, bibl.
     Reports preliminary findings of comparative fertility
     surveys in Panama City, Rio de Janeiro and San José based
     on sample of 2000 women each aged 20-50 years, irrespec-
     tive of marital status, regarding women's general

characteristics, pregnancy history, attitudes toward
family planning and use of contraceptives. Also examines
fertility differentials according to 8 variables. Educational level is most significant characteristic.

1034 OLIEN, MICHAEL D.
       1973 "The Double Standard of Sex Morals." In his Latin
       Americans: Contemporary Peoples and Their Cultural
       Traditions, pp. 214-18. N.Y.: Holt, Rinehart and
       Winston.
            Brief and general discussion of separate and distinct
       ideal standards for Latin American men and women, based
       on secondary sources. Cites examples of stereotypical
       behavior patterns; female activities and sexuality are
       circumscribed while men are accorded greater freedom.
       Women are cited in other parts of book as well, espe-
       cially Chapter 8, "The Urban Sector."

1034a PAIGE, KAREN E. and PAIGE, JEFFERY M.
       1973 "The Politics of Birth Practices: A Strategic
       Analysis." ASS/ASR 38:6:663-77. tables, bibl.
            Includes 21 South American indigenous groups in a
       sample of 114 societies taken from Murdock and White's
       Standard Cross-Cultural Sample to test hypotheses
       related to birth practices of both sexes. Data confirm
       that "restriction of women during childbirth and the
       husband's ritual involvement in birth are both strategies
       for asserting or defending paternity rights." Suggests
       that such practices represent a special case of bargain-
       ing mechanisms in societies without centralized
       authority.

1035 REQUENA B., MARIANO
       1968 "The Problem of Induced Abortion in Latin America."
       PAA/D 5:2:785-99. graphs, tables, bibl.
            Abortion is still the most widely used birth control
       measure in most of LA; its incidence highly influences
       fertility level. Describes and interprets problem of
       induced abortion in LA and suggests how to control it:
       methodological problems in epidemological study of it;
       magnitude, prevalence, and incidence; variations accord-
       ing to socio-economic cultural strata; additional charac-
       teristics of women who have experienced it (age, marital
       status, religion, obstetrical history, influence of
       family planning programs). Notes that differences
       within socio-economic groups are even more significant
       than national variations.

Human Sexuality, Reproduction, and Health

1035a SIMMONS, ALAN B.
1974 "Ambivalence Toward Small Families in Rural Latin America." SOBIO 21:2:127-43. tables, bibl.
Using rural fertility survey data gathered by CELADE among women in Costa Rica, Colombia, Mexico and Peru from 1968 to 1969, analyzes social definitions of "large" and "small" families; examines perceptions of advantages and disadvantages associated with family size; and develops a hypothetical model of the relationships between patterns of perceived "good" and "bad" features, different measures of family size preferences, and interest in learning about contraceptives. Reveals ambivalent attitudes toward family size.

1036 SOMOZA, JORGE L.
1965 "Trends of Mortality and Expectations of Life in Latin America." MMFQ 43:4/Part 2:219-41. tables, graphs, bibl.
Includes statistics which indicate higher life expectancy for women than men.

1037 STEPHENS, WILLIAM N.
1967 "A Cross-Cultural Study of Menstrual Taboos." In Cross-Cultural Approaches: Readings in Comparative Research, ed. by C. S. Ford, pp. 67-94. New Haven, Conn.: Human Relations Area Files Press. tables, bibl. Reprinted from GPM 64(1961):385-416.
Hypothesizes that menstrual taboos are a reflection of male castration anxiety with origins in the Oedipal complex, which is subjected to 14 tests (child-rearing practices, extensiveness of taboos, castration-suggestive incidents in folklore, etc.) Latin American groups include Aymara, Araucanians, Jívaro, Zapotec, Tarahumara. Elaboration of menstrual taboos measured by ordinal scale of Guttman type, using 15 variables.

1038 STYCOS, J. MAYONE
1973 Fecundidad en América Latina; Perspectivas sociológicas. 2nd ed. Mex., D.F.: Edit. Pax-Mexico. 328 p. tables, bibl. notes.
Collection of essays covering more than a decade of research by Stycos on population control in LA. Divided into general panorama; attitudes toward family size and family planning (e.g., "Interpersonal Influences in Family Planning in Puerto Rico"); social and cultural aspects (e.g., "Female Employment and Fertility in Lima, Peru," "Education and Fertility in Latin America"); conclusions.

1039   _____.
1968 Human Fertility In Latin America: Sociological Perspectives. Ithaca, N.Y.: Cornell Univ. Press. 318 p.
tables, graphs, bibl. f/notes.
Collection of articles on various aspects of fertility
and birth control in several Latin American countries
which have appeared in other publications.

1040   _____.
1965 "Needed Research on Latin American Fertility:
Urbanization and Fertility." MMFQ 43:4/Part 2:299-323.
tables, bibl.
Suggests further research on urbanization and fertility
in LA. Migrants and working women are of particular
importance.

1041   _____.
1965 "Opinions of Latin-American Intellectuals on Population Problems and Birth Control." AAPSS/A 360:11-23.
Presents arguments of national leaders in excerpts
from speeches, articles and reports along with voting
patterns on WHO and UN legislation for technical assistance on birth control in order to demonstrate that main
opposition comes from Marxists, nationalists and liberals
rather than the Church. However, negative attitudes are
shifting toward the positive as a result of population
increase, financial and technical assistance from the US,
and reconsideration by the Church of its position.

1042 STYCOS, J. MAYONE, et al.
1971 Ideology, Faith and Family Planning in Latin America.
Studies in Public and Private Opinion on Fertility Control. N.Y.: McGraw-Hill Book Co. 418 p. illus.,
tables, graphs, notes.
Collection of articles on the controversy over family
planning in LA, mostly on Colombia but with information
on other countries. Although discussion is focussed
on ideological and religious issues, relates to women
in terms of attitudes toward them and their reproductive
function.

1043 TALAMÁS de KITAIN, IRENE
1956 "La mujer en la medicina." FL 30:60/61/62:197-206.
Provides background remarks on women in medicine
throughout the world since ancient times before noting
specifics for LA. Begins with female practitioners
among the Aztecs and names the first graduates in medicine, dentistry, and pharmacy as well as specialists
for individual countries.

261

Human Sexuality, Reproduction, and Health

1044 TATUM, HOWARD J.
        1968 "Research on Physiological Aspects of Reproduction."
        MMFQ 43:3/Part 2:121-54. table, bibl.
           Presents survey of current research on the physiology
        of reproduction in many centers throughout LA, naming
        the most prominent institutions and individuals.

1045 TIETZE, CHRISTOPHER
        1958 "Human Fertility in Latin America." AAPSS/A 5:316:
        84-93. tables.
           Well researched and documented article on fertility
        levels and trends, prospect for a future decline, pat-
        terns of reproduction and the social and psychological
        factors associated with them. Statistical tables
        included.

1046 WHITEHEAD, LAURENCE
        1968 "Altitude, Fertility and Mortality in Andean
        Countries." LSE/PS 22:3:335-46.
           Reviews studies in same journal by Stycos (#1163),
        Heer (#1028) and James (1966, 20:1) which hypothesize on
        what affects fertility rates among Indian and mestizo
        women in Peru, Bolivia and Ecuador. Suggests that
        instead of unusually low level of fertility, there is an
        exceptionally high level of mortality because of a lack
        of modern medical practices. Predicts that improved
        health standards will result in population growth and
        aggravation of already existing social problems.

1047 YOUNG, FRANK W. and BACDAYAN, ALBERT A.
        1967 "Menstrual Taboos and Social Rigidity." In Cross-
        Cultural Approaches: Readings in Comparative Research,
        ed. by C. S. Ford, pp. 95-110. New Haven, Conn.: Human
        Relations Area Files Press. tables, bibl. Reprinted
        from UP/E 4(1965):225-40.
           Using a sociogenic approach and a scale for measuring
        the degree of institutionalization of menstrual taboos
        in society, authors view menstrual taboos as public
        restrictions of behavior throughout a woman's life in
        sub-communities where male dominance and solidarity
        exist within a framework of social rigidity. Included
        are the Aymara, Jívaro, Tarasco, Araucanians, and
        Tarahumara.

MIDDLE AMERICA

Mexico

1048 Asociación Pro Salud Maternal de México
      1974 "Si el Papa me mantiene los hijos . . ." BDSLM/
      CIDHAL 4:4:46-49.
           Survey taken to determine public opinion on Humanae
      Vitae of Pope Paul VI in 1968 reveals strong reaction by
      lower-income women to Pope's edict against contraception.
      Women firmly stated they would continue to use birth
      control pills. Rhythm was found ineffective and economic
      deprivation more pressing than ecclesiastical dictum.
      Women generally felt lack of true understanding on
      Pope's part because of his wealth.

1049 BRITO VELÁZQUEZ, ENRIQUE M.
      1971 ¿Quién escucha al Papa? Sondeo efectuado sobre las
      actitudes ante la Encíclica Humanae Vitae. Mex., D.F.:
      Inst. Mexicano de Estudios Sociales. 199 p. tables.
           Presents findings of a survey taken in Monterrey,
      Guadalajara and the Federal District to determine effect
      of the Pope's 1968 Humanae Vitae encyclical on the atti-
      tude and behavior of couples regarding family planning
      and contraceptive usage. Comparison between 1965 and
      1969 indicated an increase of persons in favor of and
      practicing birth control.

1050 _____.
      1969 "La fecundidad según status socio-económico.
      Análisis comparativo de las ciudades de México y Buenos
      Aires." CM/DE 3:2:156-85. tables, bibl.
           See ARGENTINA for annotation.

1051 BROWN, JACK
      1963 "Some Changes in Mexican Village Curing Practices
      Induced by Western Medicines." III/AI 23:2:93-120.
      tables, bibl.
           Carried out in San Nicodemo and Harmonía, *mestizo*
      communities in Tlaxcala, Mexico, examines adaptations of
      a *curandera* upon introduction of Western medicine.
      Describes Doña Luisa and her methods of classifying,
      diagnosing and treating illnesses. Points out mainte-
      nance of traditional values through economic, socio-
      cultural, and psycho-linguistic ways. Makes detailed
      comparison between *curandera* and doctor.

Human Sexuality, Reproduction, and Health

1052 BURNIGHT, ROBERT G.; WHETTEN, NATHAN L. and WAXMAN, BRUCE D.
1956 "Differential rural-urban fertility in Mexico."
ASS/ASR 21:1:3-8. tables, bibl.
Using 1950 census data and fertility ratio as a
measurement, points out variations in fertility among
different states of Mexico due to differences in urbanization. Suggests that variation in age composition is
probably a result of migration. Concludes that differential effect of urbanization affects fertility in Mexico
and Western industrialized countries similarly, with
urban dominance serving to significantly reduce fertility
ratio.

1053 CORWIN, ARTHUR F.
1964 "Mexico Resists the Pill." Nation 198:20:477-80.
Participant of a group which studied Mexican attitudes
toward birth control quotes 6 prominent Mexican men,
5 of whom opposed contraception. Tries to determine
why more support for birth control is lacking. Looks at
role of cult of motherhood, mestizo nationalism,
religion and machismo.

1054 _____.
1963 Contemporary Mexican Attitudes Toward Population,
Poverty and Public Opinion. Latin American Monographs,
25. Gainesville, Fla.: Univ. of Fla. Press. 54 p.
tables, bibl.
Based on questionnaires and interviews conducted among
several occupational and social groups, examines Mexican
attitudes toward birth control, sexual behavior and
population growth in Monterrey. Discusses family dynamics and the mother image.

1054a DAVIDSON, MARIA
1973 "A Comparitive Study of Fertility in Mexico City
and Caracas." SOBIO 20:4:460-72. tables, bibl.
See VENEZUELA for annotation.

1055 ELU de LEÑERO, MARÍA del CARMEN, ed.
1971 Mujeres que hablan: implicaciones psico-sociales en
el uso de métodes anticonceptivos. Mex., D.F.: Inst.
Mexicano de Estudios Sociales e Inst. Nacional de la
Nutrición. 214 p. tables, graphs, bibl. f/notes.
Reports findings of interviews with 200 women who
attended Clinic for Studies of Human Reproduction in
Mexico City. Explores antecendents and motivations for
family planning; its consequences on family life; attitudes of women regarding contraceptive measures.

Includes discussion of problem of population growth in
Mexico; a socio-economic profile of families who practice
birth control; and 2 contributions on the relationship
between men's occupation and family planning and between
female employment and the family (see Zetina Lozano
(#1377) and Romero Aguilar, Lourdes (#1073a).

1056   FABREGA, HORACIO, JR. and METZGER, DUANE
        1968 "Psychiatric Illness in a Small Ladino Community."
        Psychiatry 31:4:339-51. bibl. f/notes.
        Investigates psychiatric illness within a socio-
        cultural context in Tenejapa, Chiapas. Local informants
        provided data on native conceptions of psychiatric ill-
        ness, beliefs regarding its causes, and descriptive mani-
        festations distinguishing different disturbances.
        Verbatim account of 3-month state of madness endured by
        60-year-old woman illustrates social context and impli-
        cations of such illness in community: crisis was
        resolved by intervention of neighbors and leaders rather
        than by segregation of individual.

1056a   HALBERSTEIN, ROBERT A.
        1974 "Mortality Patterns in Cuanalan, Mexico: 1866-1970."
        SOBIO 21:3:256-71. maps, tables, graph, bibl.
        Using data from the municipal registry since 1866,
        questionnaires, and census materials from Cuanalan in
        the state of Mexico, attempts to interpret trends in
        age at death, infant and childhood mortality, survivor-
        ship and cause of death in terms of several ecological
        and cultural variables influencing the community.
        Results are presented for both women and men.

1057   HICKS, W. WHITNEY
        1974 "Economic Development and Fertility Change in Mexico,
        1950-1970." PAA/D 11:3:407-21. tables, bibl.
        Attempts to separate out causal mechanisms of Mexico's
        high population growth. Explores relationship between
        economic development, mortality decline, and fertility
        rate. Considers data for female literacy and relation-
        ship of education to fertility. Concludes that drastic
        reduction in fertility rate must come from combination
        of forces currently operative with government's recent
        support for family planning clinics and its efforts to
        improve child and maternal health.

1058   _____.
        1966 "A 'Reproductive Function' for Young Women in
        Mexico." UWI/SES 15:2:121-25.

Human Sexuality, Reproduction, and Health

Estimates effect of socio-economic variables (urbanization, literacy, wage rates) on fertility by using cross-
sectional 1960 census data for 32 states of Mexico.
Findings indicate significant positive correlation
between urban/rural variable and number of children ever
born, negative correlation for literacy rate, and no
significant correlation between wage rate and dependent
variable.

1059   HINTON, THOMAS B.
        1955 "The Seri Girls' Puberty Rite at Desemboque, Sonora."
        AAHS/K 20:4:8-11.
        Describes 4-day puberty rite which author partially
        witnessed in 1953 in main Seri settlement, fishing
        village of Desemboque, Sonora.

1060   KELLER, ALAN
        1971 "Mexico City: A Clinic Dropout Study." SFP 2:9:
        192-96. tables.
        Reports on study which coded and analyzed clinic data
        and included interviews with women at 5 clinics in
        Mexico City in order to follow up on acceptors of family
        planning practices who discontinue their clinic visits.
        Oral and injection patients are more inclined than IUD
        users to discontinue effective contraceptive practices.

1061   KELLER, ALAN; RABAGO de RODRÍGUEZ, AURORA and CORREU, SERGIO
        1974 "The Mexican Experience with Postpartum/Postabortion
        Programs, 1970-1972." SFP 5:6:195-200. tables.
        The Foundation for the Study of Population (FEPAC)
        began several programs in Mexican hospitals to offer
        information on family planning and contraception to
        women who had given birth or had an abortion. Reports
        on acceptance rates, characteristics of acceptors and
        nonacceptors, reasons for their choice, etc. Concludes
        that such programs are probably the most efficient means
        of promoting family planning. Based on interviews with
        214 women and program dropouts and clinic records.

1062   KELLY, ISABEL TRUESDELL
        1965 Folk Practices in North Mexico: Birth Customs, Folk
        Medicine, and Spiritualism in the Laguna Zone. Latin
        American Monographs, 2. Austin: Univ. of Tex. Press.
        166 p. table, bibl.
        Based on fieldwork in mestizo Torreón area of Coahuila
        (1953), describes beliefs and practices related to con-
        ception, pregnancy, parturition, postnatal care, and
        breastfeeding; folk medicine practioners (witches, curers,
        spiritualists, etc.); "unnatural" and "natural"

266

illnesses; remedies, luck and magic. Discusses relationship of modern folk medicine and magic in Laguna zone to
ancient Mexican and European practices. Appendices provide data on local spiritualism and herbs.

1063 _____.
1956 Santiago Tuxtla, Veracruz: Culture and Health.
Mex., D.F.: Inst. of Inter-American Affairs. 212 p.
tables, map, bibl.
Based on fieldwork (1955) in an urban town in the
Mexican state of Veracruz. In addition to general
ethnographic notes, concentrates on health, sex, and
reproduction: midwife, curer, sorcerer, supernatural
illnesses, marriage, menstruation, conception, pregnancy,
birth, postnatal care, abortion. Provides accounts by
female native informants and statistics on birth rate,
population, stillbirth. Also refers to women's important
role in the local economy and their recreational
activities.

1064 _____.
1955 "El adiestramiento de parteras en México, desde el
punto de vista antropológico." III/AI 15:2:109-17.
Suggests that local conditions be studied before
planning for a training project in midwifery because the
midwife's status is a basic point of reference and
varies according to region and because it is advisable
to examine local cultural patterns related to pregnancy,
birth and postnatal care.

1065 LARKIN, MARGARET
1966 "As Many As God Sends? Family Planning in Mexico."
Nation 203:16:508-11.
Discusses changing parental attitudes toward ideal
family size; describes traditional birth control methods,
such as prolonged nursing, selling children or giving
them to a relative, rhythm and abortion; examines governmental and Church attitudes; and cites organizations
which educate public in family planning.

1066 MADSEN, CLAUDIA
1968 "A Study of Change in Mexican Folk Medicine."
Contemporary Latin American Culture, by M. S. Edmonson,
C. Madsen, and J. F. Collier, pp. 89-137. Middle Ameri-
can Research Inst., Publication 25. New Orleans:
Tulane Univ. bibl.
Field research carried out in Tepepan, Xochimilco,
D.F. 1962-63. Covers curanderos, witches, love magic

Human Sexuality, Reproduction, and Health

> spiritist and spiritualist curing, illnesses, home
> remedies, pregnancy and childbirth, providing case
> examples of female practitioners and patients.

1067   METZGER, DUANE and WILLIAMS, GERALD E.
        1963 "Tenejapa Medicine I: The Curer." UNM/SWJA 19:2:
        216-34. tables.
           Explores role of the curer in Tzeltal-speaking commu-
        nity of Tenejapa, Chiapas, stressing attributes and
        performances which define the role as well as form the
        basis for evaluating curers and choosing one over
        another. Although male curers are more numerous than
        female ones, detailed description is applicable to
        either sex. Based on data from 7 informants.

1068   O'NELL, CARL W. and SELBY, HENRY A.
        1968 "Sex Differences in the Incidence of *Susto* in Two
        Zapotec Pueblos." UP/E 7:1:95-105. tables, bibl.
           Fieldwork by O'Nell in San Marcos Tlapazola and by
        Selby in Santo Tomás Mazaltepec supported basic assump-
        tion that *susto*, classified as a folk illness, represents
        an important culturally and socially sanctioned mechanism
        of escape and rehabilitation for persons suffering from
        intra-culturally induced stress resulting from failure
        in sex role performance. Discusses socialization of boys
        and girls and behavior of men and women. Evidence indi-
        cates that women are more likely to experience role
        stress because their sex roles are more narrowly defined
        than those for men and because they have fewer outlets
        for escape from that stress. Consequently, women are
        more susceptible to and experience *susto* more frequently.

1069   PADILLA PIMENTEL, MIGUEL
        1969 El noviazgo y la virginidad femenina. Mex., D.F.:
        Edit. Novaro. 108 p. bibl.
           Using the results of a limited survey among several
        hundred young women and men workers, students et al. in
        Mexico City, discusses changing attitudes and behavior
        with respect to relationships (engagements) and sexuality.
        Considers cult of female virginity an obstacle to love
        which, among Mexicans, is a consequence of vindictive
        aggression against the female figure and the necessity
        of asserting masculinity.

1070   PEÑA GÓMEZ, ROSA MARÍA
        1970 Edad de la menarquia en tres grupos de niñas
        mexicanas. Depto. de Investigaciones Antropológicas.
        Publicaciones, 24. Mex., D.F.: Inst. Nacional de
        Antropología e Historia. 84 p. illus.

Compares onset of menstruation among 3 groups of
Mexican girls (high altitude and sea level, rural and
urban) to determine if difference exists between rural
and urban areas and if altitude above sea level is an
important factor.

1071 "El pueblo habla."
1973 BDSLM/CIDHAL 3:3:5-11.
Reproduced from Contacto (April 1973), bimonthly publication from Mexican Social Secretariat. Series of
opinions on birth control by working class women in
Mothers' Circles in Mexico City. See in conjunction
with Zenteno article (#1086).

1072 RAINWATER, LEE
1964 "Marital Sexuality in Four Cultures of Poverty."
WRU/JMF 26:4:457-66. bibl. f/notes.
Patterns of marital sexuality in Mexico, Puerto Rico,
England and the US demonstrate notable similarities
in sentiments of lower class spouses toward sexual experiences and expectations about sex role performances by
conjugal partner. Hypothesizes that in societies
experiencing marked segregation of husband/wife role
relationship, it is less likely that a couple will develop a close sexual relationship or that the wife will
encounter sexual relations as satisfying.

1073 ROBINSON, WARREN C. and ROBINSON, ELIZABETH H.
1960 "Rural-Urban Fertility Differentials in Mexico."
ASS/ASR 25:1:77-81. tables, bibl. f/notes.
Using census data from 1930, 1940 and 1950 and fertility and marital ratios, examines urban-rural fertiltiy
differentials and trends in Mexico. Concludes further
urbanization or industrialization will reduce birth rate.

1073a ROMERO AGUILAR, LOURDES
1971 "Relación de la ocupación masculina y algunos
aspectos de la planeación familiar." In Mujeres que
hablan, ed. by M. del C. Elu de Leñero, pp. 135-63.
Mexico, D.F.: Instituto Mexicano de Estudios Sociales,
Instituto Nacional de la Nutrición. tables.
Analyzes attitudes of 300 Mexican women in relation
to birth control as influenced by their position as
wives and the socio-economic status of their husbands
(laborers, service workers, employees). Concludes that
husband's occupation and income must be taken into
account in family planning programs since they are closely
related to wife's access to media, goods and services
and her resulting behavior and satisfaction with life.

Human Sexuality, Reproduction, and Health

1074   ROSS, FREDERICK U.
       1970   "Mexico Ambivalent on Birth Control." CCY
       87:47:1428-29. illus.
          Despite very high birth rate (cites statistics),
       Mexico was only nation to oppose a resolution supporting
       birth control at a Latin American medical conference in
       1969. Gives official position as well as women's views
       in support of and attendance at birth control clinics.
       Sketches development of family planning movement in
       Mexico and future prospects.

1075   ROTHMAN, ANA MARÍA
       1969   La participación femenina en actividades económicas
       en su relación con el nivel de fecundidad en Buenos
       Aires y México. Serie C, no. 108. Santiago: Centro
       Latinoamericano de Demografía. 40 p. tables, diagram,
       bibl. f/notes.
          See ARGENTINA for annotation.

1076   SELBY, HENRY A.
       1974   Zapotec Deviance. The Convergence of Folk and Modern
       Sociology. Austin: Univ. of Tex. Press. 166 p. illus.,
       table, maps, bibl.
          Fieldwork carried out in traditional Zapotec community
       in Oaxaca (1965-71); 2 out of 6 informants interviewed
       were women. Demonstrates interactionist approach to
       deviance. Examines in detail ideologies, sexual devi-
       ance and witchcraft (practiced by both sexes). Defines
       general dimensions of Zapotec value system and how they
       in turn define categories of kinship, drawing examples
       from both sexes. Believes women experience greater
       oppression by the value system than men, since the for-
       mer bear a heavier moral burden and since their "work is
       more crucial, unrecognized, and less rewarded."

1077   SULLIVAN, THELMA D.
       1969   "Embarazo y parto: costumbres, supersticiones y
       técnicas prehispánicas de los aztecas y su supervivencia
       en México." III/A 29:285-93. bibl.
          Discussion of pregnancy and birth practices, super-
       stitions and pre-Hispanic techniques based on 16c. and
       17c. Nahuatl and Spanish sources. Illustrates their
       persistence in present-day Mexico by referring to the
       texts of Madsen, Redfield and Lewis and data from an
       informant: e.g., breast-feeding for a year or more is
       still considered quite important. Believes these tradi-
       tions have survived because they are fundamental cultural
       concepts and beliefs created and conserved by women,
       "the most traditional human beings."

1078   SULLIVAN, THELMA D., trans.
        1966 "Pregnancy, Childbirth, and the Deification of the
        Women Who Died in Childbirth. Texts from the Florentine
        Codex, Book VI, Folios 128v - 143v." UNAM/ECN 6:63-95.
        Paleography of Florentine Codex texts in parallel
        columns of Nahuatl and English, which deal with Aztec
        beliefs and practices regarding pregnancy and childbirth:
        hiring of midwife and her acceptance of case; midwife's
        rules for pregnant woman to observe during final months;
        pre-parturition treatment by midwife; operation to remove
        dead child and save mother; account of woman who dies
        in childbirth and is deified. Believes these texts are
        not only pre-Cortesian medical data, but also reflection
        of Nahuatl concept of Woman. Women giving birth were
        equated with warriors going into battle. Explanatory
        footnotes.

1079   THOMPSON, RICHARD W. and ROBBINS, MICHAEL C.
        1973 "Seasonal Variation in Conception in Rural Uganda
        and Mexico." AAA/AA 75:3:676-86. tables, bibl.
        Using data from monthly birth records (1963-70) of
        Amealco, Queretaro, assesses complex interrelationship
        between socio-cultural and climatic variables and sea-
        sonal variations in conception and birth in rural Mexico
        (and Uganda). Challenges Nurge's hypothesis by demon-
        strating with product-moment correlations that a negative
        association exists between months of increased physical
        activity and workload and sexual activity and possibil-
        ities for conception. Suggests that urban migration and
        temperature be examined as additional variables with
        potential causal efficacy.

1080   VALDIOSERA BERMAN, RAMÓN
        1973 El lesbianismo en México. Mex., D.F.: Eds.
        Asociados. 157 p. illus., bibl.
        Fashion designer purports to present "objective"
        study (!) of lesbianism as more of a social than a
        medical problem. Considers lesbians sick, neurotic
        women who become addicted to their sexual vice because
        of a lack of affection! Offers 31 accounts of Mexican
        women from several social classes (1949-73), obtained
        1st, 2nd and 3rd hand, in which they recount horrible
        and often traumatic experiences they had with men when
        young and pleasure and happiness they found with other
        women.

1081   van KEEP, PIETER A. and RICE-WRAY, EDRIS
        1973 "Attitudes toward Family Planning and Contraception
        in Mexico City." SFP 4:11:305-09. tables.

271

Human Sexuality, Reproduction, and Health

> Reports on the attitudes toward family planning and
> contraception held by Mexican women attending the
> Asociación Pro-Salud Maternal clinic compared to those
> of the general female population in Mexico City. Inter-
> views with 750 women revealed a greater inclination
> toward family planning among the clinic sample and an
> unexpected high rate of approval among the city sample.
> Women aged 21-30, with a higher educational level and
> from higher socio-economic groups indicated greatest
> approval.

1082 VARGAS G., LUIS ALBERTO and MATOS M., EDUARDO
      1973 "El embarazo y el parto en el México prehispánico."
      UNAM/AA 10:297-310. illus., plates, bibl.
      A presentation of concepts, practices and views re-
      garding pregnancy and childbirth by pre-Hispanic culture
      in Mexico before the Spanish conquest. Based on Sahagún's
      observations and collection of data among the Nahuatl,
      and his examination of the Codices and secondary sources.

1083 ZÁRATE, ALVÁN O.
      1967 "Differential Fertility in Monterrey, Mexico: Pre-
      lude or Transition?" MMFQ 45:2/Part 1:93-108. tables,
      bibl.
      Reports findings of investigation of fertility dif-
      ferentials among socio-economic subgroups in Monterrey,
      Mexico. Unusual aspect of the study is that survey was
      conducted among men rather than women, but the economic
      activity of their wives in relation to fertility level
      is discussed.

1084 _____.
      1967 "Fertility in Urban Areas of Mexico: Implications
      for the Theory of the Demographic Transition." PAA/D
      4:1:363-73. tables, bibl. notes.
      Using Mexican census and vital registration data
      (1940-60), tests whether urban fertility is inversely
      related to proportion of urban population employed in
      secondary sector of economy and whether changes in urban
      fertility are inversely related to changes in proportion
      of that same population. Findings do not support hypoth-
      eses. Fertility change variation is explained more by
      city growth rates and changes in proportion literate than
      percentage in secondary sector. Economic development
      has increased instead of reduced fertility.

1085 _____.
      1967 "Some Factors Associated With Urban-Rural Fertility
      Differentials in Mexico." LSE/PS 21:3:283-94. tables.

Uses 1960 census data for 23 urban and rural areas in
Mexico for correlation analysis. Findings point to
relationship between urban-rural fertility differentials
and differentials in age at marriage, percentage married,
physical availability of marital partners, all of which
are associated with urban growth. Suggests that changes
in urban population composition may favor higher and
lower fertility rates.

1086 ZENTENO, ARNALDO
1974 "It is Good, But a Sin." In An Anthology on Women
in Latin America, pp. 32-38. 1st special issue of
BDSLM/CIDHAL. Spanish version: 1974 "Limitar naci-
miento es bueno, pero es pecado!" BDSLM/CIDHAL 4:3:3-8.
Observations by enlightened Mexican priest on problems
related to birth control as noted in Mothers Circles in
a working class neighborhood in Guadalajara. Women
manifest deep concern for economic and educational welfare of their children and see advantage of birth control, but they also believe it is a sin, children are
sent by God, marriage is for having children rather than
loving a husband, and dialogue between partners is
impossible.

Guatemala

1087 GENDELL, MURRAY; MARAVIGLIA, MARIA NYDIA and KREITNER, PHILIP C.
1970 "Fertility and Economic Activity of Women in
Guatemala City, 1964." PAA/D 7:3:273-86. tables, bibl.
Utilizing data from 5% census sample in Guatemala City
(1964), demonstrates that economically active women, in
particular domestic servants, had lower cumulative fertility than inactive women, partly because many of the
former had not married nor had children. Cross tabula-
tion and regression analysis reveal that for all women
fertility is more strongly associated with age, marital
status, and educational level than activity status.
"Live-in" domestics had considerably lower fertility
rates than "live-out" ones because employers prefer
single or childless women. Confirms thesis that in LA
relatively low fertility associated with economic activity is prevalent in large, urban, more modern economic
and social sectors.

1088 GILLIN, JOHN
1948 "Magical Fright." Psychiatry 11:4:387-400. bibl.
f/notes.

Human Sexuality, Reproduction, and Health

Describes the *susto* complex and its cultural setting
in the eastern Guatemala community of San Luis Jilotepeque
as well as treatment. Assesses personality structure of
male curer and female patient (63 year old Pokomán Indian)
through the use of life sketches, Rorschach, and opinions
of community members: schizophrenic curer and hypochondriacal, compulsive, insecure, anxious, frustrated, re-
pressed and intellectually dual woman. Offers comparative
ethnographic data on *susto* for Peru and Middle America
and suggests that this psychiatric syndrome in various
Latin American folk cultures is defined by or a product
of the cultural and social structure, with a concomitant
system of treatment.

1089   GONZÁLEZ, NANCY L. SOLIEN
       1963   "Some Aspects of Child-Bearing and Child-Rearing in
       a Guatemalan Ladino Community." UNM/SWJA 19:4:411-23.
       table, bibl.
          Based on interviews with 102 mothers in Ladino town
       of San Antonio La Paz, near Guatemala City, describes
       health resources, pregnancy and childbirth, breast-
       feeding and weaning, infant and child diet, sickness
       and disease.

1090   HINSHAW, ROBERT; PYEATT, PATRICK and HABICHT, JEAN-PIERRE
       1972   "Environmental Effects on Child Spacing and Popula-
       tion Increase in Highland Guatemala." UC/CA 13:2:216-30.
       map, tables, graphs.
          Using comprehensive birth-interval data from 3 Indian
       communities around Lake Atitlán during a 35-year period,
       attributes declining birth rate to declining mortality
       rate and physiological constraints of nursing-induced
       postpartum amenorrhea. Analyzes secular and community
       variations in spacing of children according to differing
       levels of concern with reproduction.

1091   Instituto Centro Americano de Población y Familia (ICAPF)
       1972   Fecundidad en Guatemala. Guat.: ICAPF. 709 p.
       tables, graphs.
          Collection of 15 essays by different authors on various
       aspects of fertility in Guatemala: 1967-68 survey on
       socio-cultural conditioning; family structure of marginal
       groups; sexual behavior; knowledge of and attitudes
       toward contraception; attitudes of the medical profession
       and national leaders; etc.

1092   PAUL, LOIS
       1974   "The Mastery of Work and the Mystery of Sex in a
       Guatemalan Village." In Women, Culture and Society,

ed. by M. Z. Rosaldo and L. Lamphere, pp. 281-99.
Stanford: Stanford Univ. Press. bibl.

Based on sporadic living experiences in San Pedro,
Lake Atitlán since 1941, uses "body concepts relating to
women's work and to sex and reproduction" to understand
how Pedranas see themselves and their position in society.
Concludes that while both men and women are considered
masters in their own sphere of work, they are not equal
in matters of sex. Symbolic and social importance of
women's productive work is contrasted by weak self-
concept of a woman's body, which is dominated by men in
sex and by mysterious forces in menstruation and pregnancy. Describes socialization of girls and various
stages of life cycle, especially in relation to
reproduction.

1093 SAQUIC CALEL, RASALÍO
      1970 "La familia indígena y la planificación familiar."
      GIIN/GI 5:3/4:91-100.
      Provides general sketch of the indigenous family in
Guatemala (e.g., selecting a mate; civil, religious or
ritual marriage; consensual union; family organization;
functions of the father, mother, and children; clothing;
family planning). Interviews with 14 women, around age
32, at 3 Centers of Family Orientation in 3 municipalities revealed that there is good acceptance of birth
control among indigenous women.

El Salvador

1094 GÓMEZ, CARLOS J.
      1965 Estudio económico y social de la familia del area
      metropolitana de San Salvador, agosto 1964. San
      Salvador. 171 p. tables.
      Data compiled on 2,255 women (20-50 years old) in
San Salvador (1964) reveals that gap between knowledge
of birth control methods and practice of family planning
techniques is a factor of greater importance among
poorly educated classes, regardless of degree of reli-
giousness. Joint study by National Council of Economic
Planning and Coordination, Ministries of Economy, Labor
and Social Prevision, Population Council and Cornell
University.

1095 HENRÍQUEZ de PAREDES, QUERUBINA
      1974 "Un dilema: la educación sexual." BDSLM/CIDHAL
      4:2:3-7. table.

275

Human Sexuality, Reproduction, and Health

> Lists several conclusions of sociological study (1970) by member of Salvadorean Democratic Association about national attitudes toward sexuality of parents of secondary school students. Information on sexuality has generally been inadequate and learned late and sometimes incorrectly. Sexual activities are initiated at an earlier age by men than by women and considered a pleasant experience by more men; but for women sexual initiation is immediately tied with reproduction whereas for men there is a 5 year lapse between the two.

Honduras

1096 MUNDIGO, AXEL
> 1970 "Scarcity and Family Planning in Honduras." CJSR 5:2:102-18. tables, bibl.
> Using data from fertility and family planning survey (212 women, 106 men) in 1 of Tegucigalpa's poorest areas (1968), explores whether "an environment of scarcity inhibits successful family planning." Notable material and social-psychological differentials are related to practices and attitudes surrounding family planning. Results indicate more female participation in family decision-making among contraceptive users and importance of husband-wife communication and agreement for successful family planning.

Costa Rica

1097 AMADOR GUEVARA, JOSÉ, et al.
> 1966 Nuestro problema demográfico. San José, C.R.: Ministerio de Salubridad Pública, Sección de Comunicaciones del Departamento Educación Sanitaria. 26 p. tables, graphs, bibl.
> Comments on abortion as a public health problem in Costa Rica, providing some 1960's statistics.

1098 GONZÁLEZ-QUIROGA, ALBERTO
> 1968 "Attitudes Toward Family Planning in Turrialba, Costa Rica." MMFQ 46:3/Part 2:237-55. tables, graphs, bibl.
> Reports on family planning attitudes and practices in rural Costa Rican community, comparing husbands and wives.

1099   MICHIELUTTE, ROBERT, et al.
        1973   "Consensual and Legal Marital Unions in Costa Rica."
        YU/IJCS 14:1/2:119-28. tables, bibl.
            Defining consensual union as a co-residential, non-
        legal sexual and social liaison, examines characteristics
        of Costa Rican women in consensual and legal unions,
        emphasizing reproductive behavior. Data obtained from
        6 family planning clinics, where 1500 white and Indian
        women (15-49 years of age) were randomly interviewed;
        women's knowledge of contraception and reproduction and
        attitudes toward birth control were scored. Notes sig-
        nificant differences in 20 out of 27 variables, with
        characteristic patterns emerging according to social
        class, but similar reproductive behavior in women of
        both kinds of unions. Class and race not defined.

1099a   _____.
        1973   "Factors Associated with Utilization of Family
        Planning Clinics in Costa Rica." SOBIO 20:2:160-72.
        tables, bibl.
            Questions if factors correlated with interest in fam-
        ily planning are also related to clinic attendance or
        if family planning clinics appeal only to limited sub-
        group of women interested in family planning. Also
        looks for differences between women who drop out of
        clinics and those who remain active. Based on inter-
        views with almost 1500 primarily low-income women in
        areas served by 6 clinics in Costa Rica.

1100   _____.
        1973   "Early Sexual Experiences and Pregnancy Wastage in
        Two Cultures." CFS/J 4:2:225-38. tables, bibl.
            Examines several aspects of early sexual experience--
        age at first intercourse, at first marriage, at first
        conception, and when first learned of contraception--in
        relationship to pregnancy wastage among low-income black
        females in North Carolina and primarily low-income white
        and Indian females in Costa Rica. Generally weak support
        found for hypothesis in either group.

1101   ONAKA, ALVIN T. and YAUKEY, DAVID
        1973   "Reproductive Time Lost Due to Sexual Union Dissolu-
        tion in San José, Costa Rica. LSE/PS 27:3:457-65.
        tables.
            Using 1964 CELADE fertility survey data, attempts to
        measure amount of reproductive time lost as a combined
        result of widowhood, separation and divorce and to ex-
        plain variations in that lost time. Findings reveal
        approximately 10% lost due to break-up of sexual unions;

Human Sexuality, Reproduction, and Health

and loss was 3 times greater in consensual than legal
unions. Discrepancy explained through examination of
social background characteristics. Suggests that attention be given to consensual unions as a predictor of
future trends in Latin American fertility.

1102   ORSO, ETHELYN
        1970 Hot and Cold in the Folk Medicine of the Island of
        Chira, Costa Rica. Monograph and Dissertation Series,
        1. Baton Rouge, La.: La. State Univ., Latin American
        Studies Inst. 100 p. tables, diagrams, bibl.
            Field work carried out (1967, 1968-69) for an analysis
        of the hot-cold system of folk medicine on the Island of
        Chira, Costa Rica. Cites 14 case examples of illnesses
        and cures involving girls and women; also discusses men-
        struation, pregnancy, childbirth. Two types of curing
        specialists are midwives and masseurs(euses).

1103   REYNOLDS, JACK
        1973 "Costa Rica: Measuring the Demographic Impact of
        Family Planning Programs." SFP 4:11:310-16. tables,
        bibl.
            Application of model (demographic and program analysis)
        to measure impact of Costa Rica's family planning program
        on fertility. Data indicate that the program did not
        play a major role in the decline of fertility between
        1959 and 1969, since many women dropped out, among other
        reasons.

1104   SANDERS, THOMAS G.
        1973 Population Perception and Policy in Costa Rica.
        Field Staff Reports: South America: Mexico and Carib-
        bean Area Series, 1. Hanover, N.H.: American Univer-
        sities Field Staff. 16 p. illus., tables, map, bibl.
        notes.
            Overview of population development in Costa Rica
        deals in great part with factors responsible for growing
        family planning and "demographic awareness," describing
        programs and results of various studies. However, a
        recent survey among female participants in public health
        clinics indicates a negative response to the orientation
        talk and procedures of the family planning programs.

1105   WAISANEN, F. F., et al.
        1966 A Survey of Attitudes Related to Costa Rican Popula-
        tion Dynamics. San José, C.R.: Programa Interamericano
        de Información Popular of the American Int'l. Assoc. for
        Economic and Social Development. 189 p. tables, bibl.

Research conducted in Costa Rica (1965-66) under AID contract provides data at national sample level with respect to cultural, economic, social and psychological factors (and communication) that relate to favorability or unfavorability toward family planning and induced abortions. Data demonstrate favorable attitudes among 64% of total sample population of 1500. Appendix includes annotated bibliography of international literature on family planning, analysis design, index construction, and interview schedule with data.

SOUTH AMERICA

Venezuela

1105a DAVIDSON, MARIA
       1973 "A Comparative Study of Fertility in Mexico City and Caracas." SOBIO 20:4:460-72. tables, bibl.
       Using 1963-64 CELADE fertility survey data, compares variations in fertility among women in Mexico City and Caracas considering such factors as age at marriage, education and labor force status of woman, occupation of husband, religiosity, and ideal and desired number of children. Analysis indicates that cumulative fertility of ever-married women in Mexico City was higher than of women in Caracas.

1106 _____.
       1969 "Some Demographic and Social Correlates of Fertility in Venezuela." IASI/E 27:105:587-601. tables.
       Examination of trends and differentials in fertility in Venezuela using 1950 and 1961 census data and relating fertility to marital status of women, age at birth of first child, urban-rural residence and education. Latter demonstrates negative or inverse relationship to fertility in both urban and rural areas, with lower fertility rates in urban areas. Notes increase in fertility rate from 1950 to 1961.

1107 GUTIÉRREZ ALFARO, PEDRO A., et al.
       1955 La obstetricia en Venezuela. Ensayo histórico. Caracas: Edit. "Ragón." 576 p. illus., tables, graphs, plates, bibl.
       Comprehensive compendium of historical, medical, and folkloric information on obstetrics in Venezuela--beliefs, practices, practitioners--from pre-conquest to contemporary times. Extensive bibliography.

Human Sexuality, Reproduction, and Health

1108 RAMÍREZ ROMERO, RAMIRO
       1966 La mujer destinada por el sexo. Madrid: Edit.
       Mediterráneo (EDIME). 545 p.
       Based on author's clinical experience as an obstetri-
       cian, venereologist and gynecologist in Venezuela, dis-
       cusses birth control, sexual development, frigidity,
       promiscuity, prostitution, masturbation, etc., from a
       physiological/psychological perspective. Cites specific
       cases and provides a dictionary of terms.

1109 SUÁREZ, MARÍA MATILDE
       1974 "Etiology, Hunger, and Folk Diseases in the Vene-
       zuelan Andes." JARES 30:1:41-54. map, table, bibl.
       Based on empirical data obtained from 30 males and 40
       females, aged 15-70, in El Morro, Mérida (1971, 1972),
       establishes etiological categories and explains curative
       treatments of folk disease. Assigns "hunger" and "cold"
       diseases to the natural category and folk diseases re-
       sulting from injurious effect of magical or supernatural
       powers to prenatural category.

1110 WATSON, LAWRENCE C.
       1973 "Marriage and Sexual Adjustment in Guajiro Society."
       UP/E 12:2:153-61.
       Continuation of previous study (See Watson, #1111)
       addresses itself to the problem of "negative sexual fixa-
       tion" as a result of severe sexual socialization. De-
       scribes female sexual behavior in marriage and accounts
       for the lack of anticipated conflict and anxiety through
       an explanation of 4 socio-cultural factors which lead to
       female sexual adaptation. Sex can be used as a commodity
       to obtain important concessions from one's husband.
       Records women's reactions to sexual activities.

1111 _____.
       1972 "Sexual Socialization in Guajiro Society." UP/E
       11:2:150-56. bibl.
       Maintains that severe socialization of female sexual
       behavior among the Guajiro Indians functions as a sta-
       bilizer of marriage and thus helps to create basis for
       establishing political alliances for the support and
       security of the matrilineage. Describes the socializa-
       tion process and consequent personality traits, and the
       relationship between sex, marriage and politics. Based
       on field research (1964-65) in the Guajiro Peninsula of
       Colombia and Venezuela.

Colombia

1112 AGUIRRE, ALFREDO
  1966 "Colombia: The Family in Candelaria." <u>SFP</u> 2:11:1-5.
  bibl. f/notes.
   Based on data collected from 100 couples in a family
  planning program in semi-rural Candelaria in the Cauca
  Valley, discusses most important effects which demographic and socio-cultural problems are having on this
  community, on family structure, and on the individual;
  the role of the physician; and changes in attitudes.
  Offers descriptive data on women, abortion, infant mortality, use of contraceptives, etc. Concludes that
  greater knowledge of sex education and technical information accompanied by family planning practices will help
  to alleviate growing demographic problem.

1113 ALZATE, HELI
  1974 "A Course in Human Sexuality in A Colombian Medical
  School." <u>ME/J</u> 49:5:438-43. tables, bibl.
   Describes sexuality course for sixth-semester medical
  class of Caldas University (Manizales, Colombia), composed of 32 males and 7 females. Questionnaire administered pre- and post-program to evaluate impact of
  instruction on students' sexual knowledge and attitudes
  revealed significant improvement.

1114 Asociación Colombiana de Facultades de Medicina
  1965 <u>Boletín del 2º Seminario Sobre Demografía</u>. Bogota.
  433 p. tables, graphs, bibl.
   Collection of papers read at second Seminar on
  Demography (Medellin, 10-13 October 1965) includes
  socio-demographic investigations, studies on abortion
  in several cities, fertility and sexual attitudes,
  family planning, etc., all pertaining to Colombia; and
  comments, discussions, recommendations.

1115 BAILEY, JERALD
  1973 "An Evaluative Look at a Family Planning Radio
  Campaign in Latin America." <u>SFP</u> 4:10:275-78. tables,
  bibl.
   Considers the effect of radio campaigns on initial
  acceptance of family planning at 16 Profamilia clinics
  in Colombia (1969-1972). Concludes that there was a
  substantial impact on the number of women who accepted
  a contraceptive method in the clinic.

Human Sexuality, Reproduction, and Health

1116 BAILEY, JERALD; LÓPEZ-ESCOBAR, GUILLERMO and ESTRADA E.,
ALCIDES
1973 "A Colombian View of the Condom." SFP 4:3:60–64.
tables, bibl.
Drawing data from a 1969 national KAP survey and a
1970 survey of the commercial sector, discusses the use
of the condom for contraceptive purposes in Colombia.
Findings indicate that a large number of people, especially women, were unaware of it. Supply problems of
and status ambivalence about the condom exist.

1117 CORREA, PATRICIA; JARAMILLO, ISA de and UCRÓS, ANAMARÍA
1972 "Influencia de la educación sexual en el nivel
de información y en las actitudes hacia la sexualidad."
RLP 4:3:323–34. tables, bibl.
Studies the level of information and attitudes of
2000 (500 of each sex, according to whether or not they
had received sex education) Colombian high school students toward sexuality in general as well as specific
aspects of it. Findings indicate that women without
sex education have the healthiest attitudes toward sex,
suggesting that for them sex education is influenced by
and reinforces prejudices and taboos. In general, female
students are slightly better informed than males; concepts of masculinity and femininity are deformed; and
religion plays a detrimental role in adequately, accurately, and unbiasedly educating people in sex.

1118 CRUZ BETANCOURT, CARMEN INÉS
1974 La apertura al cambio en la población rural.
Publicación 3. Bogota: ASCOFAME, División de Estudios
de Poblacion. 84 p. tables, bibl.
Analyzes results of national fertility survey for rural
sample (2736 women, 15 to 49 years old). Concludes that
acceptance of new behavior patterns is produced in differentiated form according to level of aspirations,
attitudes or conduct, which are conditioned by educational level, exposure to contact with other communities,
interpersonal communication, etc.

1119 ESTRADA E., ALCIDES, et al.
1974 Características socio-demográficas de las mujeres
colombianas. Encuesta nacional de fecundidad: parte
urbana. Publicación 4. Bogota: ASCOFAME, División de
Medicina Social y Población. 85 p. map, graphs, tables.
Descriptive report uses findings of Colombian national
fertility survey for urban sample of 2590 women (15 to
49 years old). Looks at socio-demographic characteristics of the women and of their unions; knowledge and

use of contraceptive methods; fertility level and
differentials.

1120 _____.
1973 Resultados Generales. Encuesta Nacional de
Fecundidad. Publicación 1. Bogota: ASCOFAME, División
de Estudios de Población. 305 p. maps, tables.
Contains almost 200 tables demonstrating the findings
of a national survey measuring knowledge, attitudes and
behavior of Colombian women of reproductive age (15 to
49) regarding fertility and family planning in rural
and urban areas.

1121 _____.
1972 Características socio-demográficas de las mujeres
colombianas. Encuesta nacional de fecundidad: parte
rural. Publicación 2. Bogota: ASCOFAME, División
de Medicina Social y Población. 95 p. tables, graphs,
maps.
Descriptive report uses findings of Colombian national
fertility survey for rural sample of 2736 women (15 to
49 years old). Looks at socio-demographic characteristics of the women and of their unions with men; ideals,
motives, and attitudes toward number of children and
use of contraceptives; knowledge and use of family
planning; fertility level and differentials.

1122 GUERRERO, RODRIGO
1965 "Family Planning." CRW/A 112:19:665-66.
Doctor at sex education center in Cali explains the
family planning program there and makes observations on
the male and female patients in it: their ignorance
about conception, attitudes toward virility and female
fidelity. Supports rhythm method, taking official
church position on birth control.

1123 HARTFORD, ROBERT B.
1971 "Attitudes, Information, and Fertility in Medellin,
Colombia." In Ideology, Faith and Family Planning in
Latin America, ed. by J. M. Stycos, pp. 296-317. N.Y.:
McGraw Hill. tables, graphs.
Based on survey (1966) among 200 women, currently
mated (15-49 years old), and stratified into 28 categories of equal size, provides data on attitudes, practices
and knowledge related to marital fertility and fertility
control in Medellin. Concludes that despite current
state of contraception and its effects, significant
changes in fertility are forthcoming.

Human Sexuality, Reproduction, and Health

1124   JARAMILLO GÓMEZ, MARIO
        1968 "Medellín: A Case of Strong Resistance to Birth
        Control." PAA/D 5:2:811-26. tables, graphs.
            Studies phenomenon of intense desire for public family
        planning services coupled with institutional resistance
        to it in Medellín. Refers to series of 13 specific
        situations in which leaders and the population discussed
        the most important aspects of this conflict (e.g.,
        women's opinion, ideal of large family, Church opposition
        to research). Concludes that factors which favor a
        successful program are economic prosperity, excellent
        health services, veneration of maternity and fertility;
        those which hinder family planning are Church influence,
        and exaggerated puritanism in social life.

1125   JARAMILLO GÓMEZ, MARIO, et al.
        1968 Regulación de la fecundidad. Conocimientos,
        actitudes y prácticas de la población colombiana.
        Bogota: ASCOFAME, División de Estudios de Población.
        2 vols. graphs, tables, bibl.
            Includes "First Comparative Evaluation of Pilot Ser-
        vices in Family Planning," "Attitudes of Medical Profes-
        sors Toward Demographic Growth and Methods of Birth
        Control in Colombia," "Attitudes and Uses Regarding
        Family Planning in Bogota," "National Plan of Fertility
        Survey," "Relationships Between Social Mobility and
        Fertility in Bogota," "Patterns of Fertility in Bogota,"
        "Fertility Survey of Medellin" et al.

1126   JOHNSON, ELIZABETH L.
        1971 "Lower Income Mothers in Bogota." In Ideology,
        Faith and Family Planning in Latin America, ed. by
        J. M. Stycos, pp. 318-38. N.Y.: McGraw Hill. tables.
            Presents findings of a study conducted at the Instituto
        Materno Infantil of the Hospital San Juan de Dios in
        Bogota among 97 lower-class women, currently mated,
        20-35 years old, presently living in the capital, with
        at least one child and expecting another. Describes
        sample (birthplace, education, employment if any, employ-
        ment of husband, average income, living conditions); and
        its social relationships (kinship, compadrazgo, friend-
        ship) to determine their functions for the care and
        support of children; institutions for sharing child care;
        child care in special situations; and attitudes toward
        family size. Concludes that striking relationship exists
        between educational level and both salience of family
        size problems and willingness to practice birth control;
        no relationship exists between family size attitudes

and marital status and between frequency of church atten-
dance and willingness to practice birth control; etc.

1127 LÓPEZ, ALVARO
      1968 "New Techniques to Estimate Fertility and Mortality:
      The Case of Colombia." MMFQ 46:3/Part 2:75-85. tables,
      bibl.
            Analysis of national census data reveals increase of
      7-8 years in life expectancy at age 5 for Colombian
      women, 1938-51 and 1951-64.

1128 _____.
      1967 "Some Notes on Fertility Problems in a Colombian
      Semi-Urban Community." PAA/D 4:2:453-63. tables, bibl.
      notes.
            Using fragmentary fertility data from 100 women (in
      legal or consensual union) in Candelaria (1965), poses
      several questions regarding mating patterns and union
      stability, fertility and birth spacing, contraception
      and frequency of sexual relations, and fecundability
      under conditions of variable coital frequency. Also
      considers religion and attitudes toward contraception.
      Does not arrive at conclusions but points to areas for
      future analysis.

1129 LUCENA SALMORAL, MANUEL
      1970-71 "Notas sobre la magia de los guahibo." ICA/RCA
      15:131-69.
            Based on data gathered in the Commissary of Vichada
      (1964-65) among the Guahibo Indians, describes the role
      of magic in the life cycle from conception to death in
      the section on magic-religious practices. Includes
      notes on pregnancy, postnatal restrictions on mother,
      puberty rites for girls and marriage.

1130 MENDOZA-HOYOS, H.
      1968 "Research Studies on Abortion and Family Planning in
      Colombia." MMFQ 46:3/Part 2:223-36. tables, bibl.
            Summarizes research in Colombia on abortion and family
      planning. Abortion appears to increase parallel to
      strong rural-urban migratory trends. Believes determin-
      ing factor in general fertility is change in couples'
      attitudes favoring family planning rather than transitory
      use of contraceptive method.

1131 PRESS, IRWIN
      1971 "The Urban Curandero." AAA/AA 73:3:741-56. bibl.
            Reviews existing literature on curanderos. Based on
      data for a comparative study of curer and hospital clinic

Human Sexuality, Reproduction, and Health

patients in Bogota (1967), questions utility of peasant-
derived stereotype of curers and describes 5 (2 of them
women) and their practices. Concludes that there is no
particular urban curer "type," but rather an "urban
curanderismo complex," of which the variety and quality
of overall services offered are enumerated.

1132   PRIETO DURÁN, RAFAEL and CUCA TOLOSA, ROBERTO
        1966   Análisis de la encuesta de fecundidad en Bogotá.
        Monografía 19. Bogota: Centro de Estudios Sobre
        Desarrollo Económico, Univ. de los Andes. 166 p.
        tables.
            Presents findings of 1964 fertility survey among 2257
        women (20 to 50 years old) in Bogota. Married women
        have more children and the longer the relationship the
        greater the number of children. Analyzes relationship
        between various social, economic and cultural factors
        and fertility and considers opinions and attitudes
        related to family formation and development. Similar
        to Santiago survey.

1133   Primera Conferencia Nacional sobre Familia, Infancia,
        Juventud.
            1970   Bogota. 575 p. illus., ports., map.
            Presents results of and many presentations given at
        a conference held under the auspices of UNICEF,
        Colombia's Ministry of Public Health, National Department
        of Planning and the Colombian Institute of Family Welfare
        (Bogota, 2-7 March 1970). Covers sex and procreation;
        social organization, sexual relations, fertility and
        planning in working-class families of Bogota; Catholic
        morality and demographic politics; sex education in the
        university; prostitution; homosexuality; single mother-
        hood; etc.

1134   RIQUELME, MARCIAL ANTONIO
        1970   "Organización social, relaciones sexuales,
        fertilidad y planificación en las familias de clase baja
        en Bogotá." CPES/RPS 7:18:80-97. tables.
            Attempts to shed light on social organization and fer-
        tility of 50 lower-class families in *barrios* of southern
        Bogota, based on participant observation, recorded con-
        versations, questionnaire and psychological test admin-
        istered to 50 men, 46 women. Describes structural
        variables and organization of daily family life. Con-
        siders attitudes and experiences in sexual relations,
        fertility, family planning, and contraceptives.

1135   RODRÍGUEZ L., JORGE
        1941 "Sexualidad." AEE 4:9:37-38. tables.
        Compilation of 1940 birth statistics from department
      of Antioquia to determine influence of age of parents
      in sex of their children. More boys than girls were
      born when wife was older than husband.

1136   SCHULTZ, T. PAUL
        1969 Population Growth and Internal Migration in Colombia.
      Memorandum RM-5765-RC/AID. Santa Monica, Ca.: The
      Rand Corp. 104 p. tables.
        Study sponsored by US AID and RAND for policy formula-
      tion in Colombia. Part 1 considers determinants of fer-
      tility and population growth. Using 1964 census data,
      finds negative correlation between birth rates and such
      environmental characteristics as female labor force
      participation and child and adult education. Rural or
      urban residence, agricultural activity, wage increase,
      and previous migration to community are not significant.
      Part 2 estimates and analyzes internal migration pat-
      terns using 1951 and 1964 census data and develops an
      interregional migration model. Tables provide data by
      sex.

1137   SIMMONS, ALAN B.
        1971 "Projective Testing for Ideal Family Size." In
      Ideology, Faith and Family Planning in Latin America,
      pp. 339-59. N.Y.: McGraw Hill. illus., tables, bibl.
      notes.
        Suggesting that survey studies on preferences for
      family size and attitudes toward family planning have
      provided an incomplete, and perhaps even false, picture,
      discusses and utilizes projective technique to measure
      tendencies in family size preferences in Bogota (1966).
      Focuses on social-status differences among 83 mated
      women, 19-49 years old, with a control group of unmar-
      ried high school girls, 16-19 years old. Findings sup-
      port 1964 CELADE survey and also indicate that
      lower-status women are most aware of burden created by
      many children in poor families; high school girls are
      least aware of the problems.

1138   SIMMONS, ALAN B. and CARDONA GUTIÉRREZ, RAMIRO
        1974 "Colombia: Stages of Family Planning Adoption,
      1964-1969." SFP 5:2:42-49. tables, bibl.
        Analyzes rates of change in family planning acceptance
      in Colombia based on surveys conducted in urban, semi-
      urban and rural districts in 1964 and 1969. Concludes
      that family planning practices by women have increased

287

Human Sexuality, Reproduction, and Health

significantly, especially in Bogotá, partially as a
result of better education. However, traditional elements linger in the spread of withdrawal among the less-
educated in urban centers and the near absence of
contraception among such women in rural areas.

1139   ____.
          1973 Family Planning in Colombia. Changes in Attitude and
          Acceptance, 1964-69. IDRC-009e. Ottawa, Canada: Int'l.
          Development Research Center. 30 p. tables, bibl.
             Evaluation of Colombia's progress through stages in
          family-planning adoption focuses on changes in knowledge
          of contraception, attitudes, and practices during a
          period (1964-69) of extensive public discussion on family
          planning and of program activity in Bogota. Based on
          1964 and 1969 survey data, concludes that substantial
          changes took place and fertility fell significantly, but
          contraceptive practice is still basically restricted to
          urban populations. Findings suggest a series of specific
          stages.

1140 TORRES NIETO, CARLOS
          1973 Programa de estudios comparativos de aborto inducido
          y uso de anticonceptivos en América Latina. Bogotá,
          1972. Metodología. Bogota: ASCOFAME División de
          Estudios de Población. 63 p. tables, bibl.
             Detailed description of methodology used for a compar-
          ative study on provoked abortion and use of contracep-
          tives in LA, providing statistics for Colombian women.

1141 WATSON, LAWRENCE C.
          1973 "Marriage and Sexual Adjustment in Guajiro Society."
          UP/E 12:2:153-61.
          See VENEZUELA for annotation.

1142   ____.
          1972 "Sexual Socialization in Guajiro Society." UP/E
          11:2:150-56. bibl.
          See VENEZUELA for annotation.

1142a CHEN, KWAN-HWA, WISHNIK, SAMUEL M. and SCRIMSHAW, SUSAN
          1974 "Effects of Unstable Sexual Unions on Fertility in
          Guayaquil, Ecuador." SOBIO 21:4:353-59. tables, bibl.
             Based on a 1971 survey of approximately 2,000 lower
          income urban families, examines the impact of union
          stability (increased reproductive time lost and greater
          number of unions entered into by an individual during
          her/his lifetime) on fertility in Guayaquil.

Ecuador

1143   COWAN, RACHEL
       1971 "Ecuador: Birth-Controlling the People." Ramparts
       10:4:20-23. illus.
       Personal impressions of birth control problems in
       Ecuador derived from experience as Peace Corps volunteer
       in family planning clinic in Guayaquil. Without faith
       in their own government or US government to provide a
       better social and economic future, Ecuadorian women and
       men lack incentive to voluntarily limit size of their
       families. Notes resentment against US imperialism, dis-
       regard of religious beliefs and intrusion into privacy.
       Remarks on inhumanity of the doctors. Illustrates with
       the experiences of 2 women friends, one who did avail
       herself of the clinic and another who didn't, as repre-
       sentative of different attitudes and behaviors and the
       position of women in Ecuadorian society.

1144   Ecuador. División de Estadística y Censos
       1967 Encuesta de fecundidad, levantada en las principales
       ciudades y en algunas parroquias rurales del país.
       Quito: División de Estadística y Censos. 255 p.
       tables.
       In 72 tables, presents findings of a fertility survey,
       conducted in Ecuador in 1967. Includes information on
       educational level, economic situation, marital status,
       number of children, pregnancies and abortions, attitudes,
       etc. of women in the sample.

1145   MERLO J., PEDRO
       1971 Ecuador: Análisis de la encuesta de fecundidad
       urbana y rural realizada en el año 1967-1968. Serie C,
       no. 133. Santiago: · Centro Latinoamericano de Demo-
       grafía. 32 p. tables.
       Based on survey conducted among approximately 6500
       women in urban and rural Ecuador, estimates fertility
       levels and trends according to various demographic,
       socio-economic and cultural factors and reports attitudes
       and opinions related to desired family size, family
       planning, knowledge and use of contraceptive methods,
       all according to the socio-economic-cultural character-
       istics of the women interviewed. Reveals notable differ-
       ence between the sierra and the coast.

1146   SANDERS, THOMAS G.
       1971 Family Planning in Ecuador. Field Staff Reports:
       South America: West Coast Area Series, 18:3. Hanover,
       N.H.: American Universities Field Staff. 8 p.

Human Sexuality, Reproduction, and Health

Discusses history of family planning programs in
Ecuador. The Church has not emerged as a force of opposition. Despite lack of consistent data, provides estimates of major demographic characteristics. Notes that
migrants into urban areas have disproportionately been
women who become domestic servants and street venders.
Reports results of an investigation of fertility characteristics in Quito and Guayaquil conducted in 1965.

1146a ABELSON, ANDREW E., BAKER, THELMA S. and BAKER, PAUL T.
       1974 "Altitude, Migration, and Fertility in the Andes."
       SOBIO 21:1:12-27. tables, graphs, bibl.
       Examines relationship between hypoxia and reduced fer-
       tility of high Andean populations. Using retrospective
       reports of reproductive life histories of 241 women
       (nonmigrants resident at high and low altitudes and
       migrants to low altitude from birthplaces of both high
       and low altitude) of Peru's Tumbo Valley, concludes that
       altitude appears to be the most significant factor
       affecting an increase in fertility among downward
       migrants from high to low altitude.

Peru

1147   ADURIZ, JOAQUÍN
       1969 Así viven y así nacen: estudio psicosocial de los
       condicionamientos de fecundidad en los migrantes pro-
       vincianos de Lima-Callao. Cuadernos de DESCO, A-3.
       Lima: Centro de Estudios y Promoción del Desarrollo.
       57 p.
       According to the Handbook of Latin American Studies
       35(1973):8409, this is a qualitative study of the psycho-
       logical mechanisms behind motivational aspects of fer-
       tility among rural-urban migrants in Lima and Callao.
       Transcribes personal story of Gregorio and Sofía to
       illustrate these mechanisms.

1148   BRADSHAW, B. S.
       1969 "Fertility Differences in Peru: A Reconsideration."
       LSE/PS 23:1:5-20. tables, bibl. notes.
       Challenges Stycos' findings on a difference in fertil-
       ity rate between women in Spanish-speaking and Indian
       areas. Concludes that average number of children ever
       born per woman, as reported in 1940 census, far under-
       states true levels of current fertility in departments
       containing major Indian concentrations in Peru.

1149   Centro de Investigaciones Sociales por Muestreo (CISM)
        1967 La fecundidad en el área metropolitana de Arequipa.
        Estudio de una encuesta de hogares, agosto - septiembre,
        1965. Lima: Ministerio de Trabajo y Comunidades,
        Servicio del Empleo y Recursos Humanos. 38 p. tables,
        graphs.
            Based on 1940 and 1961 census data and a 1965 survey
        among 1486 persons in Arequipa, examines evolution of
        fertility, influential factors (e.g., migration, educa-
        tion, religion), ideal family size and desires for more
        children. Concludes, among other things, that migration
        appears to delay formation of a family.

1150   ESTEVA FABREGAT, CLAUDIO
        1970 "Medicina tradicional, curanderismo y brujería en
        Chinchero (Perú)." EEHA/AEA 27:19-60.
            Field research conducted in 1969 near Cuzco, Peru.
        Includes description of traditional medical practices
        related to pregnancy and birth (9 p.). Witchcraft is
        practiced by both sexes.

1151   GIUNTA de STIGLICH, TERESA
        1973 Algunos aspectos de la educación sexual en Lima
        Metropolitana. III. Encuestas sobre actitudes, conoci-
        mientos y comunicación sobre educación sexual de los
        maestros. Lima: Centro de Estudios de Población y
        Desarrolo (CEPD). 44 p. tables, graphs, bibl.
            Presents findings of a survey among 200 male and female
        primary and secondary school teachers in Lima. In addi-
        tion to socio-economic characteristics of the sample,
        describes their religiosity and attitudes toward sex
        education. Concludes, among other things, that teachers
        are more positive toward communicating information on
        sex to students in coed and boy's schools than in girls'
        schools.

1152   _____.
        1972 Algunos aspectos de educación sexual en Lima Metro-
        politana. II. Encuesta sobre actitudes, conocimientos
        y comunicación en los padres de familia. Lima: Centro
        de Estudios de Población y Desarrollo (CEPD). 16 p.
        graphs, bibl.
            The findings of a similar survey conducted among stu-
        dents (ages 7-17) correspond to those of a survey among
        parents: e.g., parents impart more information on sex
        to sons than to daughters. In general, parents res-
        ponded that their children should be informed about
        menstruation, pregnancy, sexual relations and family
        planning.

Human Sexuality, Reproduction, and Health

1153 GONZÁLEZ, VIOLETA
1971 Peru: Migración, educación y fecundidad en los estratos sociales bajos de Lima metropolitana. Serie C, no. 131. Santiago: Centro Latinoamericano de Demografía. 33 p. tables, bibl. f/notes.
Reviews literature on relationship between migration, education and fertility. Using data from Survey II on Immigration to Metropolitan Lima (1965-66), confirms hypothesis that younger female migrants demonstrate lower fertility than native urban women of the same age while the inverse is true for older women. Educational level further confirms this conclusion.

1154 HALL, M-FRANÇOISE
1965 "Birth Control in Lima, Peru: Attitudes and Practices." MMFQ 43:4/Part 1:409-38. graphs, tables, bibl.
Reports results of questionnaire administered to 500 women, aged 20-39, in Lima, for pregnancy histories and contraceptive practices. Findings indicated high rate of abortion on all socio-economic levels, especially among upper- and middle-class women, who also practiced contraception widely. All groups favored family limitation.

1155 _____.
1965 "Family Planning in Lima, Perú." MMFQ 43:4/Part 2: 100-16. tables, graphs, bibl.
Shorter version of study reported in MMFQ 43:4/Part 1: 409-38.

1156 McCLUNG, JEAN
1969 Effects of High Altitude on Human Birth: Observations on Mothers, Placentas, and the Newborn in Two Peruvian Populations. Cambridge, Mass.: Harvard Univ. Press. 150 p. tables, graphs, bibl.
Pilot investigation of 100 births in Cuzco and in Lima to identify important variables in decreased birth weight at high altitude. Findings indicate no depression of maternal fertility but significant increase in child mortality is caused by fetal hypoxia rather than racial or nutritional differences among the mothers.

1157 La Maternidad Voluntaria
1972 "La maternidad voluntaria." BDSLM/CIDHAL 2:3:45-47.
Excerpts from pamphlet guide put out by group of women in Lima who believe contraception is only a partial solution to the problem of women's participation in the liberation of LA, not an answer to underdevelopment.

Considering that it is every woman's right to have information on female sexuality and birth control methods,
provides such data.

1158   MORENO, DARÍO and DONNEL, ERIC
        1971 El sexo y el hombre peruano. El sexo y la mujer
        peruana. Lima: Eds. Peisa. 2 vols. in 1.
           Providing case examples for both sexes, discusses
        sexual problems of Peruvian men and women. Considers
        inadequate sexual education, repressive traditional con-
        cepts of sex, marriage and sex, prostitution, machismo,
        etc.

1159   PATCH, RICHARD
        1970 Attitudes toward Sex, Reproduction and Contraception
        in Bolivia and Peru. American Universities Field Staff
        Reports. West Coast South America Series. 17:11.
        Hanover, N.H.: American Universities Field Staff. 10 p.
           Based on residence and field studies in Bolivia and
        Peru since 1951, discusses sexual attitudes underlying
        population growth. Dense population patterns result
        from particular attitudes toward sex and reproduction
        which cause a high birth rate, in turn checked by a high
        rate of infant mortality and low life expectancy. Con-
        siders machismo, male dominance and the double standard,
        use of contraceptive measures, value placed on reproduc-
        tion, legitimacy vs. illegitimacy, premarital and extra-
        marital sex practices, autoeroticism, and religion.
        Cites several nonsexual reasons for predicting a
        Malthusian nightmare and notes absence of statistics due
        to scant, contradictory and hypothetical data available.

1160   Peru. Oficina Nacional de Estadística y Censos.
        1969 Informe de la encuesta de fecundidad en El Agustino.
        Lima. 129 p. map, tables, graphs, bibl.
           Presents findings of a survey among 1,000 women
        (ages 15-49) in Lima's low-income district of El Agustino
        to determine level, trends, and characteristics of fer-
        tility. Median age of mostly immigrant women of low
        educational level is 28.5 years, with very low level of
        productive employment, higher fertility rate than in
        Metropolitan Lima and lower incidence of abortion.
        Economic activity and religious observance are not sig-
        nificant factors, but a negative relationship exists
        between fertility and educational level and indices for
        socio-economic status and aspirations for children.

Human Sexuality, Reproduction, and Health

1161 ROY, KRISHNA
1969 "Aspectos saltantes del estudio de fecundidad en "El Agustino." CEPD/EPD 3:4:8p.
Summarizes findings of a fertility survey conducted in the Lima *barriada* El Agustino: population growth and economic consequences, comparison of urban infrastructure between metropolitan Lima and El Agustino, demographic and socio-economic characteristics of the sample, determining causes in fertility (demographic, socio-economic, and cultural variables; abortion; family size preferences; knowledge, attitudes and use regarding contraceptive methods).

1162 STYCOS, J. MAYONE
1965 "Female Employment and Fertility in Lima, Peru." MMFQ 43:1:42-54. tables, graph, bibl.
Survey among almost 2,000 currently-mated women in Lima reveals no clear-cut relation between fertility and employment status. Class comparison made. Analysis repeated in Chimbote indicated even more homogeneous attitudes toward family size. Concludes that employment status is more often a consequence rather than a cause of marital fertility.

1163 _____.
1963 "Culture and Differential Fertility in Peru." LSE/PS 16:3:257-70. tables, bibl.
Analyzes regional data on fertility from 1940 Peruvian census for a variety of social and demographic characteristics and surveys monographs of Peruvian communities for aspects of norms and behavior patterns for a comparison between Indian and *mestizo* cultures. Concludes that a negative relation exists between social variables (urbanization, literacy, and speaking Spanish) and motherhood while a positive relation occurs to fertility of mothers, especially with regard to speaking Spanish: highest fertility in Spanish-speaking rural areas; lowest in Indian urban areas. Interprets differential mating patterns as the cause; permissiveness of sexual conduct in Indian areas.

1164 VERMUNT, KORNELIUS; MERCADO, HILDA and ALCÁNTARA, ELSA
1971 Opiniones y actitudes frente a la procreación en el estrato bajo de Lima Metropolitana. Lima: Centro de Investigaciones Sociales, Económicas, Políticas y Antropológicas (CISEPA), Pontificia Universidad Católica del Perú. 212 p. tables, graphs, bibl.

Based on survey taken among 484 lower-class women in
Lima (1967), describes sample according to socio-economic
characteristics, which are analyzed in relation to fertility; explains fertility differences through motiva-
tional and attitudinal factors; and analyzes data on
family planning, knowledge and use of contraceptive
methods, and abortions. Appendices include information
on sample, structure of family authority, conjugal
communication, family relations, migration patterns,
etc. and questionnaire. Several conclusions are that
negative relation exists between fertility and level of
urbanization, education (beyond primary) reduces fertility level, patriarchal authority structure decreases
when woman attains a secondary or higher educational
level, man's attitude is significantly more influential
in number of children that a family will have, etc.

1165 VILLAVICENCIO, VÍCTOR LUCIO
      1966 La vida sexual del indígena peruano. Lima. 110 p.
      Based on primary and secondary sources, describes
      sexual practices and beliefs of Indians in Peru from
      the Inca Empire to the 20c.: concept of love, courtship,
      trial marriage, marriage, sexual rights of godfather,
      female virginity, submission and fidelity, abortion,
      incest, concubinage, venereal diseases, aphrodisiacs,
      etc.

1165a WELLIN, EDWARD
      1956 "Pregnancy, Childbirth, and Midwifery in the Valley
      of Ica, Peru." CCHE/HIDHC 4:1-51.
      Abbreviated version of memorandum from project spon-
      sored by WHO in collaboration with Peru's Ministry of
      Public Health and Social Welfare amply describes folk
      beliefs and practices surrounding pregnancy, childbirth,
      and midwifery in the Ica Valley. Also considers abor-
      tion, food patterns, availability of and attitudes toward
      hospital facilities, economics of childbirth, incorpora-
      tion of modern elements. Concludes that although native
      midwifery in rural Ica is vital and functioning, the
      encroachment of modern medicine and increased occupa-
      tional and educational opportunities in urban areas is
      leading to a decline of popular medicine and a change
      in attitude toward traditional practices.

Human Sexuality, Reproduction, and Health

Bolivia

1166   Centro de Estudios de Población y Familia (CEP)
       1969 Condicionamientos socio-culturales de la fecundidad
       en Bolivia. La Paz. 198 p. illus., map, tables,
       graphs, bibl.
       Based on 1968 survey conducted among 2468 women (15-50
       years old) in the departments of La Paz, Cochabamba and
       Santa Cruz, examines levels and tendencies of fertility;
       values, attitudes, motivations, behavior, and opinions
       regarding fertility, family, and social change; and
       level of knowledge, use, and attitudes regarding birth
       control methods.

1167   LLANO SAAVEDRA, LUIS
       1971 Fecundidad diferencial y anticoncepción en el área
       urbana de La Paz. La Paz: Centro de Estudios de
       Población y Familia (CEP). 53 p. tables, graphs, bibl.
       Using only the data on the department of La Paz from
       the 1968 CEP survey Condicionamientos socio-culturales
       de la fecundidad en Bolivia, (#1166) considers a variety
       of variables in testing 6 hypotheses on fertility. Con-
       cludes, among other things, that women born in an urban
       area demonstrate lower fertility rates than rural women.
       Educational level is a determinant for lower fertility,
       but economic activity is not.

1168   PATCH, RICHARD
       1970 Attitudes Toward Sex, Reproduction and Contraception
       in Bolivia and Peru. American Universities Field Staff
       Reports. West Coast South America Series 17:11. Hanover,
       N.H.: American Universities Field Staff. 10 p.
       See PERU for annotation.

Paraguay

1168a   CERISOLA, ELSA
        1968 "Fecundidad diferencial en la República del Paraguay,
        según condición de ruralidad y nivel de instrucción de
        la mujer." CPES/RPS 5:12:34-52. tables, bibl. f/notes.
        Based on 5% sample of 1962 Paraguayan census data,
        attempts to evaluate relation between number of live
        births per woman and age group; historical tendency of
        rural and urban fertility; differences in fertility
        according to region and educational level of the woman.
        Points out limitations of the data and concludes that
        urban-rural differential is influenced by age at marriage,
        higher percentage of permanently unmarried women and

concentration of women with higher educational level
in urban areas.

1169   Seminario Nacional de Planificación Familiar. 2nd, Asunción,
        1969.
        1970 Población y planificación familiar en el Paraguay.
        Asunción: Centro Paraguayo de Estudios de Población.
        161 p. tables.
            Reproduces 12 papers presented at the second National
        Seminar on Family Planning on medical, social, political,
        and educative aspects of family planning in Paraguay;
        includes abortion, women's attitude and socio-cultural
        and emotional factors conditioning it, sexual education,
        maternal mortality, etc.

1170   "Training of Empiric Midwives."
        1956 BIND 16:1:82-85.
            Brief notice from Boletín de la Oficina Sanitaria
        Panamericana (September 1955) reports on a Paraguayan
        training program for midwives (Guaraní-speaking Chaé)
        who attend women in childbirth without any professional
        preparation other than tradition and experience. In
        English and Spanish.

Chile

1171   ARMIJO, ROLANDO and MONREAL, TEGUALDA
        1965 "Epidemiology of Provoked Abortion in Santiago,
        Chile." In Population Dynamics, ed. by M. Muramatsu
        and P. Harper, pp. 137-60. Baltimore, Md.: Johns
        Hopkins Press. tables, graphs, bibl. Spanish version:
        1964 "Epidemiología del aborto provocado." Santiago,
        documentos. Santiago: Escuela de Salubridad.
            Summarizes data on abortion in Chile and attempts to
        define the magnitude and most pertinent factors and
        variables of induced abortion, female attitudes toward
        family planning and use of contraceptives, and habits
        and attitudes related to women's intimate life. Based
        on a 1961 survey among 1890 women, aged 20 to 44, in
        Santiago, concludes, among other things, that "economic
        reasons and ignorance of birth control methods appear to
        be the basic explanation for the alarming trend of pro-
        voked abortion" and low income groups demonstrate a
        tendency toward sexual life at an earlier age, but such
        a trend exists in all social brackets.

Human Sexuality, Reproduction, and Health

1172 _____.
        1965 "The Problem of Induced Abortion in Chile." MMFQ
        43:4/Part 2:263-80. tables, bibl.
        Reports comparative results on the incidence of abor-
        tion in several areas of Chile. Concludes that it is a
        major health problem; that rates are high among women
        aged 20-34, married women, women with up to 3 children,
        and women of low income groups; that medically unquali-
        fied persons induce most abortions; and that the most
        important reasons behind its use are related to economic
        situations, health, large family, conjugal problems and
        illegitimacy.

1173 ARMIJO, ROLANDO and REQUENA B., MARIANO
        1968 "Epidemiological Aspects of Abortion in Chile." PHR
        83:1:41-48. tables, bibl.
        Critically reviews methods of approach employed in
        raw data and preliminary, community retrospective, and
        prospective studies, studies of abortion as a hospital
        problem, and evaluation of control measures. All indi-
        cate provoked abortion as a major health problem in
        Chile.

1174 Centro para el Desarrollo Económico y Social para América
        Latina (DESAL, Santiago)
        1970 Fecundidad y anticoncepción en poblaciones
        marginales. B.A.: Eds. Troquel. 365 p. tables, graphs.
        Presents and discusses findings of a family and fertil-
        ity survey conducted among lower-income groups in San-
        tiago by the Centro Latinoamericano de Población y
        Familia (CELAP), 1966-67. Describes socio-economic
        characteristics of the female sample, attitudes toward
        marriage and family, aspects of birth control, and fam-
        ily structure characteristics. Also includes comparative
        results for male spouses.

1175 DA VANZO, JULIE
        1972 The Determinants of Family Formation in Chile 1960:
        An Econometric Study of Female Labor Participation,
        Marriage and Fertility Decisions. R-830-AID. Santa
        Monica, Ca.: Rand Corp. 134 p.
        Based on 1960 census and wage data, develops and tests
        an econometric model using two-stage least square regres-
        sions. Resulting equations indicate a positive relation-
        ship to the male wage but a negative one to the female
        income. Suggests that a decline in fertility, a usual
        side-effect of development, results from the increased
        cost of children. Attempts to explain fertility as a
        function of economic choice within a household.

1176   FAÚNDES-LATHAM, ANÍBAL; RODRIGUEZ-GALANT, GERMÁN and
       AVENDAÑO-PORTIUS, ONOFRE
           1968 "Effects of a Family Planning Program on the Fertil-
           ity of a Marginal Working-Class Community in Santiago."
           PAA/D 5:1:122-37. tables, graph.
               Describes methodology, sample, and results of a re-
           search project in the San Gregorio community of Santiago
           (1965-66) on the effects of a family planning program on
           birth and abortion rates, maternal-child mortality and
           morbidity, and related social and psychological variables.
           Notes a fertility decline after 13 months.

1177   _____.
           1968 "The San Gregorio Experimental Family Planning Pro-
           gram: Changes Observed in Fertility and Abortion Rates."
           PAA/D 5:2:836-45. graphs, tables.
               Based on data from a research and action family plan-
           ning program at San Gregorio, a marginal working-class
           community in Santiago, observes changes in fertility and
           abortion rates since 1964. A decrease indicates effec-
           tiveness of program in fertility decline. Hypothesizes
           about decline in abortion.

1178   GALL, NORMAN
           1972 Births, Abortions and the Progress of Chile. Field
           Staff Reports: West Coast South America Series 19:2.
           Hanover, N.H.: American Universities Field Staff. 10 p.
               Reports on the achievements and failures of the various
           family planning programs which have significantly reduced
           Chile's birthrate since 1964, and the causes and nature
           of their present crisis. Appendix contains text of 2
           taped interviews with a middle-class housewife and a
           woman living in a squatter settlement, which reveals
           the trauma of reproductive problems; both women had a
           history of multiple abortions.

1179   GREBE, MARÍA ESTER and SEGURA, JOSÉ
           1974 Psiquiatría folklórica de Chile: estudio antro-
           pológico de seis enfermedades vigentes." AFSM/APPAL
           20:5:367-82. tables, bibl.
               Using 2 samples in random correlation: 100 men and
           100 women to study prevalence; and 40 men and 20 women
           for descriptive analyses, 6 well-known diseases within
           folkloric psychiatry were studied: fright, jealousy,
           temper tantrums or epileptic seizures, depression, agi-
           tation, and bewitchment or alcoholic deprivation. Women
           evidenced a slightly greater occurrence of all but jeal-
           ousy and agitation. When chronic symptoms appear, common
           recourse is to consult a woman healer. Conducted among
           in-patients at José Joaquín Aguirre Hospital in Santiago.

Human Sexuality, Reproduction, and Health

1180   HALL, M.-FRANÇOISE
      1971 "Family Planning in Santiago, Chile: The Male View-
      point." SFP 2:6:143-47. tables, bibl. f/notes. 1970
      "Male Use of Contraception and Attitudes Toward Abortion:
      Santiago, Chile, 1968." MMFQ 48:2/Part 1:   145-66.
      tables, bibl.
         Survey conducted among 4 socio-economic strata of men
      in Santiago and 3 levels in a rural village questioned
      marital experience with contraception, attitude toward
      abortion and family planning education and marital and
      nonmarital sexual relations. Concludes that ignorant
      or misinformed men retard acceptance and use of modern
      contraceptive methods among women.

1181   KATTAN, LIDIA, et al.
      1973 "Características del alcoholismo en la mujer y
      evaluación del resultado de su tratamiento en Chile."
      AFSM/APPAL 19:3:194-204. tables, bibl. notes.
         Describes findings of comparative study (1966) among
      50 female and 49 male working-class alcoholics attending
      the Psychiatric Hospital of Santiago. The women were
      less educated, with a higher incidence of inveterate
      alcoholism and psychopathological disorder, and a greater
      numer of heavy drinkers in their immediate environment.

1182   LOMNITZ, LARISSA
      1969 "Patrones de ingestión de alcohol entre migrantes
      Mapuches en Santiago." III/AI 29:1:42-71. table, bibl.
         Based on interviews with 48 Mapuche migrants (15 women,
      25 men) ranging in age from 18 to 33, domestic servants,
      and housewives, concludes that women who drink exces-
      sively are severely judged. According to the informants,
      as a result of migration, Mapuche women are acting like
      Chilean women. Notes factors contributing to alcoholic
      consumption among these migrants and characteristics of
      their drinking patterns.

1183   "La píldora entre los adolescentes, en Chile."
      1972 BDSLM/CIDHAL 2:3:60-63.
         Excerpted from article about the use of the pill, in
      the Colombian periodical Presencia. A survey among
      100 middle-class high school girls, 15-17 years old, in
      Santiago, reveals that they all know about oral contra-
      ceptives, but greater sexual liberty is not necessarily
      a consequence.

1184   PLANK, STEPHEN J. and MILANESI, MARÍA LUCILA
      1973 "Fertility in Rural Chile." SOBIO 20:2:151-59.
      tables, graph, bibl.

Based on census data and interviews with 3,528 women
of reproductive age in 15 rural communities in Chile,
describes demographic conditions and family planning
attitudes and practices prior to a study on the effects
of family planning programs on natality and health.

1185   REQUENA B., MARIANO
1969 "Chilean Program of Abortion Control and Fertility
Planning: Present Situation and Forecast for the Next
Decade." In Fertility and Family Planning: A World
View, ed. by S. J. Behrman, L. Corsa, Jr., and
R. Freedman, pp. 478-89. Ann Arbor, Mich.: Univ. of
Mich. Press. tables, bibl.
Describes the state of family planning in Chile during
the 1960's and notes that induced abortion and contra-
ceptive usage had a greater impact on the fertility level
than other variables. Predicts future trends.

1186   _____.
1965 "Social and Economic Correlates of Induced Abortion
in Santiago, Chile." PAA/D 2:33-49. tables, bibl.
Describes one part of a larger study in Santiago to
measure the effects of a program to control induced
abortion. Midwives interviewed 580 women of fertile
age from a working-class neighborhood for following
factors: incidence of induced abortion, age, civil
status, educational level, occupation, religion and
religious practices, environment, obstetrical history,
sexual conduct. Among other things, concludes that
Catholic women risk abortion as frequently as non-
religious women and even more so than Protestant women.
Civil status, educational level and frequency of sexual
relations are not significant variables. An unskilled
manual worker evidences a higher rate of risk than a
housewife, white-collar worker or professional.
A higher percentage of induced abortion exists among
women of lower socio-economic strata than among total
population of Santiago.

1187   _____.
1965 "Studies of Family Planning in the Quinta Normal
District of Santiago: The Use of Contraceptives."
MMFQ 43:4(Part 2):69-99. tables, bibl.
Midwives interviewed 448 women of childbearing age,
of a lower socio-economic stratum in Santiago for a
pilot study on contraceptives. Reports data on method
and prevalence of birth control practiced, information
on contraception and its source, attitudes toward offer
of free contraceptives and type chosen.

Human Sexuality, Reproduction, and Health

1188   REQUENA B., MARIANO and MONREAL, TEGUALDA
      1968 "Evaluation of Induced Abortion Control and Family
      Planning Programs in Chile." MMFQ 46:3(Part 2):191-222.
      tables, graphs, bibl.
      Reviews family planning statistics from hospitals and
      clinics in Santiago (1931-66) to assess their accomplish-
      ments, and summarizes their combined effect upon the
      birth rate. Notes increase in induced abortion.

1189   RODRÍGUEZ M., GUILLERMO
      1966 "Algunos aspectos de la actividad física y del
      deporte en la mujer." CEF/R 33:129:28-35.
      Attempts to determine influence of physical education
      on women, given their particular physiology, and whether
      sports are detrimental to women. Analyzes relationship
      between exercise and age, physical activity and menstrua-
      tion, and pregnancy, birth and sports. Notes favorable
      and unfavorable aspects of physical education on women.

1190   SALINAS, JUAN and GATICA, EDUARDO
      1960 "Fecundidad y actitudes relativas a la formación de
      la familia en Santiago de Chile." UC/B 15:44-49.
      tables.
      Preliminary report on 1959 study of differential birth
      in Santiago using data from 2455 women, aged 20 to 50,
      for a 3-fold analysis: importance of several demographic,
      social, cultural, economic, and psychological factors
      affecting fertility; levels and tendencies of fertility
      according to socio-economic condition; and determinations
      of fertility measures in different groups of women. Some
      of the initial unanalyzed and uninterpreted results are
      that voluntary sterility increases with educational or
      economic level; a high percentage of married women are
      engaged in remunerated employment; the ideal number of
      children is around 4 but the real number is different.

1191   TABAH, LEÓN
      1963 "A Study of Fertility in Santiago, Chile." JMFL
      25:1:20-26. tables.
      Presents results of 1959 survey among nearly 2000
      women, aged 20 to 25 years, in Santiago. Considers
      socio-economic factors, employment of women, urban migra-
      tion, family formation, opinions on ideal family size,
      religion, abortion, and birth control. Concludes that
      Santiago is in a transitional stage: opposition to
      birth control is declining while conditions favorable to
      a decrease in births are increasing.

1192   TABAH, LEÓN and SAMUEL, RAÚL
       1962 "Preliminary Findings of a Survey on Fertility and
       Attitudes Toward Family Formation in Santiago, Chile."
       In Research in Family Planning, ed. by Clyde V. Kiser,
       pp. 263-304. Princeton, N.J.: Princeton Univ. Press.
       tables.
          Detailed provisional report on preliminary findings of
       1959 survey among nearly 2000 women, aged 20 to 50,
       interviewed for data for a 3-fold analysis: relative
       importance of various demographic, social, cultural,
       economic and psychological factors influencing fertility;
       fertility levels and trends according to socio-economic
       criteria; and determination of fertility measurements.

1193   VIEL V., BENJAMÍN
       1967 "Family Planning in Chile." SR/J 3:4:284-91.
       tables, graphs.
          Briefly reports on a study created to measure the
       effectiveness of contraceptive devices distributed to
       women in Santiago (1964-66) and provides national data
       on birth rates, infant mortality and abortion.

1194   WEEKS, JOHN R.
       1969 "Urban and Rural Natural Increase in Chile." MMFQ
       48:1:71-89. tables, bibl.
          Considers urban-rural differences in the rate of
       natural increase in Chile between 1952 and 1960. Attrib-
       utes rise to mortality decline and fertility increase,
       the latter resulting from a lowering of age at marriage,
       an increase in proportions marrying, and a general ten-
       dency of women to bear more children. A pronatalist
       government policy and a reduction in female labor force
       activity and female mobility are other influential
       factors.

Argentina

1195   AGÜERO BLANCH, VICENTE ORLANDO
       1968 Las remedieras de Malargüe. Inst. de Antropología,
       27. Cordoba, Arg.: Univ. Nacional de Córdoba. 34 p.
       map, plates.
          Study carried out in Department of Malargüe in Argen-
       tine province of Mendoza, where 70 practicing "healers"
       (remedieras) were interviewed for details on their be-
       liefs and curing practices, especially in matters of
       love, sexual relations, pregnancy, and the couvade, but
       also for such illnesses as measles and cataracts. The

Human Sexuality, Reproduction, and Health

majority are women, well respected by the villagers and preferred to any doctor with a university degree.

1196   BRITO VELÁSQUEZ, ENRIQUE M.
        1969 "La fecundidad según status socio-económico.
        Análisis comparativo de las ciudades de México y Buenos
        Aires." CM/DE 3:2:156-85. tables, bibl.
        Attempts to provide schematic view of demographic evo-
        lution in LA. Using 1964 CELADE survey data, analyzes
        SES as a differential in fertility among women of Mexico
        City and Buenos Aires as representing respectively the
        highest and lowest fertility of 7 Latin American cities.

1197   CICOUREL, AARON VICTOR
        1974 Theory and Method in a Study of Argentine Fertility.
        N.Y.: John Wiley. 212 p. tables, bibl.
        Focuses on methodological and theoretical issues in the
        study of fertility, using Argentina as a case example.
        Provides detailed picture of families interviewed and
        textual analysis of their responses on sexual unions.
        Also includes traditional tables indicating socio-
        economic characteristics of sample and attitudes related
        to family planning.

1198   HENRY, JULES
        1949 "The Social Function of Child Sexuality in Pilagá
        Indian Culture." In Psychosexual Development in Health
        and Disease, ed. by P. H. Hoch and J. Lubin, pp. 91-101.
        N.Y.: Greene and Stratton. bibl.
        Explains the social function of child sexuality among
        the Pilagá Indians of Argentina, in contrast to North
        American culture. Notes differences in male and female
        roles in child play, gives examples of homo- and hetero-
        sexual activities, and considers their functions.

1199   MAFUD, JULIO
        1966 La revolución sexual argentina. Nueva Biblioteca de
        Cultura Social. Buenos Aires: Edit. Américalee. 133 p.
        bibl.
        Attempts to determine new patterns or norms in modern
        Argentine sexual relations, based on surveys taken in
        Buenos Aires and its environs. Attributes incompatibil-
        ities between the sexes to different social trajectory
        of men and women. Discusses superficial changes (e.g.,
        dress, make-up, language, cigarette smoking) as a kind
        of masculinization of women; the role of modern media in
        changing sex models; and lingering patterns of traditional
        behavior and ambivalences in female independence, sexual
        relations, marriage, etc. Part 2 is more clinical, with

respect to knowledge and practice of sex. Popular
rather than scientific study.

1200 MINUCHIN de ITZIGSOHN, SARA, et al.
1973 "Grupo familiar y matrimonio en una área rural."
III/AI 33:3:783-800. bibl.
Because of the problem a migratory group faces in its
need for health care, a questionnaire was administered
to patients in the Health Center of Isla Maciel (province of Buenos Aires) soliciting information regarding
menstruation, fecundity, pregnancy, labor, birth, abortion, etc. Describes several practices and beliefs
related to pregnancy and newborn babies.

1201 Primera Plana, Buenos Aires
1964 "Sex and the Argentine Man." Atlas 7:3:143-45.
Taken from Primera Plana's survey among 71 men in
Buenos Aires regarding the consistency in their beliefs
on sexuality and adherence to their own moral code,
presents findings such as: ostentatious virility is the
prime mover in their sexual relations. The ideal woman
and ideal wife are one and the same and should be submissive, beautiful, intelligent, friendly, and home-
loving. Points out that Don Juanism, machismo, and
under-estimation of women are the dominant characteristics deeply rooted in minds of Argentine men.

1202 ROTHMAN, ANA MARÍA
1969 La participación femenina en actividades económicas
en su relación con el nivel de fecundidad en Buenos
Aires y México. Serie C, no. 108. Santiago: Centro
Latinoamericano de Demografía. 40 p. tables, diagram,
bibl. f/notes.
Using CELADE's comparative fertility survey data,
analyzes relationship between female labor force participation and fertility, according to variables concerning
family size as well as individual family, and social
structures. Concludes that differences in fertility
between economically active and inactive women are related to different age at marriage and use of contraceptives, and that for Mexico, urbanization without general
development does not necessarily lead to lower fertility.

1203 _____.
1967 La fecundidad en Buenos Aires según algunas características demográficas y socio-económicas. Serie
Población y Sociedad, 48. B.A.: Inst. Torcuato Di
Tella. 60 p. tables, graphs.

Human Sexuality, Reproduction, and Health

Based on CELADE survey data for Greater Buenos Aires, analyzes fertility according to women's marital status, occupation, educational level, place of birth, and husband's occupation and also considers age at marriage and use of contraceptives as possible intervening variables in differential fertility. Reveals relatively low fertility level.

1204 SAKS, MICHAEL J.; EDELSTEIN, JANE; DRAGUNS, JURIS G. and FUNDA, TOBA A. de
1970 "Social Class and Social Mobility in Relation to Psychiatric Symptomatology in Argentina." SIP/RIP 4:2:105-21. tables, bibl.
Through interviews with patients and/or relatives and hospital records, collected biographical and symptom data on 68 men and 49 women at several public psychiatric institutions in and around Buenos Aires and Córdoba. Presents distribution of symptoms, differentiated according to socio-economic group, sex and variables such as father's class level, patient's occupational level and mobility. Some results: Upwardly mobile women and those of stable occupational level tend toward passivity, with active coping style dominant among downwardly mobile women. Premarital sexual adjustment is a source of problems in high socio-economic class.

1205 SHERWELL, ANA MARÍA
1929 "The Mothers' Club of Argentina." PAU/B 63:5:474-76.
Describes the activities and publications of the Club de Madres, founded in Buenos Aires during first decade of 20c. to reduce infant mortality and save mothers.

1206 SLONINSKY, TEODORO
1965 Crianza y desvíos humanos. Buenos Aires: Eds. Troquel. 320 p. bibl.
Although remarks on puberty, sexuality, frigidity, male and female homosexuality, psychosis, psychopathy, and delinquency are general, there are case examples of Argentine women and men from the National Hospital of Neuropsychiatry, National Neuropsychiatric Hospital for Women, Penal Institute of the Devoted Villa et al., relating everything back to an individual's upbringing and family situation (e.g., lack of affection).

1207 SOMOZA, JORGE L.
1968 "Fertility Levels and Differentials in Argentina in the Nineteenth Century." MMFQ 46:3(part 2):53-73. tables, graphs, bibl.

Using national census data, estimates level of fertility in Argentina around 1895 and assesses fertility
differentials by region, place of birth, and literacy.

CARIBBEAN

Puerto Rico

1208   BELCHER, JOHN C. and CRADER, KELLY W.
        1974 "Social Class, Style of Life and Fertility in Puerto
        Rico." SF 52:4:488-95. tables, bibl.
            Using household survey data from 3 agricultural areas
        in Puerto Rico (1966), examines relationship between
        fertility, social class and life styles. Factor analy-
        sis includes 43 behavioral items (e.g., wife's employ-
        ment outside home) reflecting cultural alternatives.
        Middle-class syndrome, male dominance, agricultural
        self-sufficiency and evening leisure are 4 initial
        characterizations of life-style components. Concludes
        that combined style of life and social class approach
        systematically differentiates fertility patterns.

1209   BOUVIER, LEON F. and MACISO, JOHN J., JR.
        1968 "Education of Husband and Wife and Fertility in
        Puerto Rico." UWI/SES 17:1:49-59. tables.
            Based on 1960 census data, reports on analysis of
        effects on fertility of husband's and wife's education
        in Puerto Rico. Findings agree that fertility is uni-
        versely related to women's increased education. However,
        concludes with hypothesis that it is inversely related
        to increased education of both spouses.

1210   CARLETON, ROBERT O.
        1965 "Labor Force Participation: A Stimulus to Fertility
        in Puerto Rico." PAA/D 2:233-39. tables.
            Special tabulation of 1960 population census reveals
        marked positive correlation between economic activity
        and level of education of married women in metropolitan
        San Juan. Hypothesizes that only those women whose
        education qualifies them for particular jobs are able
        to overcome husband's opposition to their working and
        shows that women with some university education, as
        opposed to high school graduates, have lower fertility
        rates (between ages of 35 and 44). Eliminating effect
        of economic activity differential, married university
        women have more children than high school graduates.
        Suggests explanation for this phenomenon.

Human Sexuality, Reproduction, and Health

1211 COMBS, J. W., JR. and DAVIS, KINGSLEY
1951 "The Pattern of Puerto Rican Fertility." LSE/PS
4:4:364-79. graphs, tables.
Examination of demographic data for Puerto Rico
(1890-1948) suggests that increasing urbanization will
help to lower fertility rates.

1212 GODLEY, FRANK H.
1968 "La fecundidad y el nivel educacional - Puerto Rico,
1962." IASI/E 26:99:256-84.
Presents and interprets statistics on the education of
parents with children born in 1962 in Puerto Rico. Annual fertility rates tend to decrease among women of
increasing levels of education, but only near beginning
or end of childbearing age. Birth rates are relatively
high for women aged 20 to 34 of intermediate and high
educational levels. Cites possible factors to account
for this.

1213 HATT, PAUL K.
1952 Backgrounds of Human Fertility in Puerto Rico: A
Sociological Survey. Princeton, N.J.: Univ. of
Princeton Press. 511 p. tables.
Reports on a field study of social and socio-
psychological factors related to fertility in Puerto
Rico (1946-47). Describes methodology; general patterns
of social conditions and attitudes; socio-economic
status; age, sex, and rural-urban differences; factors
affecting family growth; etc. Concludes that although
Puerto Rican fertility is high, attitudes and values
favorable to low fertility are widespread; predicts a
trend toward lower fertility. Number of adults interviewed included 6,187 men and 7,085 women.

1214 HILL, REUBEN; BACK, KURT W. and STYCOS, J. MAYONE
1957 La estructura de la familia y la fertilidad en
Puerto Rico." UPR/RCS 1:1:37-66. tables.
Reports findings of 1953-54 survey on Puerto Rican
attitudes and behavior surrounding birth control among
lower-class spouses married less than 20 years: rural
consensual unions most favorable toward small families;
birth control users less satisfied with general life
conditions; wife less likely satisfied sexually in families practicing contraception for long time.

1215 HILL, REUBEN and STYCOS, J. MAYONE
1955 "Intrafamily Communication and Fertility Planning in
Puerto Rico." RSS/RS 20:3/4:258-71. tables.

Findings indicate low interspousal communication in Puerto Rico, barriers to which are wifely modesty and respect for husband. Families with best communication are most likely to practice birth control.

1216 JAFFE, A. J. and AZUMI, K.
1960 "The Birth Rate and Cottage Industries in Under-developed Countries." UC/EDCC 9:1:52-63. tables, bibl. f/notes.
Demonstrates relationship between female fertiltiy and activity in cottage industries. Puerto Rico and Japan are used to illustrate that employment in a non-agricultural industry at or near the residence of women, under favorable conditions for combining household and work tasks, is conducive to higher fertility than if woman worked away from her home. Recommends introducing industries using female labor outside the home to help lower rate of population growth.

1217 KANTNER, JOHN F. and STYCOS, J. MAYONE
1962 "A Non-Clinical Approach to Contraception. Prelim-inary Report on the Program of the Family Planning Asso-ciation of Puerto Rico. In Research in Family Planning, ed. by C. V. Kiser, pp. 573-90. Princeton, N.J.: Princeton Univ. Press. tables, bibl. f/notes.
Preliminary report on Puerto Rican program to dis-seminate contraceptive knowledge and methods in the home and on the motivations of women enlisted in program as users of Emko. Part 2 describes women involved in the program. Notes 30% rise in level of contraception.

1218 KING, MARGUERITE N.
1948 "Cultural Aspects of Birth Control in Puerto Rico." WSU/HB 20:1:21-35. table, graph, bibl. f/notes.
Presents fertility statistics and case examples of 13 women in Lajas, a rural community in Puerto Rico, a typical example of population problems. Concludes that widespread use of birth control is hampered by basic living conditions, inhibiting psychological attitudes, and cultural factors.

1219 MACISO, JOHN J., JR.; BOUVIER, LEON F. and RENZI, MARTHA JANE
1969 "Migration Status, Education and Fertility in Puerto Rico. 1960." MMFQ 47:2:167-87. tables, bibl.
Based on special tabulations of 25% sample of ever-married, spouse-present women derived from 1960 census of Puerto Rico, draws 2 hypothetical models: young mi-grants into San Juan are better educated than non-migrant urban counterparts and may be more innovative; in

Human Sexuality, Reproduction, and Health

comparison to urban residents, older migrants are poorly educated, have larger families, and may reflect more traditional values regarding family size.

1220 MACISCO, JOHN J., JR.; BOUVIER, LEON F. and WELLER, ROBERT H. 1970 "The Effect of Labor Force Participation on the Relation Between Migration Status and Fertility in San Juan, Puerto Rico." MMFQ 48:1:51-70. tables, bibl.
Using special tabulations of Puerto Rico's 1960 census, examines interrelations between rural-urban migration, labor force activity, and fertility. Concludes that both female labor force participation and migration from rural areas to San Juan are associated with lower fertility.

1221 MYERS, GEORGE C. and MORRIS, EARL WALKER 1966 "Migration and Fertility in Puerto Rico." LSE/PS 20:1:85-96. tables.
Using special tabulations of 25% sample of ever-married women in 1960 Puerto Rican census, considers 3 categories of marital status--legal; consensual; widowhood, divorce, separation--and suggests that fertility during child-bearing age for Puerto Rican women tends to be depressed by migration, although by itself it does not account for fertility differences by marital status.

1222 MYERS, GEORGE C. and ROBERTS, JOHN M. 1968 "A Technique for Measuring Preferential Family Size and Composition." EQ 15:3:164-72. graphs, tables, bibl.
In a group of 18 Puerto Rican women, recently married and with no children, most expressed their preference for 2 children of each sex, followed by one of each.

1223 PRESSER, HARRIET B. 1973 Sterilization and Fertility Decline in Puerto Rico. Population Monograph Series, 13. Berkeley, Ca.: Univ. of Ca., Inst. of Int'l. Studies. 211 p. tables, bibl.
A revised doctoral thesis, this monograph describes and analyzes sterilization as a method of birth control in Puerto Rico. Includes a historical account of social conditions leading to the adoption and diffusion of this practice and a detailed empirical analysis of character-istics of sterilized and non-sterilized women. Based on Master Sample Survey of 1965, hospital and clinic records, and personal interviews. Concludes with a comparison between Puerto Rico and other developing countries, con-sidering the island as a unique case.

1224 _____.
      1969 "The Role of Sterilization in Controlling Puerto
      Rico's Fertility." LSE/PS 23:3:343-61. tables, bibl.
      f/notes.
         Using data on 1,071 women (20-49 years old) from 1965
      Master Sample Survey of Health and Welfare in Puerto
      Rico, suggests increasing prevalence and earlier timing
      of sterilization since mid-1950's as highly influential
      in notable decline in marital and total fertility between
      1950 and 1960. Hypothesizes that induced abortion among
      young women and contraceptive practices by women of all
      ages may be important secondary factors, along with
      marital instability, which account for extended age
      range (20-44) of fertility decline.

1225 RAINWATER, LEE
      1964 "Marital Sexuality in Four Cultures of Poverty."
      WRI/JMF 26:4:457-66. bibl. f/notes.
      See MEXICO for annotation.

1226 ROGLER, LLOYD H. and HOLLINGSHEAD, AUGUST B.
      1961 "The Puerto Rican Spiritualist as a Psychiatrist."
      UC/AJS 67:1:17-21. bibl.
         Concludes that persons in lower class of San Juan rely
      on spiritualist beliefs and practices as a therapeutic
      outlet for mental illnesses. Provides illustrations
      from interviews with mentally ill persons, persons with
      no mental illness, and spiritualist mediums (females).
      One woman went to a session complaining of her husband's
      infidelity; another took her husband to a medium so that
      he would stop accusing her of infidelity.

1227 ROGLER, CHARLES
      1946 "Morality of Race Mixing in Puerto Rico." SF
      25:1:77-81.
         Discusses Spanish dominance over blacks in Puerto
      Rico; some functional aspects of Spanish culture;
      Spanish, Puerto Rican and interracial sex mores; mixed
      racial marriages; and differences according to socio-
      economic status.

1228 SCOTT, JOSEPH W.
      1967 "Sources of Social Change in Community, Family, and
      Fertility in a Puerto Rican Town." UC/AJS 72:5:520-30.
      tables, bibl.
         Tests general hypothesis raised in The Family and
      Population Control by Hill, Stycos and Back on correla-
      tion between 2 typologies of families--equalitarian and
      patriarchal. Findings from small town in Puerto Rico

Human Sexuality, Reproduction, and Health

undergoing social and economic change indicate that
employment and education of wives under particular circumstances were correlated with new emerging family
organization and subsequent decline in number of children per family. Equalitarian-type families reported
lowest fertility ratios; patriarchal-type reported
highest. Working and non-working married women were
interviewed.

1229   STYCOS, J. MAYONE
        1955 Family and Fertility in Puerto Rico. A Study of the
        Lower Income Group. N.Y.: Columbia Univ. Press. 332 p.
        illus., tables, bibl.
           First part of 3-stage project on human fertility in
        Puerto Rico emphasizes "sexual norms, character structure,
        the fertility belief system, and birth control practices
        as they are involved in and influenced by the family."
        Traces life history of the family and discusses differ-
        ential status ideologies of the sexes, child rearing
        practices, courtship, early marriage and consensual
        union, marital relations, attitudes toward fertility
        and birth control. Based on detailed questionnaire
        administered to 140 married women and men from lower-
        class villages.

1230   _____.
        1954 "Female Sterilization in Puerto Rico." EQ 1:2:3-9.
        tables.
           Post-partum sterilization, begun in Puerto Rico in
        1930's has proved a very popular birth control method.
        Discusses background of sterilization, frequency of its
        use, characteristics of sterilized women, effect of this
        method on fertility, attitudes toward its use, and its
        future in Puerto Rico.

1230a   _____.
        1954 "The Pattern of Birth Control in Puerto Rico." EQ
        1:3:176-81. tables, bibl. f/notes.
           Explores factors influential in a continuing high rate
        of fertility in Puerto Rico and gives some indication of
        the extent and effectiveness of birth control practice
        among urban and rural women. Based on studies conducted
        by Social Science Research Center of the University of
        Puerto Rico.

1231   _____.
        1953 "La dinámica del control de la natalidad en la clase
        baja de Puerto Rico." UNAM/RMS 15:1:37-65. tables.

Interviews with 72 lower-class couples with children
in the countryside, small town, and city of Puerto Rico
reveal that traditional ideal of large family has dimin-
ished but a rapid fertility decline is not likely. Religion and ignorance are not, contrary to public opinion,
major factors against limiting family size; principal
obstacles include superstitions about danger of contraceptives; hostility, suspicion and lack of communication
between spouses; and psychological barriers on men's
part.

1232 ____.
    1952 "Family and Fertility in Puerto Rico." ASS/ASR
    17:5:572-80.
    Describes and analyzes salient characteristics of
Puerto Rican family. Sees discrepancy in lower-class
families between low fertility aspirations and high
fertility performance as a result of wide gulf between
the sexes, which is aggravated at the time of marriage
and which continues in a breakdown of adequate interspousal communication. Certain individual and institutional mechanisms become operative: sexual denial and
sterilization to reduce fertility; extended family and
compadrazgo to ease burden of already existing high
fertility within family.

1233 STYCOS, J. MAYONE; BACK, KURT and HILL, REUBEN
    1957 "Interpersonal Influence in Family Planning in Puerto
    Rico." TWCS/T 8:212-21. tables.
    Deals with sources of personal influence concerning
fertility control among a sample of lower-class Puerto
Ricans. Discusses 3 topics: "(1) the extent of interpersonal communication on birth control; (2) the sources
of influence and information; (3) the possible differential effects of these sources on fertility control
behavior."

1234 ____.
    1956 "Contraception and Catholicism in Puerto Rico."
    MMFQ 34:2:150-59. tables.
    Attempts to show to what extent religion affects be-
liefs concerning fertility and birth control in Puerto
Rico, based on surveys of 3 different samples: 1,000
households; 888 mothers of less than 7 years of education; and intensively interviewed 72 lower-class women
and their mates.

Human Sexuality, Reproduction, and Health

1235   _____.
         1956 "Problems of Communication Between Husband and Wife
         on Matters Relating to Family Limitation." HURE 9:2:
         207-15. tables.
         Based on intensive interviews with 72 lower-class hus-
         bands and wives and 3,000 short interviews in Puerto
         Rican public health clinics and hospitals, findings
         indicate that large proportion never discuss desired
         family size. Suggests that lack of communication
         results from tendency of each spouse to assume other's
         lack of concern, failure to share knowledge of birth
         control methods, and inclination to either not practice
         methods or use them ineffectively. Female modesty and
         male dominance cause this situation.

1236   THIMMESCH, NICK
         1968 "Puerto Rico and Birth Control." WRU/JMF 30:2:252-
         62.
         Charts progress of the birth control movement in
         Puerto Rico since a League for Birth Control was orga-
         nized by Dr. Lanauze Rolón in Ponce in 1925, through
         the 1937 legislation opposed by the bishops, and
         Celestina Z. Zalduondo's directorship of the Family
         Planning Association of Puerto Rico, organized in 1954.
         Also follows relationship of Roman Catholic Church to
         this movement.

1237   VÁZQUEZ CALZADO, JOSÉ L.
         1973 "La esterilización femenina en Puerto Rico." UPR/
         RCS 17:3:281-308. illus., tables, bibl. f/notes.
         Analyzes historical tendencies and socio-economic fac-
         tors associated with voluntary sterilization of women in
         Puerto Rico. Presents data from other studies since
         1939 and from a survey by School of Public Health
         (University of Puerto Rico) among 634 women (up to age
         49) in 1968, using demographic and socio-economic vari-
         ables along with such factors as knowledge and use of
         contraceptive measures. An interesting result: more
         husbands (82.9%) were satisfied with the woman's having
         been sterilized than the women themselves (63.9%),
         because women wanted more children, especially if they
         remarried after widowhood or divorce.

1238   _____.
         1968 "Fertility Decline in Puerto Rico: Extent and
         Causes." PAA/D 5:2:855-65. tables.
         Studies fertility changes since 1899 and believes
         interplay of factors--urbanization, education, standard

of living, etc.--and family planning efforts in Puerto
Rico have been responsible for significant decline in
fertility.

1239   WELLER, ROBERT H.
        1968 "The Employment of Wives, Role Incompatibility and
        Fertility: A Study Among Lower- and Middle- Class Resi-
        dents of San Juan, Puerto Rico." MMFQ 46:4:507-26.
        tables.
            Attempts to evaluate effect of role incompatibility on
        relationship between fertility and employment of married
        women. Findings bear out hypothesis that "the greater
        the incompatibility between the roles of mother and
        worker, the greater the differential fertility behavior
        of workers and women not in the labor force."

1240   WING, WILSON M.; TAYBACK, MATTHEW and GAMBLE, CLARENCE J.
        1958 "Birth Control in a Rural Area of Puerto Rico." EQ
        5:3:154-61. tables.
            Describes fertility control services for individual
        families in a rural area (1950-57) and results on
        efficacy.

Cuba

1241   LARA MENA, MARÍA JULIA de
        1958 "La medicina y la mujer." SCHM/R 1:2:1-9. illus.
            Part of a larger work on women's role in medicine in
        many countries since 380 A.D., traces history of women
        in Cuban medicine, beginning with Mariana Nava, a curer,
        in 1612, and ending with Laura Carvajal, an ophthalmolo-
        gist, who died in 1914.

1242   _____.
        1940 Salud y belleza. Divulgaciones científicas sobre
        anatomía, fisiología, patología, higiene y estética
        de la mujer. Havana: Casa Ed. "La Propagandista."
        663 p., illus., ports, clr. plate, diagrs.
            A kind of hygiene textbook reflects attitudes toward
        and of women regarding their physical appearance in
        Cuba during first 3 decades of 20c. Chapter headings
        include "The Secret of a Beautiful Figure"; "Is Your
        Body Well Proportioned?"; "The Evolution of Beauty in
        Cuba"; etc.

Human Sexuality, Reproduction, and Health

Dominican Republic

1243   STYCOS, J. MAYONE and MUNDINGO, AXEL
         1974   "Motivators Versus Messengers: A Communications
         Experiment in the Dominican Republic."   SFP 5:4:130-33.
         tables.
             Reports on an experiment formulated to decrease drop-
         outs and increase acceptors of family planning in Santo
         Domingo in 1971.   The campaign included 14 female moti-
         vators who made house-to-house visits and a male messen-
         ger to deliver letters to women, encouraging them to
         attend a local clinic.   Concludes that individual case-
         worker approach is costlier without greater effective-
         ness.   No difference in acceptance rate was noted between
         pamphlet and motivator approaches.

PSYCHOLOGY

This section includes studies on *machismo* and *marianismo* as exaggerated but practiced patterns of male and female behavior; on sex roles, differences, behavior, and conflict; on values, attitudes, orientation, and identity; and national character studies. Only those studies which also tested or interviewed a female sample are included; and only those national character and *machismo* studies which make sufficient reference to women or analyze the female personality as well are cited.

For additional citations which relate to psychology or psychiatric health, see HUMAN SEXUALITY, REPRODUCTION, AND HEALTH. For many items on behavior, conflicts, and socialization within the family setting, see MARRIAGE AND THE FAMILY, a category which includes much psychological material on women with the context of the family, especially in their role as wife and mother. See also the GENERAL category.

SPANISH AMERICA - GENERAL

1244   ADOLPH, JOSÉ B.
             1971 "The South American Macho: Mythos and Mystique."
             UNESCO/I 21:1:83-92.
                 Summarily traces roots of Latin American morality,
             which he considers basically anti-sexual. Sketches 2
             standard cinema types--tango man and *charro*; notes impact
             of neo-liberalism and radicalism; and claims that most
             rampant and uncouth *machismo* exists among middle and
             lower classes because of men's sense of alienation in
             society and occupation.

1245   BALTRA, LIDIA
             1972 "Los mitos de la hombría." S/HM 5:58:26-31.
             illus.
                 Discusses *machismo*, defined as an oppressive ideology
             which divides individuals into superior or inferior,

Psychology

according to their sex. Looks at historical antecedents, and the patriarchal family, *machismo* in the character of Don Juan, the Buenos Aires man, the Mexican *charro*, the Chilean man, and the feminine image. Uses social science literature, folklore and drama verses.

1246 GEYER, GEORGIE ANN
1971 "Machismo or the Unromantic Latin." In her The New Latins. Fateful Change in South and Central America, pp. 86-103. Garden City, N.Y.: Doubleday and Co.
Sees *machismo* as major factor holding back Latin American progress. Subjective and generalized statements.

1247 LLANOS y ALCARÁZ, ADOLFO
1876 La mujer en el siglo diez y nueve; hojas de un libro originales. Lima: Librería Hispano-francesca. 368 p.
First published in 1865, includes instructions as to how women should behave, with generalizations about different stages of female life cycle which reflect 19c. stereotypes: "good daughter," "old maid" (considered an abortion of nature), "good wife," etc.

1248 PALAU de NEMES, GRACIELA
1974 "Machismo." OAS/AM 26:4:2-7.
Begins with etymology of the term *machismo*, noting differences in meaning according to epoch and region, and traces its appearance and significance in the writings of Sor Juana, "Concolorcorvo," Octavio Paz, Sarmiento, Mario Vargas Llosa, Rómulo Gallegos, Martínez Estrada and Manuel Puig. For the most part, these writers exalt manliness and virility while emphasizing passive, weak, and defensive aspects of women. Concludes that *machismo* has evolved from being a local and regional trait to a national one and a code of life.

1249 ROMERO-BUJ, SEBASTIÁN
1970 "Hispanoamérica y el machismo." MN 46:28-32.
Defines *machismo* as a misunderstood, exaggerated, and false virility which varies according to society and epoch. Discusses LA's particular brand; its manifestation in literature; and its historical, environmental and psychological roots.

1250 STEVENS, EVELYN P.
1973 "Machismo and Marianismo." Society 10:6:57-63.
Describes characteristics of *machismo* and *marianismo*, the secular cult of femininity derived from worship of the Virgin Mary. The latter pattern of attitudes and

behavior provides women with great power as spiritually superior beings, which is why they have not taken steps to change the status quo but rather cooperate in pressuring men to conform to the *macho* stereotypes.

1251 _____.
    1973 *"Marianismo*: The Other Face of *Machismo* in Latin America." In Female and Male in Latin America: Essays, ed. by Ann Pescatello, pp. 89-101. Pittsburgh, Pa.: Univ. of Pittsburgh Press. bibl. notes.
    Focuses on dynamic interplay between *machismo*, the cult of virility, and its counterpart, *marianismo*, the cult of female spiritual superiority, tracing historical antecedents in archaeology, mythology, and religion and its development in America since the Conquest. Discusses alternative models to this ideal of womanly behavior and concludes that despite changes in *mestizo* society, Latin American women are not yet prepared to surrender their own chauvinism because of its advantages.

1252 YORBURG, BETTY
    1974 "Spain and Latin America." In her Sexual Identity: Sex Roles and Social Change, pp. 124-34. N.Y.: John Wiley and Sons.
    Very general picture of "extreme sex typing" in Latin culture, briefly discusses *machismo*, legal status of women. Continuing traditional values, as exemplified in several episodes quoted from Lewis' Five Families, are contrasted with examples of modern Mexico City women. Based on secondary sources.

MIDDLE AMERICA

Mexico

1253 ALEGRÍA, JUANA ARMANDA
    1974 Psicología de las mexicanas. Serie: Cuarta Dimensión. Mex., D.F.: Edit. Samo. 187 p.
    Attempts to present psychological portrait of Mexican women by tracing roots in history: Aztec religion and society; Doña Marina, *mestizaje*, Sor Juana, la Llorona, Virgin of Guadelupe, 3 women of the Independence era, women during 1910 Revolution. For contemporary times discusses *machismo*, stereotypical feminine behavior (abnegation, servility, sexual attitudes, motherhood, family), and historical, economic, religious and psychological reasons behind continuation of submissive

319

Psychology

conduct. Based on secondary sources, but no bibliography included.

1254 ARAMONI, ANICETO
1972 "Machismo." Psychology Today 5:8:69-72.
Machismo is Mexico's disturbed response to the "universal quest for individuation, dignity and relatedness." Discusses cause, range and goal of machismo, women's position as a sex object to be despoiled or as a venerable trio (mother, sister, Virgin). Illustrates with lyrics and anecdotes.

1255 _____.
1961 Psicoanálisis de la dinámica de un pueblo. Mex., D.F.: UNAM. 321 p.
Attempts to understand the psychology of the Mexican by tracing the historical development of the male and female character since pre-Conquest times. Considers Aztec religion and mythology, Spanish chivalry and Mexican charrería, the corrido and ranchera song, female figures such as doña Marina, Virgin of Guadalupe, la Adelita, Mother and others in Mexican history, women's important role as well as ambivalence toward her, machismo and its effects on women. Concludes that in pre-Cortesian Mexico a matriarchal order had been destroyed and substituted by male supremacy. Characteristics of Aztec society and Mexico today reflect admiration of woman as a goddess (or virgin) with a consequent fear of explicit and occult powers but also a secondary position relative to men in the affairs of the culture.

1256 BATT, CARL
1969 "Mexican Character: An Adlerian Interpretation." IP/J 25:2:183-201. bibl.
Reviews Samuel Ramos' and Octavio Paz' interpretations of Mexican national character. Uses Oscar Lewis' and his own observations to describe it from an Adlerian perspective. Emphasis is on the cult of manliness (masculine protest, violence and alcoholism, weakness and fear), women's role (female martyr complex and defiance), and childhood situation (pampering, neglect, parental roles). Believes Latin family and tradition are more influential in forming Mexican inferiority complex than historio-cultural situation.

1257 BÉJAR NAVARRO, RAÚL
       1968 El mito del mexicano. Fac. de Ciencias Políticas y
       Sociales. Serie Estudios, no. 1. Mex., D.F.: UNAM.
       163 p. bibl.
          Analyzes an extensive bibliography of studies on Mexi-
       can national character by nationals and foreigners, out-
       lining the major ideas of each writer, many of which
       relate to the psychology of Mexican women and male-female
       relations. Concludes that, while useful, these studies
       have limited scientific validity.

1258 BUSHNELL, JOHN H.
       1958 "La Virgen de Guadelupe as Surrogate Mother in San
       Juan Atzingo." AAA/AA 60:2:261-65.
          Suggests that Virgin of Guadalupe fulfills intensely-
       felt need for a mother figure by villagers, especially
       men, of San Juan Atzingo in south central Mexico.
       Describes social relationships in Ocuilteca community
       as atomistic and representative of affect starvation.
       In their attempt to recreate a satisfying child-parent
       relationship, villagers turn to comforting and permissive
       Virgin, who is only exception to demanding, fear-
       inspiring and authoritarian qualities of God. Women are
       less emotionally involved than men in worship of Virgin.

1259 Centro de Estudios de la Juventud de México, D.F.
       1971 "La soltera en la Ciudad de México, D.F." BDSLM/
       CIDHAL 1:2:1-10.
          Reports some results of 1970 survey carried out among
       232 unmarried women, aged 15-25, asking their opinions
       on young single women who have sexual relationships, use
       of artificial contraceptive methods, marriage or free
       union, divorce or separation, Church's position on birth
       control, etc. Pro and con arguments broken down by
       working group (students, secretaries, sales clerks et
       al.).

1260 CHÁZARO, GABRIEL
       1964 De la mujer; ensayo. Col. Suma Veracruzana. Serie
       Ensayo. Tucubaya, Mex.: Edit. Citlaltepetl. 23 p.
       port.
          Short essay replete with stereotypical generalizations
       about women in terms of frailty, tears, insecurity,
       illogicalness, cruelty, inferiority, etc.

1261 DÍAZ-GUERRERO, ROGELIO
       1974 "La mujer y las premisas histórico-socioculturales
       de la familia mexicana." RLP 6:1:7-16. tables, bibl.

Psychology

Reports some of the findings of study carried out among male and female grade and high school students of Federal District. Presents data pertinent to changes in Mexican females between 1959 and 1970, when a questionnaire of socio-cultural premises was administered: differences between attitudes about male/female relations, women's role in Mexican society and parent/child relations of girls attending co-ed schools and those of girls in sex-segregated schools. Concludes that 1960's produced a number of changes, with mass media being a prime vehicle of information: women feel less controlled by male authority or superiority; they want to become more independent in terms of work; they are less prone to blindly obey parents.

1262 _____.

1973 "Interpreting Coping Styles Across Nations From Sex and Social Class Differences." IJP 8:3:193-203. tables, bibl.

Questionnaire administered to 8 national samples (including Mexico) of 400 14-year-old children of 2 social classes and sexes measured active/passive orientation to life situations. Males scored significantly higher than females in coping style. Appendix includes "Views of Life" measure of 17 subsyndromes (e.g., positive versus negative self-concept, independence versus interdependence, etc.).

1263 _____.

1968 Estudios de psicología del mexicano. 3rd ed. Mex., D.F.: Edit. Trillas. 205 p. bibl. English translation: 1975 Psychology of the Mexican: Culture and Personality. The Texas Pan American Series. Austin, Tex.: Univ. of Tex. Press. 171 p. tables, graphs, bibl.

Collection of studies dealing with the effects of culture upon personality. Includes "Neurosis and the Mexican Family Structure" (See Díaz-Guerrero, R., #842); "Mental, Personal and Social Health in Mexico City," which concludes from a survey that maladjustment or neurosis is definitively greater in Mexican women than men; comparison of respect among Mexican and US male and female college students, including a table on the cosmos of respect among Mexican females, who receive greater respect from Mexican males than do US women from US men; socio-cultural premises and attitudes regarding male and female roles and the family.

1264   DÍAZ-GUERRERO, ROGELIO and LARA TAPIA, LUIS
        1972 "Diferencias sexuales en el desarrollo de la
        personalidad del escolar mexicano." RLP 4:3:345-51.
        tables, bibl.
           Reports observable sex differences for 7 out of 21
        variables in application of Holtzman's Ink Blots to
        442 grade school boys and girls. Sees role of Mexican
        mother (especially abnegation) as crucial center for
        maintaining certain cultural and behavioral norms, par-
        ticularly syndrome of passivity. Men are more active
        than women.

1265   FROMM, ERICH and MACCOBY, MICHAEL
        1970 Social Character in a Mexican Village: A Sociopsy-
        choanalytic Study. Englewood Cliffs, N.J.: Prentice-
        Hall. 303 p. tables, bibl.
           Studies social character of Mexican peasant through
        an analysis of interrelations and interactions between
        emotional attitudes and socio-economic conditions.
        Explores 6 factors: adulthood vs. adolescence; exploit-
        ativeness vs. non-exploitativeness; productiveness vs.
        unproductiveness; hoarding vs. receptive modes of assim-
        ilation; masculinity vs. femininity; and mother-centered
        vs. father-centered orientations. A chapter on sex and
        character focuses on traits distinguishing men from
        women. Results challenge ideal of patriarchy: 20% of
        the families are headed by women and 48% are dominated
        by women even though 2/3 of husbands appear to fit
        patriarchal model as dominant.

1266   GECAS, VICTOR; THOMAS, DARWIN L. and WEIGERT, ANDREW J.
        1973 "Social Identities in Anglo and Latin Adolescents."
        SF 51:4:477-84. tables, bibl.
           TST (20 Statement Test) was used to measure 4 social
        identities (family, peer, gender, religion) among male
        and female high school adolescents in Mexico, Puerto
        Rico, and US. Sex was most salient identity in all
        groups. For Latin females, hierarchy was gender, reli-
        gion, family, peer, in descending order. Notes greater
        cross-cultural than cross-sex similarity.

1267   GIRALDO, OCTAVIO
        1972 "El machismo como fenómeno psicocultural." RLP
        4:3:295-309. illus., bibl.
           Using Oscar Lewis' study on Mexican families, views
        machismo as a Hispanic cultural characteristic partic-
        ularly prevalent in Mexico. In light of Adlerian theory,
        interprets male behavior patterns of exaggerated manli-
        ness, aggression, valor, sexual license, emotional

323

Psychology

aloofness, physical dominance, and alcoholism as compo-
nents of an inferiority complex. Various cultural ideas
and child-rearing practices teach and foster *machismo*
syndrome: female submission, virginity, genital filth
of women, etc.

1268 GÓMEZ ROBLEDO, JOSÉ
1962 Psicología del mexicano. Motivos de perturbación
de la conducta psico-social del mexicano de la clase
media. Cuadernos de Sociología. Biblioteca de Ensayos
Sociológicos. Mex., D.F.: UNAM, Inst. de Investigaciones Sociales. 108 p. graphs.
Reports and interprets findings of psychological
testing of 230 men and 255 women of the Mexican middle
class of various occupations and age groups. In evalu-
ating sex differences, concludes that men are more disturbed than women because actual life conditions affect
them more adversely.

1269 GONZÁLEZ PINEDA, FRANCISCO
1961 El mexicano: psicología de su destructividad.
Monografías Psicoanalíticas, 7. Mex., D.F.: Edit.
Pax-México, Asociación Psicoanalítica Mexicana. 268 p.
Study of aggression in the Mexican character provides
a psychological portrait of the Mexican woman in her
various roles as daughter, fiancée, wife, mother,
virgin, sex object, etc. and describes ambivalent attitude toward women in marked dichotomy between "good"
and "bad" ones. See "La agresión en la mujer" (pp. 119-
82). See "La niña" (pp. 115-18) for a concise illustration of reactions to the birth of a female child.

1270 HERNÁNDEZ MICHEL, SUSANA
1971 "Algunas características de la mujer mexicana de
clase media." RMCP 17:65:99-105.
Middle class Mexican women of today face role conflict:
active social and economic life vs. home and family only.
Sketches characteristics of women who work outside home,
who do not work, and who carry out public and domestic
roles. Concludes that middle class women and men are
poorly educated to cope with socio-economic system in
which they live; that employment itself is not an end to
these conflicts; and that problem is one of traditional
vs. modern values. Makes no indication of having conducted a survey.

1271 HEWES, GORDON
1954 "Mexicans in Search of the 'Mexican': Notes on
Mexican National Character Studies." AJES 13:2:209-23.
Good summary of contributions made by Mexican writers
to Mexican national character studies plus a composite
picture of Mexican personality based on their writings.

1272 LANGNER, THOMAS S.
1965 "Psychophysiological Symptoms and the Status of
Women in Two Mexican Communities." In Approaches to
Cross-Cultural Psychiatry, ed. by J. M. Murphy and A. H.
Leighton, pp. 360-92. Ithaca, N.Y.: Cornell Univ.
Press. tables, bibl. notes.
A psychological screening questionnaire was administered in 1959 to two samples representing 3 socio-
economic groups in Mexico City and Tehuantepec. Findings
presented by sex, age, residence, income and education
suggest that women whose status is closer to that of the
men in the community report fewer psychophysiological
symptoms; women of all income groups report more complaints than men in either city; and women's attitudes
in favor of sexual equality are not related to their
sexual status or number of symptoms.

1273 LORETO HERNÁNDEZ, MARGARITA
1961 Personalidad (?) de la mujer mexicana. Mex., D.F.:
Impresora Galve. 157 p. bibl.
National character study on Mexican women, along the
lines of Ramírez et al. Traces historical roots, compares male and female personalities, dissatisfaction vs.
resignation and a passive maternal temperament. Considers the woman-mother vs. the man-child. Briefly
describes particular situation of women in 7 classes and
different kinds of working women; and discuss feminism
superficially. Concludes that women must recognize
their own worth, raise their consciousness and break
the vicious circle.

1274 MACCOBY, MICHAEL
1970 "Methods of Studying Mexican Peasant Personality:
Rorschach, TAT and Dreams." CUA/AQ 43:4:225-42.
Using dreams, Rorschach and TAT, attempts to understand personality of Macaria Gómez, a 60-year-old
woman of Tzintzuntzan, Michoacán, and to compare
strengths and weaknesses of each method. Her responses
on Rorschach reveal uncertainty of sexual identity and
rejection of inferior female role.

Psychology

1275 _____.
1967 "On Mexican National Character." AAPSS/A 370:63-73.
bibl. f/notes.
Based on socio-psychological research with Erich Fromm
since 1960 in *mestizo* village in Morelos, considers
several social, economic, and historical determinants of
Mexican character, character being defined as "a structure of underlying motives, interrelated and relatively
unchanging after childhood." Using projective questionnaires, Rorschach, TAT, and participant observation with
900 villagers, confirms that conflict between the sexes
is the most crucial determinant of Mexican psychopathol-
ogy, one which is both historically rooted and fostered
by contemporary economic trends. Standard pattern is
that men, in their attempt to impose patriarchal ideal,
are thwarted by resentful women. Males then adopt role
of compulsive masculinity while maternal figures really
possess power within the family. However, majority of
Mexican villagers are not representative of these traits;
many are loving and productive. Believes social behavior
is insufficiently explained by character; socio-economic
reality is also influential. Includes consideration of
Mexican intelligentsia's view of national character.

1276 MACCOBY, MICHAEL: MODIANO, NANCY and LANCER, PATRICIA
1964 "Games and Social Character in a Mexican Village."
Psychiatry 27:2:150-62. bibl. f/notes.
An analysis of games played by boys and girls revealed
that sex differences reflected greater differences in
the social character of women and men in a Mexican village. Girls' games are more structured and orderly,
and refer to danger from the male world; girls also take
turns being leader and accept authority.

1277 MEBANE, DONATA and JOHNSON, DALE L.
1970 "A Comparison of the Performance of Mexican Boys and
Girls on Witkin's Cognitive Tasks." SIP/RIP 4:3/4:227-
39. tables, bibl.
Study conducted among 87 Mexican boys and girls (aged
9-13) attending school in working class neighborhood in
Monterrey used Children's Embedded Figure Test, Draw-a-
Person Test, and child rearing/daily experience questionnaire to test Witkin's hypotheses regarding variation
of sex differences in cognitive style according to type
of culture and women's role in it. Findings revealed
Mexican boys and American girls were more field independent than Mexican girls. Confirms that in highly sex-
role differentiated society, girls are more field
dependent. Questionable sample and measurement.

Middle America - Mexico

1278   NELSON, CYNTHIA
       1967 "Analysis of World View in a Mexican Peasant Village:
       An Illustration." SF 46:1:52-60.
         TAT's were administered to 19 women and 11 men in
       Erongaricuaro, *mestizo* village in Michoacán, to test
       cognitive orientation. Findings indicate deep concern
       over dependency, success through submission, strong empha-
       sis on duty and obligations, and fear of separation.

1279   PAZ, OCTAVIO
       1962 The Labyrinth of Solitude. Life and Thought in
       Mexico. Trans. by L. Kemp. N.Y.: Grove Press. 212 p.
         National character study by well known Mexican poet
       and intellectual traces roots of typical Mexican behav-
       ior. Deals with *machismo* and how it relates to women.
       Describes general characteristics of Mexican women,
       passivity appearing as main trait. Explains meaning of
       La Chingada and discusses Sor Juana.

1280   RAMÍREZ, SANTIAGO
       1968 El mexicano: psicología de sus motivaciones. 5th
       ed. Monografías psicoanalíticas, 1. Mex., D.F.: Edit.
       Pax-Mexico. 262 p. illus., bibl.
         Beginning with colonial heritage of the Spaniards' neg-
       ative valuation of indigenous woman as a sexual servant,
       analyzes psychology of Mexican men and women--their roles
       and attitudes: e.g., ambivalence toward the mother,
       who is adored and hated simultaneously. Sees the Mexican
       Revolution as only form in which women were finally able
       to express their repressed sexuality: to be women, not
       only mothers. *Machismo* is the insecurity of masculinity.
       The absence of father figure is very notable in family
       organization. Motherhood is women's outlet for tensions
       and frustrations derived from her rejection by father,
       world of men and social world. Discusses masculine/
       feminine dichotomy of active/passive and 3 tendencies
       of Mexican family in terms of mother/child, father/
       child relations.

1281   REYES NEVARES, SALVADOR
       1971 "El machismo en México." BDSLM/CIDHAL 1:2:21-32.
       Originally appeared in Mundo Nuevo 46(1970):14-19.
         Defines *machismo* and discusses its female counterpart,
       hembrismo, since *machismo* doesn't affect man by himself
       but in relation to woman; commercialization of both
       tendencies, and the need to change this duality by break-
       ing down such antitheses as friend and enemy, Indian and
       Spaniard to unite Mexico and eliminate the basis for
       machismo.

Psychology

1282 RODRÍGUEZ BAÑOS, ROBERTO; TREJO de ZEPEDA, PATRICIA and
SOTO ANGLI, EDILBERTO
1973 Virginidad y machismo en México. Mex., D.F.:
Edit. Posada. 187 p. bibl.
Referring to such well-known analysts of the Mexican
psyche as Paz, Aramoni, Ramos, Ramírez et al., explores
historical roots of machismo in Mexico from pre-Conquest
times through the 1910 Revolution, considering social,
economic, and political conditions favoring its development. Section on contemporary era includes questions
and responses regarding attitudes toward machismo, virginity, sexual relations, motherhood, etc. among 4
small groups of young middle-class males and females in
urban center. Concludes that formulas for solving
serious problem of cults of virility and virginity in an
underdeveloped nation must exist within a restructuring
of development model, or the shift from capitalism to
socialism.

1283 SIMON, KATE
1971 "Machismo." In her Mexico: Places and Pleasures,
rev. ed., pp. 44-49. N.Y.: World Publishers.
Traveler's personal impressions of machismo as "the
scourge of Mexico," an indoor and outdoor sport. Origins of macho character lie in Indian pride and fatalism,
strong latent homosexuality, etc. Stereotypical
description.

1284 STEVENS, EVELYN P.
1965 "Mexican Machismo: Politics and Value Orientation."
UU/WPQ 18:4:848-57.
Sees relationship between cult of virility and Mexican
political system: politics, sphere of male activities
and values, calls for facade of toughness and intran-
sigence; however, behind it exists a flexibility which
curbs a relapse into bloody warfare or anarchy--male
politicians play "the role of 'feminine' maneuvers."

1285 STROSS, BRIAN
1967 "The Mexican Cantina as a Setting for Interaction."
KAS/P 37:58-89. illus.
Describes social interaction in a Mexican cantina,
where according to Mexican definitions, a participation
category of women is found. Also distinguishes among
types of men who frequent cantinas. Discusses behavior
cycles of participants, rules followed, and role of
cantina in Mexican culture for both sexes.

1286   VILLASEÑOR, IRENE
         1965 "Psicología del mexicano." RMP 1:6:544-55.
         Outlines several hypotheses on the Mexican personality
         as expounded by Bermúdez, González Pineda, Díaz Guerrero
         et al.: male supremacy in the home; female feelings of
         inadequacy, resignation and dependence on men; female
         role as passive, self-abnegating, unequal, weak, etc.
         Presents traditional picture of differences and conflicts
         between women and men in Mexico.

1287   WHITING, BEATRICE and EDWARDS, CAROLYN P.
         1974 "A Cross-Cultural Analysis of Sex Differences in the
         Behavior of Children Aged Three Through Eleven." In
         Culture and Personality: Contemporary Readings, ed. by
         R. A. LeVine, pp. 188-201. Chicago: Aldine Publishing
         Co. tables, bibl. Reprinted from: 1973 JSP 91.
         Investigates validity of stereotypes of sex differences
         among children (3-11 years old) in 6 cultures, 1 of
         which was Juxtlahuaca, Mexico. Results suggest existence
         of universal sex differences in this age group, but they
         are less consistent and major than assumed and may be
         explained by socialization pressure through task assign-
         ments and viewed as differences in style more than intent.
         Observes 4 major areas of behavior: dependency, passiv-
         ity, nurturance and aggression.

Guatemala

1288   ZAVALA de AQUINO, CAROLINA
         1966 Estudio sobre valores realizado en una muestra de
         mujeres guatemaltecas que solicitaron ingresar en la
         Universidad de San Carlos de Guatemala, en los años
         1960-1963. Guatemala: Univ. de San Carlos de Guatemala,
         Facultad de Humanidades, Depto. de Psicología. 44 p.
         graphs, tables, bibl.
         Using values study of Allport, Vernon and Lindzey as a
         measurement, considers theoretical, economic, esthetic,
         social, political and religious values (as conceived by
         Edward Spranger) manifested among women who applied to
         study in different disciplines at the University of San
         Carlos of Guatemala between 1960 and 1963. Findings
         indicate order of values in decreasing importance as
         follows: to find truth and be sociable; law of economy
         or least effort; union to the beyond in religious faith;
         obtaining power; impression and expression of form.

Psychology

Panama

1289 BROWN, BERTHA B.
1968 "Notes on the Study of Machismo." FSU/NA 13:19-30.
bibl.
Begins with a discussion of the Spanish cultural heritage which underlies prevalence of *machismo* in America
today and comments on its manifestations among Panamanian
males (who are neither Indian nor West Indian) in sexual
activities and politics. Points out several areas in
need of further investigation and the real and ideal
role of Panamanian women. Based on secondary sources.

SOUTH AMERICA

Venezuela

1290 WATSON, LAWRENCE C.
1974 "Defense Mechanisms in Guajiro Personality and Culture." JARES 30:1:17-34. table, bibl.
Using structured methods of observation and inter-
viewing, Rorschach and TAT tests among 7 male, 7 female
Guajiro Indians evaluates 5 defense mechanisms (projec-
tion, displacement, reaction formation, repression and
introjection) in Freud's psychoanalytic formulation to
determine their relevance to psychological processes in
a non-Western cultural setting. Provides specific
examples of Guajiro women. They often deal with threat-
ening sexual feelings through reactive behavior. Concludes that all the mechanisms prevail but differ in
importance; are manifested in a well-defined culturally
determined form; group themselves around the most
conflict-ridden systems of behavior in the culture; and
vary in use according to age, sex, class, and occupation.

Colombia

1291 ARDILA, ALFREDO, et al.
1971 Psicología y problemas sociales en Colombia. Eds.
"La Rana y el águila." Tunja: Univ. Pedagógica y
Tecnológica de Colombia. 155 p. illus., tables, bibl.
Using TAT and Rorschach tests, three studies were
carried out in Pereira, Colombia to determine correlation between certain psychological traits and social
groups. The first, administered to 642 men and women,
indicated, among other things, the existence of exces-
sively conflict-ridden sexuality. The second,

administered to 59 women and men, revealed that men had
been more psychologically affected by *la violencia* but
women demonstrated greater fear of physical danger. The
third describes socio-cultural aspects of prostitution
and analyzes principal psychological characteristics of
28 prostitutes.

1292   DUSSAN de REICHEL-DOLMATOFF, ALICIA
       1954 "Características de la personalidad masculina y
       femenina en Taganga." ICA/RCA 2:2:87-113.
          Based on field research (1946-50) in racially mixed
       fishing village on Colombia's Caribbean coast, where the
       economic system is based on a strict division of labor
       (men fish, women sell fish) and family organization is
       monogamous concubinage, describes process of socializing
       individuals according to his or her sex from infancy to
       25 years of age. Schematically presents characteristics
       of male and female personality in 3-fold aspect: real,
       functional, ideal. Findings indicate that women form
       the most acculturated sector of the society, economically
       dominating the men; and cultural equilibrium is estab-
       lished by controlling social aggression in men and
       allowing its free expression in women. Women relate to
       the "out-group" on a daily basis and represent "progres-
       sive" tendencies while men are reduced to relations with
       the "in-group." Men are expected to be generous, honest,
       composed, collaborative, cohesive, and controlled while
       women are expected to be aggressive, competitive, emo-
       tional, jealous, avaricious, egotistical, dishonest, and
       gossipy.

1293   HARKESS, SHIRLEY
       1973 "Pursuit of an Ideal: Migration, Social Class, and
       Women's Roles in Bogotá, Colombia." In Female and Male
       in Latin America: Essays, ed. by A. Pescatello,
       pp. 231-254. Pittsburgh: Univ. of Pittsburgh Press.
       tables, bibl.
          Contrary to expectations, survey conducted among mi-
       grant women in a working-class neighborhood and a very
       poor *barrio* in Bogotá (1969) indicates similarity in
       response. Traditional ideals persist in role relation-
       ships, in politics, educational aspirations for children
       of both sexes, occupational aspirations for oldest daugh-
       ter, family power and authority. Longer urban residence
       does not necessarily imply greater modernity; transition
       from traditional to modern is not linear in this case.

Psychology

1294   WATSON, LAWRENCE CRAIG
         1974 "Defense Mechanisms in Guajiro Personality and Cul-
         ture." JARES 30:1:41-54. map, table, bibl.
         See VENEZUELA for annotation.

1295   WHITTEN, NORMAN E., JR.
         1974 "Ritual Enactment of Sex Roles in the Pacific Low-
         lands of Ecuador-Colombia." UP/E 13:2:129-43. illus.,
         bibl.
           Focuses on sex roles and rituals among the lower-class
         black population of the Pacific lowland running from
         Buenaventura, Colombia to Esmeraldas, Ecuador. Describes
         variations in enactment of sex roles in several ritual
         contexts (secular: cantina, saloon, curralao, marimba
         dance; sacred) and relates them to household, kinship
         network, community, and inter-community maintenance.
         Good descriptions of male/female interaction. Male role
         provides continuity in Afro-Hispanic culture while female
         role provides stability through household permanence.

1296   _____.
           1970 "Personal Networks and Musical Contexts in the
         Pacific Lowland of Colombia and Ecuador." In Afro-
         American Anthropology: Contemporary Perspectives, ed.
         by N. E. Whitten, Jr. and J. F. Szwed, pp. 203-18. N.Y.:
         Free Press. illus. Also in: 1968 MAN 3:1.
           Analyzes the symbolic expression of interpersonal net-
         works through activities within musical contexts among
         the lower-class black population of the Pacific Litoral
         of Colombia and Ecuador. Deals specifically with the
         "categorical relationship" of female sexual solidarity.
         Discusses 5 musical contexts to illustrate how such a
         relationship is symbolically presented, reinforced and
         built and to point out how these musical contexts support
         the development of personal networks which are flexible
         in a fluctuating money economy. Interesting observations
         on male/female relations.

1297   WILLIAMSON, ROBERT C.
         1968 "Social Class and Orientation to Change: Some Rele-
         vant Variables in a Bogotá Sample." SF 46:3:317-28.
         tables.
           Conducted among 229 lower- and middle-class residents
         of Bogota, tests hypotheses about social participation,
         traditionalism vs. rationality, past- vs. future-
         orientation, and mobility and adjustment to determine
         class variance with respect to social involvement and
         receptivity to change. Findings indicate a higher de-
         gree of social participation among middle-class

interviewees than among lower-class subjects. Questions
were asked about birth control, mobility and satisfaction
with status quo, attitudes toward Colombian societal
institutions, kinship and friendship networks, etc.
60% of the respondents were women.

1298   ____.
         1964 "University Students in a World of Change: A
         Colombian Sample." SOSOR 48:4:397-413. tables.
            Reports findings of study among male and female uni-
         versity students in Bogota (See Williamson, #1299).
         "The woman student appears to be less adequately social-
         ized within society at large and in the university sys-
         tem. She has peripheral and desultory contact with the
         professions and has only partial knowledge of political
         events. Her entry into given professions such as medi-
         cine and dentistry is no better if no worse than in the
         US. Her religious and social life is considerably more
         restrained than that of the male or her counterpart
         abroad but even there, change is in the air."

1299   ____.
         1962 El estudiante colombiano y sus actitudes. Un
         análisis de psicología social en la Universidad Nacional.
         Monografías Sociológicas, 13 Bogota: Univ. Nacional de
         Colombia, Facultad de Sociología. 76 p. tables.
            Based on interview sample of 460 male and 150 female
         university students in Bogota, using sex as a variable,
         finds that women are more family-oriented with respect
         to residence patterns and values; more indifferent to,
         ignorant of and conservative in politics; less optimistic
         about the future; and more restricted in social partici-
         pation. Other variables include social class, career
         choice, and age.

Ecuador

1300 LARREA BORJA, PIEDAD
         1968 Habla femenina quiteña. Quito: Edit. Casa de la
         Cultura Ecuatoriana. 70 p. illus., facsims.
            Unique essay identifies interesting traits character-
         istic of female speech, especially coloquial, in high-
         land Ecuador. Notes the affective tones and psychological
         conditions expressed in everyday, popular, familiar
         idioms. Points out influence of indigenous language in
         quichuismos.

Psychology

1301   WHITTEN, NORMAN E., JR.
1974 "Ritual Enactment of Sex Roles in the Pacific Lowlands of Ecuador-Colombia." UP/E 13:2:129-43. illus.,
bibl.
See COLOMBIA for annotation.

1302   _____.
1970 "Personal Networks and Musical Contexts in the
Pacific Lowlands of Colombia and Ecuador." In Afro-
American Anthropology: Contemporary Perspectives, ed.
by N. E. Whitten, Jr. and J. F. Szwed, pp. 203-18.
N.Y.: Free Press. illus.
See COLOMBIA for annotation.

Peru

1303   ADOLPH, JOSÉ B.
1970 "La emancipación masculina en Lima." MN 46:39-41.
Brief, tongue-in-cheek examination of male sex roles
in Lima, considered a "feminine" city. Believes men of
Lima are not ready to deal with women on a level of
equal sexual conditions.

1304   ARAMBURÚ LECAROS, HELENA
1949 Lo que piensan las mujeres (primera parte). Lima:
Ed. Médica Peruana. 373 p.
Reproduces 100 inquiries sent to column of same title
in the Lima daily El Comercio by women and the replies
by author, covering 27 June 1947 to 27 February 1948, on
a wide range of subjects (passion, general psychology,
philosophy, pedagogy). Similar to "Dear Abby."

1305   ROTONDO, HUMBERTO
1970 "Personalidad básica, dilemas y vida de familia de
un grupo de mestizos." In his Estudios sobre la
familia en su relación con la salud, pp. 48-101. Lima:
Univ. Nacional Mayor de San Marcos. tables, bibl.
Using biography form, interview, anthropological data,
and A. Kardiner's concept of the "emerging" cholo, describes basic personality of 80 (40 women, 40 men) low-
income residents of Barrio de Mendocita in Lima and
analyzes some influential factors in its formation.
Concludes that principal traits correspond to a syndrome
of oral pessimism: inclination toward depression, feelings of dependency, insecurity, inferiority and low
self-esteem, fear, envy, hypochondriacal attitudes,
aggressiveness and hostility (especially toward women).
Possible causes are an inconsistent and ambivalent

mother figure, distant or absent father figure, disintegration of one's family, oral problems (especially
regarding breastfeeding), and tensions between the sexes.
Women are not trusted; they are feared and under-
appreciated.

1306   STEINMANN, ANNE and FOX, DAVID J.
          1969 "Specific Areas of Agreement and Conflict in Women's
          Self-Perception and Their Perception of Men's Ideal
          Woman in Two South American Urban Communities and an
          Urban Community in the United States." WRU/JMF 31:2:
          281-89. tables, bibl. f/notes.
             See ARGENTINA for annotation.

Bolivia

1307   AILLÓN RÍOS, LUZ
          1970 "Un dilema de la mujer boliviana: ¿madre o
          profesional?" IBEAS/EA 1:3:55-68. bibl.
             Using role theory as conceptual framework, looks at
          influence of socialization process of educating Bolivian
          woman, her self-identity, her roles, her peer group in
          the conflict of roles experienced as a professional and
          as a mother at the same time. Discusses organization
          and function of the family and role theory. Refers to
          data on students at the Universidad de San Andrés, La
          Paz, 1960's. Compares characteristics of professional
          women and women of lower class.

Chile

1308   WILLIAMSON, ROBERT C. and SEWARD, GEORGENE H.
          1971 "Concepts of Social Sex Roles Among Chilean Adoles-
          cents." HUDE 14:3:184-97. tables, bibl.
             On the basis of a 12-point semantic differential scale,
          210 Chilean male and female adolescents responded on
          their concepts of ideal woman and man, mother, father,
          and self-image. Reveals significant differences between
          the sexes in rating traits of men and women, but they
          are not greater than for US and German samples. Girls
          tend to idealize parents and women more than boys do.

Psychology

Argentina

1309   BRUMANA, HERMINIA
       1936 Cartas a las mujeres argentinas. Santiago: Eds.
       Ercilla. 260 p.
       Using the vehicle of answers to letters from women,
       discusses problems, defects, virtues, concerns, etc.
       of Argentine women to reveal "the roots of their person-
       ality." Presents personal impressions, observations,
       opinions, and advice. Includes some comments on Chilean
       women too.

1310   COCONI de SEDACA, DEBORA
       1973 La mujer y su mundo. B.A.: Junta Bautista de
       Publicaciones. 2 vols.
       A kind of handbook advising women how to be in our
       changing times. Considers why women were created, the
       nature of their function, their role as wife/server,
       getting rid of fears, accepting life's circumstances,
       women's relationship with the Church and God, their
       husband, children, relatives, neighbors, friends, and
       fellow workers. Biblical passages used liberally.

1311   CORTADA de KOHAN, NURIA
       1970 "Un estudio experimental sobre el machismo." RLP
       2:1:31-54. tables, bibl.
       Analyzes origin of Latin American machismo in a social
       and historical context and relates it to southern Euro-
       pean cultural traditions. Administering a battery of
       psychological tests and socio-economic questionnaire to
       20 university students and 13 workers from slum areas
       of Buenos Aires, found students less "machista" and
       authoritarian than workers.

1312   GIBERTI, EVA
       1970 Los argentinos y el amor. Col. Tiempos Modernos.
       Buenos Aires: Edit. Merlin. 109 p.
       Based on professional experience as clinical psycholo-
       gist and sexology teacher, offers psychological inter-
       pretation of Argentine men and their way of loving.
       Views inscriptions on the backs of buses, agressive
       street flattery, the pick-up, and bachelor farewell
       parties as characteristics of an exhibitionism and vio-
       lence particular to a certain type of Argentine man.
       Discusses influence of home life, peer group and mass
       media in socialization; infidelity and adultery; marital
       relations; and places for quick sex. Notes change in
       men and women: men now ask help of women, whereas pre-
       viously they only turned to a man. Draws on letters

written by both sexes. Relevant for male attitudes
toward women.

1313   JOFRE BARROSO, HAYDÉE M.
        1970 "La mujer argentina." MN 46:42-50.
           Discusses the many contradictions that accompany wo-
        men's gains since the end of the 19c. Looks at problems
        of women in different classes (from prostitute to aris-
        tocrat) and concludes that the average Argentine woman
        is satisfied with the successes she has achieved but
        does not know how to reach a balance in her life. Sug-
        gests that a fundamental task is the elimination of the
        taboo about masculine tenderness toward women.

1314   KINZER, NORA SCOTT
        1973 "Women Professionals in Buenos Aires." In Female
        and Male in Latin America: Essays, ed. by A. Pescatello,
        pp. 159-90. Pittsburgh, Pa.: Univ. of Pittsburgh Press.
           Reveals the lives of 125 professional women in Buenos
        Aires to demonstrate how they overcame confines of Latin
        American society and how several variables interplayed
        to achieve "male" success and "female" fulfillment.
        Sees social class as important in reduction of role con-
        flict. Suggests that these Latin American women may
        serve as viable role models for North American feminists.

1315   MAFUD, JULIO
        1967 "El machismo en la Argentina." MN 16:72-78.
           Analyzes machismo in Argentina: its origins in the
        conquest and gaucho life on the pampa and its manifesta-
        tion in literature and language. Discusses the psychol-
        ogy of this behavior, the overriding importance of
        friendship, the dichotomous spheres of men and women,
        and changes.

1316   STEINMANN, ANNE and FOX, DAVID J.
        1969 "Specific Areas of Agreement and Conflict in Women's
        Self-Perception and Their Perception of Men's Ideal
        Woman in Two South American Urban Communities and an
        Urban Community in the United States." WRU/JMF
        31:2:281-89. tables, bibl. f/notes.
           Using an inventory of 34 statements on feminine values,
        examines women's perception of domestic role vs. public
        role, among 460 Caucasian middle-class women in New York
        City, Buenos Aires, and Lima, ranging in age from 18 to
        50, in occupation from university student to non-working
        housewife. Identifies and describes homogeneity and con-
        flict in responses among 3 groups: agreement in self-
        concept in men's ideal of women in terms of submissive

Psychology

position of wife to husband; conflict in terms of children and self-achievement.

Puerto Rico

1317 GECAS, VICTOR; THOMAS, DARWIN L. and WEIGERT, ANDREW J.
      1973 "Social Identities in Anglo and Latin Adolescents."
      SF 51:4:477-84. tables, bibl.
      See MEXICO for annotation.

1318 LEAVITT, RUBY ROHRLICH
      1974 The Puerto Ricans: Culture Change and Language
      Deviance. Viking Fund Publications in Anthropology,
      no. 51. Tucson, Ariz.: Univ. of Ariz. Press for the
      Wenner-Gren Foundation for Anthropological Research.
      268 p. tables, bibl.
          To determine validity of theory that stuttering is a
      deviant linguistic response to socio-cultural stress, a
      speech screening test was administered to 2 sample popu-
      lations, each of 10,000 boys and girls of mostly lower
      socio-economic migrant families in San Juan and New York.
      Findings indicate higher incidence of stuttering among
      boys in both places. However, in San Juan, much higher
      incidence of stuttering among females reflects greater
      stress for females where matrifocal families and con-
      sensual unions prevail and where there is far less satis-
      factory role and status for girls. Does not bear out
      original hypothesis about greater stress in New York.

1319 MIRANDA de JESÚS, FREDESWINDA and CÓRDOVA, ANA A.
      1964 "Características psico-sociales del estudiante de
      primer año de la Universidad de Puerto Rico, Río Piedras,
      1960-61." RMP 1:4:368-80. tables, bibl.
          Reports on study of 130 first year male and female
      students at the University of Puerto Rico using tests
      such as Raven's Progressive Matrices to evaluate intel-
      ligence, personality, vocational interests, language and
      vocabular skills. Findings indicate males evince better
      emotional adjustment and control, objectiveness, and
      greater freedom from infantileness and anxiety. In the
      hierarchy of values, females place more importance on
      esthetics than do men, but demonstrate less interest in
      politics than men.

1320   NUTTALL, RONALD L.
        1972 Do the Factors Affecting Academic Achievement Differ
        By the Socio-Economic Status or Sex of the Student? A
        Puerto Rican Secondary School Sample. Final Report.
        ERIC - ED 064 465. 110 p. tables, graphs, bibl.
            A sample of 2500+ secondary school students in Baymon
        Norte, Puerto Rico was measured and statiscally analyzed
        to study the association of certain variables with
        academic achievement. Findings indicate that high
        achievers tend to have, among other things, accepting
        mothers. High achieving girls were less authoritarian,
        dogmatic, and test anxious, giving fewer false but
        socially desirable responses and being more group depen-
        dent. Low-achieving girls were more self-sufficient.

Cuba

1321   FOX, GEOFFREY E.
        1973 Honor, Shame, and Women's Liberation in Cuba: Views
        of Working-Class Emigré Men." In Female and Male in
        Latin America: Essays, ed. by A. Pescatello, pp. 273-90.
        Pittsburgh, Pa.: Univ. of Pittsburgh Press. bibl.
        notes.
            Explains machismo in terms of complex cultural tradi-
        tion of "honor and shame." Revolutionary changes in
        status of Cuban women have resulted in strong, even hos-
        tile reactions by men who are unwilling to make the
        transition and resentful at Castro regime for provoking
        it. Interviews with émigré working-class Cuban women
        revealed sex role attitudes as an important factor in
        their counterrevolutionary position; they used different
        moral standards for judging women and men.

1322   OLESEN, VIRGINIA
        1969 "Leads on Old Questions from a New Revolution:
        Notes on Cuban Women." NYAS/A 175:880-97.
            Contribution to a workshop on the impact of "free
        choice" on female life styles and self determinations
        focuses on changes in Cuba. Contrasts situation of women
        before and after 1959. Concludes that although there
        is a much wider range of choices, a number of tensions
        have also arisen because emphasis is still placed on the
        family, old values and patterns. Based on Granma,
        Cuban films, novels, government publications, statements
        in print and in person, and retrospective statements
        from émigrés.

Psychology

Dominican Republic

1323   LANZ, GREGORIO
      1972   "Machismo en la República Dominicana." BDSLM/CIDHAL
      2:2:41-48.
      Deals with male and female roles before and after
      marriage. Analyzes socialization process which breeds
      machismo, according to historical models, culture of
      poverty, traditional culture. "*Machismo* is indissolubly
      tied to the concept of man, accepted by women, in which
      the masculine sex is superior to the fragile sex and
      therefore a man is allowed to act with a liberty not
      permitted to women."

ECONOMIC LIFE

This section covers female participation in the labor force
(agricultural, industrial, commercial, professional; marketing;
domestic service). Entries consider working conditions, wages,
disparities between men and women workers, opportunities for and
impediments to employment, unemployment, labor union activity, and
women's involvement in the processes of migration and development.

Items on traditional, unremunerated activities within the domestic
sphere, or the division of labor by sex, are included in this section, but for much additional information see this aspect of women's
economic activities in ETHNOGRAPHIC MONOGRAPHS/COMMUNITY STUDIES;
and for notes on weaving, see THE ARTS. Labor legislation affecting
women constitutes a subsection in the LAW category. Although a
profession, prostitution is dealt with in the literature more often
in legal terms than as a strictly economic activity; it is treated
as a crime and regulated by legislation. Entries on prostitution
are part of the subsection Female Delinquency and Penal Institutions
of the LAW category. Articles concerned with women's role conflict
(mother vs. worker) can be found in PSYCHOLOGY and MARRIAGE AND THE
FAMILY. For the influence of labor force participation on fertility,
see HUMAN SEXUALITY, REPRODUCTION, AND HEALTH. For additional notes
and statistics on female labor force participation in studies covering a variety of topics, see the GENERAL category. For economic
aspects of marriage (e.g., dowries), see MARRIAGE AND THE FAMILY.
For a theoretical discussion of defining female labor force participation, see PERSPECTIVES ON WOMEN'S LIBERATION. [1, 2, 3]

---

[1] For a discussion of the problem of and attempts at defining female
labor force participation, and the effect of development on women's
status, see section III of my article, "Women in Latin America: The
State of Research, 1975," LARR 11:1 (1976).

[2] For additional information on women and development, see two publications prepared by the American Association for the Advancement
of Science in conjunction with the UN International Women's Year
Conference in Mexico City (June 1975): A Guide to the Study of Women

Economic Life

SPANISH AMERICA - GENERAL

1324   BOSERUP, ESTER
       1970   Woman's Role in Economic Development. London:
       George Allen and Unwin. 283 p. tables, maps, graphs,
       bibl.
          Early effort to analyze women's role in economic
       development discusses changing patterns of female labor
       force participation in LA, Asia and Africa in the vil-
       lage, town and rural/urban transition. Notes role of
       education and effect of modernization on women's status.
       Based on census and survey data and an extensive
       bibliography.

1325   CANNON, MARY M.
       1942   "Women Workers in Argentina, Chile, and Uruguay."
       PAU/B 76:3:148-54;76:5:246-51. illus. Also as: 1942
       Women Workers in Argentina, Chile, and Uruguay. Bulle-
       tin of the Women's Bureau, 195. Wash., D.C.: US Dept.
       of Labor, Women's Bureau. 15 p. tables, bibl.
          Report by Inter-American representative of the Women's
       Bureau of the US Department of Labor based on six-month
       survey in 1941, provides fairly comprehensive picture
       of female employment in Chile, Argentina and Uruguay.
       Summarizes findings on working conditions, wages, nur-
       series, trade unions, women's associations, educational
       opportunities, labor legislation. Although industrial
       work is emphasized, the professions, agriculture, per-
       sonal service, home manufacturing and business are also
       noted. Makes use of government publications and census
       data.

1326   CHACKIEL, JUAN
       1969   América Latina: participación en la actividad
       económica por sexo y grupos de edades, 1960. Serie C,
       no. 117. Santiago: Centro Latinoamericano de
       Demografía. 40 p. tables, graphs.

---

in Development, an annotated bibliography, and Women in Development:
Where are They?, a collection of the proceedings of the seminar on
women in development; Washington, D.C.; Overseas Development Council,
1976.

[3] For additional references see Suzanne Nicolas, Bibliography on
Women Workers/Bibliographie sur le travail des femmes (1861-1965).
International Labour Office, Central Library and Documentation Branch,
Bibliographical contributions, no. 26. Geneva: International Labour
Office, Central Library and Documentation Branch.

Based on national census data, deals with labor force
participation in LA by sex and age, comparing countries
and groups and countries, and considering demographic
and socio-economic factors in the level of participation.

1327   COLLVER, ANDREW and LANGLOIS, ELEANOR
        1962   "The Female Labour Force in Metropolitan Areas, An
        International Comparison." UC/EDCC 10:4:367-85.
        graph, tables.
            Considers general trends of development of female labor
        force, some if its effects, and some sources of resis-
        tance to it. Analyzes 1950's census data on women's
        employment rates and the composition of the female labor
        force in the metropolitan populations of 38 countries
        (12 of LA). Discusses women's employment at different
        levels of economic development; it is seen as a positive
        contribution to economic production but a negative one
        to human fertility. Concludes that women's participation
        in "certain kinds of paid work outside the home" in-
        creases with economic development, along with a number
        of subsequent changes in the family system.

1328   Commission on the Status of Women
        1970 Participation of Women in the Economic and Social
        Development of their Countries. E./CN.6/513/rev.1.
        N.Y.: United Nations Economic and Social Council.
            Secretary General's report contains revised analysis
        of replies received from member governments in the UN
        to the questionnaire on the "role women play in the
        economic and social development of their countries, the
        degrees of priority which should be given to the contri-
        bution of women to the various areas of national
        economic and social development, the problems encountered
        in those areas, possible ways of surmounting those prob-
        lems, and the kinds of assistance that might be
        required." Nine Latin American countries replied. Also
        includes analysis of replies from 36 non-governmental
        organizations.

1329   ELIZAGA, JUAN C.
        1974 "The Participation of Women in the Labor Force of
        Latin America: Fertility and Other Factors." ILO/R
        109:5/6:519-38. tables.
            Notes level of female labor force participation in
        LA as among the lowest world-wide and examines marital
        status, education, income and structure and stage of
        economic development, while holding fertility as a con-
        stant, as factors affecting low rate of economic activ-
        ity of women. Concentrates on urban female population

Economic Life

of childbearing age engaged in non-agricultural activities. Concludes that the rate could increase if educational standards improved, the economy modernized and
changed structurally and family size decreased. Uses
1960 and 1970 national census data plus CELADE census
sample data.

1330 _____.
1965 "Internal Migrations in Latin America." MMFQ 43:
4/Part 2:144-65. tables, bibl.
Discussion of internal migratory movements in LA
includes sex differential. Statistics indicate heavier
female than male migration, especially in Central America
and particularly in major urban nuclei.

1331 ELIZAGA, JUAN C. and MELLON, ROGER
1971 "Factores que inciden en la participación femenina."
In their Aspectos demográficos de la mano de obra en
América Latina, pp. 78-89. Santiago: Centro Latinoamericano de Demografía. tables, graph, bibl.
In addition to principal factors (age, school atten-
dance, social security) affecting both male and female
labor force participation, which are dealt with in the
same chapter, this section specifically considers influences particular to women's participation: urbanization,
educational level, marital status, fertility and cultural
factors. The book itself contains much statistical information on female economic activities throughout LA
based on national census data.

1332 GENDELL, MURRAY and ROSSEL U., GUILLERMO
1968 "The Trends and Patterns of the Economic Activity of
Women in Latin America During the 1950's." IASI/E
26:100:561-76. tables.
Revision of document (DCAA / Doc. 21) prepared for the
14th Annual Assembly of IACW (Montevideo, November 1967).
Based on unadjusted national census data, reports on the
number of economically active women in LA during the
1950's: their age, residence, marital status, educational
level, and occupational categories. Notes generally low
rates of labor force participation and describes faults
in the data.

1333 GIL, ELENA
1970 "La mujer en el mundo de trabajo." In Tres temas de
la América Latina, hoy, by J. L. Vega, E. Gil, and
W. V. Costanza, pp. 19-26. Col. Seminarios y Documentos.
San José, C.R.: Centro de Estudios Democráticos de
América Latina.

Lecture given at "Seminario Latinoamericano sobre Responsabilidad Política de la Mujer en América Latina" (21 August 1970) at CEDAL. Briefly comments on Flora Tristán, 19c. labor organizer; the economic situation of women in 3 classes in the Andean countries and women in the Atlantic countries, using the OAS Classification (1958); discrimination; and population explosion. Some statistics.

1334   GOMES del REY de KYBAL, E.
        1959 "Womanpower - Untapped Resource for Latin America's Economic Growth." NBW 38:4:8-9.
        Raises question as to whether Latin American economies will be able to absorb increased population and increased female workers simultaneously. To compete, women must become better equipped and specialized. Suggestions made on how to achieve that end. 1950's statistics cited.

1334a   International Labour Office
        1972 "Women's Bureaux in Ministries of Labour." ILO/R 105:5:481-82.
        Summary of conclusions and recommendations of a Regional Seminar on the Role of Women's Bureaus in Ministries of Labour, held in Buenos Aires in May, 1971 through cooperation of OAS and Argentine government. It was noted that various factors influence the incorporation of women into economic life of LA: insufficient employment opportunities, traditional attitudes, discrimination, inadequate vocational guidance and child care facilities, and inaccessibility of better-paying professions.

1335   _____.
        1968 Equal Pay for Work of Equal Value. Report by the International Labour Office. N.Y.: UN Economic and Social Council, Commission on the Status of Women. 45 p.
        Progress report on the application of the principle of equal remuneration for male and female workers for labor of equal value. Lists those countries which have ratified the Equal Remuneration Convention (No. 100) of 1953 and the Discrimination (Employment and Occupation) Convention (No. 111) and dates of ratification; and summarizes major national developments with respect to implementation of equal pay for equal work. Cites 14 Latin American countries.

Economic Life

1336 _____.
1956 "Women's Employment in Latin America." ILO/R 73:2:
177-93.
Using census data from the 1940's and 1950's, describes
the female labor force in LA. Discusses factors affecting occupational distribution, work conditions and terms
of employment (maternity protection, regulation of night
work, unhealthy or heavy work, wages), and concludes that
the main problems are closely interrelated and call for
special measures in vocational guidance and training,
employment and social welfare.

1336a _____.
1955 "Seminar on the Utilisation of Women's Work in Latin
America." IL/ILO 13:10:437-42.
Reports on seminar on women's work in Latin America
held under auspices of International Labour Organization
in Lima (6-17 December 1954). Describes purpose and
agenda, organization of work, report of the seminar,
general conclusions, employment services, vocational
training and guidance, labor legislation, technical
assistance.

1337 MICHAELSON, EVALYN JACOBSON and GOLDSCHMIDT, WALTER
1971 "Female Roles and Male Dominance Among Peasants."
UNM/SWJA 27:4:330-52. tables, bibl.
Analyzes 46 peasant communities to explore ideal and
real female roles, the economic setting of peasant andro-
centrism, and its effect on male/female relations. Discusses sexual dominance and the division of labor, social
relationships in a patrilineal household, bilateral
inheritance, and male dominance. Concludes that an
association exists between strong male dominance and
control of basic agricultural production; this relationship does not erode even when women have important non-
agricultural roles. Suggests close connection exists
between social structure and intrafamilial life and
machismo syndrome results from increased economic power
of women in bilateral families, which also creates
brother-sister rivalry.

1338 MURDOCK, GEORGE P. and PROVOST, CATERINA
1973 "Factors in the Division of Labor by Sex: A Cross-
Cultural Analysis." UP/E 12:2:203-25. tables, bibl.
Emphasis is on factors governing the assignment of
particular tasks to men or women rather than on the
consequences of the division of labor. An assessment
of ethnographic sources indicates absence or presence
of 50 activities in 185 societies (35 in LA). Discusses

factors such as masculine or feminine advantage, qualities of raw materials, sequential series, fixity of
residence et al.

1338a NERLOVE, SARA B.
1974 "Women's Workload and Infant Feeding Practices: A
Relationship with Demographic Implications." UP/E 13:2:
207-14. tables, bibl.
Includes several Latin American indigenous groups in
a sample of 83 societies taken from Murdock and White's
Standard Cross-Cultural Sample to test hypothesis that
"women who begin supplementary feeding of their infants
before the age of one month participate to a greater
degree in the subsistence activities of agriculture,
hunting, fishing, and animal husbandry than do women who
begin supplementary feeding of the infants after one
month." Concludes that child care responsibilities may
be adjusted to accommodate mother's subsistence
activities.

1339 Organización Regional Interamericana de Trabajadores
(ORIT-CIOSL)
1961 Seminario Interamericano para la Mujer Sindicalista,
1st, México. 41 p.
Summarizes the talks and discussions of the first
Interamerican seminar on women in unions, held in Mexico,
4 - 16 December 1961. Themes on women workers include
application of labor laws; role in labor movement; problems as head of household; technical, political and
union training; social, economic, political and cultural
problems.

1340 ORTEGA, ANTONIO
1967 Proyección de la poblacion economicamente activa de
los paises de América Central. Serie C, no. 98.
Santiago: Centro Latinoamericano de Demografía. 40 p.
tables, graphs.
Based on projections, approximates the economically
active population of the Central American countries by
age and sex for 1960-80. Much statistical information.

1341 SAFILIOS-ROTHSCHILD, CONSTANTINA
1971 "A Cross-Cultural Examination of Women's Marital,
Educational and Occupational Options." AC 14:1/2:96-113.
tables, bibl. notes.
Examining official data available on women's marital,
educational and occupational behavior throughout the
world, makes correlations between women's options to

Economic Life

not marry, to work after marriage, enroll in college,
and enter "masculine" occupations and the level of
economic development of a country. GNP used as standard
for level. Data not consistent throughout. Appendix.

1342 SANTA CRUZ OSSA, ELVIRA
      1927 "Latin American Women as Industrial Workers."
      PAU/B 61:3:259-64. Also in Revista Chilena (June 1926).
      An advocate of economic independence for women argues
      that women's trade-unions are essential to achieve that
      end and discusses the many ways they can remedy evils
      existing in employment.

1343 VAN DEN BOOMEN, JOSEPHUS
      1972 Algunos aspectos de la actividad económica de la
      mujer en la América Latina. Serie A, no. 3. Santiago:
      Centro Latinoamericano de Demografía. 42 p. tables,
      graphs.
      Hypothesizes on social and economic factors which
      influence female labor force participation in LA. On
      the basis of national census data, the limitations of
      which are noted, discusses economic and demographic
      aspects of women's participation, noting that it is
      lower and less uniform than men's from country to country
      and by age.

1344 WARD, BARBARA E.
      1972 "Women and Technology in Developing Countries."
      Technos 1:1:3-8. Reprinted from UNESCO/I 15:1(1970).
      Discusses impact of technology on women's life styles
      in terms of transportation, education, rural-urban migra-
      tion, medicine; and negative aspects.

1345 "Women and Labor in Latin America."
      1945 PAU/B 79:4:206-10. illus., ports.
      Reports on the visit by four women labor officials from
      Brazil, Chile, Mexico and Puerto Rico for a 3-month pro-
      gram of study and observation in the US. Describes
      their activities and reproduces comments on women's labor
      conditions and legislation in their respective countries.

1346 No entry

1347 No entry

1348 YOUSSEF, NADIA HAGGAG
      1974 Women and Work in Developing Societies. Population
      Monograph Series, no. 15. Berkeley: Institute of Int'l.
      Studies. 137 p. tables, bibl.

Based on latest available census data for LA and
Middle East, analyzes and interprets comparative differences in female participation in nonagricultural employment and explains them through an analysis of social
organization and culture of the 2 areas. Concludes that
"economic development does not affect behavior except
in terms of social organization" and "no one distinctive
institutional arrangement conduces to a large-scale work
involvement of women." In LA both increased educational
opportunities and economic pressures serve to hasten
greater female labor force participation.

1349   _____.
        1972 "Differential Labor Force Participation of Women in
        Latin America and Middle Eastern Countries: The Influ-
        ence of Family Characteristics." SF 51:2:135-53.
        tables, bibl.
        Attempts to explain significant differential in Latin
        American and Middle Eastern women's nonagricultural
        labor force participation rates by evaluating relative
        importance of marital and fertility characteristics.
        Suggests necessity of comparing family and kinship
        organization of both societies, particularly the role
        played by kinship unit in system of social control.

MIDDLE AMERICA

Mexico

1350   ALVARADO, RICARDO
        1970 "México: proyecciones de la población total
        (1960-2000) y de la población economicamente active
        (1960-1985)." UNAM/RMS 32:5:1173-1209. tables, graphs,
        bibl.
        Variables of sex and age used in 32 tables projecting
        population and economically-active persons from 1960
        to 1985 and 2000. Compares births and deaths registered
        between 1960 and 1965.

1351   ANTUÑANO, ESTEVAN de
        1837 Ventajas politicas, civiles, fabriles y domésticas
        que por dar ocupación también a las mujeres en las
        fábricas de maquinaria moderna que se están levantando
        en México, deben recibirse. Puebla: Oficina del
        Hospital de San Pedro. 8 p.
        Argues that modern machinery makes it possible for
        family to work together without having to rely solely on

Economic Life

father. Points out advantages and contends that a woman
alone at home or out on the street runs a greater risk
than working side by side with men. Provides examples
of families who work in 2 factories--age and income of
each member.

1351a ARIAS GALICIA, FERNANDO
1964 "Una encuesta sobre intereses laborales en algunos
grupos de trabajadores de México, D.F.: ITAT/R 22:7-69.
tables, bibl.
Reviews psychology of the Mexican woman and man according to well-known national character studies; and tests
8 hypotheses related to workers' attitudes, interests,
and motivation. Administered a questionnaire to 260
male and female workers, single and married, unionized
and non-unionized, in 4 businesses, the findings of
which indicate a different order of priorities regarding
one's work situation between men and women.

1352 ARIZPE S., LOURDES
1975 Indígenas en la ciudad de México. El caso de las
"Marías." Mex., D.F.: SEP/SETENTAS. 157 p. illus.,
map, tables, bibl.
Descriptive study analyzes interaction of individual
and structural factors characterizing migration of
Mazahua and Otomí to Mexico City, where they become
street vendors of fruit, seeds or sweets. Views break
with traditional role and appearance as consequence of
marginalization and husband's inability to support
family. Persistent cultural identity of "Marías" is
not ultimate determinant of their situation. Based on
field research in 4 indigenous communities, census data,
and 1971 survey of street vendors.

1353 BEALS, RALPH L.
1975 The Peasant Marketing System of Oaxaca, Mexico.
Berkeley: Univ. of Ca. Press. 419 p. tables, maps,
figures, graphs, bibl.
Women figure in but are not the special focus of this
detailed anthropological monograph on the extensive
traditional marketing system of Oaxaca and the impact
upon it by modern industrializing economy of Mexico.
Concludes, among other things, that system is unique in
multiplicity of economic roles open to participants.
Includes extensive appendices.

1354 BOYNTON, YSOBEL
1945 "Señoritas Come Down From Their Balconies." NBW
24:1:10, 23-24. ports.

The revolution of 1910 brought about changes in Mexican
social traditions, one of which was the adoption of
careers among daughters of the aristocracy. Article
describes the enterprising activities of 3 of these
women.

1355 DOMÍNGUEZ, ANA E. and SÁNCHEZ MORALES, AURELIA GUADALUPE
1973 "Reflexiones sobre las mujeres en México." BDSLM/
CIDHAL 3:3:45-63.
Mexican women represent a mosaic of rural and urban,
Indian and *mestizo*, social classes, cultures, and
regions, which must be taken into account to avoid generalizations. To understand their social status, it is
important to consider transition between pre-Hispanic
epoch and imprint of Conquest and changes after the 1910
Revolution. Discusses results of survey about women and
work within and outside home in rural and urban context.

1356 Encuentro de Mujeres. Grupo de Trabajo: "La mujer en el
trabajo."
1972 "La mujer y el trabajo." PC 1:12:35-39. illus.
Problems related to economic role of Mexican women
stem from 3 areas of work in which they predominate:
family-organized agricultural production; domestic
work; salaried labor. Describes exploitation in each
area. Calls for radical changes on economic level as
well as in myths and values. Suggests collectivization
of land, equal division of household tasks, creation
of public dining rooms and laundromats, and union organization of women workers.

1357 FABREGA, HORACIO JR.
1971 "Begging in a Southeast Mexican City." SAA/HO 30:
3:277-87.
Behavior of beggars was observed systematically in
San Cristóbal, Chiapas. Females constituted 40% Latinos,
10% Indians, and tended to fall into oldest age category.
They also had smallest proportion of persons with physical handicap. Discusses reasons for begging, social perceptions related to begging, behavior of beggars, social
and psychological implications of begging. Suggests
certain factors which influence small proportion of
females in sample.

1358 GONZÁLEZ SALAZAR, GLORIA
1974 "Participación laboral y educativa de la mujer en
México." BDSLM/CIDHAL 4:3:14-22.
Despite advances toward legal equality of the sexes,
sex discrimination persists in traditions and customs;

Economic Life

socio-economic conditions limit and even deny gains
achieved in women's rights in many areas. Examines
census data on labor force participation and educational
levels of Mexican women, pointing out gains as well as
problems.

1359 _____.
1972 "La mujer: condiciones estructurales y educación."
In Reforma educativa y "apertura democrática", by
Fernando Carmona et al., pp. 106-24. Col.: Los Grandes
Problemas Nacionales. Mex., D.F.: Edit. Nuestro
Tiempo. bibl. f/notes.
Discusses limited labor force participation of Mexican
women, citing structural and cultural factors and pointing out varied position of women according to socio-
economic class (e.g., "liberated" bourgeois women at the
expense of superexploited domestic servants). Considers
education as important means for overcoming inferiority
and discrimination. Mass media need to be purged of
the narrow, traditional image of women which is projected in perpetuation of female backwardness; legal
equality must be enforced; and women's role as a
rational, thinking being rather than as a passive
appendix of man must be recognized. Women must be incorporated into the popular struggle to attain structural
changes necessary for a just and egalitarian society.
Some census statistics cited.

1360 HERNÁNDEZ, ANA MARÍA
1940 La mujer mexicana en la industria textil. Mex.,
D.F.: Tipografía Moderna. 160 p. bibl.
History of women's involvement in Mexico's textile
industry from colonial times to present discusses first
workers' organizations, congresses, and strikes, first
revolutionary organization of women, individual female
fighters, federations, unions, laws, contracts, etc.

1361 International Labour Office
1946 "Employment of Women on Mexican Railways."
ILO/R 54:5/6:372.
Very brief notice about the recognition of women's
right to work in shops or general duties of Mexican
national railway by the 6th Congress of the Mexican
Trade Union of Railway Workers (Mexico City, August
1946). Women claimed they had undertaken "men's jobs"
during WWII and wished to be able to continue to do so.

1362   IWÁNSKA, ALICJA
       1966   "Division of Labor Among Men and Women in a Mazahua
       Village of Central Mexico." Sociologus 16:2:173-86.
       Describes division of labor by sex among Mazahua
       Indians in central Mexico in early 1960's, based on
       fieldwork and secondary sources. Hypothesis is supported
       that interchangeability of female and male roles is
       freer from tensions and conflicts in society which has
       strong conscious and well-defined goals but more diffi-
       cult in social group lacking such corporate goals. Con-
       cludes that "organic solidarity" based on sharing of
       community objectives--preservation of Mazahua culture
       and acceptance of technological progress--is reflected
       in serene, enthusiastic, and cheerful interchange of
       sex roles, especially in emergencies.

1363   JOPLING, CAROL F.
       1974   "Women's Work: A Mexican Case Study of Low Status
       as a Tactical Advantage." UP/E 13:2:187-95. table,
       bibl.
       Based on fieldwork (1969, 1970-71), compares shirt-
       making and huarachi-making industries in Zapotec market
       town of Yalálag, Oaxaca. Suggests that rapid and suc-
       cessful development of former industry is directly
       related to its employment of women, which means it lacks
       prestige and notice. Women are not as affected by polit-
       ical or social considerations and can be more flexible.
       Guesses at direction industry will take.

1364   LLACH, GUILLERMINA
       1956   "La enfermera y la trabajadora social." FL 30:60/
       61/62:223-34.
       Mexican lawyer cites important role of nurses and
       social workers in national life. Traces development of
       both professions, beginning with midwife among the
       Aztecs, and names establishments concerned with providing
       training and/or service.

1365   MERCADO, ISABEL
       1970   "Trabajadoras auxiliares del hogar en México."
       BDSLM/CIDHAL 1:1:51-57.
       Taken from report prepared for Promoción Popular in
       Mexico City, presents picture of problematic situation
       of women working as domestic servants: migration;
       origin; cultural, social, economic, moral, legal, and
       employment aspects. Concludes that these women are
       generally young, illiterate migrants from neighboring
       states or outlying regions of the capital who work long
       hours for low pay without labor legislation to protect

Economic Life

them. Based on interviews with the workers, housewives, members of religious organizations and employment agencies, et al.

1366 "Mexican Women, Their Struggle in the Worker's Movement." 1972 ALA 1:3:10-11. illus.
Interview with 25-year-old Mexican factory worker by North American woman in Cuernavaca, in which she discusses her organizing activities to raise consciousness of women, oppression of workers and future of the struggle. Advocates overthrow of government and abolishment of private property.

1367 Mexico. Comisión investigadora de la situación de la mujer y de los menores trabajadores. Depto. del Trabajo.
1936 Informe sobre las labores de la Comisión investigadora de la situación de la mujer y de los menores trabajadores. Mex., D.F. 83 p. fold. tables, fold. diagrams.
Findings of Commission's survey of 2,835 female workers in 208 small factories or workshops (talleres) reveal tremendous exploitation. Gives brief summary of each place of work. Cites Labor Department's efforts in favor of female workers. Includes questionnaire.

1368 MORENO CONTRERAS, CARMEN
1959 "Consideraciones generales sobre la mano de obra femenina en México." ITAT/R 8:106-21.
Analyzes female worker as a subject of labor legislation and as an economic factor, her situation in relation to society and family and in field of human relations. Discussion divided into: historical notes on evolution of female labor; typically female jobs; transformation of domestic activities into industrial ones; female workers within corporate structure; female work in Aztec society, the colony, Independence and Reform eras; advances resulting from 1910 Revolution.

1369 PLATTNER, STUART
1972 "Occupation and Marriage in a Mexican Trading Community." UNM/SWJA 28:2:193-206. tables, graphs, bibl.
Based on fieldwork in small town in Chiapas (1967-68, 1970), analyzes limited traditional occupational choices available to men and women. Ranks in descending order of remuneration and prestige and briefly describes 5 male and 4 female occupations. Stresses economic motives over status as overriding consideration in determining patterns of occupation and marriage choices, but notes

that desire for both increased income and prestige does
exist. Women are pork traders, shopkeepers, produce
traders, home specialists and servants.

1370 POZAS, ISABEL H. de
      1959 "La posición de la mujer dentro de la estructura
      social Tzotzil." UNAM/CPS 5:18:565-75.
        Challenges what she considers to be unprofessional
      observations about inferior position of indigenous women.
      Believes that although equality is not total, it is
      invalid to say Tzotzil women are inferior. Prefers to
      analyze position of the sexes in terms of group's eco-
      nomic structure, which demands a tight interdependence
      of men and women.

1371 ROJAS GONZÁLEZ, FRANCISCO
      1950 "La familia rural mejicana y su industria doméstica."
      Congreso Nacional de Sociología, 1°. Estudios Socio-
      lógicos, pp. 69-76. Mex., D.F.: UNAM, Inst. de Inves-
      tigaciones Sociales.
        General description of the peasant family in Mexico.
      Considers major cohesive factor to be work whether in
      agriculture or in the home. Lists women's activities
      and notes that the division of labor is chronological
      more than sexual and that after completing the day's
      agricultural tasks, men help women in heavier chores.
      Many young women from rural areas migrate to the cities
      for domestic service employment.

1372 ROJAS PÉREZ, ALFONSO
      1964 "El salario de la mujer y su función social como
      madre." MSTPS/R 11:11/12:19-21.
        Discusses Mexico's obligation to promote and conserve
      the physical, mental and social health of the working
      woman, especially because of her function as a mother,
      and the measures necessary to insure the protection of
      women during and after pregnancy.

1373 ROYER, FANCHÓN
      1949 "Working Women of Mexico." AAFH/TAM 6:2:167-72.
        Although more Mexican women have entered the labor mar-
      ket since the 1910 Revolution, economic independence has
      not necessarily led to social independence. Girls and
      women live with their families and are chaperoned.

1374 TAX, SUSAN
      1966 "Actividad de desplazamiento en Zinacantan." In
      Los zinacantecos: un pueblo tzotzil de los altos de

355

Economic Life

Chiapas, ed. by E. Z. Vogt, pp. 298-312. Col. de Antropología Social, 7. Mex., D.F.: Inst. Nacional
Indigenista. English original: 1964 "Displacement
Activity in Zinacantan." III/AI 24:2:111-21. bibl.
Based on fieldwork in Chiapas highlands, examines inter-
relationship between Zinacantecan social etiquette,
interpersonal tensions and cultural emphasis on industri-
ousness. Discusses positive value placed on work; male
and female activities; areas of tension in social life,
especially ambivalence surrounding sexual relations
(women are considered sexually aggressive and highly
desirable, yet somehow dangerous and powerful); and
social manners. Women's work is individual; men's is
corporate. Using energy displacement model, views
activities such as women's constant daily chores and
weaving as displacement of tension into productiveness
between periods of leisure allowed during fiestas.

1375   VALDIVIA, MARÍA ANGELA
       1973 "La larga marcha de las obreras de 'Medalla de
       Oro'." CM/SS 580(21 March):II-IV. illus.
       Exposé of devious methods to reduce work force of
       1400 women in 1971 to 830 in 1972 at Medalla de Oro fac-
       tory in Monterrey. Points out union leaders' complicity
       with factory owners; describes workers' march to Mexico
       City, the difficulties encountered and other related
       events into 1973.

1376   "Wages of Woman Workers in Mexico."
       1921 MLR 12:5:79-80.
       Cites Mexico's Labor Department's report showing
       women workers' need for minimum wage. Provides wage
       statistics in different industries along with recommended
       increases.

1377   ZETINA LOZANO, GUADALUPE
       1971 "El trabajo de la mujer y su vida familiar." In
       Mujeres que hablan: implicaciones psico-sociales en el
       uso de métodos anticonceptivos, ed. by M. del Carmen
       Elu de Leñero, pp. 164-83. Mex., D.F.: Inst. Mexicano
       de Estudios Sociales. tables.
       Using data from investigation carried out by the Clinic
       for the Study of Human Reproduction of the National
       Institute of Nutrition, analyzes relationship between
       women who work for pay and their family life, focusing
       on women's triple function as worker, wife and mother,
       to determine level of conjugal satisfaction. Also con-
       siders education and salary of sample. Concludes that

women who don't work are in a better position, although
women who do work have greater autonomy in decision-
making.

Guatemala

1378   ALONSO, JOSÉ ANTONIO
       1973 "La mujer guatemalteca en 1973: de 'inferioridad'
       a 'explotación': el trabajo de la mujer casada fuera
       del hogar en la ciudad de Guatemala." URL/ES 10:15-36.
       tables, bibl.
          Departing from premise that marriage is primarily an
       economic institution, concludes that women will not
       have equal relations with their spouse until they effec-
       tively contribute to the economic maintenance of the
       family with their own income. Rejects Freudian psycho-
       analysis and Parsonian functionalism for interpreting
       Guatemalan women's dependence but accepts conflict for
       theoretical framework and Engels' perspective that
       enslavement of women arose with private property. Inter-
       viewed urban sample (90 families) of economically privi-
       leged minority, divided into groups of married working
       and non-working women (1972).

1379   BREMME de SANTOS, IDA
       1972 "El chocolate en Mixco." III/AI 32:2:523-27.
          Reproduces series of recipes to prepare chocolate as
       used by some women of Mixco and mentions other products
       they make to augment their income. The old women con-
       tinue to follow traditional formula with few modifica-
       tions but the young women have eliminated certain
       ingredients and steps, supposedly resulting in lower
       quality of chocolate.

1380   REINA, RUBEN C.
       1972 "Markets and Marketing." In his Chinautla, a
       Guatemalan Indian Community. A Study in the Relationship
       of Community Culture and National Change, pp. 68-74.
       Middle American Research Series, Publication 24. New
       Orleans, La.: Tulane Univ., Middle American Research
       Inst. map, bibl. f/notes.
          Based on fieldwork (1955-56) among the Pokomam Indians
       and Ladinos of Chinautla, notes women's activities as
       village potters, and vendors in the Guatemala City mar-
       kets and the role of the regatonas or locatarias (city
       saleswomen or middlewomen), who comprise a powerful
       guildlike organization since the 16c. Describes their

Economic Life

aggressive manner and economic and political function.
On page 98 points out that the position of Chinautla
woman remains stable because of her economic independence. Originally issued in 1960.

1381 RODRÍGUEZ, AÍDA and SCHKOLNIK, SUSANA
1974 Chile y Guatemala: Factores que afectan la
participación femenina en la actividad económica. Serie
C, no. 156. Santiago: Centro Latinoamericano de
Demografía. 31 p. tables, bibl.
See CHILE for annotation.

Honduras

1382 QUEZADA, F. VENTURA
1958 "Problemas del servicio doméstico en Honduras."
ET/T 1:9:13-14.
Brief discussion of domestic service in Honduras notes
high illiteracy rate and low salaries. Because of various problems inherent in this occupation, it is necessary
to pay greater attention to the education of servants.
Mentions night school course provided by Ministry of
Labor for 70 female students.

Panama

1383 BROWN, JUDITH K.
1970 "Sex Division of Labor Among the San Blas Cuna."
CUA/AQ 43:2:57-63. bibl.
Despite the introduction of white contact and economic
change from subsistence agriculture to a cash crop, the
importance of women's economic role among the San Blas
Cuna Indians of Panama has persisted intact. Based on
ethnographies, travel accounts and secondary sources,
examines this fact in historical perspective, beginning
with earliest description of Cuna sex division of labor
by a 17c. observer.

1384 RAM, BALI
1971 "Net Internal Migration by Marital Status For
Panama: Females 1950-1960." UWI/SES 20:3:319-33.
Uses census survival ratio method to estimate net
migration of females over 15 years of age by marital
status in Panama (1950-60). Discusses development of
this methodology. Concludes that province of Panama
is only one to experience substantial net migration.
Single females demonstrate out migration at an early

age and immigration at a later age. Married and widow
migrants outnumber single ones.

1385   VALDELAMAR, EMILIA
        1974 "Mujeres panameñas participando en el trabajo."
        BDSLM/CIDHAL 4:3:60-61. illus.
            Notes increased participation by women in Panamanian
        labor force, but limited representation in higher posts
        commanding greater wages. Attitudes toward and of women
        are still influenced by traditions, cultural values,
        superstitions and taboos, which limit women's advancement
        despite economic and educational gains.

SOUTH AMERICA

Venezuela

1386   ALMOINA de CARRERA, PILAR
        1961-62 "Apuntes sobre formas tradicionales populares de
        trabajo de la mujer venezolana." AVF 10/11:7:269-75.
        illus.
            Using data collected by Folklore Institute, considers
        tasks carried out by women in non-urban areas in terms
        of 3 categories: domestic chores, economically produc-
        tive work, and social collaboration. Describes how and
        where these activities are executed for weaving, ceram-
        ics, food preparation, laundering, adornment of crosses
        and altars, and carving of *anima*. Additional pages
        illustrate women at various tasks.

1387   WATSON-FRANKE, MARIE-BARBARA
        1974 "A Woman's Profession in Guajiro Culture: Weaving."
        ICAS/A 37:24-40. illus., bibl.
            Based on field trip in Venezuela, 1972, presents data
        on the female profession of weaving among the Guajiro
        Indians: its importance to the culture, textile tech-
        niques, socialization and instruction, the period of
        seclusion, homosexual weavers, taboos and charms.

Colombia

1387a   CARDONA GUTIÉRREZ, RAMIRO and ECHEVERRÍA ALARCÓN, GILDA
        1971 "Estudio descriptivo-exploratorio sobre migración y
        familia." CPES/RPS 8:20:115-27. tables, graphs, bibl.
        f/notes.
            Reports preliminary findings related to variable of
        migration among a sample of women aged 15 to 49 in 3

Economic Life

Colombian cities (Cali, Cucuta, Armero). Considers population size of city of origin, migration in stages, age at arrival to the city, length of stay in the city, distance covered in migration. Concludes, among other things, that female migrants to Cali had traveled the greatest distance; that the majority of female migrants arrived when younger than 30 years old, etc.

1388   Centro de Estudios Sobre Desarrollo Económico (CEDE)
       1968 Empleo y desempleo en Colombia. Bogota: Univ. de
       los Andes, Facultad de Economía. 315 p. tables, graphs,
       bibl.
       Series of technical essays exploring various aspects of
       employment and unemployment in Colombia includes women
       in the statistical data and analyses throughout. An
       essay on the relationship between employment and fertility concludes that women confined only to housework
       have, on the average, a greater number of children than
       those who are economically active and women who work
       outside the home have less children than those who work
       within the home.

1389   _____.
              1968 Encuestas urbanas de empleo-desempleo. Barranquilla,
       Bogotá, Bucaramanga, Cali, Ibagué, Manizales, Medellín
       y Popayán. Apéndice estadístico. Bogota: Univ. de los
       Andes, Facultad de Economía. n.p. tables.
       Presents over 300 tables on the male and female work
       force in 8 Colombian cities for 1967 (except Cali, 1968):
       occupation, marital status, salary; length of unemployment, age, kind of job sought, place of origin.

1390   ECHEVERRÍA ALARCÓN, GILDA and CARDONA GUTIÉRREZ, RAMIRO
       1973 La variable distancia en la migración a tres ciudades
       colombianas (un ensayo metodológico). Bogota: ASCOFAME.
       31 p. graphs, tables.
       Based on 1969 survey of 1026 middle- and lower-class
       women (15 to 49 years old) of Cali, Cucuta and Armero,
       analyzes their migration in terms of distance covered
       and suggests a technique of measurement. Concludes that
       the city of origin and attraction generated by city of
       destination are the determining factors.

1391   FIERRO, MARCO F.
       1973 Algunos problemas relacionados con la migración
       interna en Colombia. Documento CEDE no. 003. Bogota:
       Centro de Estudios Sobre Desarrollo Económico, Univ. de
       los Andes. 181 p. tables, graphs, bibl.

Based on CEDE survey data since 1944, studies characteristics of migrants to urban Colombia, causes of their
migration, and the effect of migrants on their place of
origin and destination. Provides breakdown by sex.
Analyzes relationship between migration and the labor
market.

1392 GARCÍA N., CARLOS
      1970 Características de los inmigrantes en cinco ciudades
      de Colombia: Bogotá, Bucaramanga, Manizales, Medellín
      y Popayán. Serie P, No. 6. Bogota: Centro de Estudios
      Sobre Desarrollo Económico, Univ. de los Andes, Facultad
      de Economía. 177 p. tables, bibl.
      Based on survey of 545 men and 388 women in 5
      Colombian cities, makes comparative analysis of several
      characteristics of migrants: place or origin and point
      of departure, pattern and causes of migration, age of
      arrival at city, educational level, how decision to
      migrate is made, whether migration is an individual or
      family move. Considers sex differentiation throughout.
      Among other things, concludes that matters relating to
      work constitute the principal reason for migrating,
      among men as well as women.

1393 IBERO, NORMA
      1952 La señorita empleada. Bogota?: Talleres Gráficos
      de la Penitenciaría Central. La picota. 59 p.
      Superficially traces history of education and employ-
      ment of women in Colombia. Reproduces legal dispositions
      in favor of female workers.

1394 JUNGUITO, ROBERTO, et al.
      1970 Análisis de la estructura y evolución de la fuerza
      de trabajo colombiana 1938, 1951 y 1964 y proyecciones
      de la población economicaments active 1965-1985.
      Bogota: Centro de Estudios Sobre Desarrollo Económico,
      Univ. de los Andes, Facultad de Economía. 177 p.
      tables, graphs, bibl.
      Comparative analysis of the Colombian labor force based
      on census data of 1938, 1951, and 1964; approximation
      of economically active population for 1965-85; and
      analysis of principal structural characteristics of the
      work force (distribution by economic activity sector,
      occupation, and occupational position).

1395 MALLOL de RECASENS, MARÍA ROSA
      1962 "Estudio del ritmo de vida en una pequeña comunidad
      urbana." ICA/RCA 11:189-237. illus., tables, bibl.

Economic Life

Based on a survey among families of several socio-
economic groups (workers, middlemen, businessmen, employees, unemployed persons) in Puerto Colombia, near
Barranquilla, analyzes the 24-hour schedule of men and
women. In order to clarify the sociological problems
that exist for mothers with regard to the attention and
education of their children and the differential consequences resulting from women's work at home and on the
outside, takes into account not only a woman's daily
schedule but the kind of work she does, reasons for
working and aspirations, domestic and family activities,
assistance from other family members, causes of fatigue,
opportunities to rest, etc. Includes comparative figures
for male/female salaries. Concludes that there is a
tendency away from the extended and toward the nuclear
family. Family instability is tied to changes in women's
status, which has improved upon availability of remuner-
ated work.

1396   RINCÓN, OVIEDO
       1954 "El trabajo femenino en Colombia." CGR/ED 3:8:299-
       307. illus.
       Decries lack of statistics on women and employment in
       Colombia's Ministry of Labor, citing the few and only
       available data, obtained from the departments of
       Cundinamarca and Antioquia. Lists several arguments
       about female employment in Colombia and explains them
       within the national context. Notes complete absence of
       statistics on home industry, in which large number of
       women are engaged. Discusses problems of and solutions
       for working women, beginning with a call for analysis
       and statistics of female employment, comparison of male/
       female wages, equal pay for equal work, etc.

1397   SALAZAR VALENCIA, DIEGO
       1971 "Estudio de los ingresos familiares: análisis de
       resultados." DANE/BME 283:81-92. tables.
       Taken from a national household survey, presents data
       on incomes broken down by sex and rural/urban residence.
       Women who live in rural zones are the least remunerated
       and most unemployed.

1398   SÁNCHEZ, ANTONIO MARÍA
       1957 "Mujeres que trabajan." CGR/EC 12:35:443-54.
       illus., tables, graphs.
       In response to crying need (See O. Rincón #1396) for
       statistical data on female employment in Colombia, a
       survey was undertaken by this journal's research depart-
       ment. Limited to workers in private enterprise (office

and administration), presents results of 636 interviews
using questionnaire on period of employment, educational
level by salary, recreational interests by educational
level, motivations for employment, marital status, age,
etc. Concludes that purely economic reasons motivated
these women to work and their educational level limited
them from assuming positions of greater responsibility.

Ecuador

1399   Centro de Análisis Demográfico.   Junta Nacional de Planifica-
       ción y Coordinación Económica.
           1974 Estimación del subempleo en el área urbana del
           Ecuador, 1968. Quito. 49 p. tables, graphs.
               Using 1968 household and 1962 census data measures
           and analyzes underemployment in urban Ecuador. Considers
           factors of age, educational level, migration, occupation,
           branches of economic activity, occupational category
           providing breakdown by sex. Findings indicate that
           unemployment is approximately the same for both sexes
           and that women demonstrate higher rates of underemploy-
           ment, chiefly because they earn lower wages than men.

1400   KLUMPP, KATHLEEN
           1970 "Black Traders of North Highland Ecuador." In Afro-
           American Anthropology: Contemporary Perspectives, ed.
           by N.E. Whitten, Jr. and J. F. Szwed, pp. 245-62. N.Y.:
           The Free Press.
               Deals with the ecological and ethnic contexts of trad-
           ing in the Chota Valley of north highland Ecuador and
           on a national scale; and considers the marketing system
           at local level of intracommunity exchange. Focuses on
           the nature of interpersonal relationships between buyers
           and sellers in a large urban marketplace in Quito.
           Traders are black women from Chota.

1401   NETT, EMILY M.
           1966 "The Servant Class in a Developing Country:
           Ecuador." UM/JIAS 8:3:437-52.
               Brings out importance of additional category--the
           servant class--which has generally been ignored in anal-
           yses of political and economic factors in social change
           in developing countries; and assesses future of this
           group in Ecuador. Concludes that urbanization, national-
           ization, communications, mechanization and devaluation
           of personal service add up to change, while psychological
           impediment in master-servant relations makes elimination

Economic Life

of servant class difficult. On the whole does not differentiate according to sex, but briefly describes female servant's tasks.

Peru

1402 BONO, AGOSTINO
1974 "Juana Washes Clothes . . . and Hopes." N/UNICEF
82:4:29-31. illus.
Describes a mother's hard life in a Lima slum and the worsening conditions caused by too rapid migration to urban areas. Notes limited employment options for women.

1403 CANNON, MARY M.
1947 Women Workers in Peru. Bulletin no. 213. Wash., D.C.: US Dept. of Labor, Women's Bureau. 41 p. illus., tables.
Based on 1943 survey and 1940 census data, Chief of Internal Division of US Women's Bureau, reports on women workers in Peru. Covers women in manufacturing plants, home industry, commerce, professions; workers' organizations; wages; labor and social legislation; vocational and trade schools; and women's organizations.

1404 CÁRDENAS VARGAS de MATTO, MORAYMA
1945 "Encuesta realizada en 100 familias de empleadas en servicio doméstico particular." SS 3:3:133-35.
Survey taken among 100 domestic servants in Lima to determine their socio-economic situation, which was found deficient in health, remuneration, culture, and rights. Covers marital status, educational level, place of origin, salary, etc.

1405 CARPIO, LOURDES
1974 "Las mujeres campesinas en el Perú." BDSLM/CIDHAL
4:2:31-42. illus. Also in 1973 "La mujer campesina: una alarmante postergación." Fichas de ISAL 4:46:19-26.
1970 PED 1:3:9-17. illus.
Women constitute a majority in the rural, basically indigenous, population of Peru and engage in agriculture as a primary or secondary occupation, and in other activities to supplement family income, even though their participation rates in census data are low. Despite their important role, women are marginalized in relation to community government, public administration and social life and their integration into the rural and national economy is characterized by exploitation and obstacles

to equal participation. Suggests structural conversion
of society to a non-capitalist system, making specific
recommendations regarding women.

1406   CASTRO, MERCEDES
        1972 "La nueva situación de las empleadas de casas parti-
        culares." Rikchay 2:3:36-38.
             From the point of view that the ontological vocation
        of a student must be kept in mind in the kind of educa-
        tion that person receives, looks at the socio-economic
        conditions of 30 young women students/domestic servants.
        Notes general characteristics and transcribes brief
        biography of one woman.

1407   Centro de Estudios de Participación Popular (CENTRO)
        1974 ¿Cómo vive la mujer trabajadora en el Perú? and
        Situación y aspiraciones de la mujer trabajadora en el
        Perú. Lima: Sistema Nacional de Apoyo a la Movilización
        Social (SINAMOS). 166 p. and 23 p.
             Collection of interviews with 15 working-class women
        (street vendors, agriculturalists, prostitutes, house-
        wives, factory workers, etc.) in urban and rural Peru
        regarding their work, personal lives, and political
        consciousness. With a synthesis of Peruvian women's
        situation: socio-cultural, legal, political, and eco-
        nomic aspects of rural environment, labor, domestic ser-
        vice, prostitution, and housewifery; offering suggestions
        to alleviate women's problem.

1408   Centro de Investigaciones Sociales por Muestreo (CISM)
        1968 Aspectos sociales y económicos de la Ciudad de
        Moyobamba. Encuesta de hogares. Lima: Servicio del
        Empleo y Recursos Humanos. 41 p. tables.
             Based on a survey of 298 households in Moyobamba,
        Department of San Martín, presents socio-economic data
        on 833 women and 744 men: marital status, education,
        migration, age, living aspects, occupation, income,
        work hours, agricultural activity, opinions on community
        services.

1409   CHAPLIN, DAVID
        1967 The Peruvian Industrial Labor Force. Princeton,
        N.J.: Princeton Univ. Press. 324 p. tables, bibl.
             Based on national census data, other government sta-
        tistics and reports, data gathered from 13 textile mills
        in Lima, Arequipa and near Cuzco, and biographies of
        3918 workers (1958-59), demonstrates that the Peruvian
        textile industry did not develop in the classic western
        pattern, concentrating on variables of age, sex,

Economic Life

birthplace and previous occupation. Considers female
workers throughout, noting a reverse trend in their
labor force participation despite an increase in urbanization since 1940. Appendices contain vignettes of the
plants and parent firms and discussion of methodological
problems.

1410　GARCÍA, JOSÉ URIEL
　　　 1959　"Sumas para la historia del Cusco. III." CAM 106:
　　　 5:152-86. illus., bibl.
　　　　 For the Inca monument in Cuzco called Aclla-Huasi or
　　　 "House of the Chosen Women," Indian girls cloistered
　　　 since adolescence were selected for their beauty in ser-
　　　 vice of the dominant class, classified according to 4
　　　 categories of skin and hair color, and exploited as
　　　 workers in a highly specialized division of tasks in
　　　 weaving, cooking, dancing, etc., while required to lead
　　　 a celibate life. Describes who these women were, how
　　　 and why they were selected, what they had to do, what
　　　 their work signified, and how they contributed to eco-
　　　 nomic production. Concludes with a discussion of changes
　　　 in this female labor once the Spaniards conquered the
　　　 Incas.

1411　GURRIERI, ADOLFO
　　　 1971　"La mujer joven y el trabajo." In Estudios sobre la
　　　 juventud marginal latinoamericana, by A. Gurrieri et al.,
　　　 pp. 66-194. Mex., D.F.: Siglo XXI Editores. tables,
　　　 bibl. f/notes.
　　　　 Valuable examination of occupational problems particu-
　　　 lar to young women of Lima's low income sector, preceded
　　　 by analysis of evolution of female labor force participa-
　　　 tion within the context of Peru's social structure.
　　　 Using census for 1940 and 1961, demonstrates paradoxical
　　　 phenomenon of reduced female labor activities despite
　　　 national economic expansion. Based on interviews with
　　　 311 economically active women, aged 19-30, living in 2
　　　 low-income barrios (1968), provides information on kinds
　　　 of jobs they have and how they were obtained; problems
　　　 encountered at work and causes of job stability or rota-
　　　 tion; future occupational perspectives, etc. Appendix,
　　　 prepared by J. González and E. de la Vega, further anal-
　　　 yzes interview data on 6 specific points. Concludes that
　　　 this group's occupational situation is confining, but
　　　 within it are certain possibilities for mobility, with
　　　 education serving as an initial door-opener.

1412   MYERS, SARAH K.
        1971-72   "Lazos culturales de los habitantes de barriadas
        con su tierra andina."   IBEAS/EA 2:3:115-36.   tables,
        bibl.   f/notes.
            Identifies characteristics of *mestizo*, Quechua and
        cholo migrants to Lima who continue to maintain cultural
        ties with their place of origin.   Describes trips made
        by 6 migrants (2 women) and makes bivariate and multi-
        variate analysis of migrants who return and those who
        don't.   Those who return are important agents of western
        cultural diffusion between city and countryside.   Based
        on fieldwork (1969-70) for socio-linguistic study on
        language shift from Quechua to Spanish among migrants.

1413   "Peruvian Women Take to the Air."
        1946   GRLO 21:5:28-29.   illus.
            Brief report on the entry of 15 Peruvian women (aged
        21-26) into Panagra (Pan-American Grace Airways) as the
        stewardesses on an international airline on South
        America's west coast.   Describes the women chosen for
        the job and the training they received.

1414   RUTTÉ GARCÍA, ALBERTO
        1973   Simplemente explotadas.   El mundo de las empleadas
        domésticas de Lima.   Lima: DESCO, Centro de Estudios
        y Promoción del Desarrollo.   164 p.   facsim., tables,
        bibl.
            Exploratory study of relationship between socio-
        cultural environment and behavioral characteristics of
        domestic servants in Lima, based on biographies of 5
        women (à la Oscar Lewis), information from employers and
        students, and secondary sources.   Provides descriptive
        part on migration, work conditions, and development of
        critical consciousness of these women.   Part 2 hypothe-
        sizes on psycho-social implications of domestic servitude
        as a system of domination (insecurity, authoritarianism,
        superiority/inferiority complex, identification with
        oppressor).   Appendix includes study by Marcial Rubio
        on Peruvian legislation affecting domestic workers.

1415   SALAZAR, JULIA
        1967?   Peru: Proyección de la población economicamente
        activa, 1960-1980.   Serie C, no. 88.   Santiago: Centro
        Latinoamericano de Demografía.   28 p.   tables, graphs.
            Based on projections, estimates the size of the
        Peruvian labor force by sex and age for 1960-80.   Pre-
        dicts an increase in economic activity of women.   Much
        statistical information.

Economic Life

1416   SARA-LAFOSSE, VIOLETA
        1972 "La condición femenina en el Perú (1)." Rikchay 2:
        3:32-35; (2) 1:4:37-39.
        Using 1961 census data, proves inequality between men
        and women in Peru in a discussion of female occupations,
        classified into 5 categories and considered in light of
        status accorded by society and in relation to male jobs.
        Concludes that female participation is very minor in
        occupations of greater prestige and responsibility but
        major in auxiliary or secondary jobs, such as domestic
        service. Offers data on male/female differences in
        language ability, education, and literacy, and in sala-
        ries. Concludes that lower level of education impedes
        women from moving into better employment; and a mentality
        which postulates masculine superiority as a justification
        of women's inferior condition of frustration and exploi-
        tation and of her "innate" destiny to perform exclusively
        domestic sphere activities is also an important
        hindrance.

1417   SISKIND, JANET
        1973 "Tropical Forest Hunters and the Economy of Sex."
        In Peoples and Cultures of Native South America. An
        Anthropological Reader, ed. by D. R. Gross, pp. 226-40.
        Garden City, N.Y.: Doubleday/The Natural History Press.
        bibl.
        Based on field research (1966-67) among the Sharanahua
        Indians in Peru's Amazon basin, hypothesizes that the
        scarcity of women is a culturally contrived means to
        induce competition between men and thus provide incentive
        for hunting. Demonstrates that in a hunting and agricul-
        tural population, when protein resources are the limiting
        factor and the responsibility for providing them falls
        on the men, while the women are the primary producers of
        agricultural and gathered crops, an artificially induced
        mechanism (few women) causes social tensions and motiva-
        tions for raiding.

1418   SMITH, MARGO
        1973 "Domestic Service as a Channel of Upward Mobility
        for the Lower Class Woman: The Lima Case." In Female
        and Male in Latin America: Essays, ed. by A. Pescatello,
        pp. 191-207. Pittsburgh, Pa.: Univ. of Pittsburgh
        Press. tables, bibl.
        Based on field research in Lima (1967-70), provides a
        good description of domestic servants--their background,
        working conditions, etc. Considers domestic service an
        effective mechanism for perpetuating and reinforcing

the social structure, accommodating some rural migrants, acculturating provincial women to an urban environment, and providing an opportunity for upward socio-economic mobility within the lower class. Emphasizes latter aspect.

1419 URBANO, ENRIQUE O.
1972 "Intercambio de mujeres y estructuras familiares. A propósito del caso de Pillpinto." IPA/AP 4:121-33.
Using Pillpinto (in the Department of Cuzco) as a case example, develops thesis that women are a good or property item among indigenous commercial landless class. Women represent an economic value in their role as reproducer of children, who then fulfill the double function of accruing economic goods and achieving higher social status for the family. A repressive ideological system positions women into ideal of woman-mother, an object of men's desire, without sexual desires of their own.

Bolivia

1420 FERNÁNDEZ, GUMERSINDA and SEVILLANO, NORMA
1970 "Bolivia: análisis de la situación actual y general de la mujer." BDSLM/CIDHAL 1:2:60-63.
Describes dismal situation of Bolivian women as mothers and workers—as slaves to husbands, children, and employers. Considers married, single and divorced women; women in commerce, domestic service, bars and restaurants, factories and mines; lack of union participation.

1421 FORTÚN, JULIA ELENA
1972 "La mujer aymará en Bolivia." III/AI 32:3:935-47.
National Director of Anthropology in Bolivia provides breakdown of tasks performed by Aymará men and women. Women are active in all areas except purchasing; men do not sell goods, except cattle, clean house or take care of children. Cites need for programs to improve living conditions. Some Aymará have contested validity or accuracy of Fortún's information.

1422 _____.
1964 "La mujer aymará. Algunos problemas relacionados con su incorporación." Abril 2:50-59.
Includes 3 1/2 page chart of division of labor between women and men: sowing, cultivating, animal husbandry,

Economic Life

commerce, house construction, acquisitions, other
activities. Concludes from the above that women directly
participate in agriculture and that their position is
much more closed to cultural change. Points out problems of agricultural programs of *mejoramiento* and makes
recommendations, particularly with respect to education.

Paraguay

1423　CANNON, MARY M.
　　　1946 Women Workers in Paraguay. Bulletin of the Women's
　　　Bureau, 210. Wash., D.C.: US Dept. of Labor, Women's
　　　Bureau. 16 p. illus., table.
　　　　Report on survey conducted by Chief of Women's Bureau's
　　　International Division. War transformed Paraguay into
　　　a "land of women," where women have had to work for the
　　　survival of the nation. Discusses Guaraní and Spanish
　　　heritage; industrial resources; women in industry (occu-
　　　pations, wages, working conditions, trade unions, etc.),
　　　home manufacture (*ñandutí* lace), agriculture, and the
　　　professions; social security legislation; and women's
　　　organizations.

Chile

1424　DUCCI de SANTA CRUZ, MARÍA ANGÉLICA and ILLANES de SOTO, MARTA
　　　1973 "El trabajo: ¿nuevo destino para la mujer chilena?"
　　　C/F 1:2:84-88.
　　　　Summarizes study, prepared by the Instituto Laboral
　　　y de Desarrollo Social of Chile's Ministry of Labor,
　　　on the labor force participation of 292 working mothers,
　　　aged 14 to 65, of different socio-economic groups in
　　　Santiago (See #1425). Analyzes factors which influence
　　　their ability to work and causes which could explain
　　　slight increase in women's incorporation into Chile's
　　　production. Concludes that while women are desirous and
　　　capable of working, conditions do not permit full
　　　participation.

1425　DUCCI de SANTA CRUZ, MARÍA ANGÉLICA; GILI de JIMÉNEZ,
　　　Margarita and ILLANES de SOTO, MARTA
　　　1972 El trabajo. ¿Un nuevo destino para la mujer
　　　chilena? Santiago: Inst. Laboral y de Desarrollo
　　　Social, Ministerio de Trabajo y Previsión Social. 204 p.
　　　tables, bibl.
　　　　Reports and analyzes findings of a survey among 292
　　　mothers (14 to 65 years old) with dependent children in

370

Greater Santiago to determine positive and negative factors affecting their ability to enter the labor force and
to explain small increment in female employment in Chile.
Measures characteristics, opinions and attitudes related
to women's confrontation with employment as both an
individual and member of a family (e.g., age, education,
training, family size, economic situation, mate's attitude). Concludes women's access to employment is impeded
by their responsibilities as mother, wife and house-
keeper. Economic reasons rather than self-fulfilment
motivate women to work. Inadequate education and training restrict women to limited work alternatives. Social
and family prejudices resulting from cultural factors,
internalized through socialization, represent a negative
factor. Recommends that an entity be specifically concerned with women's situation and investigate it to
determine what is women's role in society so as to avoid
individual frustration and social maladjustment. Additional 54 p. include questionnaire, international classification of occupations and other material.

1426 ELIZAGA, JUAN C.
      1966 "A Study of Migration to Greater Santiago (Chile)."
      PAA/D 3:2:352-77. tables.
         Presents the most significant results of a 1962
      CELADE survey on migration into the Santiago area: there
      are 3 female migrants for every 2 male migrants; 51% of
      the women arrive when between 15 and 29 years of age;
      migrant women are less educated but more active econom-
      ically than native men; 80% of female migrants but 56%
      of native men are laborers; migrant women demonstrate
      lower fertility rates than native women. Discusses last
      place of residence, previous mobility, initial age of
      migration history, factors of migration, differential
      aspects of city life of migrants.

1426a GAMBOA de ALVARADO, GRACIELA; CUELLO de MATELUNA, HAYDÉE and
      PETIT ALCAÍNO, ALICIA
      1956 "El trabajo de la mujer en la industria y sus
      consecuencias." JBS/SS 30:2:3-28.
         Presents results of an investigation among 10 industries
      in Chile in which women work and of a comparative study
      of 100 families, equally divided by working and non-
      working wives. Given that women have had to abandon
      their domestic chores in order to engage in industrial
      activities, the study focuses on why this has happened,
      what repercussions industrial work by women has had, and
      what role Social Service ought to play with respect to

Economic Life

resulting problems. Synthesizes history of female labor
in Chile and principal legal dispositions which favor
the industrial workers. Concludes that women's employment outside the home is disadvantageous for women's
physical and mental health and for the family's well
being.

1427　INFANTE GARMENDIA, INÉS
　　　　1940　"Estudio comparativo del trabajo de la mujer en la
　　　　fábrica en el año 1939." JBS/SS 14:1:1-58. tables,
　　　　bibl.
　　　　　　Comparative study of 50 factory workers and 50 women
　　　　who work at home in Santiago. Questionnaire elicited
　　　　information on marital status, age, educational level,
　　　　salary, health, children, kinds of tasks, religion,
　　　　opinion about marriage, entertainment, etc. Concludes
　　　　that difficult economic situation constitutes major
　　　　reason for women to work. Suggests measures to better
　　　　their conditions. Also cites relevant legislation.

1428　LAMPEREIN, LINA VERA
　　　　1936　Trabajo femenino. Santiago: Imprenta "El Esfuerzo."
　　　　64 p. bibl.
　　　　　　University of Chile thesis discusses various aspects
　　　　of female labor in 20c. Chile--salary, hours, night
　　　　work, maternity protection, etc.--as reflected in legis-
　　　　lation and criticisms against female employment. Con-
　　　　cludes that, in spite of evolution of women as useful
　　　　members of society, women's place is still in the home.

1429　MacAULIFFE, ANA
　　　　1950　"Desempeño profesional de la visitadora social."
　　　　JBS/SS 24:1:3-17.
　　　　　　Sent to the second Pan American Congress of Social
　　　　Work (Rio de Janeiro, 1949) and based on a larger study
　　　　of women social workers in Peru, outlines the fundamen-
　　　　tals of the profession, functions and methods of social
　　　　work and workers. This journal contains other articles
　　　　related to training of social workers, congresses,
　　　　organizations, graduate theses related to women, work,
　　　　family life, crime, etc.

1430　RIBEIRO, LUCÍA and BARBIERI, M. TERESITA de
　　　　1973　"La mujer obrera chilena. Una aproximación a su
　　　　estudio." CRN/CEREN 16:167-201.
　　　　　　Attempts to describe the basic problems found among a
　　　　small group of Chilean women who confront on a daily
　　　　basis those tensions which originate through production

and reproduction. Analyzes the occupational structure of
Chile and the responses given by employers and female
workers resulting from interviews about the principal
problems created by female employment.

1430a RODRÍGUEZ, AÍDA and SCHKOLNIK, SUSANA
       1974 Chile y Guatemala: Factores que afectan la partici-
       pación femenina en la actividad económica. Serie C,
       no. 156. Santiago: Centro Latinoamericano de Demo-
       grafía. 31 p. tables, bibl.
           Using census data for Chile (1960) and Guatemala
       (1964), applies regression and correlation analysis to
       establish statistically significant associations between
       age, marital status, number of children, level of educa-
       tion, and place of residence and female participation in
       economic activities. Concludes that as a whole, age,
       number of children and educational level account for
       almost one half of total variation of economic partici-
       pation rates for married women and women in consensual
       union; this does not hold for unmarried females.

1431   SIMONE, JOSÉ A. de
       1970 "En favor del acceso de la mujer a carreras técnicas."
       Revista de Educación 24/25:72-75.
           Outlines project in favor of making technical careers
       (chemistry, textiles, electronics, telecommunications,
       etc.) accessible to women in Chile in collaboration with
       UNESCO. Reports antecedents, objectives, participation,
       orientation, and development of project since 1969.

Argentina

1432   Argentine Republic. Ministerio de Comunicaciones
       1950 Revista de Correos y Telecomunicaciones 14:159/160.
       96 p. illus.
           Entire issue dedicated to women who work, especially
       women in the post office and communications operations.
       Some notes on conquest of rights, such as suffrage, but
       basically a tribute to women workers and Eva Perón.

1433   Argentine Republic. Secretaría de Estado de Trabajo.
       Dirección Nacional de Recursos Humanos. Oficina Nacional de
       la Mujer
       1969? Realidad económica social de la mujer trabajadora.
       B.A. 66 p. fold. map, fold. forms.
           Useful compendium of official statistics on women's
       labor force participation in Argentina; efforts to pro-
       mote greater capacitation among women; and results of a

Economic Life

1967 survey conducted among 60 business establishments, 14 unions, and 1197 female workers on labor and union activity and training, as well as personal aspects of the women. Concludes that single women constitute largest female segment of Argentina's labor force, many of them coming from the interior.

1434 Argentine Republic. Secretaría de Estado de Trabajo. Dirección Nacional de Recursos Humanos. Dept. Socio-Económico. División Estadísticas Sociales.
1969 Incidencia salarial y ocupacional de la mano de obra femenina en las convenciones colectivas de trabajo. Buenos Aires. 9 p. tables, graphs.
     In order to evaluate Argentina's economically active female population, annual series (1954-1969) of wages were compiled, keeping in mind the level of women's hourly wages, comparison with men's remunerations and the total number of agreements and beneficiaries by production sector (commerce, services and manufacturing). On all levels in all years women's wages were not equal to men's.

1435 BOUZÓN de TERZANO, EMILIA BEATRIZ
1973 "El trabajo de la mujer casada." In La familia, by José Ignacio Cafferata et al., pp. 287-307. Cordoba, Arg.: Taller Ed. de la Univ. Nacional de Córdoba. bibl.
     Discusses undervaluation, mechanization and rationalization of domestic tasks; women in Argentina's labor force (using 1960 census data) and the particular position of married women; arguments on psychological, historical and biological factors which influence their fluctuating participation and why they are not valid today; OIT norms and Argentine legislation regarding maternity protection for working women; part-time employment; problems of reentry into labor market. UNESCO data indicate fewer educational opportunities for women; UN and OIT data conclude that women's professional preparation is far from satisfactory even in developed nations. The Department of the Woman was established in Argentina in 1958 to investigate these problems and act on them. Insists that women's mission in life is not tied exclusively to marriage and maternity and conflict between home and work need not exist. Lists documents of international organizations.

1436 CACOPARDO, MARÍA C.
1969 Argentina: Aspectos demográficos de la población economicamente activa, en el período 1869-1895. Serie C,

no. 118. Santiago: Centro Latinoamericano de Demografía. 25 p. tables, graphs, bibl.

Using adjusted national census data, estimates levels of labor force participation by sex and residence in Argentina for 1869-95. Concludes that high levels of female participation fell markedly because of decreased economic activity for all ages, resulting from socio-economic factors, especially urbanization for women.

1437 DRIMER, ALICIA K. de and DRIMER, BERNARDO
1953 "El servicio social de asistencia doméstica. I-V." RCE 41:40/Serie 3:99-136. bibl.

Discusses social, educative, health and labor advantages of a social service which provides domestic assistance for housewives who are unable to attend to tasks and children at home because of illness or other infirmity. Considers antecedents of such a service in several non-Latin countries and makes a comparison in terms of finances, legislation, organization, work conditions, and professional training. Describes its possible adaptation in Argentina along these lines, suggesting that it be free for poor families and on a sliding scale for others.

1438 GIL, ELENA
1970 La mujer en el mundo del trabajo. Buenos Aires: Eds. Libera. 129 p. tables, graphs, bibl. f/notes.

Divides discussion of female labor into general historical background; distribution of female labor force by country, age, and branch of economic activity; the role of education, especially vocational, and unions; organizations and conferences dealing with question of female workers. Although applied to worldwide situation, study emphasizes the Argentine case, including statistics and notes on relevant legislation; with some remarks on LA as well.

1439 GONELLA, NIEVES
1969 "Participación de la mujer en la empresa." UNC/R 10:1/2:267-82.

Makes observations on women's participation in the Argentine economy, citing census data, problems, advances, prejudices, etc. Believes total female liberation is conditional upon women's economic independence.

1440 GREGORIO LAVIÉ, LUCILA de
1945 "Proyeccion del trabajo femenino en el futuro del país." ECAR/R 44:326:403-04.

Economic Life

It is absurd to impede women from working; that does
not contribute to depopulation. National Constitution
of Argentina makes no distinction according to sex.
Suggests how to orient women in work to carry out
nation's needs after WWII.

1441   GUIDO, FRANCISCO ALBERTO
        1972 La mujer en la vida sindical argentina. B.A.:
        Ministerio de Cultura y Educación, Centro Nacional de
        Documentación e Información. 15 l.
            Although women have integrated well into labor force
        in greater numbers, this is not reflected as well in
        union participation. Explores reasons for "absence" and
        briefly traces evolution of unions since 1945. Suggests
        6 aspects of women's role in unions for investigation
        and action.

1442   HERMITTE, ESTHER
        1972 "Ponchos, Weaving, and Patron-Client Relations in
        Northwest Argentina." In Structure and Process in
        Latin America: Patronage, Clientage and Power Systems,
        ed. by A. Stricken and S. M. Greenfield, pp. 159-77.
        Albuquerque, New Mex.: Univ. of New Mex. Press. tables,
        bibl.
            Examines system of patronage and clientage among women
        weavers of Huarco, in the province of Catamarca, through
        4 variables which order relationships: 1) weaving
        ponchos is a significant economic commodity; 2) this
        skill is considered women's work; 3) acceptable male
        activities are limited by ecological factors; 4) other
        acceptable male activities exist outside the community.
        Constructs a typology of weavers based on access to
        resources. Concludes that the woman weaver as chief
        economic provider in the home and as socializing agent
        of future weavers has increased decision-making power in
        the domestic group; the nuclear family is thus not the
        only productive unit; and by controlling a significant
        skill in the local economy, these women participate in
        patron-client relations with substantial community
        figures.

1443   HOLLANDER, NANCY CARO
        1973 "Women: The Forgotten Half of Argentine History."
        In Female and Male in Latin America: Essays, ed. by
        A. Pescatello, pp. 141-58. Pittsburgh, Pa.: Univ. of
        Pittsburgh Press. bibl. notes.
            Attempts to redress injustice of largely unwritten
        history of Argentine women by demonstrating contributions
        made by them to the country's economic and political

life. Analyzes incorporation of women into labor force
and reaction to it. Evaluates mobilization of women
within Peronist movement (1945-55). Examines census
data, legislation and secondary sources.

1444 "The Inner Forum."
1941 Commonweal 35:2:54.
Feature on the Federación de Asociaciones Católicas de
Empleades, which is composed of 25 vocational organizations and whose major purpose is to achieve a better
understanding between capital and labor. Founded by
Bishop Miguel de Andrea of Temnos, it is a leading
women's organization in Argentina.

1445 LEBAN de CAVIA, LUCÍA N.
1974 "Women as Non-valued Human Resource in the Rural
Environment." An Anthology on Women in Latin America,
1st special issue of BDSLM/CIDHAL, pp. 59-64. illus.
Spanish version: 1974 "La mujer como recurso humano
no reconocido en el medio rural." BDSLM/CIDHAL 4:3:
42-48.
Considers the problems of the campesina: lack of
coverage by protective legislation, no wages for labor.
Emphasizes situation of female migrant workers. Cites
1960 census data for Argentina but generalizes dilemma
for LA and lists recommendations proposed by the IACW
at its 14th annual assembly for the integration of
female migrant workers.

1446 MARPONS, JOSEFINA
1938 La mujer en el trabajo. Col. Contemporáneos.
Santiago: Eds. Ercilla. 300 p.
Discusses various aspects of women as workers: double
shift, sexual differences rather than inequality, reasons
for working, age, civil status, salary, protective legislation, work at home, family, feminism, etc. Related to
situation in Argentina, with references to other Latin
American countries.

1447 "La migración de las jóvenes del interior a Buenos Aires,
encuesta."
1967 AEST 582:217-27.
Reports on the first results of a survey carried out
by the University of Salvador to determine motives for
rural-urban migration among young Argentine women and
their difficulty in adjusting to the urban center. Data
and impressions derived from various institutions dealing
with these women (e.g., Obra de Protección a la Joven,

Economic Life

Colegio Nuestra Señora de la Misericordia). Concludes
that motivation level depends on socio-economic and
educational level and former residence zone.

1448   MUZZILLI, CAROLINA
      1913 "El trabajo femenino." MSA/BM 2:15/16:65-90.
      Early, informative study on working women in Argentina
at the beginning of the 20c. based on observations in
factories, work experience as a sales clerk, and national
census data (1910). Provides statistics on women working
in factories, small shops and at home (salaries, daily
production, costs in different branches of shoe and
clothing manufacturing). Discusses women employed in
offices, telephone system, at cash registers, and as
vendors. Part 2 deals with existing protective labor
legislation, reform project presented to the Senate and
Chamber of Deputies, civil and penal laws approved by
Congress, resolutions and actions in favor of working
women advanced by various congresses and groups, and
suggestions for further improvement.

1449   RÍOS, RAÚL ARTURO
      1969 "Valoración del ama de casa." UNC/R 10:1/2:197-207.
      Analyzes women's role in the market economy of Argen-
tina, distinguishing it from that in former subsistence
economy on landed estates. While some women are
directly involved in the development of Argentina
through their role as workers or executives and business-
persons, housewives too play an active, if indirect, role
in the family sector by making decisions about consump-
tion and savings of income.

1450   STÁBILE, BLANCA
      1962 "La mujer en la vida económica argentina." IT/R
65:2:135-52. English version: 1962 "The Working
Woman in the Argentine Economy." ILO/R 85:2:122-28.
      Based on experience in the National Directorate of
Safety and Social Welfare of the Ministry of Labor, provides an overview of women workers in the Argentine
economy: distribution of occupations, differences from
male labor force, problems of equal remuneration and
child care facilities, labor legislation. Suggests that
obstacles can be overcome by vocational and technical
training, protective laws, and participation in professional organizations, trade unions, non-governmental
women's groups, and politics. Cites some statistics and
legislation.

1451   VENTURA, OVIDIO
        1944 "Consecuencias económicas y sociales del trabajo
        femenino." ECAR/R 43:313:203-08. bibl.
            Claims that when women work, the moral and numerical
        force of the family is adversely affected and thus makes
        society vulnerable. Considers this to be one of capital-
        ism's most difficult problems. WWII greatly influenced
        increased female labor force participation (1935-41,
        56% of industrial sector was female). Discusses economic
        and moral causes and consequences of this "acute" prob-
        lem and suggests possible solutions.

CARIBBEAN

Puerto Rico

1452   HERNÁNDEZ-ALVAREZ, JOSÉ
        1968 "Migration, Return and Development." UC/EDCC 16:4:
        574-87. tables.
            Detailed tabulation and analysis of 1960 Puerto Rican
        census material. Tables include information on female
        migrants: age, employment status, occupation, educa-
        tional level. Rate of labor force participation among
        female return migrants was lower than corresponding
        measure for Puerto Ricans living in US.

1453   McBRIDE, NINA LANE
        1917 "Women Workers of Puerto Rico." ISR 17:12:717-19.
        illus.
            Decries the low wages and bad working conditions of
        Puerto Rican women employed in cigar and canning facto-
        ries, coffee and cane fields, telephone operations and
        domestic service. Applauds efforts to organize into
        unions and/or strike for better pay.

1454   WELLER, ROBERT H.
        1968 "An Historical Analysis of Female Labour Force Par-
        ticipation in Puerto Rico." UWI/SES 17:1:60-69. tables,
        graphs.
            Examines trend and pattern of female labor force par-
        ticipation in Puerto Rico. Traces post-1940 decline to
        decrease in such traditional forms of employment as
        domestic service, needlework, etc.; but observes an
        increase in non-traditional labor. Maintains that no
        necessary relation exists between industrialization and
        such increases nor is marital status related to employ-
        ment status. Rather, the relation is with gainful
        employment outside the home.

Economic Life

Cuba

1455 BENGLESDORF, CAROLLEE
1974 "The Frente Femenino." CR 4:2:27-28. illus.
Describes the Feminine Front as a secretariat within
the Confederation of Cuban Workers (CTC) whose function
is to deal with problems of women in work centers—objective conditions preventing full integration into labor
force and attitudes limiting acceptance of women as
workers. How the organization functions illustrates
revolutionary Cuba's way of conceptualizing and solving
social problems.

1456 BENGLESDORF, CAROLLEE and HAGEMAN, ALICE
1974 "Emerging from Underdevelopment: Women and Work."
CR 4:2:3-12. illus., graph, bibl.
Points out that basic need of Cuban revolutionary
process to integrate women into struggle out of underdevelopment in their capacity as workers. Describes
economic and educational situation before the Revolution
and charts transition toward incorporation of women into
labor force in 2 stages: 1959-70, 1970-74. Discusses
problems of women workers and government attempts to
ameliorate them through day care centers, laundry service, housing projects, Shopping Bag Plan, and Maternity
Law of 1974. Concludes with optimistic outlook for
increased sharing of household responsibilities and
child-rearing by both sexes. Includes female labor force
participation statistics for 1953 and 1973.

1457 _____.
1974 "Mujer y trabajo en Cuba: dando el paso al frente."
BDSLM/CIDHAL 4:4:3-7.
Abbreviated version of article written in English in
Cuba Review (#1456).

1458 CORDOVA y CORDOVÉS, EFRÉN
1957 "Trabajo de la mujer." In his Derecho laboral
cubano, vol. 1, pp. 343-50. Havana: Edit. Lex.
Discusses justifications elaborated for special regulation of female labor; international agreements; Cuban
legislation: women's right to equality in employment and
to certain privileges, particular reasons for not being
fired, specific obligations imposed on businesses hiring
women, prohibition of night and dangerous work, sanctions
for not complying with these legislative provisions.

1459   "CTC Resolutions."
>1974 <u>CR</u> 4:2:17-18. illus.
>Cites resolutions regarding women and work adopted by the XIIIth Congress of the Confederation of Cuban Workers (CTC) in Havana (11-15 November 1973). They refer to women's incorporation into work and job turnover, resolutions 47 and 48 of the Ministry of Labor, the second Conference of Working Women, and the Feminine Front (an auxiliary commission of the secretary assigned by trade union local to see that things are carried out in interest of women workers).

1460   "Cuba¡ si! But Sexual Division of Labor . . .?"
>1972 <u>ALA</u> 1:3:14-16. bibl. notes.
>Cites the many areas in which sexual discrimination has been eliminated in Cuba--labor, education, military, family planning--but also points out persistent division of labor along sex lines due to cultural biases. Notes serious consequences of sexual division in labor force for the Revolution. Uses newspaper articles.

1461   FERNÁNDEZ SAVIO, HUMBERTO
>1966 "Proyecta el regimen castrocomunista crear campos de trabajo forzados para mujeres." <u>AIP/C</u> 139:7-9.
>Exile denunciation of Castro's plans to incorporate more women into Cuban labor force, calling the Unidades Militares de Ayuda a la Producción (MAP) concentration camps.

1462   GUZMÁN CASANOVA, ESTHER
>1956 "Working Women." <u>OAS/AM</u> 8:11:36.
>Quote from Guzmán, Cuban attache in Washington, on changes in the status of women since Cuba became a republic in the areas of education, employment and professions. Cites individual women's accomplishments.

1463   LEIGH, BESSIE
>1969 "Woman's Place in Cuba." <u>Comment</u> 7:47:750-51.
>Brief report on female labor force participation in Cuba in Communist weekly review.

1464   MARTÍNEZ BARRAQUÉ, CARLOS
>1966 "Fidel 'libera' a las mujeres para que vayan a trabajar al campo y ayuden a mejorar la economía." <u>AIP/C</u> 108:3-5.
>Exile denunciation of Castro's plan to incorporate more women into the labor force. Quotes Cuban government officials' statements.

Economic Life

1465 PURCELL, SUSAN KAUFMAN
      1973 "Modernizing Women for a Modern Society: the Cuban
      Case." In Female and Male in Latin America: Essays,
      ed. by A. Pescatello, pp. 257-71. Pittsburgh, Pa.:
      Univ. of Pittsburgh Press.
         Discusses women in pre- and post-revolutionary Cuba
      and changes in their status as Cuba moves from a tradi-
      tional to modern society. The modernization of Cuban
      women is considered in the context of Castro's goals for
      the country as a whole. Purcell believes Castro regime
      has not made it a goal of utmost priority when it did
      not fit into development goals, only when traditional
      behavior hindered achievement of other higher priority
      aims. Cites aspects of lingering traditional behavior.
      Based on secondary sources.

1466 ROMAN, GEORGINA
      1956 "The Women Workers of Cuba and Labour Throughout
      the World." FLW 7:70:22-24.
         Although Cuban labor legislation affords same rights
      and obligations to men and women, women are still
      exploited through ignorance or cowardice; they are afraid
      to join unions. Calls for equal opportunities, more
      education, etc.

Dominican Republic

1467 NORVELL, DOUGLASS G.
      1969 "Food Marketing in an Urban Place in the Dominican
      Republic." UPR/CS 9:3:104-10. bibl. f/notes, illus.
         Study conducted in spring 1966 describes consumer
      income and shopping patterns, fresh produce and marketing
      systems, of Santiago, second largest city of Dominican
      Republic. Although a relatively efficient marketing
      system, it has its problems. Solutions suggested.
      Brief notes on the market women.

LAW

This section is comprised of works which deal with women as a subject under law--civil, criminal, labor, agrarian, etc. It does not include items which are specifically concerned with women's political rights, especially suffrage, which are considered in the category POLITICS AND 20th CENTURY REVOLUTIONARY MOVEMENTS. It does include items on women's legal position in colonial as well as contemporary society, as a member of a family or as a national citizen, as an offender or an offended (e.g., as the object of sexual crimes).

The LAW category is divided into three subsections: General Legal Status; Female Delinquency and Penal Institutions; Employment Legislation. Although an economic activity, prostitution is generally studied as a crime subject to government regulation. Publications on prostitution range from distressed cries over its contribution to the moral decay of society to legal, economic, psychological, sexual, and health aspects of the profession and its practitioners. However, for facility in approaching this subject, all items on prostitution, whatever the aspect or perspective, are grouped in LAW and cross-referenced into other subject categories where appropriate. Together with items on abortion as a crime and other aspects of female delinquency, and penal institutions for women (including *recogimientos* or *casas de recogidas*), entries on prostitution form the subsection FEMALE DELINQUENCY AND PENAL INSTITUTIONS. Although labor laws directly affect women's economic activity, entries discussing protection legislation for women workers and government agencies charged with their enforcement have been separated from the ECONOMIC LIFE category to facilitate consideration of women as a subject under law. These items form the subsection Employment Legislation.[1] All other. items pertaining to women's legal position form the subsection General Legal Status.

----

[1] For additional entries on employment legislation see Suzanne Nicolas, Bibliography on Women Workers/Bibliographie sur le travail des femmes (1861-1965). International Labour Office, Central Library and Documentation Branch, Bibliographical contributions, no. 26. Geneva: International Labour Office, Central Library and Documentation Branch.

Law - General Legal Status

Information on marital arrangements and divorce, when not of a strictly legal nature (e.g., colonial divorce cases were an ecclesiastical rather than civil affair), can also be found in the MARRIAGE AND THE FAMILY category. Although there are innumerable publications dealing with marriage, family and divorce laws, in general, they have not been considered for this bibliography. Studies focusing on abortion as a practiced birth control method can be found in HUMAN SEXUALITY, REPRODUCTION AND HEALTH. Additional notes on women's legal position in indigenous and other ethnic groups can be found in ETHNOGRAPHIC MONOGRAPHS/COMMUNITY STUDIES and the pre-Conquest period of HISTORY BEFORE 1900; on efforts or movements to gain women's rights in PERSPECTIVES ON WOMEN"S LIBERATION and POLITICS AND 20th CENTURY REVOLUTIONARY MOVEMENTS; and in the GENERAL category.

GENERAL LEGAL STATUS

SPANISH AMERICA - GENERAL

1468   ALVAREZ VIGNOLI de DEMICHELI, SOFÍA
        1969 "Condición juridica de la mujer en Latinoamérica."
        UNC/R 10:1/2:105-24.
        See URUGUAY for annotation.

1469   BIDONE VILLANUEVA, CLARA AMALIA
        1948 Los derechos de la mujer y el niño en la constitu-
        ciones americanas. B.A.: Talleres Graficos "Garrot."
        10 p.
        Briefly reviews constitutional articles referring to
        the family, maternity, women, and children in 12
        countries.

1470   CRAWFORD, HENRY PAINE
        1936 "Civil Rights of the Latin American Woman." PAU/B
        70:7:541-48.
        Citing relevant legislation from Argentina, Brazil,
        Cuba, Mexico and Nicaragua, informs on the women's civil
        rights with respect to nationality and equality, domi-
        cile, property and personal rights, rights of action and
        testamentary disposition, and custody of minors.

1471   GESCHE MULLER, BERNARDO and MERINO REYES, ROLANDO
        1947 "Conveniencia de uniformar las legislaciones
        americanas en lo relativo a la nacionalidad de la mujer
        que se casa con extranjero." UC/RD 15:62:425-38. bibl.

Presented at the 5th Inter-American Conference of Lawyers (Lima, 1947), comparative study of Latin American
legislation regarding the nationality of married women
concludes that 2 diametrically opposed systems exist.
Explains each one and suggests that uniformity of such
legislation be organized on the basic premise that neither marriage nor divorce should alter the nationality
of married persons.

1472   LEÓN BARADIARÁN, JOSÉ
       1947 "Nacionalidad de la mujer casada." DCP/R 11:1/2/3:
       28-32.
       Paper presented at 5th Inter-American Conference of
       Lawyers (Lima, 1947) briefly compares Latin American
       legislation regarding a married woman's nationality and
       concludes that uniformity be adopted on the criterion
       that marriage and divorce should not influence the
       nationality of a married person.

1473   MARSÁ VANCELLS, PLUTARCO
       1970 La mujer en el derecho político. Pamplona, Spain:
       Eds. Univ. de Navarra. 494 p. bibl.
       Study and compendium of women's legal rights worldwide,
       divided into 4 major topics: women in doctrine, legis-
       lative evolution of women's rights, women's rights in
       international organizations and in national states
       (human, political, electoral, office-holding, social,
       family and labor protection). Good source for cross-
       cultural comparison of women's legal status. Includes
       extensive bibliography.

1474   NELSON, LINDA
       1972 "La economía del hogar en la reforma agraria."
       B/DRA 4:3:279-87.
       Suggests that integral change of rural structure cannot
       be effected without the participation of peasant women,
       who have not been taken into account by agrarian reform
       laws. Points out ways in which home economics can con-
       tribute to the objectives of agrarian reform, how peas-
       ants can benefit from the programs, and how they can be
       implemented, considering 5 essential areas: diet and
       physical; mental; family management; improvement in
       family and communal relations; participation of peasants
       in local and national decision-making.

1475   OTS CAPDEQUÍ, JOSÉ MARÍA
       1946 "La condición jurídica de la mujer." In his El
       estado español en las Indias, 2nd ed., pp. 115-40.
       Mex., D.F.: Fondo de Cultura Económica. bibl. f/notes.

Law - General Legal Status

Good summary of legislation contained within the
Recopilación de 1680 affecting women in colonial America,
especially during 16c. and 17c. Begins with juridicial
capacity of Spanish women, especially regarding their
passage to America, and covering regulations restricting
the work of Indian women, their freedom or slavery. Also
discusses laws related to sharing of honors derived
from one's husband's office, office-holding, the establishment of *recogimientos* and the right to *encomiendas*
or chieftainships. Notes more vigorous application of
penal code to women in matters of propriety.

1476   _____.
        1934   Instituciones sociales de la América española en el
        período colonial. Biblioteca Humanidades, Facultad de
        Humanidades y Ciencias de la Educación, Universidad de
        La Plata, 15. La Plata, Arg.: Imprenta López. 269 p.
        bibl. f/notes
        See chapters 5 and 6 for a well-documented study of
        legal dispositions affecting marriage and the family and
        the juridical capacity of women, covering all racial
        groups during the colonial period. Includes passage of
        Spanish women to America, widows, orphans, slavery,
        tribute system, public office, property and inheritance,
        dowries, education, chieftainships, religion, penal sys-
        tem. Concludes that laws effective in the Indies merely
        referred back to and ratified Castilian law despite
        social and geographical differences between the two
        areas.

1477   _____.
        1930   "El sexo como circunstancia modificativa de la
        capacidad jurídica en nuestra legislación de Indias."
        CEH/AHDE 7:311-80.
        Documented analysis of legislation pertaining to women
        in the Indies during colonial period. See his 1934
        work (#1476).

1478   _____.
        1917-1920   "Bosquejo histórico de los derechos de la mujer
        casada en la legislación de Indias." LJ/RG 131:185-206,
        324-39; 132:162-82; 133:5-33, 222-38; 137:139-53, 339-62.
        Based on archival research, valuable extensive study
        documents the legal and social life of women in the
        Indies during the precolonial and colonial periods, as
        well as of women in Spain as background information.
        Probably the most comprehensive scholarly work available
        on the subject.

1479   PENA BUSTOS, MARTA ELENA
        1969 "La condición de la mujer a nivel de los organismos
        internacionales." UNC/R 10:1/2:475-522. bibl.
        Details specific actions of the UN, OAS, their special
        organisms and non-governmental international organiza-
        tions to promote the social and legal equality of women.

1480   SECO CARO, CARLOS
        1958 "Derecho canónico particular referente al matrimonio
        en Indias." EEHA/AEA 15:1-112. bibl. f/notes.
        Lengthy, detailed analysis of canon law on marriage,
        the problem of its application in the Indies (colonial
        America) and matrimonial privileges and dispensations
        there in general.

1481   TILLETT, GLADYS A.
        1964 "Existing Law and Measures to Improve the Status of
        Women in the Western Hemisphere. UN Seminar on the Sta-
        tus of Women in Family Law, Bogotá, Colombia, December
        3-17, 1963." USDS/B 51:1309:128-32.
        US representative reports on discussion of existing
        law and practice, and measures to improve women's status
        in America. Cites participants, agenda items, hemisphe-
        ric problems, and follow-up suggestions. Concludes that
        UN regional seminars are useful instruments for open
        exchange of information.

1482   US Dept. of Labor. Women's Bureau
        1948 Women in Latin America: Legal Rights and Restric-
        tions. Wash., D.C. 8 p. illus., map. Reprinted with
        revisions from WLJ, winter 1948.
        Reprint of principal parts of speech given by Mary
        Cannon at 48th Annual Meeting of National Association of
        Women Lawyers (Cleveland, Ohio, 19 September 1947) incor-
        porating legal data from IACW. Briefly sketches histor-
        ical background; discusses legal status of married women
        with respect to property, business, adultery, suffrage
        and women in the professions and politics. Map of LA
        indicates where national or municipal suffrage was
        granted and where bills were pending in 1948.

1483   WELLS, WILLIAM C.
        1925 "Women's Property Rights in Latin America." PAU/B
        59:3:232-40.
        Informative discussion of the origins of as well as the
        divergencies themselves between English and Spanish laws
        related to women's property rights before and after mar-
        riage. Notes recent developments in LA and the US.

Law - General Legal Status

1484   ZIMMERMAN, MARY H.
       1954   "The Contractual Capacity of Married Women in the
       Americas."   MSBJ 33:7:27-36.   illus.
       Comparative study of contractual capacities (according
       to 8 categories) of married women, and their capacity or
       legal lack thereof, in 20 American republics, derived
       chiefly from 1954 Martindale-Hubbell's Law Directory.

MIDDLE AMERICA

Mexico

1485   Alianza de Mujeres de México
       1953   La situación jurídica de la mujer mexicana.   Estudios
       Jurídicos.   Mex., D.F.   195 p.
       Collection of articles and speeches by court ministers,
       professors, lawyers and other functionaries on 6 basic
       subjects: women and private rights, female sciences,
       work rights, agrarian rights, political constitution,
       and juridical statute.

1486   CHÁVEZ de VELÁZQUEZ, MARTHA
       1956   "La mujer y la Reforma Agraria."   FL 30:60/61/62:
       235-44.
       Describes land ownership in relation to women during
       the precolonial, colonial and independence eras and the
       double personality of agrarian law: collective and indi-
       vidual.   Analyzes the Agrarian Code to demonstrate how
       it does not deal equally with women, of whom more
       requirements are demanded, and argues for necessary
       revisions which would comply with women's constitutional
       and civil rights.

1487   COLLIER, JANE FISHBURNE
       1973   Law and Social Change in Zinacantan.   Stanford, Ca.:
       Stanford Univ. Press.   281 p.   illus., plates, tables,
       bibl.
       Although women figure throughout this study of
       Zinacantan, Chiapas, Mexico, where "law is a language
       used by individuals to interpret and manipulate their
       social environment," women predominate in the chapters
       on marital disputes, which are the most frequent con-
       flicts in this Tzotzil township, and courtship disputes.
       They include a description of an average woman's life
       cycle, an analysis of disputes concerning wife beating,
       adultery and divorce; a description of courtship prac-
       tices and analysis of courtship disputes.   Case examples
       are provided.   Other kinds of conflicts, witchcraft cases
       and aggressive acts are also discussed.

1488   COSENTINI, FRANCESCO
        1930 Declaración de los derechos y obligaciones civiles
        de la mujer. Proyecto para la protección de la mujer
        y del hogar. Biblioteca del Inst. Americano de Derecho
        y Legislación Comparada. Studios y documentos, 1. Mex.,
        D.F.: Edit. "Cvltvra." 31 p.
            Reproduces text of legal project which, among other
        things, grants equal juridical capacity to Mexican
        women, including retention of citizenship even if married
        to a foreigner. Other laws refer to marriage, separa-
        tion, divorce, paternity.

1489   EZETA, REMEDIOS A.
        1956 "La mujer mexicana ante el Derecho." FL 30:60/61/62:
        135-46.
            Analyzes Mexican law to determine whether women enjoy
        same civil, public, and political rights as men. Con-
        cludes that women's legal capacity is equal to men's in
        the Civil, Penal and Commercial Codes, and the Constitu-
        tion, except in 3 instances, which author considers to
        women's advantage.

1490   GARCÍA, GENARO
        1891 Apuntes sobre la condición de la mujer. Mex., D.F.:
        Cía. Limi. de Tipografía. 80 p.
            Early defense of women's equal rights in Mexico demon-
        strates that the inequality of women is not a natural
        phenomenon. Analyzes, article by article, the Constitu-
        tion, Civil and Commerce Codes to expose flagrant viola-
        tion of women's rights as citizens.

1491   GÓMEZ LARA, CIPRIANO
        1965 "El delito de violación en el matrimonio." UNAM/DPC
        6:61-81. bibl. f/notes.
            Discusses crime of rape as delineated in Mexico's
        Penal Code: e.g., legal nature of sexual relations
        between conjugal partners concludes that marriage is
        not sufficient reason for wife to be without penal pro-
        tection against a brutal husband; concubines and prosti-
        tutes are protected. Partners should have right to
        decide whether or not to have sex since legal equality
        of the sexes exists.

1492   GONZÁLEZ DÍAZ LOMBARDO, FRANCISCO
        1967 "La familia, el concubinato y la seguridad social."
        MSTPS/R (ser. 6) 14:3:31-40.
            Discusses family and marriage; relatives; divorce;
        equality of children before the law; concubinage and

Law - General Legal Status

civil legislation, Federal Labor Law, Social Security
Law, law of ISSSTE; the wife, concubine and economic
dependence. Summarizes final conclusions and considerations of Mexican laws affecting these topics.

1493 GONZÁLEZ SALAZAR, GLORIA
1969 "Situación juridica de la mujer en Mexico." In La
mujer y los derechos sociales, by I. M. de Navarrete,
apéndice 1, pp. 105-23. Mex., D.F.: Eds. Oasis.
Brief exposition of movement for women's civil and
political rights from the first Feminist Congress in
Yucatán (1915) to complete suffrage throughout Mexico
(1953); and of women's position in labor legislation
from a two-fold perspective--woman as a worker equal to
men and woman in her double role as mother/worker.

1494 GRAUE, DESIDERIO
1966 "Panaroma jurídico para la proteccion de la familia
en México." Criminalia 32:8:490-511.
Same as 1965 article (#1495).

1495 _____.
1965 "Consideraciones sobre algunos aspectos jurídicos
del régimen familiar en México." Criminalia 31:7:376-96.
Summarizes principal legal disposiciones which refer to
the family in Mexico: private and public rights with
regard to marriage, divorce, children, women.

1496 Mujeres en Acción Solidaria: Pascual, Dulce María; Peraza
Landero, Rocío; Rascón, Maria Antonieta and Tovar, Rosalinda
1974 "Un punto de vista sobre las reformas a los artículos
4 y 5 de la Constitución. Hacia la dualidad." CM/SS
1114(30 Oct):V-VII.
This was to be presented to public audience on October
14 to Mexican Chamber of Deputies' commission analyzing
presidential initiative of September 18 regarding legal
equality between men and women. M.A.S. disputes proposed constitutional reforms. Concludes that women and
men are not equal, but it is desirable to equalize opportunities of both sexes, for man is not the model woman
should adopt. Given the basics for full development,
woman will impose her own perspective on history.

1497 NADER, LAURA
1964 "An Analysis of Zapotec Law Cases." UP/E 3:4:404-19.
Briefly analyzes content of law cases adjudicated
during one month in Zapotec town. Reveals patterned out-
comes for specific classes of complaints: e.g., women

regularly take their husbands to court and the authority
of male head of household is often overruled by elected
town officials. It is possible to compare ideal and
real patterns of behavior, e.g., between husband and
wife, by reviewing law cases.

1498   NADER, LAURA and METZGER, DUANE
          1963 "Conflict Resolution in Two Mexican Communities."
          AAA/AA 65:3:584-92.
             Investigates alternative strategies employed by hus-
          bands and wives in 2 communities of Oaxaca and Chiapas
          to resolve conflicts between them. Among the 2 legal
          subsystems of family and court, 2 sets of factors
          influence distribution, strength, and availability of
          authority: "differential availability of scarce goods
          such as food, sex, and family inheritance to married
          and single individuals;" and "degree to which institu-
          tionalized political organization concerns itself with
          the legal aspects of marriage."

1499   OYARZÚN, MARÍA del ROSARIO
          1956 "La mujer y la justicia." FL 30:60/61/62:185-95.
             Mexican lawyer reviews position of women in Mexican
          legislation (agrarian reform, commerce, family, social
          security, labor, etc.), noting almost total equality.
          However, points out that not all Mexican women enjoy
          full justice, especially indigenous and working class
          women. Educated women have responsibility of helping
          those women less prepared and knowledgeable about their
          rights.

1500   REGER, MURIEL
          1948 "María Lavalle Urbina: Supreme Court Judge." MAR
          16:4/5:37.
             Short sketch on only woman judge in a Mexican
          Supreme Court with 24 male judges. She is especially
          concerned with penal reforms in Mexico City, juvenile
          delinquency and the problems of women in Mexican prisons.

1501   SHONTZ, ORFA JEAN
          1927 "Land of 'Poco Tiempo'," A Study in Mexican Family
          Relationships in a Changing Social Environment." The
          Family 8:3:74-79.
             Discusses various aspects of marriage in Mexican Civil
          Code: definition of, impediments to, reciprocal rights
          and duties, dowry, support, child custody, divorce,
          birth records, etc. Cites case studies. Suggests that
          through growing freedom Mexican women will probably
          change the Code.

WOMEN IN SPANISH AMERICA

Law - General Legal Status

1502 SPOTA VALENCIANA, ALMA L.
1967 La igualdad jurídica y social de los sexos; filosofía, sociología e historia. Mex., Edit. Porrúa.
318 p. bibl.
Only the last chapter deals specifically with Mexican
women--their rights and social situation. Other chapters
deal with the question of equality of the sexes; history
of prejudice and discrimination against women; feminist
thought and movements; UN activities in this area.

1503 VILLA de BUENTELLO, G. SOFÍA
1921 La mujer y la ley. Pequeña parte de la obra en
preparación titulada "¡La esclava se levanta!" Estudio
importantísimo para la mujer que desee su emancipación
y para el hombre amante del bien y la justicia. Mex.,
D.F.: Imprenta Franco-Mexicana. 218 p. port.
Analyzes Mexican legal codes and the Law of Domestic
Relations to point out the inequalities which exist
against women. Argues forcefully for women's equal
rights in all arenas (family, politics, economy, etc.).

Guatemala

1504 CARRILLO, ALFONSO
1940 La mujer guatemalteca y su situación jurídica. San
José, C.R.: Imprenta Lehmann. 14 p.
Then Guatemalan Minister to Costa Rica concludes from
the Civil Code that, except for the lack of suffrage,
women in Guatemala enjoy absolute equality with men, and
certain privileges as mothers.

El Salvador

1505 RIVAS, PEDRO GEOFFROY
1963/67 "La justicia salvadoreña en el siglo XVIII."
MNDGJ/A 11:37/41:61-70.
Reproduction of documents related to legal suit (1791)
involving a *mulata* virgin and soldier accused of breaking
his promise to marry her after they had sexual relations.

Honduras

1506 BLANCO, FRANCISCO J., ed.
1955 La mujer ante la legislación hondureña.
Tegucigalpa: Talleres Tipo-Litográficos "Aristón."
203 p.

Compilation of dispositions affecting women, as contained within the various codes, decrees, laws, and
regulations of Honduras (e.g., Labor Law for Women and
Minors, Agrarian Law, Civil Code, Constitution.).

1507   MENDOZA de BARRET, OFELIA
       1949 "Posición jurídica de la mujer hondureña." Norte
       9:8:43. ports.
       Very briefly runs down legal position of women in
       Honduras; Constitution grants almost total equal rights
       but no political rights.

Nicaragua

1508   BORGE de SOTOMAYOR, AMELIA
       1953 La mujer y el derecho. León, Nic. 87 p. bibl.
       Universidad Nacional de Nicaragua thesis provides
       mixed bag of information: legal situation of women in
       pre-Columbian and colonial America, in Nicaragua, in
       various codes; feminism worldwide; legislative changes
       in Uruguay, Mexico, Costa Rica, Guatemala, etc. granting
       equality or suffrage; feminist movement in Nicaragua;
       countries where women hold public office; international
       organizations and conferences for women's rights.
       Appendix reproduces declarations of those groups.

Panama

1509   CHIARI, EDUARDO
       1918 "Situación jurídica de la mujer casada en Panamá."
       Revista Nueva 5:5:842-68.
       In favor of reform then under consideration for Pana-
       manian Civil Code which would permit women to manage
       their own property with absolute independence from their
       husband. Draws comparative study of women's legal posi-
       tion in civil codes of European and Latin American
       countries. Demonstrates why separation of property
       would be advantageous.

SOUTH AMERICA

Colombia

1510   ARCILA GONZÁLEZ, ANTONIO
       1959 El delito sexual en la legislación colombiana.
       Complementada con un estudio sobre psicopatías sexuales.
       2nd ed. Bogota: Eds. Caravana. 320 p. bibl.

Law - General Legal Status

Comprehensive analysis of sexual crimes in Colombian
legislation discusses honor, rape, prostitution, incest,
bigamy, transvestism, homosexuality and other sexual
"deviations." Appendix reproduces penal dispositions
related to crimes against sexual liberty and honor and
against the family.

1511   CHAVARRIAGA MEYER, JOSÉ LUIS
      1940 Derechos y reinvindicaciones de la mujer colombiana.
      Bogota: Edit. ABC. 492 p. bibl.
      Detailed thesis on legal condition of Colombian women,
preceded by long discussions about women in antiquity
and modern times: women in colonial America; heroines
of the Colombian Independence movement; Colombian women
writers since the 19c.; history of education in Columbia
since Independence era, including statistics and documents. Elaborates on Colombian women's political and
civil emancipation: antecedents and evolution of legal
position, legislation, constitutional and civil reforms
proposed to establish equality, arguments in favor of
liberation. Concludes that the proposed reforms will
establish independence for Colombian women, but insists
upon necessity of providing excellent education for them
and awakening their political consciousness. Based on
primary and secondary sources.

1512   Colombia. Ministerio de Hacienda y Crédito Público.
      1967 or 1968 Proyecto de ley por la cual se modifican y
adicionan las leyes 45 de 1936, 83 de 1946 y otras disposiciones legales sobre filiación; se crea el Instituto
de Bienestar Familiar; se organiza la campaña de protección de la madre y al niño; y se dictan otras disposiciones. Bogota: Dirrección de Información de la
Presidencia. 67 p.
      Reproduces legal text projecting modifications of and
additions to Civil Code with respect to paternity; the
relegation of functions of various organizations into one
institute; mothers' pensions; and obligatory social work
for women in Colombia who have completed 4 years of
secondary school, to be carried out between the ages of
18 and 25 in various institutes and centers.

1513   GÓMEZ GARZÓN, SOLEDAD
      1958 "Reformas legales que la mujer debe pedir ante las
cámaras legislativas." UNI 14:123-34.
      Argues for reform of Colombian laws which discriminate
against women, laws which reflect one morality for
women and a separate, more privileged one for men: e.g.,
154 of the Civil Code cites as reasons for divorce

adultery by women but concubinage by men; and 539 of the
Civil Code denies women the right to administer the
possessions of a dissipated husband. Also cites irregu-
larities and inconsistencies of laws referring to penal
punishment for infidelity and homicide; and discrepancy
between written law and actual behavior (e.g., women
earn lower salaries for performing same tasks as men
despite a law prohibiting sex discrimination, and more
women are illiterate than men despite law which stipu-
lates free and obligatory education for all.

1514   JARAMILLO ARBELAEZ, DELIO
        1944 "La mujer diferenciada, es una realidad en pugna
        con la ley." UA/U 64:489-99.
        Provoked by adverse public reactions to the appointment
        of a female judge, reflects on and protests the discrim-
        inatory position which women occupy as a result of
        unequal laws and conservative opinions. By virtue of
        being female, women remain on the same level as crimi-
        nals, children, and the demented. Despite recent pre-
        occupation of Colombian legislation with granting greater
        freedom to women, a kind of separation has resulted.
        Advocates earlier, freer, and easier marriages to combat
        prostitution and sexual commerce.

1515   LÓPEZ, J. EMILIO
        1964 "Capacidad de la mujer para el ejercicio de la tutela
        y curatela." UA/ED 23:65:79-82.
        Cites modifications in Colombian legislation which
        grant women equal civil and political rights; and argues
        that women should also enjoy complete rights as guardians
        of children and/or incapacitated individuals.

1516   OCHOA RESTREPO, GUILLERMO
        1963 "Licencia marital." UA/ED 22:64:223-31.
        See ARGENTINA for annotation.

1517   PINZÓN, GABINO
        1952 "Capacidad de la mujer casada para el comercio."
        UNI 3:173-82.
        Argues that, contrary to what many persons believe,
        married women's commercial capacity is not incompatible
        with marital power or jurisdiction. Colombian Law 28
        confers upon women the capacity to enter into contracts
        and obligations, thereby modifying or reducing the insti-
        tution of marital power.

Law - General Legal Status

1518   SOLARTE HURTADO, DANIEL
          1961 "La mujer colombiana ante la ley civil." UCAU/R
          28:7-60.
            Discusses classification of women in Colombian Civil
          Code: legal situation of single and married women,
          comparing previous laws to present reforms; society of
          property between conjugal partners; marital power or
          dominion; dissolution of conjugal society; separation of
          property; divorce, etc. Itemizes new legislation of a
          project presented by Senator Esmeralda Arboleda de
          Uribe in 1959, discussing importance of project, debate
          surrounding it in Congress, and objectives of the new
          law.

1519   STRAVE HAKER, RICARDO
          1945 "Divorcio y segundo matrimonio verificados por
          colombiano en país extranjero, en su aspecto penal."
          REJAV 23:115:303-14.
            Based on the Civil and Penal Codes, Code of Canon Law
          and of Penal Proceedings, discusses divorce and second
          marriage contracted in another country by Colombians.
          Argues that those who commit crime of divorce and bigamy
          outside of Colombia should be prosecuted.

Ecuador

1520   COELLO GARCÍA, ENRIQUE
          1967 "La familia y la propiedad en la Constitución de
          1967." UCE/A 95:350:123-47.
            First part discusses marriage. Since in essence men
          and women are equal, laws referring to equality mean
          acquiring and exercising rights, as contained in preamble
          to new Constitution of 1967. However, present legisla-
          tion assumes an inequality exists and therefore protects
          the weak. For example, marriage is not founded on abso-
          lute equality of men and women since latter represent
          weak element in it and a difference in attitude exists
          toward the sexes with respect to premarital or extra-
          marital relations. Although women have rights in the
          social, political, cultural and economic spheres, they
          participate less frequently than men because they are
          limited by maternity and their nature (weak, fearful,
          sentimental, etc.). Compares legislation to pre-1967 and
          discusses family, children, and private property.

1521   FERNÁNDEZ MÁRQUEZ, CÉSAR
          1962 "Proyecto de reforma al Código Civil." UCE/A 18:3:
          239-53.

Describes project of reforms to Ecuador's Civil Code
to enable married women to administer their own property,
listing reasons why they should have this right. Other
reforms relate to the domicile of married women, heredi-
tary rights, legitimacy of children, etc.

1522   RENDÓN de MOSQUERA, ZOILA
      1949 "La mujer en los diversos organismos humanos."
      MPSQ/PS 22:150-62.
      Very briefly traces evolution of the family since pre-
      historic times and looks at legal position of women in
      various Latin American countries, emphasizing Ecuador:
      married women, adultery, abortion, sexual crimes, etc.
      Suggests measures to protect mother and child: instruc-
      tion in the factory as to child care, dining room where
      working mothers could breast feed, etc.

1523   VILLEGAS D., RODRIGO
      1962 "La situación de la mujer casada en la legislación
      ecuatoriana." UA/ED 21:61:11-19.
      Discusses incapacity of a married woman to engage in
      certain legal acts and contracts without her husband's
      authorization; and cites evolution of modifications in
      Ecuadorian legislation to ameliorate this form of women's
      inferiority.

Peru

1524   ALZAMORA VALDÉZ, MARIO
      1955 "La mujer peruana ante el derecho." CA/RF 42:2:
      285-96.
      Somewhat rambling discussion cites Peruvian law rele-
      vant to women--protective legislation, equal rights and
      obligations. Notes restrictions for women in Civil
      Code of 1852 in effect until 1936.

1525   COOPER, H. H. A.
      1973 "The Law Relating to Sexual Offenses in Peru."
      AJCL 21:86-123. bibl. f/notes.
      Very informative and interesting review of Peruvian
      law related to sexual offenses discusses rape, statutory
      rape, indecency, seduction, personal injury resulting
      from rape, forgiveness, and prostitution (sexual
      exploitation).

1526   CORNEJO CHAVEZ, HECTOR
      1947 "La invalidez del matrimonio en el derecho peruano."
      UNAR/R 19:25:21-73.

Law - General Legal Status

Legal analysis of Peruvian legislation (Civil Code)
pertaining to marriage: cases in which marriage is
illicit, null and void, or can be annulled. Does not
make distinctions for women, but is relevant in that it
deals with a contract into which women enter.

1527   CUADROS E., RAÚL
        1951 Los derechos de la mujer; divulgación de la ley.
        Lima: Escuela Tipográfica Salesiana. 109 p.
        Explains the rights of women in Peruvian legislation:
        during engagement and marriage, upon dissolution or
        annulment of marriage or death of husband, divorce, with
        respect to extramarital sexual relations, abortion, and
        employment.

1528   ECHECOPAR H., CARLOS
        1938 "The Civil and Political Status of Women in Peru."
        PAU/B 72:8:462-64.
        Notes changes in civil status of Peruvian women when
        the new Civil Code was enacted in 1936: civil rights,
        marital partnership, management, financial affairs,
        divorce, illegitimate children, right of inheritance.
        Women's political rights at that time did not include
        full suffrage or public officeholding.

1529   PATRÓN FAURA, PEDRO
        1972 Legislación de la mujer peruana; prontuario. Normas
        contenidas en la Constitución, en los códigos y en otras
        disposiciones relacionadas con la mujer y en especial
        con las madres de familia, con las maestras y las
        empleadas y obreras al servicio del Estado o de empresas
        particulares. 3rd. ed. Lima. 120 p. bibl.
        Comprehensive collection of those legal dispositions
        related to women, as contained in Peru's Constitution,
        Civil and Penal Codes, Agrarian Reform, Public Employees'
        Legislation, etc. Includes a list of national and inter-
        national women's organizations in Peru and affiliates
        of the National Council of Women throughout the world.

1530   SARA-LAFOSSE, VIOLETA
        1968? La ley de reforma agraria (no. 17716) y sus impli-
        caciones en la estructura familiar. Publicaciones
        CISEPA: Documentos de trabajo, 3. Lima: Centro de
        Investigaciones Sociales, Económicas, Políticas y
        Antropológicas, Pontifica Universidad Católica del Peru.
        12 p.
        Analyzes effect of agrarian reform law on each member
        of peasant family. It favors married men and discrimi-
        nates against women because they can manage land only

when recognized as head of family, i.e., if she is a
single mother, widow, divorcée, or separated, and living
with her children. However, only 33% belong to this
category; 51% are farmers' wives; 15% are agricultural
workers whose husbands are not farmers. Concludes that
because the law does not favor women in agricultural
labor, they wind up in occupations and dedication to the
home, which reinforce their dependence and diminish
their status. Suggests modification consistent with
family structure.

Bolivia

1531   ABELLI, SRA. LUIS de
          1932 "The Status of Women in Bolivia." MPM 44:6:550-52.
             Wife of former Bolivian Minister to US sees Bolivia
          as one of the last of the Latin American countries where
          women are awakening to their need for independence.
          Mentions fight for legal rights, efforts of Ateneo
          Femenino since 1924, and outstanding professional women.
          Attributes less action of Bolivian women to united family
          life, certain degree of contentment, and indifference
          to politics.

1532   GALLARDO, BENJAMÍN H.
          1925 Reintegración de los derechos civiles de la mujer.
          La Paz: Talleres "La República." 57 p. ports.
             Condemns inferiority of women in Civil Code of Bolivia,
          whose origin is the Napoleonic Code; proposes a reinte-
          gration of women's civil rights according to Brazil's
          Civil Code, which he considers the most modern, scien-
          tific, and methodical; and describes project to grant
          equal civil rights to women. Disagrees that women are
          physiologically inferior to men.

1533   SALAZAR, MARIO E.
          1951 "La mujer en la legislación boliviana." EJPS/R
          3:2/3:208-11.
             Points out inferior position of women in Bolivian
          legislation, derived from Napoleonic Code, and recommends
          that women be made equal in constitutional, civil,
          penal and other legislation, that they be economically
          independent of husbands and have equal control over
          their children.

1534   TERRAZAS TORRES, CARLOS
          1955-1956 "La capacidad jurídica de la mujer." UMSA/RD
          7/8:25/26:15-22.

Law - General Legal Status

Formulates law project outlining legal equality between married persons. According to then present Civil Code, upon marriage women converted from legally capable to incapable individuals.

1535 URQUIDI, JOSÉ MACEDONIO
1946 "Derechos de ciudadanía femenina. La reforma instaurada en la Constitución boliviana." UNT/RJ 8:35:137-43.
Names many individuals who helped bring about legislative reform of Bolivian women's rights and reproduces articles from Constitution of 1938 incorporating such changes as women do not lose their nationality when marrying a foreigner.

1536 _____.
1937 La condición jurídica o situación legal de la mujer en Bolivia. 3rd ed. Cochabamba: La Aurora. 112 p. Also in: 1933 DERIN/R (30 September):44-134; (31 December):244-85.
Responds to 6th Panamerican Conference questionnaire on paternal and marital rights, public relations, sexual crimes as dealt with in the Bolivian Constitution, Civil, Penal and Commercial Codes. Cites new legislation (1936) on women's civil rights as well as the legal and economic system of conjugal society as well as other relevant decrees. Includes another questionnaire by American Institute of International Law and Carnegie Foundation for purpose of preparing a study on civil and political equality of women in America for 7th Inter-American Conference.

Paraguay

1537 GASPERI, LUIS de
1957 De la igualdad civil de los sexos en el derecho comparado; explicación y crítica de la ley no. 236. Buenos Aires: Talleres Gráficos Lucania. 243 p. bibl. f/notes.
Legal explication on women's civil rights in Paraguay, with references to legal status of women in other countries written by one of the members of the commission appointed by the Executive Branch to edit a project on women's civil rights in Paraguay. Explains confusions and contradictions which arose in that commission's work when law no. 236 was decreed on 6 September 1954.

Chile

1538   ARTEAGA INFANTE, CLAUDIO
       1922   La mujer chilena, esclava de la ley. Santiago:
       Edit. "Minerva." 85 p. bibl.
          Examines Chilean Civil Code of 1855 to point out legal
       situation of single and married women and argues for re-
       form to eliminate legal enslavement of women, especially
       husband's authority over wife's goods and property.
       Also examines women's position in the Penal and Commerce
       Codes and Civil Process.

1539   CAFFARENA de JILES, ELENA
       1947   ¿Debe el marido alimentos a la mujer que vive fuera
       del hogar conjugal? Santiago: Eds. de la Univ. de
       Chile. 297 p. bibl.
          In Part 2, feminist lawyer analyzes in detail problem
       of food obligation between conjugal partners who live
       together or are separated, temporarily or definitively
       divorced, or whose marriage is annulled. Considers
       problem in relation to Chilean Civil Code, doctrine,
       and jurisprudence; discusses actual cases.

1540   _____.
          1944   Capacidad de la mujer casada con relación a sus
       bienes. Santiago: Imprenta Universitaria. 83 p.
          Feminist lawyer summarizes and explains different
       marital regimes to which married women are subject in
       Chilean legislation. Concludes that conjugal society
       regime should be replaced and article 171 of the Civil
       Code should be revoked. Urges women and their organiza-
       tions to demand a law project which establishes full
       capacity for married women.

1541   GALLO CHINCHILLA, MARGARITA
       1945   La mujer ante la legislación chilena, derechos
       político y social. Col. Síntesis del Derecho Chileno,
       2. Santiago: "Gutenberg" Impresores. 160 p. bibl.
          University of Chile thesis examines position of Chilean
       women with respect to their constitutional rights (nation-
       ality, citizenship, public power, etc.), position of
       different parties regarding women's rights, protective
       labor legislation, unions, domestic service, and much
       more. Also names women's organizations fighting for
       rights and female unions.

Law - General Legal Status

1542 REBORA, JUAN CARLOS
1938 La familia chilena y la familia argentina. Univ.
Nacional de la Plata, Arg. 191 p.
See ARGENTINA for annotation.

1543 VEGA A., JULIO ALBERTO
1900 Necesidad de reformar la condición jurídica de la
madre e hijos ilegítimos. Santiago: Imprenta de
Enrique Blanchard-Chessi. 20 p.
Argues for better legislative protection for lower
class women who have become pregnant without being married. Notes that Chilean Civil Code does not obligate
the men to provide women with anything, no distinction
being made as to whether the sexual act was with or
against her will. Recommends several reforms in favor
of the woman.

1544 ALVAREZ VIGNOLI de DEMICHELI, SOFÍA
1973 Igualdad jurídica de la mujer. Alberdi, su precursor en América. Textos legales vigentes. Buenos
Aires: Eds. Depalma. 59 p.
See URUGUAY for annotation.

1545 AMALLO, HORACIO SILVERIO
1955 El divorcio; comentario a la ley no. 14.394 y a sus
instituciones: regimen de menores, ausencia y ausencia
con presunción de fallecimiento, bien de familia,
indivisión forzosa de bienes hereditarios, edad para
contraer matrimonio. Buenos Aires. 105 p.
Upon approval of passage of reform allowing for dissolution of marriage in Argentina, discusses the law,
congressional projects for its implementation, pro and
con arguments, first court decision on divorce, comparative legislation, and other items cited in title.

1546 ANASTASI, LEÓNIDAS
1938 Derechos civiles de la mujer; conferencia patrocinada
por la Unión Argentina de Mujeres. Buenos Aires: Unión
Argentina de Mujeres. 34 p.
Argues in favor of maintaining legal and economic
equality for women as decreed in law 11.357 which, at
the time, was being considered for reform to reduce such
equality. Defends many other Argentinians unanimously
in favor of the law and attacks those in favor of "re-
forming" it to the disadvantage of women, by putting
them more under husband's control. Provides statistics
on working women.

1547 BORDA, GUILLERMO A.
    1955 Tratado de derecho civil argentino: familia.
    Buenos Aires: Edit. Perrot. 2 vols. bibl. f/notes.
    Treatise on Argentine civil law covers marriage (reli-
    gious, civil, concubine); impediments to its celebration
    (natural, social, and moral conditions) and consent;
    annulment; effects of marriage on persons (legal equal-
    ity, rights and obligations) and on property (dowry,
    conjugal society, etc.); divorce; dissolution of mar-
    riage. Includes specific references to women.

1548 GARCÍA BELAUNCE, CÉSAR A.
    1963 "Prohibición de matrimonio entre españoles y
    americanos (1817)." IDRL/R 14:47-58.
    Documented study of Argentine decree (1817) prohibiting
    marriage between American women and Spanish men without
    formal governmental permission. Concludes that decree,
    first legislation in matters of matrimony enacted by the
    State, was contrary to canon law but was neither anti-
    clerical nor anti-religious, rather a result of political
    motives related to the war for independence. Non-white
    women were not equally affected.

1549 GUASTAVINO, ELÍAS P.
    1969 "La mujer en el derecho civil argentino." UNC/R
    10:1/2:43-70.
    Discusses 5 cycles in the evolution of women's civil
    rights in Argentina (1810-1967), ratification of the
    Interamerican Convention (1948) on women's civil rights
    in America and its effect on married women, and the
    application of international law on the internal legal
    system of Argentina.

1550 MIGLIORINI, INÉS CANDELARIA
    1972 Los derechos civiles de la mujer en la República
    Argentina. B.A.: Centro Nacional de Documentación e
    Información Educativa. 34 p.
    Good synthesis of evolution of women's civil rights in
    Argentina from the colonial era to 1972. Despite legis-
    lative changes, male prerogatives still exist in the
    Civil Code. Suggests modifications to achieve full
    equality of married women.

1551 OCAMPO, VICTORIA
    1969 "La condición inhumana." Sur 318:10-16.
    Reflects on discrimination against women. Ties to-
    gether a Japanese film about a woman during feudal
    times, incidents in the life of Vita Sackville-West, an
    article in the Buenos Aires daily La Prensa (19 April

Law - General Legal Status

1969), and the death of a friend, Dorothy Whitney
Elmhirst. Elaborates on woman as an object (as in the
film): inability to obtain a passport in one's own (as
opposed to married) name, automatic labelling of a child
with father's surname, prohibition of returning to maiden
name after a divorce, denial of a passport to a woman
who marched in a parade for female suffrage. Concludes
with 1968 UNESCO publication of declarations regarding
equal rights for women.

1552 OCHOA RESTREPO, GUILLERMO
1963 "Licencia marital." UA/ED 22:64:223-31.
Discusses marital license (necessity of married women,
of legal age, to obtain permission from husband in order
to carry out certain legal acts) as derived from Roman
law, noting its inclusion and subsequent modification in
Colombian and Argentine legislation.

1553 RÉBORA, JUAN CARLOS
1938 La familia chilena y la familia argentina. Univ.
Nacional de La Plata. Biblioteca Interamericana, 1.
La Plata, Arg. 191 p.
Studies the evolution of the American family, especially
in Argentina and Chile, from a legal perspective, considering the subordination of single and married women
within the family and charting the reforms emancipating
them from tutelage under father or husband. Analyzes
family and marriage in the civil codes of both countries.
Cites the development of education for women and employment possibilities as important factors contributing to
their independence.

Uruguay

1554 ALVAREZ VIGNOLI de DEMOCHELI, SOFÍA
1973 Igualdad jurídica de la mujer. Alberdi, su precursor en América. Textos legales vigentes. Buenos
Aires: Eds. Depalma. 59 p.
Lawyer/senator discusses 1946 Uruguayan law which
grants civil rights to women; makes some comparisons
with laws affecting women in the rest of LA; and cites
Alberdi as a precursor of legal equality for all, regardless of race, sex or religion. Contains documentary
appendix on Argentine and Uruguayan legislation reflecting women's civil rights.

1555   _____.
      1969 "Condición jurídica de la mujer en Latinoamérica."
      UNC/R 10:1/2:105-24.
         Examines civil rights of women in Uruguay, as decreed
      in 1946 (includes legal text); and compares them to
      women's rights in Latin American countries in terms of
      5 categories which determine women's status: *patria
      potestas*, patrimonial autonomy, separation of property,
      domicile, and civil capacity.

1556   _____.
      1946 Derechos civiles de la mujer, antecedentes parla-
      mentarios. Serie "Jurídicas y Sociales," vol. 1.
      Montevideo: Edit. Alfa y Omega. 480 p.
         Reproduces the entire 23-year parliamentary process
      which led to the passage of reforms regarding women's
      civil rights in Uruguay (1946). Part 1 covers action in
      the Senate, part 2 in the House of Representatives,
      part 3 in the General Assembly; part 4 is the text of
      the law passed. An appendix contains additional data.

1557 BAYARDO BENGOA, FERNANDO
      1957 Sobre delitos sexuales. Montevideo. bibl. f/notes.
         Collection of lectures examining sexual crimes in the
      Uruguayan Penal Code: rape, seduction, incest, etc.
      Each section broken down into 9-part analysis.

1558 BRUM, BALTASAR
      1923 Los derechos de la mujer. Reforma a la legislación
      civil y política del Uruguay. Montevideo: José María
      Serrano. 204 p.
         Discusses and explains the details of the 1923 reform
      project to grant equal political and civil rights to
      women in Uruguay, as presented to the Congress; and re-
      produces relevant passages in the Civil, Penal, Civil
      Process, Commerce and Military Codes, as they were, how
      they should be modified, and why. Also cites additional
      reforms.

1559 COUTURE, EDUARDO J.
      1947 "La ley 10.783, sobre derechos de la mujer. Sus
      aspectos procesales." DJA/R 45:8:197-228. bibl.
      f/notes.
         Detailed examination of law 10.783, passed in 1846,
      granting equal civil rights to women in Uruguay. Dis-
      cusses significance and antecedents of the law, concept
      of capacity, dissolution and liquidation of conjugal
      society, judicial solution of conjugal conflicts, etc.

Law - General Legal Status

1560 FRUGONI, EMILIO
1940 La mujer ante el derecho. Montevideo: Edit. Indo-
Americana. 279 p.
Collection of diverse speeches and articles defending
equal rights for women in Uruguay. Includes a report
and project on women's civil rights presented in the
Senate, debate over segregation of the sexes in education and the founding of a university for women, divorce,
infanticide, abortion, prostitution, and political rights.

1561 IRURETA GOYENA, JOSÉ
1932 "Delito de rapto." In his Delitos contra la libertad
de cultos, rapto y estado civil, pp. 46-122. Montevideo:
"Casa A. Barreiro y Ramos."
Series of 6 lectures which provide detailed legal analysis of rape in the Uruguayan Penal Code, with comparisons made to European codes.

1562 PINTO de VIDAL, ISABEL
1951 El batllismo precursor de los derechos civiles de la
mujer. Montevideo: Talleres Gráficos BM. 125 p.
Compilation of parliamentary antecedents initiated by
José Battle y Ordoñez in favor of women's civil rights
in Uruguay. Includes author's articles related to the
1930 law which appeared in El Día.

1563 Uruguay. Cámara de Senadores. XXXIIIª Legislatura.
1939 Derechos civiles de la mujer. Montevideo: Imprenta
Nacional. 98 p.
Records the Uruguayan Senate sessions (1938) wherein
project to amend the Civil Code in those aspects pertaining to women was presented. Discusses motives for
proposing such changes, general considerations, social
reality, and need for and moral significance of reform.
Examines proposed changes of 20 articles.

1564 _____. Laws, statutes, etc.
1939 Derechos civiles de la mujer. Montevideo: Imprenta
Nacional. 98 p.
Reproduces law project in Uruguayan Senate regarding
civil rights of women of age, married women, women's
work, etc., with arguments explaining proposed reforms
and final version which was passed in 1938.

1565 VASCONCELLOS, AMÍLCAR
1947 La mujer ante el derecho positivo uruguayo.
Montevideo: Organización Taquigráfica Medina. 91 p.
Ordered compendium of Uruguayan legislation affecting
women in the following areas: patria potestad; marriage;

406

inheritance; pensions and retirement; maternity; Penal
Code; Constitution; civil rights; guardianship; last will
and testament; and social laws. Concludes that general
orientation of Uruguayan positive law has been to grant
women a maximum of rights, civil and political, as well
as protection to mothers.

CARIBBEAN

Puerto Rico

1566 Comisión de Derechos Civiles
      1973 La igualdad de los derechos y oportunidades de la
      mujer puertorriqueña. San Juan, P.R. 496 p. illus.,
      tables, bibl.
         Civil Rights Commission reports on all aspects of
      women and the law in Puerto Rico. Covers constitutional
      bases, analysis of present situation, access to formal
      education opportunities, participation of women in labor
      force and professional sector, and family rights. Pro-
      vides biographical synopsis of 31 distinguished Puerto
      Rican women from Chieftain Yuisa of the early 1500's to
      poets, educators, journalists, feminists, politicians
      et al. of the 19c. and 20c. Extensive, valuable
      bibliography.

1567 E.E.
      1916 "El feminismo." In Puerto Rico y sus hombres;
      bocetos biográficos y artículos científicos consagrados
      a los agricultores y comerciantes, ed. by V. Gautier,
      pp. 5-7. Ponce, P.R.
         Briefly discusses legislation passed in favor of
      Puerto Rican women.

1568 GONZÁLEZ DEL VALLE, AMBROSIO
      1968 "La mujer casada comerciante: problemas jurídicos
      que plantea esta situación." RDP 7:27:219-24.
         Analyzes article 6 of the Puerto Rican Commerce Code,
      which appears to allow women equal rights with respect
      to engaging in commerce or industry, thus overriding the
      authorization of one's husband as stipulated in article
      91 of the Civil Code; in fact, however, conditions of
      inequality do exist.

1569 HERRERA, SYLVIA
      1965 "La mujer casada y la acción por daños y prejuicios."
      UPR/RJ 34:3:397-42.

407

Law - General Legal Status

> Raises question as to whether women should be able to sue for damages suffered during marriage. Discusses legal aspects, conflict about public policy regarding proposed legislation; and illustrates with examples from comparative law.

1570   MALARET y YORDÁN, AUGUSTO
        1908 "Condición jurídica de la mujer puertorriqueña."
        NT 8:120:321-29.
        Upon independence from Spain and subsequent domination by North America, Puerto Rico greatly modified the Spanish Civil Code to reflect increased legal emancipation of women. Points out these changes, such as women are no longer legally represented by their husbands but by their own person, and they are no longer solely culpable of adultery as grounds for divorce.

1571   SIMON, JOHN L.
        1971 "The Virginity Cult in the Civil and Criminal Law of Puerto Rico." UPR/RJ 40:1:103-20.
        Psychiatrist studying law in Puerto Rico is concerned with the equal treatment of women before the law, with particular emphasis on the removal of the seduction statute. Virginity is objectified as a legal value; as such, it establishes harmful comparisons among women and renders them an inferior sex by the law. Neither does the code increase respect for the institution of marriage or protect the men and women forced into marriage. Urges legal doctrines which raise the level of relationships between the sexes rather than objectify aspects of human beings.

1572   VANEGAS, J. D.
        1942 "La personalidad jurídica de la mujer nicaragüense."
        Ateneo 30:154:70-74.
        The Nicaraguan Civil Code of 1904 put an end to husband's control over wife's property and goods, and established divorce.

Cuba

1573   FIGUERAS y GONZÁLEZ, JESÚS A.
        1945 Posición jurídica de la mujer. Monografías jurídicas,
        49. Havana: Jesús Montero Edit. 105 p.
        Briefly analyzes causes and goals of feminism; considers philosophical fundamentals of activity and education; and traces evolution of women's rights in Cuban

legislation in 20c. Appendix reproduces the relevant articles from 1940 Constitution, Civil and Commerce Codes, Law of July 18, 1917, and the Suárez Rivas Project.

1574   LE RIVEREND BRUSONE, EDUARDO
         1945 El derecho de la mujer casada. Biblioteca Jurídica de Autores Cubanos y Extranjeros, 93. Havana: Jesús Montero, Ed. 333 p. bibl. f/notes.
         Prize-winning work notes that although Cuban constitution of 1940 establishes absolute equality between the sexes, problems and inequality continue to exist. Part 1 discusses capacity of married women, modifications and transition. Appendix analyzes law project presented to Congress in 1945, which he finds very inadequate. Detailed footnotes.

1575   MARTÍNEZ, JOSÉ AGUSTÍN
         1940 La mujer en el Código Nuevo; conferencia pronunciada en la "Alianza Nacional Feminista". Monografías Jurídicas, vol 26. Havana: Jesús Montero, Ed. 22 p.
         Examines articles interpreted as protective measures for women in Cuba's New Code of Social Defense (1938): female physiological condition, defense of one's honor, abortion as a crime, pimping and prostitution, and abduction or rape.

1576   PICHARDO, HORTENSIA
         1969 "La liberación de la mujer." In Documentos para la historia de Cuba, vol. 2, pp. 411-16. Havana: Inst. del Libro.
         Reproduces, from Gaceta Oficial, 2 laws which partially liberated Cuban women from male domination: 1) Law of 18 July 1917 conceded to women patria potestas over their children, regardless of remarriage or widowhood, and the right to administer and/or dispose of their property, whether dowry or otherwise, and 2) law establishing divorce.

1577   RANDALL, MARGARET
         1974 "Introducing the Family Code." CR 4:2:31.
         Excerpt from afterword in her Cuban Women Now (1974; #2202). Following an ideological campaign for more than 2 years, official discussions of the Family Code draft indicate proposals to advance a workable equality between women and men regarding housework, child care, marriage, divorce, child support, etc.

Law - General Legal Status

1578 _____.
1974 "Women in Cuba, An Interview With Margaret Randall."
Plexus 1:10:5.
Interviewed by Diane and Sarah of the Venceremos Brigade, Randall cites 2 laws indicative of change in Cuba:
1) anti-vagrancy law makes it a crime for either sex not
to work; 2) maternity law provides excellent coverage
and flexibility before, during, and after pregnancy.
Notes family law under consideration, dealing with ille-
gitimacy and divorce. Also discusses changing roles and
attitudes among women and men regarding household responsibilities, marriage, machismo.

FEMALE DELINQUENCY AND PENAL INSTITUTIONS

SPANISH AMERICA - GENERAL

1579 CHAUVIN, CHARLES
1974 "La prostitución en América Latina." BDSLM/CIDHAL
4:2:53-63.
Personal observations on prostitution in Colombia,
Chile, Peru and Brazil, which he sees as a consequence
of population growth, economic stagnation, racial tensions and crazy urbanization. Cites statistics without
references. Discusses prohibition versus regulation of
prostitution. Quotes several LA social scientists.

1580 DÁVALOS y LESSÓN, PEDRO
1909 La prostitución en la ciudad de Lima. Lima:
Imprenta La Industria. 97 p.
See PERU for annotation.

1581 ILLICH, IVAN
1971 "¿Abolición de las leyes sobre el aborto?" BDSLM/
CIDHAL 1:1:3-10.
Talk given by founding member of CIDOC in Cuernavaca,
pointing out why the Church must take the initiative in
providing a liberal abortion law. A realistic birth
control policy is especially crucial for the poorest
sector of the Latin American population. Women should
be able to plan their families without having to resort
only to abortion.

1582 LÓPEZ-REY y ARROJO, MANUEL
1964 "El delito de aborto en España y América Latina."
UNAM/BIDCM 17:49:31-81. tables, bibl. f/notes.

Discusses several categories of abortion (with consent, *honoris causa*, therapeutic, eugenic, et al.) and demonstrates that penal regulation of abortion in Spain and LA is a legal incongruence because it is not responsive to contemporary needs on a legal or social level. Includes late 1950's/early 1960's statistics related to abortion as a crime.

1583   RODRÍGUEZ-SOLÍS, ENRIQUE
1921?   Historia de la prostitución en España y América.
Madrid: Biblioteca Nueva.   335 p.
Information on prostitution in Spain may serve as background for its occurrence in America.   Includes only brief notes on Cuba and Puerto Rico in the 19c.   Useful more as background.

1584   SCHWARTZ, KESSEL
1973   "The Whorehouse and the Whore in Spanish American Fiction of the 1960's."   UM/JIAS 15:4:472-87.   bibl.
Spanish American society and the primal drives of its people are reflected in the fictional theme of prostitution.   Describes psychological characteristics of prostitutes, where the profession is practiced, its social and economic importance, and its relation to Catholicism, philosophical preoccupations and male/female interaction. Considers 19c. and 20c. Spanish American fiction of several countries and concludes that contemporary writings emphasize the sexual frustrations and compulsions as well as the insecurities and alienation of modern society.

MIDDLE AMERICA

Mexico

1585   AGUILAR GARCÍA, LEOPOLDO
1973   El aborto en México y en el mundo.   Mex., D.F.: Costa-Amic.   121 p.   illus., tables, bibl.
Part 1 cites laws from Mexican Penal Code as it affects abortion; discusses abortion as a social and public health problem; demonstrates incidence of abortion in statistics from 3 hospitals; lists general characteristics of women who abort.   Part 2 is a comparative review of laws on abortion throughout the world.   Concludes that women who abort the most have had more than 3 children, live in urban centers, and are 21-25 years old; bourgeois women attend private clinics while proletariat women suffer complications from relying on witches, midwives, spiritualists and self-induced abortion, and wind up in public hospitals.

Law - Female Delinquency and Penal Institutions

1586 FERNÁNDEZ DOBLADO, LUIS
1963 "El Ministerio Público y el tráfico inmoral con
personas." Criminalia 29:9:606-10.
Discusses activities of Public Ministry in prevention
of, search for, and prosecution of crimes related to
"white slavery." Names 4 principal forms of intervention
in prostitution by State. Makes 3 recommendations to
third Interamerican Congress of Lawyers.

1587 GÓMEZ VÍVEROS, CLEMENCIA, et al.
1965 "El Centro de Reclusión número dos del Distrito
Federal." Criminalia 31:3:110-23. tables, bibl.
Presents results of questionnaire administered (July
1964) to 100 female delinquents at detention center in
Mexico City regarding moral, family, legal, economic,
and personal aspects. Most of the women were held because of prostitution. Provides 2 case studies.

1588 GRAUE DÍAZ GONZÁLEZ, DESIDERIO
1950 "La prostitución en la Ciudad de México, causas y
efectos sociales." Congreso Nacional de Sociología, 1º.
Estudios Sociológicos, pp. 131-59. Mex., D.F.: UNAM,
Inst. de Investigaciones Sociales. bibl.
Considers legal and social aspects of prostitution in
Mexico; describes its practice in 8 kinds of locales
(brothel, night club, restaurant-bar, etc.) in the capital; analyzes 33 possible general and particular causes
for its incidence; and discusses 7 social effects. Calls
for repression and elimination of prostitution.

1589 LARA y PARDO, LUIS
1908 La prostitución en México. Estudios de Higiene
Social. Librería de la viuda de Ch. Bouret. 266 p.
tables.
Uses Inspección de Sanidad 1904-06 statistics and other
official data to present picture of prostitution in
Mexico at turn of the century, including socio-economic
and psychological aspects, regulations, and a discussion
of venereal disease.

1590 Michoacan, Mexico. Laws, statutes, etc.
1923 Reglamento de la prostitución. Morelia, Mex.:
Tipografía de la Escuela de Artes y Oficios. 20 p.

Reproduces text of law regulating prostitution in the
state of Michoacan, Mexico; corresponds to no. 80 of the
"Periódico Oficial."

1591　MURIEL de la TORRE, JOSEFINA
　　　1974　Los recogimientos de mujeres: respuesta a una
　　　problemática social novohispana. Serie de Historia
　　　Novohispana, 24. Mex., D.F.: UNAM, Inst. de Investi-
　　　gaciones Históricas. 260 p. illus., plates, bibl.
　　　　Valuable contribution to the history of women in colo-
　　　nial Mexico demonstrates how the Spanish government,
　　　the Church and society dealt with such problems as
　　　prostitution, the lack of well-paying work for women,
　　　abandonment, marriage, divorce, widowhood, being single
　　　and needing to find a husband. Recogimientos were estab-
　　　lished to protect and help women who lived in a society
　　　which denied them equal rights and to correct and punish
　　　women who were sentenced by various tribunals in New
　　　Spain as part of the Crown's protectionist policy toward
　　　women and its efforts to maintain public morality. Based
　　　on archival research, covers several kinds of these in-
　　　stitutions in Mexico City and the provinces: how they
　　　were founded and for what purpose, its residents and the
　　　kind of life they led there. Introductory chapters de-
　　　scribe women's general situation (prostitution, legal
　　　condition, economic possibilities and means of living)
　　　in the Hispanic world during the 16c.

1592　RAMÍREZ de ARELLANO, JUAN JOSÉ
　　　1895　La prostitución en México. Leyes y reglamentación
　　　a que debe sujetarse en beneficio de la salubridad
　　　pública. Mex., D.F.: Oficina Tipografía de la
　　　Secretaría de Fomento. 21 p.
　　　　Read at a session of the Medical Society "Pedro
　　　Escobedo," discusses existing regulation of prostitution
　　　in 19c. Mexico and noting deficient data on practicing
　　　prostitutes, suggests additional measures for greater
　　　control.

1593　ROEBUCK, JULIAN and McNAMARA, PATRICK
　　　1973　"Ficheras and Free-lancers: Prostitution in a
　　　Mexican Border City." PP/ASB 2:3:231-44. bibl.
　　　　Based on interviews with public health officials,
　　　police, taxi drivers, and prostitutes in a Mexican
　　　border city, develops a typology of prostitution bars.
　　　Describes existing conditions which reveal prostitution
　　　as a flourishing and relatively stable occupation. Pro-
　　　vides a collective profile of registered prostitutes.

Law - Female Delinquency and Penal Institutions

1594   ROLDÁN, FRANCISCO F.
        1892 La ramera arrepentida. Ligeros apuntes sobre la
        prostitución y sus consecuencias. Historia única en su
        genero, dedicada a la sociedad femenina en general y a
        la prostituida en particular. Poema que deben de tener
        de precisión por ser de suma importancia todas las
        personas que constituyen el sexo femenino. Mex., D.F.:
        "La Europea" de R. Arquero y cía. 26 p.
        Uses verse form to illustrate dignified and orderly
        expression of affection and to expose ugliness and
        immorality of prostitution, exhorting all prostitutes to
        repent and all women to preserve their modesty and honor
        as precious jewels.

1595   SOLÍS QUIROGA, HÉCTOR
        1964 "La prostitución en México hasta 1957." Criminalia
        30:4:271-77.
        Defines legal concepts used in relation to prostitu-
        tion and describes situation in Mexico since 1939:
        where practiced, causes, legislation, prevention,
        rehabilitation.

1596   TUDELA de la ORDEN, JOSÉ
        1971 "La pena de adulterio en los pueblos precortesianos."
        IGFO/RI 31:123/124:377-88. illus.
        Commentaries on paintings and texts of codices and
        Relación de Michoacán in their depiction and explanation
        of adultery among the Aztecs, Tarascans and Yopes in
        pre-Conquest Mexico. Severity of punishment varied by
        group, sex, and class. Women are depicted quartered,
        strangled, burned alive, decapitated and left to ven-
        geance of husband.

1597   VILLELA, ENRIQUE
        1951 "Sobre prostitución en México." Congreso Nacional
        de Sociología, 2o. Estudios Sociológicos, pp. 217-29.
        Mex., D.F.: UNAM, Inst. de Investigaciones Sociales.
        bibl. f/notes.
        Discusses federal regulation of prostitution in Mexico,
        health and social consequences, efforts to change the
        situation; Ciudad Juarez as a case example; recommenda-
        tions for a program to repress and prevent prostitution.

El Salvador

1598   LÓPEZ, CÉSAR EMILIO
        1954 "Nuestro problems social de la prostitución."
        Ateneo 42:202:32-54.

414

South America - Venezuela

Based on 35 years of experience as head of Women's
Section in Psychiatric Hospital, Hospital of Profilaxis
and private medical practice, discusses social problem
and sexual phenomenon of prostitution. Considers definition and general history of prostitution: social,
economic and ethical factors, biological determinants,
influence of illiteracy, delinquency of regulations.
Believes prostitution is not a crime but a biological-
social phenomenon; 1 obstacle to resolving it is double
standard in sexual matters. Defends women's right to
choose or reject motherhood. Prohibition is ridiculous
because poverty must be combated before prostitution
can be eradicated.

Nicaragua

1599   MONTALBÁN, LEONARDO
        1958 "La prostitución aborígen en Nicaragua." MIIN/NI
        3:22:34-39.
        Brief notes on prostitution among indigenous people of
        Nicaragua, based on comments by Oviedo in his Historia
        general y natural de las Indias, by Columbus in a letter
        to the Spanish crown, and by Bernal Díaz for Mexico.

1600   NAVAS y BARRAZA, JUAN M.
        1967 La educación sexual; estudio de la sexualidad en
        Nicaragua, en Centroamérica, y en Rubén Darío. Managua.
        299 p. bibl.
        Collection of comments and statistics on prostitution,
        sex, sexual education, sex-linked crimes, marriage, con-
        traceptive measures. Includes results of several surveys
        taken in Managua among prostitutes, boys, and married
        persons; and a chapter on theme of sexuality in Ruben
        Darío's poetry.

SOUTH AMERICA

Venezuela

1601   COVA GARCÍA, LUIS
        1962 "Criminalidad femenina en nuestro medio."
        Criminalia 28:10:629-30.
        Personal opinion on rising crime rate among women
        attributes increase to greater complication of women's
        life. No longer confined to family and school but
        obligated to earn a living under difficult socio-
        economic conditions, women are following in the steps
        of men.

Law - Female Delinquency and Penal Institutions

1602 GODOY FONSECA, PABLO
1911 La prostitución. Caracas: Tipografía Americana.
15 p.
Deplores rampant prostitution and general state of
moral decay in Caracas and calls for strict regulation
of the profession to avoid disease and corruption of
minors. Mothers are responsible for social corruption
because they are the persons closest to children from
the start; therefore, it is imperative to teach women
to be mothers, to have a concept of virtue and pure
morality in their hearts.

1603 MAYORCA, JUAN MANUEL, hijo
1967 or 8 Introducción al estudio de la prostitución.
Caracas. 187 p. bibl.
Section pertaining to prostitution in Venezuela includes statistics from other studies and from data for
1961 in Intelligence Service of Municipal Police in
Caracas. Makes legal recommendations to stem tide of
prostitution and in appendix reports on efforts of a
volunteer organization to rehabilitate prostitutes.
Glossary contains criminal terms used in Chile, Mexico,
Venezuela and Spain.

1604 RISQUEZ, FERNANDO
1959 Investigación integral de un grupo representativo de
la delincuencia femenina en Venezuela. Caracas:
Ministerio de Justicia. 459 p. + 329 p. illus., map,
tables, graphs, plates, bibl.
Reports, in English and Spanish, results of an 11-
member team (anthropologist, psychiatrist, neurologist,
et al.) under Risquez' direction which sought to explore
within the causes, implications and repercussions,
criminal acts committed directly or indirectly by women
in Venezuela. Carried out in the Penitentiary and
Women's Jail in Los Teques, in the state of Miranda,
project discloses advantages and disadvantages of jail;
anthropological data, socio-economic characterisitcs,
and sexual life of the prisoners; psychiatric interviews
and conclusions for 50 individual cases; and other kinds
of information.

Colombia

1605 HERNÁNDEZ CARRILLO, JORGE
1947 La mujer delincuente en Colombia. Bogota: Edit.
Centro-Instituto Gráfico Ltda. 208 p.

Proposes to look for specific factors leading to
female delinquency in Colombia and for a penitentiary
reform program, but cites no statistics or references.
Part 2 considers prostitution, sexual crimes, passion and
crime, female sexual psycopathy; and readaptation.

1606   PÉREZ, LUIS CARLOS
        1947 "Apuntes para una interpretación de la delincuencia
        femenina en Colombia." UNC 10:209-28. tables.
        Believes phenomenon of female criminality should be
studied from a naturalist point of view rather than with
legal dogmas. Criticizes dominant theories surrounding
origin of punishable acts by women and briefly examines
their application to situation in Colombia. Does not
agree that women rebel against laws and society created
by men; economic, organic or psychic factors cause
women to commit prostitution, abortion and infanticide.
Neither are women, by nature, more or less delinquent
than, nor physically and mentally inferior to, men.
They are not less capable of conceiving and executing
crimes nor do they evince more perversions. Discusses
theories on prostitution and delinquency. Colombian
statistics (1938-46) demonstrate kinds of crimes and
their frequency as committed by women: 14 times less
often than by men. Parents and a masculine culture
place women in a position in which they are destined to
only raise children and keep house; education is denied
to them more frequently. As a result, women try to
escape their environment. Concludes that it is imperative to free women through a culture which gives them
equal rights and in which they can be responsible for
their own actions.

1607   SEPÚLVEDA NIÑO, SATURNINO
        1970 La prostitución en Colombia; una quiebra de los
        estructuras sociales. Bogota: Edit. Andes. 204 p.
        illus., tables, bibl.
        Claims that no one else has undertaken a systematic
study of prostitution in Colombia, for it has been a
taboo. Using data from National Police and Ministry of
Justice (1959-67) and a case study of 160 prostitutes in
Puerto Berrío, hypothesizes on cultural, social and
economic factors which determine predisposition to prostitution, possibilities for its disintegration, and
alternatives of change (systems of control, societal
attitudes, models of change in sexual cultural code,
socio-economic structure, norms and sanctions). Criticizes society and Church rather than blaming the women

Law - Female Delinquency and Penal Institutions

> or accusing them of uncontrollable sexual desires. Also makes reference to situation in Bogota, Medellin, Popayan.

1608   TORRES, HERNANDO and GONZÁLEZ, CLARA
1972 "La mujer y la delincuencia." DANE/BME 247:81-111. tables, graphs, bibl.
Valuable statistical portrait and analysis of female delinquency, economic activity, and education in Colombia (1951-70), utilizing national census data. Part 1 deals with women's incorporation into the labor force, providing breakdown by sector, occupation, region, level of income, rates of under- and unemployment, and educational level of women workers. Part 2 deals with three kinds of criminality (apparent, legal, threatened). Provides comparative figures for men throughout. Concludes that restrictions on women in the economy and education limit their sphere of action and are related to traditional cultural values which define women's status in the community. Low rate of female delinquency reflects general situation of greater passivity and dependence and stricter controls; but increases in female labor force participation and education are paralleled by increases in female criminality.

Ecuador

1609   BARRERA B., JAIME
1943 La mujer y el delito. Tesis doctoral. Quito: Imprenta de la Universidad. 172 p. bibl. Also in: UCE/A (October/December 1942):115-280.
Develops unsubstantiated thesis relating women's biology and psychology to female delinquency, using arguments by European and Latin American writers. Discusses prostitution and abortion. Also examines the Ecuadorian Penal Code for articles relevant to women and regulations governing women in the national penitentiary and public jail of Quito; and reproduces data from the Institute of Criminology on 39 female criminals. Makes references to situation in other Latin American countries.

Peru

1610   DÁVALOS y LESSÓN, PEDRO
1909 La prostitución en la ciudad de Lima. Lima: Imprenta La Industria. 97 p.

Taking the regulationist (as opposed to the abolition-
ist) position, describes the state of prostitution in
Lima at the beginning of the 20c. and recommends a
project to regulate the trade as an anti-veneral measure.
Fairly enlightened view of prostitutes as women who are
not criminals or nymphomaniacs but mothers who have to
raise their children however they can. Also includes
notes on prostitution in Chile, Mexico, Cuba, and
Argentina.

1611 HERNÁNDEZ AGUILAR, ZOILA
1968 "Rasgos psicológicos predominantes en las madres
prostitutas." In La familia, la infancia y la juventud
en el desarrollo nacional, pp. 373-93. Lima. tables.
Reports results of interviews, questionnaires, and
psychological testing among 50 prostitutes/mothers in an
anti-venereal clinic (age, marital status, abortions,
educational level, residence, present family/living
arrangements, economic situation, psychological characteristics, etc.). Sees prostitution as a psychological
disturbance.

1612 ISMODES CAIRO, ANÍBAL
1968 "Prostitución en Lima." In La familia, la infancia
y la juventud en el desarrollo nacional, pp. 349-72.
Lima.
Sets up typology of prostitution in Lima and reports
findings of a questionnaire administered to 400 prostitutes (origin, age, marital status, children, educational level, reasons for entering the profession, etc.).
Concludes that most powerful cause is the inability to
be socialized and integrated into society as a result
of familial and social frustrations.

1613 RAMOS ALVA, ALFONSO
1972 La socialización delictiva de la mujer: caso peruano.
Lima: Eds. Deara. 195 p. tables, bibl.
Seeks to explain rise in female delinquency by referring to process of socialization. Sample includes total
population (122 in 1970) of the Centro de Reeducación,
Taller y Escuela para Mujeres of Chorrillos, which was
narrowed down to 40 case studies. Looks at their educational level, age, income, family situation, nature of
their crimes. Concludes that women's crime results from
social status, that becoming delinquents allows women
the means to live artificially at a different level to
gain higher social status.

Law - Female Delinquency and Penal Institutions

Paraguay

1614   Paraguay. Laws, statutes, etc.
        1896 Ordenanza y decreto reglamentario de la prostitución
        en el municipio de la capital. Asunción. 16 p.
        Reproduces text of ordinance and regulation of
        Asunción, Paraguay governing prostitution.

Chile

1615   KLIMPEL ALVARADO, FELICITAS
        1946 "Estudio comparativo de la delincuencia femenina en
        Chile y en la Argentina." CPC/R 7:83:11-15.
        See ARGENTINA for annotation.

1616   _____.
        1946 La mujer, el delito y la sociedad. B.A.: Edit.
        El Ateneo. 385 p. tables, bibl.
        See ARGENTINA for annotation.

1617   _____.
        1942 La mujer ante el hombre y el derecho penal.
        (Sociología y criminología). B.A.: Edit. Celta. 96 p.
        tables, bibl.
        Thesis from University of Chile studies female delin-
        quency from a feminist perspective. Women are victims
        of social and biological factors which determine their
        committing crimes. Points out injustices in Chilean
        Penal Code and examines crimes considered "female."
        Provides statistics on women in correctional houses in
        Santiago (1936-40) and several case histories. Concludes
        that delinquent women have a low cultural and intellec-
        tual level, working at home or as domestic servants;
        they commit crimes without premeditation and principally
        between ages of 20 and 30; etc. Calls for immediate
        revision of Penal Code.

1618   LAVAL M., ENRIQUE
        1935 "La Casa de Recogidas." ACH/B 3:6:353-63.
        Interesting account of the troubled and difficult
        founding of the Casa de Recogidas, petitioned for by
        the Real Audiencia in 1704 in reaction to the active and
        uncontrolled prostitution in Santiago. In the late
        1730's it was run by a group of Jesuit beatas (Colegio
        de Esclavas de Jesús). Provides information on the
        beatas' functions, attitudes toward prostitutes, the
        vicissitudes of maintaining the Casa until it was closed
        in 1810 by the government junta. Based on primary
        sources.

WOMEN IN SPANISH AMERICA

1619 MANRÍQUEZ BUSTOS, EDMUNDO
      1963 Protección penal de la vida humana en su primera
      etapa. Facultad de Ciencias Jurídicas y Sociales de la
      Univ. Católica de Chile: memoria 5. Santiago: Edit.
      Jurídica de Chile. 84 p. bibl.
        Detailed legal explication of abortion and infanticide,
      including arguments by other writers, with respect to
      problems implicit in the crime, comparison between Chilean
      and foreign legislation, and analysis of Christian think-
      ing about the meaning and value of human life.

1620 SCHEPELER RAVEAU, MANUEL
      1967 El delito de aborto. Univ. Católica de Chile.
      Facultad de Ciencias Jurídicas, Políticas y Sociales.
      Memoria, 18. Santiago: Edit. Jurídica de Chile.
      103 p. bibl.
        Strictly legal analysis of abortion, limited to an
      exegesis of articles 342 to 345 of the Chilean Penal
      Code.

1621 ALBARRACÍN, ROBERTO
      1936 "La delincuencia femenina, sus cifras, sus causas."
      PRL/B 2:7:17-23. tables.
        Looking over Argentine police statistics of 1934 and
      1935, makes comparison between women and men and hypo-
      thesizes on possible causes of lower criminality among
      women. Suggests establishment of houses to reform and
      educate female delinquents for a better life.

1622 BÁTIZ, ADOLFO
      19--? Buenos Aires, la ribera y los prostíbulos in 1880.
      Buenos Aires: Eds. AGA-TAURA. 121 p.
        Also published in Paris, 1908. Subcommissioner in
      Buenos Aires police department holds governmental sys-
      tems and legislative structures responsible for problems
      of prostitution. Considers himself a Marxist. Based on
      observations in late 19c. Argentina and readings. No
      substantial data; personal impressions.

1623 BERETERVIDE, JUAN JOSÉ and ROSENBLATT, S.
      1934 Glándulas endocrinas y prostitución. Buenos Aires:
      Librería y Edit. "El Ateneo." 254 p. illus., bibl.
        Presents findings of clinical study among 110 prosti-
      tutes in Buenos Aires, using questionnaire and physical
      examinations. Discusses environmental conditions
      (economy, family, education, etc.); puberty, menstrua-
      tion, sexual excitability and libido; initiation into
      sexual relations, menopause, and physiological/psycho-
      logical aspects of the sample, relating all these

Law - Female Delinquency and Penal Institutions

    factors to their exercising the profession of prostitu-
tion. Draws conclusions related to their endocrine system and other glands or organs.

1624 Boletín del Patronato de Recluídas y Liberadas
      1933-1948
      Bulletin of the Buenos Aires institution which took
care of imprisoned and released women has many articles
on women as delinquents. Began publication in 1933,
ended in 1948.

1625 GIMÉNEZ, ANGEL M.
      1930 La reglamentación de la prostitución y la represión
      de la trata de blancas ante la justicia penal. Proyecto
      de ley presentado a la Cámara de Diputados en la sesión
      del 20 de junio de 1917. Sociedad "Luz," Univ. Popular,
      serie 2, vol. 6, no. 110. Buenos Aires: Imprenta "La
      Vanguardia." 52 p.
      Explication of project to modify Argentine law 9143
and discussion of prostitution in Buenos Aires since the
19c., citing statistics from 1889 to 1915. Modifications
presented to the Chamber of Deputies and Senate provide
for punishment of men engaged in pimping.

1626 GOLDAR, ERNESTO
      1971 La "mala vida." La historia popular. Vida y
      milagros de nuestro pueblo, 20. Buenos Aires: Centro
      Ed. de América Latina. 114 p. illus., plates.
      Sees rise of prostitution in Argentina as a result of
the country's precapitalist structure in the 19c.--few
industries, flood of immigration and notes changes in
it after 1930 as a result of cultural change as Argentina passed through new stage of industrialization and
internal migration. Utilizing literature, secondary
sources and some statistics, provides colorful description of prostitution in Buenos Aires from latter part
of 19c. to middle of 20c.: what the "bad life" was
like; differences between "local" and "imported" prostitutes; organized prostitution by Polish leaders; and
legal aspects.

1627 GONZÁLEZ LEBRERO, RODOLFO A.
      1945 "El Asilo de Corrección de Mujeres de Buenos Aires."
      PP/R 10:35/38:23-34.
      Discusses history of correctional institutions for
women in Buenos Aires since the 17c., and various aspects
of the Correctional Asylum for women--physical structure
and internal organization (objectives, personnel, work

activities, instruction, discipline, post-imprisonment assistance). Concludes with a critique of the system and recommends construction of a new penal establishment. Some documentation.

1628 KLIMPEL ALVARADO, FELÍCITAS
     1950 Carceles de mujeres. B.A.: Talleres Gráficos de Dirección General de Institutos Penales de la Nación. 127 p. tables, fold. plans, bibl. f/notes. Originally published in 1947 Revista Penal y Penitenciaria (Buenos Aires) 12:43/46.
     Decries deplorable situation of female prison system in Argentina, which unlike male system, is very neglected. Provides history of penal establishments for women and describes jails in individual provinces. Citing principal defects of jails, recommends and explains reforms for an alternative system, a reformatory of women, which she outlines in detail. Also discusses social assistance for those women who are released and organization of Patronato de Recluídas y Liberadas in Buenos Aires.

1629 _____.
     1946 "Estudio comparativo de la delincuencia femenina en Chile y en la Argentina." CPC/R 7:83:11-15.
     Extracted from her larger study (#1630). Existing penal institutions are deficient in meeting needs of female delinquents, in whom a new consciousness should be created. Society and its laws treat these women unjustly and without understanding.

1630 _____.
     1946 La mujer, el delito y la sociedad. B.A.: Edit. El Ateneo. 385 p. tables, bibl.
     With a feminist perspective and based on observations of women in the Casa Correccional de Mujeres in Santiago and on criminological cards in the Dirección General de Institutos Penales in Buenos Aires, studies in detail the problems of female delinquency. Important work which concludes that "the society we live in is male conceived. That's why every kind of law is nothing other than the thought of men, directed to obtain for them the greatest advantages, without taking into account the characteristics and rights of women."

1631 MADANES, DOLORES
     1947 "La mujer en el Código Penal argentino." DP/R 3:1:55-67. bibl. f/notes.
     Examines position of women in Argentine Penal Code. Discusses theories propounded by Klimpel and Bunge.

Law - Female Delinquency and Penal Institutions

Concludes that sex always plays a role, but in function
and in relation to circumstances surrounding the criminal
act.

1632   PAREJA, ERNESTO M.
       1937 La prostitución en Buenos Aires. Factores antropoló-
       gicos y sociales - su prevención y represión - policía
       de costumbres. Buenos Aires: Edit. Tor. 235 p. tables,
       bibl.
       Only last chapter specifically deals with prostitution
       in Buenos Aires in its legal aspects: Constitution,
       national legislation, administrative jurisdiction,
       measures of prevention and repression. Includes statis-
       tics from 1928 to 1934: prostitutes' nationality, age,
       civil status, years of residence, etc.

1633   SANGUINETTI, MANUEL JUAN
       1940 "Antecedentes de la cárcel de mujeres en Buenos
       Aires." PP/R 5:15:27-34.
       Using documents, traces historical antecedents of the
       women's jail in Buenos Aires, beginning with a bishop's
       request to the King to establish a recogimiento for poor
       and orphaned young women in late 17c. and ending with
       English occupation of the establishment in 1807.

Uruguay

1634   ALBANELL McCOLL, EDUARDO
       1932 Legislación sobre proxenetismo y delitos afines
       (leyes nos. 5520 y 8080). Montevideo: Imprenta
       Nacional Colorada. 159 p. bibl.
       Introduction and early chapters present varying
       opinions surrounding prostitution: whether or not it is
       a crime, regulation system, related crimes, social danger,
       etc. Believes prostitution is incorrectly identified as
       a crime though it may be considered a vice. Remainder
       of book traces evolution of and explains Uruguayan
       legislation related to prostitution, beginning with
       1889 Penal Code. Extensive, explanatory, bibliographical
       notes.

1635   LUISI, PAULINI
       1948 Otra voz clamando en el desierto. (Proxenetismo y
       reglamentación). 2 vols. Montevideo.
       Gathers together her various publications and discourses
       from 40 years of fighting, on a national and international
       level, for abolition of prostitution. Includes trans-
       criptions of international conferences and agreements

on procuration, legal projects, leagues and associations
working for abolition, in Uruguay and elsewhere.

CARIBBEAN

Puerto Rico

1636   RODRÍGUEZ CASTRO, JOSÉ
      1892   Infanticidio. Causa contra Isidora Giral. Informe
      médico-legal. Ponce, P.R.: Imprenta "El Telégrafo."
      19 p.
        According to Bibliografía puertorriqueña (Barcelona,
      1934) of Géigel y Zenón and Morales Ferrer, this pamphlet
      is a medical-legal report of a case in which "an unhappy
      mother under the irresistible impulse of an attack of
      madness, strangles" her own son. Law considers it infan-
      ticide; medicine finds it the result of a functional
      imbalance, which relieves the mother of any
      responsibility.

Cuba

1637   CASTELLANOS, ISRAEL
      1929   La delincuencia femenina en Cuba. Estadísticas
      judiciales, penitenciarias y clínicas. Gráficas
      criminológicas. vol. 2. Havana: Imprenta "Ojeda."
      133 p. plates, port., tables, graphs, bibl.
        Compendium of statistical data on female delinquents
      in Cuba, 1862-1927. Discusses aspects of female crimes,
      including factors of age, civil status, and race. Uses
      some comparative statistics in order to demonstrate very
      low rate of crime among Cuban women. More than 100
      tables and graphs. See also vol. 1, Caracteres biológi-
      cos de la cubana normal y delincuente, and vol. 3,
      Indices filiativos y álbum identoscópico.

1638   HENRÍQUEZ, ENRIQUE C.
      1970   Crímenes de la brujería. La sugestión criminal en
      los ignorantes fanáticos. B.A.: Eds. Depalma. 229 p.
      bibl.
        Includes several Cuban cases of crime, resulting from
      witchcraft and hypersensitivity to superstitions, in
      which women were both culprits and victims.

Law - Female Delinquency and Penal Institutions

1639 RAGGI AGEO, ARMANDO M.
1941 "La mujer y el delito." Criminalia 7:7:437-48.
Reprinted from the Revista del Colegio de Abogados
de la Habana.
Speech given at the Alianza Nacional Feminista in
Havana manifests alarm at increased rate of female delinquency in Cuba, tracing curve with statistics from 1862
to 1939. Emphasizes association between female sexual
cycle and crime, noting that the Code of Social Defense
allows for reduced responsibility during menopause
changes, pregnancy, post-partum illness, and
menstruation.

EMPLOYMENT LEGISLATION

SPANISH AMERICA - GENERAL

1640 ANDERSON, MARY
1935 "What the Americas Are Doing for the Woman Worker."
PAU/B 69:7:521-35. illus.
The Director of the Women's Bureau of the US Department
of Labor summarizes basic efforts by Latin American
countries to establish legal standards for women workers
and to enact general labor legislation in their benefit.
Notes women at childbirth, night work, occupations pro-
hibited or regulated for women, hours of work, annual
holiday with pay, wages, industrial home work, compensation, additional measures for social security.

1640a International Labour Office
1940 "Second Labour Conference of American States."
ILINFO 73:9:182-88.
Includes brief section on committee concerned with the
employment of women and children in America.

1640b _____.
1939 "Protection of Women Home Workers in Latin America."
ILINFO 72:6:159-61. bibl. f/notes.
Briefly describes protective measures taken for women
home workers in Argentina, Colombia, Uruguay, and the
Dominican Republic.

1640c _____.
1939 "Protection of Maternity in Latin America." ILINFO
69:1:3-4. bibl. f/notes.
Summarizes measures taken for the protection of maternity in Argentina, Chile, Colombia, and Mexico.

1641   "Laws for Latin-American Wage-Earning Women."
        1940 USDLWB/WW 20:6:5-6.
        Brief rundown on labor legislation affecting Latin
        American women with respect to dangerous or unhealthy
        occupations, hours, and wages. Difficulty of enforcement
        noted.

MIDDLE AMERICA

Mexico

1642   CIVEIRA TABOADA, MIGUEL
        1967 "Documentos de la Nueva España. Disposiciones para
        que la mujer pueda trabajar en el comercio." BSHCP/B
        13:358:10-11.
        Taken from Richard Konetzke's Colleción de documentos
        para la historia de la formación social de Hispanoaméri-
        ca, 1495-1810, vol. 3, pp. 767-71 (Madrid, 1962), repro-
        duces 1799 document which permitted women to engage in
        commerce. Recounts process whereby Council of the
        Indies granted permission to Viceroy of New Spain in
        response to a widow's petition to be able to sell her
        embroidery work without being impeded by union workers.
        Indicates attitudes toward women's economic activities
        and conflict with men in unions.

1643   GÓMEZ R., GUDELIA
        1965 "Atribuciones y funcionamiento del Departamento de
        Protección al Trabajo de Mujeres y Menores." MSTPS/R
        12:1:31-34.
        Discusses functions and actions of Mexican Department
        of Protection for Female and Child Labor, beginning with
        formation, in 1936, of Investigating Committee of Situa-
        tion of Women and Child Workers.

1644   Mexico. Laws, statutes, etc.
        1934? Regulations Governing Unhealthy or Dangerous
        Labours for Women and Minors. Mex., D.F.? 18 numb. 1.
        tables.
        Typewritten translation from the Diario Oficial
        (11 August 1934), of legislation forbidding certain
        kinds of work by women and minors in Mexico. A series
        of tables lists prohibited forms of labor, reasons for
        their prohibition, and establishments where minors and
        women may be employed subject to specific conditions,
        citing those conditions and reasons for them.

Law - Employment Legislation

1645   "Real cédula sobre aumento de jornales."
       1934 MAGN/B 5:3:406-14.
           Collection of documents (Real Audiencia, vol. 33)
           related to Spanish crown's decree in 1804 regarding
           increase in daily wages of Indian laundresses in rural
           New Spain and difficulties in carrying out that
           disposition.

1646   "Reglamento de labores peligrosas e insalubres para mujeres
       y menores."
       1960 MSTPS/R 7:7/8:63-69.
           Law regulating dangerous and unhealthy work for
           women and minors in Mexico: for example, it is prohib-
           ited to employ women and minors under 16 years of age in
           subterranean or submarine work.

Guatemala

1647   GONZÁLEZ PINEDA, HÉCTOR
       1964 El trabajo de la mujer en la legislación laboral
           guatemalteca. Guatemala: Univ. de San Carlos, Facultad
           de Ciencias Jurídicas y Sociales. 73 p. bibl.
           Before discussing Guatemalan laws which affect female
           labor, thesis traces historical antecedents of women's
           work; biological, economic, historical and other factors
           which influence female employment; special protection
           for women workers; and employment of women with family
           responsibilities.

1648   QUIÑÓNEZ CASTILLO, ZOILA
       1958 "El trabajo industrial a domicilio y el trabajo
           domestico de la mujer." MTBS/R 1:2:20-32.
           Defines work at home and domestic service, their
           advantages and disadvantages, and regulations governing
           these activities as stipulated in Guatemala's Labor
           Code. Discusses protection afforded these workers by
           Institute of Social Security and methods for controlling
           application of legislation related to women's work in
           these two areas.

Costa Rica

1648a International Labour Office
           1951 "Equal Remuneration in Costa Rica." IL/ILO 5:9:344.
           Reports that Inspectorate General of Labor in Costa
           Rica ruled (January 1951) that women and children
           employed in agriculture be paid the same minimum wages
           as male workers.

SOUTH AMERICA

Colombia

1649   Colombia. Ministerio de Trabajo.
        1953 El trabajo de la mujer; disposiciones legales.
        Bogota: Imprenta Nacional. 51 p.
        Gathers together Colombian legislation referring to
        women workers, divided according to protection for mater-
        nity, domestic service, work at home, work of minors,
        plus other relevant decrees and resolutions.

1650   International Labour Office
        1944 "Maternity Protection in Colombia." ILO/R 49:6:678.
        Order no. 972 of 14 December 1943 was issued in
        Colombia as a result of Complaints to the Ministry of
        Labor that industrial establishments employing over 50
        women were evading a provision of the Child Welfare Act
        No. 48 (1924) which requires that they provide day
        nurseries for working mothers' children.

1650a   _____.
        1939 "Maternity Protection in Colombia." ILINFO 70:12:
        823-24. bibl. f/notes.
        Provides brief details on system of maternity protec-
        tion for women workers in Colombia: e.g., Department of
        Maternity and Child Protection within the Ministry of
        Labor, Hygiene and Social Welfare.

Ecuador

1651   "Condiciones de trabajo de la mujer en el Ecuador."
        1939 E/BIESE 1:4:86-88.
        Summarizes situation of working women in Ecuador on a
        legislative level. Despite lack of ratification of
        various international agreements, Ecuador has incorpo-
        rated some aspects, as evidenced in articles 86 to 94
        of the Labor Code, reproduced here: e.g., women are
        prohibited from working in preparation or sale of
        liquor.

1652   International Labour Office
        1938 "Pro Section of Wages of Women and Young Persons in
        Ecuador." ILINFO 68:5:147-48.
        Reminder by Ecuador's Department of Labor's Coast
        Division to heads of commercial and industrial enter-
        prises regarding minimum wage for women and young people,
        explaining application of the 2/3 rate.

Law - Employment Legislation

Peru

1653 CORONADO S., PEDRO P.
1935-1937 "Exposición y crítica de la legislación peruana
sobre trabajo de mujeres y menores de edad." CA/RF
22:4/5/6:280-88; 23:1/2/3/4/5/6:102-08; 23:10/11/12:
589-611; 24:4/5/6:233-44.
Detailed, comprehensive analysis of 20c. Peruvian
protective legislation of working women and minors.
Covers maternity, hours, child care, conditions, etc.
Concludes with a discussion of the application and
inspection of these laws and 40 suggestions for reform.

1654 LEÓN de IZAGUIRRE, VIRGINIA
1960 Legislación del trabajo: la mujer trabajadora.
Lima. 33 p. illus.
Comprehensive pamphlet by Peruvian lawyer, early member
of APRA, and frequent exile, traces development of labor
legislation for women in Peru, taken from a course given
at the Autonomous Syndical School of Lima. Cites 23
separate laws, resolutions and decrees pertaining to
female labor and protection they provide in terms of
rest, hours, vacations, accidents, etc.; and briefly
discusses position of women working in agriculture,
domestic service, fishing industry, textiles, home manufacture, and barbasco industry of the jungle. Also mentions administrative organs charged with carrying out
protective legislation.

1655 "Ley no. 2851 de noviembre 23 de 1918, trabajo de los niños y
mujeres por cuenta ajena."
1942 LP/R 3:28:1783-87.
Reproduces Peruvian law no. 2851, which regulates
employment of women and minors. Prohibits night work,
longer than 8-hour work days, etc.

Bolivia

1656 International Labour Office
1944 "Employment of Women in the Bolivian Mining Industry."
ILO/R 49:6:678.
In order to supplement the insufficient number of male
workers for expansion of mining operations in Bolivia,
a legislative decree provided that women could work
longer hours and night shifts, and earn double and over-
time, but must not be employed underground or in heavy
work.

Chile

1657   International Labour Office
            1954 "New Maternity Protection Act in Chile." IL/ILO
            11:1:493-95. bibl. f/notes.
                Describes Act promulgated in Chile (24 November 1953)
            which amends provisions (leave before and after confine-
            ment, maternity benefit, grounds for dismissal, transfer
            to light work, penalties) related to maternity protection
            in Part III of the Labor Code.

1657a   _____.
            1938 "Night Work of Women in Chile." ILINFO 68:5:147.
                Quotes Chile's Department of Social Welfare's circular
            regarding legal provisions for women's night work.

1657b   _____.
            1936 "Chile 2. Decree: Maternity." Legislative Series,
            1934. Part I, pp. 354-58. Geneva: Int'l Labour Office.
                Translation of decree no. 349 approving regulations for
            the administration of Part III of Book II of Chile's
            Labor Code (19 April 1934). Stipulates protection of
            working mothers and regulation of day nursery at the
            place of work.

1658   Jubilación de la mujer. Jubilación de la funcionaria según
            la ley no. 10343 de 1952; jubilación de la empleada particular
            y obrera. Según la ley 14687 de 1961; leyes y reglamentos
            sobre protección a la maternidad; leyes y reglamento sobre la
            asignación familiar.
            1962 Santiago: Eds. "Gutenberg." 64 p.
                Both the 1962 and 1965 (#1660) versions cover the same
            Chilean legislation affecting retirement of women,
            maternity, working mothers, etc., but have different
            concluding sections. Useful for analyzing legal position
            of working women and mothers in Chile.

1659   No Entry

1660   Previsión de la mujer: jubilación de la funcionaria según la
            ley no. 10343 de 1952; jubilación de la empleada particular
            y obrera según la ley 14687 de 1961; leyes y reglamentos sobre
            protección a la maternidad; leyes y reglamentos sobre la
            asignación familiar y prenatal; normas sobre revalorización de
            pensiones y nuevos beneficios para asegurados. Actualizada
            para 1967.
            1965 Santiago: Eds. "Gutenberg." 64 p.

Law - Employment Legislation

Update of 1962 publication: Jubilación de la
mujer . . . (#1658), compendium of laws which affect
retirement of women, as well as protective legislation
for maternity, the mother who works, etc.

1661   "Protective Legislation for Working Women in Chile."
        1927 MLR 25:2:73-74.
        Cites provisions of Chile's legislative decree 442
        (1925) regarding the employment of working mothers in
        industry and commerce.

Argentina

1662   DEL CAMPO, GUILLERMINA
        1969 "Oportunidad y protección en el trabajo." UNC/R
        10:1/2:93-104.
        University lecture points out that Argentine women
        have the right to engage in and administer the salary
        resulting from any job which is considered "proper,"
        usually by a father or husband. Discusses protective
        legislation for women workers and makes comparisons to
        other Latin American countries.

1663   GUEVARA, RAFAEL EDUARDO
        1972 La mujer y la seguridad social en la legislación
        argentina. B.A.: Centro Nacional de Documentación e
        Información Educativa. 45 p.
        Discusses evolution of protective legislation for
        women and their rights to social security in Argentina.

1663a   International Labour Office
        1948 "The Right to Maternity Benefits in Argentina."
        ILO/R 58:1:97-98. bibl. f/notes.
        Outlines Supreme Court judgment of 1 October 1947
        which "declared that all women workers have an inviolable
        right to maternity benefit under compulsory insurance..."
        in Argentina.

1663b   _____.
        1939 "Employment of Married Women in Argentina." ILINFO
        69:1:9-10. bibl. f/notes.
        Approved by Argentine Chamber of Deputies (28 September
        1938), Bill to prevent dismissal of women workers on the
        ground of marriage is repeated from Boletín Oficial de
        la República Argentina (10 October 1938).

1664   MARTÍNEZ VIVOT, JULIO JOSÉ
        1964 Trabajo de menores y de mujeres. Estudios de
        Derecho Social, 3. Buenos Aires: Eds. Depalma. 222 p.
        bibl.
            Traces antecedents, evolution and present state of
        Argentine legislation affecting the employment of minors
        and women. Chapter 4 deals with female labor (protective
        legislation, night work, wages, time off, married women,
        etc.); 5 covers protective legislation for working
        mothers (time off for pregnancy, birth, breast-feeding;
        social security, subsidies and benefits, etc.); 6 synthe-
        sizes respective existing legislation in other Latin
        American and some European countries.

1665   SCIARRA de ARICÓ, MARÍA ANTONIETA
        1969 "Realidad social y jurídica de la mujer que trabaja."
        UNC/R 10:1/2:71-92.
            Makes observations on the social and legal reality of
        women who work, considering the Argentine case in partic-
        ular, but also briefly referring to other Latin American
        countries.

CARIBBEAN

Cuba

1666   LENS y DÍAZ, EDUARDO C.
        1948 La mujer ante el contrato de trabajo. Havana:
        Edit. Lex. 54 p. bibl.
            Analysis of women's position in Cuban labor
        legislation.

1667   "Maternity Law."
        1974 CR 4:2:15. illus.
            Reproduces law no. 1263 on the maternity of working
        women, which took effect in January 1974. Possibly the
        most far-reaching maternity law in the world, it sanc-
        tions absence from work for bearing children and provides
        optimal conditions for this function.

1668   MATTHEWS, H. FREEMAN
        1935 "Labor Code for Women in Cuba." MLS 40:1:99-100.
            Cites and explains provisions in Cuban labor code
        for women.

1669   "Protection of Women Workers in Cuba."
        1935 ILINFO 54:10:325-26; 54:11:362-63.

Law - Employment Legislation

Cites important provisions for protection of Cuban
women workers in industry and commerce in Legislative
Decree of 16 October 1934:   night work, medical examination, home work and minimum wage, health protection,
right to work, and enforcement measures. Outlines principal changes made by other Legislative Decrees in 1934
regarding employment of women before and after
childbirth.

Dominican Republic

1670   International Labour Office
       1949 "Domestic Workers in the Dominican Republic." IL/ILO
       2:7:303-04.
       Translation of Act no. 1982 adopted on 9 April 1949 in
       the Dominican Republic to replace other legislation.
       Defines domestic workers as "persons who devote them-
       selves habitually and continuously to cooking, serving,
       cleaning and other occupations connected with the home
       or other place of private residence or non-commercial
       charitable institutions . . ." Also includes treatment,
       penalties and general provisions.

HISTORY BEFORE 1900

Although revolutionary movements occurred before the 20th century and historical events have taken place in the 20th century, for facility in handling the quantity of material, the social and political history of Spanish America before 1900 constitutes the category HISTORY BEFORE 1900 and after 1900 constitutes POLITICS AND 20th CENTURY REVOLUTIONARY MOVEMENTS.

This section focuses on women's participation in Indian civilizations prior to the arrival of the Spaniards; in the conquest and colonization of America (including anecdotes about colonial life, the process of race mixing or *mestizaje*, slavery, Indian uprisings, etc.); in the movements for Independence from Spain; and in the Republican era or the 19th century. The material is thus chronologically divided into 4 historical periods: pre-Conquest times (before the 16th century); the Conquest and colonial period (roughly 16th through 18th centuries); Independence era (roughly the first quarter of the 19th century); and the 19th century, when most of the colonies became Latin American republics. A fifth sub-category, General, is comprised of those items which consider women in two or more historical periods.

Although it is a notorious fact that many women have become historically famous as a result of their relationship with a male public figure (lover, husband, father, brother, or son) and that more attention is focused on the man's achievement than on the women's activities, at least the names of some of those women have come down to us while the majority remain anonymous. Therefore, for the most part, information on such women as the wives of viceroys and presidents is included in this section. Manuela Sáenz, infamous for her illicit affair with Simón Bolívar, as well as admired for her revolutionary spirit and action during the struggle for independence, is included here rather than in BIOGRAPHY AND AUTOBIOGRAPHY. Although her activities carried her to several countries, entries on her life can be found under Ecuador, where she was born. Because there are five or more items on Manuela Sáenz, and two Colombian Independence heroines (Policarpa Salavarrieta and Antonia Santos Plata), they are listed separately after general works on Ecuador and Colombia respectively.

435

WOMEN IN SPANISH AMERICA

Women's involvement in public life, particularly in the 19th century, through charitable organizations and other institutions of social welfare, such as the Sociedad de Beneficencia de Buenos Aires, is considered in the HISTORY BEFORE 1900 category. After 1900 such items are considered in POLITICS AND 20th CENTURY REVOLUTIONARY MOVEMENT.

Unfortunately, there is a tendency in many publications of this section to be *homenajes* more than strictly factual accounts, to describe individual heroines and upper class women than women as a collective or generic force of different socioeconomic groups. In the Spanish American literature, paeans to self-sacrifice--that ultimate of female virtues called *abnegación* (e.g., losing one's sons or other male kin for the cause of independence) abound while descriptions of women's active involvement (e.g., manufacturing cannon fodder, setting up first aid stations, sewing uniforms, relaying message, securing provisions, spying, and even fighting) are often wanting.[1]

Although not American-born, Eliza Lynch and Empress Carlotta are included in the HISTORY BEFORE 1900 section because their role in Spanish American political life warrants it. For women associated with such prominent men as O'Higgins, Hostos, Sarmiento, and Portales, see BIOGRAPHY AND AUTOBIOGRAPHY. Other historical figures, such as la Quintrala, la Güera Rodríguez, and La Perricholi, are located in BIOGRAPHY AND AUTOBIOGRAPHY and THE ARTS respectively.

For publications on the colonial family, see MARRIAGE AND THE FAMILY; on women's legal status during the colonial period, see LAW; on educational and religious activities of women during the colonial and Republican eras and the State's part in institutions which fostered them, see EDUCATION and MAGIC, RELIGION, AND RITUAL; on women's cultural or literary activities before the 20th century, see LITERATURE, MASS MEDIA AND FOLKLORE.

---

[1] For a discussion of the treatment of women in the historiography of Latin America, see Asunción Lavrín's "Historia y mujeres en América Latina" (item 1673) and Louisa Hoberman's "Hispanic American Women as Portrayed in the Historical Literature: Type or Archetypes?" (item 1672).

SPANISH AMERICA - GENERAL

1671 BLOMBERG, HÉCTOR PEDRO
1933 Mujeres en la historia americana. B.A.: Librerías
Anaconda. 264 p.
Collection of 36 vignettes of Indian, Spanish and Latin
American women noteworthy for their literary, religious,
heroic, charitable or romantic deeds from the Conquest
through the 19c. Also includes 7 sketches of female
protagonists in novels and an appendix covering women
during Rosas' reign in Argentina. Legendary quality of
some accounts and lack of proper citation make the information suspect.

1672 HOBERMAN, LOUISA S.
1974 "Hispanic American Women as Portrayed in the Historical Literature: Type or Archetypes?" RI 4:2:136-47.
bibl. f/notes.
Good overview of the portrayal of Hispanic American
women in Spanish language sources on the colonial period,
Independence era and the 19c. Concludes that a diverse
group of women—from the warrior to the teacher—are
presented as strong and independent, yet they also possess qualities of femininity.

1673 LAVRÍN, ASUNCIÓN
1974 "Historia y mujeres en América Latina." BDSLM/CIDHAL
4:4:9-18.
Good summary of state of historiography on women in
LA. Suggests a collective history of all women, rather
than only portraits of unique and celebrated figures who
represented exceptions to the rule of acceptable female
behavior. Indicates new questions, sources and
approaches. Cites reasons for lack of information and
historical perspective and calls for alliance between
social sciences and history. Reviews ideal of femininity in pre-Hispanic America and Renaissance Spain and
attempts to determine the myth or reality of the resulting ideal during the colonial period.

1674 LEWIS, WILLIAM F.
1973 "Women in Hispanic History." In Women in History,
ed. by D. Shepherd, pp. 92-106. L.A.: Mankind Publishing Co. illus., ports.

History Before 1900 - General

General review of outstanding female figures in Latin
American history since the Conquest--from Doña Marina
to Manuela Saénz--based on secondary sources, but without bibliographical notes.

1675 PARRA, TERESA de la
1961 Tres conferencias inéditas. Caracas: Eds. Garrido.
158 p.
Collection of 3 lectures (Bogotá, 1930) by acclaimed
Venezuelan novelist and aristocrat in which she expresses
her impressions of women in LA from the Conquest to Independence. Divided into 3 large groups: women of the
Conquest, of the colony, and of the Independence era.
She introduces her lectures as a historical review of
female abnegation in LA and the hidden and happy influence women have exercised from the Conquest to Independence. No references, but based on her own readings of
chronicles and literature, anecdotes by family members
and personal remembrances. Considers writers, nuns,
patriots, and women in Bolivar's life for example.

1676 REDONDO, SUSANA
1952 "La mujer en la vida y en la cultura americana."
A 37:73-82.
Attempts to review women's historical and literary
participation in LA from the Conquest to the 20c.: role
of Spanish and Indian women during Conquest and colonization; social life in the colony; 17c. decadence and
Independence movement activities; woman as an inspiration
in literature and 19c. and 20c. writers. No references.

1677 RODRÍGUEZ-SOLÍS, ENRIQUE
1898 La mujer española y americana (su esclavitud, sus
luchas y dolores). Reseña histórica. Madrid: R.
Alvarez. 256 p.
Scattered references to the American woman, but basically deals with the history of women in Spain. Useful
only as background notes.

1678 VIDARRETA de TJARKS, ALICIA
1969 "Participación de la mujer en el proceso histórico
latinoamericano." UNC/R 10:1/2:153-80. bibl.
Survey of women in the history of LA from Conquest to
present times, citing notable exceptions to the norm
that women's sphere of action was confined to private
sector: Indian princess (Anacaona); governor (Isabel de
Bobadilla); translator and guide (Doña Marina); nuns
(Sor Juana, Santa Rosa); actress (Micaela Villegas);
participants in Independence movements.

MIDDLE AMERICA

Mexico

1679 GUILLÉN de NICOLAU D'OLWER, PALMA
       1956 "La mujer en la historia de México." FL 30:60/61/62:
       23-44.
         Defines four kinds of heroines in Mexico's history and
       traces their appearance and activities from the indige-
       nous women of pre-Hispanic times and the Conquest to the
       writers and philanthropists of the colonial period and
       the patriots of the Independence and 1910 revolutions.

1680 PALAVICINI, LAURA
       1960 "La mujer en la historia de México." Combate 2:13:
       47-52.
         Traces the position of women in the history and society
       of Mexico from pre-Hispanic times to the 1960's. Consid-
       ers women's activities, education, religiosity, etc.
       during distinct historical periods (e.g., Conquest,
       Porfiriato) and takes class structure into account.

1681 Partido Revolucionario Institucional (PRI)
       1953 Heroínas de México; homenaje del P.R.I. a la mujer
       mexicana. Mex., D.F. 115 p. ports.
         Sketches well known women in Mexico's history from
       colonial times to 1910 Revolution: Sor Juana, Josefa
       Ortiz de Domínguez, Manuela Taboada de Abasolo, Leona
       Vicario, Rita Pérez de Moreno, Carmen Serdán et al.

Guatemala

1682 FERNÁNDEZ HALL de ARÉVALO, TERESA
       1969 "Figuras femeninas en la historia de Guatemala."
       SGHG/A 42:1/4:324-42. illus.
         Presents several outstanding female figures in
       Guatemala's pre-Hispanic and Conquest times, beginning
       with Ixmucané, the grandmother of the Moon, and other
       women who appear in the Popol Vuh; Indian women who had
       relationships with early Spanish conquistadors; conclud-
       ing with Spanish and Creole women.

Nicaragua

1683 CORONEL URTECHO, JOSÉ and MEJÍA SÁNCHEZ, ERNESTO, eds.
       1966 "La mujer nicaragüense en los cronistas viajeros."
       RCPC 75:2-23. bibl. Also in: 1964 MIIN/NI 6:38:11-52.
       bibl.

History Before 1900 - General

Utilizing eight early chronicles and 14 19c. travel accounts (English and French), presents panorama of details on Nicaraguan women--their activities and attributes--from the 16c. to 20c. Quotes are grouped according to headings such as beauty, love and marriage, dress, work, witchcraft.

SOUTH AMERICA

Venezuela

1684 REYES, ANTONIO
1956 "Influencia de la belleza femenina en la historia y la economía venezolana." Revista Shell 5:8:58-63. illus.
Very brief sketches of Venezuelan women, from the Indian Urimare at the time of the Conquest to Josefina Revenga de Gómez during the first quarter of 20c., who were acclaimed for their physical beauty and/or participation in public life, as wives of presidents or as leaders in their own right (e.g., Aldonza Manrique). No documents or historical references cited.

Colombia

1685 DUQUE BETANCUR, FRANCISCO
1967 "La mujer en la historia de Antioquia." In his Historia del departamento de Antioquia; epócas del descubrimiento y conquista, colonia, independencia y república, pp. 1081-1101. Medellin: Asamblea Departamental de Antioquia. bibl. f/notes.
Compendium of most well-known women in Antioquia's history since the Conquest includes some biographical data and a brief review of women's education (lists schools, where and when founded). Cites distinguished women of contemporary times--professionals, benefactor, nun--as well.

Peru

1686 BEDOYA VILLACORTA, ANTOLÍN
1958 "La actuación patriótica de las mujeres peruanas en la guerra de la independencia." CEHMP/R 11:13:1-10.
Recounts female heroism in the Indian uprisings in Cuzco in 1781 and 1814 and in Independence activities during first quarter of 19c. Some documentation.

1687 CORNEJO BOURONCLE, JORGE
1949 Sangre andina: diez mujeres cuzqueñas. Cuzco:
H. G. Rozas Sucesores. 270 p.
Documents the heroic and integral participation of 8
women of Cuzco in the Inca struggle against other indigenous and Spanish groups until 1784; the controversial
story of "La Mariscala," Pancha Gamarra; and the successful entry of Trinidad M. Enríquez into the University
of Cuzco in 1875 as the first female student to study
law.

1688 MATTO de TURNER, CLORINDA
1954 Tradiciones cuzqueñas. Leyendas, biografías y
hojas sueltas. 4th ed. 2 vols. in 1. Col. de Autores
Cuzqueños, 2. Cuzco: Eds. de la Univ. Nacional del
Cuzco, Dept. de Extensión Cultural. bibl. notes.
Includes prologues and biographical notes of 1884 and
1917 editions. Collection of short pieces, which hover
between being legend and history, on Peruvian society,
especially in Cuzco, of the colonial period and early
Republican years. Based, in part, on archival and
parish documents, relates incidents involving nuns,
upper class women and Indians. Also contains short
biographies on Francisca Zubiaga de Gamarra and María
Ana Centeno de Romainville and a criticism of the deficient and superficial education for women in 19c. Peru.

1689 PALMA, RICARDO
1930-39 Tradiciones peruanas. Madrid: Espasa-Calpe.
6 vols. illus.
A mixture of history and legend comprises basis of
these chronicles or anecdotes of life in Peru during
three periods--Conquest, Viceroyship or Colony, Republic--
by celebrated 19c. Peruvian writer. First published in
4 series between 1872 and 1877, they contain many stories
of prominent as well as unknown female figures in Peru's
history. See D. Bazán Montenegro for analysis of female
characters in the Tradiciones peruanas (#291).

1690 PRIETO de ZEGARRA, JUDITH
1965 Así hicieron las mujeres del Perú. Lima: Talleres
Gráficos "E.R.V." 146 p. illus., port., bibl.
Based on archival research and secondary sources,
traces important participation of women in various
Indian uprisings of 18c., and Wars of Independence in
first quarter of 19c. Cites individual and collective
action of hundreds of women, including nuns, reproducing
letters and documents from ample bibliography.

441

WOMEN IN SPANISH AMERICA

History Before 1900 - General

1691 _____.
1965 "Contribución de las mestizas a la emancipación del Perú." L/RH 28:149-53.
Documented review of female participation in the Túpac Amaru movement, 1783 uprising in Huarochirú, 1795 protests in Pausa and Ferreñafe against viceregal decrees, Lima salons, 1814 revolt of Mateo Pumacahua, and during San Martín's epoch as economic and conspiratorial assistants. Proposes to Congreso sobre el Mestizaje (Lima, 1965) that women's contribution be included in textbooks and that their exemplary lives be recognized and publicized.

1692 PUGA, MARIO A.
1952 "La mujer en el Perú." CAM 62:2:152-74.
Moved to reveal the true position of women in past and present Peruvian society because they have been traditionally denied, misunderstood, and undervalued, discusses women's role in the Tawantinsuyo (Inca empire), colonial times, and after independence was achieved, up to participation in the Aprista movement. Documented.

Paraguay

1693 CENTURIÓN, CARLOS R.
1939 La mujer paraguaya de la historia. Asunción: Imprenta Ariel. 13 p.
Very superficially sketches women's role in Paraguay's history, from Conquest to present, paying tribute to collaboration of Indian and Creole women in forging the country. Urges that women's efforts be recognized and that female suffrage be enacted.

1694 URBIETA ROJAS, PASTOR
1962 La mujer paraguaya (esquema historiográfico). Col. Paraguay. Asunción. 81 p. illus.
Potpourri of names and anecdotes of women in the Conquest, Independence movement, War of the Triple Alliance and other wars; charity; education; and various arts and professions of Paraguay. Lacks reference notes or bibliography in order to follow up on the many women mentioned.

Chile

1695   PICÓN-SALAS, MARIANO and FELIÚ CRUZ, GUILLERMO
       1933   Imagenes de Chile. Vida y costumbres en los siglos
       XVIII y XIX a través de testimonios contemporáneos.
       Santiago: Edit. Nascimento. 339 p. plates, bibl.
          Beautifully illustrated compendium of excerpts from a
       very extensive bibliography of 18c. and 19c. travel
       accounts which comment on life and society in Chile.
       Women are mentioned throughout, but especially in the
       following items: "Araucanian Women," "Marriage Among
       the Araucanians," "Women of Chiloé," "The Colonial Cus-
       tom of Dowry," "Attire of Chilean Women Around 1822,"
       "Convent of Nuns," "Feminine Education in the Colonial
       Epoch," et al.

Argentina

1696   BERTOLÉ de CANÉ, CORA MARÍA
       1970   El amor. Buenos Aires: Ministerio de Cultura y
       Educación. 56 p. ports.
          Uses a different approach--the theme of love--in the
       history of women in Buenos Aires. Recounts episodes of
       romance: María Dávila and the conquistador Pedro de
       Mendoza; other women during the Conquest, colony and
       Independence movement; Mariquita Sánchez de Thompson;
       Camila O'Gorman; women in Sarmiento's life, et al. No
       references.

1697   DUARTE, MARÍA AMALIA
       1969   "La mujer en la historia argentina." UNC/R
       10:1/2:127-51. bibl. f/notes.
          Although it begins with Isabel de Guevara, co-founder
       of Buenos Aires, this review of women's participation in
       Argentina's history concentrates on the 19c.: the Eng-
       lish invasions and Independence movement; dress style;
       education; salons; cottage industries; journalism; the
       pampa. Offers the women in dictator Rosas' family as
       example of strong and influential women and cites Juana
       Paula Manso de Noronha, well-known educator who worked
       with Sarmiento for popular and women's education, and
       co-education. Based on secondary sources and some news-
       paper material.

1698   MEYER ARANA, ALBERTO
       1942-44   "La beneficencia en Buenos Aires." SS/A
       I,6:1/4:63-94;II,7:1/4:171-219;III,8:1/2:37-71.

History Before 1900 - General

Briefer version of his 2 volume work on charity and social work in Buenos Aires since the 16c., originally appeared as volume 3 of the General Census of the City of Buenos Aires (1909). Discusses individuals as well as organizations and institutions engaged in charitable activities, referring to both sexes. Includes some information on women's education.

1699 _____.
    1911 La caridad en Buenos Aires. Buenos Aires. 2 vols. illus., ports., bibl. notes.
    History of public and private charity works and organizations in Buenos Aires from 1535 to early 20c. Includes chapters on the Sociedad de Beneficencia, Colegio de Huérfanas, Hospital de Mujeres, and other institutions, some specifically directed at girls and women, and the many women involved in charitable activities; and some notes on women's education.

1700 SOSA de NEWTON, LILY
    1967 Las argentinas de ayer a hoy. B.A.: Librería y Edit. L. V. Zanetti. 237 p. bibl.
    Traces evolution of women's role in the history of Argentina from the Spanish women who helped found and colonize Buenos Aires to female participation in the Independence movement, women during the dictatorship of Rosas and the latter half of the 19c. Also includes individual chapters on the evolution of education for women, journalists and writers, women in the arts and sciences, and women as workers, all of which begin with the colonial period, and a chapter on the early feminist movement of the 20c. Based mostly on secondary sources, provides good synthesis, although emphasis is heavier on upper class.

1701 VILLAFAÑE CASAL, MARÍA TERESA
    1958 La mujer en la pampa (siglos XVIII y XIX). La Plata, Arg.: A. Domínguez e Hijo. 104 p. illus., plates, bibl.
    Focuses attention on the different kinds of women in the Argentine pampa of the 18c. and 19c.: women who accompanied soldiers; captive women or booty; rural women (landowners, peasants, sharecroppers); folk medicine practitioners (curanderas); mail carriers; and the schoolteacher. Uses newspapers, diaries, documents, literature and other historical materials to provide a kind of composite picture of women's lives at that time: their roles, education, attitudes toward them, etc. Includes glossary of terms referring to women.

CARIBBEAN

Puerto Rico

1702   RIVERA, RODOLFO OSVALDO
       1942   La mujer puertorriqueña.   Managua: Tipografía
       Guardián. 7 p.
       Very brief and unspecific account of women in history
       of Puerto Rico from Indians during days of Columbus to
       professionals of today, presented at "Panamerican Round
       Table."

PRE-CONQUEST

1703   ANTON, FERDINAND
       1973   Woman in Pre-Columbian America. Trans. from the
       German by M. Herzfeld, rev. by G. A. Shepperson. N.Y.:
       Abner Schram. 200 p. illus., map, plates, bibl.
       More than 100 beautiful illustrations of predominantly
       clay figures portraying women's position in pre-Columbian
       society accompany a synoptic text, based on 150 primary
       and secondary sources since the 16c. Discusses women in
       Tlatilco, Colima, Moche, Maya, Aztec and Inca civiliza-
       tions: life cycle, education, marriage, childrearing,
       clothing, food preparation, prostitution, sexual aspects
       of religion, goddesses, rulers' wives, etc. Erroneously
       assumes matriarchies existed because matrilineality was
       noted by early chroniclers.

1704   COCCA, ALDO ARMANDO
       1963   "La mujer en las culturas americanas." In his
       Ginecocracia (El gobierno de las mujeres), pp. 79-88.
       B.A.: Bibliográfica Omeba.
       Based mostly on secondary sources, discusses women's
       position in pre-Columbian cultures in Peru, Middle
       America and Argentina, but provides no convincing ex-
       planation for statement that matriarchal regime and
       gynecocratic governments existed.

1705   HELLBOM, ANNA-BRITTA
       1967   La participación cultural de las mujeres indias y
       mestizas en el México precortesiano y post-revolu-
       cionario. Monograph Series, 10. Stockholm:
       Etnografiska Museet. 304 p. illus., bibl.
       Part A, based on Sahagún's writings and Codices
       Mendoza and Florentine, provides a comprehensive, de-
       tailed overview of women's position and role in late
       pre-Hispanic Central Mexico. Covers economy, ideology,

445

History Before 1900 - Pre-Conquest

politics, social life, education, individual life cycle,
sex roles, religion, morality, domestic life, etc.
Part B is a parallel, though less ample description of
women in post-revolutionary Mexico and a comparative
evaluation of women's active cultural participation in
both epochs. Concludes that social rather than cultural
changes caused deterioration of women's position.

1706 HERNÁNDEZ, JOSÉ ALFREDO
1947 "Estancia y prestancia de la mujer peruana del
Imperio." UA/U 84:555-68. Also in: 1953 A 41:2:17-24.
Using the writings of Betanzos, Morúa, Pedro Pizarro,
el Inca Garcilaso de la Vega, and Guamán Poma, describes
the life of the royal wives of the Incas--where and how
they lived, their origins, activities, costume, education. Compares male and female wedding clothes.

1707 HERNÁNDEZ RODRÍGUEZ, ROSAURA
1965 "Las señoras reales de Tlatelolco." UNAM/ECN
5:107-14. illus., bibl.
Summarizes history of Tepanec (Azcatpotzalco)--derived
royal family which reigned in Tlatelolco during latter
part of 14c. and 15c. Includes those women who figured
importantly in creating this royal line among the Mexicas
through marriage.

1708 LEÓN-PORTILLA, MIGUEL
1958 "La mujer en la cultura náhuatl." MIIN/NI 3:21:5-13.
Also in his Siete ensayos sobre cultura náhuatl,
pp. 95-115. Ediciones Filosofía y Letras, 31. Mex.,
D.F.: UNAM, Dirección General de Publicaciones.
Examines and reproduces parts of codices, indigenous
texts and chronicles to demonstrate that condition of
women in pre-Hispanic Mexico was different than in present times. Considers esteem or appreciation of women,
ideal of femininity, and female participation in religious life. Verses in Spanish describe young girl,
adult woman, mother, old woman, healer and seamstress,
and give advice to brides.

1709 LOMELÍ QUIRARTE, JOSEFINA
1946 "Condición social de la mujer." In México pre-
hispánico: culturas, deidades, monumentos. Antología
de Esta Semana, This Week, 1935-1946, pp. 804-21.
Mex., D.F.: Edit. Emma Hurtado. illus.
Discusses the position of women in Aztec society; their
education or socialization, marriage, childbirth, religious instruction, slavery, and sacrifice. Women were
subject to a strict moral code. Appears to be based on
Sahagún.

1710 MORLEY, SYLVANUS GRISWOLD
      1956 The Ancient Maya. Rev. by G. W. Brainerd. 3rd ed.
      Stanford: Stanford Univ. Press. 494 p. illus., maps,
      tables, bibl.
         Comprehensive history of Maya civilization includes
      information on women in Chapter 10, "Life of the Common
      People" (birth, child-naming, puberty, marriage, dress,
      daily activities, sickness, death, burial, the hereafter),
      and in Chapter 11, "Religion and Deities" (goddesses,
      ceremonies). There are also notes on women as spinners
      and weavers and as participants in religious ceremonies.

1711 SOUSTELLE, JACQUES
      1962 The Daily Life of the Aztecs on the Eve of the
      Spanish Conquest. Trans. by P. O'Brian. Daily Life
      Series. N.Y.: Macmillan Co. 319 p. illus., bibl.
         Contains much information on many aspects of female
      life in Aztec society: priestesses, weavers, healers,
      midwives, goddesses, widows; position in society; mar-
      riage, adultery, divorce, polygamy; dress; education;
      childbearing, family life, etc. Based on codices and
      early histories.

1712 SPINDEN, HERBERT J.
      1933 "Indian Manuscripts of Southern Mexico; Woman's
      Position in Ancient Mexico." Annual Report of the Board
      of Regents of the Smithsonian Institution, pp. 437-439.
      illus.
         Looks at various aspects of woman's social position
      among the Olmec, Zapotec and Mixtec of southern Mexico
      in pre-columbian times as depicted in the Bodley, Selden
      and Zouche codices of England and the Vienna Codex of
      Austria: militant feminism; legality of descent through
      female line and of succession to the Throne; monogamy and
      polygamy; dynastic mating. See also preceding pages
      (pp. 434-37) on the history of princess Six Monkey, a
      woman recognized as capable in both martial and marital
      situations. Discusses question as to whether codices
      provide historical data on real beings or narrations on
      deities.

1713 THOMPSON, JOHN ERIC
      1954 The Rise and Fall of the Maya Civilization. The
      Civilization of the American Indian. Norman, Okla.:
      Univ. of Okla. Press. 287 p. illus., maps, bibl.
         Contains less information of women than Morley's study
      (#1710). References to women in daily round of activ-
      ities and marriage.

History Before 1900 - Pre-Conquest

1714   VEGA, JUAN JOSÉ
          1967 "Dos notas sobre el ciclo matriarcal en el Antiguo
          Perú." DCP/LR 31:2:281-96. bibl.
             Tries to make a case for the existence of matriarchy
          and Amazon women in ancient Peru by pulling together
          fragments from the writings of various Spanish chroni-
          clers and Indian legends or traditions. Describes belli-
          cose activities and inheritance of governmental positions
          as (unconvincing) proof.

1715   ZURITA, ALONSO de
          1963 Life and Labor in Ancient Mexico; The Brief and
          Summary Relation of the Lords of New Spain. Trans.
          and with an intro. by B. Keen. New Brunswick, N.J.:
          Rutgers Univ. Press. 328 p. illus., maps.
             Spanish *oidor* replies to list of articles sent by
          King requesting information on tribute system. Describes
          life and labor under Aztec rule and during critical
          first 50 years after the Conquest. Includes information
          on women of all classes--customs, practices, attitudes,
          marriage, childbirth, roles and conduct, divorce, etc.

CONQUEST AND COLONY

SPANISH AMERICA - GENERAL

1716   ACOSTA de SAMPER, SOLEDAD
          1957 "Las esposas de los conquistadores. Ensayo
          histórico." AHVC/B 25:108:140-54.
             To demonstrate role played by Spanish women as a
          civilizing influence in the Conquest, discusses back-
          ground and accomplishments of wives of several conquis-
          tadors (Diego Colón, Cortés, Alvarado, Valdivia,
          Robledo et al.). Based on early chronicles and secon-
          dary sources.

1717   BORGES, ANALOLA
          1972 "La mujer-pobladora en los origenes americanos."
          EEHA/AEA 29:389-444. bibl. f/notes.
             Based on chronicles and documents, outlines crucial
          collaboration of the "woman-populator" in the conquest
          of America and establishment of Hispanic-American society.
          Focuses more on common or anonymous women than on com-
          panions of celebrated male figures. Discusses reasons
          determining female emigration from Spain, activities
          during early years of conquest, importance of marriage
          and its economic aspects, difficulties of widows and

orphans, female protests against laws and officials,
elements of bravery, danger and tragedy, economic and
social problems of creole and *mestizo* women.

1718 CÁRCER y DISDIER, MARIANO de
      1953 "Las mujeres de Castilla en la conquista." In his
      Apuntes para la historia de la transculturación indo-
      española, pp. 69-91. Publicaciones del Instituto de
      Historia, Serie I, no. 28. Mex., D.F.: Instituto de
      Historia. illus., plates, bibl.
         Believes Spanish women and their contributions are
      unjustly forgotten: self-denying martyrs, founders of
      Christian homes in America, educators of children at
      home, cooks and nurses for soldiers. Cites specific
      women as well as episodes in order to honor women's
      participation in colonization of America. Other sections
      describe kitchens and dining rooms, the legend and his-
      tory of Virgin of Guadalupe, story of chocolate and
      anecdotes about women's involvement with it.

1719 DELGADO, JAIME
      1967 "La mujer en la conquista de América." In Homenaje
      a Jaime Vicens Vives, vol. 2, pp. 101-11. Barcelona:
      Univ. de Barcelona, Facultad de Filosofía y Letras.
         Considers the participation of Indian and Spanish
      women in the conquest of America, commenting on the most
      outstanding figures, especially Doña Marina. Believes
      Spanish women were motivated not only by the prospect
      of a husband or to accompany one and Spanish men joined
      with Indian women not only for physical motivation but
      also for politico-socio-economic reasons. Based on
      16c. writings.

1720 FERNÁNDEZ DURÓ, CESAREO
      1902 La mujer española en Indias. Madrid: Tipografía
      de la viuda de M. Tello. 40 p.
         One of the earliest commentaries focusing on the female
      experience in the conquest and colonization of America.
      Notes the scarcity of Spanish women in the early years
      and royal measures taken to facilitate and increase
      their emigration. Cites examples of women famous for
      special feats or accomplishments during that difficult
      time. Praises the greatness of the Spaniards in con-
      quering America and of the mothers who bore such men.

1721 GIMÉNEZ CABALLERO, ERNESTO
      1971 Las mujeres de América. Col. Ensayo. Madrid: Ed.
      Nacional. 445 p.

History Before 1900 - Conquest and Colony

        Exclamatory vindication of the rapist role of Spanish
conquistadors. Although demure with their own men,
Indian women gave themselves willingly to the Spaniards
because they knew they were engendering a new race, men
like Martí and Bolívar. Malinche's supreme destiny was
to be *mestizadora* of America. Relates tales about the
Indian princess Ñusta, Doña Marina, Lucía Miranda et al.
Of dubious historical merit.

1722   KONETZKE, RICHARD
        1946 "El mestizaje y su importancia en el desarrollo de
la población hispano-americana durante la época
colonial." IGFO/RI 7:23:7-44. bibl. f/notes.
        Well-documented discussion of early (16c.) race rela-
tions (between Spanish men and Indian women), citing
laws, attitudes and particular cases. Although sexual
relations were effected through abduction, rape, booty,
and offerings demonstrating friendship and compliance,
believes violence of the Conquest and white men's power
and authority to exploit the indigenous population were
not the only causes.

1723   _____.
        1945 "La emigración de mujeres españolas a América
durante la época colonial." RIS 9:123-50.
        An examination of Spanish laws indicates that the
Crown actually favored and encouraged emigration of
women to America, which is confirmed by figures registered in 1509-38 that show 10% of emigrating population
was female, with more single than married women. Points
out reasons for and ordinances to insure this policy.

1724   MÖRNER, MAGNUS
        1967 "The Conquest of Women." In his Race Mixture in the
History of Latin America, pp. 21-25. Boston: Little,
Brown, and Co. illus., maps, bibl.
        Views Spanish conquest of the Americas as, in a way,
the conquest of women. Discusses concubinage, intermarriage, and Church and Crown policies and laws. Illustrations include women.

1725   O'SULLIVAN - BEARE, NANCY
        1956? Las mujeres de los conquistadores; la mujer española
en los comienzos de la colonización americana (aportaciones para el estudio de la trasculturación). Madrid:
Cía. Bibliográfica Española. 383 p. illus., maps,
bibl. f/notes.

Spanish America - General

Traces the movements of Spanish women in the conquest
of America in all their activities to bring to light
the role they played in colonization, through an examination of chronicles. Limited to the 16c., study divided
according to region or province.

1726 PINTO, CARLOS
      1902 "La mujer española en Indias." DHL/R 13:397-403.
      Attempts to supplement Fernández Duró's essay on
      Spanish women in the Indies (#1720), by adding several
      names, and sources of them. Claims that Fernández Duró
      restricted his study to *virreinas*, *comendadoras* and
      generalísimas of the Pacific. Quotes letter by Ana de
      Guevara to Queen of Spain (1560) which indicates vital
      role played by women in saving Buenos Aires community
      from extinction.

1727 PITTALUGA FATTORINI, GUSTAVO
      1946 "América." In his Grandeza y servidumbre de la
      mujer. La posición de la mujer en la historia, pp. 609-
      60. B.A.: Edit. Sudamericana. bibl. notes, ports.
      Women's position in the history of America is illus-
      trated with sections on Doña Marina, Garcilaso de la
      Vega's Indian mother, the role of women in introducing
      wheat and quinine, and Mexican society during Sor Juana's
      lifetime. Uses primary and secondary sources.
      (Includes women in North America in this chapter.)
      "*Mestizaje* is, in its magnitude, an exclusive phenomenon
      of the American continent.

1728 RIVAS, RAIMUNDO
      1944 "Una virreina de Santa Fe y México nativa de Buenos
      Aires." ANH/B 17:145-59.
      Based on documents, does not pretend to reconstruct
      the biography of Juana María de Pereira y González
      (b. B.A., 1738), wife of the Viceroy of Santa Fe and
      Mexico. More details on the viceroy; it appears that
      she was a dutiful, cultured wife who did not distinguish
      herself in public life.

1729 ROSENBLAT, ANGEL
      1954 La población indígena y el mestizaje en América.
      B.A.: Ed. Nova. 2 vols. illus., plates, bibl.
      f/notes.
      Volume 2, "El mestizaje y las castas coloniales,"
      based on an extensive bibliography of primary and secon-
      dary sources, studies race mixing throughout America and
      its importance in the evolution of the population, and

History Before 1900 - Conquest and Colony

the development of a caste system (as colonial society became more structured). Informative for an understanding of women's participation in the construction of a new society.

1730 SCHURZ, WILLIAM
1954 "The Woman." In his This New World: The Civilization of Latin America, pp. 276-338. N.Y.: E. P. Dutton and Co. bibl. notes.
Compact and informative, but anecdotal chapter in general survey book covers Indian women (appearance, bearing, relationship with Spanish men) and Spanish women in the Conquest and colony (early arrivals, cultural influence, "la limeña"). Notes economic activities of women of all classes; briefly sketches 5 unusual women; cites factors weakening family structure and influencing women's status in the 20c. Based on early chronicles, travel accounts, and secondary sources.

1731 TORRE REVELLO, JOSÉ
1927 "Esclavas blancas en las Indias occidentales." UNFFL/BIIH 6:34:263-71. f/notes.
Collection of documents, located in Archivo General de Indias in Seville, referring specifically to the slave trade involving white Christian women during the early 16c. Royal cédulas reflect pro and con positions regarding shipment of these women to America. Detailed footnotes.

1732 VILLAFAÑE CASAL, MARÍA TERESA
1964 "La mujer española en la conquista y colonización de América." CH 59:175/176:125-42. bibl. notes.
Reviews laws pertaining to Spanish women in early America; briefly describes several women of the 1500's, their contributions to colonization, and heroic acts. Good notes.

1733 WEISS, SARA C.
1974 "Oh, Those Amazon Women!" R/C 6:3:11-17. illus., map.
Traces legend of Amazon women to its 16c. origins in the chronicles of early Spaniards, quoting extensively from the account of Friar Gaspar de Carvajal, who accompanied Francisco de Orellana's voyage down the Amazon. Does not believe in historical reality of an Amazon race or nation.

MIDDLE AMERICA

Mexico

1734   BENAVENTE, FRAY TORIBIO de (MOTOLINÍA)
       1951   History of the Indians of New Spain. Trans. and
       ann. with a bio-bibliographical study of the author by
       F. B. Steck. Documentary series, v. 1. Wash., D.C.:
       Academy of American Franciscan History. 358 p. illus.,
       ports., bibl.
          Although Motolinía visited America in 1524, this his-
       tory was written from 1536 to 1541. It includes obser-
       vations on Indian marriage practices, goddesses, feasts
       and sacrifices, temple women, childbirth/naming/care,
       education of girls, incidents of particularly virtuous
       women. Obvious religious bent of author.

1735   CLEMENCE, STELLA RISLEY, contributor
       1930   "Deed of Emancipation of a Negro Woman Slave, Dated
       Mexico, September 14, 1585." HAHR 10:1:51-57.
          Spanish transcription and English translation of
       notary's copy of deed emancipating black female slave,
       preceded by interpretative discussion regarding several
       claims of ownership of her by Cortés' family as well as
       by majordomo's widow in a 1585 law-suit in Mexico.

1736   DÍAZ del CASTILLO, BERNAL
       1963   The Conquest of New Spain. Trans., with an intro.
       by J. M. Cohen. Penguin Classics, L123. Baltimore, Md.:
       Penguin Books. 412 p. maps.
          Although considered the most informative--i.e., with
       respect to women's participation--of the 16c. chronicles
       recounting conquest of Mexico, it is sorely lacking in
       details of social life. On the whole, more attention
       is given to battles and horses than to women. Also
       known as Historia verdadera de la conquista de la Nueva
       España and available in many editions.

1737   FERNÁNDEZ del CASTILLO, FRANCISCO
       1920   Doña Catalina Xuárez Marcayda, primera esposa de
       Hernán Cortés y su familia. Datos tomados de la obra
       inédita Biografías de conquistadores de México y Guate-
       mala. Mex., D.F.: Imprenta Victoria. 194 p. port.,
       plates, facsims., fold. geneal. charts.
          Contains interesting notes on family members of Hernán
       Cortés' first wife, founding of convents in Mexico, and
       marriages.

History Before 1900 - Conquest and Colony

1738 ICAZA, FRANCISCO A. de
1923 Conquistadores y pobladores de Nueva España;
diccionario autobiográfico sacado de los textos
originales. Madrid: Imprenta de "El Adelantado de
Segovia." 2 vols.
Collection of self-identifying statements by men and
women who conquered and settled New Spain in 16c., based
on early chronicles and many documents. Out of 1385
items, more than 90 are women. Primary source material
on early Spanish female population.

1739 LEONARD, IRVING
1944 "Conquerors and Amazons in Mexico." HAHR 24:4:561-
79. bibl. f/notes.
Reviews appearance of persistent legend regarding war-
like Amazon women in chronicles, documents, and literature of 16c. Europe and America. Interesting but
unresolved question.

1740 LÓPEZ de MENESES, AMADA
1948 "Tecuichpochtzin, hija de Moteczuma (¿1510?-1550)."
IGFO/RI 9:31/32:471-95. facsims., bibl. f/notes.
Well-documented account of most well-known of
Moctezuma's daughters: her several marriages with Aztec
princes and Spanish soldiers, her affair with Cortés and
their daughter Leonor, her other children, her struggle
to retrieve ownership of Tacuba and Crown's decrees
related to it, her last will and testament. Other women
also cited in way of explanation. Important as an
example of the civil and economic situation as well as
scarcity of women right after the Conquest. Includes
genealogical data.

1741 MARSHALL, C. E.
1939 "The Birth of the Mestizo in New Spain." HAHR 19:
2:161-84. bibl. f/notes.
Well-documented article contains information about
women and their role in race mixing during colonization
process. Cites laws which influenced number of women in
New Spain, mixed unions, and socio-economic factors
contributing to mixed population. Intermarriage with
indigenous population was seconded by Church and Crown.

1742 NÚÑEZ ORTEGA, ANGEL
1885 "Virreinas de Nueva España." In his Varios papeles
sobre cosas de México, pp. 211-15. Brussels. Also in:
Revista Nacional de Letras y Ciencias 2(1889):494-96.
Lists names of vicereines and consorts of viceroys of
New Spain, including 2 wives of Cortés (41 women in all).

1743   NÚÑEZ y DOMÍNGUEZ, JOSÉ de JESÚS
      1950 La virreina mexicana, dona María Francisca de la
      Gándara de Calleja. Mex., D.F.: Imprenta Universitaria.
      399 p. illus., ports., coats of arms, facsims., fold.
      plan, bibl.
        Biography of one of the few Mexican-born vicereines,
      Maria Francisca de la Gándara de Calleja, concentrates
      mostly on the viceroy. Her role was as lady of the
      house. Prologue notes other wives of New Spain's
      viceroys. Documented.

1744   O'CROULEY, PEDRO ALONSO
      1972 A Description of the Kingdom of New Spain, 1774.
      Trans. and ed. by S. Galvin. San Francisco: John
      Howell. 148 p. illus., plates.
        Beautifully illustrated description of New Spain in
      latter half of 18c. Color plates depicting racial mix-
      tures and classes of Indians are useful for observing
      dress and hair styles, and male and female activities.
      Scattered references to women throughout: marriage
      ceremony, modes of dress, fecundity, tasks, child-
      carrying, etc. One chapter devoted to history of Virgin
      of Guadalupe.

1745   ORTEGA MARTÍNEZ, ANA MARÍA
      1945 Mujeres españolas en la conquista de México. Mex.,
      D.F.: Imprimio Vargas Rea. 63 p. bibl. f/notes.
        Succinct essay brings to light those Spanish women who
      participated in conquest and colonization of New Spain
      in early 16c. (1519-40), using chronicles, Columbus'
      letters, and other documents. Briefly sketches 10 and
      mentions others.

1746   ROMERO de TERREROS y VINENT, MANUEL
      1919 Ex antiquis: bocetos de la vida social en la Nueva
      España. Guadalajara: Eds. Jaime. 248 p. ports.
      Also: Mex., D.F.: Edit. Porrua, 1944.
        Interesting comments on social life and customs in
      New Spain from 1540 to 1810. Section one contains 13
      vignettes of vicereines.

1747   SALAS, ALBERTO M.
      1958 "Crónica del mestizaje en Yucatán y la Nueva España."
      CAM 101:6:141-72.
        Race mixing in Yucatán began with survivors--Jerónimo
      de Aguilar and Gonzalo Guerrero--from Valdivia's cara-
      velle on its way to Santo Domingo. Quotes descriptions
      of Indian women (general appearance and demeanor, dress,

History Before 1900 - Conquest and Colony

education). Ordered and official gift-giving of women
to Spaniards ended brutally with the Noche Triste; thereafter, rape, slavery and liberal procreation ensued.
Indigenous women served as decisive element of agreement
and unification between two cultures. Well-documented.

1748 VALLE-ARIZPE, ARTEMIO de
1933 Virreyes y virreinas de la Nueva España. Primera
serie y segunda serie. Leyendas, tradiciones, y
sucedidos del México virreinal. Madrid: Biblioteca
Nueva. 2 vols.
Collection of anecdotes about life and people in
colonial Mexico (1540-1810) includes stories about
several vicereines as well as other women.

Doña Marina

1749 BENÍTEZ, FERNANDO
1952 "The Story of a Girl Slave Who Wished to End Her
Slavery." In his In the Footsteps of Cortés, pp. 89-97.
N.Y.: Pantheon Books.
Brief, almost melodramatic account of Doña Marina,
Cortes' interpreter, diplomat and lover during Conquest.
Remarks on exaggerated emphasis on her symbolic role as
traitor, from which term malinchismo was derived, and
considers her instead an instrument of fate. Her personal tragedy was one of remaining a slave despite her
important contributions. No references. Translated
from La Ruta de Hernán Cortés.

1750 DEL CASTILLO, ADELAIDA R.
1974 "Malintzin Tenépal: A Preliminary Look into a New
Perspective." EF 1:2:58-78. bibl.
Believes negative portrayal of Doña Marina in history
of Mexico is due to misinterpretation of her role and
misogynistic attitude. Interprets her role as one of
faith in a supernatural force and commitment to spiritual
obligations. Considers Quetzalcoatl; Aztec religion;
political environment of Aztec empire at time of Conquest; condition of Indian peoples under Aztec rule;
Marina's personal life, actions in Conquest, and motivations. Epilogue discusses Octavio Paz' position on
la Malinche and la Chingada. Based on secondary sources
and 16c. chronicles.

1751   GARCÍA ICAZBALCETA, JOAQUÍN
        1942 "Doña Marina." In his Opúsculos y biografías,
        pp. 67-73. Biblioteca del Estudiante Universitario, 38.
        Mex., D.F.: Eds. de la Univ. Nacional Autónoma.
           Renowned Mexican historian discusses several disputed
        points about Doña Marina, important aid and translator
        to Cortés, particularly her origins and her name. Based
        on early chronicles and secondary sources.

1752   GARCÍA SOMONTE, MARIANO
        1969 Doña Marina, "La Malinche". Mex., D.F.: EDIMEX,
        202 p. illus., plates, bibl.
           Based on extensive bibliography of primary and secon-
        dary sources, including archival research, details Doña
        Marina's important participation in the conquest of
        Mexico and the little known about her personal life.
        Believes she was not a traitor to her people.

1753   GÓMEZ de OROZCO, FEDERICO
        1942 Doña Marina, la dama de la Conquista. Vidas
        Mexicanas, 2. Mex., D.F.: Eds. Xochitl. 190 p.
        bibl. notes.
           Biography of Doña Marina, the Indian woman who aided
        Cortés in the conquest of Mexico, reads almost like a
        novel.

1754   GONZÁLEZ RUIZ, FELIPE
        1945 Doña Marina (la india que amó a Cortés). 2nd ed.
        Col. Ariadne. Serie I. Biografías, Epistolario,
        Anecdotario, no. 6. Madrid: Eds. Morata. 231 p.
           An account of Doña Marina's life and important parti-
        cipation in the conquest of Mexico. Believes it is
        absurd to reproach her efforts as collaboration in the
        destruction of her race. No bibliography or notes but
        cites early chronicles.

1755   KRÜGER, HILDE
        1948 Malinche; or, Farewell to Myths. Trans. by the
        author. N.Y.: Arrowhead Press Books for Storm Publish-
        ers. 103 p. front., bibl. Spanish original: 1944
        Malinche; o el adiós a los mitos. Mex., D.F.: Ed.
        Cultura. 91 p.
           Using early chronicles and secondary sources, a non-
        historian portrays Doña Marina as an extraordinary per-
        sonality and considers the figure of Malinche the last
        myth of the Aztecs, gone with the demise of their empire.

History Before 1900 - Conquest and Colony

1756 MENÉNDEZ, MIGUEL ANGEL
      1964 Malintzín en un fuste, seis rostros y una sola
      máscara. Populibros "La Prensa," 60. Mex., D.F.:
      "La Prensa." 228 p. bibl.
      Challenges Bernal Díaz' account of Doña Marina's
      origin by explaining slavery in pre-Cortesian times.
      Investigates her history through 6 names or identities
      by which she is known: Malin, Malina or Malinalli;
      Malinalli Tenepal; Marina la Lengua; Marina la de Cortés;
      Malintzin; Doña Marina de Jaramillo. Concludes with
      Malinche, name used to refer to deception and disillu-
      sionment experienced as a result of her complicity in
      Conquest. *Malinchismo* means total submission of the
      intimate essence of one's nationality to a foreigner.

1757 RODRÍGUEZ, GUSTAVO A.
      1935 Doña Marina. Mex., D.F.: Imprenta de la Secretaría
      de Relaciones Exteriores. 75 p. illus., plates, ports.,
      geneal. table, bibl.
      Prologue claims this version of Doña Marina's story is
      the most documented and complete to date (1935) because
      author studied Náhuatl and archeology in addition to
      history for data. Investigates her name, birthplace,
      life before Conquest and after seige of Tenochtitlán,
      legend surrounding her after death, geographical places
      named after her. Includes genealogy of her descendents
      with Cortés.

1758 ROMERO, RAMÓN
      1954 "Doña Marina, la gran señora de América." MIIN/NI
      2:3:5-17. port.
      Brief account of Doña Marina and her role in the con-
      quest of Mexico, based mostly on Bernal Díaz' account
      (#1736).

1759 SECO, CARLOS
      1948 "Doña Marina a través de los cronistas." IGFO/RI
      9:31/32:497-504. bibl. f/notes.
      Portrait of Doña Marina, Cortés' invaluable guide and
      interpreter during Spanish conquest of Mexico, based on
      16c. chronicles. Presents varying statements regarding
      her origin, name, relationship with Cortés, and marriage
      to one of his soldiers.

Guatemala

1760 RECINOS, ADRIÁN
      1958 "Doña Leonor de Alvarado, hija del primer gobernador
      de Guatemala." In her Doña Leonor de Alvarado y otros
      estudios, pp. 9-58. Univ. de San Carlos de Guatemala,
      Edit. Universitaria, 25. Guatemala: Edit. Universitaria.
      bibl. f/notes.
         Corrects errors of José Milla's historical novel, La
      hija del Adelantado, with historical details based on
      documents and chronicles. Daughter of Pedro de Alvarado
      (Governor and Captain General of Guatemala) and Tlaxcalan
      princess baptized Luisa, Doña Leonor was born in
      Guatemala in 1524, marries Pedro Portocarrero (Spanish
      official and later mayor of capital of Guatemala),
      becomes a widow, marries Francisco de la Cueva, and dies
      in 1584.

1761 _____.
      1958 "Dona María de Horozco, dama de doña Beatriz de la
      Cueva." In her Doña Leonor de Alvarado y otros
      estudios, pp. 79-97. Univ. de San Carlos de Guatemala,
      Edit. Universitaria, 25. Guatemala: Edit. Universi-
      taria. illus., plate.
         Beatriz de la Cueva (wife of Pedro de Alvarado, Gover-
      nor and Captain General of Guatemala) brought 20 young
      women of noble Spanish families to Guatemala. During
      a stop in Santo Domingo (1539), María de Horozco and
      Columbus' grandson Luis fell in love. Recounts details
      of incipient romance, obstacles to marriage, and later
      developments. View Luis Colón as capricious man who
      could give rein to his desires once his mother died,
      and María de Horozco as a woman of her times--i.e.,
      resigned to do the will of others. Cites documents pub-
      lished in Otto Schoenrich's The Legacy of Christopher
      Columbus.

Honduras

1762 "Auto."
      1956 SGHH/R 34:10/11/12:25.
         Reproduces document in which Mayor of Tegucigalpa
      demands that a runaway mulatto woman be returned to her
      mistress, in 1678.

History Before 1900 - Conquest and Colony

Nicaragua

1763   BONHAM, MILLEDGE L., JR.
        1934 "A Trio of American Heroines." PAU/B 68:10:708-711.
        Includes brief notes on Rafaela Herrera y Urdiate's
        heroic defense of the Castillo de la Purísma Concepción,
        on the San Juan River in Nicaragua, against the English
        in 1762.

1764   "Documentos relativos a la heroína doña Rafaela de Herrera y
        Sotomayor."
        1945 NAGH/R 7:2:1-21.
        Reproduces documents (1780-1907) located in Spanish
        and Costa Rican archives regarding Rafaela de Herrera
        y Sotomayor: filiation; heroic deeds (operating cannon
        at Castillo de S. Juan de Nicaragua in 1764 in service
        of Spanish king against England); poverty as a widow;
        royal decree granting her a pension; property and
        inheritance.

1765   PALMA MARTÍNEZ, ILDEFONSO
        1948 Rafaela de Herrera o la Niña de Nicaragua. Managua:
        Edit. La Nueva Prensa. 62 p. illus., bibl.
        Using historical sources, presents novelized version
        of the heroine who helped defend the Castillo de la
        Purísima Concepción against the English in 1764 when
        they were at war with Spain. Related documents from
        Archivo General de Indias are reproduced in appendix.

1766   PASOS, JOAQUÍN
        1968 "Origen e interpretación de la mujer nicaragüense."
        RCPC 90:54-57.
        Nacaraguan poet discusses María de Peñalosa, daughter
        of governor Pedrarias Dávila, as exemplary Nicaraguan
        woman of colonial era because of two essential qualities
        as the basis of her personality: "cleanliness of soul"
        (religious conviction) and "cleanliness of blood" (lack
        of racial mixing).

1767   SALVATIERRA, SOFONÍAS
        1937 "La Costa de los Mosquitos. Episodio de doña María
        Manuela Rodríguez." NAGH/R 2:2:105-29.
        Documented narrative relates curious episode in history
        of Indian/Spanish/English relations in late 18c.
        Nicaragua: María Manuela Rodríguez, a 10-year-old girl,
        was taken prisoner (1782) from Juigalpa by Meskito chief
        Yarrincee and added to his collection of women. Charts
        her life among Indians and attempts to subdue them by
        marrying a chief. She escapes with a friar in 1789.

South America - Colombia

Panama

1768   CASTILLERO R., ERNESTO J.
       1937 "La viuda de Balboa y su trágico destino. (Carta
       de Don Ernesto J. Castillero R. al Director del 'Bole-
       tín')." APH/B 5:14:395-402.
          Corrects erroneous statements made by Máximo Soto Hall
       in no. 12 of the Boletín regarding daughter of Pedrarias
       Dávila in early 16c.

SOUTH AMERICA

Venezuela

1769   ACOSTA SAIGNES, MIGUEL
       1967 Vida de los esclavos negros en Venezuela. Caracas:
       Hesperides. 410 p. illus., fold. maps, bibl.
          Documented social history on all aspects of the life of
       black slaves in Venezuela from 16c. to 18c. based on
       archival research. Women figure throughout, but espe-
       cially in chapters on domestics (work activities, inter-
       racial sexual relations, witchcraft) and on marriage
       (objections and obstacles, legal disputes). Extensive
       bibliography on slavery in LA.

1770   MACHADO de ARNAÒ, LUZ
       1962 "Doña Isabel Manrique: primera gobernadora de la
       provincia venezolana." VANH/B 45:180:567-71. bibl.
          Based on various chronicles of conquest and coloniza-
       tion period, refers to first woman who governed the
       province of Venezuela during 1st 3rd of 16c.--Isabel
       Manrique, wife of Marcelo de Villalobos, 1st oidor,
       fiscal and president of audiencia of Santo Domingo;
       Isabel, her daughter Aldonza, and granddaughter Marcela
       inherited title to continue governing.

Colombia

1771   ACOSTA de SAMPER, SOLEDAD
       1892 "La mujer española en Santafé de Bogotá." ESMO 4:
       40:161-68.
          Brief but informative notes on women in the conquest
       and colonization of Colombia, based on 16c. and 17c.
       chronicles. Names and provides some biographical data
       on early Spanish women settlers and recounts several
       incidents of violence committed against women by their

History Before 1900 - Conquest and Colony

husbands or brothers for capricious reasons. Some women
knew how to read: they instructed their own children
and others'. Some helped to found convents (e.g., La
Concepción, 1593).

1772 ARCINIEGAS, GERMÁN
1937 "La fronda genealógica." In his América, tierra
firme; sociología, pp. 143-66. Santiago: Eds. Ercilla.
Based on secondary sources, offers a series of 8 anecdotes about women in colonial Colombia: ill-fated
romances, scandals, business dealings of a governor's
wife, Lebrón's expedition from Santa Marta to Santa Fe
de Bogota, predictions of Juana García, a black woman
called witch.

1773 CARVAJAL, MARÍA de
1932 "Una carta de la viuda de Jorge Robledo al Rey."
HA/B 19:224:639-40.
Reproduces letter (Tunja, 10 December 1547) from María
de Carvajal to the Spanish king, requesting the return
of her usurped estates because she was afflicted with
debts which her husband, killed by Benalcazar, incurred
while a marshal in the King's service.

1774 CORTÉS ALONSO, VICENTA
1967 "Los esclavos domésticos en América." EEHA/AEA 24:
955-83. bibl. f/notes, plates.
Based on archival research names and describes the
origins, conditions, activities, and goods of the
slaves (mostly female) owned by renowned chronicler Juan
de Castellanos who lived in Tunja, Colombia during the
16c.

1775 HERNÁNDEZ de ALBA, GUILLERMO
1938 "Mujeres en la colonia." In his Estampas santa-
fereñas, pp. 1-27. Bogota: Edit. ABC. illus., bibl.
Potpourri of notes about women in Nueva Granada from
the Conquest to Independence: women of various Indian
groups; Spanish women in the 1540 expedition of
Jerónimo Lebrón; scandals of Santa Fe; founding of convents and convent school, Colegio de la Enseñanza
(1771), and more. Bibliography indicates archival
research, but Argentine historian Furlong disputes accuracy of accounts.

1776 _____.
1933 "La mujer santafareña en la colonia." Registro
Municipal 53:22:719-26. illus., ports.

Quoting Juan de Castellanos and others, provides superficial and exclamatory picture of women in Colombia
during the colonial period, from the Indian women who
related to the Spaniards during the Conquest to María
Clemencia Caycedo who founded the first school for girls
in Bogota, Colegio de la Enseñanza, in the 18c.

1777   OTERO MUÑOZ, GUSTAVO
        1936   "Figures femeninas de la colonia." Conferencias de
        la Academia Colombiana de Historia, pp. 79-111. Bogota:
        Academia Colombiana de Historia.   bibl.   f/notes.
            Based on secondary sources, this potpourri of notes on
        women during colonial times begins with anecdotes on
        several notable women of 16c. New Granada (Dorotea
        Zequeira, María de Carvajal, the Indian Catalina); gives
        a fictional account of Catalina de Erauso, the Nun-
        Ensign; discusses 3 literary nuns (Sor Juana, Sor Ursula
        Suárez, and la Madre Castillo); and considers the estab-
        lishment of 1st educational center for women in Bogota,
        La Enseñanza (1782), especially its second prioress,
        Madre Petronila Cuéllar and her writings.

1778   POSADA, EDUARDO
        1909   "Apostillas."   HA/B 5:55:371-72.
            Reprinted from El Nuevo Tiempo, corrects statements
        about Spanish women in New Kingdom of Granada: Isabel
        Romero, first Spanish woman there, was the wife of
        Francisco, not Juan, Lorenzo, both of whom arrived in
        the Lebrón (others say Lugo) expedition of 1540;
        Eloísa, not Elvira, Gutiérrez was first woman to make
        wheat bread in Santa Fe de Bogota.   Refers to Padre
        Simón, Castellanos, Groot, Piedrahita.

1779   RESTREPO SÁENZ, JOSÉ MARÍA
        1959   "Ni marichuelas ni mari-chulas (apuntes insignifi-
        cantes)."   HA/B 46:531/533:133-36.
            Explores data on women mentioned in novel by Viceroy
        Solís as inheritors in the heroine's will.   Documents
        attest to existence of María Josefa de la Cueva y Ospina
        and Petronila de Ospina.   Archival research yielded
        documents relating to a litigation (1780) resulting
        from their being vulgarly called marichuelas; they were
        mulatas.   Other documents reveal that additional quarrels
        took place earlier about similar namecalling because of
        color.   Points out that term was maruchuela and not
        marichuela.

History Before 1900 - Conquest and Colony

1780 ____.
1914 "El virrey Amar y su esposa." HA/B 9:104:451-70.
Includes very brief but documented sketch of Francisca
Villanova y Marco, wife of Viceroy Amar. Quotes one of
her letters (1812).

1781 RIVAS, RAIMUNDO
1920 "Amores de Solís." HA/B 12:143:660-84. ports.
Attempts to uncover mystery surrounding woman whose
name (la Marichuela) was linked to Viceroy Solís of New
Granada during second half of 18c.: her real name (María
Lugarda de Ospina), how they may have met, problems he
had as a result, her life and education in Real Convento
de las Clarisas and why she left it and was subsequently
exiled to Usme. Includes correspondence. Nothing con-
clusive because of lack of documents.

1782 ROJAS GÓMEZ, ROBERTO
1926 "La esclavitud en Colombia." In his Marieta, Jesús
Nazareno . . ., pp. 271-306. Bogota: Aguila Negra Edit.
Reproducing documents from Colombia's National Archive,
presents a portrait of the suffering of slaves in New
Granada from the 16c. to 1805, with equal space devoted
to female slaves and slaveholders: cruelty and punishment, branding, infanticide, separation of families,
attempts at freedom.

1783 ROMERO, MARIO GERMÁN
1963 "Mujeres indias de don Joan de Castellanos." BCB 6:
10:1509-16. bibl.
Analyzes verses of 16c. chronicler Castellanos for
information on the multiple role of Indian women as
interpreter, spy, servant, soldier and companion of the
Spanish conquistadors. Cites particular incidents and
Indian women.

1784 ____.
1962 "Mujeres españolas de la conquista en don Joan de
Castellanos." BCB I, 5:10:1293-1304; II, 5:11:1432-45.
bibl. notes.
Analyzes the verses of 16c. chronicler Castellanos
for information on the participation of Spanish women in
the Conquest. Names specific women and describes in
detail Inés de Atienza and the celebrated expedition
in search of El Dorado. Also mentions second category
of women during this epoch--solteras or single women--
citing specific examples. Documented.

1785 VELÁSQUEZ, ROGERIO
1962 "La Gaitana del pacífico." BCB 5:3:285-87. bibl.
f/notes.
Deals with the conquest of the Pacific part of Colombia by Payo Romero, against whom a successful resistance movement was organized by the mother of Tama, the *cacique* who ruled Guapí to Buenaventura. Compares her to la Gaitana of Tolima and the black woman of the Independence movement, María Antonia Ruíz. Documented.

Ecuador

1786 PHELAN, JOHN LEDDY
1967 "The Sinners and the Saint." In his The Kingdom of Quito in the Seventeenth Century; Bureaucratic Politics in the Spanish Empire, pp. 117-95. Madison, Wis.: Univ. of Wis. Press. bibl. notes.
Describes moral climate or "baroque Catholicism" of 17c. Quito. Contrasts licentious sexual conduct of its chief magistrate, Antonio Morga, with saintly charitable life of Mariana de Jesús. Portrait of license and scandal among upper-class Spaniards and creoles based on archival research and secondary sources.

Peru

1787 BOWSER, FREDERICK
1974 The African Slave in Colonial Peru, 1524-1650.
Stanford: Stanford Univ. Press. 439 p. illus.,
tables, bibl.
Well-documented history of black slavery in Peru during early colonial period based on extensive archival research. Women do not appear in a separate section but are considered throughout. Includes much data on women as slaves and slaveholders and as manumitted persons; race relations among Spanish, Indian and blacks; occupational activities; population figures; marriage and family life.

1788 BROMLEY SEMINARIO, JUAN
1957-58 "Virreinas del Perú." L/RH 23:64-84.
Based mostly on secondary sources, provides brief notes on the 14 (out of 22) vicereines who went to Peru with their husbands, the viceroys, and on the 8 who remained in Spain. Also comments on widower viceroys and lists those who were bachelors and ecclesiastics.

History Before 1900 - Conquest and Colony

1789 _____.

1955-56 "El Capitán Martín de Estete y doña María de Escobar 'La Romana', fundadores de la Villa de Trujillo del Perú." L/RH 22:122-41.

María de Escobar and her first husband, Martín de Estete, accompanied Pedrarias Dávila and his wife, María de Bobadilla y Peñaloza, on the 1514 voyage to Darien. They also joined Pedro de Alvarado's difficult and tragic 1534 expedition to Ecuador and Peru, of which she was one of few female survivors. Together, he as Lieutenant Governor of the Chimú region, they founded Trujillo, next to Chanchán. Among Gonzalo Pizarro and his men she was called "the Roman" for her strong spirit and action. She was also considered introducer of wheat into Peru and coauthor of a 1544 rebellion against Peru's first viceroy, Blasco Núñez de Vela. After her third marriage, she died childless in 1576. Cites no references, but appears to be documented.

1790 BUSTO DUTHURBURU, JOSÉ ANTONIO del

1965 "Una huérfana mestiza: la hija de Juan Pizarro." L/RH 28:103-06. bibl. notes.

Based on archival sources, provides data on the Inca noblewoman, Ynquil Coya, whom Juan Pizarro kidnapped and hid from Manco Inca in Cuzco in 1535. They had a daughter, Francisca, who even after Pizarro's death was recognized as such and attended to by Spanish and Indian relatives. Although her mother remarried, she remained single until death.

1791 _____.

1965 "La mestiza del Capitán Hernando de Soto, su familia y los lienzos del Virrey Toledo." L/RH 28:113-17. bibl. f/notes.

Provides biographical data on Leonor Tocto Chimbo, Inca princess with whom Hernando de Soto lived in Cuzco and Lima (1536) and on their daughter, Leonor de Soto, who was raised in the home of well-known Spanish matron María de Escobar when de Soto left for Florida and who married García Carrillo, a Spaniard with whom she had 5 children. Based on archival sources.

1792 _____.

1965 "La primera generación mestiza del Perú y una causa de su mal renombre." L/RH 28:67-79. bibl. f/notes.

Psychosociological portrait of first generation of Peruvian *mestizos*, born of Spanish soldier fathers and Indian mothers. Interesting picture of the Indian mother--raped or seduced, weaving, heartwarming, uncultured, giving, affectionate, etc.

1793   DESCOLA, JEAN
         1968   Daily Life in Colonial Peru, 1710-1820.   Trans. from
         the French by M. Heron.   N.Y.:   Macmillan.   273 p.
         illus., maps, bibl.
         Potpourri of information on life in colonial Peru,
         especially in 18c. Lima.   Part 3 covers stages of life,
         illegitimate children, family life, socialization of
         girls, marriage, hygiene and disease (e.g., venereal and
         cancerous), food preparation and sale, clothing, coif-
         fures and perfumes, and "gallantry" (from flirting to
         concubinage).   Part 4, on civic, economic and cultural
         life, includes some information on conventual life.
         Concludes with story of Micaela Villegas--la Perricholi--
         actress/mistress of Viceroy Amat.   Based on travel ac-
         counts and secondary sources.

1794   HARTH-TERRÉ, EMILIO
         1973   Negros e indios.   Un estamento social ignorado del
         Perú colonial.   Lima: Librería-Edit.   Juan Mejía Baca.
         171 p.   bibl.   f/notes.
         Archival investigation demonstrates an unusual aspect
         of black slavery--its practice by the Indian community--
         during Peru's viceregal period.   Cites many cases of
         Indian women as slave owners and of black women as slaves
         throughout text.   Includes a chapter on interracial sex
         relations.

1795   _____.
         1965   "El mestizaje y la miscegenación en los primeros años
         de la fundación de Lima."   L/RH 28:132-44.
         Examines and interprets First Book of Baptisms from the
         Archive of the Sagrario of the Cathedral of Lima
         (1538-48) as a document which attests to immediate eth-
         nic integration in Lima.   Looks at terms used to denomi-
         nate mother (and father) of the child, indicating ethnic
         identity and kind of relationship between the parents,
         geographical origin, whether slave or not, etc.   Cites
         specific examples.   Appendices indicate number of bap-
         tismal documents according to ethnic identity and list
         Spanish surnames of fathers of *mestizo* children.

1796   LOCKHART, JAMES
         1968   "Spanish Women and the Second Generation."   In his
         Spanish Peru, 1532-1560:   A Colonial Society, pp. 150-70.
         Madison, Wis.:   Univ. of Wis. Press.   bibl.
         Based on archival and secondary sources, attempts to
         determine number of Spanish women in Peru in 16c. and
         describes variety in their social status.   Notes impor-
         tance of family and regional ties, emphasizing marriage,

History Before 1900 - Conquest and Colony

and significant and influential role of *encomenderos'*
wives in the social and economic continuity of colonial
society. Discusses *mestizo* children and women's economic
activities (property ownership, prostitution, midwifery,
innkeeping, food preparation, etc.). Sees Spanish women's greatest contribution in their cultural influence
exerted on the urban population and in their responsibility for the existence of a second Spanish generation.

1797   Mártires y heroínas (Documentos inéditos del año de 1780 a 1782)
       1945   Intro., additions, notes and comments by F. A. Loayza.
       Los Pequeños Grandes Libros de Historia Americana, serie
       I, tomo IX. Lima: Librería e Imprenta D. Miranda.
       205 p. illus.
       Reproduces unpublished documents (including much cor-
       respondence), from the Archivo General de Indias in
       Seville, concerning 3 women who instigated and abetted
       the last Inca uprising (1780-83). For their insurrec-
       tionist activities, Cecilia Túpac Amaru and Micaela
       Bastidas, sister and wife respectively of José Gabriel
       Túpac Amaru, and Tomasa Titu Condemayta, *cacique* of
       Arocos, were whipped and/or condemned to death.

1798   MIRÓ QUESADA, AURELIO
       1965   "Ideas y proceso del mestizaje en el Perú." L/RH
       28:9-23.
       Introduction to collection of papers presented at the
       Congreso sobre el Mestizaje (Lima, 1965) discusses race
       mixing in America since 1492; laws affecting marriage
       between Indian women and Spanish men in 16c.; race mix-
       ing in Peru mentioning several such unions) from colo-
       nial times to the present, citing restrictions, attitudes,
       legislation and census data with respect to *mestizo*
       population.

1798a NOGUERA V., ARMANDO
       1971   "Micaela Bastidas Puyucahua." CEHMP/R 19:186-90.
       According to Historical Abstracts 20A (1974):2037,
       deals with "Micaela Bastidas de Condorcanqui, heroine
       of Peruvian independence, and wife and collaborator of
       the *cacique* Tupac Amaru (pseud. José Gabriel Condorcanqui)
       She was executed with her husband and sons in 1871."

1799   PITTALUGA, GUSTAVO
       1946   "Las mujeres, el trigo y la quina." REVA 6:16:77-80.
       The planting of wheat, whose first harvest in America
       took place in Lima, is attributed to María de Escobar or
       Inés Muñoz de Alcántara in 1535, depending on which
       chronicler one reads. It was also a woman, the Countess

of Chinchón, who came upon quinine, a substance the
Indians would not give the Spaniards. Linné named the
Peruvian tree Chinchona after her.

1800   ROMERO, CARLOS A.
        1906 "La virreina gobernadora." L/RH 1:1:39-59. bibl.
        Relates appointment of Conde de Lemos as Viceroy of
        Peru (sent by Spain in 1667), arrival with his family,
        and their reception. Recounts how his wife, Ana de
        Borja, Condesa de Lemos, handled the reins of government
        very well in various instances from 4 June to 3 November
        1668 while he was in Puno regarding an Indian rebellion.
        He died in 1672; she left for Spain in 1676 and died in
        1706. Includes genealogical data on their 5 children
        (2 girls, 3 boys). Documented.

Bolivia

1801   QUESADA, VICENTE GREGORIO
        1945 Escenas de la vida colonial en el siglo XVIII.
        Crónicas de la Villa Imperial de Potosí. Biblioteca
        Enciclopédica Argentina, 3. Buenos Aires: Edit.
        Huarpes. 241 p.
        Collection of legends about different incidents which
        supposedly took place in Potosí in late 16c. and 17c.
        in which several women are featured. "Doña Leonor
        Fernández de Córdoba" recounts ill-fated end of herself,
        her husband, and the woman who harbored unrequited love
        for him. Based almost entirely on chronicles of Viceroy
        Toledo's reign in Martínez y Vela's Anales de la Villa
        Imperial (La Paz, 1939).

Paraguay

1802   GANDÍA, ENRIQUE de
        1936 "Una expedición de mujeres españolas al Río de la
        Plata en el siglo XVI." ANH/BJHNA 8:117-31.
        Sees historical importance of an expedition of Spanish
        women to Asunción in 1550 as the beginning of coloniza-
        tion in the La Plata region and as an explanation of the
        origin of many aristocratic Argentine and Paraguayan
        families. Describes the long navigation and land trek,
        women who participated, romances and marriages that
        developed. Documented archival research.

History Before 1900 - Conquest and Colony

1803 GARCÍA VARGAS, LUCY ETEL
1974 "Doña Mencia Calderón." FAH/N 259:25.
Short but interesting account of Doña Mencia Calderón's
long and arduous journey with her daughters and other
young women from Spain to Asunción (1550-56), where they
were to help populate the colony. This Spanish matron
became grandmother of founder of University of Córdoba
and Bishop of Tucumán and of Hernandarias.

1804 PLA, JOSEFINA
1972 "La familia esclava." In her Hermano negro. La
esclavitud en el Paraguay, pp. 88-102. Madrid:
Paraninfo. bibl.
Documented study on slavery in Paraguay from the 16th
to early 19th c., based on archival research, includes
a chapter on the slave family but refers to women in
other sections as well, and as part of religious communities. Appendix of documents.

Chile

1805 "Documentos para el estudio de la sociedad colonial (Cartas
de . . . doña Francisca de Paula Verduzo de Carrera, de doña
María Luisa Ezterripa de Muñoz de Guzmán y de Tomás de Figueroa."
1911 SCHG/R 1:2:219-94.
The first letter (9 March 1796), written by Ignacio de
Carrera's wife to her sister-in-law Damiana de Carrera,
discusses family members. The second letter (31 December
1803), addressed to Dolores Araoz y Carrera, a friend of
María Luisa Ezterripa, thanks her for some gifts of food
and mentions family events. The third letter (20 April
1810), written to Damiana de Carrera, expresses a
father's joy that his son has chosen her daughter to be
his wife. Footnotes identify persons mentioned in these
communications among aristocratic colonial families.

1806 MAY, STELLA BURKE
1930 The Conqueror's Lady, Inés Suárez. N.Y.: Farrar
and Rinehart. 331 p. illus., bibl.
Romanticized biography of the Spanish woman, Inés
Suárez (1512-80), who accompanied Pedro de Valdivia in
the conquest and settlement of Chile, but later married
one of his captains, Rodrigo de Quiroga, who became
governor of Chile. Epilogue contains translated documents from Archive of the Indies and National Library
in Santiago.

South America - Argentina

1807   MELLAFE, ROLANDO
        1959 La introducción de la esclavitud negra en Chile.
        Tráfico y rutas. Estudios de Historia Económica Amer-
        icana, Trabajo y Salario en el Período Colonial, 2.
        Santiago: Univ. de Chile. 293 p. tables, bibl.
        Well-documented history of black slavery in Chile
        during the colonial period, especially 16c. and 17c.,
        based on archival research. Does not provide a wealth
        of information on women slaves, but cites population
        figures and contains scattered references.

1808   OPAZO MATURANA, GUSTAVO
        1941 "Doña Inés Suárez." ACH/B 8:16:141-55.
        Born in Estremadura, Spain and widowed before the age
        of 30, Inés Suárez (1507-76) embarked for America with
        her niece in 1537. She accompanied Pedro de Valdivia
        and his soldiers from Cuzco in 1540 for Chile. When
        sentenced to exile and loss of her properties or to
        marriage in 1549, she decided to marry Rodrigo de
        Quiroga in 1550.

1809   SABAT PEBET, MARÍA MATILDE G. de
        1950 "Presencia de la mujer española en la conquista
        chilena." RENAC 48:144:376-94. bibl. f/notes.
        Concentrates on the first Spanish woman in Chile,
        Inés Suárez, who accompanied Pedro de Valdivia in his
        military expedition from Cuzco to Chile in 1540 and,
        with her husband Rodrigo de Quiroga, governed in
        Concepción. Mentions several other less outstanding
        women.

Argentina

1810   CABRERA, PABLO
        1925 "Acción gubernamental y privada en pro de las hijas
        de familia durante la colonia." In his Cultura y
        beneficencia durante la colonia, vol. 2, pp. 133-47.
        Tesoros del Pasado Argentino. Córdoba, Arg.: Est.
        Gráfico La Elzeviriana. bibl. f/notes.
        Based on documents, indicates private and governmental
        efforts made for young women in colonial Córdoba such as
        willing money for dowries so that they could marry and
        providing the Colegio de Huérfanas de Santa Teresa de
        Jesús.

1811   LASSAGA, RAMÓN J.
        1917 Una santafacecina virreyna del Río de la Plata.
        B.A.: Talleres Gráficos de L. J. Rosso y cía. 77 p.

WOMEN IN SPANISH AMERICA

History Before 1900 - Conquest and Colony

Biography of American-born vice-reine of the La Plata region, Rafaela Francisca Vera Muxica de del Pino (1756-1820) abounds in verbiage rather than information.

1812 SABOR VILA de FOLATTI TORNADU, SARA
1957 "La mujer americana en las invasiones inglesas al Río de la Plata (1806-1807)." UNL/U 34:149-167.
Based on unpublished documents from Archivo General de la Nación in Buenos Aires, extols the valor and good of American women in the English invasions (1806-07). Amplifies information in her 1949 article (#1813) and includes 6-page appendix of documents.

1813 _____.
1949 "Actuación de la mujer en las invasiones inglesas al Río de la Plata." UNL/U 22:295-306.
The participation of Argentine women in the reconquest of Buenos Aires from English forces (1806-07) is supported by documentation which demonstrates the assistance they provided not only in encouraging the men and attending to their wounds, but in collecting funds and necessary materials and actually fighting against English soldiers. Uses the case of Manuela Hurtado de Pedraza (la Tucumanesa) to illustrate heroism of Argentine women: she was awarded title and salary of Infantry Ensign by royal decree of Spanish king for her valiant action. Includes documents and notes relating to her and other women.

Uruguay

1814 PEDEMONTE, JUAN CARLOS
1943 Hombres con dueño. Crónica de la esclavitud en el Uruguay. Montevideo: Edit. Independencia. 156 p. illus.
Contains some useful information on black female slaves in Uruguay in second half of 18c. and first half of 19c. in the reproduction of notices from newspapers and official papers referring to sales and flights (escape).

CARIBBEAN

Puerto Rico

1815 SZASZDI, ADAM
1967 "Apuntes sobre la esclavitud en San Juan de Puerto Rico, 1800-1811." EEHA/AEA 24:1433-77. tables, graph, bibl. f/notes.

Using parish and notarial records, studies several aspects of slavery in the municipality of San Juan, Puerto Rico, 1800-1811. Notes greater number and higher price of female slaves, who were needed for all kinds of domestic work. Mulatto women were even more expensive. Detailed footnotes cite many individual cases of female slaves and slave owners. Also concludes that in the city marriage among slaves was discouraged by owners.

1816 TÍO, AURELIO
1971 "Doña Leonor Ponce de León, la Primera Dama de Puerto Rico." APRH/B 2:7:21-26.
Talk given at Club Cívico de Damas of San Juan, Puerto Rico about Juan Ponce de León's wife, whom he brought from Spain in 1509, and the family they raised. Believes she exercised moral and cultural influence through her exemplary conduct; for women, as moral guardians of men, bridge the past with the present, serving as an anchor of the family over generations.

Dominican Republic

1817 VERGES VIDAL, PEDRO LUCIANO
1938 Mujeres célebres de América. Juana de Sotomayor, heroína dominicana. 3rd ed. Ciudad Trujillo: Edit. "Caribes." 98 p. port., bibl. f/notes.
Celebrates the heroism of Juana de Sotomayor, who dressed as a man and took up arms to fight against the English invasion of 1655 against La Española (now Dominican Republic).

INDEPENDENCE ERA

SPANISH AMERICA - GENERAL

1818 "Cartas de mujeres."
1933 VANH/B 16:62:332-98.
Interesting collection of 89 letters dated 1822 to 1828 from 14 Latin American cities and Paris written by Manuela Sáenz, Belén Aristeguieta and many other women, including nuns, covering personal family matters, politics, gratitude, and many requests for financial and other forms of assistance (e.g., widow's pension); majority addressed to Bolívar.

WOMEN IN SPANISH AMERICA

History Before 1900 - Independence Era

1819   CATURLA BRÚ, VICTORIA de
       1945   La mujer en la independencia de América. Biblioteca
       de Historia, Filosofía y Sociología, 22. Havana:
       Jesús Montero. 198 p. ports., bibl.
       Includes nine eulogistic chapters on female participa-
       tion in the Independence movements of LA, beginning with
       the precursors and also covering women in the life of
       Simón Bolívar. Attempts to break down erroneous concept
       of women as conservative, reactionary, and opposed to
       change by nature. Sketches dozens of women and their
       personal contributions.

1820   Las ilustres americanas. De la influencia de las mujeres en
       la sociedad; y acciones ilustres de varias americanas.
           1826   Reprinted in Caracas: Imprenta de Domingo Navas
           Spinola. 59 p. bibl. f/notes.
       Very early paper on women's role in the Independence
       movement, especially in SA. After lengthy paean to
       feminine virtues and examples from other cultures and
       epochs, notes specific events and individuals, remarks
       on women's contributions by virtue of their "nature,"
       and commends their valiant efforts. An article from the
       Observador Caraqueño, 48, recounts cruelties by Spaniards
       against patriotic women in Venezuela and Colombia,
       1813-23.

1821   MACHADO RIVERO, EDUARDO
       1966   "Bolívar Galante." SBV/R 25:86:38-42.
       Portrays Simón Bolívar as a lady's man, recounting
       several women who figured in his social life and quoting
       several letters to demonstrate his gallantry.

1822   PÁEZ, ADRIANO
       1869   "Heroínas y patriotas americanas. La ilustre
       colombiana Antonia Santos. Narración de su fin trájico,
       precidida de una introducción." BA/R 16:61:87-112.
       bibl. notes.
       Introduction by A. Zinny provides notes on female
       participation in the Independence movements in several
       Latin American countries. Reproduces a letter (B.A.,
       1812) in which women offer their financial and spiritual
       support; and narrates Antonia Santos' involvement in the
       Socorro action in Colombia and her tragic death.

1823   ROMERO de VALLE, EMILIA
       1944   "Mujeres famosas de la independencia de América."
       PAU/B 78:4:210-17.
       Brief paragraphs describe the collaborative efforts of
       twelve women in the independence of their respective

countries: María Parado de Bellido, Juana Azurduy de
Padilla, Javiera Carrera, Leona Vicario, Domitila García
Doménico de Coronado, et al.

MIDDLE AMERICA

Mexico

1824 CARRERA STAMPA, MANUEL
1961 "Heroínas de la guerra de Independencia." BSHCP/B
232:1, 7.
Column entitled "Conciencia de México" briefly recounts contributions made by 8 women to Mexico's Independence movement. Others are mentioned. Based on
some primary sources.

1825 CASTILLO LEDÓN, AMALIA C. de
1938 Discurso pronunciado el día 16 de septiembre de
1938, frente a la Columna de Independencia. Mex., D.F.:
Edit. México Nuevo. 10 p.
Mexican feminist reviews active participation of women
in Mexico's Independence and their achievement of political and civil rights.

1826 ECHÁNOVE TRUJILLO, CARLOS A.
1945 Leona Vicario: la mujer fuerte de la Independencia.
Vidas Mexicanas, 21. Mex., D.F.: Eds. Xochitl. 190 p.
illus., facsims., plates, ports., bibl.
Recounts the life of aristocratic Mexican woman (1789-
1842) who directed espionage service from her home and
provided supplies and money for the Independence movement. Documented.

1827 FERNÁNDEZ de LIZARDI, JOSÉ JOAQUÍN
1955 Heroínas mexicanas: María Leona Vicario, Mariana
Rodríguez Lazarín, María Fermina Rivera, Manuela Herrera
y otras. Biblioteca de Historiadores Mexicanos. Mex.,
D.F.: Vargas Rea. 35 p.
Biographical sketches of principal heroines of Mexico's
Independence movement by well-known 19c. Mexican writer.

1828 GARCÍA, GENARO
1910 Leona Vicario: heroína insurgente. Mex., D.F.:
Museo Nacional de Arqueología, Historia y Etnología.
210 p. clr. front., plates, ports., maps, facsims.,
bibl. f/notes.
Using primary sources (some of which are reproduced in
appendix), attempts to expand on three 19c. biographies of

History Before 1900 - Independence Era

Leona Vicario de Quintana Roo (1789-1842) which empha-
sized only her collaboration in Mexico's Independence
movement. Includes chapters on her origins and early
life, religiosity, education, marriage, and insurrectionist activities.

1829   JIMÉNEZ TRAVA, ANTONIA
       1960 "La mujer en la independencia y en la revolución."
       UY/R 2:12:59-64.
         Very brief sketches of heroines in Mexico's Indepen-
       dence movement and 1910 Revolution: Mariana Rodríguez
       del Toro de Lazarín, María Leona Vicario, Sára Pérez de
       Madero; others are mentioned in passing.

1830   LEAL C., MARÍA LUISA
       1949 "Mujeres insurgentes." MAGN/B 20:4:543-604.
         Reproduces interesting documents (sworn declarations,
       confessions, correspondence) regarding insurrectionist
       activities of Mexican women (1811-1817) and charges of
       treason brought against them. Demonstrates that women
       were openly involved in the Independence movement and
       were invariably accused of additional crimes (e.g.,
       seduction of a troop, illicit relations with a leader,
       etc.) in order to depreciate their honor and reputation.
       Refers to women other than such famous heroines as Leona
       Vicario and Gertrudis Bocanegra.

1831   MENDIETA ALATORRE, MARÍA de los ANGELES
       1961 La mujer en la revolución mexicana. Biblioteca del
       Inst. Nacional de Estudios Históricos de la Revolución
       Mexicana, 23. Mex., D.F.: Talleres Gráficos de la
       Nación. 175 p. illus., bibl.
         Discusses participation of Mexican women in the Reform
       and Independence movements and in the 1910 Revolution
       (precursors, participants, and those who continued the
       struggle through political demands for legal rights and
       through social service). Survey to investigate women's
       opinion on the Revolution with respect to women failed
       because of insufficient response. Reviews laws passed
       in favor of women and provides statistics to demonstrate
       improvement of women's lives. Deals with consequences
       of female participation and traces women in Mexican
       culture, stories, novels, and plastic arts. Appendix
       includes additional relevant material.

1832   MUÑOZ y PÉREZ, DANIEL
       1961 "Doña Gertrudis Bocanegra y Doña María Luisa
       Martínez." BSHCP/B 216:1, 3.

Column entitled "Conciencia de México" discusses activities of 2 women from Michoacán who participated in Independence movement. Both were executed. Based on secondary sources and newspapers.

1833 _____.
    1961 "Manuela Medina." BSHCP/B 232:1.
        Column called "Heroínas Mexicanas" reviews Juan Nepomuceno Rosáins' (Morelos' secretary) diary of operations and several historical and biographical works for data on Manuela Medina, an Indian woman born in Texcoco, who was given title of captain because of her military service in the Independence movement.

1834 _____.
    1961 "Tomasita Estévez." BSHCP/B 232:7.
        Column called "Heroínas Mexicanas" briefly describes María Tomasa Estévez of Salamanca, Guanajuato with respect to her activities for independence as an agent of several insurgent leaders and seductress of royalist soldiers over to patriotic cause, for which she was executed. Based on Iturbide's military diary and document sent to Viceroy Felix María Calleja (1814).

1835 ROMERO de TERREROS, MANUEL
    1951-52 "La condesa escribe." CM/HM 1:456-67.
        Reproduces, with only minor omissions, a dozen examples from extensive epistolary collection of María Josefa Rodríguez de Pedroso de la Cotena y Rivas Cacho, Countess of Regla, Marquess of Villahermosa de Alfaro, and Countess of San Bartolomé de Xala, an aristocratic woman of viceregal Mexican society who lived into the era of Independence. The letters reveal her personal impressions of historical events from 1812-1816--displeasure with difficult times and royalist sentiments--and her harshness in dealing with employees.

1836 RUBIO SILICEO, LUIS
    1929 Mujeres célebres en la independencia de México.
        Mex., D.F.: Talleres Gráficos de la Nación. 74 p. plates, ports.
        Recounts the patriotic participation of more than 15 heroines in the Mexican Independence movement in individual sketches. Reproduces some correspondence but does not cite references.

History Before 1900 - Independence Era

SOUTH AMERICA

Venezuela

1837 AVILES PÉREZ, LUIS
      1937 "Anotaciones sobre María Antonia Bolívar." HA/B
      24:268:88-102.
         Examines correspondence between Simón Bolívar and his
      sister (1777-1842) to present a picture of her character
      and the influence she exerted on the Liberator in her
      role as sister, informant and adviser in political
      affairs.

1838 BOLÍVAR, MARÍA ANTONIA
      1950 "María Antonia Bolívar." VANH/B 33:131:319-27.
         Reproduces document (Havana, 17 April 1817) in which
      Bolívar's older sister swears to 11 items acknowledging
      her support of the royalists when Venezuela was fighting
      for independence from Spain and another (Curacao, 28
      August 1816) in a similar vein, in which she decries
      the horrors and vicissitudes she witnessed and suffered
      during the Revolution, and pleads her case for reentry
      to Caracas with her family and for restitution of her
      property and goods.

1839 _____.
           1930 "Protesta de doña María Antonia Bolívar." VANH/B
      33:132:457-58.
         Reproduces document (18 August 1837) in which Bolívar's
      older sister protests legal action taken against her
      with respect to a payment made to Micaela Matos relating
      back to a *letra de cambio* made in 1810 by Bolívar. She
      ends her protest with a remark about the weakness of
      her sex.

1840 "Cartas de las Montilla."
      1949 VANH/B 32:126:199-202.
         Reproduces 4 letters (1821) from Venezuelan National
      Archive written by Dolores Montilla de Delpech and her
      sister Ignacia Montilla, exiled in Paris, to Carmen
      Palacios Obelmejías and her sister Josefa Palacios de
      Vega, indicating refusal to cooperate in the movement
      for independence from Spain.

1841 CLEMENTE TRAVIESO, CARMEN
      1964 Mujeres de la independencia (seis biografías de
      mujeres venezolanas). Mex., D.F.: Talleres Gráficos
      de Mexico. 364 p. bibl.

Portraits of 6 women involved in Venezuela's Independence movement: Isabel Gómez, a midwife and mother of General Manuel Piar; Josefa Joaquina Sánchez, wife of revolutionary leader José María España; Eulalia Ramos Sánchez, Coronel Chamberlain's wife; Concepción Mariño, who transported arms for the patriots; Teresa Heredia; Josefa Camejo, Coronel Juan Nepomuceno Briceño Méndez' wife. Includes documentary appendix.

1842 DOMÍNGUEZ, LUIS ARTURO
1959 "Datos históricos sobre la heroína coriana Doña Josefa Camejo." VANH/B 42:165:26-28.
Reproduces article by Rodrigo Rodríguez which appeared in the Caracas periodical La Calle (18 May 1956). Born in 1791 in Pueblo Nuevo, capital of Falcón, Josefa Venancia de la Encarnación was educated by nuns. She is known for her celebrated manifesto declaring incorporation of province of Coro into Republican movement. Refers reader to 3 other articles.

1843 IRIBARREN-CELIS, LINO
1959 "Investigaciones históricas. La heroína Josefa Camejo como figura del procerato venezolano de la independencia." VANH/B 42:165:24-25.
Very brief notes on the enthusiastic participation of Josefa Camejo, of Paraguaná, province of Coro, in the Venezuelan Independence movement.

1844 LECUNA, VICENTE
1949 "María Antonia Bolívar." VANH/B 32:126:146-57. port.
Bolívar's sister was the only member of the family who steadfastly maintained allegiance to Spain, for which she was granted a pension from Madrid. She was also given safe conduct when the republics lost in 1816 and she was in danger because of her brother's activities. Includes 9 pages of documents related to these incidents and excerpts from 2 letters to the Liberator.

1845 LOZANO y LOZANO, FABIO
1929 "Bolívar, la mujer y el amor." HA/B 17:202:655-68. bibl.
Deals with Bolívar's attitude toward women (they are superior to men), relationships with many (Spanish wife, Fanny du Villars of France, Manuela Saénz of Ecuador), and actions (e.g., granting pensions to widows out of his salary). Documented.

WOMEN IN SPANISH AMERICA

History Before 1900 - Independence Era

1846 MUÑOZ, PEDRO JOSÉ
1966 "Homenaje a Doña Luisa Cáceres de Arismendi."
VANH/B 49:194:168-75.
Typical long-winded tribute to women of upper-class
family that supported Venezuela's Independence movement,
with no facts.

1847 _____.
1964 "Informe acerca de la consulta hecha a la Academia
por el señor Ambrosio Castro de Higuerote, acerca de la
señora Eulalia Ramos Sánchez de Chamberlain." VANH/B
47:187:437-39.
Correctly identifies Venezuelan Independence heroine
as Eulalia Ramos Sánchez de Chamberlain, not Eulalia
Buroz, and provides some biographical data as well as a
brief account of her activities during the movement,
including exile.

1848 PAIVA PALACIOS, CARMELO
1972 "Biografía de Eulalia Buroz." VANH/B 55:220:670-78.
bibl.
Brief biography of Independence heroine (1796-1817)
of patriotic republican family. Married at 16, to avoid
persecution she fled to the woods, where she gave birth
to a girl who died soon thereafter. Captured in 1813,
she escaped to Cartagena and Haiti. When her second
husband shoots himself in a convent where they were
hiding with 1400 other persons, she shoots a Spanish
official, for which her body was mutilated and dragged
by a horse. Other accounts identify her as Eulalia
Ramos Sánchez de Chamberlain.

1849 SORIANO LLERAS, ANDRÉS
1957 "Una desconocida heroína venezolana." VANH/B
40:157:108-09.
As an octegenarian, Mariquita Figuera embraced the
cause of independence for Venezuela despite her ties to
a royalist family. Captured by Morales, she was publicly
whipped and decapitated. No references or documents.

1850 VARGAS, FRANCISCO ALEJANDRO
1946 "Heroínas venezolanas de todos los tiempos. Eulalia
Ramos Sánchez de Chamberlain." VFA/R 1:1:38-40. illus.
Describes hardships experienced by heroine of Venezuelan Independence movement who was a fugitive from
the royalists.

Colombia

1851 AGUDELO, ELADIO
1965 "Doña Mercedes Abrego (apuntes para su biografía)."
HA/B 52:604/605:99-133. illus., facsims.
Documented notes on the Independence heroine of
Cucuta which clarify her biography (name, family, why
and how she was executed, etc.), but do not describe
her as an individual.

1852 BUENDÍA N., JORGE
1948 "Las primeras heroínas de Colombia." HA/B 35:404/
406:428-33. facsim.
Discusses episode in which 4 women died for trying to
get the president of Popayán, Joaquín Caicedo y Cuero,
and others out of prison by dressing as soldiers, in
1812: Luisa Góngora, Domitila Sarasti, Andrea Velasco,
Dominga Burbano. When plan was denounced, they were
condemned to death.

1853 CAMACHO de GÓMEZ, BERTHA
1960 "La mujer en la guerra de la independencia." CEST
29:258/262:108-15.
Cites many Colombian women and the specific deeds which
have earned them fame as heroines of the Independence
movement. Briefly considers those women not of the
upper class who nobly sacrificed their lives and lists
the women who held salons—a meeting place for revolutionary leaders—in their homes from Buenos Aires to
Mexico.

1854 CORREA, RAMÓN C.
1962 "Las mujeres de la independencia." REPB 48:219/220:
1220-46.
Similar to his earlier article of same title (#1856).
Based on secondary sources, but including some correspondence, praises the many women who contributed to the
Independence movement in Colombia and cites additional
examples of female heroism in Venezuela, Peru and
Ecuador. Includes women of all classes in various episodes and activities.

1855 _____.
1956 "Una mujer de la independencia, nacida en el Puente
de Boyacá." REPB 42:188/189:197-98.
Suggests that a plaque of bronze or marble be made to
commemorate the patriotic act of a peasant woman,
Estefanía Parra, who in 1819 indicated the easiest cross-
ing of the Boyacá River to Rondón so that his regiments

History Before 1900 - Independence Era

could attack the Spaniards, cause them to flee and
thereby open the roads to Bogotá for Bolívar's troops.

1856 ____.
1932 "Mujeres de la independencia." REPB 12:100:31-56.
Suggests that the importance of women in the struggle
for independence began in 1780, with the rebellion of
Tupac Amaru in Peru and the movement of the Comuneros
in Colombia, rather than in 1810. Quoting primary and
secondary sources, describes female participation in the
struggle since 1810, concentrating basically on Colombia,
but also mentioning several heroines of Venezuela and
Ecuador. Many women were imprisoned and executed because
of their pro-Independence sentiments and activities.

1857 ____.
1903 "Doña Simona Duque." HA/B 1:12:656-62.
In 1819, Simona Duque contributed her jewels and 5 sons
to Colombian Independence leader Coronel Córdoba, who
later wrote a note to the government commending her sons'
service and requesting a widow's pension for her, which
General Santander, vice-president, decreed. Quotes note
and decree and reproduces her letter (1820) declaring
she could take care of herself. Upon a priest's insis-
tence, she finally accepted the pension, and lived until
the age of 102. Based on verbal communications with her
son, Captain Andrés Alzate, and other family members;
and data from historian Groot.

1858 CORTÉS VARGAS, CARLOS
1937 "Magnanimidad de Bolívar." HA/B 24:274:497-500.
Points out Bolívar's magnanimity in a series of 6
letters (1821) he dictated to provide pensions for
widows out of his own salary; a 7th refers to completion
of his order.

1859 CUERVO, LUIS AUGUSTO
1950 "Las mujeres del 20 de julio." Vida 35:11-16.
illus.
Briefly sketches patriotic participation of 4 aristocratic Colombians (Josefa Baraya, Petronila Lozano,
Gabriela Barriga, Melchora Nieto) in the independence
activities of July 20, 1810. Quotes some primary
sources.

1860 ____.
1942 "La esposa de Nariño." HA/B 29:332/333:538-43.
bibl.

South America - Colombia

Magdalena Ortega y Meza (b. 1762) married Antonio
Nariño in 1785 and became a faithful wife who helped
him in Colombia's struggle for independence. Includes
letters from her to him and from her to Queen María
Luisa (of Carlos IV) requesting her husband's freedom.

1861 DÍAZ, CARLOS ARTURO
1968 "Las mujeres de la independencia." HA/B 55:645/647:
361-72.
Acknowledging that historians have neglected women's
contribution to history, lists several reasons why a
serious analysis has not been made and offers notes on
women's participation in Colombia's struggle for independence (1816-19) in recognition of female patriotism
and sacrifice. Supposedly based on archival research,
names women who aided guerrillas; suffered imprisonment,
persecution, exile, economic ruin, and execution; and
became widows of patriots. Mentions such well-known
heroines as Policarpa Salavarrieta as well as women of
the *pueblo* and how they helped the cause.

1862 DÍAZ DÍAZ, OSWALDO
1965 "Homenaje a doña Magdalena Ortega de Nariño.
Colocación de una placa commemorativa (discurso)."
HA/B 52:606/608:411-19.
Pays tribute to Magdalena Ortega, wife of Nariño,
whom she helped in his campaign for Colombia's independence. No references, but quotes correspondence.

1863 FEBRES CORDERO, LUIS
1912 "Abrego Mercedes. Datos históricos de Cúcuta."
HA/B 7:84:745-48.
A search for documents and oral history proved futile
in the case of the heroine of Cúcuta, who was decapitated
by the Spanish royalists in 1813; however, according to
tradition, she was born between 1770 and 1775 in San
Cayetano or Cúcuta.

1864 FORERO, MANUEL JOSÉ
1965 "De cómo doña Magdalena Ortega tomó la pluma para
defender a Nariño (Capítulo de la vida de doña Magdalena
la Precursora)." BCB 8:6:874-76.
Nariño's wife wrote to the Spanish Crown (19 January
1796) imploring for better treatment of her husband. He
escaped from the Spanish Court 2 months later, and was
able to return to Granada.

History Before 1900 - Independence Era

1865 ____.

> 1962 "Un episodio de la vida de doña Magdalena Ortega,
> esposa de Nariño." BCB 5:6:677-80.
> Relates incident in which Nariño's wife defended
> Viceroy Amar and his wife Francisca Villanova (13 August
> 1810), right after independence was proclaimed, when
> crowds were anxious to punish them for the deficiencies
> and mistakes of public administration in New Granada.
> Provides some biographical data on Magdalena Ortega and
> on the Colegio de la Enseñanza, including the 1785 roster
> of pupils.

1866 GARCÍA VÁSQUEZ, DEMETRIO

> 1958 "La esposa del prócer Joaquín de Cayzedo y Cuero."
> AHVC/B 26:113:527-35. port.
> Juana Camacho (1784-1849), an aristocrat, married
> Joaquín Cayzedo y Cuero, a patriot, in 1805. She was
> widowed and deprived of her property. In a letter (1821)
> to Ignacio Herrera, she requests his help in restoring
> her estate Cañasgordas, which was used as a quarter and
> infirmary, and obtaining a scholarship for her son to
> attend colegio. She is cited with other women for their
> contribution to and suffering in the Independence
> movement.

1866a GÓMEZ LATORRE, ARMANDO

> 1970 "Simona Duque, un ejemplo espartano de la indepen-
> dencia." AAH/RH 26:211:374-77.
> According to Historical Abstracts 20A(1974):2006,
> sketches the life of Simona Duque de Alzate, heroine of
> the independence of New Granada."

1867 GÓMEZ MEJÍA, CARMEN de

> 1968 "Mujeres en la historia de la independencia
> colombiana." CEST 37:269:42-51.
> Quotes Bolívar's words to the heroic women of Socorro
> and briefly describes role played by 13 Colombian women
> in the Independence movement. Except for Manuela Sáenz,
> being a mother or wife is sufficient for inclusion in
> list of heroines.

1868 IBÁÑEZ, PEDRO I. [sic] PEDRO M.

> 1910 "Bocetos biográficos." HA/B 6:63:147-57.
> Offers few biographical details but concentrates on
> well-known episodes which made Policarpa Salavarrieta,
> Antonia Santos, Mercedes Abrego and Rosa Zárate heroines
> of Colombia's Independence movement. Reproduces some
> documents and quotes family versions of the episodes
> and other witnesses.

1869 IBÁÑEZ, PEDRO M.
      1903 "Mercedes Abrego." HA/B 2:15:148-50.
      Very brief biographical sketch of a heroine of the
      Independence movement in Colombia. Relates the episode
      of her execution, as told by one of her grandsons,
      Narciso Reyes. Without trial she was decapitated in the
      presence of 2 of her sons, who were then jailed for
      crying over her death.

1870 IBÁÑEZ, PEDRO M. and CARREÑO T., MANUEL
      1913 "Tres heroínas mártires." REPB 1:12:443-55.
      Biographical notes on 3 heroines of the Independence
      movement in Colombia, for the edification of the students
      of the Escuela Normal and 8 colegios in the department
      of Boyacá: Policarpa Salavarrieta, Antonia Santos, and
      Mercedes Abrego. Emphasizes their deeds or acts which
      made them heroines. Based on primary and secondary
      sources.

1870a MELO LANCHEROS, LIVIA STELLA
      1971 "Participación de la mujer en la revolución del 20
      de julio de 1810." AAH/RH 26:212:63-85. bibl.
      According to Historical Abstracts 20A(1974):2009,
      "stresses the participation of women in the revolution
      of 20 July 1810 and offers biographical data on Josefa
      Antonio Baraya de Sanz de Santamaría de Montoya."

1871 MONSALVE, JOSÉ DOLORES
      1929 Mujeres de la independencia. Biblioteca de Historia
      Nacional, 38. Bogotá: Imprenta Nacional. 343 p.
      ports., bibl. notes.
      Refers to several hundred women in this documented and
      comprehensive early history of female participation in
      Colombia's Independence movement.

1872 PACHECO, LUIS EDUARDO
      1949 "Mercedes Abrego. Apuntamiento sobre la mártir
      cucuteña." HA/B 36:411/413:188-91.
      Research in an ecclesiastical archive yielded documents
      (1779) which uncover certain facts about the heroine
      from Cúcuta: name, birth date and place, family.

1873 PÁEZ PUMAR, MAURO
      1970 "Dolores Vargas de Urdaneta, arquetipo de mujer."
      SBV/R 30:100:192-96.
      At the age of 15, Dolores Vargas París Recaurte headed
      a group of 20 young women in a tribute to Bolívar and the
      Liberation Army in 1819 when they entered Bogota. She
      married one of Bolívar's officers, Rafael Urdaneta, in

History Before 1900 - Independence Era

1822. After a period of exile and being left a widow
with children who later became top government officials,
she spent her remaining years in Caracas, engaged in
charity work.

1874   POSADA, EDUARDO
       1920 "Apostillas." HA/B 13:147:175-76.
       A few paragraphs about the 15 women who organized an
       uprising against the Spanish government in the streets
       of Bogotá (20 July 1810).

1875   REYES S., ERNESTO
       1955 "Las heroínas de Tenza (Boyacá)." REPB 41:179/180:
       3217-20.
       Uninformative eulogy pays homage to the heroines of
       Tenza for their patriotic sacrifices in the war for
       independence. Names 4 women who were shot--Genoveva
       Sarmiento, Juana Ramírez, María de los Angeles Avila
       and Salomé Buitrago.

1876   RIASCOS GRUESO, EDUARDO
       1967 "La madre colombiana." AHVC/B 35:143/145:3-9.
       Based on secondary sources, pays tribute to the mothers
       of many male figures famous in Colombia's struggle for
       independence. Describes only one episode, that of
       Margarita Urrea de Hoyos and Spanish brigadier Sámano
       (Popayán, 1816). Quotes Bolivar's greeting to heroines
       of Socorro and their response to him.

1877   RIBÓN, SEGUNDO GERMÁN de
       1956 "Historia y no leyenda. La Marquesa de Torre Hoyos
       y la llegada de don Pablo Morillo a Mompox." HA/B
       43:501/503:425-57.
       Born into upper-class Spanish society in Mompox,
       Columbia (1779), the Marchioness of Torre Hoyos inherited
       her marquisate from her father because there were no
       sons. Provides genealogy of her and her husband's
       families. Describes her wealth, their mansion, etc.
       Disputes Rafael Sevilla's account which suggests that
       it is more legend than historical fact that she enter-
       tained General Morillo at her home. She fled to
       Jamaica with other royalists during Independence move-
       ment. Considers her second marriage, last will and
       testament, and death in 1848.

1878   ROJAS RUEDA, JOSÉ MANUEL
       1963 "Damas santandereanas que bailaron con el Libertador,
       Simón Bolívar." AHVC/B 30:131:77-79.

WOMEN IN SPANISH AMERICA

Reports on Bolívar's visit to Socorro on his way to Angostura (4 October 1819), the grand reception given him there, and the upper-class women who remember him; also, his visit to Barichara (9 October 1819).

1879 "Señoras patriotas confinadas e hijas del pueblo desterradas en 1816."
    1916 HA/B 10:119/120:733-35.
    Copies of original documents which list the women who were imprisoned and exiled in 1816 by the Spanish Royalists. One list indicates to what town they were exiled from Bogotá; another indicates sentences given to women, e.g., 6 months of sewing, cleaning the streets until the end of the year.

1880 SOLÍS MONCADA, JOSÉ
    1933 "A la sombra de Clío, heroínas de América en la guerra magna." AAH/RH 12:133:317-31.
    Beginning 11 December 1811 and ending with 18 March 1820, lists by dates in each intermediate year, brief paragraphs on the women executed in various parts of Colombia for their activities in the Independence movement, citing reasons why.

1881 SOTO HALL, MÁXIMO
    1934 "Las tertulias de la independencia en casa de doña Manuela Sanz de Santamaría de González Manrique." SEND 2:7/8:60-64.
    Portrays Doña Manuela, a wealthy, aristocratic woman of Santa Fe de Bogota, seated in her parlor (8 August 1819) reflecting back to when that same room was a cultural center for Colombian society and recalling the well-known participants of the meetings which took place, the talks they gave, the literature they read and family members who had convened there. No references.

Policarpa Salavarrieta

1882 ARCINIEGAS, GERMÁN
    1956 "La Pola y la juventud romántica del historiador Mitre." HA/B 43:499/500:296-309.
    Relates Argentine historian Mitre and period of romanticism in which he lived to the heroic figure of Policarpa Salavarrieta, a symbol of the peasant woman in the 19c. Narrates her experience relaying messages between Bogotá and the plains during the Independence movement, being captured and executed. Also recounts incident in theater history when the 1st dramatic piece

History Before 1900 - Independence Era

about her was presented in Bogotá. Quotes verses from
Mitre's play in which she appears.

1883   CORREA, RAMÓN C.
        1967 "Policarpa Salavarrieta." REPB 252/253:2829-35.
        Documented notes establish birth date and origins of
        Policarpa Salavarrieta, heroine of Colombia's Indepen-
        dence movement. Relates her capture from home of Andrea
        Ricaurte de Lozano by Spaniards and execution in 1817,

1884   CURREA de AYA, MARÍA
        1939 "Women of America: I. Policarpa Salvarrieta
        (Colombia)." PAU/B 73:10:583-85. illus., port.
        Very briefly describes the patriotic activities of
        La Pola during Colombia's Independence movement and her
        day of execution.

1885   LENIS, ANDRÉS J.
        1959 "Policarpa Salavarrieta." AHVC/B 27:115:180-89.
        Encomium to Colombian heroine of Independence who died
        at the gallows in 1817. Uses secondary sources.

1886   MOORE, EVELYN
        1953 "Girl of the Underground. La Pola, Heroine of
        Colombia's Struggle for Independence." OAS/AM 5:2:
        20-22, 27-28. illus., ports.
        Narrates Policarpa Salavarrieta's involvement in the
        Colombian underground resistance movement in 1817. She
        located patriot conscripts in the Spanish army and helped
        them to escape, for which she was executed at age of 22.
        Quotes Andrea Ricaurte (whose home was the center of
        underground activities) and Gen. José Hilario López (who
        became President in 1849). Includes a summary of Rafael
        Marriaga's fictional version of her life, which was dis-
        counted because it lacked documentation.

1887   "Policarpa Salavarrieta, 'la guerrillera colombiana'."
        1963 CRED 9:37/38:55-60.
        An account of Policarpa Salavarrieta's participation
        in Colombia's independence and her subsequent execution.
        Describes setting in which she was born and raised.

1888   POMBO, RAFAEL
        1962 "Policarpa Salabarrieta." BCB 5:8:992-95.
        Reprint of article which appeared in El Correo Nacional
        (20 July 1894), referring to specific biographical data
        about this heroine of the Colombian Independence
        movement.

South America - Colombia/Policarpa Salavarrieta

1889   POSADA, EDUARDO, ed.
       1923 "Policarpa Salavarrieta." HA/B 14:163:399-401.
       Reproduces several paragraphs about La Pola's role
       (along with her lover) in Colombia's Independence move-
       ment and her execution as a result of it, taken from
       La flor colombiana, biblioteca escogida de las patriotas
       americanas o colección de los trozos más selectos en
       prosa y verso (Paris, 1826).

1890   _____.
       1915-17 "Policarpa Salavarrieta." HA/B 9:106:577-86;
       9:107:655-64; 9:108:759-63; 11:124:245-56.
       Reprinted from La Información (Bogota periodical) and
       his Los mártires, well-documented discussion of Policarpa
       Salavarrieta, heroine of Colombia's Independence move-
       ment: her execution (14 November 1817); name and anagram
       La Pola; dramas dealing with her patriotic efforts; son-
       nets and song written in her memory. Offers supplemental
       notes to biographical data provided by others.

1891   QUIJANO, ARTURO
       1927 "Discurso del académico Señor Don Arturo Quijano en
       la festividad organizada por la Academia en honor de la
       Pola (6 de agosto)." HA/B 16:188:465-71.
       Includes statements about Policarpa Salavarrieta and
       her execution by a witness of her trial and chronicler
       (Caballero), Bolívar's Venezuelan biographer (Larrázabal)
       and minister (Restrepo), and by Ibáñez.

1892   RESTREPO SÁENZ, JOSÉ MARÍA and ORTEGA RICAURTE, ENRIQUE
       1949 "Policarpa Salabarrieta." HA/B 36:414/416:355-68.
       ports.
       Finds fault with Rafael Marriaga's version (Una
       heroína de papel) of the life, actions and thoughts of
       La Pola, Independence heroine of Colombia. Disputes 2
       points in particular--her origins and private customs
       (as well as work)--of which another account is provided
       through various documents and reports by other writers.

1893   RICAURTE, ANDREA
       1935 "Relación de la heroína Policarpa Salavarrieta, su
       prisión y su muerte." SEND 3:12:390-92.
       Reproduces document which recounts Policarpa
       Salavarrieta's involvement in Colombia's Independence
       movement from 1809 to 1817 as related by her friend
       Andrea Ricaurte to her son in 1875. Ricaurte's home was
       a center for organizing resistance against the royalists.

WOMEN IN SPANISH AMERICA

History Before 1900 - Independence Era

1894 ROJAS GÓMEZ, ROBERTO
1926 "La mujer en la independencia; estudios históricos."
In his Marieta, Jesús Nazareno . . ., pp. 307-42.
Bogota: Aguila Negra Edit.
Using ecclesiastical and official government documents
located in Colombia's National Archive and Library, as
well as secondary sources, reconstructs a brief
biography/history of the illustrious heroine of the
Independence movement, Policarpa Salavarrieta. Reproduces documents, letters and other primary information
in the text.

1895 SALDANHA, E. de
1918 "Detalles desconocidos sobre la Pola." HA/B 12:133:
15-23.
Offers some details about Policarpa Salavarrieta,
heroine of Colombia's independence: regarding her
death, as cited in Coronel Hamilton's Travels Through
the Interior Provinces of Colombia (London, 1827) and
in the Biblioteca americana (London, 1820); regarding her
birthplace, as listed in a 19c. pamphlet, Notas
biográficas; regarding her imprisonment and trial, as
related in a letter by Lorenzo María Lozano (Bogota,
1875) and an account by Andrea Ricaurte (Bogota, 1875).

1896 SILVA HOLGUÍN, RAÚL
1968 "Una historia de amor y heroismo." AHVC/B 35:146/
148:228-37.
Biographical sketch of Policarpa Salavarrieta
(1795-1817), heroine of Colombia's Independence movement
emphasizes her love for Alejandro Sabaraín, her fiancé,
an activist in the same struggle, for which they were
both condemned to death by the Spanish royalists.

1897 UMAÑA, ENRIQUETA de
1969 "La criolla. Bogota: Eds. Tercer Mundo. 210 p.
bibl.
Novelized biography of the brief life of Colombian
Independence heroine Policarpa Salavarrieta (i.e.,
Polonia Salevarrieta Ríos), based mostly on secondary
sources. She was condemned to death in 1817 by the
royalists for her insurrectionist activities. Prologue
indicates a more historically rigorous text would have
been preferable to this version in which history and
fantasy are mixed.

Antonia Santos Plata

1898 DÍAZ, CARLOS ARTURO
1969 "La heroína Antonia Santos Plata." HA/B 56:657/659:
385-94.
Eulogy honors guerrilla fighters of Socorro, Colombia,
and other male and female patriots, singling out Antonia
Santos Plata, who assisted guerrillas against the
Spaniards (1816-19) by providing supplies, directing
attack operations, acting as a center for communications,
and spurring on others to help in the struggle. She was
executed in 1819.

1898a GUTIÉRREZ VILLEGAS, JAVIER
1969 "La heroína Antonia Santos." UNIPOB 31:108:285-88.
Sketches the life of Colombian independence heroine
Antonia Santos (1782-1819). Based on secondary sources,
particularly on a study by Luis M. Cuervo, which is not
cited with either title or publishing data.

1899 MARTÍNEZ DELGADO, LUIS
1969 "Elogio de las mujeres de la independencia y de la
heroína Antonia Santos Plata." HA/B 56:657/659:369-83.
Based on secondary sources, recounts revolutionary
activities of Antonia Santos Plata between 1816 and
1819, when she was executed. Describes her family
background and setting of her involvement in the Independence movement. Her family's estate, "El Hatillo" in
Socorro, was the center for guerrillas of Coromoro. For
more complete story see Rodríguez Plata (#1901) and
J. D. Monsalve (#1900).

1900 MONSALVE, JOSÉ DOLORES
1919 "Antonia Santos." HA/B 12:140/141:451-71. port.,
facsim.
Notes on Antonia Santos Plata, heroine and martyr from
the department of Santander who died at the hands of
Spanish authorities (28 July 1819) because of her involvement in the Independence movement. Her house was a center of communications and supplies. Mentions other
heroines as well.

1901 RODRÍGUEZ PLATA, HORACIO
1969 Antonia Santos Plata (genealogía y biografía).
Biblioteca de Historia Nacional, 110. Bogota: Edit.
Kelly. 261 p. illus., facsims., plates, ports, bibl.
Based on extensive archival research, provides detailed
genealogy of Antonia Santos Plata (1782-1819) and historical account of Socorro resistance against Spanish

History Before 1900 - Independence Era

control--Independence activities which this Colombian
heroine supported and was executed for in 1819.

1902 ROJAS RUEDA, JOSÉ MANUEL
1956 "Antonia Santos, símbolo de las virtudes de un
pueblo heróico." AHVC/B 24:105:224-34.
Documented sketch of the Santander heroine who was
condemned to death (28 July 1819) by the royalist
forces for her participation in Colombia's Independence
movement. Her home, El Hatillo, was the center for the
guerrillas of Coromoro, of which her brother was one of
the leaders. Ten days after her execution, freedom was
announced in Boyacá.

Ecuador

1903 BARRERA, ISAAC J.
1942 "Documentos históricos. Doña Rosa Zárate y don
Nicolás de la Peña." EANH/B 22:59:103-18.
Collection of documents which trace the fugitive trail
of the Ecuadorian patriots Nicolás de la Pěna and his
wife Rosa Zárate from December 1812 when the Independence
revolution was quashed by the Spanish in Quito until
their execution in 1813. Reproduces her will.

1904 CASTILLO, ABEL ROMEO
1951 "Viuda y madre de héroes, Doña Manuela Garaycoa de
Calderón." CCE/CHA 1:2/3:252-56. port.
Typical example of honoring a woman because the men in
her family were heroes: wife of patriot Coronel Francisco Calderón, shot by Spanish royalists in Ibarra
(1812); mother of Captain Abdón Calderón Garaycoa, who
died heroically in Pichincha (1822).

1905 MONROY GARAÍCOA, GUSTAVO
1930-31 "La gloriosa." CIH/B 1:1:32-34.
Reprint of article which appeared in El Telégrafo
(Guayaquíl, 17 December 1930) in response to curiosity
about a certain "gloriosa" who appears in Bolívar's
letters to the Garaicoa family. Explains that she,
Carmen de Garaicoa y Llaguno, was the sister of author's
great-grandmother, and was one of the young women chosen
to crown Bolívar upon his triumphant arrival in
Guayaquíl (1832). She also danced with and was crowned
by Bolívar.

South America - Ecuador/Manuela Sáenz

1906   TOVAR y R., ENRIQUE D.
        1943 "Los promártires de Quito: D. Nicolás de la Peña
        y doña Rosa Zárate. (Datos rectificatorios y apuntes
        sobre su descendencia)." ACH/B 10:24:51-58.
            Thanks José Ignacio Vernaza for his article on this
        Ecuadorian couple and their pro-Independence activities;
        refers to the few historians who have written about
        them, especially about her; introduces data to supplement
        and correct Vernaza's; and concludes with genealogy of
        their descendents.

Manuela Sáenz

1907   ALVARADO, V. R.
        1956 "Primer centenario de la muerte de Manuela Sáenz
        (23 de noviembre: 1856-1956)." CUAG 7:14:8.
            Manuela Sáenz was not only Simon Bolívar's lover, she
        was also a revolutionary woman with a life of her own
        who made valuable contributions to the cause of South
        American independence and unity of emerging nations.

1908   BAILY LEMBECK, JORGE
        1927 "La verdadera Manuelita Sáenz." HA/B 16:187:389-98.
            Reproduces favorable chapter dedicated to Manuela
        Sáenz in the transcribed memoirs of Juan Bautista
        Boussingault, traveler, writer, naturalist, friend of
        Humboldt, and one of Bolívar's coronels (published in
        1903).

1909   BORJA, LUIS FELIPE
        1946 "Epistolario de Manuela Sáenz." EANH/B 26:68:228-46.
        Also in: 1946 VANH/B 29:116:443-63.
            Collection of 19 letters (1841-53) from Manuela Sáenz
        to Roberto de Ascásubi in which she reveals her patriotic
        sentiments and love for Ecuador, friendship with notable
        countrymen, life in exile, prejudice against her, finan-
        cial difficulties, etc. Also includes 2 letters, from
        Luis de Saa (1839), a lawyer persecuted for revolutionary
        participation in Ecuador, and from Cayetano (1847), who
        advised her to dress in mourning clothes upon death of
        her husband.

1910   BOULTON, ALFREDO
        1962 "Breve iconografía de Manuela Sáenz." Revista Shell
        11:45:30-33. illus.
            Describes and reproduces 4 portraits of Manuela Sáenz
        in order to establish her physiognomy. Notes that since
        women's activities were restricted to the home during

History Before 1900 - Independence Era

colonial and republican times, few females emerged as
outstanding public figures in their own right; portraits
of viceroys, kings, governors, and their wives as well as
some nuns were more abundant.

1911 _____.
1953 "Un retrato de Manuelita Sáenz." VANH/B 36:142:
161-63. port.
Tries to compose a picture of what Manuela Sáenz looked
like, quoting writers who described her physical appearance and manner. Her enemies depicted her as a harpy;
her admirers, as a beauty. Provides reproduction of
1833 portrait, painter unknown.

1912 CAPO, JOSÉ MARÍA
1956 Bolívar, su maestro y su amante. Habana: Edit.
Lex. 128 p. illus., plates, ports., facsim.
The third part, pp. 87-128, is a briefly sketched portrait of Manuela Sáenz and her relationship with Simón
Bolívar. Believes she was not his shadow or a mere
passing figure in his life, but a quick and courageous
woman who saved his life and rejected a life of opulence
for persecution because of her strong beliefs. Cites
some references in text, but no notes or bibliography.

1913 CASTELLANOS, RAFAEL RAMÓN
1966 "Manuelita Sáenz y Don Antonio de la Guerra." El
Libertador 139:445-47.
Describes the last few months of Manuela Sáenz's life
in Paita, Peru and the Venezuelan who was with her
during that time. Quotes from von Hagen's La Amante
Inmortal.

1914 CHIRIBOGA N., ANGEL ISAAC
1952 "Manuela Sáenz, la libertadora del Libertador."
VANH/B 35:139:278-81. illus.
Extremely brief biographical sketch of Manuela Sáenz,
preceded by brief discussion of comments made for and
against her by other writers. See instead his earlier
article (#1915).

1915 _____.
1942 "Manuelita Sáenz, la libertadora del Libertador."
EANH/B 22:60:216-35.
Based on documents and correspondence (some reproduced
here), traces life history of Manuela Sáenz (1796-1859),
born illegitimately in Quito to a Spanish father and
Ecuadorian mother; married off to an Englishman, James

Thorne, whom she left; decorated by San Martín for her
participation in the struggle for independence; disdained
for her illicit affair with Bolívar, whose life she
saves; exiled from Colombia for taking up his cause
there; and exiled from Ecuador because of general fear
of her revolutionary fervor and acts. She died in
Paita, Peru, where she was visited and admired by such
prominent men as Garibaldi.

1916   CORREA, RAMÓN C.
     1961   "Doña Manuelita Sáenz."   REPB 47:215/216:1080-98.
     illus., ports.
       Based on secondary sources and reproducing some cor-
respondence with Bolívar, biographical sketch of Manuela
Sáenz concentrates on their love relationship and how
she saved his life in Bogotá. Not accurate in information on her early life and marriage to Thorne.

1917   "Documentos inéditos. Sumaria información para averiguar los
hechos escandalosos con que Manuela Sáenz ha tratado de
perturbar el orden público."
     1960   HA/B 47:547/548:373-402. facsim.
       Interesting collection of documents from Colombian
Academy of History which shed light on a particular
episode in the life of Manuela Sáenz. Reproduces letters, declarations, statements, etc. beginning with a
complaint on 9 July 1830 to the Municipal Mayor of
Bogotá that she was disturbing the peace and should be
arrested.

1918   DUEÑAS YBARRA, CÉSAR A.
     1948   "La libertadora del Libertador."   SS/RBN 2:109-37.
       Summarizes material on the life of Manuela Sáenz and
her relationship with Simón Bolívar, previously published by Alfonso Rumazo González.

1919   FLORES y CAAMAÑO, ALFREDO
     1953   "Origen de Manuela Sáenz."   EANH/B 36:143:342-46.
       Part 1 uses various documents to demonstrate that
Angel Isaac Chiriboga inaccurately attributed the position of "Oidor Español de la Real Audiencia de Quito"
to Simón Sáenz de Vergara, father of Manuela. Part 2
deals with statement which attributes certain words to
General Daniel Florencio O'Leary, but which were actually
written by Manuela to Venezuelan General Juan José Flores
(author's grandfather). Reproduces letter, which reflects style of a determined and forceful woman who
does not mince words in her own defense.

History Before 1900 - Independence Era

1920   LECUNA, VICENTE
        1956 "Papeles de Manuela Sáenz." SBV/R 16:53:443-70.
        Introduction to compilation of documents and letters
        from the collection of Juan Bautista y Soto attempts to
        disprove various inaccurate stories about both Simón
        Bolívar and Manuela Sáenz, regarding certain military
        activities, possible love affairs with other persons,
        etc. Deplores practice of passing off as historical
        fact the chatter of contemporaries. See #1921 for
        details on documents.

1921   _____.
        1945 "Papeles de Manuela Sáenz." EANH/B 28:112:494-525.
        Interesting collection of documents and correspondence
        preceded by attempt to disprove certain falsehoods about
        Bolívar and Sáenz. Includes 3 letters from her to her
        husband Thorne, denying any possibility of returning to
        him; to General O'Leary, recounting how she saved
        Bolívar's life on 25 September 1828; and to Colombian
        consul in Peru, complaining about forceful entry into
        her house and her imprisonment in convent of Zazarenas
        (1827). Documents indicate purchase of female slave,
        sale and later repurchase of male slave, freedom granted
        to female slave, request for a loan, purchase and value
        of goods, and support by patriotic and liberal women.
        They also disprove legend that she accompanied Bolívar
        in battle in Peru. Brief, but useful explanatory notes.

1922   El Libertador
        1956 15:115. illus., ports.
        Entire issue dedicated to memory of Bolívar, and to
        Manuela Sáenz for having saved his life (25 September
        1828). Includes illustrations and reproduces materials
        from programs in her honor.

1923   LUQUE, MARIO
        1959 "Manolita Sáenz." Turquino 28:38-44.
        Favorable sketch of Manuela Sáenz as an individual of
        transcendental attitudes and decisions and as the pri-
        vate counselor of her lover Bolívar. No references.

1924   MASUR, GERHARD
        1949 "El Libertador es inmortal. Una carta desconocida
        de Manuela Sáenz." EANH/B 29:74:277-80. Also in:
        1949 "The Liberator is Immortal - An Unknown Letter of
        Manuela Sáenz." HAHR 29:3:380-83. bibl. f/notes.
        Transcribes letter from Manuela Sáenz to her English
        friend Dundas Logan, written from Guaduas, Colombia
        (November 1830), where she was recuperating from an

illness which precluded her joining Bolívar in Barranquilla. Briefly discusses her personality, relationship with Bolívar and abandonment of her husband, and interprets the missive.

1925   MATA, GONZALO HUMBERTO
        1959   Refutación a "Las cuatro estaciones de Manuela, los amores de Manuela Sáenz y Simón Bolívar," biografía por Victor W. von Hagen. Cuenca, Ecua. 156 p.
        Vehemently and passionately challenges von Hagen's biography of Manuela Sáenz as a calumnious and falsified version of history. Refutes von Hagen's text page by page to expose lack of factual basis. Appendix continues scathing denunciation and intimates that the biography was programmed for the film industry.

1926   _____.
        1956   "Manuelita Sáenz: la mujer - providencia de Bolívar." SBV/R 16:53:471-94.
        Uses different approach in telling story of Manuela Sáenz and Simón Bolívar. Addresses himself to her as in a letter. Lists no references but quotes correspondence. Eulogistic and superfluously sentimental rather than scholarly.

1927   _____.
        1947   "Manuelita Sáenz, la libertadora es quiteña." EANH/B 27:70:306-12.
        Disputes contentions of other writers that Manuela Sáenz was born in Paita, Peru and claims she is Quito-born. Refers to and quotes historians who contest or confirm his opinion, but provides no birth or baptismal certificate which would definitively prove his thesis. She was illegitimate daughter of Simón Sáenz de Vergara and María Aizpuru.

1928   MIRAMÓN, ALBERTO
        1939   "La vida ardiente de Manuelita Sáenz." In his Los septembrinos, pp. 147-300. Bogotá: ABC.
        Portrays Manuela Sáenz as a woman given over to passion and pleasure, promiscuity and licentiousness. Sees her relationship with Bolívar as based on sensuality and as a compensation for her illegitimate birth and lack of social status. Fails to credit her as an important historical figure in her own right, criticizing her political involvement after saving Bolívar's life. Believes her tremendous fidelity to Bolívar redeems and absolves her sinful soul! Reproduces some correspondence.

History Before 1900 - Independence Era

1929 NARVÁEZ, JAIME de
1967 "Manuela Sáenz, una vida para el amor." El Libertador 140:38-40.
Begins with first encounter of Simón Bolívar and Manuela Sáenz (16 June 1822), when he triumphantly marched into Quito after the Battle of Pichincha; describes her temperament and liberationist ideas for the colonies; quotes remembrances of her by visitors to Bolívar's Quinta; briefly recounts incidents in which her foresight saved Bolívar's life in Bogotá; and ends with her exile from Nueva Granada after his death.

1930 NICHOLAS, ALISON
1970 "To Plow the Sea (Manuela Sáenz, Mistress of Simón Bolívar [1797-1856] and the Quinta de Bolívar)." In her Consorts and Castles. The Story of Three Women and Their Homes, pp. 77-152. N.Y.: Vantage Press, Inc.
In popular style, relates story of Manuela Sáenz and Bolívar. Cites no references.

1931 PÉREZ CONCHA, JORGE
1943-1944 "Manuela Sáenz, Libertadora del Libertador." América 18:75/76:286-99; 18:77:411-30; 19:78:76-94. bibl. f/notes.
Traces early life of Manuela Sáenz, intense relationship with Simón Bolívar, and her patriotic activities. Reproduces correspondence and incompletely cites some sources in footnotes.

1932 POSADA, EDUARDO
1928 "La Libertadora." HA/B 17:196:237-50.
Reproduces documents related to and describes an incident involving Manuela Sáenz in Bogotá in 1830 and her exile 3 years later. She was accused of wanting to disturb public order and tranquility with her "scandalous and criminal" deeds in favor of Bolívar after he was no longer leader.

1933 _____.
1925 "La Libertadora." HA/B 15:169:17-38. bibl. f/notes.
Excellent early (originally published in Revista Nacional, Buenos Aires, 1900 and Trofeos, Bogotá, 1908) account of Manuela Sáenz in which author allows correspondence and other primary source material to tell her story without unnecessary embellishment. She comes across as a strong-willed, forceful, spirited, capable and independent woman who was unswerved by society's opinions of her "scandalous" behavior and ideas. She

was considered "masculine" because of her temperament,
language, use of men's clothing for horseback riding,
and ability to wield a sword and pistol.

1934　QUIJANO, FÉLIX ANTONIO
　　　　1932　"Carta de Manuela Sáenz." HA/B 19:219:207.
　　　　　　Reproduces letter (no date, no place, possibly Bogotá)
　　　　by Manuela Sáenz to Minister of the Interior, Alejandro
　　　　Osorio, regarding an accusation made against her about
　　　　papers and books of Simón Bolívar which she possessed.
　　　　Demonstrates her strong will and determination not to be
　　　　overcome by authorities.

1935　RUMAZO GONZÁLEZ, ALFONSO
　　　　1962　Manuela Sáenz, la libertadora del Libertador. 6th
　　　　ed. Caracas: Edime. 231 p. bibl.
　　　　　　Straightforward biography of Manuela Sáenz (1796-1859),
　　　　based on primary and secondary sources, provides sympa-
　　　　thetic portrait of a courageous, generous, willful,
　　　　clever, and irresistible woman of formidable character.

1936　_____.
　　　　1956　"Momentos culminantes en la vida de Manuelita Sáenz."
　　　　UCV/CU 58:77-84.
　　　　　　Briefly focuses on several significant episodes in
　　　　Manuela Sáenz's career: flight from the convent of
　　　　Catalina in Quito and her first romance; active partici-
　　　　pation in San Martín's triumph in Lima, which earned
　　　　her medal of "Caballeresas del Sol" at age of 23; rela-
　　　　tionship with Bolívar; "scandalous" acts in Bogotá which
　　　　saved his life; and friendship with Simón Rodríguez, his
　　　　teacher. Quotes from correspondence but cites no
　　　　references.

1937　_____.
　　　　1941　"Manuelita Sáenz, la libertadors del Libertador."
　　　　SBV/R 3:8:79-86.
　　　　　　Complimentary biographical sketch of Manuela Sáenz
　　　　which later becomes full length biography: her early
　　　　life, brief period in a convent, incompatible marriage,
　　　　encounter with Bolívar, exile and death in Paita. Quotes
　　　　other writers and her correspondence.

1938　SAN CRISTOVAL, EVARISTO
　　　　1958　Vida romántica de Simón Bolívar; Manuela Sáenz, la
　　　　libertadora del Libertador. Lima: Ministerio de
　　　　Guerra, Servicio de Prensa, Propaganda y Publicaciones
　　　　Militares. 56 p. plates, ports., bibl.
　　　　　　Favorable portrait of Manuela Sáenz and her relation-
　　　　ship with Bolívar also summarizes other women in his

History Before 1900 - Independence Era

life and reproduces his letters to her. Incorrectly
assumes hers to him are unavailable. Interesting addition is that General Juan José Flores took up her defense in Ecuador's Congress (1837). Reproduces
safe-conduct she was granted but which she refused.

1939 von HAGEN, VICTOR WOLFGANG
1954 "Testamento de Jaime Thorne y pleito con Manuela
Sáenz sobre devolución de su dote." HA/B 41:479/480:
574-86.
Reproduces documents which reveal the litigation in
which Manuela Sáenz was involved in Lima because she
could not collect the dowry returned to her in Thorne's
will; and which form part of a larger collection published by von Hagen, The Documentary History of Manuela
Sáenz. Unable to collect the money, she spent her
remaining years in penury in Paita.

1940 _____.
1952 The Four Seasons of Manuela, a Biography: The Love
Story of Manuela Sáenz and Simón Bolívar. N.Y.: Duell,
Sloan and Pearce. 320 p. clr. port., maps, bibl.
Claims to be an exhaustively and thoroughly researched
and documented biography of Manuela Sáenz and her relationship with Bolívar during the Independence movement
but reads, in the author's words, "like some Baroque
romance." Dwells on her illegitimate birth and feminine
wiles. See Mata (#1925) for a vehement refutation of
von Hagen's version.

Peru

1940a LA PEÑA CALDERÓN, ISABEL de
1971 "La mujer peruana en la emancipación." CEHMP/R
19:112-22.
According to Historical Abstracts 20A(1974:2034, provides "biographical notes on various women who participated actively in Peruvian independence: Tomasa Titu
Condemayta, Cecilia Tupac Amaru, Marcela Castro, Manuela
Maticorena, Manuela Rodríguez, Brígida Silva de Ochoa,
Ventura Calamaqui, Trinidad Celis, María Andrea Parado
de Bellido, Bartolina Sisa, and three members of the
Toledo family whose first names are not given."

Bolivia

1941 ABECIA, VALENTÍN
1937 "Heroínas chuquisaqueñas en la guerra de la
independencia." SGS/B 31:327/332:3-20. bibl.

Written in 1909, provides notes on 9 heroines of the Bolivian Independence movement: e.g., Juana and Mercedes Cuiza suffered whiplashings and had their tongues cut out and hands cut off because they were sisters of a guerrilla; Juana Azurduy de Padilla fought alongside her husband and received title of lieutenant coronel in 1816.

1942 CRESPO, LUIS S.
 1925 Doña Vicenta Juaristi Eguino. His series, Las mujeres del tiempo heróico, 2. La Paz: Imprenta Renacimiento. 107 p. illus., ports., bibl. notes.
 Based on documents and secondary sources, provides biographical sketch of Vicenta Juaristi Eguino (1785-1857), an upper-class woman of La Paz whose house became a center of Independence activities and whose wealth supported the army and factory where women clandestinely manufactured cartridges and cannon balls, as well as bought her way out of exile sentences.

1943 GANTIER, JOAQUÍN
 1973 Doña Juana Azurduy de Padilla. 2nd ed. La Paz: Edit. y Librería Icthus. 281 p. bibl.
 Based on primary and secondary sources, narrates the life of Juana Azurduy de Padilla (1780-1862), who fought alongside her husband in the Bolivian rebellion against Spanish rule (1809-25). When he died, she fought with the gaucho Güemes in Argentina, where she was named lieutenant coronel by the government in 1816. Draws parallel between historical epochs and periods in her life: childhood and youth during the colony, and adulthood during Independence wars; her forgotten heroism during the organization and consolidation of the republic (1824-48), her sad and penurious old age and death during the administrations of Belzu and Linares (1849-62).

1944 GIANELLO de GÜLLER, MARÍA ZORAYDA
 1966 Guerrillera. Realidad, leyenda y mito de "La Coronela de los Andes" Juana Azurduy de Padilla. Buenos Aires: Edit. Nueva Impresora. 206 p. bibl.
 In introduction, author does not claim to be an historian but to have become interested in the story of Independence heroine Juana Azurduy de Padilla after suffering a depression and to have consulted the president of the Historical Institute "Sucre," Joaquín Gantier, biographer of same heroine. Author requests wives and mothers read her undocumented account.

WOMEN IN SPANISH AMERICA

History Before 1900 - Independence Era

1945   La heroína del Alto Perú: Vicenta Juaristi de Eguino.
        1943 Mujeres de América. La Pax. 31 p. illus., facism,
        port.
        Collection of brief talks on upper-class woman of La
        Paz who greatly contributed to Bolivia's Independence
        movement, in commemoration of her offering a golden key
        to Bolívar when he entered La Paz in 1825 and of the
        naming of a school after her.

1946   RAMALLO, MIGUEL
        1919 Guerrilleros de la independencia: los esposos
        Padilla. La Paz: González y Medina. 310 p. bibl.
        f/notes.
        Although emphasis is on Manuel Asensio Padilla, there
        is information on Juana Azurduy de Padilla and her role
        in the military campaigns during Bolivia's struggle for
        independence from Spain (1809-25). In 1816 she was con-
        ferred title of lieutenant coronel by the Argentine gov-
        ernment. For all her heroism and bravery, she died a
        very humble death. Includes appendix of 20 documents.

1947   URQUIDI, JOSÉ MACEDONIO
        1918 Bolivianas ilustres. Estudios biográficos y
        críticos. Primera parte. Las heroínas de la libertad
        patria. La Paz: Escuela Tipográfica Salesiana. 294 p.
        ports., facsims., plates. Reprinted in: 1967
        Bolivianas ilustres. Las guerrilleras de la independencia.
        Estudios biográficos y críticos. Col. Popular. 2ª
        Serie. vol. 6. La Paz: Ed. José Camarlinghi. 238 p.
        Based mostly on secondary sources, provides more than
        30 sketches, of varying length and detail, on Bolivian
        women who participated in the Independence struggle;
        divided according to city. Emphasizes Juana Azurduy de
        Padilla, lieutenant coronel in the patriotic forces, and
        includes appendix of documents related to her death and
        descendants. Also appended is 10-page piece, "Las
        mujeres y el 'melgarejismo'," which includes a letter
        (1865) written and signed by long list of women in de-
        fense of private and public rights and liberties.

Chile

1948   GARCÍA LYON, VIRGINIA
        1948 "Tres mujeres en la historia de Chile." ACH/B
        15:39:49-68.
        Moving narration of the hardships which Javiera Carrera
        and her sisters-in-law Mercedes Fontecilla and Ana María
        Cotapos endured and the role they played through their

involvement with the Carrera brothers in the struggle
for the independence of Chile as well as the conflict
with other leaders of the movement. Begins with 1812
revolutionary celebration and ends with the death of
José Miguel in 1821 and Javiera's return from exile in
Montevideo in 1824. Quotes correspondence.

1949   GREZ, VICENTE
       1966 Las mujeres de la independencia. Col. Historia y
       Documentos. Santiago: Empresa Editora Zig-Zag. 124 p.
          19c. journalist, novelist and government functionary
       pays tribute to the heroines of Chile's Independence
       movement. Covers Javiera Carrera, Luisa Recabarren,
       Agueda Monasterio de Lattapiat, Mercedes Fontecilla
       (wife of José Miguel Carrera), Paula Jara Quemada and
       several others, noted for their contributions either in
       the salons they held, money they gave, or in their brav-
       ery, sacrifice and imprisonment. Based on correspondence,
       newspaper articles, travel accounts, and secondary
       sources.

1950   HURTADO, MANUEL A.
       1885 "Doña Paula Jara-Quemada." BA/NR 13:289-94.
          Briefly praises contributions of Paula Jara Quemada,
       Chilean aristocrat, to Independence movement and philan-
       thropic activities after independence was won.

1951   "Papeles de doña Javiera de Carrera."
       1913-1915 SCHG/R 6:10:168-89; 7:11:197-220; 8:12:423-35;
       9:13:454-61; 10:14:334-41; 11:15:57-68; 12:16:407-14;
       13:17:240-45. bibl. f/notes.
          Collection of some documents and much correspondence
       (1810-17) related to the involvement of the Carrera fam-
       ily in Chile's Independence movement--family matters,
       economic affairs, politics, exile and imprisonment, etc.
       Includes explanatory footnotes about persons and events
       mentioned in the letters from Javiera Carrera to her
       husband Pedro Díaz de Valdés, from him to her father,
       from her sister-in-law Ana María Cotapos, from her
       brothers José Miguel and Juan José, etc.

1952   "Papeles de la familia Carrera."
       1911 SCHG/R 1:3:389-403.
          Eight letters to Javiera Carrera, from her father
       Ignacio de Carrera written in 1817 and 1818, plus a
       letter from him to Ana María Cotapos de Carrera, married
       to his son Juan José, regarding family problems, his
       sons' imprisonment in Mendoza because of involvement in
       Chile's Independence movement and disputes with its
       other leaders.

History Before 1900 - Independence Era

1953   "Proceso por correspondencia subversiva contra doña Ana María
       Cotapos, doña Rosa Valdivieso, pbro. don José de la Peña, don
       Tomás José de Urra y José Conde. 1817-1818."
       1918   SCHG/R 25:29:249-79; 26:30:90-124; 27:31:93-151.
       Reproduces correspondence, declarations, and confes-
       sions (1817-18) related to José Miguel Carrera in
       Montevideo and individuals (e.g., his sister, his wife
       and her mother) in Santiago and State accusations against
       them related to suggested subversion of the Chilean
       government and assassination of O'Higgins, San Martín
       and Monteagudo. They were sentenced to exile or
       confinement.

Argentina

1954   BATTOLLA, ELVIRA REUSMANN de
       1910   El libro de oro de la mujer americana. Páginas
       immortales (Episodios, anécdotas, acciones históricas).
       B.A.:   Imprenta A. de Martino. 188 p. illus., plates,
       bibl.
       In a series of 40 anecdotes, recounts heroic acts of
       Argentine women during the English Invasions (1806-07)
       and Independence wars (1806-30). Includes patriotic
       efforts of women of several other South American coun-
       tries during Independence era. Based on secondary
       sources, newspaper and magazine articles.

1955   BERNARD, TOMÁS DIEGO
       1941   Mujeres en la epopeya sanmartiniana. Col. "Ayer y
       Hoy." B.A.:   Edit. Sopena Argentina. 153 p. bibl.
       Based on secondary sources and correspondence, provides
       portraits of the 4 women--mother, sister, wife and
       daughter--who influenced the life of San Martín, hero
       of the Independence Movement. Includes the maxims he
       wrote for the social education of his daughter Mercedes.

1956   GARGARO, ALFREDO
       1956   "Las joyas de las damas mendocinas no fueron donadas
       para el Ejército de los Andes." A/H 2:5:63-75.
       Illustrating with a series of letters which refer to
       donations made by the people of Mendoza, contends that
       money derived from the women's jewels were used toward
       equipping a squadron against a possible Spanish expedi-
       tion and not toward forming the Army of the Andes (1815).

1957   GUERRERO, CÉSAR H.
       1960   El aporte de la mujer sanjuanina a la gesta
       libertadora del Gral San Martín. Archivo Histórico y

South America - Argentina

Administrativo. Eds. Especiales. Serie C, no. 1. San
Juan, Arg. 49 p. ports.
Improved-upon version from his Patricias sanjuaninas
(1943; #1958). Transcribes 1815 document listing women,
their jewels and value, contributed to General San
Martín; 1816 document indicating voluntary donations of
mules, horses, saddles and other trappings. Other
monetary contributions are also documented.

1958 _____.
1943 Patricias sanjuaninas. B.A.: Talleres Gráficos de
L. López y Cía. 259 p. illus., plates, ports., facisms.,
bibl.
Based on archival research and secondary sources, documents the financial contributions of women of San Juan,
Argentina to the May Revolution from 1812 to 1819, and
their charitable works. Also describes their notable
efforts in the fields of art, letters, music, and cultural life. Provides a series of 32 sketches of outstanding San Juan women in history of Argentina, from
Theresa de Ascensio de de Mallea, daughter of an Indian
chieftain who married a Spanish captain, to 19c. educators. Almost exclusively concerned with upper-class
women.

1959 IBARGUREN, CARLOS
1956 "La capitana María Remedios del Valle, madre de la
patria." In his En la penumbra de la historia argentina,
2nd ed., pp. 9-17. Buenos Aires: Unión de Eds. Latinos.
S.R.L.
Sad chapter in the life of a woman who had fought in
Belgrano's army since 1800. In 1827 she was a beggar
and food vendor who scrounged for leftovers at convents.
When her heroism was finally recognized and taken up as
a cause in the legislature by General Viamonte, she was
granted the salary of infantry captain. Because political disturbances impeded her receiving the pension, she
continued begging for alms and died an indigent and forgotten old woman.

1960 LEVENE, RICARDO
1940 Discurso pronunciado por el doctor Ricardo Levene
en el acto de la distribución de premios a la virtud en
el Teatro Colón, mayo 27 de 1940. B.A.: Imprenta de
la Escuela de Artes y Oficios del Asilo de Huérfanos.
30 p.
Founder of Argentina's public library system quotes
prominent figures (Belgrano, San Martín, Rivadivia,
Monteagudo) in Argentina's history to affirm that one of

History Before 1900 - Independence Era

the proposals of the Revolution of 1810 was the moral
and social liberation of women. Also commends the
Sociedad de Beneficencia for its important efforts in
social welfare.

1961   PALCOS, FANNY
       1951 La mujer y su destino, meditaciones - estampas.
       B.A.: Edit. Elevación. 298 p. port.
       Three essays deal with Argentine women in the 1810
       Revolution (e.g., as spies), with a brief sketch of
       Mariquita Sánchez; Sor Juana Inés de la Cruz; and La
       Camelia, a periodical for women which appeared in
       Buenos Aires in 1852.

1962   YANI, JOSÉ IGNACIO
       1916 "Algunas mujeres argentinas de las que cooperaron en
       la obra de la Independencia." CEHA/NH 1:11:34-35, 37.
       Names the many women who cooperated in the fight for
       independence in Argentina during the years of the English
       invasions before 1810 and up to 1814. They fought side
       by side with the men, contributed monies, jewels and
       property, their men, and spiritual support. Based on
       primary and secondary sources.

Uruguay

1963   GARCÍA, FLAVIO A.
       1960 "María Leoncia de Hispanoamérica." IGFO/RI 20:79:
       103-13.
       Analyzes historical qualities of the verses of María
       Leoncia Pérez Rojo, Spanish wife of naval captain José
       María de Aldana y Malpico, who remained in Montevideo
       while her husband and son were elsewhere engaged in
       their careers. For her unpatriotic activities and
       support of King Ferdinand VII during wars for indepen-
       dence she was imprisoned. Comments on her socio-political
       criticism. Original document of verses in Spanish
       archive.

CARIBBEAN

Dominican Republic

1964   ALFARI DURÁN, VETILIO JOAQUÍN
       1945 "Mujeres de la Independencia." CUDOC 3:25/26:1-43.
       Brief but factual, rather than impressionistic, bio-
       graphical sketches of 14 women who helped in the

Dominican Republic's Independence movement in communications, supplies and provisions, sewing, etc. Documented.

NINETEENTH CENTURY OR REPUBLICAN ERA

MIDDLE AMERICA

Mexico

1965   CALDERÓN de la BARCA, FRANCES
        1970 Life in Mexico: The Letters of Fanny Calderón de la
        Barca. With New Material from the Author's Private
        Journals. Ed. and ann. by H. T. Fisher and M. H. Fisher.
        Garden City, N.Y.: Anchor Books, Doubleday and Co.
        834 p. illus., maps, ports., plates, bibl.
           Beautifully illustrated and scholarly edition of the
        letters (originally published in 1843) of Fanny Calderón
        de la Barca, a Scotswoman married to Spain's first minis-
        ter to Mexico (1840-41). The letters and journal entries
        span 1839 to 1842, from Havana to arrival in New York.
        Replete with observations on all aspects of women's
        lives in Mexico during her 2 years' residence and trav-
        els. Detailed historical notes explain and elaborate
        on Fanny's account.

1966   CORTI, EGON CAESAR COUNT
        1928 Maximilian and Charlotte of Mexico. Trans. from the
        German by C. A. Phillips. N.Y.: Alfred A. Knopf. 2
        vols. illus., plates, facsims., ports., bibl.
           Based on the private archives of Maximilian, views the
        Emperor as a man of a weak physical constitution, fantas-
        tic mind, and kindly but self-willed nature who overesti-
        mated his own powers; and the Empress Carlotta as a
        young wife, primed in the ambitious ideas of her father,
        who helped her husband even to the point of madness.
        They were artisans of their own fate, given to carrying
        out their desires and ambitions through an unsuccessful
        reign in Mexico (1864-66).

1967   HASLIP, JOAN
        1972 The Crown of Mexico: Maximilian and His Empress
        Carlotta. N.Y.: Holt, Rinehart and Winston. 531 p.
        illus., plates, geneal. tables, bibl.
           Based on archival research, presents readable history
        of Carlotta and Maximilian, European royalty who reigned
        as Empress and Emperor of Mexico (1864-66). Although
        not a Mexican woman herself, Carlotta did interact with
        Mexican women, especially in the court circle.

WOMEN IN SPANISH AMERICA

History Before 1900 - Nineteenth Century or Republican Era

1968   HERNÁNDEZ, JULIA
        1958   "Mujeres en torno a la Constitución de 1857."
        MSEP/LP 20:33:2-19.
        Using historical data and popular verses, argues for
        the influence of Mexican women on the Reform period
        which led to the Constitution of 1857. Notes indirect
        influence of Josefa Juárez and Margarita Maza, sister
        and wife respectively of Benito Juárez.

1969   IBARRA de ANDA, FORTINO
        1944   Carlota. La emperatriz que gobernó. Vidas Mexicanas,
        18. Mex., D.F.: Eds. "Xochitl." 192 p. illus., ports.
        Also: 1958   Carlota (infidelidades de Maximiliano).
        Mex., D.F.:   Populibros "La Prensa." 221 p.
        Favorable biography of the Belgian princess (1840-1927)
        who became empress of Mexico (1864-66). Focuses on her
        mentality, tracing her ambitious steps through success
        and failure in politics as well as in her emotional life.
        Sees her as a victim in European intentions to institute
        a monarchy in America, yet also the only individual brave
        and clever enough to seize the opportunity by influencing
        Maximilian, whom she married in 1857, to accept the throne.
        Quotes extensively from her correspondence and cites sec-
        ondary sources in text, but there are no bibliographical notes.

1970   ITURRIBARRÍA, JORGE FERNANDO
        1958   "Una marquesa nos divisa." CM/HM 8:2(30):192-207.
        bibl. f/notes.
        Commentary on Fanny Calderón de la Barca's diary and
        travel account Life in Mexico (#1965), in which she
        describes Mexican society from 1839-1942 when her hus-
        band served as Spain's first minister to independent
        Mexico. She included many observations on women of all
        classes.

1971   MENDIETA ALATORRE, MARÍA de LOS ANGELES
        1972   Margarita Maza de Juárez. Epistolario, antología,
        iconografía y efemérides. Mex., D.F.: Comisión Nacional
        para la Conmemoración del Centenario del Fallecimiento
        de don Benito Juárez. 238 p. illus., ports., facsims.,
        bibl.
        Documented biography of Margarita Maza de Juárez
        (1826-71) presents her as President Juárez' most faithful
        collaborator and loving, abnegated companion. Consists
        of notes on girls' education in 19c. Mexico and the
        social significance of the Juárez-Maza marriage, a chro-
        nological outline of her life, family documents,
        epistolary collection (1861-67), genealogical data, and
        a collection of periodical articles published in Mexico
        during January 1871 referring to her death.

1972   MIQUEL i VERGÉS, JOSÉ MARÍA
        1962 "Pepita Peña y la caída de Bazaine." CM/HM 11:4(44):
        546-74. ports.
        Portrait of Josefa Peña, Mexican woman who married
        Marshall Bazaine during reign of Maximilian and Carlota,
        when she was 17 and he 54. She is presented as more
        energetic and knowledgeable of political affairs than
        Francisca Agüero, who married General Prim. After help-
        ing her husband escape from prison she returned to a
        poor and unacclaimed life in Mexico, where she died in
        1900.

1973   ____.
        1955 "La mexicana Francisca Agüero, esposa de Prim."
        CM/HM 4:4(16):544-73. illus., plates, ports.
        Based on correspondence, portrays Francisca Agüero,
        wealthy Mexican woman living in Paris who married Spanish
        General Prim in 1856, as self-abnegating, faithful but
        suffering wife of man old enough to be her father. Con-
        cludes she had absolutely no political, but some personal
        and linguistic, influence on Prim, who engaged in revo-
        lutionary exploits which constantly separated them.

1974   RODRÍGUEZ, RICHARD and RODRÍGUEZ, GLORIA L.
        1972 "Teresa Urrea: Her Life, As It Affected the Mexican-
        United States Frontier." El Grito 5:4:48-68. illus.,
        ports., bibl.
        Recounts the life of Teresa Urrea, born of a poor
        Yaqui Indian woman and a Mexican landowner, as a curer
        in Mexico and the US, who was accused of encouraging
        Indian uprisings against Porfirio Díaz in the 1890's.
        Based on newspaper articles, government documents and
        secondary sources.

1975   ZENDEJAS, ADELINA
        1962 La mujer en la Intervención Francesa. Col. del
        Congreso Nacional de Historia para el Estudio de la
        Guerra de Intervención. Sociedad Mexicana de Geografía
        y Estadistica. Sección de Historia, 11. Mex., D.F.:
        Edit. Libros de México. 108 p.
        Biographical sketches of 12 women--traitors and
        heroines alike--who were actively involved during the
        French Intervention in Mexico (1833-67), as well as
        anecdotes and comments about this period in Mexican his-
        tory to demonstrate that women manifest a clear revolu-
        tionary consciousness during struggle.

WOMEN IN SPANISH AMERICA

History Before 1900 - Nineteenth Century or Republican Era

SOUTH AMERICA

Venezuela

1976   "Cartas de Soledad Soublette."
        1949 <u>VANH/B</u> 32:126:169-98.
        Reproduces correspondence of Soledad Soublette de
        O'Leary from 1854 to 1869 on family news, problems,
        daughters in *colegio*, politics, and upper-class society
        in Bogotá, where she was while her brother was exiled
        in Santa Marta and his children in Chile.

1977   REYES, ANTONIO
        1955 <u>"Presidentas" de Venezuela (primeras damas de la
        República en el siglo XIX). Matronas que fueron honor
        para la patria y blasón de la República. (Rigurosamente
        históricas).</u> 2nd ed. Caracas: Imprenta Nacional.
        231 p. illus., facsims., ports., plates.
        Provides portraits of 17 women, the wives of the
        presidents of Venezuela in the 19c., including some
        biographical data but very little information about
        their historical role. No references.

Colombia

1978   ARIAS ARGÁEZ, DANIEL
        1945 "Las esposas de los ciudadanos que ejercieron el
        poder en la República de Cundinamarca." <u>HA/B</u> 32:365:
        355-56.
        Lists the 10 wives of 12 presidents (2 were bachelors)
        who governed Republic of Cundinamarca, established
        constitutionally in 1811 after the last viceroy (Amar)
        left Colombia in a state of anarchy.

1979   _____.
        1944 "Esposas de los ciudadanos que han ejercido el poder
        en Colombia." <u>HA/B</u> 31:361/362:1103-05.
        Lists the wives of the presidents of Colombia from
        Simón Bolívar (1819) to Darío Echandía (1944).

1980   CHAMBERLAYNE PICKETT, JAMES
        1945 "Las mujeres de Colombia en 1830." <u>REVA</u> 3:7:96-107.
        American diplomat's impressions of Colombian society
        and customs in its first year as a republic. Comments
        on race and physical appearance (describing on the whole
        white women), education ("all read and write"), marriage,
        clothing, activities ("many women smoke" but they rarely
        ride horses), occupations (housewives, storekeepers,

510

nuns, weavers, etc.), religiosity and character. Notes
that some women are very rich while their husbands are
very poor because a woman's estate is inviolable and
cannot be used to pay a husband's debts without her consent. Ends with brief account of Policarpa Salavarrieta,
Independence heroine.

1981   SEIJAS, RAFAEL FERNANDO
     1945 "Dolores Vargas de Urdaneta." VANH/B 28:111:312-20.
     Melodramatic brief biography of Dolores Vargas de
Urdaneta (1800-78), daughter and granddaughter of two
upper-class patriots who died at Morillo's hand fighting
for independence of Colombia from Spain, and wife of
General Urdaneta, friend and fellow soldier of Bolívar
who went on to become president of Colombia. From 1833
on she lived in Venezuela, where her husband was appointed
Plenipotentiary Minister in Spain and France. She
founded and directed the Casa de Beneficencia until her
death. Appears to be reprint of 1878 pamphlet published
by the Imprenta de la Tribuna Liberal in Caracas.

Ecuador

1982   ESCALA, VICTOR HUGO
     1944 "Mujeres ecuatorianas. La Generalita." América
19:79/80:257-59.
     Briefly recounts heroic deeds of Marietta de
Veintemilla, who at the age of 22 defended her uncle
General Ignacio de Veintemilla against a conspiracy in
1822. In 1883 she fought with soldiers against an
uprising to overthrow her uncle's dictatorship, for
which she was wounded, imprisoned and eventually exiled
to Peru, where she was recognized as a military heroine
and where she wrote a defense of her uncle's government.
Cites no references.

1983   TOBAR DONOSO, JULIO
     1947 "Cartas de la viuda de Rocafuerte." EANH/B 27:69:
129-32.
     Two letters addressed to Roberto de Ascásubi by
Baltazara Calderón de Rocafuerte, wife of President
Rocafuerte in which she manifests her concern over the
political situation in Ecuador while she is in Lima
(1846, 1849). Brief explanatory notes introduce the
correspondence.

WOMEN IN SPANISH AMERICA

History Before 1900 - Nineteenth Century or Republican Era

Peru

1984   CORNEJO BOURONCLE, JORGE
       1948 "Francisca Zubiaga." UNCFL/RL 1:2:37-92.
       Biography of Francisca Zubiaga Bernales de Gamarra,
       La Mariscala, who is seen as superior being in her mili-
       tary and political career in 19c. Peru. Reproduces
       letter and will, but based on secondary sources.

1985   LASTRES, JUAN BAUTISTA
       1945 Una neurosis célébre. El extraño caso de "La
       Mariscala," Francisca Zubiaga Bernales de Gamarra. Lima:
       Empresa Periodística. 276 p. plates, ports., facsims.,
       bibl. f/notes.
       Historical-psychiatric study of Peruvian woman who had
       a lively but short-lived military and political career
       in the early years of Republican Peru. Diagnosis of her
       personality as resulting from epilepsy was later refuted
       by Carlos E. Paz Soldán. Based mostly on secondary
       sources, relates Flora Tristán's interview with La
       Mariscala; reproduces several documents and verses re-
       lated to her.

1986   _____.
       1944 "Flora Tristán y sus entrevistas con La Mariscala,
       el centenario de la muerte de Flora Tristán y la paleo-
       neuro-psiquiatría republicana." HH 2:16:16-17, 20-21.
       illus., ports.
       Based mostly on Flora Tristán's Peregrinaciones de una
       paria (#56), recounts the meeting of 2 Peruvian women of
       strong personality and fame, one for her military/
       political career, the other for her efforts in favor of
       workers and women. Believes these visits revealed
       Pancha Gamarra's difficulties as an epileptic (which
       was later refuted).

1987   _____.
       1942 "La enfermedad de La Mariscala." Peruanidad 2:4:
       267-72.
       Historical-medical essay attempts to clarify physical
       characteristics and illness of infamous Francisca
       Zubiaga Bernales de Gamarra in order to explain her
       "markedly anti-social attitudes." Claims about her
       epilepsy not substantiated; later refuted. Includes
       biographical data.

1988 _____.
1941-1942 "La enfermedad de la Mariscala." UNMSM/RC
43:437:507-18; 43:438:615-30; 44:439:3-25. port., bibl.
Psycho-pathological study of the life, temperament and
illness of Francisca Zubiaga Bernales de Gamarra, who
briefly dominated the political scene in Peru in 19c.,
as an explanation of her emotional alterations, which he
attributes to her epileptic constitution. Relying mainly
on Flora Tristán's observations, conclusions are not
based on concrete evidence.

1989 NEUHAUS RIZO PATRÓN, CARLOS
1967 Pancha Gamarra, la Mariscala. Lima: Francisco
Moncloa Eds. 153 p. port., bibl. notes.
Carefully documented biography of Francisca Zubiaga
Bernales de Gamarra (1803-1835) attempts to present an
objective portrait of a woman whose strong and dominant
behavior was highly criticized as violent, arbitrary,
and offensive to her sex. Cloistered with her sisters
in a Lima convent, she escaped to marry Agustín Gamarra
and accompany him on a military expedition to Bolivia,
where she fought in the battle. She substituted for him
as prefect of Cuzco while he fought in the north and
served as counsel to him while he was president of
Peru (1830-34), going so far as to expel the vice-
president. Refutes Flora Tristán's comments in her
Peregrinaciones de una paria (#56).

1990 RADIGUET, MAXIMILIEN RENÉ
1958 Las limeñas según Radiguet, un artículo traducido y
publicado en Arequipa en el año 1847. Lima. 18 p.
illus.
Reprint of Spanish translation of French article
(which first appeared in La Ilustración, vol. 6) which
was published in 3 parts in El Crepúsculo, an Arequipan
periodical, in 1847. Known for his travel account,
Souvenirs de l'Amerique Espagnole, Radiguet presents his
impressions of women in Lima in the 1840's, focusing
especially on the creoles, noting how they dress and
spend their time. Also refers to women of other racial
groups.

Paraguay

1991 BARRETT, WILLIAM E.
1938 Woman on Horseback. The Biography of Francisco
López and Eliza Lynch. N.Y.: Frederick S. Stokes Co.
360 p. bibl. notes.

History Before 1900 - Nineteenth Century or Republican Era

Portrays Anglo-Irish mistress (1835-86) of Paraguayan
dictator Francisco López as a clever, active and intelligent woman in a 19c. love affair in which both partners
aided each other in power plays. Sheds light on attitudes
toward women and Lynch's relations with Paraguayan,
especially upper-class, women. Appendix of notes indicates extensive research using primary and secondary
sources (newspaper material, official and personal correspondence, etc.).

1992   CRUZ, JOSEFINA
        1960   Doña Mencia la Adelantada.   B.A.:   Edit. La Reja.
        276 p.
        Novelist indicates that archival research in Spain and
        South America forms the basis of this novelized biography
        of Mencia Calderón, who left Seville in 1550 with 50
        Spanish women for Asunción, where they finally arrived
        after five years of hardships (shipwreck, Indian attacks,
        capture, etc.). Her grandson became the 3rd bishop of
        Tucuman, Arg. and founder of the University of Córdoba;
        another, Hernando Arias de Saavedra, became first gover-
        nor of the La Plata territories.

1993   DECOUD, HÉCTOR FRANCISCO
        1939   Elisa Lynch de Quatrefages.   Buenos Aires: Librería
        "Cervantes."   J. Suárez.   232 p.   ports., bibl.   f/notes.
        Biography of Eliza Lynch (1835-86) and her relationship
        with Paraguayan dictator Francisco Solano López by a
        member of a family formerly prominent in Paraguayan
        politics, with an ax to grind. Portrays her as López'
        "adulterous concubine," a beautiful but perverse, vicious,
        cruel, and domineering seductress who robbed the country
        of its private and public wealth. Based on personal
        knowledge, information from acquaintances, documents
        and other writers.

1994   FLORES G. de ZARZA, IDALIA
        1970-1971   "La mujer en la epopeya nacional."   IFIH/A 1:
        9-45.   bibl.
        Reproduces public recognition of individual and collec-
        tive efforts of women in Paraguay's War of the Triple
        Alliance (1864-70) which appeared in varous issues of
        El Semanario, government decrees, and the First American
        Assembly of Women (24 February 1867); women's public
        thanks to López, their hero, in 1866; and general
        heroism and patriotism of the women. Documented.

1995   MASSARE de KOSTIANOVSKY, OLINDA
          1970 La mujer paraguaya: su participación en la Guerra
          Grande. Asunción: Talleres Gráficos de la Escuela
          Técnica Salesiana. 125 p. illus., facsim., bibl.
            Based on memoirs and other personal sources, newspaper
          articles, poetry and documentary war accounts, traces
          female participation in Paraguay's War of the Triple
          Alliance (1864-70) against Brazil. They contributed
          jewels and other valuables; coordinated efforts from
          capital to interior; helped in hospitals, kitchens,
          cleaning and use of arms; worked in shops and the fields;
          organized shelters for orphans. Includes very brief
          sketches of several heroines.

1996   PALLARÉS de MUSSI, MARÍA GRACIELA
          1970-1971 "Heroinas de la epopeya nacional." IFIH/A
          1:99-108. bibl.
            Gathers together comments on female heroism and patrio-
          tism in Paraguay during the War of the Triple Alliance
          (1864-70) which appeared in 3 periodicals--La Estrella,
          El Centinela, and El Semanario--at that time, and in
          several other sources.

1997   YOUNG, HENRY LYON
          1966 Eliza Lynch. Regent of Paraguay. London: Anthony
          Blond Ltd. 196 p. bibl.
            Biography of Anglo-Irish mistress (1835-86) of
          Francisco López, dictator of Paraguay, presents Eliza
          Lynch as a shrewd, ruthless, determined yet cultured and
          intelligent woman. She organized a regiment of women,
          1st of its kind since ancient Greece, during War of the
          1860's; aided López in running the country and carrying
          out war; and became Regent of Paraguay while López was
          at war scene. Includes some interesting notes on women
          in Paraguayan upper-class and slave society. Based on
          primary and secondary sources. Highly criticized as
          inaccurate, fanciful and fictional.

Argentina

1998   BERNARD, TOMÁS DIEGO
          1962 "Mercedes de San Martín de Balcarce y la Sociedad
          de Beneficencia de Buenos Aires. Episodios desconocidos."
          A/H 7:27:131-35.
            Based on documents, presents an episode in the history
          of the Sociedad de Beneficencia of Buenos Aires (1856),
          an upper-class women's charitable organization founded
          by Rivadivia in 1823 to benefit the public, direct and

History Before 1900 - Nineteenth Century or Republican Era

inspect girls' schools; and a portrait of San Martín's daughter Mercedes, known for her kind and charitable nature. A letter from then President Señorita de las Carreras requests her participation in the Society as a correspondent member from Paris; a reply confirms her acceptance. Includes biographical data on Mercedes and her family, both endowers of gifts to the Society.

1999 CAIROLI de LIBERAL, IRMA
      1963 Eulalia Ares (Revolucionaria y gobernadora) 1809-1884.
      B.A.: Edit. Goyanarte. 254 p. port., bibl.
      Based on archival documents (reproduced in appendix), and other primary and secondary sources, provides a biography of Eulalia Ares de Vildoza (1809-84) of Catamarca, who in 1862 led a group of women dressed in masculine garb to take over the barracks, attack the governor's house and make him flee the province. She took charge of the government, organized a plebiscite, and handed over command to the elected person.

2000 CORREA LUNA, CARLOS
      1923 Historia de la Sociedad de Beneficencia. Buenos
      Aires: Talleres Gráficos del Asilo de Huérfanos.
      2 vols. in 1. 298 p.
      Documented history of the Sociedad de Beneficencia (1823-1923), a charitable institution founded by Rivadivia for the purpose of involving upper-class Argentine women in public life and in State functions. It directed and inspected girls' schools, hospitals, orphan asylums, etc. Includes extensive footnotes and appendix of documents.

2001 DELLEPIANE, ANTONIO
      1957 "La hija del dictador." In his El testamento de
      Rosas, part 2, pp. 53-92. Buenos Aires: Edit. Oberón.
      bibl.
      Documented biography of Manuela de Rosas y Ezcurra (1817-98), daughter of Argentine dictator Juan Manuel de Rosas. Considers her puberty and adolescence the period in which she was being prepared for public life and her youth the period spent accompanying her father in public life (for he had delayed her marriage until she was 34 years old). Views her character as one of wax--soft and malleable--in contrast to the iron will of her parents. Covers her years in exile and happy marriage to Máximo Terrero. Manuela also appears in parts 1 and 3, which refer to her father's will and testament and many documents.

South America - Argentina

2002 _____.
1923 Dos patricias ilustres. B.A.: Imprenta y Casa
Editora "Coni." 272 p. ports., facsims., bibl.
f/notes.
Collection of lectures, given in Library of National
Council of Women and published in pamphlet form by
Argentine press, on the lives and activities of 2 patriotic and philanthropic aristocratic women who were also
known for their salons: María Sánchez de Mendeville
(1786-1868) and Carmen Nobrega de Avellaneda (1838-99),
wife of President Nicolás Avellaneda. Based on some
documents and much correspondence. Appendix includes
judicial documents related to Thompson's attempts to
marry María Sánchez against her father's wishes.

2003 ESTRADA, MARCOS
1965 "Catalina Godoy, soldado de la tropa de línea en la
lucha por la organización nacional." ANH/B 38:2:161-80.
bibl.
Catalina Godoy enlisted in militia line in campaign of
Entre Ríos (1873), passing for a man in order to accompany her husband. She was a "woman-soldier," not a
"cuartelera" or "woman of the troop." Cites all the
battles she engaged in; she continued fighting in other
fronts until 1877. Documented.

2004 _____.
1962 Martina Chapanay. Realidad y mito. Buenos Aires:
Imprenta Varese. 207 p. illus., plates, map, ports.,
bibl.
Narrates life story of legendary female bandit Martina
Chapany within historical context of 19c. Argentina.
Born in 1800 to a Zonda Indian chief and white mother,
she learned "masculine" skills (e.g., hunting, trading)
from her father. She fought on Quiroga's side in 1820's
and early 1830's, operated with bandits, and participated
in defense of province of San Juan (early 1840's) in the
cavalries of Benavídez and Peñaloza. Includes appendix
of documents.

2005 GARRIGÓS de VON der HEYDE, ZELMIRA
1964 Memorias de mi lejana infancia (El Barrio de la
Merced en 1880). Buenos Aires: Talleres Gráficos de
la Cía Impresora Argentina. 206 p. illus., parts.,
plans, facsims., bibl. f/notes.
Zelmira Zarrigós' (1872-1957) recollections of her
childhood in Buenos Aires provide a personal portrait
of upper-class life in late 19c. Argentina. She

History Before 1900 - Nineteenth Century or Republican Era

describes the homes she lived in, her family members,
clothing worn, customs observed, holidays, outings and
entertainment, her educational experience at the Colegio
Norteamericano, and businesses and other families (including the Mitres) of the neighborhood. Appendices
include genealogical and biographical data and a description of Buenos Aires in 1882 by A. Taullard. Footnotes
explain references to individuals in the text.

2006 GIUSTI, ROBERTO F.
1926 "Manuelita Rosas." Nosotros 20:204:103-14. bibl.
Praises Argentine historian Ibarguren for his monograph
on Manuelita Rosas (#2008), daughter of the 19c. dictator.
Notes psychological contradiction between her character
and her parents': her moderation, gentility and sweet-
ness vs. father's hardness and egotism and mother's sus-
picious nature and lack of distinction.

2007 GONZÁLEZ ARRILI, B.
1951 "Mujeres en la historia argentina: Delfina de Velia
de Mitre." Revista Cubana 28:138-42.
Brief sketch of wife of Argentine President Bartolomé
Mitre (1821-1906) as a faithful companion and firm
support of the home. She turned to translating famous
works as well.

2008 IBARGUREN, CARLOS
1933 Manuelita Rosas. Edición definitiva. Buenos Aires:
Librería y Edit. "La Facultad" de Juan Roldán y cía.
172 p.
Well-documented biography of Manuelita Rosas (1817-98),
daughter of Argentine dictator Juan Manuel de Rosas.
Paints portrait of her family life and setting of tyranny
perpetrated by her parents. Not wanting to be a part of
her father's barbaric, grotesque, and bufoonish political
scene, she did not participate until 1838, when her
mother died. She became the dictator's companion and
caretaker, utilized as his diplomatic and political
agent; presented as the antithesis of her mother. She
was amiable, noble and pious. She marries Máximo Terrero
against her father's wishes while exiled in England.
Narration ends with death of Rosas in 1877. Includes
detailed chapter notes and her epistolary collection
from 1852 to 1875.

2009 MEYER ARANA, ALBERTO
1923 Las primeras trece; Las beneméritas de 1828; Matronas
y maestras; Alrededor de las huérfanas; and Rosas y la
Sociedad de Beneficencia. Buenos Aires: Imprenta de
Gerónimo Pesce. bibl. f/notes.

Documented 5-volume historical essay on the Sociedad
de Beneficencia, the well-known charity organization
founded by Rivadivia in 1823 and directed by upper-class
Argentine women. Deals with the founding, the original
13 members, the institutions under the Society's care
and direction, dictator Rosas' part in it, etc.

2010 MORALES GUIÑAZÚ, FERNANDO
1943 "Caridad, beneficencia y asistencia social." In his
Historia de la cultura mendocina, pp. 195-229. Biblio-
teca de la Junta de Estudios Históricos. Mendoza, Arg.:
Best Hnos. bibl.
Good chapter on women's charitable organizations in
Mendoza since 1857--how they were created and what kinds
of activities they engaged in. Includes St. Vincent de
Paul, Correctional Jail, School of Social Workers, House
for the Protection of Working Mothers, etc.

2011 Origen y desenvolvimiento de la Sociedad de Beneficencia de la
Capital, 1823-1912.
1913 Buenos Aires: M. Rodríguez Giles. 521 p. illus.,
graphs, tables, ports., floor plans.
Traces history of important women's charity organization, the Sociedad de Beneficencia of Buenos Aires, from
1823 to 1912. Contains documents related to its founding, statutes of the organization, descriptions of its
dependents (e.g., Colegio de Huérfanas, schools, hospitals)--when they were founded, their functions, administration, etc.--; statistics on finances and people
involved; and notes on women founders, activities, etc.

2012 SÁNCHEZ ZINNY, E. F.
1941 Manuelita de Rosas y Ezcurra. Verdad y leyenda de
su vida. B.A.: Imprenta López. 459 p. bibl. f/notes.
Based on archival research, detailed biography of
dictator Rosas' daughter (1817-98) Manuela, reveals her
image as a sweet "Angel of Mercy" to be nothing more than
a legend. Believes facade of her kind and good nature
was Juan Manuel de Rosas' way of using his daughter as
an intermediary in national politics and international
intrigue. Comparative portrait of passive and mediocre
woman behind a ruthless and fear-inspiring dictator.

2013 Sociedad de Beneficencia de la Capital, Buenos Aires
1910? República Argentina. Album histórico de la Sociedad
de Beneficencia de la Capital. 1823-1910. Buenos Aires:
144 p. illus., plates, plans, ports.
Illustrated album on the Sociedad de Beneficencia, a
well-known upper-class women's charity organization in

WOMEN IN SPANISH AMERICA

History Before 1900 - Nineteenth Century or Republican Era

Buenos Aires: documents related to its foundation in 1823, lists and portraits of founding members, statistics on the Society's efforts in education and other areas of social welfare, benefactors, descriptions and photos of institutions under their charge (e.g., Casa de Huérfanas)

Uruguay

2014 FERREIRA, MARIANO
1920 "La mujer uruguaya en la Beneficencia Pública."
IHGU/R 1:1:99-116.
Social welfare by female volunteers in Montevideo began in 1843 when the Sociedad Filantrópica de Damas Orientales was created with 16 founding women whose principal goal was to establish a hospital for army casualties. Cites formation of other charitable groups and their female members and activities, decrees related to their founding and functioning. Concludes with 1910 law which drastically modified public assistance.

CARIBBEAN

Cuba

2015 ALFONSO Y GARCÍA, RAMÓN MARÍA
1920 Reseña histórica de la Casa de la Beneficencia y Maternidad de la Habana en el año 1917. Havana: Imprenta y Papelería de Rambla, Bouza y cía. 62 p. plates.
Interesting and factual history of charitable institution in Cuba, founded in 1792 to care for poor and orphaned girls (and boys).

2016 BETANCOURT, ANA
1968 "Recuerdos de la Guerra de los Diez Años: datos biográficos sobre Ignacio Mora, escrita por Ana Betancourt. Presentación y notas por Aleida Plasencia."
FCE/R 10:1:61-91. illus., bibl.
Early Cuban feminist (she demanded equal rights for women at the Assembly of Guaimaro in 1869) recounts experience with her insurrectionary leader husband (1868-71) and her exile. She refused to urge her husband to surrender even though she was put before a firing squad.

2017 CAMACHO, PANFILO D.
1947 Marta Abreu: una mujer comprendida. Havana: Edit. Trópico. 223 p.

520

Paean to Marta Abreu (1845-1909), a wealthy Cuban woman acclaimed for her philanthropic activities, especially in her native city of Villa Clara, and along with her husband, for her promotion and financial support of the revolutionary movement led by Martí. Indicates archival research and use of secondary sources.

2018   CASANOVA de VILLAVERDE, EMILIA
        1874 Apuntes biográficos de Emilia Casanova de Villaverde escritos por un contemporáneo. N.Y. 224 p. port.
        The correspondence of Emilia Casanova de Villaverde, 1869-76, reflecting her patriotic fervor and action for Cuba's independence during the 10 Years' War, is preceded by an essay tracing the development of that career since 1850.

2019   CISNEROS, EVANGELINA
        1898 The Story of Evangelina Cisneros (Evangelina Betancourt Cosio y Cisneros) Told By Herself. Her Rescue by Karl Decker. N.Y.: Continental Publishing Co. 257 p. illus., plates, map, facsims., ports.
        Dramatic account of horrible imprisonment of young Cuban woman of a pro-Independence family by Spaniards in 1897, which became a cause célèbre among American and English ladies, who petitioned directly to Queen María Cristina and Pope Leo XIII to intercede in her behalf. Story related by victim herself and by her heroic rescuer Karl Decker, sent by New York Journal. Includes introductory material and history of Cuba.

2020   FIGUEREDO de PORTILLO, CANDELARIA
        1929 La abanderada de 1868. Candelaria Figueredo (hija de Perucho) Autobiografía. Havana: Comisión Patriótica "Pro Himno Nacional" a la Mujer Cubana. 32 p. ports.
        In her own words, the daughter of General Pedro Figueredo recounts her participation in the Cuban struggle for independence as flag bearer for the Bayamesa Division, and her difficulties, including exile, during that time (1868-71).

2021   HORREGO ESTUCH, LEOPOLDO
        1951 Emilia Casanova, la vehemencia del separatismo. Havana: Imprenta "El SigloXX." 65 p.
        Read before the Academy of History of Cuba, narrates Emilia Casanova's (1832-1897) efforts toward Cuba's independence from Spain. Despite her forced departure from the island, she continued to help the movement from New York, where she founded the League of the Daughters of Cuba.

Women in Spanish America

History Before 1900 - Nineteenth Century or Republican Era

2022 LOYNAZ del CASTILLO, E.
1922 "La mujer cubana, María Cabrales de Maceo." In
Epistolario de héroes, edited by Gonzalo Cabrales,
pp. 15-18. Havana: Imprenta "El Siglo XX."
Pays homage to wife of revolutionary leader Antonio
Maceo as a model for Cuban women because she helped
found clubs and resources for independence efforts.

2023 MEDEROS de GONZÁLEZ, ELENA
1942 "Women of the Americas: IV. Marta Abreu, Cuba."
PAU/B 76:1:32-35.
Discusses the extensive philanthropic activities and
patriotic assistance to Cuba's revolution in the late
19c. of Marta Abreu, a wealthy woman who became the wife
of the first vice-president of the Republic of Cuba.

2024 MERLÍN, MARÍA de LOS MERCEDES SANTA CRUZ y MONTALVO,
COMTESSE de
1844 Viaje á la Habana, por la condesa de Merlín,
precedido de una biografía de esta ilustre Cubana por
la Señorita D.ª Gertrudis Gómez de Avellaneda. Madrid:
Imprenta de la Sociedad Literaria y Tipográfica. 109 p.
Originally published in Paris as La Havane (1844),
diary kept by Cuban aristocratic woman who moved to
Europe as a girl and returned to visit the island includes her observations on black women, women of her own
family, slaveowners and slaves, and peasants. Renowned
Cuban woman poet provides biographical introduction.

2025 PONTE DOMÍNGUEZ, FRANCISCO
1933 "La mujer en la revolución de Cuba." RBC 31:2:276-
300. bibl. f/notes.
Recounts the varied patriotic efforts of women (Marina
Manresa, Emilia Casanova and many others) in Cuba's
movement for independence from Spain during latter part
of the 19c.

2026 REXACH, ROSARIO
1968 "Las mujeres del 68." Revista Cubana 1:1:123-42.
Believes women are the force behind historical change
in cultures; they can retard or push the advancement of
society by accepting or rejecting values created by men.
With this concept in mind, introduces Cuban women as
strong participants--ideologically as well as physically
active--in the Independence movement beginning in 1868.

2027 RODRÍGUEZ GARCÍA, JOSÉ A.
1930 De la revolución y de las cubanas en la época
revolucionaria. Academia de la Historia de Cuba,

Publicaciones 30. Havana: Imprenta "El Siglo XX."
147 p.
   Part 2 is an eclectic compendium of author's attitudes
about Cuban women and scattered notes on all kinds of
women from 1810 to 1899. More verbiage than historiography. Appendix includes additional remarks.

2028   SANTOVENIA y ECHAIDE, EMETERIO S.
       1944   Huellas de gloria. Frases históricas cubanas.
       2nd ed. Havana: Edit. Tropico. 268 p. ports., bibl.
          Out of a collection of 55 brief sketches on patriotic
       Cubans fighting for independence from 1868 on, organized
       according to historical phrases attributed to them,
       6 are on women: Ana Josefa de Agüero, Ana Betancourt,
       Juana de la Torre, Lucía Iñiguez, Mariana Grajales,
       Isabel Rubio. Based mostly on secondary sources.

2029   VARELA ZEQUEIRA, JOSÉ
       1882   "Estudios estadísticos. El desnivel de los sexos en
       la Isla de Cuba." RC 11:142-47. tables.
          Using statistics from 1768 to 1877 which indicate
       Cuba's population by sex and race, whether slave or free,
       expresses alarm over greater number of men. Suggests
       that only remedy to dangerous situation is the immigration of white families.

2030   VIDAURRETA CASANOVA, ANTONIO J.
       1952   "Marta Abreu de Estevez: 3 facetas de una vida
       extraordinaria." In his Un año de periodismo, pp. 12-24.
       Santa Clara, Cuba: Eds. Culturales "Publicidad." port.
          Reproduces article published in the Santa Clara daily
       La Publicidad. Praises the many charitable, educational
       and patriotic contributions made by Cuban benefactress
       in the 19c.

POLITICS AND TWENTIETH CENTURY REVOLUTIONARY MOVEMENTS

This section contains publications referring to female civic responsibilities and activities (voting, office-holding, membership in political parties, etc.); women's role in revolutionary movements in the 20th century (e.g., *soldaderas* and *guerrilleras*) as well as the effect of revolutions on women's role (e.g., changes in women's position in Cuban society); political development of individual women (e.g., Lydia Gueiler de Moller, Benita Galeana, Eva Perón); speeches by political leaders or party platforms with respect to women; public activities of wives of politicians (particularly presidents); and female suffrage, considered a political right (*derecho político*).

Women's participation in various national and international organizations and congresses, especially those interested in women's status and affairs of public concern, are viewed here as a form of involvement in public life (e.g., the IACW is a branch of the politica OAS). However, not all publications on women's organizations and conferences are included in this section. Those relating to associations with a more religious bent can be found in MAGIC, RELIGION, AND RITUAL; those relating to female participation in charitable organizations prior to the 20th century and particularly in the 19th century, can be found in HISTORY BEFORE 1900; and those concerned with a more educational purpose are located in EDUCATION.

For theoretical perspectives on women's liberation within the context of revolutionary movements, or the class struggle, and for feminist and anti-feminist arguments on women's role in public life, see PERSPECTIVES ON WOMEN'S LIBERATION. For women's role in the political life of ethnic groups and indigenous communities, see ETHNOGRAPHIC MONOGRAPHS/COMMUNITY STUDIES. For women's participation in politics and revolutionary movements prior to 1900, see HISTORY BEFORE 1900, which this section brings up to date; see that section for an explanation of this chronological division between the two categories.

Defining political participation is an important issue for determining what constitutes women's political role, especially since many Spanish American women have been enfranchised only since 1952 (Paraguay being the last to grant suffrage to women in 1961). Has the absence of voting and office-holding rights meant that women are not or have not been politically involved in their country? What activities

constitute political behavior: social welfare, strikes, land seizures,
community projects?[1]

SPANISH AMERICA - GENERAL

2031   ANZOÁTEGUI, YDERLA G.
      1953 La mujer y la política; historia del feminismo.
      B.A.:   Edit. Mendoza.   289 p.   illus., ports., bibl.
      See ARGENTINA for annotation.

2032   AROSEMENA de TEJEIRA, OTILIA
      1974 "Supplement: The Woman in Latin America: Past,
      Present, Future."   OAS/AM 26:4:s1-s16.   illus.
      President of the IACW of the OAS summarizes women's
      position in the history of Latin America, from Indian
      civilizations to contemporary society, citing outstanding
      women.   No references.   Part 2 describes the history,
      functions, and efforts of the IACW.

2033   BASSET, GRACE
      1973 "The Seminar of Latin American Women."   PA 52:30-40.
      Report in Marxist monthly on Second Seminar of Latin
      American Women in Santiago (22-28 October 1972), sponsored
      by the International Federation of Democratic Women.
      Three basic areas were focused on: women's rights;
      family rights; problems of national economic and politi-
      cal independence, of international solidarity and peace.
      Concludes that Seminar considered women's struggle
      solidly within the context of the class struggle.

2034   CANNON, MARY M.
      1943 "Women's Organizations in Ecuador, Paraguay, and
      Peru."   PAU/B 77:11:601-607.   photos.
      Rundown of different women's organizations in these
      3 countries, e.g., Acción Femenina Peruana, Unión
      Cultural Femenina, Damas Protectoras del Obrero.   Says
      they are not lecture and tea groups; they work on
      specific problems such as child health, illiteracy,
      civil rights, etc.

---

[1] For a discussion of this problem of definition, see section III
of my article, "Women in Latin America: The State of Research, 1975,"
LARR 11:1 (1976).

Politics and Twentieth Century Revolutionary Movements

2035   CHANEY, ELSA M.
        1973 "Women and Population: Some Key Policy, Research,
        and Action Issues." In Population and Politics: New
        Directions in Political Science Research, ed. by R.
        Clinton, pp. 233-46. Lexington Books. Lexington,
        Mass.: D. C. Heath and Co. bibl. f/notes.
        Evaluates central research and action issues related
        to alternative roles for women and suggests how women
        can participate in population research, policy making
        and the implementation of population programs on a
        world-wide basis with several examples for LA. Based on
        population literature since the 1960's. Poses thought-
        provoking questions.

2036   Congreso Interamericano de Mujeres. 1st, Guatemala, 1947.
        1948 Memoria del primer congreso interamericano de
        mujeres, celebrado en la capital de Guatemala, del 21 al
        27 de agosto de 1947. Guatemala: Tipografía Nacional.
        137 p. map.
        An account of the first Interamerican Congress of
        Women, in which such notables as Gabriela Mistral and
        Victoria Ocampo participated. Contains resolutions and
        speeches by different delegates related to women's rights,
        housing, democracy, amnesty for political prisoners,
        etc. Organizations representing workers, professionals,
        feminists et al were represented.

2037   "Delegates to the Pan American Conference of Women."
        1922 PAU/B 54:4:350-52. illus., port.
        Names many of the delegates designated to represent
        the governments and various organizations of NA and LA
        at the Pan American Conference in Baltimore, April 1922.

2038   ENOCHS, ELIZABETH SHIRLEY
        1939 "Echoes of the Lima Conference." Survey 75:1:39-40.
        Deals with the IACW and its unsuccessful efforts to
        get a treaty or convention on women's suffrage. The
        Mexican and US representatives were especially thwarting
        in their promotion of protective legislation for women.
        Briefly mentions future of the Commission and a resolu-
        tion regarding the creation of a social and child welfare
        center.

2039   FREDERICK, WILLIAM F.
        1970 "Two Organizations Advance Women's Status in Latin
        America." LDA 15:6:4-10.
        Discusses activities of the IACW (1928) of the OAS and
        the Overseas Education Fund (1947) of the League of
        Women Voters, 2 international organizations dedicated to

promoting a more effective role for women in the social
and economic development of LA by advancing their rights
as well as civic and social education. Cites specific
conferences, workshops, programs and projects to this
end and lists national bureaus where problems of female
labor are overseen.

2040   Inter-American Commission of Women
        1965   Historical Review on the Recognition of the Political
        Rights of American Women. Wash., D.C.: Pan American
        Union. 29 p.
            Translated from Spanish, part 2 traces inter-American
        (1923-61), international (1934-48) and national action
        toward the recognition of women's political rights in
        20 Latin American republics.

2041   JAQUETTE, JANE
        1973   "Women in Revolutionary Movements in Latin America."
        WRU/JMF 35:2:344-54. bibl.
            Discusses historical antecedents of women's role in
        modern *guerrilla* movements (1953-71), characteristics
        shared by guerrilleras, and a possible link between
        female participation in these movements and the develop-
        ment of political statements and platforms aimed at femi-
        nist issues. Concludes that strongest feminist political
        orientation has occurred in Cuba, Colombia and Uruguay.

2042   LEE, FRANCES M.
        1957   "The Progress of Women in the American Republics.
        Twelfth Assembly of the Inter-American Commission of
        Women, June 3-18, 1957." USDS/B 37:951:506-09.
            Report by US representative to IACW on 12th assembly,
        discussing participants, election of officers, employment
        of women, education and women in political office. Cites
        proposals, recommendations and resolutions.

2043   MACAYA, MARGARITA O. de
        1966   "Inter-American Commission of Women." OAS/AM 18:
        8:37-41. illus.
            Then chairwoman of IACW describes its activities and
        resolutions of the 4th Special Assembly, and notes
        suffrage dates for women in Latin American countries.

2044   MARTÍNEZ de GUERRERO, ANA ROSA S. de
        1941   "The Inter-American Commission of Women: Meeting in
        Washington." PAU/B 75:6:346-49. illus., port.
            Reports on the 3-day November 1940 general assembly of
        the Inter-American Commission of Women: names delegates,
        objectives, resolutions and future projects.

WOMEN IN SPANISH AMERICA

Politics and Twentieth Century Revolutionary Movements

2045 "Mexico's Congress of Women."
      1925 Literary Digest 86:10:20-21.
      Describes 4 "stormy" sessions of 1st International Congress of Spanish American Women (Mexico City, 1925). Cites some resolutions, on which no action was taken, and negative comments of Mexican press, which called it a failure.

2046 NEWHALL, BEATRICE
      1936 "Woman Suffrage in the Americas." PAU/B 70:5:424-28.
      Discusses the varying state of female suffrage in individual Latin American countries, citing the relevant bills and laws.

2047 Organización Continental Latinoamericana de Estudiantes.
      1972 Special issue on women. OCLAE 6:68.
      Collection of articles focusing on female participation in 20c. revolutionary movements.

2048 Pan American International Women's Committee
      1926 Procedimientos e informe de las conferencias del día de Colón celebrados en doce países americanos el 12 de octubre de 1923. N.Y.: Inter-American Press. 60 p.
      Reports on the presentations given on Columbus' birthday to demonstrate the contributions women have made to the progress of Latin American countries.

2049 Pan American Scientific Congress. 2nd, Wash., D.C., 1915-1916. Women's Auxiliary Conference.
      1921 Bulletin of the Women's Auxiliary Committee of the United States of the Second Pan American Scientific Congress in Cooperation with the International Committee. No. 1, February. Wash., D.C. 33 p. illus., port.
      Spanish and English text contains several brief reports by Latin American women leaders (e.g., Amanda Labarca, President of National Council of Women of Chile, "The Modern Feminist Movement in Chile in 1910"), plus child welfare reports from nine countries.

2050 PUGA, CARMELA, ed.
      1972 La mujer y la revolución. Discursos, entrevistas, artículos, ensayos. Col. Testimonio. Lima: Edit. Causachun. 119 p.
      Collection of short pieces on women's revolutionary participation in LA, emphasizing Cuba: excerpts from Castro's speeches; an interview with Vilma Espin, President of the FMC; "Women in the Cuban Insurrectionary Struggle from '53 to '59;" excerpts from Margaret Randall's introduction to La mujer cubana ahora; "Tania 'the guerrilla';" "The Incorporation of Christian Women in the Revolutionary Struggle;" "The Peasant Woman in Latin America." Other items consider women in the Soviet Union, Vietnam, Bulgaria and the US.

2051   RABELL, PAQUITA
       1955   "First Steps Toward Pan American Friendship."
       NBW 34:8:19, 36.
           Describes activities of the IACW and sessions on dis-
       crimination against women in education and on economic
       and social status of women.

2052   RANDALL, MARGARET
       1973   "La mujer de hoy en América Latina."   CDLA 13:76:
       108-10.
           Short report on the 2nd Latin American Congress of
       Women convened by the Women's International Democratic
       Federation (Santiago, October 1972) describes the setting
       of the Congress, the struggle of Allende's government in
       the face of strikes and the resulting scarcity of basic
       commodities. Three principal themes predominated in the
       talks and discussion: 1) women's roots, 2) family
       rights, 3) problems of national, economic and political
       independence, of solidarity of the people, and of peace.
       Portions of the final declaration of the seminar are
       reproduced.

2053   "Revolution Within the Revolution: Women in Latin America"
       1972   Special issue of ALA 1:3.
           Collection of short articles on women in revolutionary
       movements: Mexican women in workers' struggle, torture
       of *guerrilleras*, Tupamaras, politics of birth control,
       Castro speech, etc.

2054   Seminar on Participation of Women in Public Life. Bogotá,
       18-29 May 1959.
       1959   Doc. ST/TAO/HR/5. N.Y.: UN. 40 p.
           Contains general discussion of seminar in which repre-
       sentatives of 26 countries in western hemisphere partic-
       ipated: the meaning of civic rights and responsibilities;
       influence of the home; women in the community; economic,
       social, educational and legal factors affecting women's
       participation in public life; methods for increasing
       participation; activities of women's organizations, etc.
       Each section includes recommendations for the specific
       objective described, and Col. Pres. Lleras Camargo's
       address to seminar on same theme.

2055   SWIGGETT, EMMA BAIN (MRS. GLEN LEVIN SWIGGETT)
       1916   Report on the Women's Auxiliary Conference Held in
       the City of Washington, U.S.A., in Connection with the
       Second Pan American Scientific Congress December 28,
       1915 - January 7, 1916. Wash., D.C.: Govt. Printing
       Office. 72 p.

Politics and Twentieth Century Revolutionary Movements

Names the participants and activities of the Women's
Auxiliary Conference, including abstracts of papers
given at the various sessions, six of which were presented
on Latin American women (e.g., "Nursing in Cuba").

2056   US Dept. of Labor. Women's Bureau.
       1958   Political Status of Women in the Other American
       Republics. February, 1958. Notes for Reference.
       Wash., D.C. 17 p.
       Update on 1956 publication utilizing information from
       IACW, UN Commission on Status of Women, and embassies
       in Washington. Includes individual countries' summaries
       on female suffrage, and women in elected or appointed
       office and in foreign service.

2057   WARE, CAROLINE F.
       1968   "Mujeres ciudadanas." OAS/AM 20:1:30-34. illus.
       Write-up of several workshops which took place in CA,
       Bolivia, and Argentina in 1967 in which the Overseas
       Education Fund (of the League of Women Voters in the US)
       collaborated with local organizations for the purpose of
       stimulating interest and a sense of responsibility for
       community problems and teaching techniques of social
       action among the female participants, who represented
       various occupations and regions.

2058   "Women in Struggle."
       1972   NACLA/LAER 6:10.
       Collection of materials related to revolutionary
       thinking and action of women in LA.

MIDDLE AMERICA

Mexico

2059   ACEVEDO de la LLATA, CONCEPCIÓN
       1974   Yo, la Madre Conchita. Mex., D.F.: Edit. Contenido.
       207 p.
       Unannotated memoirs of Concepción Acevedo y de la
       Llata, a Capuchin nun (1891-), recount religious perse-
       cution after the Mexican Revolution. Accused with José
       de León Toral of assassinating Obregón, she spent 13
       years (1928-40) in various Mexican jails, where she
       wrote this account.

2060   BATALLA de BASSOLS, CLEMENTINA
       1960 La mujer en la revolución mexicana. Mex., D.F.
       10 p.
          Short talk given at Instituto de Intercambio Cultural
       Mexicano-Ruso relates background of Mexican Revolution
       and women's activities and education during those years.

2061   BLOUGH, WILLIAM
       1972 "Political Attitudes of Mexican Women: Support for
       the Political System Among Newly Enfranchised Group."
       UM/JIAS 14:2:201-24. tables, bibl.
          In 1959 survey (a year after first presidential vote
       by women), explores attitudes of urban Mexicans toward
       the country, Mexican Revolution, national government
       and official party. Concludes that in spite of slightly
       more negative responses by women, both sexes essentially
       held same opinion about political order regardless of
       educational level, religious feeling, or political activ-
       ity. Women's voting behavior in 1958 election did not
       fulfill fears of political disruption. Based on secon-
       dary sources.

2062   BREMAUNTZ, ALBERTO
       1937 El sufragio femenino desde el punto de vista
       constitucional. Mex., D.F.: Frente Socialista de
       Abogados. 48 p.
          Legal interpretation of articles 37, 41, 42 of the
       Mexican Electoral Law which the Frente Unico "Pro-
       Derechos de la Mujer" claimed were unconstitutional.
       Discusses Constitutions of 1857 and 1917 and female
       suffrage movement.

2063   CRUZ F., ELODIA
       1931 "Los derechos políticos de la mujer en México."
       UMEX 2:12:505-19.
          Discusses history and condition of women through the
       centuries, feminist movements and their impact on Mexico,
       laws related to citizenship and political rights.

2064   FAGEN, RICHARD R. and TUOHY, WILLIAM S.
       1972 Politics and Privilege in a Mexican City. Stanford
       Studies in Comparative Politics, 5. Stanford, Ca.:
       Stanford Univ. Press. 209 p. illus., tables, bibl.
       notes.
          Study of politics in Jalapa (1966) analyzes how govern-
       mental process systematically defuses any challenge to
       status quo and impedes conversion of citizens' problems
       into collective problems. Women were unintentionally
       overrepresented in questionnaire sample. They are seen

as marginal in community affairs, more withdrawn and
conservative, and more similar to one another across
class and educational lines. These patterns reveal
inefficacy of women in Jalapa's political life and
greater probability that men would initiate and dominate
change.

2065   FISHER, LILLIAN E.
       1942 "The Influence of the Present Mexican Revolution
       Upon the Status of Mexican Women." HAHR 22:1:211-28.
       bibl. f/notes.
          Summarizes legal changes for women in Mexico since
       1910 Revolution and women's increased participation in
       politics, education, and careers. Covers divorce law
       of 1917, labor enactments, formation of women's organiza-
       tions, suffrage, women journalists and other profession-
       als, social legislation, etc. Believes women's influence
       in Mexican history has greatly increased because 1910
       Revolution was a social rather than merely a political
       upheaval. Based on secondary sources, especially
       Bulletin of the Pan American Union.

2066   Formoso de Obregón Santacilia, Adela
       1939 La mujer mexicana en la organización social del país.
       Mex., D.F.: Talleres Gráficos de la Nación. 29 p.
          Demonstrates women's participation in history of
       Mexico, citing Malinalxochitl, Doña Marina, Sor Juana,
       Leona Vicario, and calls to women of Mexico to help
       alleviate social problems by organizing to effect change
       in legislation, prison reform, etc.

2067   GALEANA, BENITA
       1940 Benita: autobiografía. Mex., D.F.: Imprenta "Mels."
       238 p. illus., port.
          Interesting and warm memoirs of a woman from a Mexican
       pueblo who became dedicated to the class struggle as an
       activist in the Communist Party when she moved to the
       capital. Relates her childhood experiences, continuing
       working class hardships, and political activities,
       including imprisonment.

2068   GÓMEZ MAYORGA, ANA de
       1941 "El voto para la mujer." In her Tres Ensayos,
       pp. 45-78. Mex., D.F.: Páginas de Mujer.
          Either fierce vituperation against granting women the
       right to vote or total satire of arguments presented by
       men against female suffrage. Maintains that status quo
       should be conserved: women should stay in their place,
       tending to the family, keeping out of men's world, and
       not concerning themselves with politics.

2069   HANIGHEN, FRANK C.
         1932 "Señorita Gets the Vote." Commonweal 16:16:389-91.
         Very brief history of activities of outstanding women
         in Mexico--vicereines, Sor Juana, *soldaderas*, etc. Cites
         cultural, political, social and religious factors in
         women's struggle for suffrage and independence.

2070   JIMÉNEZ, LUZ
         1972 Life and Death in Milpa Alta. A Nahuatl Chronicle
         of Díaz and Zapata. Trans. and ed. by F. Horcasitas.
         The Civilization of the American Indian Series, 117.
         Norman, Okla.: Univ. of Okla. Press. 187 p. illus.
         An Indian woman's account of life in Milpa Alta, a
         village near Mexico City, during the Díaz regime and of
         the revolution which overthrew him. Presented in
         Nahuatl and English, Part 1 describes activities of the
         villagers, education, religious customs and festivities,
         legends; Part 2 relates impressions of different groups--
         Zapatistas, Carrancistas--, her exile from and eventual
         return to village in 1923.

2071   LUNA ARROYO, ANTONIO
         1936 La mujer mexicana en la lucha social. Biblioteca
         de cultura social y política. 2. sección. Definición
         y explicación de conceptos fundamentales, 3. Mex.,
         D.F.: Partido Nacional Revolucionario. 24 p. plate.
         PNR pamphlet dedicated to awakening revolutionary
         consciousness in working women of Mexico. In favor of
         female labor force participation and suffrage.

2072   MALPICA H., JOSÉ
         1930 Más allá del socialismo y el falso feminismo.
         Segundo ensayo. Col. Tabasco. Villahermosa, Tabasco:
         "La Economía." 164 p. port.
         Believes theme of feminism was derived from socialism.
         Can't understand why women want to give up "yoke of a
         home" for "yoke of work." Discusses actual situation
         of women, female vote, free love and free matrimony,
         family planning, and women in a socialist future.

2073   MARTÍNEZ DOMÍNGUEZ, ALFONSO
         1969 No podemos hablar de justicia plena mientras haya
         muchos miles de mujeres y niños abandonados. Discurso.
         Mex., D.F.: Congreso Nacional Femenil Cetemista, PRI.
         15 p. illus.
         Address by president of national executive committee
         of PRI at National Congress of Federation of Organiza-
         tions of Women Workers pays tribute to women for their
         contributions to society as mothers and workers. Although

Politics and Twentieth Century Revolutionary Movements

the Revolution of 1910 and PRI have improved women's position, there is a large percentage of unmarried mothers and illegitimate children.

2074 MENDIETA ALATORRE, MARÍA de los ANGELES
1973 "Galería de mujeres mexicanas en la revolución." UM/R 28:3:15-21. illus., ports.
Presents women in Mexican Revolution who were not only anonymous *soldaderas* and passive heroines, but who participated consciously and decisively as journalists and editors, ideologists in the political clubs, conspirators, soldiers, benefactors, nurses, founders of hospitals, companions, messengers, etc. Sketches 22 such women with some biographical data, citing their meritorious deeds. Considers article as completion to her book, La mujer en la revolución mexicana (1961; #1831), where sources are cited.

2075 _____.
1971 Carmen Serdán. Puebla: Centro de Estudios Históricos de Puebla. 259 p. illus., facsim., ports., bibl.
Attempts to provide authentic biography of revolutionary heroine Carmen Serdán (1873-1948), whose life is surrounded by much legend. Places her in political/ social context just before the Revolution; describes women's political activities and her family's active participation. Interprets Carmen's actions as a break with rigid social patterns to which women were educated at the time and as a result of her sense of social justice, not as an accident because of her family. Traces not only Carmen's acts but whole historical event. Documented. Includes her historical letter, which resulted from interview with Ignacio Herrerías before her death and in which she recounts events of November 18, 1910.

2076 "Mexican Feminists."
1936 Literary Digest 122:16:12.
One and one-fourth columns regarding Zapata's daughter, Ana María, and the Unión de Mujeres Americanas and other women's groups in Mexico demanding reform of Article 37 of the electoral law for an extension of suffrage to women.

2077 MORTON, WARD McKINNON
1962 Woman Suffrage in Mexico. Gainesville, Fla.: Univ. of Gainesville Press. 160 p. illus., port., bibl.
Using case study approach, presents well-written history of women's suffrage movement in Mexico as pieced

together from speeches, newspapers, congressional records
and several secondary sources.

2078 NAVARRETE, IFIGENIA M. de
1969 "La mujer en la sociedad moderna." Espejo
3:7:59-83. tables.
Divided into 3 parts, deals with functions of modern
women in industrial society (at home, in classroom, at
work); responsibility of the State toward women and the
family (health, social and environmental protection,
employment); and women and political participation in
different ways and at different levels. Includes some
statistics.

2079 OBERLY, MARY
1946 "From Sink to City Hall: President Alemán Forwards
Equal Rights By Permitting Them to Vote and Be Candidates
in Municipal Elections." MAR 14:12:44-46.
Alemán considers his presidential term the beginning of
women's political education. Notes progress of women in
public service, careers, university studies, employment.

2080 Partido Nacional Revolucionario (PNR). Secretaría de Acción
Agraria.
1934 La redención de la mujer mexicana por el ejido. Its
Publicaciones. Folleto, 7. 63 p. Mex., D.F.: La
Secretaría de Acción Agraria.
Political party's anticlerical position on religion's
role in tyrannizing rather than helping women. Compares
social and moral organization of Indians and Spaniards:
women enjoyed freedom, respect and well-being. Other
positions: for a large population, against capitalist
feminism.

2081 PLENN, J. H.
1936 "Forgotten Heroines of Mexico. Tales of the
Soldaderas, Amazons of War and Revolution." Travel
66:6:24-27, 60. illus.
Anecdotal article recounts the exploits and important
contributions made by the heroic soldier-women in Mexico.
Relates acts of bravery since pre-Conquest times, concentrating on 1910 Revolution. Notes anonymity of the many
women who helped sustain the fighting men with food,
companionship and clothing and wielding of firearms
themselves. Historical sources not cited, but these are
useful accounts of individual and collective heroism by
women, with good photos.

WOMEN IN SPANISH AMERICA

Politics and Twentieth Century Revolutionary Movements

2082   PONCE LAGOS, ANTONIO
        1954 Historia de las reformas a los Artículos 34 y 115
        constitucionales, que conceden ciudadanía a la mujer
        mexicana. Mex., D.F.: Talleres S. Turanzas del Valle.
        350 p. illus., ports.
            Provides background of passage of reforms to Constitu-
        tional articles which legalized female suffrage in Mex-
        ico in 1953. Includes pro and con speeches by deputies
        in 1953 legislature.

2083   RASCÓN, MARÍA ANTONIETA
        1973 "La mujer mexicana como hecho político: la
        precursora, la militante." CM/SS 569 (3 January):
        IX-XII. illus. bibl.
            Discusses women's participation in social and political
        struggles of Mexico since late 19c., instead of presenting
        static list of heroines. Considers women workers, women
        in the 1910 Revolution, growth of women's organizations
        to gain rights during several 20c. presidencies. Through
        socialist perspective, concludes that women are not going
        to change society by giving birth to more guerrillas,
        but by changing social structures which asphyxiate
        everyone's life.

2084   SÁMANO de LÓPEZ MATEOS, EVA and LÓPEZ MATEOS, ADOLFO
        1958 La mujer mexicana en la lucha social. La crónica de
        un mitin. Temas fundamentales de la campaña presidencial,
        1. Mex., D.F.: Edit. La Justicia. 40 p.
            Includes words spoken by President López Mateos and
        his wife at a meeting (26 January 1958) of the Confedera-
        ción de Trabajadores de México, press commentary, and 3
        brief studies by others on protective legislation for
        women workers in Mexico and equality of political rights,
        particularly suffrage, for women.

2085   SMITH, MARINOBEL
        1954 "Mexican Women Go to the Polls." MAR 22:5:16-17,
        31-32.
            Discusses newly-acquired right to vote, as promised by
        Ruiz Cortines in his presidential campaign. Enumerates
        organizations and outstanding women involved in fighting
        for female suffrage and in instructing women how to use
        it: founder of Mexico's University for Women, President
        of IACW, Consejo de Mujeres, etc.

2086   STARRETT, VINCENT
        1918 "Soldier-women of Mexico." OC 32:6:376-82.
            Referring to 1910 Revolution, belittles participation
        of the soldaderas as a bunch of whores following the

army around. "Poor, brutalized, generate, sloven! She is yet the most loyal and faithful part of a faithless army!"

2087 TALAMANTES, MARÍA ESTHER
    1956 "La mujer y la política." FL 30:60/61/62:109-18.
    Although Mexican law stipulates equality between the sexes and although women have collaborated in important political movements, such as the 1910 Revolution, they did not vote on a federal level until 1955. Concludes that women need to be educated about their civic rights and duties and acclaims Eugenio María de Hostos, Puerto Rican writer, as the first feminist of America, quoting extensively his ideas about women.

2088 TURNER, FREDERICK C.
    1968 The Dynamics of Mexican Nationalism, pp. 183-201. Chapel Hill, N.C.: Univ. of N.C. Press. bibl. f/notes.
    English version of article in Historica Mexicana (#2089). Scattered references to women in other parts of the book as well.

2089 _____.
    1967 "Los efectos de la participación femenina en la revolución de 1910." CM/HM 16:4(64):603-20. bibl. notes.
    Sees Mexican Revolution of 1910 as a favorable catalyst to expanding role of women in national affairs. Participation altered family, regional, ecclesiastical and strict sex role loyalty patterns. Outlines important active contributions of women, naming heroines of the Revolution; makes comparison to 19c. situation; and traces struggle for women's rights, including desire to better conditions of prostitutes. Based on newspaper articles, secondary sources, and public documents.

2090 "Woman Suffrage in Mexico."
    1921 Nation 112:2913:676.
    Quotes the argument introducing the decree and the decree itself for women's suffrage in Mexico to give an idea of the attitude toward women at that time regarding their need for the vote.

2091 "Xochimilco's Lady Mayor."
    1948 MAR 16:2:12-16.
    Reports on municipal delegate (equivalent to mayor in US terms) of Xochimilco, in Federal District, Guadalupe Ramírez: her attitudes, activities, reactions to her post, family background, educational training, problems in position, accomplishments.

Politics and Twentieth Century Revolutionary Movements

Nicaragua

2092   Comité Central Femenino Pro-voto de la Mujer de Nicaragua
        1959? Exposición del Comité Central Femenino Pro-voto de
        la Mujer de Nicaragua (adscrito a la Federación de
        Mujeres de América) a la Asamblea Nacional Constituyente,
        presentada por la doctora infieri Srita. Joaquina Vega.
        Reproduces 1950 letter to National Constituent Assembly
        from group fighting for female suffrage in Nicaragua,
        arguing that women's right to vote not be postponed any
        longer. Also includes 1949 letter from the Secretary
        of the Supreme Court of Justice outlining the rights of
        women as stated in the Constitution of 1948.

2093   DEBAYLE, LUIS MANUEL
        1933 "The Status of Women in Nicaragua." MPM 45:3:237-39.
        Acting Nicaraguan Minister to US talks of women's
        status in terms of politics, Constitutional law, nation-
        ality and Civil Code. Although hindered by pedestal
        status inherited from chivalric tradition, women have
        participated in national life through charitable organi-
        zations, nursing associations, and behind the scenes in
        politics.

2094   SEVILLA SACASA, GUILLERMO
        1939 La mujer nicaragüense ante el derecho de sufragar.
        Porqué me opuse a que se le concediera. La verdad sobre
        mi actitud en la Constituyente. Managua: Talleres
        Gráficos Pérez. 14 p.
        In response to public attack, reproduces his arguments
        in the National Constituent Assembly in 1939, against
        granting female suffrage in Nicaragua because he believes
        women lack philosophical independence and are attached to
        dogmatic religious sentiment.

Costa Rica

2095   AVIEL, JoANN
        1974 "Changing the Political Role of Women: A Costa Rican
        Case Study." In Women in Politics, ed. by J. Jaquette,
        pp. 281-303. N.Y.: John Wiley and Sons. graphs.
        Reports on the effects of 2 different educational
        (traditional and progressive) policies on women in Costa
        Rican secondary schools. Without directly focusing on
        women or their political role, the educational reform
        program implemented in 1964 effected change as a by-
        product: female participation increased inside and out-
        side school and the difference between male and female
        attitudes and skills narrowed. Concludes that although

educational reform is a useful tool to modernize and
also maintain political system, it is insufficient for
achieving equality for new entrants (e.g., women) to
system. Broader social reform must be implemented as
well and the role of the family and peer group must be
considered in political socialization of females.

2096   BLANFORD, RUTH BROWNLOW
        1955 "The Women's Vote in Costa Rica, How They Use Their
        New Franchise." OAS/AM 7:6:3-7. illus.
           Discusses women's participation in Costa Rican politics
        since suffrage was achieved (1949). Cites feminists and
        female political leaders.

2097   BONILLA de ULLOA, JANINA
        1970 "La mujer costarricense en el mundo de hoy." UCR/R
        29:81-86.
           Rundown of Costa Rican women's rights and obligations,
        especially in family role as mother. Analyzes women's
        role in home, school and community in terms of "democratic
        civic affairs." Suggests volunteerism as medium for
        raising consciousness level of women with regard to their
        social responsibility. Women should join the many organi-
        zations in Costa Rica where they could learn to utilize
        their own capacities and learn what community's neces-
        sities are.

Panama

2098   AROSEMENA de TEJEIRA, OTILIA
        1966 La mujer en la vida panameña. Panama: Edit. de la
        Universidad de Panama. 162 p.
           Collection of articles, radio talks, and speeches
        (1924-65) by well-known Panamanian educator and defender
        of women's rights, expressing concerns about role and
        status of Panamanian women since pre-Conquest times.
        Includes her opinions on professional women, problems
        of working women, absence of women in historical texts,
        etc. Notes changes in women's position and family struc-
        ture over a period of 35 years.

2099   CASTILLERO R., ERNESTO J.
        1945 "Las que fueron, 'Primeras Damas' de la República."
        La Lotería 54:15.
           Lists the wives of 24 presidents of Panama from 1904
        to 1945.

Politics and Twentieth Century Revolutionary Movements

2100   Liga Patriótica Femenina
        1945   Recomendaciones de la Liga Patriótica Femenina al
        proyecto de Constitución de 1945. Panama: La Estrella.
        27 p.
            Panama's Feminine Patriotic League offers suggestions
        backed with reasons for modifications of articles in the
        Constitution of Panama in 1945. Does not deal with
        women's issues but demonstrates female interest and
        participation in legal matters of importance on a
        national level.

2101   MIRANDA M., JULIO
        1966   "La mujer y el voto." TDM 5:28:47.
            Very briefly discusses female vote in Panama, from
        1904 Constitution to 1946, when suffrage was conceded to
        all Panamanians over 21, irrespective of sex.

2102   OLLER de MULFORD, JUANA
        1969   "Influencia de la mujer en el sostenimiento de
        nuestra independencia nacional." TDM 8:43:8, 21, 24,
        40, 51.
            Women make their impact not directly, in daring plans,
        but behind the scenes, as mothers, forming the character
        of Panama's future citizens and leaders; as teachers,
        influencing children, instilling them with patriotism.

2103   "Unión de Ciudadanas de Panamá."
        1968   TDM 7:39:8-9, 38, 44.
            Lists objectives, rules, finances, achievements and
        projects of women's civic organization founded in
        Panama in 1962.

SOUTH AMERICA

Venezuela

2104   GIL FORTOUL, JOSÉ
        1920   "El derecho electoral de la mujer." CUVE 5:13:42-48.
            Venezuelan president cites inequality of women in
        Venezuela's Civil Code and counters arguments against
        women's full participation in public life, especially
        suffrage. Liberal ideas against the concept of male
        supremacy originally appeared in his Filosofía Constitu-
        cional (1890) and were defended by him in the National
        Parliament.

WOMEN IN SPANISH AMERICA

2105   "Women and the Vote."
        1944 The Inter-American 3:8:31-32. illus.
        Quotes petition signed by more than 11,000 Venezuelan
        women directed to the Congress, urging a constitutional
        amendment for female suffrage. See BOLIVIA for addi-
        tional information.

Colombia

2106   GILLIN, HELEN N.
        1962 "The Other Half: Women in Colombian Life." In The
        Caribbean: Contemporary Colombia, ed. by A. C. Wilgus,
        pp. 234-50. Gainesville, Fla.: Univ. of Fla. Press.
        Consultant from Overseas Education Fund of the League
        of Women Voters in US relates history of founding and
        growth of its Colombian counterpart, Unión de Ciudadanas
        de Colombia (UCC), from 1957 to 1960. It was established
        as a national organization to provide newly enfranchised
        women with an opportunity to be informed about and dis-
        cuss parties and candidates so that they could become
        independent and well-informed voters. Despite cultural
        characteristics and regional and class differences,
        hindrances to group cooperation, the UCC has emerged as
        an educational asset and stabilizing influence for
        Colombian women interested in more than charity-type
        organizations--in political know-how to help solve
        national social problems.

2107   "La gran ausente."
        1970 Flash (1-15 September):10-27. illus.
        Interviews with Colombian women leaders in which they
        express their thoughts on women's situation with regard
        to politics, economy, family, prostitution, family
        planning, etc.; with a section on Colombia's congress-
        women. General consensus is that women have been "the
        great absentee" in public life, but very present when it
        comes to exploitation and the home; and that women need
        to be awakened to their role and responsibility as
        citizens.

2108   HERNÁNDEZ de OSPINA, BERTHA
        1970 El tábano. Bogota: Inst. de Estudios Socio-
        Políticos del Conservatismo Colombiano, Edit. El Globo.
        426 p.
        Collection of almost 200 short articles by Colombian
        Senator Bertha Hernández de Ospina published in the daily
        La República (1961-70) in which she expresses her opin-
        ions on such topics as laws concerning women, the

Politics and Twentieth Century Revolutionary Movements

miniskirt, female labor, women and politics, individual
women known for their historical, civic or social deeds.
Includes some autobiographical notes.

2109   PINEDA LÓPEZ, SINFOROSO
1947   Derechos y deberes constitucionales de la mujer
colombiana. Bogota: Tipografía Grillo-Libano. 36 p.
bibl.
Brief thesis from Universidad Católica Javeriana on
question of female citizenship and suffrage in Colombia
discusses constitutional reform, limitations of political
rights and public office-holding, duties, and comparative
position with respect to women in other Latin American
countries. Reproduces 1940's congressional debates and
projects for legislative reforms.

2110   QUINTANA VINASCO, ELBA MARÍA
1960? Por la plenitud de la ciudadanía de la mujer
colombiana. Estudio histórico - jurídico de la función
del sufragio femenino. Bogota: Edit. Iqueima. 234 p.
bibl.
National University thesis studies political rights
of women in 19c. Colombia, recognition of civil and
political rights of women in 20c., and the legislative
projects presented (1933-49) for suffrage. Also discusses pro/con debates, reform projects, pro-vote
efforts, etc.

2111   TORRES GIRALDO, IGNACIO
1972   María Cano, mujer rebelde. Bogota: La Rosca.
193 p. port.
Political biography of María Cano (1887-1967) and her
revolutionary efforts toward organizing Colombian
workers, which culminated in the 1928 strike against
the United Fruit Company, for which she was jailed in
1929. Reproduces some correspondence and other material
related to her political activities. In 1925 she was
acclaimed by workers as "Flor de Trabajo."

2112   TORRES RESTREPO, CAMILIO
1969   "Message to the Women." In his Revolutionary
Writings, trans. by R. Olsen and L. Day, pp. 191-93.
N.Y.: Herder and Herder.
Colombian revolutionary priest discusses inferior position of women of all classes in Colombian and under-
developed countries in general. Believes Colombian women
recognize the exploitative power of the vote. They will
be the heart of the revolution because of their greater
sentiment, sensitivity, and intuition. Sees women's

problems within the framework of a larger ideal for
society.

2113　URIBE de ACOSTA, OFELIA
　　　　1963　_Una voz insurgente_.　Bogota:　Edit. Guadalupe.
　　　　388 p.
　　　　　Fighter for women's political and civil rights for 30
　　　　years and initiator of 1st Colombian feminist publica-
　　　　tion, _Agitación Femenina_, discusses limited participation
　　　　of women in politics and reasons for it; women too
　　　　should have opportunity for joint direction of public
　　　　affairs.　Includes chapters on 20c. feminism in Colombia;
　　　　laws related to women; their economic and educational
　　　　situation; legal protection of children; and prostitu-
　　　　tion.　Also cites heroines of the Independence era and
　　　　considers Eva Perón the most outstanding female figure
　　　　of the 20c.

2114　VILLEGAS de VARGAS, LUCÍA
　　　　1970　"Misión de la mujer contemporánea."　_UA/U_ 46:176:
　　　　155-58.
　　　　　Municipal Council of Medellin held an act of recogni-
　　　　tion of the women who performed social services for the
　　　　community.　Distinguishes between women's past confine-
　　　　ment to procreation and domestic tasks or the convent
　　　　and women's contemporary entry into all activities.
　　　　Colombia has a tremendous political, economic, cultural
　　　　and social resource in its female population.　Women
　　　　have been especially significant, for example, in the
　　　　Red Cross as volunteers.　In addition to casting a vote,
　　　　women can fulfill their mission as mother, wife and
　　　　citizen by exercising responsibility in civic/political
　　　　action, voluntary social service, and in professions
　　　　which service the community.

Peru

2115　CHANEY, ELSA M.
　　　　1973　"Women in Latin American Politics:　The Case of Peru
　　　　and Chile."　In _Female and Male in Latin America_, ed. by
　　　　A. Pescatello, pp. 103-39.　Pittsburgh:　Univ. of
　　　　Pittsburgh Press.　tables, bibl.
　　　　See CHILE for annotation.

2116　　　　　.
　　　　1972　"Mujeres en la política, el caso del Perú y de Chile."
　　　　BDSLM/CIDHAL 3:1:29-39.
　　　　See CHILE for annotation.

WOMEN IN SPANISH AMERICA

Politics and Twentieth Century Revolutionary Movements

2117   FESTINI, NELLY
        1968   "Women in Public Life in Peru." <u>AAPSS/A</u> 375:58-60.
        Briefly describes participation of Peruvian women in
        public life and cites factors which contribute to low
        level of it: lack of education, economic dependence,
        legal restraints, role ambivalence, lack of support.

2118   MENESES, RÓMULO
        1934   <u>Aprismo femenino peruano (juicio-análsis); con un</u>
        <u>trabajo-base de interpretación sobre autocrítica y</u>
        <u>disciplina política</u>. Lima: Edit. Cooperativa Aprista
        "Atahualpa."   54 p.   bibl.
        Takes pride in women's faith, courage, self-abnegation
        and sacrifice and in their efforts in social work and
        the Red Cross; but also insists on the necessity of elim-
        inating some psychological defects from female Aprismo--
        frivolity, superficiality, political fetishism.
        Discusses how women need to be incorporated and how class
        deficiencies contribute to women's condition.   Briefly
        analyzes class composition in Peru and how middle-class
        women fit in.   Cites examples of political influence of
        groups of women.   Written from prison (Lima, 1933).
        Interesting for reflection of political party's attitude
        toward female participation in revolutionary class
        struggle.

2119   PORTAL, MAGDA
        1933   <u>El aprismo y la mujer</u>. Lima: Edit. Cooperativa
        Aprista "Atahualpa."   75 p.
        Discusses many aspects of <i>Aprismo</i> and women in Peru:
        creation of a female section in the party, its appeal to
        women and its minimal program for women; party position
        on female suffrage; persecution and imprisonment of
        female <i>Apristas</i>, women's assistance, hunger strike of
        1933 and other political events; deficiencies to be over-
        come, etc.   Denies that party affiliation will break
        women's ties with the home, rather a new woman will be
        created.   Appendices include additional brief essays
        defining the female <i>Aprista</i>, listing political, social,
        civil and educational rights proposed for women, discuss-
        ing women and the electoral process, and other position
        papers.

2120   ZÁRATE y PLASENCIA, FIDEL A.
        1954   <u>Los derechos políticos de la mujer peruana</u>. Lima.
        47 p.
        In response to a request by president of Peruvian Fed-
        eration of Women, lawyer discusses constitutional reform
        granting Peruvian women citizenship rights and suffrage.

Cites sexual, religious, juridical, cultural, and
economic reasons for women to vote. Analyzes certain
terms in the Constitution to demonstrate how they are
grammatically, logically and legally incorrectly
employed, thereby potentially favoring political rights
of women. Also considers progression of various civic
rights which women have gained in several stages.

Bolivia

2121 GUEILER de MOLLER, LYDIA
      1964 "Importancia de la mujer en la acción revolucionaria."
      Abril 2:39-43.
         Brief comments on women's role in the Bolivian revolu-
      tionary movement since 1952. Notes differences between
      petty bourgeois feminist groups and women's struggle
      within the class struggle for liberation.

2122 _____.
      1959 La mujer y la revolución (autobiografía política).
      La Paz. 289 p. illus., port., tables.
         Lydia Gueiler Tejada chronicles her own personal and
      political development, the revolutionary process in
      Bolivia, and the Bolivian women's movement. Part 1
      covers her political formation in the social and economic
      reality of workers and active allegiance to MNR beginning
      in 1948; 2 deals with the period between the Popular
      Insurrection of 9 April 1952 to the coup d'etat of 6
      January 1953; 3 recounts her experiences in Europe and
      a low period in the revolutionary movement; 4 discusses
      her participation in and the results of an IACW meeting
      in 1957; 5 summarizes women in the history of LA, their
      position in Bolivia, evolution of organizations for
      women's rights, and female incorporation into the polit-
      ical struggle. Concludes that Revolution cannot succeed
      without the participation of women.

2123 "La heróica vida de Monica Ertl: la guerrillera Imilla."
      1973 Bohemia 65:25:58-61. illus.
         Tribute to Monica Ertl, German-born young woman who
      abandoned her bourgeois life in La Paz in order to col-
      laborate in Che Guevera's National Liberation Army (ELN).
      Briefly sketches her life before and after conversion
      to revolutionary struggle and her death in 1973.

WOMEN IN SPANISH AMERICA

Politics and Twentieth Century Revolutionary Movements

2124   Unión de Mujeres de Bolivia (UMBO)
        1966 Orientación revolucionaria de Unión de Mujeres de
        Bolivia. Primer Congreso Nacional. La Paz: Imprenta
        y Librería Renovación. 148 p. ports.
        Collection of materials (commission reports, goals,
        regulations, and resolutions) from the 1st National
        Congress of UMBO, reflecting its doctrine and theory
        on female and national liberation in Bolivia. Includes
        discussions of the women's movement, role in politics,
        rights, working conditions, and maternity.

2125   "Women and the Vote."
        1944 The Inter-American 3:8:31-32. illus.
        Quotes lengthy editorial from La Paz newspaper, El
        Diario, regarding negative reaction to recommendation of
        Bolivian delegate at a meeting of the IACW for granting
        suffrage to Bolivian women. Paper's opinion is that
        women are not equipped to enter fully into exercising
        political rights. See VENEZUELA for additional
        information.

Paraguay

2126   AVALOS, ADOLFO
        1948 La mujer en la política. Formosa: Talleres Gráficos
        de "La Voz Popular." 35 p.
        Congratulating Argentine women on obtaining the vote,
        argues that Paraguayan women are ready for it too, as
        well as for congressional officeholding.

2127   Partido Revolucionario Febrerista. Departamento Asuntos
        Femeninos.
        1962 Ideario de la mujer febrerista. B.A.? 12 p.
        Hails the Partido Revolucionario Febrerista of
        Paraguay as a forerunner in the recognition and defense
        of women's rights and political participation; and
        describes the objectives of the Febrerista woman in
        political, educational, economic, social, moral and
        spiritual arenas.

Chile

2128   BUSSI de ALLENDE, HORTENSIA
        n.d. "Women in the Revolutionary Process in Chile."
        Wash., D.C.: Cultural Dept., Embassy of Chile. Los
        Angeles: Eds. de la Frontera. 14 p. tables.

Discusses how women have been marginalized in Chilean
society and how the socialist government of Allende
planned to incorporate them into the social, political
and economic development of the country--in community
organizations, agrarian reform, education, and industry.
Outlines goals and presents data on labor force by sex
in a series of 8 tables.

2129 CHANEY, ELSA M.
      1974 "The Mobilization of Women in Allende's Chile." In
      Women in Politics, ed. by J. Jaquette, pp. 267-80. N.Y.:
      John Wiley and Sons. bibl. notes.
          Uses Allende's socialist government in Chile as a case
      for studying the "difficulties in mobilizing women for
      social and political change at both the voter and the
      leadership levels," through an examination of the mascu-
      line perspective in print and through discussions with
      former interviewees of different political persuasions
      from author's study on women in politics. Attempting to
      understand why women have been notably absent as
      decision-makers, suggests that role of motherhood may
      account for women's inferiority in every caste and class
      since it influences their political participation in
      quantity and quality. As a result, views the female
      politician's role in Chile as that of *supermadre*, with
      her political sphere of activities as a larger *casa*.
      Reviews problem of defining models with which to analyze
      women's participation.

2130 _____.
      1973 "Women in Latin American Politics: The Case of Peru
      and Chile." In Female and Male in Latin America:
      Essays, ed. by A. Pescatello, pp. 103-39. Pittsburgh,
      Pa.: Univ. of Pittsburgh Press. tables, bibl. notes.
          Provides descriptive profile of women's professional
      and political participation trends, based on a survey
      among 167 Peruvian and Chilean women active in politics
      and government in 1967. Suggests reasons for women's
      restricted activity but does not emphasize explanatory
      and analytical dimensions. Posits image of the
      supermadre.

2131 _____.
      1972 "Mujeres en la política, el caso del Perú y de
      Chile." BDSLM/CIDHAL 3:1:29-39.
          Translated excerpts from unpublished Ph. D. thesis
      "Women in Latin American Politics: The Case of Peru and
      Chile" (University of Wisconsin, 1970). Female political

Politics and Twentieth Century Revolutionary Movements

participation has been characterized by its tentativeness and limitations to "feminine" tasks. Cites reasons why it is probably better not to encourage women to aspire to important policy-making positions. Without a fundamental change in attitudes, women's participation will continue as is—temporary and limited.

2132　CORREA MORANDE, MARÍA
1974　La guerra de las mujeres. Santiago: Edit. Univ. Técnica del Estado. 202 p. port.
The opposition's account of bourgeois female resistance to Allende's Marxist government in Chile, from his election to the presidency in 1970 to his assassination in 1973, and their participation or assistance in making his overthrowal possible.

2133　DONOSO LOERO, TERESA
1974　La epopeya de las ollas vacías. Col. Pensamiento Contemporáneo. Santiago: Ed. Nacional Gabriela Mistral. 149 p. illus., bibl.
Reports the individual and collective experiences of Chilean women during the 3-year Marxist government of Allende from the opposition's point of view. In a chatty style reviews the build-up of female power which culminated in overthrowal on September 11, 1973.

2134　GÓMEZ, EMA, et al.
1965　Mujeres en la lucha por el progreso y la felicidad. Documentos del XIII Congreso Nacional del Partido Comunista de Chile (10 al 17 de octubre de 1965). Folleto no. 5. Santiago. 50 p. port.
Collection of 11 speeches, presented at National Congress of Communist Party in Chile by female comrades representing various parts of the country, which refer to discrimination of capitalism against women, need for organized political and labor action, and importance of Mothers' Centers.

2135　MALUENDA, MARÍA M.
1973　"La Oficina Nacional de la Mujer: su primera etapa." C/F 1:2:53-57.
First director of Chile's National Office of Women briefly outlines its history, objectives, and activities (programs of health, work, community organizations, housing education, etc.).

2136　PRADO, DANDA
1973　"Mujer y política." PUFIN 7:174:17-20. illus.

Discusses historical position of men and women in politics, briefly tracing development of female suffrage up
to 1971. Considers the right to vote and be elected a
conquest of individual participation in power and politics and the 1st civic contact with contemporaries.
Nevertheless, this has not meant the modification of
women's dependent role. Discusses problem of conjugal
dependence and the need to industrialize domestic work.
Calls for feminist movement since socialism is insufficient for eliminating discrimination against women.

2137 PRENAFETA J., SERGIO
      1973 "Oficina Nacional de la Mujer: decretan la hora
      cero para el machismo." C/F 1:2:58-61.
         Short report on the activities of the National Office
      of Women (ONM) since Allende's official signing of
      Decree 1322. Interviews Rosario Castellanos, in charge
      of public relations at the ONM.

2138 SUÁREZ SILVA, JAIME
      1946 "La mujer ante el Senado de Chile." A 29:1/3:60-61.
         Reports that Chilean President Alessandri and a group
      of senators presented a law project whereby women would
      be granted full suffrage, i.e., beyond municipal elec-
      tions. Also touches upon inferior condition of women
      throughout LA, restricted to the domestic sphere despite
      their prominent participation in the Independence and
      Republican eras.

2139 VIDELA de PLANKEY, GABRIELA
      1974 "Las mujeres pobladoras de Chile y el proceso revolu-
      cionario." BDSLM/CIDHAL 4:4:19-24.
         Based on experiences as a Chilean social worker and
      journalist, analyzes female participation during the
      Allende years within the context of the class struggle.
      Cites specific examples of qualitative change effected
      by women: distribution of food and clothing, health
      campaign. Working-class women, conscious of a fundamen-
      tal change in the government's relationship with the
      people, played an important role in the most critical
      stages of Allende's government and functioned as one of
      the forces to confront reactionary activities. However,
      in the last analysis, Allende achieved very little for
      women despite some ambitious social projects (laundromats,
      artisan centers, child care, etc.).

2140 ZEITLIN, MAURICE and PETRAS, JAMES
      1970 "The Working Class Vote in Chile: Christian Democ-
      racy vs. Marxism." BJS 21:1:17-29. tables.

Women in Spanish America

Politics and Twentieth Century Revolutionary Movements

Analysis of electoral returns of the presidential elections of 1958 and 1964 in Chile's 296 municipalities proves hypothesis that the typical worker of Chile voted for FRAP (Frente de Acción Popular) candidate Allende. Since men and women vote at separate polling places, returns, broken down by sex, indicate a wide disparity in voting patterns of men and women, with women overwhelmingly against the Left.

Argentina

2141   ALVAREZ de HARVEY, DELIA
        1962   "Importancia de la incorporación de la mujer al campo de lo social." ECA 4:10:23-58. bibl.
        Includes brief history of Argentine struggle for female suffrage; declarations of Interamerican Conference (1938, 1945); Argentine laws which affect women's rights as a citizen, minor, mother, employee; women in public office; history of regulations and reforms for prostitution; women in private enterprise and public administration, etc. "Woman, by nature, is the antithesis of all that leads to war and its intrigues." Therefore, changes will have to be made so that a woman president does not have to follow constitutional rulings that the president is Commander-in-Chief of all armed forces, declares war, etc.

2142   ANZOÁTEGUI, YDERLA G.
        1953   La mujer y la política; historia del feminismo mundial. B.A.: Edit. Mendoza. 289 p. illus., ports., bibl.
        Includes a favorable biography of Eva Perón; general discussion of women and politics; history of feminism, suffrage and formation of Partido Femenino Peronista; list of national and provincial women senators and deputies elected in Argentina in 1951; and history of feminism in rest of LA.

2143   Argentine Republic. Senado de la Nación.
        1949   Congreso. Cámara de senadores. Ley María Eva Duarte de Perón, No. 13.010. Derechos políticos para la mujer. Buenos Aires. 90 p.
        Antecedents of, Senate debates regarding and text of law 13.010, passed in 1947, which grants Argentine women equal political rights.

2144   BACHEM d'ARAGON de RUIZ MORENO, LILIANE
       1967 "La mujer, antítesis del comunismo." MSA/B 44:330:
       43-56.
       Diatribe against communism, which has done nothing
       for women and vice versa. Cites Jacqueline Kennedy and
       European film stars as examples of outstanding women
       in Western society!!

2145   BERARDO, RODOLFO
       1955 "Derechos políticos de la mujer." UNC/BFDCS 19:
       2:275-90.
       Recounts feminist and anti-feminist arguments regarding
       women's entry into political life; notes change in
       Argentine politics from being a goal to a means; and
       briefly traces evolution of women's political rights in
       Argentina from the Constitution of 1853 to Law 13.010
       of 1947, which grants political equality to women.

2146   CÁCERES, Z. AURORA (EVANGELINA)
       1909? "Argentinas." In her Mujeres de ayer y de hoy,
       pp. 179-86. Paris: Casa Edit. Garnier Hnos.
       Considers collaboration of women in the social progress
       of Argentina (e.g., women's charity organizations).
       Cites writers and the Consejo Nacional de Mujeres
       (feminist group organized in 1901).

2147   COCCA, ALDO ARMANDO
       1948 Ley de sufragio femenino. Antecedentes
       parlamentarios - Ley 13.010. Disposiciones
       complementarias. B.A.: "El Ateneo." 351 p. bibl.
       Part 1 provides a detailed legal history of female
       suffrage in Argentina since 1862, distinguishing
       between municipal and national elections. Part 2 dis-
       cusses in detail law 13.010, which stipulates equal
       rights for women, and complementary legal dispositions.
       Extensive bibliography.

2148   _____.
       1947 Anteproyecto de ley de voto femenino (elevado al H.
       Congreso de la Nación el 19 de abril de 1947). B.A.:
       Edit. Bibliográfica Argentina. 175 p. bibl.
       Explication of 11 articles recommended to the Argentine
       Congress with respect to women's political rights.
       Equality of the sexes is not the basis of the argument.
       Female suffrage is conditional: e.g., women who commit
       infanticide, abortion or prostitution cannot vote.

2149   EDELMAN, FANNY J.
       1959 Conferencia nacional de mujeres comunistas, 7 y 8
       de marzo de 1959 en Rosario. B. A.: Edit. Anteo. 30 p.

Politics and Twentieth Century Revolutionary Movements

Speech, given on International Women's Day, discusses
role of Communist women in the people's struggle for
liberation, citing the Communist Party as a defender of
women's rights. Includes summary, declaration, and
resolutions of the conference.

2150 FLORIA, CARLOS ALBERTO
1972 La mujer argentina y la política. B.A.: Ministerio
de Cultura y Educación, Centro Nacional de Documentación
e Información Educativa. 27 p.
Discussion-provoking exploration of questions regarding
women and politics: Does having the vote mean women
have been able to operate in political world in same
manner as men? Has women's voting behavior substantially
modified general behavior of Argentine politics? et al.
Good synthesis of role of Argentine women in national
politics from May Revolution to Eva Perón includes analysis of writings of Argentine thinkers on this subject
and analysis of women's voting behavior, political affil-
iations and general impact.

2151 GREGORIO LAVIÉ, LUCILA de
1948 Las mujeres de América y la paz. Inst. Social.
Publicación de Extensión Universitaria, 58. Santa Fe,
Arg.: Univ. Nacional del Litoral. 19 p.
Argentine lawyer recalls the references made to woman's
mission in the consolidation of peace at various international conferences, where claims were also voiced for
women's rights, as a medium, not an end, in order to
work toward peace since the turn of the century. Concludes with description of new stage in Argentine women's
social evolution in terms of advancement in education,
employment and legal rights.

2152 HOLLANDER, NANCY CARO
1974 "Si Evita viviera." LAP 1:3:42-57. bibl.
Equal political, economic and social rights for women
were part of Peronist ideology and action. Traces historical roots of Perón's politican mobilization of
women, discussing women's fascism in Europe and class
role of women. Notes actual improvements for women
under first Peronist regime. Sees Evita as synthesis
of progressive and conservative aspects in Peronism;
discusses her role in the women's movement in Argentina,
as organizer of Peronist Women's Party, and her political
activism. Points out contradictions of Peronist feminist
ideology and leftist female activities in 1960's and
1970's. Based on Perón's words as well as secondary
sources.

2153   "In Brazil and Argentina: How Repression Treats Women."
        1972 ALA 1:3:20.
            Includes testimony of an Argentine revolutionary woman
        who was tortured with electrodes for her political
        activities.

2154   "Latin American Women March from Kitchen to Capitol."
        1936 Literary Digest 122:20:16-17.
            Delegates from Argentine women's organizations met in
        an effort to force the issue of suffrage and other
        rights for women in anticipation of the 8th Pan American
        Conference (B.A., December 1936).

2155   LEWIS, PAUL H.
        1971 "The Female Vote in Argentina, 1958-1965." CPS 3:
        4:425-41. tables, bibl.
            Using aggregate data from Argentina's elections
        (1958-65, because women and men voted in separate polling
        places), tests several generalizations about the female
        vote. Contrary to popular belief, more women than men
        voted in 1965 congressional elections. Consistent with
        popular belief, however, women as a whole tended to
        favor more conservative parties. Class differences
        influence women's voting behavior: working-class women
        are more radical than upper-class women and about as
        radical as middle-class women but more conservative than
        men of their same class. General conclusion is that
        differences between the male and female vote are not
        great.

2156   MARPONS, JOSEFINA
        1946 "La mujer en la lucha por la libertad." REVA 6:16:
        41-44.
            Notes progress of female integration in Argentine
        public life since the beginning of the 20c., when femi-
        nists campaigned for women's rights. Political upheaval
        in the 1940's sparked reaction and participation from
        women of all socio-economic groups--housewives, univer-
        sity students, nurses, Catholics, wealthy women. When
        the military government decided to grant female suffrage,
        women refused to accept it from anything but a legal
        and freely elected congress.

2157   MILBRATH, MARGARET
        1943 "Argentine Women Aid Allies." NBW 22:2:47, 57.
        illus.
            Describes activities of Ana Rosa de Martínez-Guerrero,
        then president of IACW, and those of the Junta de la
        Victoria, the largest women's organization in Argentina,

Politics and Twentieth Century Revolutionary Movements

of which she is founder--knitting, sewing, raising money
for Allies during WWII.

2158   MOREAU de JUSTO, ALICIA
1969 "Participación de la mujer en la política nacional."
UNC/R 10:1/2:283-304.
Early feminist recounts legal advances of Argentine
women from 1902 to 1947 when Perón proclaimed absolute
equality between the sexes, and political action of
women initiated by Eva Perón in 1949 when the first
National Assembly of the Feminine Peronist Movement was
inaugurated.

2159   _____.
1945 La mujer en la democracia. Buenos Aires: Librería
y Edit. "El Ateneo." 287 p. bibl.
First half studies women's efforts in Europe and the
US to integrate themselves into democracy, i.e., the
struggle for suffrage, and the role of the IACW in it.
Latter half focuses on Argentine women: evolution of
2 types--Hispano-colonial and Argentine-European--, with
statistics on women in labor force (1914-42) and education (1940-41); 20c. feminist movement with a discussion
on maternity as an obstacle to political action; 20c.
legislative action regarding women's rights; women and
politics; and women's role and influence in social evolution of humankind.

2160   La mujer ya puede votar.
1947 B.A.; Peuser. 24 p. illus., ports.
Propaganda piece to publicize role of the Peróns in
obtaining the vote for women in Argentina with the
passage of law 13.010 in 1947. Text of law and of
speeches by Juan and Eva Perón are reproduced.

2161   Las mujeres de Argentina.
1952 B.A.: Servicio Int'l. de Publicaciones Argentinas.
illus., plates, tables, map.
Account of Argentine women's struggle for equal political rights preceded by a brief review of women in history and education. Includes voting statistics. No
author or references; may be government propaganda.

2162   NAVARRO L., EUGENIO
1957 "La mujer argentina en la vida del país." CEE/DS
7:81:44-45. illus., ports.
Using 1947 census data, presents statistics on voters
in Argentina, by sex: population, average age and
probable life span, urban/rural breakdown, civil status,

religion, illiteracy rates, labor force participation.
Gives breakdown of voters in national elections of 1951
and 1954. Notes greater percentage of female votes.

2163   Partido Comunista de la Argentina. Sección Nacional de
Educación.
      1967   Problemas y luchas de las mujeres. Buenos Aires:
      Edit. Anteo. 94 p.
        Pamphlet containing 3 talks given at seminar (June
1966), organized by the National Education Section of
Argentina's Communist Party and the National Feminine
Commission of the Party, discusses 3 themes: 1) "The
Dictatorship, Social Organization of the Country and
Women's Problems" (by Oscar Révelo); 2) "Women Workers:
Their Recoveries, Organization and Struggles" (by Irma
Othar); and 3) "The National Democratic Front and Women's
Participation" (by Fanny Edelman). Item on working women
gives the most concrete information (salaries, laws,
organizational activities), while the other 2 expound on
what needs to be done and how to incorporate women's
participation and achievement of their rights.

2164   RIÉFFOLO BESSONE, JOSÉ FAUSTO
      1950   Los derechos sociales de la mujer. (Cartas a mi
      amigo Bover). Sufragismo y feminismo. Biblioteca del
      Ciudadano, 1. B.A.: Edit. "El Ateneo." 231 p.
        Using format of travel correspondence, describes to
a friend the concession of suffrage to women in Argentina
(1947), feminism and antifeminism, Juan and Eva Perón's
political position on the issue. Accepting women's
intervention in the State, he concludes with considerations on how to consolidate feminism in Argentina and
to orient female education toward that end.

2165   ROBERTSON, LIZBETH
      1945 "The Argentine Woman's Point of View." AAUW/J 38:
      2:81-86.
        Discusses concerns of leaders of Argentine women's
groups in general, and more specifically of the Federación de Asociaciones Catolicas de Empleadas, 2 social
service schools, Acción Católica, the IACW, the Women's
Division of the Department of Labor, quoting statements
by its chief and Perón; and also remarks on Argentine
view of feminism.

2166   STÁBILE, BLANCA
      1961   La mujer en el desarrollo nacional. Col. Día
      Venidero. Buenos Aires: Eds. Arayú. 235 p.

Politics and Twentieth Century Revolutionary Movements

Based on personal experience as director, narrates
history of the Dirección Nacional de Seguridad y Protección Social de la Mujer of Argentina since its formation
in 1958 for the investigation and amelioration of problems of working women. Provides statistics on women's
participation in national life in public administration,
the judiciary, unions and politics throughout the country and makes recommendations regarding women in community organizations, labor, the family and politics.
Appendix reproduces related decrees, statutes, documents,
lists of participating women, meetings held all over the
country, and members of the First National Seminar on
Participation of Women in Public Life.

Eva Perón

2167   ACOSSANO, BENIGNO
         1955 Eva Perón, su verdadera vida. Buenos Aires: Edit.
         Lamas. 158 p. illus., facsims.
            Claims to have written neither a defense of nor dia-
         tribe against Eva Perón. Believes no other female figure
         in the history of the world attained as much power as she
         was able to in the way she got it and held it. Eva Perón
         existed by virtue of Juan Perón's force but he also owed
         the height of his power to her, using her simplicity and
         courage. Believes Juan Perón capitalized on her passion
         for power. No references.

2168   BORRONI, OTELO and VACCA, ROBERTO
         1970 La vida de Eva Perón. Tomo I: Testimonios para su
         historia. Buenos Aires: Edit. Galerna. 348 p. bibl.
            Claims to be an objective account of Eva Perón's life
         without evaluating her personality as either that of
         saint or prostitute. At the end of each chapter includes
         a chronology of world events corresponding to events in
         the lives of Eva and Juan. Based on newspapers and other
         periodical literature, biographies and other secondary
         sources, and *testimonios*.

2169   ELLENA de SOTO, JULIO
         195? La acción política de Eva Perón. B.A. 31 p.
            Uncritical, laudatory evaluation of Eva Perón's polit-
         ical action, which is defined as a kind of concern for
         humanity. Cites the rights she declared for workers,
         old people, and women (suffrage).

2170   GHIOLDI, AMÉRICO
         1952 El mito de Eva Duarte. Montevideo. 78 p.

South America - Argentina/Eva Perón

A victim of Peronism, an Argentine exile denounces totalitarianism of Perón's regime from his socialist position. Scathing denouement of Eva's social welfare work, dispelling the myth that she was its creator, and pointing out details of state mechanism which fabricated it to present her as the national godmother. Draws comparisons between Eva and Doña Encarnación, wife of Argentine dictator, Manuel de Rosas. Judges Eva Perón as barely intelligent, culturally deficient, ignorant of moral and civil relations, lacking taste and self-criticism.

2171   LOMBILLE, ROMÁN J.
   1955 Eva, la predestinada. Alucinante historia de éxitos y frustraciones. Buenos Aires: Eds. Gure. 155 p.
   Sees Eva Perón as an actress her whole life in order to overcome the shame of her humble background, as a psychological battleground where the saint and the demon, the exploiter and the exploited, the executioner and the crucified fight it out. Focuses on her intervention in Argentine politics up to 1951 when she renounced her candidacy as vice president. No references.

2172   MAIN, MARY (FLORES, MARÍA)
   1952 The Woman with the Whip: Eva Perón. Garden City, N.Y.: Doubleday. 286 p.
   Portrays Eva Perón as an acquisitive, vindictive, unscrupulous, extravagant, plotting, resentful, untalented and uncultured megalomaniac. Presents her and Juan Perón as accomplices in opportunism. Despite the fact that women did not even have the right to vote let alone to hold public office, Eva Perón assumed much power and control and challenged the tradition of women's inferiority. Includes side comments on women's plight in Argentine society. Accuses Eva of lack of data in her autobiography but cites no documentation or bibliography herself.

2173   ORTIZ, DELIO
   1952 Eva Perón la inmortal. Quito: Edit. Rumiñahui. 157 p.
   Countering the publications which attack Eva Perón as an opportunist who abused power in Argentina in the 1940's, presents her as the most formidable female figure to have appeared in the world since Joan of Arc. Worships her as a heroine whose influence and messianic power could not be avoided. Presents her as Eva of America, the revolutionary, the builder, the realizer of good works, the great. Appendix contains press notices which appeared world-wide upon her death.

Politics and Twentieth Century Revolutionary Movements

2174   PAZ, CARLOS and DEUTSCH, OSCAR
        1974 Eva Perón, peronismo para el socialismo. Col.
        Argentina Popular. Buenos Aires: Eds. Del Mirador.
        93 p. bibl. f/notes.
            Through a socialist interpretation and chronological
        analysis of her speeches and writings, attempts to
        demonstrate Eva Perón's attitude and unconscious ties
        to scientific materialism (as in the thinking of Mao,
        Lenin, Marx, Engels, Che Guevara). Includes a selection
        of texts.

2175   PERÓN, EVA (DUARTE)
        1953 My Mission in Life. Trans. by Ethel Cherry. N.Y.:
        Vantage Press. 216 p. illus. Spanish version: 1951
        La razón de mi vida. Buenos Aires: Eds. Peuser. 316 p.
        illus., ports.
            In her own words, Eva Perón defends and explains her-
        self and her political actions, which she attributes to
        her indignation against social injustice. Expounds on
        her love for Juan Perón, to whom she owes all the won-
        derful things in her life, on Peronism, and on the social
        welfare work she carried out. Her attitude on women:
        "Women's happiness is not her own happiness, but that of
        others." The home is woman's great and irremediable
        destiny.

2176   _____.
        1951 Escribe Eva Perón. Buenos Aires: Eds. Argentinas.
        114 p.
            Collection of 16 of Eva Perón's articles synthesizing
        economic, social and political problems in Argentina
        and illustrating her political position with Peronism.
        Includes 2 brief pieces specifically on women: their
        present duty and responsibility, and their support for
        constitutional reform.

2177   _____.
        1949 Discurso en el acto inaugural de la primera Asamblea
        Nacional del Movimento Peronista Femenino. B.A. 31 p.
            Political rhetoric arguing for female Peronist unity,
        comparing economic, political and social situation of
        Argentine women before and after the rise of Perón, in
        order to demonstrate his contributions toward female
        liberation.

2178   _____.
        1947 Mensaje a las mujeres de América. B.A. 7 p.
            Speech given in celebration of Día de las Américas.
        Her message to women consists of: there have always

been women who helped the country and for every woman there is a place in America's history; all women should work toward peace and social justice.

2179 RODRÍGUEZ, ANGELA RINA
1949 Eva de América: Madona de los humildes. B.A.: Imprenta "Editorial Mayo." 103 p.
Journalist lavishly praises Eva Perón's social works for children, workers and old people, calling her the madonna of humble folk, samaritan of the disinherited, and angel of the workers.

2180 SEBRELI, JUAN JOSÉ
1966 Eva Perón, ¿aventurera o militante? Buenos Aires: Eds. Siglo Veinte. 157 p. bibl. f/notes.
Claims objective of this study on Eva Perón's life is to demonstrate the limitations of theories such as determinism and the cult of heroes to understand her role in Argentine history. Sees her as formed in the image of her epoch, class and country; at the same time, she formed them in her own image. Concludes that "the virtues and defects of Eva Perón are in the end those of the Argentine woman of her epoch with its immense possibilities and its limitations, and all Argentine women should look at themselves in its mirror." Includes descriptive chronological outline of her life at the end.

Uruguay

2181 FONTELA ORTEGA, LOLA
1929 Programa político para la mujer uruguaya. Montevideo: "Casa A. Barreiro y Ramos." 19 p.
Since women are representatives of the family and they could extend the home to society and since men have misgoverned, dividing society into antagonistic classes, it is incumbent on women to make the necessary modifications through practical and reasonable programs related to the national economy, commerce, political and social morals: e.g., candidates for office will belong to either party or sex; no woman under 30 may engage in prostitution under penalty of imprisonment for her and the consenting man, etc.

2182 LUISI, PAULINA, ed.
1930? La mujer uruguaya reclama sus derechos políticos. Discursos pronunciados en la Universidad en el mitín público del 5 de diciembre de 1929. Montevideo. 211 p. ports., fold. map.

WOMEN IN SPANISH AMERICA

Politics and Twentieth Century Revolutionary Movements

Includes 11 speeches given at the University in
Montevideo at a public meeting (5 December 1929) organized by The National Council of Women and the Uruguayan
Alliance of Women to argue for women's rights, especially
the vote. An appendix reproduces petitions and programs.

2183   "Never Is a Woman as Equal to a Man As When She's Behind a
       Colt 45."
       1972 ALA 1:3:17-19.
       Outlines position of the Tupamaros, the National Liber-
       ation Movement of Uruguay, on the role of women in the
       urban guerrilla movement, as stated in their Actas
       Tupamaras. Indicates need to overcome difficulties of
       role assigned to women by capitalist society in order to
       assume responsibility as a militant. Women's tasks
       include delivery of messages and objects, organization
       of work, political orientation of new members, and the
       "feminine touch."

2184   PASCAL, VINCENT de
       1949 "Uruguayan Portia." OAS/AM 1:5:7-10.
       Despite an inane introduction comparing her culinary
       skill with career ability, provides information on back-
       ground, achievements and activities of Uruguayan feminist,
       lawyer and legislator Sofía Alvarez Vignoli de Demicheli
       who has fought for women's civil and political equality
       beyond the right to vote. She was first woman to be
       elected senator in western hemisphere and first woman
       Minister Plenipotentiary to sign an international treaty.

CARIBBEAN

Puerto Rico

2185   "More Votes for Women."
       1929 Nation 128:3338:7556.
       Reports success of Puerto Rican women's fight for the
       vote. Alludes to suffrage situation in Brazil and
       Mexico.

Cuba

2186   BERMAN, JOAN
       1970 "Women in Cuba." WOM/JL 1:4:10-14.
       Written upon returning from participation in 1970
       Venceremos Brigade, discusses changes for women in
       revolutionary Cuba in terms of education, employment,

marriage, divorce, etc., as well as remnants of *machismo*
and patriarchal structure.

2187   BLANCO, MARY LOUISE
       1944   "Cuban Women Fight Inflation." PANAM 5:3:49-51.
          Discusses creation of Feminine Service for Civil De-
       fense (10 August 1942) by Dictator Batisto to prepare
       Cuban women for civilian tasks during wartime and de-
       scribes the group's activities.

2188   CARRERA y JUSTIZ, FRANCISCO
       1905   La ciencia cívica en su relación con la mujer y con
       la democracia. Estudios de Sociología Municipal.
       Havana: "La Moderna Poesía." 79 p.
          In 3 lectures given at Normal School for Teachers of
       Havana, discusses Cuba's need for civic action by women.
       Women should have political rights (the vote), partici-
       pate civically, and cooperate morally in national life.

2189   CASTRO, FIDEL
       1974   "July 26, 1974." CR 4:2:35. illus.
          Excerpts from Castro's July 26th speech commemorating
       the anniversary of the attack on the Moncada barracks:
       signals problems of women in not being recognized for
       their contribution to the Revolution; refers to very low
       percentage of women elected at grass roots level; and
       calls for their complete freedom and participation.

2190   _____.
       1972   "Women as a Revolutionary Force." ALA 1:3:12-13.
       illus.
          Excerpts from speech given by Fidel in Santiago, Chile
       (29 November 1971), in which he praises women as a deci-
       sive force in revolution. Compares role given to women
       by reactionaries and that offered by the Revolution.
       From Granma (19 December 1971).

2191   _____.
       1963   Speech to the Women. Jan. 15, 1963. N.Y.: Fair
       Play for Cuba Committee. n.p.
          Cites gains made by Cuban women in labor, education
       and other areas since 1959. Calls for continued revolu-
       tionary participation of women in struggle against
       imperialism.

2192   CHERTOV, EVA
       1970   "Women in Revolutionary Cuba." The Militant
       34:34:9-11.
          Based on lecture given (May 1970) after having spent
       6 years as an English teacher in Havana. Discusses

561

Politics and Twentieth Century Revolutionary Movements

status of women in pre-1959 Cuba and changes brought on by Castro Revolution in education, employment, child care, family, image of women. Makes appeal for Young Socialist Alliance.

2193 COLLADO y ROMERO, MARÍA
1953 "La mujer cubana en el Parlamento." In Album del Cincuentenario, 1902-1952, by Asociación de Reporteros de la Habana, pp. 123-25. Havana: Edit. Lex. ports.
Reviews female participation in the Cuban legislature from the 16th Congressional Period in 1936 when women first occupied positions in the House of Representatives, until 1948. Names individuals and the legislation they introduced. Also cites the only 2 women senators during the 1940's.

2194 FRANQUI, CARLOS
1968 The Twelve. Trans. by A. B. Teichner, N.Y.: Lyle Stuart. 190 p. Spanish version: 1966 El libro de los doce. Col. Ancho Mundo, 19. Mex., D.F.: Eds. Era. 174 p. illus.
Participants in the early struggles of the Cuban Revolution recount its history between 2 December 1956 and 28 May 1957. Celia Sánchez, Haydee Santamaría and Vilma Espin relate their experiences and interpretation of events in 3 separate chapters.

2195 GONZÁLEZ, EDELMIRA
1955 Martha Fernández Miranda de Batista. Havana. 208 p. illus., plates.
Lauds philanthropic activities of Cuban dictator Batista's wife during 1950's, recounting her social service to the people like another Eva Perón.

2196 GORDON, LINDA
1970 "Speculations on Women's Liberation in Cuba." WOM/JL 1:4:14-15.
Based on her travels in Cuba, Marxist speculates about the effect of Cuba's socialism on the situation of Cuban women. Believes "there is no feminism in Cuba today because there are neither conditions nor need for a feminist movement now."

2197 GUDJONSSON, PETUR
1972 "Women in Castro's Cuba." The Progressive 36:8:25-29.
Journalist reports his impressions of women's situation in revolutionary Cuba after an intensive tour, illustrating with satisfied and disgruntled comments by

the women themselves. Concludes that in spite of noteworthy advancements, women are still very much subject
to male domination.

2198 HERRERA, AÍDA T. de
1944 "¡Un vítor a las mujeres cubanas!" UPA/Bs
78:3:136-40. illus., port.
Names and praises the many clubs and associations
patriotically organized by Cuban women to aid the war
effort (e.g., Servicio Femenino de Defensa Civil) and to
promote peace, better living and culture.

2199 JENNESS, LINDA
1970 Women and the Cuban Revolution: Speeches by Fidel
Castro; Articles by Linda Jenness. A Merit Pamphlet.
N.Y.: Pathfinder Press. 15 p.
Collection of excerpts on women from Castro's May Day
and Santa Clara speeches: "The New Role for Women in
Cuban Society" and "Women's Liberation: The Revolution
Within a Revolution;" and 2 articles by Jenness: "The
Successful Battle Against Discrimination" and "'Lucia':
An Attack on Male Chauvinism." Cites new roles for women
and reviews 3-part feature film on women's participation
in revolutionary struggles in Cuba.

2200 LADRÓN de GUEVARA, MATILDE
1964 Diario de una mujer en Cuba; adiós al cañaveral.
3rd abr. ed. Col. Testimonios. B.A.: Seijas y
Goyanarte. 313 p.
President of the Chilean-Cuban Institute of Cultura at
the University of Chile resigned from her post in order
to witness the Cuban Revolution first hand. Narrates
her departure from Chile, a year after the July 26 movement, her imprisonment in Cuba, and her inexplicable
release.

2201 RAMOS, ANA
1971 "La mujer y la revolución en Cuba." CDLA
10:65/66:56-72. bibl. f/notes. English excerpt: 1972
"Women in the Cuban Revolution." CRC/N 2:2:3-11.
Begins with history of women's status in capitalist
society since the French Revolution, pointing out double
exploitation as worker and as woman and considering situation of women in LA by class. Part 3 recounts female
revolutionary action since the Independence movement
against Spain; analyzes women's liberation within the
context of a socialist revolution; and discusses women's
incorporation into society through 3 central themes:
1) handicap of women (as compared to men) in education

and employment, 2) national dependence on agriculture as the primary economic base in the early years of the Cuban Revolution, and 3) change in mentality. Cites some statistics.

2202 RANDALL, MARGARET
1974 Cuban Women Now: Interviews With Cuban Women and Cuban Women Now: Afterword 1974. Toronto: The Women's Press and Damont Press Graphix. 375 p. and 16 p. illus. Spanish versions: 1973 La mujer cubana ahora. vol 1. Caracas: Rocinante. 130 p. illus. 1972 Mujeres en la revolución. Margaret Randall conversa con mujeres cubanas. Col. Mínima Mayor. Historia Inmediata. Mex., D.F.: Siglo Veintiuno Eds. 356 p. illus. 1972 La mujer cubana ahora. Havana: Edit. de Ciencias Sociales, Inst. Cubano del Libro. 471 p. illus.
       Collection of interviews with more than 100 Cuban women (members of the Central Committee of the Communist Party, former prostitutes and domestic servants, foundry and refinery workers, dancers, peasants, housewives, etc.) about their lives, experiences, situations, visions, and the Revolution's effect on how women can fulfill themselves. The changing role of women is considered in the context of Cuba's specific historical and socio-economic conditions. Notes that existing "contradictions themselves speak of the transition." Afterword optimistically discusses current changes and problems since the interviews were conducted in 1971. Presently the only major, though limited, overview of women in Cuban Revolution.

2203 _____.
1974 "Women in the Cuban Revolution." WOM/JL 3:4:2-4. illus.
       Notes that major problems relating to women have been taken care of by revolutionary Cuban government, although an ideological struggle persists with respect to machismo and women still face a "second shift" of work at home.

2204 REEVES, NANCY
1960 "Women of the New Cuba." MR 12:387-92.
       Observations made upon returning from Cuba. Briefly discusses status of Cuban women before 1959 and gains achieved with the Revolution in terms of education, housing, employment, child care, and marriage.

2205 ROBB, CAROL and HAGEMAN, ALICE
1974 "Let Them Be Examples . . . ." CR 4:2:19-21. illus.

Several brief paragraphs on Rosa "la Bayamesa"
Castellanos, Ana Betancourt and Mariana Grajales, 3
women who aided and abetted the Independence movement
in 1868 against Spain, and on 10 women who have made a
contribution to the Cuban Revolution since the 1950's
(Melba Hernández, Isabel Rielo et al.).

2206 ROJAS, MARTA and RODRÍGUEZ CALDERÓN, MIRTA, eds.
1971 Tania, The Unforgettable Guerrilla. N.Y.: Random
House, Vintage Books. 212 p. illus., facsims., ports.,
map. Spanish version: 1970 Tania, la guerrillera
inolvidable. Havana: Inst. del Libro. 355 p. facsims.,
plan, ports.
Scrapbook of recollections and photographs, in the
words of those who knew her and in her own words, of
Tamara Bunke (1937-67), Argentine-born young woman who
worked for the Revolution in Cuba and died with Che
Guevara in the Bolivian jungle.

2207 ROTHKRUG, BARBARA and WHITEHEAD, SHARI
1970 "The Revolution of Cuban Women." In Cuba: 100
Years of Struggle. N.Y.: Cuba Resource Center. 6 p.
illus.
First-hand report by North American visitors on
changes in situation of Cuban women as a result of
Castro revolution. They note new mobility and independence, greater educational and employment opportunities,
political consciousness, position on birth control.
They also point out contradictions: separate jobs for
men and women, persistent double standard, etc.

2208 ROWBOTHAM, SHEILA
1974 "Colony Within the Colony." In her Women, Resistance and Revolution. A History of Women and Revolution
in the Modern World, pp. 220-33. N.Y.: Random House,
Vintage Books. bibl. notes.
Traces female participation in Cuban revolutionary
movements from Independence to Castro (paralleled by
film "Lucía"). Although much effort has been made to
overcome male/female segregation and there is a commitment to liberating women from and socializing household tasks, the material circumstances of underdevelopment
limit social experimentation and men still cling to traditional reactionary ideas. Notes contradictions in
sexual relations. Concludes that women are still a
colonized group within a colony. Mirrors literature on
Cuban women during last 10 years.

Politics and Twentieth Century Revolutionary Movements

2209 SALADO, MINERVA
1972 "Women in Revolutionary Cuba." NACLA/LAER
6:10:21-25.
Interview with the director of the Cuban Women's
Federation (FMC), Vilma Espin, regarding FMC's role,
achievements and objectives, position on feminist trends,
etc.

2210 STEFFENS, HEIDI
1974 "FMC at the Grass Roots." CR 4:2:25-26. illus.
Impressions of Federation of Cuban Women delegation in
large agricultural province Camaguey, considered most
underdeveloped area of Cuba. Outlines the structure and
operation and the functions of the various secretaries.
Author was taken on tour by Secretary General of FMC for
province.

2211 _____.
1974 "FMC: Feminine, Not Feminist." CR 4:2:22-24. illus.
Brief history of Federation of Cuban Women since it was
organized in 1960: goals, activities, concerns. It is
responsible for organizing and mobilizing women to actively participate in the Revolution and for analyzing
and solving women's problems. Includes chart diagram-
ming organizational structure.

2212 SUTHERLAND, ELIZABETH
1969 The Youngest Revolution. A Personal Report on Cuba.
N.Y.: Dial Press. 277 p. illus.
First hand observations on life in Cuba since the
Revolution include comments on and by women throughout
text. Chapter on "The Longest Revolution" (pp. 169-90)
focuses on question of male/female relations, the changing position of women, and the need for a new ideology
to supercede traditional mores. Includes a diary kept
while participating in an agricultural camp of women on
Isle of Youth.

2213 TORRES HERNÁNDEZ, LÁZARO
1973 "Presencia de la mujer en la revolución cubana."
Bohemia 65:25:100-06.
Divided in several epochs (Colony, Republic, Revolution of 1933, Batista regime, Revolution since 1959),
traces participation of women in Cuban liberation movements since 1868. Cites well-known figures and their
contributions and women's organizations.

2214   TORRIENTE, LOLÓ de la
        1963 "Una mirada a la actividad de la mujer cubana."
        UH/U 27:163:53–69.
            General overview of female participation in Cuban
        national life from 1762, when women sent a message to
        Carlos III to defend Havana against English attack
        through the 19c., during the Republic, Machado regime,
        and Socialist Cuba. Notes suffrage campaigns before
        WWI and other women's groups formed since then; active
        role of guerrillas; formation and activity of the FMC.
        Refers to "typical" female support—self-denial, sacri-
        fice, teaching, etc.

2215   VALDÉS, NELSON P.
        1974 "A Bibliography on Cuban Women in the Twentieth
        Century." CSN/BESC 4:2:31 p.
            Valuable compendium contains 568 items, some with a
        one-sentence summary, on socio-political-economic as-
        pects of women during 2 historical periods: pre-
        revolutionary Cuba (1900–58) and revolutionary Cuba
        (1959–73), with an emphasis on the latter. Subject
        headings include labor and production, social structure,
        women's emancipation, family life, sex, law, politics
        and education.

2216   Venceremos Brigade
        1971 "Women." In Venceremos Brigade: Young Americans
        Sharing the Life and Work of Revolutionary Cuba; Diaries,
        Letters, Interviews, Tapes, Essays, Poetry, by the
        Venceremos Brigade, ed. by S. Levinson and C. Brightman,
        pp. 246–72. N.Y.: Simon and Schuster. illus.
            Composite portrait of women in the Cuban Revolution
        presented through excerpts from the diaries, letters,
        interviews, tapes, essays and poetry of the first 2
        Venceremos Brigades (1969–70). Also reflects struggle
        of North American women with male chauvinism and con-
        tradictions in the liberation of Cuban women.

2217   "Women in Transition"
        1974 Special issue of CR. 4:2. bibl.
            Contains a dozen items on women in revolutionary Cuba
        with regard to labor, law, organizations, etc.

2218   YGLESIAS, JOSÉ
        1968 In the Fist of the Revolution: Life in a Cuban
        Country Town. N.Y.: Random House, Pantheon Books.
        307 p.
            North American writer of Cuban descent revisited
        Mayarí, town in northern Oriente province, for several

Politics and Twentieth Century Revolutionary Movements

months in 1967. Micro-analysis of life there includes
passing remarks on women of all ages engaged in different activities--from hotel chambermaid to doctor's
patients. Chapter on *machismo* deals with attitudes
toward women and sex, double standard, interviews with
several FMC women, and a visit to a school. Discusses
changes, dissatisfactions on a national level as well as
personal complaints and satisfactions.

2219   ZEITLIN, MAURICE
       1967 "Sex and the Single Worker." In his <u>Revolutionary</u>
       <u>Politics and the Cuban Working Class</u>, pp. 120-31.
       Princeton, N.J.: Princeton Univ. Press. bibl. f/notes.
       Based on interviews with 210 workers in Cuban indus-
       trial plant (1962), deals with effect of sex on politics--
       e.g., women's conservatism even after participating in
       labor force; and effect of marriage on politics--e.g.,
       married workers are more revolutionary than single
       workers despite their greater responsibilities.

Dominican Republic

2220   Congreso Femenino Dominicano, 2nd. Santiago de los Caballeros,
       1945.
       1945 <u>La mujer dominicana en documento trascendental</u>
       <u>proclama la reelección del Presidente Trujillo en el</u>
       <u>año 1947</u>. Ciudad Trujillo: Edit. La Nación. 524 p.
       illus.
       Five-hundred-twenty-four pages of women in favor of
       the reelection of Trujillo for 1947-52, listed by
       provinces, sections, and streets.

2221   MORITZEN, JULIUS
       1943 "Political Emancipation of Dominican Women a
       National Asset." <u>DR</u> 11:1:14-15.
       Reports on the vote granted to women by Trujillo in
       1942 and any feminism which existed on the island.

2222   _____.
       1943 "Political Emancipation of Women in the Dominican
       Republic." <u>PAU/B</u> 77:3:149-54. illus.
       Very brief history of the women's suffrage movement
       in the Dominican Republic from 1927 to 1942 when Trujillo
       granted the vote to women. Also reports on the First
       Congress of Dominican Women (January 1943), naming par-
       ticipants and resolutions.

2223   MOTA, VIVIAN M.
        1974 "El feminismo y la política en la República
        Dominicana." BDSLM/CIDHAL 4:4:50-60.
           Analyzes evolution of female political participation
        in 20c. Dominican Republic as characterized by positive
        correlation with higher educational and socio-economic
        level, fairly low level of activity except during suf-
        frage movement, and collaboration of women from dominant
        sectors of Dominican society with the system in a non-
        threatening way to their interests. Cites factors for
        lack of successful political participation of leftist or
        proletarian women. Describes political and feminist
        activities of Trujillistas and Reformistas, explaining
        why neither group can basically improve Dominican women's
        situation or liberate them.

2224   TRUJILLO, RAFAEL L.
        1941 "Proclamation by Generalissimo Rafael L. Trujillo
        Molina to the Women of the Dominican Republic. Dated
        June 5, 1941, Birth Anniversary of His Son "Ramfis."
        DR 9:4:9.
           President Trujillo promises to extend equal rights to
        the women of the Dominican Republic through constitu-
        tional reform.

PERSPECTIVES ON WOMEN'S LIBERATION

This section covers feminist and anti-feminist arguments, concern
for women's rights, feminist movements, sexist ideologies, speculations on women's liberation movements in Latin America, and theories
of women's liberation within the context of the class struggle.

For references on the fight for female suffrage, women's organizations dedicated to the improvement of women's status, and additional
items on women's liberation within the context of socio-political
movements, see POLITICS AND 20th CENTURY REVOLUTIONARY MOVEMENTS.
Educational, legal, and economic gains are treated separately in their
respective categories, EDUCATION, LAW, and ECONOMIC LIFE. For conflicts arising from women's attempts at and gains in independence and
entrance into the public sphere of activities, see MARRIAGE AND THE
FAMILY and PSYCHOLOGY. See also the GENERAL category.

SPANISH AMERICA - GENERAL

2225 ANDER EGG, EZEQUIEL; ZAMBONI, NORMA; YAÑEZ, ANABELLA TERESA;
      GISSI, BUSTOS JORGE and DUSSEL, ENRIQUE
        1972 Opresión y marginalidad de la mujer en el orden
        social machista. Col. Desarrollo Social, 14. B.A.:
        Edit. Humanitas. 206 p.
          Collection of 4 theoretical essays (sociological,
        psychosocial and philosophical) on women's oppression
        and marginality in patriarchal, or *machista*, society,
        presented at the Instituto de Acción Social y Familiar
        in Mendoza, Argentina in 1972. See items listed sepa-
        rately by author.

2226 DUSSEL, ENRIQUE
        1974 "Towards a Methodology of Women's Liberation, Latin
        American Style." An Anthology on Women in Latin America,
        pp. 3-10. First special issue of the BDSLM/CIDHAL
        October. illus.
          Views women's liberation in LA as possible only within
        the global process of liberation, not as oligarchic

feminism. The traditional family must die and a new one
be born, one in which men fully participate in daily
household activities. Proposes several methods of
action. Notes importance of listening to the voice of
ordinary, poor women.

2227 _____.
1973 "La liberación de las mujeres vista por un latinoamericano." BDSLM/CIDHAL 3:3:36-44.
The trouble with feminism, North American style, is
its error in wanting to eliminate any differences between women and men. Insists women's liberation must
take place along lines of sexual distinction. Believes
nuns are in a good position to help liberate other women
because they are free from demands and absorption by men;
however, it is necessary that they be free from all masculine ties, including the Roman curate.

2228 FOPPA, ALAIDE
1974 "Is Man So Much Dominated, After All?" In Anthology
on Women in Latin America, pp. 11-14. First special
issue of BDSLM/CIDHAL, October. Spanish version:
"Acerca del Varón Domado." BDSLM/CIDHAL 4:2:25-27.
Critique of Mexican publication of The Dominated Male,
by German-Argentine Esther Villar. Considers book con-
tradictory, annoying and partial; its arguments are
specific to and valid only for bourgeoisie, neglecting
to take into account working class women. Villar maintains that despite her profound stupidity, woman has
been able to dominate and use man to her advantage.

2229 GARCÍA GRADILLA, NATIVIDAD
1972 "Liberación de la mujer en América Latina." Summa
52:13-14. illus.
Poses set of interrogatories regarding position of
Latin American women and liberation and why women's movement (as in Europe and North America) has not occurred
in LA. Without answering questions, concludes that it
is necessary to change mentality of women and men.
Problem in LA is a matter of dependence, under-development
and a mentality produced from racist and sexist education.

2230 HENAULT, MIRTA
1973? "La mujer y los cambios sociales." In Las mujeres
dicen basta, by M. Henault, P. Morton, and I. Larguía,
pp. 13-40. B.A.: Eds. Nueva Mujer.
Argentine feminist analyzes causes of female oppression, pointing out that the most significant social

Perspectives on Women's Liberation

revolutions (Russian, Chinese, Cuban) essentially have
not altered women's situation, the result of unequal
economic development. Cites need for collectivization
of domestic sphere, elimination of private means of production and a change in women's consciousness to fight
for their own liberation. Notes radical changes in
Cuba.

2231   HENAULT, MIRTA; MORTON, PEGGY and LARGUÍA, ISABEL
       1973? Las mujeres dicen basta. B.A.: Eds. Nueva Mujer.
       130 p.
       Collection of 3 theoretical articles by 2 Argentine
       and 1 North American women on female liberation, pub-
       lished by Argentine feminist group Nueva Mujer, part of
       the Unión Femenista Argentina, as a consciousness-
       raising act. Attempts to go beyond limitations of
       Marxist theory and socialism. See individual articles
       of Henault (#2230) and Larguía (#2233).

2232   INMAN, SAMUEL GUY
       1922 "The Feminist Movement in Latin America." PAU/B
       54:4:353-62.
       Describes the development, organization, activities
       and objectives of women's movements in Argentina, Chile,
       Uruguay, Brazil and Peru. Reproduces extensive com-
       ments by Latin Americans related to the subject.

2233   LARGUÍA, ISABEL
       1973? "La mujer." In Las mujeres dicen basta, by
       M. Henault, P. Morton, and I. Larguía, pp. 71-128.
       B.A.: Eds. Nueva Mujer.
       See Larguía and Demoulin (#2234).

2234   LARGUÍA, ISABEL and DEMOULIN, JOHN
       1973 "Por un feminismo científico." BDSLM/CIDHAL
       3:4:49-61. 1972 "Toward a Science of Women's Libera-
       tion." NACLA/LAER 6:10:3-20. illus. 1971 "Hacia una
       ciencia de la liberación de la mujer." CDLA
       10:65/66:37-53.
       Various versions of an article which stresses the need
       for a scientific theory of female liberation because of
       its primordial importance in the construction of a
       classless society. In an attempt to elaborate such a
       theory, discusses differences between "visible" and
       "invisible" work, division of labor, consolidation of
       opposing sex typologies, Industrial Revolution and in-
       corporation of women into working class, domestic work
       as a second shift, women as prisoners of consumer society,

sexual liberalism, female economism, and differences
between reformist and revolutionary ideas. Agrees with
M. Benston's "political economy of women's liberation"
but insists on necessity of going beyond Marxist theory
in order to reveal housewife's role and its political
implications in a class society.

2235 "La liberación de la mujer en América Latina."
1973 Special issue of Fichas de ISAL 4:46.
Contains statistics on women in the economy and education; discussions of women's liberation and peasant
women; and reproduces statements by different women's
groups in several countries. See Moro (#2238), and
Carpio (#1405).

2236 "Liberación Femenina."
1972 Special issue of S/HM 5:58.
Very well illustrated collection of articles on women's
liberation throughout the world, including 3 essays
specific to LA. See Aravena Derpich (#2272), and Baltra
(#1245).

2237 MAÑON, DARÍO A.
1956 Orientaciones feministas para las mujeres de América.
Col. Libros para las Mujeres, 3. Mex., D.F.: Ed.
Ibero-Mexicana. 107 p.
General discussion of feminism does not refer to specific movements but suggests directions and programs
which could be followed.

2238 MORO, AMÉRICA
1973 "La liberación de la mujer latinoamericana." Fichas
de ISAL 4:46:1-18. tables.
Providing statistics from various Latin American countries, offers panorama of women's economic, educational
and juridical situation. Cites in particular women's
advances and revolutionary participation in Chile and
Cuba and women's education in Uruguay. However, notes
that everywhere women are an object, housewives, servants, etc.; they continue unliberated.

2240 "La voz de America discutiendo sobre feminismo."
1926 ND 7:6:25-27, 30; 7:8:26-28.
Interesting debate among 3 imaginary men who represent
the pessimistic, optimistic and common sense opinions
on feminism in early 20c.

573

Women in Spanish America

Perspectives on Women's Liberation

2239   STEVENS, EVELYN P.
       1973   "The Prospects for a Women's Liberation Movement in
       Latin America."   WRU/JMF 35:2:313-21.   bibl.
       Does not view Latin American women as "dupes of a
       male-dominated power-elite."   Defines the *machismo-
       marianismo* pattern of attitudes and behavior, noting its
       conscious perpetuation by Latin American women in order
       to preserve certain advantages.   Compares North American
       and Latin American male/female relations and female
       liberation within the context of social, economic, polit-
       ical and religious conditions, predicting the unlikeli-
       hood of a women's movement in LA along North American
       lines.

2241   WALSH, GEORGE
       1918   "South American Feminism, Showing Some Portraits of
       Charming South American Types."   SA 6:10:12-13.   illus.
       Portraits of "types" from several countries accompany
       comments on increasing restlessness among South American
       women, disintegration of certain traditions and estab-
       lishment of new ones.   Believes an understanding of wo-
       men is crucial to success or failure of nations engaged
       in trade and commerce with SA.

MIDDLE AMERICA

Mexico

2242   ACEVEDO, MARTA
       1972   "Sobre el sexismo mexicano; I, primeras considera-
       ciones."   CM/SS 553:VIII-IX.   illus.
       In addition to socio-economic conditions, ideology of
       sexism serves to maintain oppression of women through
       inter-relationship of cheap sex, feminine/masculine
       stereotypes, women's relegation to role in family.
       Notes lack of group identification among women because
       of isolation in nuclear home.   Suggests need for inter-
       preting personal problems on political level.

2243   ARNAIZ AMIGO, AURORA
       1965   Feminismo y femineidad.   Mex., D.F.:   Talleres
       Daniel Boldo.   223 p.   illus.
       In response to her student's question--"What is
       feminism?"--in 26 letters voices her philosophy: fem-
       inists of the past were, in general, intelligent, cul-
       tured women who never confused feminism with femininity,
       unlike those of today, who sit around cafés talking,
       smoking and drinking; conceptual thinking is alien to

female world; not fulfilling women's fundamental mission
in the home is one cause of disintegration of family
today.

2244   CAMPUZANO, FELIPE
        1973 "Antisexismo; de la liberación de la mujer como
        abolición del trabajo invisible." CM/SS 600:XIII-XIV.
        illus.
           Mexican's discussion of The Liberation of Women: Year
        Zero, a collection of essays by militant North Americans,
        Cubans, French et al., analyzing women's liberation prob-
        lem in terms of economic exploitation, which is accompa-
        nied by cultural and moral psychological oppression.

2245   CASTAÑEDA, CARLOS E.
        1951 "Sor Juana Inés, primera feminista de América."
        UA/U 104:701-17.
           Views Sor Juana's activities and writings as first
        example of feminism in America. Concentrates on develop-
        ment of and dedication to intellectual aspects in her
        life. Reply to Bishop of Puebla in 1691, who chided her
        for excessive devotion to non-religious material, ex-
        presses and defends fervent desire for women's right to
        study, write, and teach.

2246   CASTELLANOS, ROSARIO
        1950 Sobre cultura femenina. Mex., D.F.: Eds. de
        "América," Revista Antólogica. 127 p. bibl.
           Well-known Mexican writer arrives at some very negative
        conclusions: a separate female culture does not exist;
        lack of female participation in cultural processes is due
        to women's indifference toward cultural values; women
        satisfy their need to eternalize themselves through
        maternity; women have chosen the most accessible of cul-
        tural forms--literature, especially poetry and novel.

2247   Encuentro de Mujeres. Grupo de Trabajo: "Grupo 7"
        1972 "La mujer en México." PC 1:8:25-33. illus.
           Overview of women's oppressive situation in Mexico,
        particularly in role as peasant and worker. Covers
        female participation in strikes, revolution, struggle
        for suffrage, domestic service, procreation and woman
        as a sexual object, object of luxury, consumer and house-
        wife. Women have a double reason to be revolutionary:
        they are oppressed by class and by sex. It is necessary
        to consider women's struggle according to class of each
        woman.

Perspectives on Women's Liberation

2248   FERNÁNDEZ, ROSA MARTA
        1972   "La mujer mexicana y la conciencia de la opresión."
        CM/SS 563 (22 November):X-XI. illus.
            Passionate objection to situation of women as dominated
        majority subordinated to domestic sphere, oppressed by a
        sexist ideology which is reinforced through family, laws,
        institutions, education and mass media.

2249   GAMBOA A., IGNACIO
        1906   La mujer moderna. Mérida, Yucatán: Imprenta
        "Gamboa Guzmán. 136 p.
            Argues against feminism, citing divorce, women's
        organizations against marriage, and "lesbian vice" as
        more than sufficient motives to conclude that modern
        women were tending to disengage themselves from obliga-
        tions of motherhood and to give themselves over to
        sensual pleasures.

2250   HIRIART, ROSARIO
        1973   "America's First Feminist; Sor Juana Inés de la Cruz."
        OAS/AM 25:5:2-7. illus.
            Descriptive sketch of Sor Juana's life. Quotes from
        her letter to and response from the Bishop regarding
        Father Vieira and her laments for the position of women
        and their status with respect to education.

2251   LAURELL, CRISTINA
        1972   "Sobre el sexismo mexicano; II la ofensiva patriarcal
        y el movimiento de la mujer." CM/SS 553 (13 September):
        X. illus.
            Sees women's movement as a social struggle to be ana-
        lyzed within a dynamic historical context, citing its
        changing characteristics since 1906. Lances article by
        Mexican psychologist Césarman (Diorama de Excelsior,
        13 August 1972) which interprets women's liberation
        through static concept of history and sees use of con-
        traceptives as psychically disastrous to the population.

2252   MACÍAS, ANA
        1974   "The Mexican Revolution Was No Revolution For Women."
        In History of Latin American Civilization, ed. by
        L. Hanke, 2nd ed., vol. 2, pp. 591-601. Boston: Little,
        Brown.
            Brief but informative study of feminism in Mexico,
        specifically: its appearance in Yucután during latter
        part of 19c.; inconclusive efforts by national leaders
        during Revolution (1910-20) compared to radical efforts
        by Salvador Alvarado, Governor of Yucatán, to improve
        women's opportunities in education and employment, health

service for prostitutes, minimum wages and maximum hours
for domestics and to organize feminist congresses in
1916. Concludes that, although immediate results were
not forthcoming from these congresses, attended by
middle-class women divided on several issues, symbolically
it was a beginning for women who had remained reticent
and submissive for centuries.

2253 _____.
        1973 "La mujer y la revolución social mexicana."
        BDSLM/CIDHAL 3:4:3-14.
           Preliminary study on feminist movement in Mexico
        briefly examines role and condition of Mexican women
        from 16c. to 1910 Revolution, emphasizing Díaz regime
        (1876-1910); analyzes Carranza divorce law (1915) and
        its effects; and discusses feminist movement in Yucatán
        (1915-17). Contends that little was accomplished for
        Mexican women during Revolutionary leadership of Madero
        and Carranza and that any gains obtained between 1916
        and 1920 resulted from regional pressures, particularly
        in Yucatán.

2254 MAYO, ANNA
        1972 "Mexico: *mucho macho*." Ms. 1:6:116-20.
           Looks at contemporary situation of Mexican women and
        offers comments from individuals who have broken with
        traditional stereotype--ex-nun, tv director et al. Sees
        strength for a women's movement through Indian element.

2255 MILLÁN, VERNA CARLETON
        1939 "Freedom for Mexican Women." In her Mexico Reborn,
        pp. 148-69. Boston: Houghton, Mifflin.
           Sympathetic portrait of Mexican women by Anglo woman
        married to Mexican man. Considers the women "much
        superior in every respect to Mexican men." Mentions
        female participation in Mexican history, especially as
        soldaderas; different practices among indigenous groups;
        traditions inherited from Spain; problems in marriage
        and divorce; feminist movement (organizations and par-
        ticular women) and fight for citizenship and suffrage.

2256 Mujeres en Acción Solidaria
        1974 "Mujeres en Acción Solidaria." PC 2:24:50-51.
        illus.
           Succinct summary of women's movement in Mexico by
        M.A.S., which considers it a political movement in reac-
        tion to oppression from a socio-economic structure of
        exploitation. M.A.S. was originally organized as

577

Perspectives on Women's Liberation

>   Encuentro de Mujeres in November 1972, operating in
>   small consciousness-raising groups of heterogeneous women
>   in which problems facing women were discussed: abortion,
>   contraception, childcare, employment, etc. Stresses that
>   national and class differences must be considered in
>   development of program of action.

2257   RAMÍREZ GARRIDO, JOSÉ DOMINGO
>   1918 Al margen del feminismo. Col. Tabasco. Col. de
>   escritos de Ramírez Garrido, 8. Mérida, Yucatán:
>   Talleres "Pluma y Lápiz." 51 p. ports.
>   Short history of condition of women from antiquity to
>   crystallization of feminism during French Revolution and
>   to Yucatecan Feminist Congress in 1916. Ardently pro
>   female suffrage.

2258   SÁENZ ROYO, ARTEMISA ("XÓCHITL")
>   1954 Historia político-social-cultural de movimiento
>   femenino en México, 1914-1950. Mex., D.F.: M. León
>   Sánchez. 115 p. ports.
>   Dedicated to Mexican President Ruiz Cortines for hav-
>   ing granted women citizenship, contains biographical
>   sketches of women who fought for civic and political
>   rights between 1914 and 1950. Includes, in part, a
>   narrative of author's life as pioneer and precursor in
>   Mexican feminist movement, as a social worker and
>   journalist.

2259   VERA, LUZ
>   1956 "El feminismo en el México independiente." FL
>   30:60/61/62:45-57.
>   Digressive essay considers varying definitions of
>   feminism and names Mexican women who distinguished
>   themselves in different activities, not necessarily
>   specific to women's rights. Does not confine herself
>   to 20c., as indicated.

El Salvador

2260   MONTES, SEGUNDO
>   1975 "La liberación femenina." UJSC/ECA 30:316/317:
>   115-28.
>   Using a quoted interview with Susan Sontag as a jump-
>   ing off point, looks at the Old and New Testaments,
>   various declarations on human rights, the social reality
>   of women today, and world organization in order to under-
>   stand the evolution of female oppression and liberation
>   and the contemporary woman's struggle. Suggests that

the Church investigate the question of women's secondary
role as a result of divine institution or social conditions and structural pressures. Concludes that women's
struggle for liberation must be accepted by all, but
women themselves have to fight for it rather than wait
for male action.

SOUTH AMERICA

Venezuela

2261   AGUIRRE ELORRIAGA, MANUEL
      1968 "La promoción de la mujer." Sic 31:303:117-19.
        Editorial in Catholic periodical notes modern women's
rebellion against the old order--her condition as slave,
housewife and unequal--and her 20c. conquests in education, politics, employment, and professional life. Cites
discrepancies between labor laws which stipulate equal
salaries for equal work and the reality of women's situation; between the Vatican Council's declaration against
sex discrimination and its exclusively male hierarchy
and ministry; between mass media's idol image of women
and the reality of economic pressures which place them
in a dependent and inferior position. Women need to
discover themselves and their capabilities.

2262   HANNOT, TAMARA
      1974 "La mujer en Venezuela. ¿Nueva imagen o nueva
mujer?" In Valores, Estructura y Sociedad, pp. 79-113.
Caracas: Fondo Edit. Común. bibl. f/notes.
        Theoretical discussion as to whether/the Venezuelan
woman has actually changed as her participation outside
the domestic sphere has increased or whether it is
merely an image of a new woman transmitted by the mass
media. Concludes that the image is new, but not the
woman. Verification to be made with empirical data.

2263   VELÁZQUEZ, LUCILA
      1971 "Proceso y evaluación de la evolución de la mujer en
Venezuela." CP/F 237:n.p. ports.
        Despite advances in the struggle for women's liberation
(e.g., women appointed to high political positions and
directorships of hospitals), women's social status is
still characterized by 2 negative factors: domestic and
professional dependence (i.e., wage and hierarchical
discrimination). Briefly reviews conquests in field
of women's rights since 1915, when the 1st woman enrolled

Perspectives on Women's Liberation

in medical school, especially the organized movement
for suffrage, and notes increasing female university
student population.

Ecuador

2264   PAREDES de MARTÍNEZ, IRENE
        1970   Responsabilidad de la mujer en el mundo actual.
        Quito.   37 p.
        President of the National Union of Women of Ecuador
        (UNME) considers women's liberation, mostly in light of
        North American literature and discusses the general
        responsibilities of Latin American women in today's
        world not only within the family context but also in
        public life.

Peru

2265   CHANEY, ELSA M.
        1973   "Old and New Feminists in Latin America: The Case
        of Peru and Chile."   WRU/JMF 35:2:331-42.   bibl.
        See CHILE for annotation.

2266   GARCÉS, CARMELA
        1973   "Mujeres peruanas: ¿existe un imperialismo
        masculino?"   SIDI 23:782:52-59.   illus.
        Interviews 7 Peruvian women (university professor,
        lawyers, administrative assistant, leader in Peru's
        Women's Rights Movement, et al.) with respect to their
        ideas about female liberation and how to achieve it,
        relations with men, aspects of their work and life.

2267   MARTELLI, JUAN CARLOS
        1967   "La peruana: una crisalida que echa alas."   Caretas
        17:351:37-44.   illus., table.
        Asks such questions as :   Is woman really superior?
        Are women going to overpower men?   Includes a table on
        the behavior of men and women (e.g., cruel, generous,
        joking, understanding, exhibitionist, modest) and pro-
        vides some statistics on women in universities in Lima.
        Interviewed women who have their own careers, and/or
        are divorced, and a psychiatrist who discusses problems
        of the middle class.   Cartoons indicate problems for men
        with women as their equals or superiors.

Women in Spanish America

2268 "La ñusta y los concursos de belleza: ¿liberación de la
mujer? reforma de la educación?"
1974 Rikchay 1:4:40-41.
Beauty contests and commercial sales techniques utilizing women for sexual motivation in advertising prod-
ucts are based on a concept of woman as object. While
the Education Reform (general education law, article 11)
states that the education of women will be oriented
toward a reevaluation of women toward their development
and liberation, a discrepancy exists: in the name of
this same reform bill beauty contests are still being
carried on among students--El Concurso La Ñusta de la
Juventud. Decries this inconsistency.

2269 PORTUGAL, ANA MARÍA
1970 "La peruana, ¿"Tapada" sin manto?" MN 46:20-27.
Looks at women's changes and problems in 20c. Peru
after describing la tapada, the colonial archetype of
femininity, elegance, mystery, and beauty. Discusses
professionals, housewives, journalists, et al. and notes
that despite favorable statistics, the "new" Peruvian
woman has not yet emerged because antiquated socio-
economic and cultural structures still exist.

2270 PUYO D., CARLOS
1920 "Striving for Women's Rights in South America."
PASUS/PAR 2:4:14-16. port.
Interview with María L. de Palomino, Peruvian feminist
then studying at Columbia University, who wanted to
spread the word that women and men should share equally
the same rights and duties.

Paraguay

2271 LÓPEZ DECOUD, ARSENIO
1902 Sobre el femenismo. Asunción: Imprenta de Luis
Tasso. 68 p.
Summary of 5 articles which appeared in Asunción
daily La Patria (June, 1901) synthesizes feminist ideas
of several European writers in order to inform the
Paraguayan public of "the very noble idea of obtaining
the just and well understood liberation of women."

Chile

2272 ARAVENA DERPICH, SONIA
1972 "Escalada femenina en Chile." S/H 5:58:52-55. illus.

Perspectives on Women's Liberation

Cites gains made by Chilean women in education; feminist movement for civil and political rights (1915-1949); continued legal discrimination against women; women's incorporation into work force in 20c.; organizations which make possible women's participation in solving her problems related to family; and problem of lingering *machismo*.

2273 BAMBIRRA, VANIA
1972 "The Chilean Woman . . ." In New Chile, by NACLA, pp. 34-36. Berkeley and N.Y.: North American Congress on Latin America. illus.
Translated excerpts from Punto Final (22 March 1971). Compares struggle for women's liberation in dependent and developed capitalist countries, stating that in the latter, where the class struggle has not been contracted, it is not sensible to isolate specific social sectors from the general struggle of the oppressed classes. Discusses problems specific to Chilean women. Concludes that, despite their gains and a few exceptions to the rule, they are still subjected to the condition of "object."

2274 _____.
1972 "Women's Liberation and Class Struggle." Trans. by L. Krebs and B. Bayer. RPE/R 4:3:75-84. Spanish version: 1972 "Liberación de la mujer y lucha de clases: una tarea de hoy." PUFIN 151:10-15.
Synthesis of lecture to Federation of Students at the University of Concepción (October 1971) discusses attitudes of Chilean bourgeoisie regarding women and their liberation, as expressed in the press. Maintains that capitalism is incapable of promoting a real women's liberation because it is so exploitative. Points out possibility of ending exploitation of women by industrializing the domestic economy under socialism/communism. Outlines basic short term goals: full judicial equality, and legalization of rights to abortion, divorce, etc., and the implementation of public services, day care centers, all day schools, laundromats, collective restaurants and so on. Sketches 3 basic family types and woman's role in each: bourgeois, petty bourgeois, proletarian. Believes the women's struggle must be directed by the working class because it exists within the class struggle, and women's liberation is not a struggle against men.

2275   _____.
        1971 "La mujer chilena en la transición al socialismo."
        Suplemento de PUFIN 5:133:8 p. illus.
           Comments on recent Assembly of Communist Women of
        Chile, posing questions as to necessity of considering
        problems specific to women within the overall class
        struggle and why the Chilean left has not dealt with
        them. Defines those problems, discussing Margaret
        Benston's Marxist analysis of female exploitation in a
        capitalist society and Chilean women's position as an
        object. Points out that women's liberation strategy in
        dependent countries must be different than the "special
        sector" politics adopted in developed nations. Concludes
        with suggestions on what it will take to create a society
        of new women and men.

2276   CHANEY, ELSA M.
        1973 "Old and New Feminists in Latin America: The Case of
        Peru and Chile." WRU/JMF 35:2:331-43. bibl.
           Utilizing background information and survey data from
        a study on women political leaders in Peru and Chile to
        provide a history of the struggle for female suffrage,
        notes limited benefits and reasons for failure of early
        feminism and cites the following conditions to explain
        the unlikelihood of feminist militancy in LA in contem-
        porary and near future times: chivalresque and coquett-
        ish aspects of male/female relationships which undercut
        overt competition and confrontation; *supermadre* syndrome;
        traditional ideas on feminine behavior; some status
        achievement by middle- and upper-middle-class women;
        little female solidarity across class lines; and a
        servant class.

2277   GANNON, ISABEL and RIBEIRO, LUCÍA
        1972 "Chile: creciente desconcierto para enfrentar a la
        mujer." BDSLM/CIDHAL 2:4:15-16.
           Notes from introduction and conclusion of article
        which appeared in no. 13 of Cuadernos de la Realidad
        Nacional of CEREN, Santiago, commenting on well-known
        feminist works of Greer, Millet et al. Concludes that
        the search for women's liberation needs to be taken in
        the context of elaborating a politics which incorporates
        women in the process of socialism; whose final goal is
        the liberation of men and women.

2278   GISSI BUSTOS, JORGE
        1972 "Mitología de la femineidad." In Opresión y
        marginalidad de la mujer en el orden social machista,

WOMEN IN SPANISH AMERICA

Perspectives on Women's Liberation

> by E. Ander Egg et al., pp. 125-73. Col. Desarrollo
> Social, 14. Buenos Aires: Humanitas. bibl. f/notes,
> tables. Also in: 1972 CRN/CEREN 11:n.p. 1972
> BDSLM/CIDHAL 2:3:24-28.
> Using a psycho-social approach, explores problems
> related to women, men and society in terms of myths
> about the sexes (femininity vs. masculinity), and certain
> aspects of social structure, socialization, ideology and
> social change. Concludes that women must fight for
> their liberation and that by doing so will also exert
> an indirect pressure for the transformation of society:
> i.e., when men can no longer find refuge in a pervasive
> sexist ideology which defines male-female relations as
> superior-inferior respectively, they will have to con-
> front their own inferiority in relation to those who run
> society and demand their liberation too.

2279 LABARCA HUBERTSON, AMANDA
> 1951 "Sobre el movimiento femenino chileno." LLTC/R 7:
> 25:96-103.
> Outlines women's movement in Chile from its organiza-
> tion in 1915 to the promulgation of Decreto-Ley Maya
> in 1925, the struggle for more rights in the 1930's and
> 1940's, and the tasks still at hand.

2280 _____.
> 1947 Feminismo contemporáneo. Santiago, Zig-Zag. 242 p.
> bibl.
> Collection of various writings, by Chile's foremost
> educator of women, many of which are related to the
> history of feminism in Europe and NA, with some notes
> on Chile and other Latin American countries. For Chile
> also considers how women voted in the early 1940's,
> education, nursing, professionals, etc.

2281 _____.
> 1944 "Trayectoria del movimiento feminista en Chile."
> INS 2:5:61-63.
> Brief history of feminism in Chile from the 1st affir-
> mation of their equality with men in 1870 by Máximo Lira
> and Jorge Mennadier, the development of an educational
> system for women, the fight for legal rights and suf-
> frage, up to the National Congress planned as a reunion
> of all Chilean women (from union workers to university
> professors).

2282 _____.
> 1934 ¿A dónde va la mujer? Santiago: Eds. Extra. 262 p.

Collection of lectures, studies and articles on feminism, education and women's organizations in Chile (and
non-Latin American countries) written between 1914 and
1934.

2283 RICHARD, MARÍA ELSA
      1973 "Tres opiniones sobre la realidad de la mujer
      chilena de hoy." C/F 1:2:62-81.
         Interviews 3 Chilean women--working-class mother, uni-
      versity educated mother and nun/educator--on questions
      regarding female liberation, machismo, work outside the
      home, male/female differences, femininity, etc. All 3
      believe women are capable of much more than what they
      have been doing as housewives and are doubly oppressed
      by the social structure and an ideology of machismo.

2284 VIDAL, VIRGINIA
      1972 La emancipación de la mujer. Nosotros Los Chilenos,
      30. Santiago: Ed. Nacional Quimantú. 94 p. illus.,
      bibl.
         Comprehensive summary of historical process and con-
      temporary situation of women's liberation in Chile, from
      the 1st female doctor in 1886 to the role of Mothers'
      Centers today, concentrating especially on proletarian
      women (urban, peasant, indigenous). Covers MEMCH, edu-
      cation, employment, legal status, child care, domestic
      service, marital and sexuality problems, mass media,
      political participation, machismo, participation in
      struggles of the proletariat (strikes, unions, land
      seizure), etc.

Argentina

2285 ABELLA de RAMÍREZ, MARÍA
      1965 Ensayos femenistas. 2nd. ed. Montevideo: Edit.
      El Siglo Ilustrado. 206 p. port.
         Collection of diverse articles, letters, brief
      accounts, stories, some of which appeared in newspapers,
      related to didactic and feminist ends, originally pub-
      lished as En pos de la justicia (La Plata, 1908).
      Includes topics which range from women's honor, educa-
      tion, aspirations, liberation and political rights to
      domestic tasks, divorce, motherhood, free thinking and
      religion. In 1906 author proposed a 17-article minimal
      program advocating the vindication of women's rights.

Perspectives on Women's Liberation

2286   BULNES, EDGARDO
        1933   "La reintegración de la mujer a la humanidad."   In
        his Dos ensayos políticos, pp. 49-69.   Buenos Aires:
        Edit. Claridad, "Ciencias Sociales."
            Various institutions (e.g., *patria potestas*, levirate)
        were imposed on women through the will and violence of
        men.   Cites legislation in several countries, including
        Argentina, to demonstrate position and restrictions of
        married women.   Disagrees that eliminating such limita-
        tions would spell the disorganization of family life and
        anarchy of society.   Argues for women's rights to be
        integrated into, rather than separated out of, humanity.
        Believes in women's ability to take their place and
        exercise their freedom.   There is no need to hold them
        with reins.

2287   LILLO CATALÁN, VICTORIANO
        1929   "Sexo, feminismo y derecho."   BA/RA 23:66:188-93.
            Feminism is the aspiration of modern women to have
        equal legal, political and economic rights.   Women should
        be granted suffrage.

2288   OCAMPO, VICTORIA
        1936   La mujer y su expresión.   Buenos Aires: Eds. Sur.
        67 p.
            Title refers to radio-telephonic talk aired in
        Argentina and Spain in which Victoria Ocampo, well-known
        Argentine writer, magazine editor and cultural leader
        calls for better instruction of women and equal respect
        for their freedom.   Brief collection of articles express-
        ing her ideas and proposals for the advancement of women
        in Argentina and worldwide.   Women should assume their
        responsibilities and rights without waiting for the help
        of men.   For too long they have conceded to men's mono-
        logue ("don't interrupt me"), denying their own need
        to express themselves, they grow up with an inferiority
        complex which impedes their expression, literary or
        otherwise.

2289   QUESADA, ERNESTO
        1899   La cuestión femenina; discurso pronunciado en el
        acto de clausura de la Exposición Femenina, en el
        pabellón de Argentina, el 20 de noviembre de 1898.
        Buenos Aires: Imprenta de Pablo E. Coni e Hijos.   46 p.
            Calls for studying problem of emancipating women.   Not
        all women marry and make a home; in fact, women do work.
        Cites Argentine census data for 1895.   Reviews "feminist"
        movement in Western world since 17c.   Recommends equal

educational opportunities for the purpose of equal
employment opportunities and economic independence of
women and the concession of political rights. Praises
efforts of female charity associations, such as the one
which set up the exhibit where this talk was given, but
encourages them to go further.

2290   RÉBORA, JUAN CARLOS
    1929   La emancipación de la mujer (el aporte de la juris-
    prudencia). Buenos Aires: Librería y Edit. "La
    Facultad," de Juan Roldán y cía. 285 p.
        Legal dissertation on the emancipation of women
    divided into 2 parts: 1) development of a feminist
    movement, covering its direction and rhythm in Europe
    and Argentina; 2) repercussions of the movement on the
    situation of married women, covering civil rights and
    influence on the nature of marriage in terms of personal
    relations between spouses, unity of the home, patrimonial
    relations, etc.

2291   STROZZI, ADA
    1932   "Feminism in Argentina." PAU/B 66:8:565-67. illus.,
    photos.
        Discusses feminist activities in Argentina, beginning
    with the founding of the Centro Feminista in 1906 and
    efforts directed toward civil rights and suffrage for
    women. Names leading feminists and organizations up to
    1930.

2292   TELLO, W.
    1919   "El feminismo argentino." DHL/R 63:456-59.
        Sees men and women as 2 very different sexes that
    complement each other physically and psychically. A
    world ruled only by men would be a disaster because of
    a lack of morality and humanitarianism, while a world
    governed only by women would be a failure because of an
    excess of sentimentalism. Women's basic destiny is to
    educate children, man, and humanity. However, public
    life and home life are not incompatible. Supports fe-
    male suffrage and access to public positions so that
    women can effectively assist in socializing the world.

2293   VILAR, ESTHER
    1972   The Manipulated Man. N.Y.: Farrar, Straus and
    Giroux. 184 p.
        Translated from German and published in 19 countries,
    this diatribe against women by an Argentine-born medical
    doctor of German parents portrays the female sex as a

Perspectives on Women's Liberation

> lot of ugly, dumb, unfeeling, nonworking parasites who
> have craftily manipulated and enslaved men, their supe-
> riors, to expend their talents and energies to the bene-
> fit of women. A vitriolic, unsubstantiated argument
> which appears to capitalize on the women's movement for
> personal gains.

2294   YÁÑEZ, ANABELLA T., ed.
       1973 Acerca de la mujer en el proceso de liberación.
       Col. Aportes Protagónicos. Documento de Trabajo No. 1.
       Mendoza, Arg.: Edit. I.A.S.Y.F. 100 p. bibl.
          Kind of handbook of the Centro de Investigación de
       la Mujer which grew out of the Instituto de Acción
       Social y Familiar in Mendoza, Argentina in 1969. Part
       1 outlines consciousness-raising/discussion groups on
       such themes as "Woman is Alienated," "Women and Advertis-
       ing," "Toward Liberation." Part 2 contains material
       used for discussing problems of women's liberation
       (e.g., excerpts from Engels, summary of Castilla del
       Pino's book on The Alienation of Woman, a piece on
       motherhood, etc.).

2295   ZICARI, JULIO de
       1926 Los derechos de la mujer argentina. (Una novela,
       algunos estudios y opiniones sobre la condición civil y
       política de la mujer). Buenos Aires: Edit. Claridad.
       63 p. ports.
          Discussion in support of women's rights movement in
       Argentina comments on the 7 major points proposed by
       the Asociácion Pro Derechos de la Mujer, mentions other
       organizations and individuals involved in this struggle,
       and outlines the political and economic rights women
       should have.

Uruguay

2296   VAZ FERREIRA, CARLOS
       1945 Sobre feminismo. 2nd ed. Buenos Aires: Edit.
       Losada. 137 p.
          Series of lectures, given before 1914 at the University
       of Montevideo but not published until 1933, in which
       Uruguayan lawyer, writer, philosopher, and professor
       attempts to analyze the problems surrounding feminist-
       anti-feminist fight of his time: political capacity
       of women or female suffrage; civil capacity or social
       activity, access to education, public office, profes-
       sions and careers; relations between the sexes and

family organization; similarities and differences between
women and men. Draws distinction between feminism of
equalization and that of compensation. Does not agree
with total equality because women's primordial mission is
perpetuation of the species.

2297 VAZ FERREIRA de ECHEVARRÍA, SARA
1963 Sobre Vaz Ferreira. (Vida, obra y actuación).
Fascículo 1. Lo moral en la vida y en la obra de Carlos
Vaz Ferreira. Montevideo. 31 p. facsim., bibl.
f/notes.
Daughter of Uruguayan lawyer, writer, law and philosophy professor provides explication of his work and attitudes on feminism as expressed in Sobre feminismo (1933;
#2296) and based in part on her personal experience.
Updates his series of lectures to include his changing
opinions until he died.

CARIBBEAN

Puerto Rico

2298 FERNÁNDEZ CINTRÓN, CELIA and RIVERA QUINTERO, MARCIA
1974 "Bases de la sociedad sexista en Puerto Rico." RI
4:2:239-45.
Demonstrates how in Puerto Rico male domination and
female subordination are generated through socialization
in the family and at school, perpetuated through the
capitalist system, and preserved through governmental and
other organizations. Briefly reviews female participation in Puerto Rico's economy since 1899. Concludes that
only full participation in political and economic life
will bring full equality between the sexes.

Cuba

2299 BARINAGA y PONCE de LEÓN, GRAZIELLA
1931 El feminismo y el hogar. Havana. 15 p.
Cuban feminist effectively counters arguments of male
anti-feminists to allay their fears about what would
happen once women were given the vote and equal rights.

2300 CAMARANO, CHRIS
1971 "On Cuban Women." Science and Society 35:1:48-58.
A member of first contingent of Venceremos Brigade
comments on progress of women's liberation in Cuba from
the destruction of an exploitative political system

Perspectives on Women's Liberation

rife with racism and chauvinism to the creation of a
material base which deinstitutionalized male chauvinism
and precipitated greater assimilation of women into
labor force and to the socialization of domestic work
and legislative changes. Despite both obvious, immediate and subtle, long-range effects, attitudes and
values still need decolonization.

2301   POGOLOTTI, GRAZIELLA
       1974 "Revolución, lucha de clases y condición femenina."
       CDLA 14:82:169-71.
          Emphasizes importance of taking into account histor-
       ical, social and economic context in theories of women's
       liberation because although the subordination of women
       cross-cuts all social classes, peasant and working class
       are doubly exploited; this is essential when assessing
       female participation in revolutionary struggle. Based
       on her own experience in Cuban Revolution and a reading
       of Randall's La mujer cubana ahora (#2202), which she
       considers a "rich and suggestive panorama of the Cuban
       woman today" but also deficient in an understanding of
       how exploitation and discrimination against women are
       produced in each social class in industrialized as well
       as underdeveloped nations.

2302   SABAS ALOMÁ, MARIBLANCA
       1930 Feminismo. Cuestiones sociales - crítica literaria.
       Havana: Edit. "Hermes." 235 p.
          Collection of 41 previously published short critical
       essays and letters reflecting Cuban journalist's strong
       support of feminism. Notes importance of women's eco-
       nomic independence, the "stupidity" of linking a woman's
       honor with her husband's, the hypocrisy of marriage and
       adultery, differences between upper- and lower-class
       women, the necessity of equal rights, and much more.

2303   SPRINGER, MARY ELIZABETH
       1923 "The Feminist Movement in Cuba." PAU/B 57:6:580-90.
       illus., ports.
          Briefly traces the development of the Cuban feminist
       movement from 1899 to 1923, when the First National
       Congress of Women took place. The complete program of
       that congress is reproduced.

Dominican Republic

2304   "Feminismo balaguerista: A Strategy of the Right."
        1974 NACLA/LAER 8:4:28-32. illus., bibl. notes.
              Uses the Dominican Republic as a case study to illus-
        trate how the lack of a feminist movement imbued with
        a revolutionary ideology leads to elitist feminism and
        its use by reactionary political forces. Discusses
        Trujillista (of the 1930's and 1940's) and Balaguerista
        (since 1966) feminists, pointing out how their compat-
        ibility with the existing social, political, and economic
        systems precludes liberation. Concludes that "role of
        feminism must be to mobilize women in the class struggle
        for socialist revolution."

GENERAL – MISCELLANEOUS

This is a kind of catch-all category for those works which deal
with a variety of topics, considering social, economic, political,
educational, cultural, psychological, legal, religious or literary
aspects of women within one work; or those works which are of an
unspecific nature, not clearly fitting into the major subject categories to which the bulk of the entries are assigned. These items
are cross-referenced into the several subjects which are covered in
the one publication.

SPANISH AMERICA - GENERAL

2305   BROWN, G. M. L.
          1906 "Women of Spanish America." Canadian Magazine
          27:4:321-28. illus.
          One man's early 20c. impressions of Latin American
          women in words and photos. Makes broad generalizations
          about upper class women: exclusive and excessive inter-
          est in dress above all else; slovenliness; meager educa-
          tion, lack of practical education and art; medieval
          customs of Moorish seclusion and mourning restrictions.
          Useful only as North American view which helped foster
          stereotypes.

2306   BUITRÓN, ANÍBAL
          1966 "La mujer latinoamericana." RCPC 75:27-29.
          Ecuadorian anthropologist gives very general descrip-
          tion of LA women's economic, social and cultural situa-
          tion, according to whether indigenous or of lower,
          middle or upper class. No references.

2307   _____.
          1956 "Situación económica, social y cultural de la mujer
          en los países andinos." III/AI 16:2:83-92. Also in:
          1956 A 49:1/3:52-57.
          Based on personal observations, provides very general
          picture of the economic, societal, and cultural condition

592

of women in Ecuador, Peru, and Bolivia, considering 4
distinct groups: Indian; lower class; middle class;
upper class. Unsubstantiated generalizations.

2308   CERNI, HORST MAX
        1974   "Setting New Sights for Latin America's Women."
        N/UNICEF 82:4:36-39. illus.
            Reflects views expressed by 3 prominent professional
        Latin American women who participated in UNICEF staff
        meeting (Paraguay, 1974): irresponsible fatherhood,
        machismo and *hembrismo*, lack of education, limited em-
        ployment opportunities, need for more employment
        benefits.

2309   COOPER, CLAYTON SEDGWICK
        1918   "Women of South America." Travel 30:3:25-28, 45.
        illus.
            Early 20c. traveler's stereotypical impressions of
        South American women with respect to participation in
        history, the economy, politics, customs and clothing
        styles, etc. Although the photographs portray women
        of several classes, written comments appear to be re-
        stricted to upper class women. Concludes that Argentine
        women lead the way into the modern world, but "in their
        new-found freedom are advancing a little too fast for
        their spiritual good"!

2310   GEYER, GEORGIE ANN
        1970   "The New Women." In her The New Latins. Fateful
        Change in South and Central America, pp. 235-58.
        Garden City, N. Y.: Doubleday and Co.
            Overview of women in Latin American history from the
        conquest on. Notes changes in this century in status
        and life style. Touches lightly on Cuban situation,
        the Church, upper-class women, courtship, birth control,
        suffrage, etc.

2311   GINER, P.
        1905   Mujeres de América. Barcelona: Guarner, Taberner
        y Cía. 230 p.
            Series of 14 sections, each on women of a particular
        country or region, relating generalizations about Latin
        American women by race and/or class. No indication of
        sources.

2312   GUIJARRO, MIGUEL, ed.
        1872-1876 Las mujeres españolas, portuguesas y americanas
        tales como son en el hogar doméstico, en los campos, en

General - Miscellaneous

el templo, en los espectáculos, en el taller y en los
salones. Descripción y pintura del carácter, costumbres,
trajes, usos, religiosidad, belleza, defectos, pre-
ocupaciones y excelencias de la mujer de cada una de
las provincias de España, Portugal y Américas españolas.
Vol. 3. Madrid: Imprenta y Librería de D. Miguel
Guijarro. plates.
   Contains brief sketches on women in the Spanish
American countries, according to what is indicated in
the title. Useful as 19c. impressions.

2313   KINZER, NORA SCOTT
      1974 "Sexist Sociology." CSDI/M 7:3:48-59.
         A witty diatribe on some of the shortcomings of social
science research and attitudes on Latin Americans in
general, on women in particular, using her own study on
professional Argentine women for illustration.

2314   MAY, STELLA BURKE
      1923 Men, Maidens, and Mantillas. N.Y.: The Century Co.
      362 p. front., plates, ports., fold. map
         North American women's impressions of Latin American
women of all classes and races engaged in all kinds of
activities, based on a year-long trip from Mexico to
Brazil. Considers courtship, family relations, work,
leisure, and any manifestations of feminism. Notes
Moorish influence as well as changes in early 20c.
Believes Latin American and North American women are
different geographically and racially but not
psychologically.

2315   MIRÓ, CARMEN A.
      1964 "The Population of Latin America." PAA/D
      1:1:15-41. tables.
         Using census data, presents statistical picture of
Latin America's population by sex: density, urban-
rural distribution, composition, labor force participation, birth and death rates, migration tendencies.
Rural-urban migration stands out as general characteristic of all countries, producing significant demographic
and consequently fertility changes.

2316   ORTIZ de MACAYA, MARGARITA
      1970 "Mujer, desarollo social y educacional en América
      Latina." BDSLM/CIDHAL 1:1:59-62.
         Excerpts from talk given by Costa Rican ambassador.
Explains discrepancy in the development of the US and
LA and their different attitudes toward women as stem-
ming from difference in incentives of immigrants and in

legal systems they brought with them. Discusses role
of international agencies and need for more educational
and technical preparation of women.

2317   PESCATELLO, ANN, ed.
        1973 Female and Male in Latin America: Essays.
        Pittsburgh, Pa.: Univ. of Pittsburgh Press. 342 p.
        tables, bibl.
           Collection of 12 essays by social scientists of several
        disciplines, using various methodologies. Divided into
        3 major areas--images and realities of female life; women
        in history and contemporary perspective; future prospects
        (action and reaction in the Cuban case)--the essays
        range in topic from literary archetypes, *marianismo* and
        politics to professionals and domestic servants and cover
        8 Latin American countries. An extensive, unannotated
        bibliography provided in addition to bibliographic notes
        of each essay. For individual articles See Jaquette
        (#265); Flora (#263); Stevens (#1251); Chaney (#2130);
        Hollander (#1443); Kinzer (#1314); Smith (#1418); Tancer
        (#2388); Harkess (#1293); Purcell (#1466); Fox (#1321).

2318   PESCATELLO, ANN
        1972 "The Female in Ibero-America: An Essay on Research
        Bibliography and Research Directions." LARR 7:2:125-41.
        bibl.
           The first introductory essay on women in LA as a field
        for research, discussing the problems plaguing the field
        and recent studies attempting to deal seriously with the
        subject. Includes a briefly annotated bibliography.

2319   RAMOS MEJÍA, MARÍA ELENA
        1951 "La mujer en nuestro mundo. II - Así es la vida
        hispanoamericana." MH 37:39-40. illus.
           General remarks on who the Latin American woman is,
        from the days of the Conquest to modern times, citing
        well-known names. Believes one cannot speak seriously
        of a feminist movement in LA because the women know
        that their femininity becomes complete only when they
        join with a man.

2320   SCHULTZ CAZENUEVE de MANTOVANI, FRYDA
        1963 "La mujer latinoamericana." Cuadernos 70:47-52.
           Very general remarks on Latin American women referring
        to early history, education, and several types (actress,
        teacher, intellectual). Just one writer's impressions.

General - Miscellaneous

2321   SIGNORELLI de MARTÍ, ROSA
          1967   "Spanish America."   In Women in the Modern World,
          ed. by R. Patai, pp. 192-208.   N.Y.:   The Free Press.
              Provides general overview of women in Spanish America:
          traditional past, urban/rural differences as a result of
          the economy in each sector, legal and social position,
          trends in education, sex mores, marriage and the family,
          occupations and organizations.

2322   STEWART, C. ALLAN
          1957   "Widening Horizons for Women in Latin America."
          USDS/B 36:935:860-62.
              Address given before Miami Women's Club (16 April,
          1957) summarizing heroic story of women in early America
          (Indian women who helped conquistadors and governors),
          participation in public affairs (women office holders),
          educational progress, IACW, and an exchange program of
          visiting Latin American women leaders.

2323   "Women in Latin America."
          1973   Special section in WRU/JMF 35:2.   Edited by Nora
          Scott Kinzer.
              See Kinzer (#1029); Chaney (#2265); and Cohen (#471).

MIDDLE AMERICA

Mexico

2324   Alianza de Mujeres de México
          1956   Conferencias sustenadas durante el año de 1956.
          Mex., D.F.   99 p.
              Collection of 6 speeches given on feminism in Mexico,
          women in history of Mexico, women in national life, and
          other aspects by woman judge, municipal president of
          Tlaxcala et al.

2325   CASTILLO LEDÓN, AMALIA C. de
          1951   "La mujer mexicana ante el mundo."   ID/R 7:57-58.
              Then President of IACW briefly reviews women in Mexico's
          history from colonial to revolutionary times, their
          condition and economic/political participation today at
          luncheon given by Feminine Christian Association of
          Washington, D.C.

2326   DOMÍNGUEZ, JULIETA
          1960   Pensamiento y acción de la mujer mexicana.   Ciclo
          Presidente López Mateos, 17.   Mex., D.F.   72 p.   illus.,
          ports.

Middle America - Mexico

Superficial reflections on women's participation in history of Mexico from pre-Conquest to contemporary times, citing heroines of revolutionary movements, incorporation of women into civic, cultural and social life in 20c., and professional women with university degrees, in government posts, etc.

2327 FLORES, ANA MARÍA
1961 "La mujer en la sociedad." In La vida social, vol. 2 of México; cincuenta años de revolución, pp. 327-49. Mex., D.F.: Fondo de Cultura Económica. tables.
Discusses women in Mexican society before the Revolution, beginning with the Aztecs, and during the revolutionary epoch: what women have done to obtain rights; advances in education and employment; principal contemporary women's groups; how women live today. Considers different classes, indigenous as well as mestiza, rural and urban women.

2328 FOLAN, WILLIAM J.
1967 "Don- and doñaship terminology in Mérida, Yucatán, México." III/AI 27:1:119-29.
Investigates use of don and doña among persons of same or different social class and age in Mérida, providing Spanish background and examples also from Guatemala and a Mexican-American town in Texas.

2329 GRUENING, ERNEST
1928 Mexico and Its Heritage. N.Y.: The Century Co. 728 p. front., plates, ports., fold. map, bibl.
Section on women in Mexico (pp. 623-31) discusses social status, the 1910 Revolution, lack of political rights, superiority of indigenous women. Mentions women in other sections. Outdated general survey quotes other writers.

2330 MORRIS, BERENICE T. and SIGNAIGO, FLORENCE I.
1944 The Status of Women in Mexico. Wash., D.C.: US Office of the Coordination of Inter-American Affairs. 16 p. tables, bibl.
Describes economic conditions, legal status, marriage and divorce, education, organizations, legislation, women in industry.

2331 NAVARRETE, IFIGENIA M. de
1969 La mujer y los derechos sociales. Mex., D.F.: Eds. Oasis. 204 p. illus., plates, tables, graphs.

597

General - Miscellaneous

> Includes a discussion of female participation in the
> educational system, economy, and politics of Mexico,
> citing mostly 1960's statistics. Appendix 4 lists over
> 100 national women's organizations. See also González
> Salazar (#1493) for women's legal rights in Mexico.

2332 NICHOLSON, IRENE
1960 "Women in Mexico." GM 32:8:408-16. illus.
General notes on contemporary condition of Mexican
women of all classes as witnessed by an English woman
and discussed with several women. Includes some historical points.

2333 ROBLES de MENDOZA, MARGARITA
1931 La evolución de la mujer en México. Mex., D.F.:
Imprenta Galas. 113 p. port.
Former Mexican delegate to IACW discusses women in
general and Mexican women in particular: from chival-
resque tradition inherited from Europe to religious
complex to suffragism in 20c.

2334 SANZ, M. A.
1907 La mujer mexicana en el santuario del hogar. Mex.,
D.F.: Imprenta Lacaud. 3 vols. in 1.
Praises Mexican women, whether as heroines of Inde-
pendence or on the frontier, but especially as homemakers.
Describes several women from different states.

2335 SMITH, H. ALLEN
1963 "The Aphrodites of Tehuantepec." ML 39:10:73-74,
63-66.
Grossly generalizes women of Isthmus of Tehuantepec.

El Salvador

2336 JIMÉNEZ, LILIAM
1962 Condiciones de la mujer en El Salvador. Mex., D.F.:
Edit. Muñoz. 76 p.
General review of women's situation in El Salvador:
peasant; worker; domestic servant; market, commerce, and
State Office employees; nurse; teacher, university student; artist; legal conditions; women's organizations.

2337 _____.
1961 "La mujer salvadoreña. Notas y reportajes." CDLA
1:5:68-73.
See her Condiciones de la mujer en El Salvador (1962;
#2336).

Honduras

2338   Seminario Nacional de Mujeres Hondureñas, 2nd, Tegucigalpa,
        1964.
        1964 Boletín del 2° Seminario Nacional de Mujeres
        Hondureñas que estudió la condición económica y social
        de la mujer hondureña. Tegucigalpa: Ministerio de
        Educación Pública. 47 p. illus.
        Reports on various aspects of situation of Honduran
        women: education, health, employment. Includes con-
        clusions and recommendations of the group.

Nicaragua

2339   AGUERRI, JOSEFA TOLEDO de
        1935 (Reproducciones). Anhelos y esfuerzos. Managua:
        Imprenta Nacional. 205 p.
        Reproduces articles previously published in Revista
        Femenina Ilustrada, Mujer Nicaraguense (which she di-
        rected), and other periodicals and speeches given at
        schools she directed: women, feminism and femininity,
        children, morality, etc.

Costa Rica

2340   ACUÑA de CHACÓN, ANGELA
        1969-1970 La mujer costarricense a través de cuatro siglos.
        San José, C.R.: Imprenta Nacional. 2 vols.
        Gathers together an enormous amount of information on
        all aspects of women in Costa Rica from Indians in the
        16c. to active women in contemporary times. Covers edu-
        cation, politics, charitable work, literature, theatre,
        art, dance, agriculture, business, women's organizations,
        journalism, legislation, feminism, religion, etc. through
        4 centuries of Costa Rican history. Based mostly on
        secondary sources and some primary sources, including
        travel accounts.

Panama

2341   KORSI de RIPOLL, BLANCA
        1969 "Evolución social de la mujer." LNB/L 14:164:34-40.
        Educator and artist selected as Woman of the Year in
        a national poll in Panama discusses history of women on
        superficial level and Panamanian women only briefly.

WOMEN IN SPANISH AMERICA

General - Miscellaneous

Venezuela

2342 CLEMENTE TRAVIESO, CARMEN
     1951 <u>Mujeres venezolanas, y otros reportajes</u>. Caracas:
     Avila Gráfica. 183 p.
          Collection of short pieces, several based on inter-
     views by journalist, on female participation in the
     Venezuelan Independence movement and student protest of
     1928 against Gómez; with an educator, social welfare
     workers, pioneer of female journalism, nurses in public
     health, women in jail, and girls mistreated in homes.

Colombia

2343 AGUALIMPIA, CARLOS, et al.
     1969 "Demographic Facts of Colombia. The National Inves-
     tigation of Morbidity." <u>MMFQ</u> 47:3/Part 1:255-96.
     tables, graphs, map, bibl.
          A national investigation, including household surveys
     among a representative sample equivalent to 98% of
     Colombia's total population and census data, provides a
     statistical picture of the female population by age,
     urban/rural residence, education, annual income, occupa-
     tion of household head, pregnancy, fertility, abortion,
     etc.

2344 ARMAND, LUIS
     1965 "Función de la mujer en el porvenir." <u>REJAV</u>
     64:318:269-71.
          Divides women's participation/contribution in the
     future into 3 categories: social, affective, physio-
     logical. Notes that women discovered agriculture; that
     there is a need to save the family and at the same time
     permit both spouses to work and to act as educators of
     their children; and that attention must be paid to
     problem of qualifying women for employment.

2345 OSORNO CÁRDENAS, MARTA CECILIA
     1974 <u>La mujer colombiana y latino-americana. La pareja y</u>
     <u>la familia. Status, situación histórica y actual,</u>
     <u>dificultades, realización integral</u>. Medellín, Colombia:
     Tipografía Italiana - Impresos Marin. 399 p. graphs,
     bibl.
          Nun covers wide range of topics related to women in
     Colombia: the feminist struggle for equal rights,

obstacles against female liberation (myths about masculine superiority, virginity, maternity, and femininity;
prostitution; familial and cultural discrimination),
conjugal relations, family. Includes survey responses
by 50 couples each of 3 classes.

2346 RAMÍREZ de BERMÚDEZ, SONIA
1973 Estructura demográfica de la población en Colombia.
Bogota: ASCOFAME División de Medicina Social y
Población. 31 p. tables, graphs, bibl.
Statistical demographic description of Colombia's
population by sex, based on census data, considers
immigration, economic activity, age, level of growth of
regions, etc. Rate of female labor force participation
is higher in region of greatest growth.

2347 RUBIO de LAVERDE, LUCILA
1965 Perfiles de Colombia. Bogota: Edit. Guadalupe.
206 p. bibl.
Includes separate chapters on women (education, political condition, civil capacity, social service, employment); civil marriage and divorce; family planning;
prostitution; and orphanhood (mothers, children, and
centers for both) in Colombia.

2348 WILLIAMS, MRS. C. S.
1918 "Mothers of Men in Colombia." MRW 41:10:826-31;
41:12:917-20. illus.
Missionary wife's anecdotal observations on poor young
women (domestic servants and market vendors) and their
struggle to keep themselves and their children alive.
Vivid, sympathetic portrait of the plight of 7 individuals.

Ecuador

2349 ARIAS ROBALINO, AUGUSTO
1935 "Mujeres de Quito." ALMA 58:25-33.
Rambling comments on women in Quito's history:
Mariana de Jesús et al. who dedicated their lives to
religion, figures in Independence movement, writers.

Peru

2350 CÁCERES, Z. AURORA (EVANGELINA)
1909? "Peruanas." In her Mujeres de ayer y de hoy,
pp. 187-213. Paris: Casa Edit. Garnier Hnos.

General - Miscellaneous

General remarks on Peruvian women: writers and their
works; professional women; state of education for women
in very early 20c.; women's social work. No references.

2351 Centro de Estudios de Población y Desarrollo
1974 Situación demográfica de la CAP Cartavio. Diciembre
1972. Estudios de Población y Desarrollo. Serie B,
no. 3. Lima. 27 p. tables, graphs.
Presents findings of demographic survey (1972) among
member families of the Lima Cooperative Cartavio, divided into 4 strata by number of men in household. Includes data, broken down by sex and age, on population,
household composition, whether migrant or native, marital
status, educational level, economic activity, fertiltiy,
mortality.

2352 _____.
1974 Situación demográfica de la CAP Casa Grande. April,
1972. Estudios de Población y Desarrollo. Serie B,
no. 2. Lima. 22 p. tables, graphs.
Presents findings of demographic survey (1972) among
member families of Lima's Cooperative Casa Grande. Includes data on population by sex, age, migrant or
native-born, fertility, mortality, life expectancy.

2353 "Estadísticas sobre la mujer peruana."
197-? Creatividad y Cambio 15. Lima: Promoción Cultural
"Creatividad y Cambio." n.p. bibl.
Series of statistical tables on Peruvian women--
demography and fertility, educational level, economic
activity--based on governmental, household survey and
other data gathered since 1960.

Bolivia

2354 GUEILER de MOLLER, LYDIA
1961 "La mujer en Bolivia." Combate 3:18:33-41. tables.
Political activist of MNR, executive secretary of the
Alliance of Liberation of the American Woman, ex-
parliamentarian and diplomat sees situation of women in
relation to a society which continually experiences
pressures from foreign culture. Briefly sketches Bolivian women in 4 historical epochs (pre-Columbian, Conquest-
colony, Republic, and contemporary). Lists several
women's organizations fighting for women's rights since
1923. Discusses social and civil legislation affecting
women; female participation in the economy and education.

Cites 1950 and 1960 statistics. Concludes that legal
equality is insufficient without equality of opportunities, that true democracy does not exist without women's civic participation and that legislation must
establish equality of rights and obligations.

2355 OTERO, GUSTAVO ADOLFO
      1946 "Los ideales de la mujer boliviana." América
      22:85/86:314-27.
         Superficial look at Bolivian women since 1765: the
      ideal lady according to Baltazar Castiglione's El
      Cortesano; collaboration in the Independence movement;
      romantic verses in the 19c.; the establishment of
      schools for women as of 1890; various accomplished
      writers, artists, et al.

2356 RICO, HEIDI K. de
      1969-70 Páginas íntimas de la mujer boliviana. Tupiza,
      Bol.: Eds. Rico. 280 p. illus.
         Swedish woman married to Bolivian man offers a brief
      analysis of Bolivian women's social and economic situa-
      tion, describing characteristics of women of different
      social strata and situations (married or single, pros-
      titute, concubine, etc.); and a guide of social, cul-
      tural and marital preparation for the new woman, which
      includes information on reproduction, contraception,
      birth, etc., but also describes what first kiss is like!
      Illustrations are of Caucasian phenotype. No statistics
      or references; based on husband's observations.

Paraguay

2357 FERNÁNDEZ, CARMEN S.
      1940? Inquietudes de la hora. La Paz: Edit. "Sport."
      164 p.
         Paraguayan writer's reflections on several themes:
      the horror of war (mothers should inculcate their chil-
      dren with a spirit of peace); unsheltered children and
      the pedantic exhibitionism of upper-class women and
      their charitable organizations; Bolivian sculptor,
      Marina Núñez del Prado, and other Latin American women;
      conscious maternity; assistance and protection for mother
      and child; failure in marriage; female prison system and
      delinquency; economic independence of Paraguayan women;
      feminism, yes, but *marimachos*, no.

Women in Spanish America

General - Miscellaneous

2358   MacDONALD, ALEXANDER K.
           1911 "A Village Belle." In his <u>Picturesque</u>
           <u>Paraguay</u> . . . , pp. 266-67. London: Charles H. Kelly,
           plate, port.
               British traveler's very brief impressions of typical
           peasant girl in Paraguayan countryside, recounting her
           daily activities.

2359   VITTONE, LUIS
           1968? <u>La mujer paraguaya en la vida nacional</u>. Asunción:
           Dirección de Publicaciones, Imprenta Militar. 70 p.
               Sketchy, superficial collection of notes on various
           aspects of women in Paraguay: role in wars; education,
           dance, literature, art, and sports; Guaraní and peasant
           women; women's rights. Lacks depth and bibliography.

Chile

2360   CRUCHAGA de WALKER, ROSA and CALM, LILLIÁN
           1970 "¿Quién es la mujer chilena?" <u>MN</u> 46:33-38.
               Tries to provide an overall portrait of Chilean women
           today through questions and comments made at interviews
           with the director of a women's magazine, a novelist, 2
           educators/directors of girls' schools, the director of
           Social Welfare, a nun at a women's correctional institu-
           tion, a lawyer and an actress.

2361   KLIMPEL ALVARADO, FELÍCITAS
           1962 <u>La mujer chilena (el aporte femenino al progreso de</u>
           <u>Chile) 1910-1960</u>. Santiago: Edit. Andrés Bello. 304 p.
           bibl.
               Extensive and comprehensive compendium of women's
           activities in Chile from 1910 to 1960 considers women's
           legal position (Constitution, Penal, Labor, Commerce,
           and Civil Codes, and Legislation of Minors); women in
           public life (as office holders in executive, legislative
           and judicial branches, as diplomats, governors, mayors,
           etc.; campaign for suffrage); women's political partici-
           pation (as voters, party members, politicians; the
           Partido Femenino Chileno); women's economic, cultural
           and social contributions (philanthropy and social wel-
           fare; university graduates and professionals; women in
           agriculture, commerce, industry; in religion, the arts,
           literature and journalism, etc.); women and education
           (schools, educators, administrators); and international
           organizations concerned with women's issues (e.g., IACW).
           Names hundreds of individual women, organizations,

institutes, centers, etc. and their contributions to
Chile's national development.

2362   MATTELART, ARMAND and MATTELART, MICHÈLE
        1970 Juventud chilena: rebeldía y conformismo. Col.
        Problems de Nuestro Tiempo, 5. Santiago: Edit.
        Universitaria. 335 p. tables.
          Reports findings of interviews with 400 Chilean stu-
        dents and workers (rural and urban), aged 18 to 24, of
        both sexes, regarding their perceptions of social struc-
        ture; educational and occupational opportunities; rela-
        tionship to family; attitudes on religion, sexuality and
        new trends; use of mass media; well-known male and fe-
        male models; intensity of sociopolitical participation
        and commitment; and aspirations. Variation in responses
        indicates that archetype of youth is a myth imposed on
        public. Notes that young women resist concretizing
        their own liberation.

2363   _____.
        1968 La mujer chilena en una nueva sociedad: un estudio
        exploratorio acerca de la situación e imagen de la mujer
        en Chile. Trans. by I. Budge de Ducci. Santiago:
        Edit. del Pacífico. 227 p. tables, bibl.
          Most comprehensive study to date explores images of
        women as perceived by both sexes and actual situation of
        Chilean women with respect to their position in the fam-
        ily, work, social integration, attitudinal changes,
        aspirations for children, migration opportunities, and
        daily problems. Reports findings of survey conducted
        among 4 socio-economic groups in an urban setting and
        5 in rural environments. Discusses ideology of female
        liberation in regard to mobilization of Third World
        women and relationship between women and revolution.
        Includes statistical summary of educational level, eco-
        nomic activity, civil rights, and political participation
        of Chilean women.

2364   PUZ, AMANDA
        1972 La mujer chilena. Col. Nosotros los Chilenos, 22.
        Santiago: Edit. Quimantú. 95 p. illus.
          General contemporary overview of Chilean women: per-
        sonality traits by region; attitudes toward work, love
        and marriage, a home and children; difficulty with
        machismo; preoccupation with physical appearance, health
        and religion; involvement in social struggles.

General - Miscellaneous

2365 TAPPEN, KATHLEEN B.
      1944 The Status of Women in Chile. Wash., D.C.: US
      Office of the Coordinator of Inter-American Affairs,
      Research Division, Social and Geographic Section. 19 p.
      tables, bibl.
         General overview of women's situation in Chile con-
      siders marriage, family, professions, political and
      civil rights, labor and maternity legislation, employ-
      ment, women's clubs, social conditions and education.
      Provides statistics on women receiving degrees since
      1887, student enrollment, and economic activity.

2366 TORO GODOY, JULIA
      1967 Presencia y destino de la mujer en nuestro pueblo.
      Santiago: Eds. Maipo. 47 p.
         Journalist, short story writer and novelist offers
      negative but sympathetic portrait of the Chilean woman
      of the popular classes and her suffering: the lack of
      welcome the day she's born, her servile position, prob-
      lems as an unwed or married mother, as an urban or rural
      worker.

Argentina

2367 ERIKSSON, N.
      1972 "The Argentine Woman: Her Social, Political and
      Economic Role." RRP 152:3840:959-61, 985-88. tables.
         Collection of demographic, political, educational and
      economic statistics on Argentine women based largely on
      1960 census data. Notes considerable increase in female
      population since WWII but limited number of women play-
      ing active part in economic process.

2368 GARCÍA, MARTA M. de
      1957 "Women in Free Argentina." OAS/AM 9:4:32-33. ports.
         Wife of then OAS ambassador from Argentina answers
      questions about Argentine women posed by woman in
      Washington, D.C.: careers, preferred fields, restric-
      tions, political rights, interests outside the home.
      Describes several women's organizations and names leaders.

2369 GERMANI, GINO
      1955 Estructura social de la Argentina; análisis
      estadístico. Biblioteca Manuel Belgrano de Estudios
      Económicos. Buenos Aires: Edit. Raigal. 278 p.
      tables, graphs, bibl. notes.
         Using national census data, provides a statistical
      portrait of the Argentine population from 1869 to 1947.

South America - Argentina

With respect to women, the following information is available: population, rural/urban residence, marital status, nuptiality, age at marriage, number of children, birth rates, employment (domestic, industrial, etc.), literacy rates, educational levels. 110 tables and 23 graphs are accompanied by an interpretation of data.

2370　GREGORIO LAVIÉ, LUCILA de
　　　1947　Trayectoria de la condición social de las mujeres ayentinas. Inst. Social. Publicación de Extensión Universitaria, 57. Santa Fe, Arg.: Univ. Nacional de Litoral. 23 p.
　　　　Brief but factual notes about the education of women in Argentina since colonial times; their civil rights; regulation of their employment in 20c.; struggle for women's rights in 20c.; contemporary transition.

2371　LA PALMA de EMERY, CELIA
　　　1910　Discursos y conferencias de Celia La Palma de Emery, 1910; acción pública y privada en favor de la mujer y el niño en la República Argentina. B.A.: Alfa y Omega. 259 p. illus., ports.
　　　　Collection of speeches given between 1906 and 1910 in favor of protection for women and children at work, on charitable organizations run by women, and on schools established for women in Argentina.

2372　LUNGO, TERESITA D. L.
　　　1969　"Situación social de la mujer en el norte de Córdoba." UNC/R 10:1/2:467-73.
　　　　Based on 6 years' experience as a teacher in the Department Totoral of Cordobá, Argentina, briefly describes life cycle of peasant women, especially socialization of girls, and suggests certain educational, social, health and economic reforms for a better life in the countryside.

2373　PICHEL, VERA
　　　1968　Mi país y sus mujeres. Buenos Aires: Edit. Sudestada. 171 p. bibl.
　　　　Overview of women in Argentina, beginning with the first Spanish and Indian women who helped populate the colony, and noting women's participation during the English invasions and Independence movement. Briefly mentions immigration, development of education and incorporation into labor force. Charts the struggle for women's civil and political rights since the 19c. by various feminist groups. Regarding female suffrage

607

General - Miscellaneous

(approved in 1947), reproduces debates, 1951 electoral analysis and list of women candidates. Notes influence of Peronism and devotes last 10 chapters to Eva Perón: life, works, political actions, and influence in women's rights. Views her as an example of the slow but inexorable process of women's incorporation into sphere of social and political action. Based on secondary sources.

2374 SCHULTZ CAZENUEVE de MANTOVANI, FRYDA
1960 La mujer en la vida nacional. Buenos Aires: Eds. Galatea - Nueva Visión. 103 p.
Potpourri of personal views on women in Argentina: roles for women in late 19c.; writers; teachers; laborers; students; etc. Basically sketches the many kinds of women found in 19c. and 20c. Argentina--rural or urban, upper-, middle- or lower-class, landed or employed, married or single, beautiful or not. Several chapters have been published separately in periodicals.

2375 _____.
1959 "Bocetos de la Argentina: mujeres." NRCUB 1:2: 42-49.
Brief general descriptions of Argentine women, their socioeconomic status and activities: peasant woman, widow of average means, landowner, bourgeois woman, student's girlfriend, bank employee's girlfriend, and mother.

2376 _____.
1959 "La mujer de la 'Gran Aldea.' (Bocetos de la Argentina)." CAM 107:6:167-76.
Attempts to provide a portrait of women in late 19c. Argentina by describing the roles available to them: woman of politicians and doctors, lover, actress, teacher, "solitary" (old aunt or pious woman), woman of the community. Women's access to the public sphere was through a husband or lover; others became educators.

2377 Sur, Buenos Aires
1970-1971 "Encuesta." Sur 326/327/328:172-253.
Reports findings of questionnaire containing 53 items on work, religion, sexual preconceptions, education, marriage, self-image, politics, equality, etc. given to 74 women, aged 15-35, of various occupations, living in greater Buenos Aires, for their opinions regarding role, destiny, and responsibility of women. Also includes responses of 49 Argentine women writers, actresses, journalists, and other professionals to 8

questions about women's rights, sexual education, obstacles encountered in personal career, divorce, abortion, birth control, etc. Limited samples but useful and interesting for contemporary opinions.

2378   TAPPEN, KATHLEEN B.
       1944   The Status of Women in Argentina. Wash., D.C.:   US
       Office of the Coordinator of Inter-American Affairs,
       Research Division, Social and Geographic Section.   22 p.
       tables, bibl.
          General overview of women's situation in Argentina
       considers social customs, marriage, occupational opportunities, political and civil rights, suffrage activities, economic and social conditions, labor and maternity
       legislation, education, organizations working for women's
       rights, work in Buenos Aires and life in the interior.
       Provides statistics (1939-41).

Uruguay

2379   CANTWELL de BALS, EULALIA
       1947   "Mujeres del Uruguay."   BAWM/B 3:1:36-39; 3:2:55-61;
       3:3:86-93; 3:4:129-36.
          Notes on women in the history of Uruguay, social and
       philanthropic works through women's organizations, education for women and female educators since 1794, the
       feminist movement in the 20c., and women writers, artists
       and musicians. Most attention focused on women's social
       services.

2380   FERNÁNDEZ y MEDINA, BENJAMÍN
       1928   Estampas de mujeres del Uruguay. Madrid: Tipografía
       de Alberto Fontana.   23 p.
          Brief overview of women in the history, education and
       poetry of Uruguay, beginning with the Indian Liropeya.
       Based in part on traveler's impressions.

2381   MACHADO BONET, OFELIO
       1972   "La mujer en el Uruguay." In her Hacia la revolución
       del siglo. 2a parte, pp. 127-238. Montevideo: Imprenta
       Edit. "Goes." bibl.
          Uruguayan feminist and writer provides good compendium
       of notes and statistics (1960's) on women in Uruguay,
       beginning with the development of charity organizations
       and education in the 17c. Covers the suffrage movement,
       legal and educational advances, several women poets,
       labor force participation, delinquency, prostitution,

General - Miscellaneous

demographic aspects, women's associations, legislation,
etc. A separate section contains a potpourri of related
data: document on founding of 1st girls' school in
Montevideo, lists of people who have favored or promoted
women's rights, biographical sketches, resolutions, con-
gresswomen, and much more.

2382 _____.
1950 Circunstanciales II. Montevideo: Imprenta "Rosgal."
233 p.
Collection of lectures, articles, and impressions by
well-known Uruguayan feminist and writer includes 10
selections pertaining to the situation of Uruguayan
woman in 1940's, her participation in international
conferences, National Feminine Union and IACW, and poet
María Eugenia Vaz Ferreira (b. 1875).

2383 Universidad del Trabajo del Uruguay, Depto. de Orientación
y Examen Médico-Psicopedagógico. San Salvador 1674, Montevideo.
1967 "Características de la población estudiantil
montevideana de la Universidad del Trabajo." RMP 2:11:
963-94. tables.
Reports results of survey on interests and preferences
among 3246 male and female 1st year students at 14 industrial schools in Montevideo (1963). Consists of personal
data and data on family organization, parents' occupations, previous schooling, course selection, etc.; as
well as on preferences with respect to reading and entertainment. Notes age and sex differences: e.g., female
students demonstrated more varied reading interests than
males.

CARIBBEAN

Puerto Rico

2384 CADILLA de MARTÍNEZ, MARÍA
1937 "La campesina de Puerto Rico." APR/R 28:3:423-35.
illus., bibl. f/notes.
General comments on peasant women in Puerto Rico:
character, clothing, social and family life, racial
types, folk beliefs, housing, fertility, socialization,
domestic activities.

2385 PADILLA de SANZ, TRINIDAD, et al.
1923 "La mujer puertorriqueña . . ." In El libro de
Puerto Rico. The Book of Puerto Rico, edited by

E. Fernández García, pp. 812-45. San Juan, P.R.: El
Libro Azul Publishing Co. illus., ports.
  Includes 7 separate pieces in Spanish and English on
the founding, aims and tasks of women's civic and religious organizations in Puerto Rico, on several professional women (writers, musicians, etc.), on social
activities such as charity work, on the mother/wife/
grandmother role, and on the demand for equality.

2386   RIBES TOVAR, FEDERICO
        1972   The Puerto Rican Woman. Her Life and Evolution
        Throughout History. Trans. by A. Rawlings. Puerto
        Rican Heritage Series. A Plus Ultra Book, 4. N.Y.:
        Plus Ultra Educational Publishers. 253 p. illus.,
        bibl.
          Broad and general, but not in-depth survey of women in
        the history of Puerto Rico from the Taino women in the
        early days of the Conquest to contemporary times: fem-
        inine attire and scarcity of white women during colonial
        times; country life in 18c.; education; midwifery; migra-
        tion; birth control; prostitution and suffrage. Includes
        chapters on Puerto Rican women in New York and sports-
        women as well as brief biographies of poet Julia de
        Burgos, actress Rita Moreno, Sister Carmelita and Mayor
        Felisa Rincón Marrero. An illustrated section (pp. 127-
        80) contains engravings of 16c. Puerto Rico and 20c.
        photographs. Based almost entirely on secondary sources.

Cuba

2387   AGUIRRE, MIRTA
        1947   Influencia de la mujer en Iberoamérica. Ensayo.
        Havana: Imprenta P. Fernández y cía. 117 p. bibl.
          Based on secondary sources, covers specific signifi-
        cance of women as writers (Sor Juana, La Avellaneda,
        Mistral); erotic female poetry (Agustini, Storni,
        Ibarbourou); women in the history of Ibero-America
        (pre-Columbian indigenous communities to 19c. demands
        for women's rights); and women's social unfolding
        (charity work, First National Congress of Women, IACW,
        other international organizations and meetings,
        movement for women's rights).

General - Miscellaneous

Dominican Republic

2388   TANCER, SHOSHANA B.
        1973 "*La quisqueyana*: The Dominican Woman, 1940-1970."
        In Female and Male in Latin America: Essays, ed. by
        A. Pescatello, pp. 209-29. Pittsburgh: Univ. of
        Pittsburgh Press. bibl. f/notes.
            General overview of Dominican women explores interre-
        lationship between African and Hispanic traditions,
        effects of poverty upon women's role, socialization of
        women, patterns of marriage, women's ability to partici-
        pate in activities beyond "house and patio."

Unpublished Doctoral Disserations*

2389   ALGUERO, MANUEL SALVADOR
      1972 "Individual Modernity, Its Determinants and Conse-
      quences: A Study of Lower-Class Fertility in Guatemala."
      University of Illinois, Urbana. 195 p. DAI 34:2:879-A.

2390   ARNOLD, MARIGENE
      1973 "Mexican Women: The Anatomy of a Stereotype in a
      Mestizo Village." University of Florida. 190 p. DAI
      34:11:5295-B.

2391   BAILEY, SUSAN McGEE
      1971 "Political Socialization Among Children in Bogotá,
      Colombia." University of Michigan. 167 p. DAI 32:12:
      6671-A.

2392   BARBER, JANET
      1972 "Mexican *Machismo* in Novels by Lawrence, Sender, and
      Fuentes." University of Southern California. 422 p.
      DAI 33:7:3630-A.

2393   BERKEMOE, DIANE SOLOMON
      1968 "Contemporary Women Novelists of Argentina (1945-
      1967)." University of Illinois. 441 p. DAI 29:7:
      2249-A.

2394   BLANCH, JOSÉ-MARÍA
      1973 "Differential Fertility Behavior and Values in Rural
      and Semi-Urban Costa Rica." University of Southern
      California. 258 p. DAI 33:9:5315-A.

2395   BLOUGH, WILLIAM JOHN
      1967 "Political Participation in Mexico: Sex Differences

---

* See explanation of this section in the Introduction.

Unpublished Doctoral Dissertations

in Behavior and Attitudes." University of North Carolina.
260 p. DAI 28:11:4672-A.

2396 BOYD, MONICA
1971 "Occupational Mobility and Fertility in Latin
America." Duke University. 304 p. DAI 32:10:5916-A.

2397 BRANSTETTER, KATHERINE BRENDA
1974 "Tenejapans on Clothing and Vice Versa: The Social
Significance of Clothing in a Mayan Community in Chiapas,
Mexico." University of California, Berkeley. 222 p.

2398 BRIAGES, JULIAN C.
1973 "The Population of Mexico: Its Composition and
Changes." University of Florida. 366 p. DAI 35:2:
1253-A.

2399 BROWN, SUSAN E.
1972 "Coping With Poverty in the Dominican Republic:
Women and Their Mates." University of Michigan. 156 p.
DAI 33:9:4087-B.

2400 BUECHLER, JUDITH-MARÍA
1972 "Peasant Marketing and Social Revolution in the
State of La Paz, Bolivia." McGill University.

2401 CANCIAN, FRANCISCA MICAELA
1963 "Family Interaction in Zinacantan." Harvard
University.

2402 No Entry.

2403 CARRÉ, SHIRLEY KILBORN DESHON
1959 "Women's Position on a Yucatecan Henequen Hacienda."
Yale University. 270 p. DAI 26:6:2972.

2404 CHAMBERS, ERNE JEFFERSON
1973 "Los Maestros: A Study in Mexican Middle Class Life
Styles." University of Oregon. 327 p. DAI 34:12:
5788-B.

2405 CHANEY, ELSA M.
1971 "Women in Latin American Politics: The Case of Peru
and Chile." University of Wisconsin. 578 p. DAI 31:
12:6673-A.

Unpublished Doctoral Dissertations

2406 CHERPAK, EVELYN MAY
1973 "Women and the Independence of Gran Colombia 1780–1830." University of North Carolina. 374 p. DAI 34: 9:5838-A.

2407 CLASS, BRADLEY MELLON
1974 "Fictional Treatment of Politics by Argentine Female Novelists." University of New Mexico. 300 p. DAI 35: 9:6132-A.

2408 COHEN, LUCY M.
1966 "Colombian Professional Women as Innovators of Cultural Change." Catholic University of America. 203 p. DAI 27:12:4220-B.

2409 COLL, EDNA
1963 "Injerto de tema en las novelistas mexicanas contemporáneas." University of Florida.

2410 COLLVER, ORVILLE ANDREW
1964 "Birth Rates in Latin America: New Estimates of Historical Trends and Fluctuations." University of California, Berkeley. 263 p. DAI 26:11:6815.

2411 COVNEY, NORMA O'NEILL
1967 "Control of Aggression in Child Rearing in Puerto Rico: A Study of Professed Practices Used With Boys and Girls in Two Socioeconomic Urban Groups." Columbia University. 139 p. DAI 28:2:777-A.

2412 CROUSE, RUTH COMPTON
1964 "Clorinda Matto de Turner: An Analysis of Her Role in Peruvian Literature." Florida State University. 143 p. DAI 25:9:5272.

2413 CRUZ, JOSÉ ANGEL
1972 "Realismo y literatura en el cuento de la 'Generación del Cuarenta' en Puerto Rico." New York University. 846 p. DAI 33:11:6349-A.

2414 DÁVILA, DAVID
1972 "The Life and Theater of Gabriela Roepke." University of Cincinnati. 240 p. DAI 33:6:3063-A.

2415 De GRYS, MARY SCHWEITZER
1973 "Women's Role in a North Coast Fishing Village in Peru: A Study in Male Dominance and Female Subordination." New School for Social Research. 193 p. DAI 35: 3:1297-A.

Unpublished Doctoral Dissertations

2416 De MELLO, GEORGE
        1968 "The Writings of Clorinda Matto de Turner," Univer-
        sity of Colorado. 643 p. DAI 29:4:1225-A.

2417 De WINTER, ADRIAN M. THOMAS
        1971 "Family Interaction, Family Planning and Fertility
        in the City of Durazno, Uruguay." University of Wiscon-
        sin. 227 p. DAI 32:7:4114-A.

2418 DÍAZ, MAY NORDQUIST
        1963 "Tonolá: a Mexican Peasant Town in Transition."
        University of California, Berkeley. 274 p. DAI 24:10:
        3924.

2419 ECHOLS, JAMES R.
        1974 "Migration and Fertility in Tlaxcala, Mexico." Uni-
        versity of Virginia, 234 p. DAI 35:5:3138-A.

2420 ENNIS de SAGASTI, HELI ELLEN
        1972 "Social Implications of Adult Literacy: A Study
        Among Migrant Women in Peru." University of Pennsylvania.
        306 p. DAI 33:7:3789-A.

2421 FELSTINER, MARY ALEXANDRA LOWENTHAL
        1970 "The Larrain Family in the Independence of Chile,
        1700-1830." Stanford University. 284 p. DAI 31:11:
        5982-A.

2422 FIGUEROA de VALENTÍN, EDITH
        1971 "Attitudes Toward Foods of Homemakers Living in
        Tras Talleres, San Juan, Puerto Rico." Texas Technical
        University. 224 p. DAI 32:4:1745-A.

2423 FILELLA, JAMES F.
        1957 "Educational and Sex Differences in the Organization
        of Abilities in Technical and Academic Students in
        Colombia, South America." Fordham University.

2424 FOUND, RUTH ELAINE
        1971 "Dietary Adequacy and Health Behavior of Low-Income
        Families in Colombia." University of Wisconsin. 334 p.
        DAI 32:6:3461-B.

2425 FOX, LUCÍA UNGARO
        1962 "La mujer como motivo en ocho poetas representativos
        del Perú." University of Illinois. 233 p. DAI 23:8:
        2913.

Unpublished Doctoral Dissertations

2626 FRIEDLAND, ANNE BRAND
1971 "An Ethnographic Study of San Mateo Almomoloa: A
Mexican Peasant Village." University of California,
Los Angeles. 200 p. DAI 32:10:5586-B.

2427 FULLER, GARY ALBERT
1972 "The Spatial Diffusion of Birth Control in Chile."
Pennsylvania State University. 257 p. DAI 33:10:5852-A.

2428 GALLAGHER, ANN MIRIAM
1972 "The Family Background of the Nuns of Two *Monasterios*
in Colonial Mexico: Santa Clara, Querétaro; and Corpus
Christi, Mexico City (1724-1822)." Catholic University
of America. 313 p. DAI 33:2:694-A.

2429 GALLAGHER, SISTER MARY LIAM
1964 "Social Class and Social Change in the Colombian
Family." St. Louis University. 275 p. DAI 26:4:2377.

2430 GARFINKEL, LILA GONZÁLEZ
1972 "La imagen de la madre ausente en la poesía de César
Vallejo." Stanford University. 161 p. DAI 33:5:2325-A.

2431 GIMON, ALEXANDER T.
1973 "Maternal Expectancies: Effects of Their Modification on Training Behavior of Puerto Rican Mothers Toward
Their Retarded Children." Yeshiva University. 329 p.
DAI 34:9:6482-A.

2432 GROSS, JOSEPH JOHN
1974 "Domestic Group Structure in a Mayan Community of
Guatemala." University of Rochester. 181 p. DAI 35:
4:1787-A.

2433 HALBERSTEIN, ROBERT A.
1973 "Evolutionary Implications of the Democratic Structure of a Transplanted Population." University of
Kansas. 166 p. DAI 34:12:5791-B.

2434 HALE, FRANK ARTHUR
1972 "Fertility Control Policy in the Dominican Republic."
Syracuse University. 233 p.

2435 HALSTED, DAVID WRIGHT
1966 "Differences Between the Mothers of Over-Achieving
and Under-Achieving Eleventh-Grade Puerto Rican Students." Michigan State University. 168 p. DAI 27:12:
4127-A.

Unpublished Doctoral Dissertations

2436   HASS, PAULA HOLLERBACH
        1971 "Maternal Employment and Fertility in Metropolitan
        Latin America." Duke University. 540 p. DAI 32:10:
        5905-A.

2437   HELLERMAN, MYRNA KASEY
        1972 "Myth and Mexican Identity in the Works of Carlos
        Fuentes." Stanford University. 199 p. DAI 33:5:2376-A.

2438   HERNÁNDEZ, MARY FRANCES BAKER
        1963 "Gabriela Mistral and the Standards of American Crit-
        icism." University of New Mexico. 159 p. DAI 24:8:
        3324.

2439   HERNÁNDEZ-CELA, CÉSAR XAVIER
        1971 "Fertility Stress in Costa Rica." University of
        Notre Dame. 222 p. DAI 32:5:2819-A.

2440   HERNANDO, DIANA
        1973 "Casa y Familia: Spatial Biographies in Nineteenth
        Century Buenos Aires." University of California, Los
        Angeles. 761 p. DAI 34:7:4156-A.

2441   HEYMAN, BARRY N.
        1974 "Urbanization and the Status of Women in Peru."
        University of Wisconsin. 227 p. DAI 35:8:5529-A.

2442   HOLLANDER, NANCY CARO
        1975 "Women in the Political Economy of Argentina."
        University of California, Los Angeles. 357 p. DAI 35:
        10:6637-A.

2443   HUBBELL, LINDA JEAN MOULDER
        1972 "The Network of Kinship, Friendship, and Compadrazgo
        Among the Middle-Class Women of Uruapán, Michoacán,
        Mexico." University of California, Berkeley. 334 p.

2444   HUNT, M. EVA VERBITSKY
        1962 "The Dynamics of the Domestic Group in Two Tzeltal
        Villages: A Contrastive Comparison." University of
        Chicago.

2445   HUYKE-GARNER, ANA LUCIA
        1974 "Factors Affecting the Adoption of Modern Family
        Planning Techniques, As Perceived By Adult Women in
        Barranquilla, Colombia." Florida State University.
        237 p. DAI 35:7:4114-A.

Unpublished Doctoral Dissertations

2446 ICKEN, HELEN MARGARET
1962 "From Shanty Town to Public Housing: A Comparison
of Family Structure in Two Urban Neighborhoods in Puerto
Rico." Columbia University. 321 p. DAI 23:5:1488.

2447 JACKSON, JEAN ELIZABETH
1972 "Marriage and Linguistic Identity Among the Bara
Indians of the Vaupés, Colombia." Stanford University.
329 p. DAI 33:8:3435-B.

2448 JAMES, WILLIAM RUSSELL
1972 "Household Composition and Domestic Groups in a
Highland Colombian Village." University of Wisconsin.
199 p. DAI 33:7:2907-B.

2449 JOHNSON, ALLAN GRISWOLD
1972 "Modernization and Social Change: Attitudes Toward
Women's Roles in Mexico City." University of Michigan.
301 p. DAI 33:11:6471-A.

2450 JOPLING, CAROL F.
1973 "Women Weavers of Yalálag; Their Art and Its Process." University of Massachusetts. 244 p. DAI 34:4:
1348-B.

2451 KAHLEY, WILLIAM JOSEPH
1972 "Family Planning in Colombia: An Analysis of Cost
and Achievement." Pennsylvania State University. 139 p.
DAI 33:12:6538-A.

2452 KAPLAN, JOANNA OVERING
1974 "The Piaroa, A People of the Orinoco Basin: A Study
in Kinship and Marriage." Brandeis University. 420 p.
DAI 35:7:3957-8-A.

2453 KASSCHAU, PATRICIA LEE
1972 "Political Skepticism and Alienation in a Sample of
Young Mexican Children." University of Southern California. 266 p. DAI 33:7:3793-A.

2454 KINCAID, DON LAWRENCE
1973 "Communication Networks, Locus of Control, and
Family Planning Among Migrants to the Periphery of
Mexico City." Michigan State University. 178 p. DAI
34:9:6105-A.

2455 KONGAS, LEMBI
1972 "Metropolis-Satellite Relationships in Southern
Hidalgo, Mexico: The Non-Nuclear Household as an

Unpublished Doctoral Dissertations

Indicator of Economic Deprivation." University of
Michigan. 296 p. DAI 33:9:4088-B.

2456 LACOT, MARÍA SOCORRO
1962 "Freedom in Making Personal Decisions as Perceived
by Puerto-Rican Ninth-Grade Girls." Iowa State University. 206 p. DAI 23:4:1346.

2457 LAUGHLIN, ROBERT MOODY
1963 "Through the Looking Glass: Reflections in Zinacantan Courtship and Marriage." Harvard University.

2458 LAVRÍN, ASUNCIÓN IRIGOYEN
1963 "Religious Life of Mexican Women in the Eighteenth
Century." Harvard University.

2459 LITZLER, BEVERLY NEWBOLD
1968 "Women of San Blas Atempa: An Analysis of the Economic Role of Isthmus Zapotec Women in Relation to Family
and Community." University of California, Los Angeles.
183 p. DAI 29:06:1912-B.

2460 LONGRES, JOHN FRANK
1970 "Social Conditions related to the Acceptance of
Modern Medicine Among Puerto Rican Women." University
of Michigan. 182 p. DAI 31:12:6716-A.

2461 LOUSTAUNA, MARTHA OEHMKE
1973 "Mexico's Contemporary Women Novelists." University
of New Mexico. 227 p. DAI 34:5:2637-A.

2462 McKEGNEY, JAMES CUTHBERT
1959 "Female Characters in the Novels of José Rubén
Romero and Gregorio López Fuentes." University of
Washington. 600 p. DAI 20:10:4115.

2463 MARTÍNEZ-ALIER, VERENA
1970 "Marriage, Class, and Colour in Nineteenth Century
Cuba." Oxford University.

2464 MAYNARD, EILEEN
1963 "The Women of Palin: A Comparative Study of Indian
and Ladino Women in a Guatemalan Village." Cornell
University. 343 p. DAI 24:06:2216.

2465 MIDDLETON, DeWIGHT RAY
1972 "Form and Process: A Study of Urban Social Relations
in Manta, Ecuador." Washington University. 257 p.
DAI 33:3:992-B.

Unpublished Doctoral Dissertations

2466 MILLS, DOROTHY A. H.
      1955 "A Descriptive Analysis of the Morphology of the
      Diminutives 'ito', 'illo', 'ico', 'uelo', and of their
      Increments (Including Feminine and Plural Forms) as Used
      in Spanish America." University of Southern California.
      930 p.

2467 MOORE, BRIAN EDWARD ARTHUR
      1970 "Some Working Women in Mexico City: Traditionalists
      and Modernists." Washington University. 238 p. DAI
      31:7:3659-A.

2468 MORRIS, EARL WALTER
      1969 "Acculturation, Migration and Fertility in Peru: A
      Study of Social and Cultural Change." Cornell Univer-
      sity. 258 p. DAI 30:12:5543-A.

2469 MOXLEY, ROBERT LONNIE
      1970 "Differentiation of Family Structure and Interfamily
      Networks in a Highland Peruvian Community." Cornell
      University. 204 p. DAI 31:6:3068-A.

2470 MULHARE de la TORRE, MIRTA
      1969 "Sexual Ideology in Pre-Castro Cuba; A Cultural
      Analysis." University of Pittsburgh.

2471 NUTINI, HUGO G.
      1962 "Marriage and the Family in a Nahuatl-Speaking
      Village of the Central Mexican Highlands." University
      of California, Los Angeles.

2472 OJEDA, ÁQUILES PALOMINO
      1972 "Patrones matrimoniales entre los Ixiles de Chajul,
      Guatemala." University of California, Irvine. 198 p.
      DAI 33:2:542-B.

2473 OLIVER-SMITH, ANTHONY RICHARD
      1974 "Yungay North: Disaster and Social Change in the
      Peruvian Highlands." Indiana University. 522 p. DAI
      34:12:5796-B.

2474 PAUL, CATHERINE MANNY
      1967 "Amanda Labarca H.: Educator to the Women of Chile:
      The Work and Writing of Amanda Labarca H. in the Field
      of Education in Chile; Their Importance; Their Value
      in the Progress of Education in Chile." New York Uni-
      versity. 210 p. DAI 28:4:1215.

2475   PAYNE, SISTER MARY RUTH
       1967 "A Study of Value Crisis: Traditional and Modern
       Values of the Female Students at the University of San
       Andres, La Paz, Bolivia." St. Louis University. 242 p.
       DAI 28:8:3046-A.

2476   PEDRERO-NIETO, MERCEDES
       1973 "Labor Force in Mexico: A Study of Regional Varia-
       tions 1950-1960." University of Pennsylvania. 303 p.
       DAI 34:8:5350-A.

2477   PERCAS PONSETI, HELENA
       1951 "Women Poets of Argentina (1810-1950)." Columbia
       University. 424 p. DAI 12:1:70.

2478   PÉREZ, JOSÉ RAMON
       1973 "The Rate of Return to Educational Investments With
       Special Reference to Puerto Rico." University of
       Michigan. 166 p. DAI 34:8:4521-A.

2479   PRESSER, HARRIET BETTY RUBINOFF
       1969 "Sterilization and Fertility Decline in Puerto
       Rico." University of California, Berkeley. 348 p.
       DAI 30:7:3108-A.

2480   PROCTOR, PHYLLIS ANN WIEGAND
       1972 "Mexico's *Supermachos*: Satire and Social Revolution
       in Comics by Rius." University of Texas, Austin. 228 p.
       DAI 33:9:5138-A.

2481   RICO-VELASCO, JESUS ANTONIO
       1972 "Modernization and Fertility in Puerto Rico: An
       Ecological Analysis." Ohio State University. 177 p.
       DAI 33:2:839-A.

2481a SÁNCHEZ CARO, DOMINGO
       1967 "Differential Fertility in Chile: Selected Demo-
       graphic and Sociological Aspects." University of
       Florida. 181 p. DAI 29:3:978-A.

2482   SANTOS, NELLY E.
       1973 "La poesía hispánica del '90 escrita por mujeres.
       (La problemática de la trascendencia histórica de la
       mujer y su expresión poética en los dos últimos cuartos
       del siglo.)" University of Connecticut. 423 p. DAI
       34:5:2578-A.

2483   SCOTT, JOSEPH WALTER
       1963 "Sources of Change in Community, Family and

Unpublished Doctoral Dissertations

Fertility in Aibonito, Puerto Rico." Indiana University.
333 p. DAI 25:2:1396.

2484 SCHWARTZ, LOLA ROMANUCCI MANZOLILLO
1963 "Morality, Conflict and Violence in a Mexican
Mestizo Village." Indiana University. 270 p.

2485 SEDA BONILLA, EDWIN
1958 "The Normative Patterns of the Puerto Rican Family
in Various Situational Contexts." Columbia University.
191 p. DAI 18:5:1886.

2486 SERROS, ROBERT
1971 "La felicidad a través del amor, la soledad, y la
muerte en la obra literaria de María Luisa Bombal."
University of Southern California. 237 p. DAI 32:8:
4633-A.

2487 No Entry.

2488 SMITH, MARGO LANE
1971 "Institutionalized Servitude: The Female Domestic
Servant in Lima, Peru." Indiana University. 497 p.
DAI 32:9:4995-B.

2489 SOLIEN, NANCY LOUDON
1959 "The Consanguineal Household Among the Black Carib
of Central America." University of Michigan. 245 p.
DAI 19:9:3083.

2490 STEVENS, LEONARD E.
1964 "Feminine Protagonists in Manuel Galvez' Novels."
Indiana University. 420 p. DAI 26:2:1050-51.

2491 STILLWELL, WILLIAM DUNCAN, III
1969 "House of Glass: The Study of a Mexican Urban Marriage Relationship." University of Pittsburgh. 279 p.
DAI 30:6:2517-B.

2492 STINNER, WILLIAM FRANCIS
1969 "Modernization, Nuptiality and Fertility in Latin
America." Pennsylvania State University. 173 p. DAI
31:4:1910-A.

2493 SUPER, JOHN CLAY
1974 "Querétaro: Society and Economy in Early Provincial
Mexico, 1590-1630." University of California, Los
Angeles. 318 p. DAI 34:7:4175-A.

623

Unpublished Doctoral Dissertations

2494   TAGGART, JAMES MOUNSEY
           1971 "The Factors Affecting the Developmental Cycle of
           Domestic Groups in a Nahuat-Speaking Community of
           Mexico." University of Pittsburgh. 282 p. <u>DAI</u>
           32:3:1335-B.

2495   TALBOT, DOROTHY McCOMB
           1970 "Professionalization Among Student Nurses in Peru:
           A Sociological Analysis." Tulane University. 339 p.
           <u>DAI</u> 31:9:4911-A.

2496   TAYLOR, MARTIN CHARLES
           1964 "Religious Sensibility in the Life and Poetry of
           Gabriela Mistral." University of California, Los
           Angeles.

2497   THOMAS, SANDRA CAROL
           1973 "The Women of Chile and Education for a Contemporary
           Society: A Study of Chilean Women, Their History and
           Present Status and the New Demands of a Society in
           Transition." St. Louis University. 378 p. <u>DAI</u>
           35:5:2799-A.

2498   TUSA, BOBS McELROY
           1972 "The Works of Silvina Bullrich." Tulane University.
           302 p. <u>DAI</u> 33:11:6377-A.

2499   URBINA, SUSANA PATRICIA
           1972 "Cultural and Sex Differences in Affiliation and
           Achievement Drives As Expressed in Reported Dream Con-
           tent and a Projective Technique." Fordham University.
           148 p. <u>DAI</u> 33:1:432-B.

2500   WATSON, LAWRENCE CRAIG
           1967 "The Effect of Urbanization on Socialization Prac-
           tices and Personality Development in Guajiro Society."
           University of California, Los Angeles. 536 p. <u>DAI</u>
           28:4:1327-B.

2501   WELLER, ROBERT H.
           1967 "Female Work Experience and Fertility in San Juan,
           Puerto Rico. Cornell University.

2502   WHITTINGTON, JAMES ATTISON, JR.
           1971 "Kinship, Mating, and Family in the Chocó of
           Colombia: An Afro-American Adaptation." Tulane Uni-
           versity. 395 p. <u>DAI</u> 32:11:6179-B.

Unpublished Doctoral Dissertations

2503   WORTMAN, MARY ALICE
         1973   "The Concept of Machismo in the Poetry, Music, and
         Dance of the Gaucho of the Río de la Plata." University
         of Ohio.   214 p.   DAI 33:8:4279-A.

2504   YABOUR de CALDERA, I. ELIZABETH
         1974   "Evaluation of Family Planning Experimental Informa-
         tion and Education Programs at Maternidad Concepcion
         Palacios Caracas, Venezuela."   Cornell University.
         193 p.   DAI 35:7:4711-12-A.

2505   YOUSSEF, NADIA HAGGAG
         1970   "Social Structure and Female Labor Force Participa-
         tion in Developing Countries: A Comparison of Latin
         American and Middle-Eastern Countries."   University of
         California, Berkeley.   299 p.   DAI 31:7:3670-A.

2506   ZELMAN, ELIZABETH ANN CROUCH
         1974   "Women's Rights and Women's Rites: A Cross-Cultural
         Study of Womanpower and Reproductive Ritual."   University
         of Michigan.   369 p.   DAI 35:7:3969-A.

2507   ZIMMERMAN, CHARLOTTE BENEDICT
         1960   "The Meaning of the Role of Women in a Transition
         From a Civilization to a Fellaheen Social Order: A
         Study of Continuity and Change in the Maya Culture."
         St. Louis University.   312 p.   DAI 21:10:3187.

Unpublished Master's Theses*

2508   ABAT, MARY LEE
      1946   "Madame Lynch of Paraguay, Her Rise, Her Romance,
      Her Tragedy." University of Texas, Austin. 176 p.

2509   BLAKE, JOHN HERMAN
      1966   "Urbanization and Urban Fertility in Mexico, 1930-
      1960." University of California, Berkeley.

2510   BRENNAN, NANCY
      1973   "Cooperativism and Socialization Among the Cuna
      Indians of San Blas." University of California, Los
      Angeles.

2511   BULAND, JANN
      1975   "Women in Nineteenth-Century Mexico: A Preliminary
      Assessment of Their Images and Roles." Iowa State
      University of Science and Technology.

2512   CAMPANA de WATTS, LUZ ANGÉLICA
      1969   "La Perricholi, mito literacio nacional peruano."
      University of Southern California. 185 p.

2513   CANNON, EMILIE T.
      1963   "Women Characters in Works of Ricardo Guiraldes."
      Tulane University.

2514   CASTILLO, HENRIETTA AMPARO
      1939   "The Life and Works of María Enriqueta." University
      of Texas, Austin. 104 p.

2515   COVA MADURO, ANTONIO AVELINO
      1966   "The Legion of Mary: A Catholic Response to Dechris-
      tianization in Latin America." University of California,
      Berkeley.

---

*   See explanation of this section in the Introduction.

WOMEN IN SPANISH AMERICA

2516 DOHEN, DOROTHY
1959 "Two Studies of Puerto Rico." Fordham University.
155 p.

2517 ELTON, CHARLOTTE
1974 "The Economic Determinants of Female Migration in
Latin America." University of Sussex. 78 p.

2518 GARCÍA, EMILIO F.
1969 "Las personajes femeninas en las Tradiciones
Peruanas de Ricardo Palma." Tulane University.

2519 GRAY, CORDELIA
1964 "Archetypal Pattern in the Writings of María Luisa
Bombal." Tulane University.

2520 GREEN, JUDITH STRUPP
1968 "Changes in Tarahumara Women's Work from Prehistoric
Times to the Present." Tulane University.

2521 GREENE, LILA THRACE
1935 "A Study of the Women Characters of the South American Novel." University of Texas, Austin. 115 p.

2522 KRESS, DOROTHY M.
1931 "Catalina de Erauso, su personalidad histórica y
legendaria." University of Texas, Austin. 100 p.

2523 MILLER, JOHN C.
1965 "Clorinda Matto de Turner: The Apostolate of Social
Protest of a Genteel Woman of the Nineteenth Century."
University of Maryland.

2524 MILLER, VIRGINIA
1974 "The Concept of Femininity in Aztec Religion and
Culture." University of Texas, Austin.

2525 MONTENEGRO, ROSE MARIE
1970 "Periodicals for Women in Nineteenth Century Mexico."
Catholic University of America.

2526 O'HAGAN, MARYANN JOAN
1968 "The Distribution of Economically Active Women in
Major Industrial and Occupational Sectors in Latin
America." University of Texas, Austin.

2527 PASSMORE, HELEN FAY
1939 "Women Printers, Publishers, and Journalists in
Colonial Mexico." University of Texas, Austin. 124 p.

Unpublished Master's Theses

2528 RAYNES, MARÍA GUADALUPE LEAL
1960 "An Annotated Study of José Joaquin Fernández de
Lizardi's La educación de las mujeres o la quijotita
y prima." University of Texas, Austin. 115 p.

2529 SUARDIAZ, DELIA E.
1973 "Sexism in the Spanish Language." University of
Washington.

2530 SWEENEY, JUDITH L.
1973 "Immigrant Women in Argentina: 1890-1914."
University of California, Los Angeles.

2531 TILLEY, SALLY DAVIS
1965 "Women Characters in the Novels of Roberto Jorge
Payro." Tulane University.

2532 TURNER, ELSA SCHAMIS
1964 "Fertility Differences in Buenos Aires, 1960."
University of California, Berkeley.

2533 VÉLEZ, BRUNILDA
1964 "Women's Political Behavior in Chile." University
of California, Berkeley.

2534 VERLINGER, DALE E.
1973 "Gardens of Freedom: The Life and Works of Nellie
Campobello." Ohio University. 376 p.

Author Index

Spanish surnames are often cited in various forms. Wherever possible, an author's name is given in full. In those instances where it was not possible to be certain that it was the same person, variations in the name are entered. Women whose name has changed due to marriage are cited in the several names with a reference to the other forms which should be consulted. For example: Chiñas, Beverly Litzler see also Litzler, Beverly Newbold.

Subject Index

Prepared by Mary Lombardi

Extensive subject analysis of the annotations of each bibliographic entity forms the basis of the index. Within, cross-references provide access to subject interrelationships through see also references from broader to narrower terms and between related terms at similar levels. Synonyms and other unused terms are indicated through the use of see references. Also included are the titles of periodicals, and the names of persons, cities, organizations, indigenous cultures, etc. See the AUTHOR INDEX for names of authors of individual items. Alphabetising is word-by-word, except that initial articles are ignored, and except that subdivision by country follows subject subdivision. References are to item numbers.

Abduction, 840, 1575
Abella Caprile, Margarita, 164, 340, 348
Abnegation, 1253, 1675
Abortion, 1035
    as birth control method, 1035, 1581; see also subdivision by country
    comparative studies, 1023, 1030, 1040, 1585
    in indigenous cultures, 699; see also Indigenous cultures (ethnographies)
    legal aspects, 1522, 1527, 1560, 1575, 1581-82, 1585, 1619-20, 2148
    in migratory groups, 1200
    in pre-Columbian cultures, 1025, 1030
    as public health problem, 1097, 1172-73, 1585
    Argentina, 1200, 2148
    Chile, 961, 1171-74, 1176-78, 1180, 1185, 1186, 1188, 1191, 1193, 1619-20
    Colombia, 1112, 1114, 1130, 1140, 2343
    Costa Rica, 1097, 1105
    Cuba, 1575
    Ecuador, 1522, 1609
    Mexico, 1061, 1063, 1065, 1585

    Paraguay, 1169
    Peru, 1154, 1160-61, 1164, 1165a, 1527
    Puerto Rico, 1224
    Uruguay, 1560
Abrego, Mercedes, 1851, 1863, 1868-70, 1872
Abreu de Estévez, Marta, 97, 2017, 2023, 2030
Acción Católica, 655, 2165
Acción Femenina Peruana, 2034
Acculturation, 696, 921, 2468
Acevedo, Josefa, 475
Acevedo, Olga, 315
Aclla-Huasi, 1410
Acosta, Cecilio, 260
Acosta Berbeo family, 41
Acosta de Samper, Soledad, 262, 269-71, 404, 407, 409, 475
Actresses:
    Argentina, 152-53
    Mexico, 116
    Peru, 1, 12, 140-43, 1793
Acuña, Manuel, 168
Adler, María Raquel, 336
Adolescence:
    cross-cultural studies, 1031, 1266, 1308
    Chile, 1308
    Germany, 1308
    Mexico, 715, 717, 737, 1266

Castillo, la Madre, see Castillo y
   Guevara, Sor Francisca Josefa
   del
Castillo Ledón, Amalia de, 420
Castillo y Guevara, Sor Francisco
   Josefa del, 261, 273-85, 475,
   1777
Castration anxiety: mental taboos
   and, 1037
Castro, Fidel, 2050
Castro, Marcela, 1940a
Catalá de Princivalle, Emma, 555
Catalina (la India), 1777
Catamarca (Argentina), 1999
Cataracts: treatment by remedieras,
   1195
Catholic Church:
   and abortion, 1581
   on courtship, 973
   and demographic politics, 1133,
      1236
   female participation in, 578-79,
      583, 673
   influence on family of, 818, 823
   opposition to contraceptives,
      1029, 1048-49
   and society, 585, 587, 636, 646,
      690-91, 1724, 2310
   status of women and, 585, 673
   theology, 579
   (by country), see Religion
   see also Beatas; Convents;
      Guadalupanismo; Marianismo;
      Missionaries, Catholic; Nuns;
      Religion; Saints
Cayapa Indians, 776
Caycedo, María Clemencia, 474, 483,
   1776
Cayetano, 1909
Cayzedo y Cuero, Joaquín, 1866
Celis, Trinidad, 1940a
Centeno de Romainville, María Ana,
   1688
Centro de Investigación de la Mujer
   (Argentina), 2294
Centro Educacional Femenino de
   Antioquia (Colombia), 479
Ceramics, see Pottery and ceramics
Ceremonies, see Indigenous cultures
   (ethnographies); Festivals
Césarman, Fernando, 2251
Cetina Gutiérrez, Rita, 21
Chaé, 1170
Chajul (Guatemala), 903, 2472
Chalchihuitlicue, 593
Chamberlain, Coronel: wife of, 1841
Chamula, Chiapas (Mexico), 727
Chan Kom, Yucatan, (Mexico), 708,
   728, 731, 889
Chapa, Esther, 17
Chapanay, Martina, 346, 2004

Chaperonage, 775, 853, 975, 1373;
   see also Courtship
Charitable activities/institutions:
   Argentina, 84, 528, 532, 547,
      1698-99, 2010, 2146, 2289, 2371
   Bolivia, 57
   Chile, 67, 69, 2361
   Colombia, 43, 775, 1685, 1981
   Costa Rica, 2097, 2340
   Cuba, 97, 2015, 2017, 2030, 2195
   Mexico, 455, 775, 2015
   Nicaragua, 2093
   Paraguay, 2357
   Peru, 50, 498
   Puerto Rico, 91, 2385
   see also Beatas; Beaterio; Red Cross
      volunteers; Social work/workers;
      Sociedad de Beneficencia
Charrería, 1255
Charro, 1244-45
Chaves, María de, 681
Chemistry/chemists, 18, 530
Cherán, Michoacán (Mexico), 701
Chiapas (Mexico), 1369, 1498, 2397
Chibcha Indians, 770
Chibchan-speaking communities, 764
Chichicastenango (Guatemala), 745
Chieftainships, colonial, 1475-76
Child care:
   Bolivia, 505
   Chile, 2284
   Colombia, 1126
   Cuba, 570-72, 574, 1009, 1456, 2192
   Puerto Rico, 559
   see also Children
Childbirth, see Birth customs
Children:
   cross-cultural studies, 848, 980,
      985, 1262, 1287, 2049
   in indigenous cultures, 698, 1198,
      1338a; see also Indigenous cul-
      tures (ethnographies)
   legislation affecting, 1469
      Argentina, 1545, 1551, 1664,
         2286
      Bolivia, 1533
      Chile, 1657
      Colombia, 1649, 1650
      Cuba, 1576, 1667, 1669
      Ecuador, 1520-22, 1652
      Mexico, 1492, 1495, 1501, 1643-
         44, 1646
      Peru, 1528, 1653, 1655
      Uruguay, 1555, 1565
   naming, 717, 750, 1734
   nutrition, 1089
   play behavior, 848, 995, 1276
   pre-Columbian, 858-59
   sex differences, 523, 1276-77,
      1287, 1308
   sibling rivalry of, 1337

Comisión de Labor Feminil (Mexico), 602
Commerce, see Business
Common-law marriage, see Consensual unions
Communism: diatribe against (Argentina), 2144
Communist Party:
    Argentina, 2149, 2163
    Chile, 2134
    Mexico, 2067
Community studies, see Indigenous cultures (ethnographies); Mestizos; also see under names of individual cities, e.g. Cartagena (Colombia); Chinautla (Guatemala); Zamora, Michoacán (Mexico)
Compadrazgo, 1232, 2443
Compi, Lake Titicaca (Bolivia), 791
Composers, 115, 148, 151, 354, 376
Conceptionist order, 589
    Colombia, 648
    Mexico, 599, 613, 632, 635
    Yucatán, 612
Concubinage:
    during conquest, 1724
    in indigenous cultures, 699, 819; see also Indigenous cultures (ethnographies)
    legislation about, 1491-92, 1513
    Colombia, 1292, 1513
    Mexico, 1491-92
Conde, José, 1953
Condom (birth control method), 1116
Condorcanqui, see Tupuc Amaru, José Gabriel
Confederación de Trabajadores de Mexico, 2084
Conquest, see subdivision Conquest and colonial under History
Consciousness-raising:
    Argentina, 2231, 2294
    Mexico, 428, 1366, 2256
Consejo Nacional de Mujeres (Argentina), 82, 2146
Consensual unions, 808, 811, 819, 821
    Colombia, 924, 936
    Costa Rica, 912, 1099, 1101
    Cuba, 999
    Dominican Republic, 1010
    Guatemala, 1093
    Mexico, 1259
    Paraguay, 960
    Puerto Rico, 981, 1214, 1229
    Venezuela, 917
    see also Single motherhood
Contraception, see Birth control
Contractual capacities (married women), 1484, 1517

Convents:
    colonial, 170, 589
    Argentina, 354
    Chile, 318, 684, 686-88
    Colombia, 474-75, 481, 483-84, 648, 650-51, 1771, 1775, 1781
    Ecuador, 654-55, 659-60, 662
    Mexico, 446, 589-90, 595-96, 600, 604-10, 612-13, 617-18, 621-35, 639, 1737
    Peru, 669, 681
    nineteenth-twentieth centuries, 597-99, 656, 667, 695, 1949
Cordero, Alonso, 688
Córdoba (Argentina), 966, 1810, 2372
Córdoba, José María, 1857
Coromoro (Colombia), 1899, 1902
Correa Zapata, Dolores, 211
Correctional institutions:
    Argentina, 1627-30, 1633
    Chile, 1617
    see also Prisons, Recogimientos
Correo de las Damas, (Cuba), 694
Corrido, 1255
Cortés, Hernán, 1716, 1737, 1740; see also Marina, Doña
Cortés, Leonor, 1740
Costume, see Clothing
Cotapos de Carrera, Ana María, 1948, 1951-53
Cottage industry, 1216, 1697
Courtship, 820, 2310, 2314
    Catholic Church on, 973
    cross-cultural studies, 982
    indigenous, see Indigenous cultures (ethnographies)
    legal aspects, 1487, 1527
    Argentina, 973
    Chile, 319
    Colombia, 938
    Costa Rica, 758, 911
    El Salvador, 907
    Mexico, 715-16, 725-26, 944, 852, 869, 893-94, 1069, 1373, 1487
    Panama, 913
    Peru, 1527
    Puerto Rico, 975, 982-83, 996-97, 1229
    see also Marriage
Couvade, 1018, 1022, 1195
Coya, Ynquil, 1790
Crafts, 698
    Chile, 802
    Mexico, 108, 722, 731
    Middle America, 740
    Nicaragua, 757
    see also Basketry; Indigenous cultures (ethnographies); Lace work; Pottery and ceramics; Weaving
Creole women, 1548, 1717

International Congress of Spanish
American Women, 2045
International organizations, see
Women's organizations--inter-
national; Women's rights--inter-
national organizations active in
Interpersonal relations:
Colombia, 932, 1296-97
Mexico, 715, 721, 725-26
see also Female-male relations;
Parent-child relations
Interracial relations, 812, 1579
Colombia, 939
Cuba, 1001-02
Peru, 1794
Puerto Rico, 1227
see also Intermarriage; Miscege-
nation
Isaacs, Jorge and Clementina, 266
Isaacs, 'María' de, 266-67
Isla Maciel, Buenos Aires (Argentina),
1200
Ixil Indians, 903, 2472
Izquierdo, María, 121-22

Jacalteca Indians, 747
Jalacingo, Puebla (Mexico), 896
Jalapa (Mexico), 2064
Jalisco (Mexico), 849
Jara Quemada, Paula, 71, 1949-50
Jaramillo, Doña Marina, see Marina,
Doña
Jerez Aristeguieta, Miguel, 35
Jeronymite order, 617, 633
Jesús, Mariana de, 45, 655, 657-58,
661, 663, 1786, 2349
Jesús Cepeda, Teresa de, 289
Jesús María y José, Sor Catalina
Luisa de, 654
Jesús Paredes y Flores, Mariana de
see Jesús, Mariana de
Jívaro Indians, 656, 777, 779, 1037,
1047
Journalism/journalists, 169a, 221
Argentina, 80, 365, 1700
Chile, 307, 314, 2361
Colombia, 43-44
Costa Rica, 2340
Cuba, 377
Ecuador, 286
Mexico, 183, 187, 204, 206, 220,
2065, 2258, 2527
Panama, 249
Peru, 2269
Puerto Rico, 1566
see also Periodicals; Women's
magazines
Juana, Doña (Jacalteca legend), 747
Juana, Sor, see Cruz, Sor Juana Inés
de la
Las Juanas, 1

Juárez, Benito, 1968, 1971
Juárez, Josefa, 1968
Juaristi de Eguino, Vicenta, 1942,
1945
Judges, 1500, 1514, 2166
Juigalpa (Nicaragua), 1767
Junta de la Victoria (Argentina),
2157
Juvenile courts/delinquency, 931,
1500; see also Delinquency
Juxtlahuaca, Oaxaca (Mexico), 743,
873

Karinya Indians, 921
Kickapoo Indians, 733
Kindergartens, 498, 655
Kinship, 809, 820, 1349
indigenous, see Indigenous cul-
tures (ethnographies); Marriage--
indigenous
Colombia, 1297
Mexico, 2443
Venezuela, 920
see also Family; Marriage

La Paz (Bolivia), 793, 957, 1166-67,
1942, 1945, 2400, 2475
Labarca Hubertson, Amanda, 65, 74,
2049, 2474
Labor force participation, 1324,
1326-28, 1333-34, 1336, 1341,
1346-49, 1438, 1446, 1730, 2505,
2526
educational levels and, 1359-60,
1377, 1393, 1398, 1411, 1416,
1608; see also Education
fertility levels and, 1024, 1026-
29, 1032, 1038, 1040, 1327,
1329, 2436
Argentina, 1024, 1202
Chile, 1175, 1177, 1186, 1190-
91, 1194
Colombia, 1136, 1388
Costa Rica, 1024
Ecuador, 1144
Guatemala, 1087
Mexico, 1024, 1079, 1083, 1202
Peru, 1160, 1162
Puerto Rico, 1210, 1216, 1220,
1228, 1239, 2501
Venezuela, 1024
options for, 1341, 1369, 1402,
1415, 1439, 2308
pre-Columbian, 1410, 1705
projections of, 1340, 1350, 1415
role conflict with, see Role
conflict
socio-economic factors, 1326-28,
1331, 1343, 1346-49
statistics, 1324, 1326-27, 1332-
36, 1343, 1347-49, 2235, 2238
2315

Martínez, María Luisa, 1832
Martínez, Pedro, 860, 862
Martínez, Pedro Vicente, 267
Martínez de Carvajal y del Camino,
Laura, 96
Martínez-Guerrero, Ana Rosa de, 2157
Martínez Pastoriza, Benita, 79
Martyr complex, female, 842, 965,
1256
Martyrs, see Biographies; History
Maruchuelas, 1779
Marxism: women's liberation and,
2231, 2234
Marxist governments, see Allende,
Salvador; Castro, Fidel
Mary, Virgin, see *Marianismo*
Masculinity; concept of, see *Machismo*
Mass media:
influence of, 1199, 1261, 1312,
1360, 2261
Argentina, 351, 1199
Chile, 312, 2284
Colombia, 264, 925
Mexico, 184, 214, 218, 1261,
1360
see also Films; Folklore;
Fotonovelas; Literature;
Radionovelas; Television;
Women's magazines
Masturbation, 1108, 1159
Mate selection, see Chaperonage;
Courtship; Family; Marriage
Mathematics: education for, 530
Maticorena, Manuela, 1940a
Matos, Micaela, 1839
Matriarchate, 699, 1714
Matrilineality, matrilocality, etc.,
see Indigenous cultures (ethnog-
raphies); Kinship; Marriage;
Residence patterns
Matto de Turner, Clorinda, 11, 180,
293, 2412, 2416, 2523
Maximillian, 1966-67, 1969
Maya civilization, 1703, 1710, 1713
Maya cultures, 708, 720, 782, 731,
738, 740-41, 2432, 2507
betrothal, 877
children play behavior, 848
clothing, 108, 2397
literature, 839
maternity rites, 875
myth and ritual, 591, 641
see also Jacalteca Indians
Mayauel, 640
Maza de Juárez, Margarita, 1968,
1971
Mazahua Indians, 713, 1352, 1362
Mazateco, Oaxaca (Mexico), 886
Mbayá Indians, 959
Mecayapán, Veracruz (Mexico), 897
Medeiros, Paulina, 368

Medellín (Colombia), 1124-25, 1392,
1607, 2114
Media, see Mass media
Medicine, 1043
education for, 89, 425, 530, 2263
fertility rates and lack of
modern, 1046
folk, 1020, 1062, 1150, 1179
indigenous, 730, 755, 760, 799
pre-Columbian, 1078
Argentina, 530
Chile, 314
Costa Rica, 1102
Cuba, 1241
Guatemala, 755
Mexico, 730, 1062
Peru, 1150
Puerto Rico, 2460
Venezuela, 2263
see also Doctors; Healing
Medina, Manuela, 1833
Memoirs, see Autobiographies
Men, see Family; Female-male rela-
tions; Literature: images of men
in; *Machismo*; Marriage, esp. sub-
division Spousal relations;
Sexuality
Méndez de Cuenca, Laura, 211
Mendocita, Barrio de, Lima (Peru),
1305
Mendoza, Pedro de, 1696
Mendoza (Argentina), 354, 1956, 2010
Mennadier, Jorge, 2281
Mensajera, 306
Menstruation, 1019, 1037, 1047
in indigenous cultures, see
Indigenous cultures (ethnog-
raphies); Indian women
Argentina, 1200
Chile, 1189
Costa Rica, 1102
Mexico, 1063, 1070
Peru, 1152
Mental health/illness:
Mexico, 1263, 1272
Puerto Rico, 1226
see also Curers; Psychiatric
illness
Mérida, Ana, 114
Mérida, Yucatán (México), 2328
Merlín, María de las Mercedes Santa
Cruz y Montalvo, comtesse de, 94,
98, 379
Meskito Indians, 1767
Mestizaje, see Miscegenation
Mestizos, 810, 1046, 1251, 1717
Bolivia, 958
Colombia, 771
Mexico, 623, 725-26, 730, 890,
1051, 1062-63, 2390
conflict with indigenous
cultures, 709

Serviez, Manuel, 407
Sewing/seamstresses, 507, 521, 559
Sex differences:
  in children, 1276-77, 1287
  in concept of sex roles, 1308
  cross-national studies of ado-
    lescent, 523, 1308
  in dreams, 2499
  in education, 440, 477, 523,
    535, 537, 1264
  Argentina, 535, 537
  Chile, 523, 1308
  Colombia, 477, 1513
  Mexico, 440, 1264-65, 1268,
    1276-78, 1287
  Uruguay, 2383
  see also Sex roles
Sex education:
  Central America, 1012
  Colombia, 1117, 1133
  El Salvador, 1095
  Nicaragua, 1600
  Paraguay, 1169
  Peru, 1151, 1158
  see also Family planning
Sex roles:
  education for, see Education;
    Socialization
  effect of media on, 499, 1199,
    1261
  in indigenous cultures, see
    Indian women; Indigenous
    cultures (ethnographies)
  in literature, see Literature:
    images of men; Literature:
    images of women
  nineteenth century ideas, 881
  in peasant communities, 1337
  pre-Columbian, 1705
  ritual enactment of, 1295
  Argentina, 966, 1199, 1316
  Bolivia, 957
  Chile, 1308
  Colombia, 265, 931-32, 1293,
    1295
  Costa Rica, 911
  Cuba, 381, 1006-07, 1321-22
  Ecuador, 1295
  Mexico, 725, 826, 846, 867,
    1254, 1256
    conflict in, 716, 721, 1068,
      1270, 1372
    economic, 1353
    education and, 437
    in family, 856, 869, 885,
      1261, 1269
    in literature, 212
    socialization to, 842
  Peru, 265, 1303-05, 1316, 2415
  Puerto Rico, 990, 1239
  United States, 1316

  see also Double standard; Family;
    Female-male relations; Marriage;
    National character studies;
    Psychology; Role conflict
Sex roles, female, see Behavior pat-
    terns, female; Marianismo; Martyr
    complex, female; Motherhood/
    maternity; Passivity; Virgin
    cults; Virginity, female
Sex roles, male, see Behavior pat-
    terns, male; Dominance; Machismo
Sexism, ideology of:
  Chile, 2278
  Mexico, 2242, 2248, 2251, 2529
  Puerto Rico, 2298
  see also Dominance; Machismo;
    Submission; Women's liberation
Sexual crime:
  Bolivia, 1536
  Colombia, 1510, 1605
  Ecuador, 1522
  Nicaragua, 1600
  Peru, 1525
  Puerto Rico, 1570
  Uruguay, 1557
  see also Bigamy; Homosexuality;
    Incest; Prostitution; Rape;
    Seduction; White slavery
Sexual identity, 1016, 1266, 1274
Sexual license: in machismo syndrome,
    see Machismo
Sexual solidarity, female (Colombia),
    1296
Sexuality:
  attitudes toward, 694, 1031,
    1054, 1113, 1159, 1180, 1374
  conflict in, 1016, 1291
  cross-cultural studies, 1031,
    1072
  deviance, 1076
  in indigenous cultures, see
    subdivision sexuality under
    Indian women; also see Indi-
    genous cultures (ethnographies)
  medical school's course, 1113
  pre-Columbian, 1025, 1703
  psychology/physiology, 1108
  teaching, see Sex education;
    Socialization
  as theme in poetry, 1600
  Argentina, 1199, 1201, 1204,
    1206, 1312
  Bolivia, 1159
  Central America, 697
  Chile, 1180, 2284
  Colombia, 1114, 1117, 1133-34,
    1291, 1296
  Costa Rica, 1100
  Cuba, 2470
  El Salvador, 1095
  England, 1072

Migration/migrants; Social
class; Status of women; etc.
Socorro (Colombia), 1867, 1876,
1878, 1898-99, 1901
Sodomy (pre-Columbian), 1025
Sogandares, Lidia Gertrudis, 34
Solar, 999
Solar de Claro, Amelia, 74
Soldaderas, 1, 28
Argentina, 2003
Mexico, 2069, 2074, 2081, 2086,
2255
see also History
Solteras (single women), 1259, 1784
Solís, Viceroy, 1779, 1781
Sorcery, 685, 755, 1063
Sororate, 764
Sosa, Miguel de, 615
Sosa Medina, María Luisa, see
María Dolores, Rev. Madre
Bethlemita
Soto, Hernando de, 1791
Soto, Leonor de, 1791
Soto Hall, Máximo, 1768
Sotomayor, Juana de, 1817
Soublette de O'Leary, Soledad, 1976
Spanish men:
Argentina, 1548
see also Indian women, esp.
subdivision history (Conquest
and colonial)
Spanish-speaking:
Ecuador, 1300
Peru, 1163, 1412
Puerto Rico, 556, 1318
Spanish women, 1671, 1676-77
in Conquest and colonial, 817,
1475-78, 1716-21, 1723, 1725-
26, 1730, 1732
Argentina, 1726, 1810
Chile, 1805-06, 1808-09
Colombia, 1771-73, 1775-78,
1780, 1784
Guatemala, 1761
Mexico, 1738, 1745
Nicaragua, 1763-67
Paraguay, 1802-03
Peru, 1788-89, 1796
see also Creole women; *Mestizos*;
White slavery
Special Institute of Feminine Tech-
nical Education No. 1 (Peru),
494
Speech, see Language; Stuttering
Spiritualism, 1062, 1066, 1226
Spooks (Mayan), 591
Sports, 480, 567, 728, 1189
Squatter settlements (Peru), 51;
see also Migration/migrants
Statistics, see Mortality rates;
Population; also see subdivision

statistics under subjects such as:
Education; Family; Fertility;
Labor force participation; etc.
Status of women, 585, 1324, 1416,
2032, 2051-52, 2054-56, 2310
Argentina, 2378
Bolivia, 975, 2122
Chile, 2052, 2138
Colombia, 2112, 2114
Cuba, 1321-22, 1462, 1465, 2192
Mexico, 1272, 1355, 2330, 2403
Nicaragua, 2093
Peru, 1416, 2441
see also Education; Family;
Female-male relations; Labor
force participation; Legal
status; Marriage; Women
(general); Women's rights
Sterilization, 1190, 1223-24, 1230,
1232, 1237, 2479
Stewardesses (Peru), 1413
Stillbirth (Mexico), 1063
Storni, Afonsina, 165-66, 175, 342,
344, 355
and Gabriela Mistral, 327
poetry of, 169, 182, 357, 2387
Street vendors, 1146, 1352, 1380,
1407
Stuttering, 1318
Suárez, Inés de, 1, 67, 520, 1806,
1808-09
Suárez, Sor Ursula, 1777
Submission:
Mexico, 884, 1253, 1267
Puerto Rico, 989, 996, 2298
see also Dominance
Suffrage, 1482, 1493, 2043, 2046,
2056, 2159, 2310
international organizations
involved with, 2038; see also
Women's rights--international
organizations active in
Argentina, 1551, 2141-42, 2147-
48, 2154, 2156, 2160, 2164,
2287, 2291-92, 2373
Bolivia, 2125
Chile, 2136, 2138, 2276, 2281,
2361
Colombia, 2106, 2109-10
Costa Rica, 1508, 2096
Cuba, 2214, 2299
Dominican Republic, 2221-24
Guatemala, 1504, 1508
Mexico, 1493, 1508, 2062, 2068-
69, 2071, 2076-77, 2082, 2084-
85, 2087, 2090, 2247, 2255,
2257
Nicaragua, 2092, 2094
Panama, 2101
Paraguay, 1693, 2126
Peru, 2119-20, 2276

Subject Index

Peru, 1150
see also Curers; Folk medicine;
  Indigenous cultures
  (ethnographies)
Wives, see Family; Marriage, esp.
  subdivision Spousal relations
Women (general), 578, 1247, 2305-23
  Argentina, 528, 971, 1199, 1309-
    10, 1312-13, 2309, 2367-78
  Bolivia, 1420-22, 2354-56
  Chile, 521, 1309, 1695, 2360-66,
    2497
  Colombia, 932-33, 1112, 2343-48
  Costa Rica, 2340
  Cuba, 1000, 1009, 1242, 2387
  Dominican Republic, 2388
  El Salvador, 2336
  Guatemala, 1378
  Honduras, 461, 2338
  Mexico, 428, 881, 1279, 1355,
    1831, 2066, 2078, 2324-35
  Nicaragua, 2339
  Panama, 2341
  Paraguay, 2357-59
  Peru, 1405, 1408, 2350-53
  Puerto Rico, 977, 997-98,
    2384-86
  Uruguay, 2379-83
  Venezuela, 2342
  see also Behavior patterns,
    female; Family; History; Mar-
    riage; National character
    studies; Psychology; Status of
    women
Women's Auxiliary Committee/Confer-
  ence, Pan American Scientific
  Congress, 2049, 2055
Women's Bureaus (in Ministries of
  Labor), 1346
Women's International Democratic
  Federation, 2033, 2052
Women's liberation: perspectives
  on, 2225-41
  Argentina, 1439, 2285-95
  Chile, 2272-84, 2363
  Colombia, 2345
  Cuba, 2299-2303
  Dominican Republic 2304
  Ecuador, 2264
  El Salvador, 2260
  Mexico, 2242-59
  Paraguay, 2271
  Peru, 2266-70, 2276
  Puerto Rico, 2298
  Uruguay, 2296-97
  Venezuela, 2261-63
  see also Feminism; Consciousness-
    raising; Women's rights
Women's liberation movements, see
  Feminism

Women's magazines:
  female image in fiction in, 167
  nineteenth-century, 397-414
  Argentina, 351, 401-02
  Chile, 311
  Colombia, 404, 407, 409
  Cuba, 390, 397-98, 400, 1008
  Mexico, 203, 212, 399, 405-06,
    410-14
  Puerto Rico, 403, 408
  see also Journalism/journalists;
    Periodicals
Women's organizations:
  international, 1529; see also
    Women's rights--international
    organizations active in
  national, 1529
  Argentina, 1444, 2154, 2157,
    2165, 2368, 2378
  Bolivia, 503, 576, 2122, 2354
  Chile, 320, 1541, 2272, 2282,
    2361
  Colombia, 2106
  Costa Rica, 2340
  Cuba, 2198, 2209-11, 2213-14
  Dominican Republic, 2222
  Ecuador, 2034
  El Salvador, 2336
  Mexico, 580, 602, 2065, 2076,
    2083, 2331
  Nicaragua, 462
  Panama, 2103
  Paraguay, 1423, 2034
  Peru, 1403, 2034
  Uruguay, 2182, 2379, 2381
  political, see Women's rights;
    Political rights
  religious, 576, 602, 736
  vocational, 1444
  see also Mothers' Centers/Circles/
    Clubs
Women's rights:
  cross-cultural studies, 1473,
    1555, 2040, 2506
  to economic independence, 1436;
    see also Labor force participa-
    tion
  history, 2040; see also History
  international organizations active
    in, 1479, 1481, 1508, 1529,
    2151, 2316, 2361; see also
    under names of individual orga-
    nizations, e.g. Inter-American
    Commission of Women (IACW); Pan
    American Conference of Women;
    United Nations; etc.
  national organizations, 1529;
    see also Women's organizations--
    national
  Argentina, 1960, 2141, 2149,
    2151-52, 2154, 2156, 2159,
    2285-88, 2295, 2370